MARKET SHARE REPORTER

ISSN 1052-9578

MARKET SHARE REPORTER

AN ANNUAL COMPILATION
OF REPORTED MARKET SHARE
DATA ON COMPANIES,
PRODUCTS, AND SERVICES

1998

ROBERT S. LAZICH

DETROIT • NEW YORK • TORONTO • LONDON

Robert S. Lazich, *Editor*

Editorial Code & Data Inc. Staff

David Smith and Susan Turner, *Contributing Editors*
Joyce Piwowarski, *Programmer*

Gale Research Inc. Staff

Donna Wood, *Coordinating Editor*

Mary Beth Trimper, *Production Manager*
Deborah Milliken, *Production Assistant*

Cynthia D. Baldwin, *Product Design Manager*
Barbara Yarrow, *Graphic Services Supervisor*
Mikal Ansari, *Macintosh Artist*

∞™ The paper used in this publication meets the minimum requirements of American National Standard for Information Sciences—Permanence Paper for Printed Library Materials, ANSI Z39.48-1984.

This book is printed on recycled paper that meets Environmental Protection Agency Standards.

835 Penobscot Building
Detroit, MI 48226-4094

ISBN 0-7876-1460-2
ISSN 1052-9578

Printed in the United States of America

TABLE OF CONTENTS

TABLE OF TOPICS

The *Table of Topics* lists all topics used in *Market Share Reporter* in alphabetical order. One or more page references follow each topic; the page references identify the starting point where the topic is shown. The same topic name may be used under different SICs; therefore, in some cases, more than one page reference is provided.

INTRODUCTION

Market Share Reporter (MSR) is a compilation of market share reports from periodical literature. The eighth edition covers the period 1994 through 1997; while dates overlap slightly with the seventh edition, the eighth edition of *MSR* has completely new and updated entries. As shown by reviews of previous editions plus correspondence and telephone contact with many users, this is a unique resource for competitive analysis, diversification planning, marketing research, and other forms of economic and policy analysis. Features of the 1998 edition include—

- More than 2,000 entries, all new or updated.
- SIC classification, with entries arranged under 511 SIC codes.
- Corporate, brand, product, service and commodity market shares.
- Coverage of private and public sector activities.
- North American coverage.
- Comprehensive indexes, including products, companies, brands, places, sources, and SICs.
- Table of Topics showing topical subdivisions of chapters with page references.
- Graphics.
- Annotated source listing—provides publishers' information for journals cited in this edition of *MSR*.

MSR is a one-of-a-kind resource for ready reference, marketing research, economic analysis, planning, and a host of other disciplines.

Categories of Market Shares

Entries in *Market Share Reporter* fall into four broad categories. Items were included if they showed the relative strengths of participants in a market or provided subdivisions of economic activity in some manner that could assist the analyst.

- ***Corporate market shares*** show the names of companies that participate in an industry, produce a product, or provide a service. Each company's market share is shown as a percent of total industry or product sales for a defined period, usually a year. In some cases, the company's share represents the share of the sales of the companies shown (group total)—because shares of the total market were not cited in the source or were not relevant. In some corporate share tables, brand information appears behind company names in parentheses. In these cases, the tables can be located using either the company or the brand index.

- ***Institutional shares*** are like corporate shares but show the shares of other kinds of organizations. The most common institutional entries in *MSR* display the shares of states, provinces, or regions in an activity. The shares of not-for-profit organizations in some economic or service functions fall under this heading.

- ***Brand market shares*** are similar to corporate shares with the difference that brand names are shown. Brand names include equivalent categories such as the names of television programs, magazines, publishers' imprints, etc. In some cases, the names of corporations appear in parentheses behind the brand name; in these cases, tables can be located using either the brand or the company index.

- ***Product, commodity, service, and facility*** shares feature a broad category (e.g. household appliances) and show how the category is subdivided into components (e.g. refrigerators, ranges, washing machines, dryers, and dishwashers). Entries under this category cover products (autos, lawnmowers, polyethylene, etc.), commodities (cattle, grains, crops), services (telephone, child care), and facilities (port berths, hotel suites, etc.). Subdivisions may be products, categories of services (long-distance telephone, residential phone service, 800-service), types of commodities (varieties of grain), size categories (e.g., horsepower ranges), modes (rail, air, barge), types of facilities (categories of hospitals, ports, and the like), or other subdivisions.

- ***Other shares.*** *MSR* includes a number of entries that show subdivisions, breakdowns, and shares that do not fit neatly into the above categorizations but properly belong in such a book because they shed light on public policy, foreign trade, and other subjects of general interest. These items include, for instance, subdivisions of governmental expenditures, environmental issues, and the like.

Coverage

The eighth edition of *Market Share Reporter* covers essentially the same range of industries as previous editions. However, all tables are *new* or represent *updated* information (more recent or revised data). Also, coverage in detail is different in certain industries, meaning that more or fewer SICs are covered or product details *within* SICs may be different. For these reasons, it is recommended that previous editions of *MSR* be retained rather than replaced.

Changes in Coverage. Beginning with the fifth edition, *MSR*'s geographic area of coverage became North America—Canada, the United States, and Mexico. As in all past editions, the vast majority of entries are for the United States. In the first four editions of *MSR*, international data were included at greater or lesser intensity depending on availability of space. This necessitated, among other things, frequent exclusion of data organized by states or regions of the United States—which are popular with users.

In order to provide better service to users, a companion publication, called *World Market Share Reporter* (*WMSR*), is available. *WMSR* features global market share information as well as country-specific market share and/or market size information outside North America. At the same time, *MSR* features more geographical market shares in the North American area.

MSR reports on *published* market shares rather than attempting exhaustive coverage of the market shares, say, of all major corporations and of all products and services. Despite this limitation, *MSR* holds share information on nearly 5,500 companies, more than 1,650 brands, and more than 2,500 product, commodity, service, and facility categories. Several entries are usually available for each industry group in the SIC classification; omitted groups are those that do not play a conventional role in the market, e.g., Private Households (SIC 88).

Coverage by SIC has increased over the seventh edition: 511 SIC categories versus 462 last year. Variation in coverage from previous editions is due in part to publication cycles of sources and a different mix of brokerage house reports for the period covered (due to shifting interests within the investment community).

As pointed out in previous editions, *MSR* tends to reflect the current concerns of the business press. In addition to being a source of market share data, it mirrors journalistic preoccupations, issues in the business community, and events abroad. Important and controversial industries and activities get most of the ink. Heavy coverage is provided in those areas that are—

- large, important, basic (autos, chemicals)
- on the leading edge of technological change (computers, electronics, software)
- very competitive (toiletries, beer, soft drinks)
- in the news because of product recalls, new product introductions, mergers and acquisitions, lawsuits, and for other reasons
- relate to popular issues (environment, crime), or have excellent coverage in their respective trade press.

In many cases, several entries are provided on a subject each citing the same companies. No attempt was made to eliminate such seeming duplication if the publishing and/or original sources were different and the market shares were not identical. Those who work with such data know that market share reports are often little more than the "best guesses" of knowledgeable observers rather than precise measurements. To the planner or analyst, variant reports about an industry's market shares are useful for interpreting the data.

Publications appearing in the May 1996 to July 1997 period were used in preparing *MSR*. As a rule, material on market share data for 1997 were used by preference; in response to reader requests, we have included historical data when available. In some instances, information for earlier years was included if the category was unique or if the earlier year was necessary for context. In a few other cases, projections for 1998 and later years were also included.

"Unusual" Market Shares

Some reviewers of the first edition questioned—sometimes tongue-in-cheek, sometimes seriously—the inclusion of tables on such topics as computer crime, endangered species of fish, children's allowances, governmental budgets, and weapons system stockpiles. Indeed, some of these categories do not fit the sober meaning of "market share." A few tables on such subjects are present every edition—because they provide market information, albeit indirectly, or because they are the "market share equivalents" in an industrial classification which is in the public sector or dominated by the public sector's purchasing power.

Organization of Chapters

Market Share Reporter is organized into chapters by 2-digit SIC categories (industry groups). The exception is the first chapter, entitled *General Interest and Broad Topics*; this chapter holds all entries that bridge two or more 2-digit SIC industry codes (e.g. retailing in general, beverage containers, advanced materials, etc.) and cannot, therefore, be classified using the SIC system without distortion. Please note, however, that a topic in this chapter will often have one or more additional entries later—where the table could be assigned to a detailed industry. Thus, in addition to three tables on packaging in the first chapter, tables appear later on glass containers, metal cans, etc.

Within each chapter, entries are shown by 4-digit SIC (industry level). Within blocks of 4-digit SIC entries, entries are sorted alphabetically by topic, then alphabetically by title.

SIC and Topic Assignments

MSR's SIC classifications are based on the coding as defined in the *Standard Industrial Classification Manual* for 1987, issued by the Bureau of the Census, Department of Commerce. This 1987 classification system introduced significant revisions to the 1972 classification (as slightly modified in 1977); the 1972 system is still in widespread use (even by the Federal government); care should be used in comparing data classified in the new and in the old way.

The closest appropriate 4-digit SIC was assigned to each table. In many cases, a 3-digit SIC had to be used because the substance of the table was broader than the nearest 4-digit SIC category. Such SICs always end with a zero. In yet other cases, the closest classification possible was at the 2-digit level; these SICs terminate with double-zero. If the content of the table did not fit the 2-digit level, it was assigned to the first chapter of *MSR* and classified by topic only.

Topic assignments are based on terminology for commodities, products, industries, and services in the SIC Manual; however, in many cases phrasing has been simplified, shortened, or updated; in general, journalistically succinct rather than bureaucratically exhaustive phraseology was used throughout.

Organization of Entries

Entries are organized in a uniform manner. A sample entry is provided below. Explanations for each part of an entry, shown in boxes, are provided on the facing page.

1 *Entry Number.* A numeral between star symbols. Used for locating an entry from the index.

2 *Topic.* Second line, small type. Gives the broad or general product or service category of the entry. The topic for Bagged Salad Market is Salads.

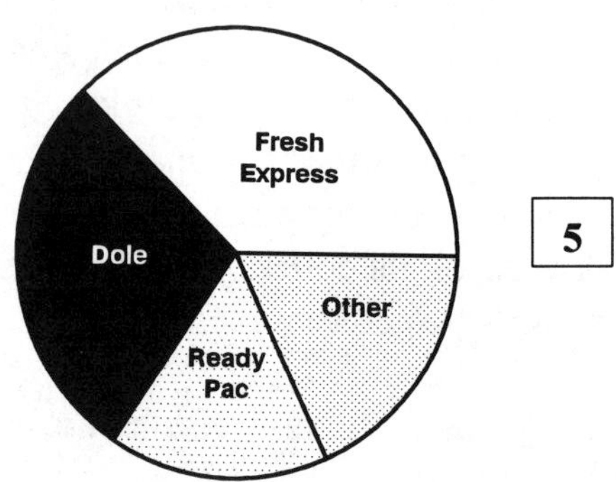

Sales are shown by brand for the year ended September 8, 1996. 6

	($ mil.)	Share
Fresh Express	$ 294.4	37.3%
Dole	223.0	28.2
Ready Pac	129.0	16.3
Other	143.6	18.2

7 8

Source: *Brandweek*, November 11, 1996, p. 25, from Information Resources Inc.

9

3 *SIC Code.* Second line, small type, follows the topic. General entries in the first chapter do not have an SIC code.

4 *Title.* Third line, large type. Describes the entry with a headline.

5 *Graphic.* When a graphic is present, it follows the title. Some entries will be illustrated with a pie or bar chart. The information used to create the graphic is always shown below the pie or bar chart.

6 *Note Block.* When present, follows the title and is in italic type. The note provides contextual information about the entry to make the data more understandable. Special notes about the data, information about time periods covered, market totals, and other comments are provided. Self-explanatory entries do not have a note block.

7 *Column headers.* Follow the note block. Some entries have more than one column or the single column requires a header. In these cases, column headers are used to describe information covered in the column. In most cases, column headers are years (1997) or indicators of type and magnitude ($ mil.). Column headers are shown only when necessary for clarity of presentation.

8 *Body.* Follows the note block or the column header and shows the actual data in two or more columns. In most cases, individual rows of data in the body are arranged in descending order, with the largest market share holder heading the list. Collective shares, usually labelled "Others" are placed last.

9 *Source.* Follows the body. All entries cite the source of the table, the date of publication, and the page number (if given). In many cases, the publisher obtained the information from another source (original source); in all such cases, the original source is also shown.

Continued entries. Entries that extend over two adjacent columns on the same page are not marked to indicate continuation but continue in the second column. Entries that extend over two pages are marked *Continued on the next page.* Entries carried over from the previous page repeat the entry number, topic (followed by the word *continued*), title, and column header (if any).

Use of Names

Company Names. The editors reproduced company names as they appeared in the source unless it was clearly evident from the name and the context that a name had been misspelled in the original. Large companies, of course, tend to appear in a large number of entries and in variant renditions. General Electric Corporation may appear as GE, General Electric, General Electric Corp., GE Corp., and other variants. No attempt was made to enforce a uniform rendition of names in the entries. In the Company Index, variant renditions were reduced to a single version or cross-referenced.

Use of Numbers

Throughout *MSR*, tables showing percentage breakdowns may add to less than 100 or fractionally more than 100 due to rounding. In those cases where only a few leading participants in a market are shown, the total of the shares may be substantially less than 100.

Numbers in the note block showing the total size of the market are provided with as many significant digits as possible in order to permit the user to calculate the sales of a particular company by multiplying the market total by the market share.

In a relatively small number of entries, actual unit or dollar information is provided rather than share information in percent. In such cases, the denomination of the unit (tons, gallons, $) and its magnitude (000 indicates multiply by 1,000; mil., multiply by 1,000,000) are mentioned in the note block or shown in the column header.

Data in some entries are based on different kinds of currencies and different weight and liquid measures. Where necessary, the unit is identified in the note block or in the column header. Examples are long tons, short tons, metric tons or Canadian dollars, etc.

Graphics

Pie and bar charts are used to illustrate some of the entries. The graphics show the names of companies, products, and services when they fit on the charts. When room is insufficient to accommodate the label, the first word of a full name is used followed by three periods (...) to indicate omission of the rest of the label.

In the case of bar charts, the largest share is always the width of the column, and smaller shares are drawn in proportion. Two bar charts, consequently, should not be compared to one another.

Sources

The majority of entries were extracted from newspapers and from general purpose, trade, and technical periodicals normally available in larger public, special, or university libraries. All told, 1,133 sources were used; of these, 370 were primary print sources, while 13 were taken from the Internet. Many more sources were reviewed but lacked coverage of the subject. These primary sources, in turn, used 750 original sources.

In many cases, the primary source in which the entry was published cites another source for the data, the original source. Original sources include other publications, brokerage houses, consultancies and research organizations, associations, government agencies, special surveys, and the like.

Since many primary sources appear as original sources elsewhere, and vice-versa, primary and original sources are shown in a single Source Index under two headings. Primary sources included in *MSR* almost always used the market share data as illustrative material for narratives covering many aspects of the subject. We hope that this book will also serve as a guide to those articles.

Indexes

Market Share Reporter features five indexes and two appendices.

- **Source Index.** This index holds 1,120 references in two groupings. *Primary sources* (370) are publications where the data were found. *Original sources* (750) are sources cited in the primary sources. Each item in the index is followed by one or more entry numbers arranged sequentially, beginning with the first mention of the source.

- **Place Names Index.** This index provides references to cities, states, and regions in North America and elsewhere. References are to entry numbers.

- **Products, Services, and Issues Index.** This index holds more than 2,500 references to products and services in alphabetical order. The index also lists subject categories that do not fit the definition of a product or service but properly belong in the index. Examples include *budgets, conglomerates, crime, defense spending, economies, lotteries*, and the like. Some listings are abbreviations for chemical substances, computer software, etc. which may not be meaningful to those unfamiliar with the industries. Wherever possible, the full name is also provided for abbreviations commonly in use. Each listing is followed by one or more references to entry numbers.

- **Company Index.** This index shows references to nearly 5,500 company names by entry number. Companies are arranged in alphabetical order. In some cases, the market share table from which the company name was derived showed the share for a combination of two or more companies; these combinations are reproduced in the index.

- **Brand Index.** The Brand Index shows references to more than 1,650 brands by entry number. The arrangement is alphabetical. Brands include names of publications, computer software, operating systems, etc., as well as the more conventional brand names (Coca Cola, Maxwell House, Budweiser, etc.)

- **Appendix I - SIC Coverage.** The first appendix shows SICs covered by *Market Share Reporter*. The listing shows major SIC groupings at the 2-digit level as bold-face headings followed by 4-digit SIC numbers, the names of the SIC, and a *page* reference (rather than a reference to an entry number, as in the indexes). The page shows the first occurrence of the SIC in the book. *MSR*'s SIC coverage is quite comprehensive, as shown in the appendix. However, many 4-digit SIC categories are further divided into major product groupings. Not all of these have corresponding entries in the book.

- **Appendix II - Annotated Source List.** The second appendix provides publisher names, addresses, telephone and fax numbers, and publication frequency of primary sources cited in *Market Share Reporter*, 8th Edition.

Acknowledgements

Market Share Reporter is something of a collective enterprise which involves not only the editorial team but also many users who share comments, criticisms, and suggestions over the telephone. Their help and encouragement is very much appreciated. *MSR* could not have been produced without the help of many people in and outside of Gale Research. The editors would like to express their special appreciation to Ms. Donna Wood (Senior Editor, Gale Research) and to the staff of Editorial Code and Data, Inc.

Comments and Suggestions

Comments on *MSR* or suggestions for improvement of its usefulness, format, and coverage are always welcome. Although every effort is made to maintain accuracy, errors may occasionally occur; the editors will be grateful if these are called to their attention. Please contact:

Editors
Market Share Reporter
Gale Research Inc.
835 Penobscot Building
Detroit, Michigan 48226-4094
Phone: (313) 961-2242 or (800) 347-GALE
Fax: (313) 961-6815

MARKET SHARE REPORTER

General Interest and Broad Topics

★1★

Beauty Treatments

Exercise Spending

A total of $4.27 billion was spent on the quest for a more attractive body.

Gym memberships	65.6%
Exercise equipment	30.6
Ab machines	3.4
Slenderizing garments	0.4

Source: *Fortune*, September 9, 1996, p. 78, from International Health, Racquet & Sportsclub Association.

★2★

Building Materials

Top Construction Material Producers - 1996

Corning
Owens-Illinois
Owens-Corning
USG
Armstrong World Industries
Schuller

Revenues are shown in millions of dollars.

Corning	$ 4,200
Owens-Illinois	3,976
Owens-Corning	3,832
USG	2,590
Armstrong World Industries	2,156
Schuller	1,552

Source: *Fortune*, April 28, 1997, p. 45.

★3★

Consumer Products

Top Product Introductions - 1996

Sales are shown in millions of dollars.

Luvs Stretch diapers	$ 435.0
Scott 1000 paper products	309.0
Pepcid AC	248.0
Nicorette gum	189.0
Baked Lays potato chips	167.0
Pampers Premium	162.0
Tagament HB/200	155.0
Bounty Medleys	126.0
DiGiorno self-rising pizza	120.0
Zantac	116.0

Source: *Bangkok Post*, May 8, 1997, p. 11, from Information Resources Inc.

★4★

Consumer Spending

Favorite Tourist Items

Data show the items purchased in the United States by foreign and domestic tourists.

Clothing	61.0%
Souvenirs	27.0
Electronics	14.0
Sports equipment	14.0
Cosmetics/toiletries	10.0
Food/gourmet stores	8.0
Jewelry	8.0
Toys	8.0

Source: *Stores*, November 1996, p. 77, from American Express.

★ 5 ★

Consumer Spending

How Canadians Will Spend Their Money

Data show how Canadians will spend money in 1997, based on a survey. RRSP stands for Registered Retirement Savings Plans.

Vacations	67.0%
RRSP	59.0
Furniture/appliances	42.0
Children's education	41.0
Investments	41.0
Home renovations	36.0
Computers	31.0
Cars	29.0

Source: *Toronto Star*, February 6, 1997, p. E1, from Royal Bank of Canada.

★ 6 ★

Consumer Spending

How We Pay for Goods - 2000

Data are estimated.

Check	42.0%
Credit/debit cards	24.0
Cash	16.0
Other	18.0

Source: *Investor's Business Daily*, December 3, 1996, p. A4, from National Data Corp. and Payment Systems Inc.

★ 7 ★

Consumer Spending

Teens' Favorite Brands

Nike
Levi's
Calvin Klein
Sony
Pepsi
The Gap
Tommy Hilfiger
Guess
Coca-Cola
Adidas

Data show the brands that teenagers ranked as "coolest" in a survey of 2,000 respondents. More than one brand or product could be cited.

Nike	42.9%
Levi's	13.3
Calvin Klein	13.2
Sony	10.4
Pepsi	10.3
The Gap	8.8
Tommy Hilfiger	8.2
Guess	7.4
Coca-Cola	7.1
Adidas	7.0

Source: *USA TODAY*, September 4, 1996, p. 2B, from Teenage Research Unlimited.

★ 8 ★

Contraceptives

Leading Contraceptive Brands

Brands are ranked by dollar sales in millions of dollars for the 52 weeks ending December 1, 1996. Total market sales reached $276,049,952. Conceptrol and Ortho-Gynol are contraceptive jellies; other listed brands are prophylactics.

	Sales ($ mil.)	Share
Trojan	$ 65.4	23.7%
Trojan-Enz	50.0	18.1
Lifestyles	29.0	10.5
Sheik	14.2	5.2
Conceptrol	11.7	4.7
Ortho Gynol II	7.9	2.9

Continued on next page.

★8★ *Continued*

Contraceptives

Leading Contraceptive Brands

Brands are ranked by dollar sales in millions of dollars for the 52 weeks ending December 1, 1996. Total market sales reached $276,049,952. Conceptrol and Ortho-Gynol are contraceptive jellies; other listed brands are prophylactics.

	Sales ($ mil.)	Share
Kling Title Naturalamb	$ 7.0	2.5%
Class Act	6.6	2.4
Fourex	6.5	2.4
Ramses Extra	6.3	2.3

Source: *Drug Topics Today*, February 17, 1997, p. 81, from Information Resources Inc.

★9★

Corporations

Leading Canadian Firms

Firms are ranked by market capitalization in millions of dollars.

Northern Telecom	$ 14,814.5
Seagram	13,731.4
BCE	13,492.4
Thomson Corp.	10,734.2
Barrick Gold Corp.	9,249.9
Royal Bank of Canada	8,901.8
Canadian Pacific	7,997.7
Imperial Oil	7,763.0
Canadian Imperial Bank	7,415.6
Bank of Montreal	6,924.0

Source: *Financial Times*, January 24, 1997, p. 35.

★10★

Correspondence

How Correspondence is Handled - 1996

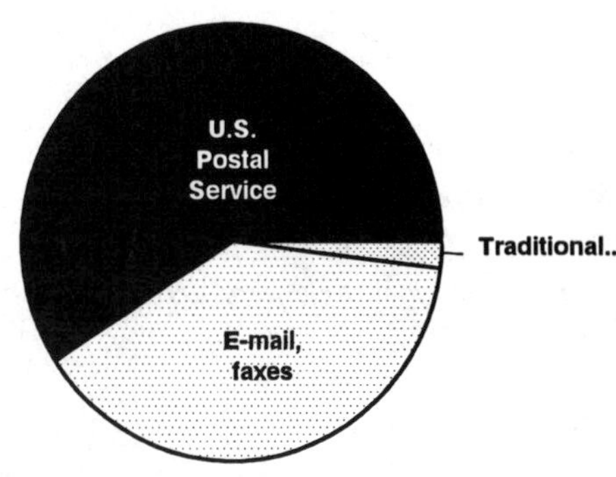

Distribution of $48 billion in services is shown in percent. The market refers to revenues from bills, statements, orders, payments, legal documents, business and personal correspondence and greeting cards.

United States Postal Service	59.0%
E-mail, faxes	39.0
Traditional competitors	2.0

Source: *New York Times*, May 15, 1997, p. C1, from United States Postal Service.

★11★

Debit Cards

Where We Use Debit Cards

Supermarkets	68.0%
Gas stations	34.0
Department stores	29.0
Fast food restaurants	6.0
Convenience stores	5.0
Other restaurants	12.0
Other	8.0

Source: *ABA Banking Journal*, September 1996, p. 45, from Payment Systems Inc.

★ 12 ★

Foreign Aid

Foreign Investment in Mexico

Data are shown by industry for January 1994 - June 1996.

Manufacturing	58.2%
Services	21.0
Commerce	10.7
Transportation & commerce	7.7
Other	2.4

Source: *Global Finance*, January 1997, p. 128, from SECOFI.

★ 13 ★

Hair Products

Hair Growth Spending

A total of $1.36 billion was spent on the quest for hair.

Hair transplants	57.3%
Wigs/toupees	29.1
Nontraditional	7.3
Rogaine	6.3

Source: *Fortune*, September 9, 1996, p. 69, from American Academy of Cosmetic Surgery and Pharmacia & Upjohn.

★ 14 ★

High Tech Firms

Largest High Tech Firms - Washington D.C.

America Online Inc.
American Management Systems Inc.
Government Technology Services Inc.
Life Technologies Inc.
Genicom Corp.

Firms are ranked by revenues in millions of dollars.

America Online Inc.	$ 1,093.9
American Management Systems Inc.	812.0
Government Technology Services Inc.	491.6
Life Technologies Inc.	310.3
Genicom Corp.	303.3

Source: *Washington Post*, April 28, 1997, p. 29.

★ 15 ★

Investment Clubs

Popular Investment Club Stocks - 1997

Data represent the number of investment clubs holding stock in each company.

Motorola	9,334
Pepisco	8,812
Merck	8,106
McDonald's	7,712
Intel	6,667
AFLAC	5,923
Coca-Cola	5,577
Lucent Technologies	4,545
RPM	4,311
AT&T	4,017

Source: *Business Week*, April 28, 1997, p. 4, from National Association of Investors Corp.

★ 16 ★

Media

Top Entertainment Companies - 1996

Revenues are shown in millions of dollars.

Walt Disney	$ 18,739
Viacom	12,084
Time Warner	10,064
Westinghouse Electric	9,401

Source: *Fortune*, April 28, 1997, p. 50.

★ 17 ★

Media

Top Media Buying Firms - Canada

Firms are ranked by estimated 1996 billings in millions of dollars.

McKim Media Group	$ 360
Initiative Media	324
Alliance HYPN/Strategem	312
Media Buying Services Ltd.	275
WPP Alliance	245
Cossette Communication-Marketing	216

Continued on next page.

★17★ *Continued*

Media

Top Media Buying Firms - Canada

Firms are ranked by estimated 1996 billings in millions of dollars.

Young & Rubicam Ltd.	$ 210
Genesis Media Inc.	176
Optimedia Canada	155
Leo Burnett Company Ltd.	145

Source: *Marketing Magazine*, December 9, 1996, p. 24.

★18★

Media

U.S. Media Consumption

The table shows the estimated hours per week devoted to various media in 1997.

Radio	20.5
Broadcast TV	19.7
Cable	11.3
Recorded music	5.7
Daily newspapers	3.1
Consumer books	2.0
Consumer magazines	1.6
Home video	1.1
Home video games	0.6
On-line/internet services	0.3

Source: *Chicago Tribune*, April 27, 1997, p. C1, from Audit Bureau of Circulation, FCC, Forrester's Research, Morgan Stanley & Co., National Cable Television Association, and Newspaper Association of America.

★19★

Media

Yellow Pages Media Firms

Firms are ranked by 1995 Yellow Pages revenues in millions of dollars.

BellSouth Corp.	$ 1,677.0
GTE Corp.	1,383.0
Bell Atlantic	1,107.7
Pacific Telesis Group	1,031.0
US West Media Group	1,026.0
SBC Communications	953.1
Nynex Corp.	943.1

Source: *Advertising Age*, August 19, 1996, p. S4.

★20★

On-line Services

Largest Events on America Online

Data show the number of attendees at auditorium events on America Online.

Michael Jackson	16,100
Oprah Winfrey	2,500
Sandra Bullock	2,035
Anthony Edwards	1,846
Steve Martin	1,829
Rosie O'Donnell	1,766

Source: *Wired*, October 1996, p. 74, from America Online.

★21★

Packaging

Top Flexible Packaging Markets

Data show the top growth markets in the next five years, based on a survey.

Fresh produce	70.0%
Drugs	45.0
Surgical, medical	43.0
Snack foods	33.0
Agricultural products, industrial chemicals	27.0

Source: *American Ink Maker*, March 1997, p. 26, from FPA Outlook Survey, 1996.

★ 22 ★
Packaging

Top Packaging Types - 1994

Shares are shown based on a $94 million market.

Paperboard	37.0%
Flexible packaging	16.0
Metal cans	13.0
Plastic bottles	6.0
Other plastics	9.0
Others	20.0

Source: *Paperboard Packaging*, May 1997, p. 10, from Bureau of the Census and Flexible Packaging Association.

★ 23 ★
Packaging

U.S. Drum Market - 2000

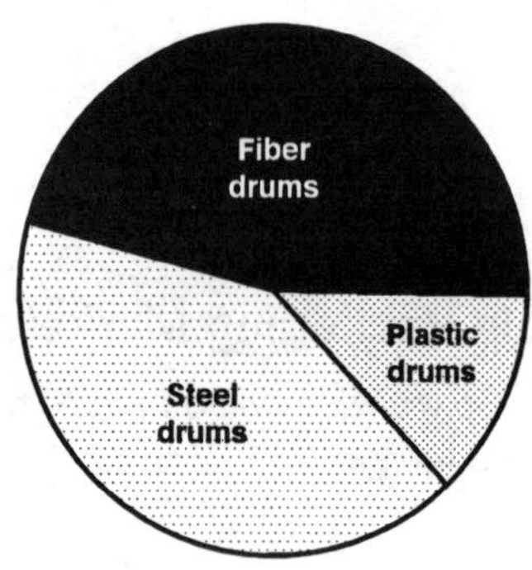

Market shares are estimated for the year 2000.

Fiber drums	46.0%
Steel drums	41.0
Plastic drums	13.0

Source: *Investext*, Thomson Financial Networks, August 6, 1996, p. 28, from Freedonia and Morgan Stanley Research.

★ 24 ★
Parking Tickets

Boston's Parking Ticket Revenues

Data show the revenues generated by parking ticket fines.

Chelsea	$ 800,000
Salem	527,000
Lynn	420,000
Malden	334,227
Everett	219,791
Revere	195,000
Beverly	170,535

Source: *Boston Sunday Globe*, November 3, 1996, p. 8, from local communities.

★ 25 ★
Patents

Patent Leaders - 1996

Data show who held the most patents.

IBM	1,867
Canon	1,538
Motorola	1,064
NEC	1,042
Hitachi	961
Mitsubishi	932
Toshiba	912
Fujitsu	868
Sony	854
Matsushita	837

Source: *Economist*, January 18, 1997, p. 5, from IFI, Plenum Data, and IBM.

★ 26 ★
Pets

U.S. Pet Population

Data are in thousands.

Cats	57,000
Dogs	52,500
Rabbits	4,600
Hamsters	1,300
Turtles	709
Lizards	314

Source: *Entrepeneur*, July 1996, p. 27, from American Veterinary Medical Association.

★ 27 ★

Private Label

Private Label Categories

Categories are ranked by mass merchandiser sales in millions of dollars.

Dog food	$ 329.4
Vitamins	240.2
Diapers	206.3
Internal analgesics	160.8
Carbonated beverages	145.3
Bottles juices	120.1
Cat food	92.4
Bottled water	91.5
Cold/sinus tablets/cough drops	83.1
Pet supplies	66.6

Source: *DM*, July 1996, p. 1, from Information Resources Inc. and Private Label Manufacturers Association.

★ 28 ★

Private Label

Private Label Health/Beauty Products

Dollar shares are shown in percent.

Cotton balls	39.0%
Vitamins	34.2
First aid treatment	23.6
Moist towelettes	22.9
Cold/allergy relief	20.0
Internal analgesics	18.6
Misc. health treatments	16.6
Mouthwash	16.3
Nasal sprays	15.6

Source: *Supermarket Business*, November 1996, p. 58, from Private Label Manufacturers Association.

★ 29 ★

Private Label

Top Private Label Items

Sales are shown in millions of dollars for the 52 weeks ended December 29, 1996.

Ice cream	$ 975.6
Carbonated beverages	856.0
Frozen plain vegetables	740.1
Sugar	689.8
Canned vegetables	645.3
Cold cereals	531.8
Bottled juices	480.2
Canned/bottled fruit	471.3
Cookies	444.1
Frozen juices	419.7

Source: *Supermarket News*, March 17, 1997, p. 46, from Information Resources Inc.

★ 30 ★

Promotional Products

Top Employee Incentive Gifts by Category

Categories are shown based on premium industry sales in 1995. The market reached $8.937 billion; an average corporation spends $244,000 a year on merchandise incentives and gifts.

Wearables	23.4%
Writing instruments	12.1
Glassware/ceramics	10.0
Calendars	8.9
Recognition awards, clocks and watches	7.8
Business accessories	6.4
Other	31.4

Source: *Advertising Age - Supplement*, May 1997, p. A4, from Promotional Products Association International.

★ 31 ★

R&D

R&D Expenditures - 1997

1997 research funding is shown by source based on the $192 billion forecast.

Industry	62.8%
Federal Government	32.4
Colleges & universities	3.2
Other nonprofit institutions	1.7

Source: *American Ceramics Society Bulletin*, February 2, 1997, p. 33, from Battelle.

★ 32 ★

R&D

Top R&D Spenders - 1995

Firms are ranked by R&D (research & development) expenditures in millions of dollars. The top 100 firms spent $77.2 billion.

General Motors	$ 8,387.9
Ford	6,509.0
IBM	5,227.0
AT&T	3,718.0
Lucent Technologies	2,697.0
Hewlett-Packard	2,302.0
Motorola	2,197.0
Johnson & Johnson	1,634.0
Pfizer	1,442.4
Chrysler	1,400.0

Source: *Assembly*, August 1996, p. 11, from *Inside R&D*.

★ 33 ★

R&D

Who Performs R&D - 1997

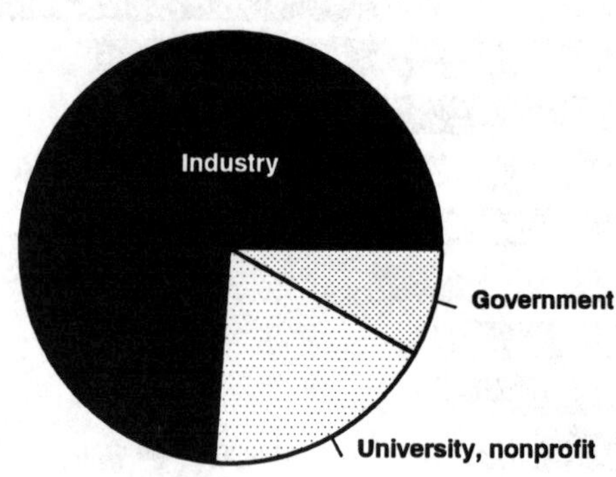

Industry	73.4%
University, nonprofit	18.2
Government	8.4

Source: *R&D Magazine*, January 1997, p. 12, from Batelle.

★ 34 ★

Roofing

Commercial Roofing Market

Data are for 1995.

Single-plies	40.5%
Built-up roofing	23.5
Modified bitumen	16.1
Metal	6.0
Other	13.1

Source: *Building Operating Management*, May 1996, p. 10, from National Roofing Contractors Association.

★ 35 ★

Scented Products

Home Fragrance Market

Distribution of the $600 million market is shown in percent.

Candles	56.0%
Potpourri	27.0
Specialty room products	6.0
All other	11.0

Source: *Soap/Cosmetic/Chemical Specialties*, January 1997, p. 78, from Kline & Company Inc.

★36★

Transportation

How Freight is Shipped

Rail	40.6%
Truck	27.2
Pipelines	17.7
Ships	14.1
Air	0.4

Source: *USA TODAY*, October 16, 1996, p. B1, from Association of American Railroads.

★37★

Volunteerism

Sources of American Volunteers

Data show the percent of volunteers coming from various kinds of organizations. Note that one volunteer may be a part of more than one group.

Church	60.0%
Workplace	20.4
School or college	13.5
Fraternal group or service club	11.5
Informal social group	7.1
Another volunteer group	12.8
Other	6.3

Source: *Wall Street Journal*, April 23, 1997, p. A20, from Gallop Organization for the Independent Sector.

★38★

Weddings

U.S. Weddings Market

The market was valued at over $32 billion.

Receptions	$ 6,600
Rings	3,300
Tableware	1,200
Dresses	604

Source: *Working Woman*, May 1997, p. 33.

★39★

Windows

Replacement Window Market - 1996

Shares of the 21.8 million unit market are shown in percent.

Vinyl	43.0%
Wood	40.0
Aluminum	17.0

Source: *Do-It-Yourself Retailing*, March 1997, p. 71, from American Architectural Manufacturers Association and National Wood Window and Door Association.

★ 40 ★

Produce (SIC 0100)

Supermarket Produce Sales

Item	Share
Apples	10.4%
Potatoes	7.0
Tomatoes	6.9
Citrus fruits	6.3
Bananas	5.9
Lettuce	5.8
Onions	3.0
Celery	1.9
Carrots	1.5
Mushrooms	1.5
Corn	1.2
Wild bird seed	0.7
Floral	0.4
Other vegetables	35.0
Other fruit	12.5

Source: *Supermarket Business*, October 1996, p. 28.

★ 41 ★

Corn (SIC 0115)

Corn Production by State

Data are in thousands of acres in 1996.

	(000)	Share
Kentucky	1,300	1.6%
North Carolina	1,000	1.2
Tennessee	770	1.0
Mississippi	630	0.8
Georgia	580	0.7
Louisiana	550	0.7
South Carolina	400	0.5
Alabama	310	0.4
Arkansas	200	0.2
Florida	140	0.2
Other	74,475	92.7

Source: *Farm Journal*, September 1996, p. 36, from United States Department of Agriculture.

★ 42 ★

Corn (SIC 0115)

Iowa's Corn Production

Data are in bushels per acre in 1996.

Central	151
North Central	147
Northwest	147
Northeast	139
West Central	139
East Central	137
Southeast	129
Southwest	125
South Central	112

Source: *Wallace's Farmer*, January 1997, p. 9, from Iowa Agricultural Statistics and United States Department of Agriculture.

★ 43 ★

Corn (SIC 0115)

Top Seed Corn Producers - North America

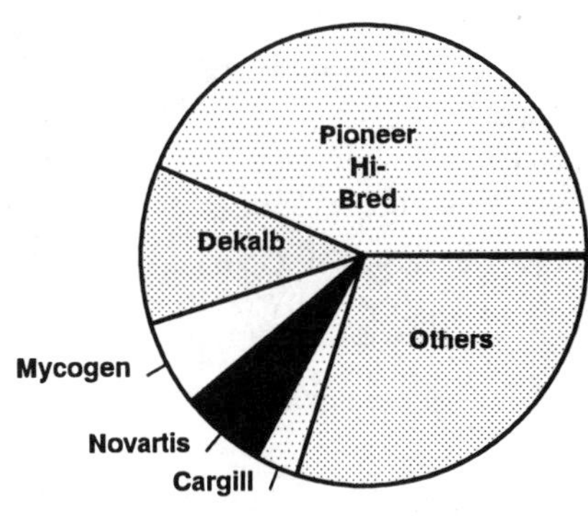

Company shares for the 1996 market are shown in percent.

Pioneer Hi-Bred	44.0%
Dekalb	11.0
Mycogen	6.0
Novartis	6.0
Cargill	3.0
Others	30.0

Source: *Investext*, Thomson Financial Networks, January 14, 1997, p. 3, from PHB, SEEDB, and GKB estimates.

★ 44 ★

Corn (SIC 0115)

Top Sweet Corn Growers

Firms are ranked by acreage.

Hundley Farms Inc.	9,055
P.J. Taggares Co.	5,560
Hartung Brothers Inc.	5,434
R.C. Hatton Inc.	4,500
Turek Farms	3,598
Suwannee Farms	3,075

Source: *American Vegetable Grower*, October 1996, p. 10.

★ 45 ★

Soybeans (SIC 0116)

Iowa's Soybeans Production

Data are in bushels per acre in 1996.

Central	47
Northwest	47
Northeast	46
North Central	46
East Central	45
West Central	43
Southeast	42
Southwest	37
South Central	34

Source: *Wallace's Farmer*, January 1997, p. 9, from Iowa Agricultural Statistics and United States Department of Agriculture.

★ 46 ★

Soybeans (SIC 0116)

Top Soybean Producers - North America

Company shares for the 1996 market are shown in percent.

Pioneer H-Bred	17.0%
Asgrow	11.0
Dekalb	8.0
Novartis	8.0
Stine Seed Co.	4.0
Others	52.0

Source: *Investext*, Thomson Financial Networks, January 14, 1997, p. 3, from PHB, SEEDB, and GKB estimates.

★ 47 ★

Tobacco (SIC 0132)

Top Tobacco States

The four states shown account for more than 85% of tobacco production. States are ranked by 1995 cash receipts in millions of dollars.

North Carolina	$ 1,050.0
Kentucky	636.5
Tennessee	233.4
Virginia	174.9

Source: *American Banker*, August 30, 1996, p. 6, from States' Department of Agriculture and United States Department of Agriculture.

★ 48 ★

Potatoes (SIC 0134)

Top Potato Producing States - 1996

Idaho
Washington
Oregon, Wisconsin
Colorado, North Dakota
Minnesota
Maine
Other

States are ranked by potato production in billions of pounds. Total production reached 44.1 billion pounds.

	(bil.)	Share
Idaho	14.0	31.7%
Washington	9.5	21.5
Oregon, Wisconsin	3.1	7.0
Colorado, North Dakota	2.9	6.6
Minnesota	2.5	5.7
Maine	2.1	4.8
Other	10.0	22.7

Source: *USA TODAY*, May 29, 1997, p. B1, from U.S. Agriculture Department.

★ 49 ★

Vegetables (SIC 0161)

Bagged Lettuce Revenues

Revenues are shown in millions of dollars by year.

1996	$ 1,100
1995	889
1994	577
1993	312

Source: *USA TODAY*, November 13, 1996, p. B1, from International Fresh-Cut Produce Association and Information Resources Inc.

★ 50 ★

Vegetables (SIC 0161)

Top Bean Producers

Firms are ranked by acreage.

Hartung Brothers Inc.	8,961
Navajo Agricultural Products Industry	8,728
DiMare-Homestead	4,400
Thomas Produce Co.	3,900
Charles H. West Farms Inc.	2,728

Source: *American Vegetable Grower*, October 1996, p. 11.

★ 51 ★

Vegetables (SIC 0161)

Top Lettuce Producers

Firms are ranked by acreage.

Tanimura & Antle	19,030
Bruce Church Inc.	18,658
Nunes Vegetables Inc.	9,300
D'Arrigo Bros. Co. of California Inc.	9,100
Merrill Farms	6,262

Source: *American Vegetable Grower*, October 1996, p. 11.

★ 52 ★

Vegetables (SIC 0161)

Top Melon Growers

Firms are ranked by acreage.

Martori Farms	6,700
Dresick Farms Inc.	3,800
Starr Produce Co.	3,800
Griffin & Brand Inc.	3,750
Rosseau Farming Co.	1,900

Source: *American Vegetable Grower*, October 1996, p. 10.

★ 53 ★

Vegetables (SIC 0161)

Top Tomato Producers

Firms are ranked by acreage.

Pacific Tomato Growers Ltd.	14,053
DiMare-Homestead	9,560
Six L's Packing Co.	9,000
NT Gargiulo	6,000
Nobles Farms Inc.	4,000

Source: *American Vegetable Grower*, October 1996, p. 10.

★ 54 ★

Vegetables (SIC 0161)

Top Vegetable Growers - North

Hartung Brothers Inc.
A & W Farms
Paramount Farms Inc.
Heartland Farms Inc.
Charles H. West Farms Inc.
Empire Farms Inc.
Wysocki Farms Inc.
Okray Family Farms
Torrey Farms Inc.
Anthony Farms Inc.

Firms are ranked by acreage. Potatoes are the most commonly produced vegetable in this region, followed by sweet corn.

Hartung Brothers Inc.	22,415
A & W Farms	8,168
Paramount Farms Inc.	7,100
Heartland Farms Inc.	6,970
Charles H. West Farms Inc.	6,788
Empire Farms Inc.	5,500
Wysocki Farms Inc.	5,343
Okray Family Farms	5,282
Torrey Farms Inc.	4,600
Anthony Farms Inc.	4,450

Source: *American Vegetable Grower*, October 1996, p. 18.

★ 55 ★

Vegetables (SIC 0161)

Top Vegetable Growers - Southeast

Firms are ranked by acreage. Tomatoes are the most commonly produced vegetable in this region, followed by potatoes.

A. Duda Sons Inc.	30,000
Dimare-Homestead	17,370
Pacific Tomato Growers Ltd./Triple E. Produce	17,067
Six L's Packaging Co.	13,550
Hundley Farms Inc.	11,724
Thomas Produce Co.	10,175
Zellwin Farms Co.	8,815
Mecca Farms Inc.	8,005

Source: *American Vegetable Grower*, October 1996, p. 18.

★ 56 ★

Vegetables (SIC 0161)

Top Vegetable Growers - Southwest

Firms are ranked by acreage. Lettuce and onions are the most commonly produced vegetable in this region, followed by potatoes.

Navajo Agricultural Products Industry	16,108
Griffin and Brand Inc.	10,450
Marton Farms	7,700
Sharyland Plantation	6,435
Greer Farms	5,900
Rousseau Farming Co.	5,780
J.S. McManus Produce Co.	5,150
Pasquinelli Produce Co.	4,939
Starr Produce Co.	4,900
Holden Wallace Inc.	3,990

Source: *American Vegetable Grower*, October 1996, p. 18.

★ 57 ★

Vegetables (SIC 0161)

Top Vegetable Growers - West

Firms are ranked by acreage. Lettuce is the most commonly produced vegetable in this region, followed by potatoes.

Grimmway Farms	35,040
Tanimura & Antle	32,443
Bruce Church Inc.	21,632

Continued on next page.

★ 57 ★ *Continued*

Vegetables (SIC 0161)

Top Vegetable Growers - West

Firms are ranked by acreage. Lettuce is the most commonly produced vegetable in this region, followed by potatoes.

D'Arrigo Bros. Co. of California Inc.	20,090
Boskovich Farms Inc.	16,550
Blaine Larsen Farms	16,200
P.J. Taggares Co.	15,625
Dresick Farms Inc.	13,950
Rio Farms	13,300
AgriNorthwest	13,000

Source: *American Vegetable Grower*, October 1996, p. 18.

★ 58 ★

Watermelons (SIC 0161)

Top Watermelon Harvesting States

States are ranked by acres of watermelons harvested.

Texas	47,500
Georgia	35,000
Florida	33,000
California	17,200
South Carolina	11,000
North Carolina	9,300
Oklahoma	9,000
Alabama	8,000
Arizona	6,800
Indiana	6,600
Mississippi	6,500
Missouri	5,400
Maryland	2,800
Lousiana	2,500
Arkansas	2,400

Source: *American Vegetable Grower*, April 1997, p. 54, from U.S. Department of Agriculture Economic Research Service.

★ 59 ★

Berries (SIC 0172)

Top Berry Growers

Companies are ranked by total acreage devoted to berry production.

Cherryfield Foods Inc.	8,400
Jasper Wyman & Sons	7,009
Northland Cranberries Inc.	2,299
Merrill Blueberry Farms Inc.	2,063
A.D. Makepeace Co.	1,475
Atlantic Blueberry Co.	1,320
Haines & Haines Inc.	1,115
Gargiulo Inc..	1,085
Reiter Affiliated Companies	820
Adkin Blue Ribbon Pkg. Co. Inc.	800

Source: *Fruit Grower*, August 1996, p. 12.

★ 60 ★

Grapes (SIC 0172)

Leading Grape Growers

Companies are ranked by total acreage devoted to grape production.

Delicato Vineyards/San Bernabe Vineyards	12,520
Simpson Farm Co.	12,004
Giumarra Vineyards Corp.	10,000
Golden State Vintners	9,500
Beringer Wine Estates	7,033
Dole Food Company Inc.	7,000
Sun World	6,871
Wine World Estates	6,667
E & J Gallo Winery	6,200
McCarty Co.	6,200
Vino Farms Inc.	5,409
Met West Agribusiness	5,400

Source: *Fruit Grower*, August 1996, p. 12.

★ 61 ★

Grapes (SIC 0172)

Virginia's Grape Acreage by County

	Acres	Share
Orange	200	14.9%
Fauquier	171	12.8
Albemarle	169	12.6
Loudon	128	9.5
Madison	119	8.9
Westmoreland	55	4.1
James City	49	3.7
Shenandoah	48	3.6
Rappahannock	44	3.3
Augusta	35	2.6
Nelson	35	2.6
Frederick	31	2.3

Continued on next page.

★ 61 ★ *Continued*

Grapes (SIC 0172)

Virginia's Grape Acreage by County

	Acres	Share
King George	30	2.2%
Floyd	28	2.1
Other	199	14.8

Source: http:// www.reap.vt.edu/reap/hor7-1htm, February 1995, p. 2.

★ 62 ★

Nuts (SIC 0173)

Leading Nut Growers

Companies are ranked by total acreage devoted to nut production.

Paramount Farming Co./Paramount Citrus	36,409
Diamond Agraindustries	8,619
Dole Food Company Inc.	8,300
Farmland Management Services	8,202
Ka'U Agribusiness Co. Inc.	6,415
Farmers Investment Co.	6,293
Lassen Land Co.	5,610
Braden Farms Inc.	5,388
Pecan Valley Nut Company	4,500
Premiere Partners Ill/Westchester Group Inc.	4,078
McFarms of Hawaii Inc.	3,800
Capital Agricultural Property Services Inc.	3,610

Source: *Fruit Grower*, August 1996, p. 12.

★ 63 ★

Fruit (SIC 0174)

Apple Production by State - 1996

States are ranked by production in thousands of 42-lb. bushels. The most popular variety was the red delicious. Total production reached 255.56 million bushels.

	(000)	Share
Washington	133,333	52.2%
New York	25,000	9.8
California	22,619	8.9
Michigan	19,643	7.7
Pennsylvania	9,524	3.7
Virginia	7,619	3.0
Oregon	4,405	1.7%
North Carolina	4,286	1.7
Idaho	4,048	1.6
West Virginia	2,857	1.1
Other	22,226	8.7

Source: *American Fruit Grower*, September 1996, p. 7, from United States Department of Agriculture.

★ 64 ★

Fruit (SIC 0175)

Top Apple & Pear Growers

Companies are ranked by total acreage devoted to apple and pear production.

Brewster Heights Packing	5,150
Naumes Inc.	4,763
Stemilt Management Inc.	4,603
Evans Fruit Farms	4,482
Broetje Orchards	4,000
Fruit Hill Orchards Inc.	3,148
Capital Agricultural Property Services Inc.	3,117
Bowman Agricultural Enterprises LLC	3,100
Northwestern Fruit & Produce Co.	2,999
Borten & Sons Inc.	2,674
Fowler Brothers Inc.	2,195
National Fruit Product Co. Inc.	2,015

Source: *Fruit Grower*, August 1996, p. 11.

★ 65 ★

Fruit (SIC 0175)

Top Peach States

Data show millions of pounds produced in 1994.

California	632
South Carolina	250
Georgia	175
New Jersey	75
Michigan	10

Source: *American Fruit Grower*, October 1996, p. 16.

★ 66 ★

Fruit (SIC 0175)

Top Stone Fruit Growers

Companies are ranked by total acreage devoted to stone fruit production.

Gerawan Farming	4,600
Lane Packing Co.	4,000
Sun World	3,531
California Fruit Packing	3,162
Taylor Orchards	3,054
Evans Farms	2,952
J.W. Yonce & Sons Farms Inc.	2,675
Fowler Packing Co. Inc.	2,660
Thiara Brothers Orchards	2,275
ITO Packing Co. Inc.	2,263

Source: *Fruit Grower*, August 1996, p. 11.

★ 67 ★

Floriculture (SIC 0181)

Green Goods Market - 1996

Shares shown are based on a $17.81 billion retail market.

Evergreens	39.6%
Shade/flowering trees	17.9
Bedding/garden plants	16.5
Flowering plants	11.3
Fruit/nut plants	7.5
Foliage plants	4.5
Bulbs	2.7

Source: *Nursery Retailer*, February/March 1997, p. 65.

★ 68 ★

Floriculture (SIC 0181)

L&G Sales by State

California
New York
Texas
Pennsylvania
Illinois
Ohio
Michigan
Florida
New Jersey
Massachusetts
Other

The leading states are ranked by lawn and garden (L&G) sales in millions of dollars.

	Sales ($ mil.)	Share
California	$ 7,349.0	10.3%
New York	5,712.0	8.0
Texas	4,326.0	6.1
Pennsylvania	3,782.0	5.3
Illinois	3,618.0	5.1
Ohio	3,474.0	4.9
Michigan	2,964.0	4.2
Florida	2,878.0	4.0
New Jersey	2,359.0	3.3
Massachusetts	1,860.0	2.6
Other	32,908.0	46.2

Source: *Nursery Retailer*, February/March 1997, p. 66.

★ 69 ★

Floriculture (SIC 0181)

Lawn/Garden Sales by Segment

Distribution is shown based on sales of $22.2 billion.

Lawn products	34.2%
Landscaping	24.8
Flower gardens	9.5
Vegetable gardens	6.3
Insect control	4.5
Indoor plants	4.1
Other products	16.7

Source: *New York Times*, September 28, 1996, p. 23, from National Gardening Association.

★70★

Floriculture (SIC 0181)

Top Flower Gardening Markets

The top markets are shown as a percentage of households with gardens.

Eugene, OR	42.3%
Bangor, Maine	42.2
Eureka, CA	41.7
Glendive, Montana	41.7
Medford/Klamath Falls, OR	41.7
Portland, OR	41.7

Source: *USA TODAY*, May 12, 1997, p. D1, from Polk.

★71★

Floriculture (SIC 0181)

U.S. Flower/Plant Imports

Data show the source of $532 million in imports in 1995.

Colombia	61.0%
Netherlands	13.0
Ecuador	9.0
Costa Rica	5.0
Other	12.0

Source: *Journal of Commerce*, July 25, 1996, p. 1, from Global Trade Information.

★72★

Seeds (SIC 0181)

Grass Seed Production - 1995

Total production reached 559.13 million pounds in 1995. Distribution is shown by type.

	(000)	Share
Perennial ryegrass	170,365	59.6%
Tall fescue	83,733	29.3
Kentucky bluegrass	13,920	4.9
Chewings fescue	8,259	2.9
Red fescue	3,561	1.2
Creeping bentgrass	3,478	1.2
Colonial bentgrass	2,715	0.9

Source: *Grounds Maintenance*, August 1996, p. 10, from Extension Economic Information Office, Oregon State University.

SIC 02 - Agricultural Production - Livestock

★ 73 ★

Cattle (SIC 0211)

Montana Cattle Breeds

Figures show the leading breeds, based on a survey.

Breed	Share
Angus	35.0%
Hereford	23.0
Red Angus	12.0
Angus Cross	9.0
Black Angus	9.0
Hereford-Angus	8.0
Other	4.0

Source: *Montana Business Quarterly*, Autumn 1996, p. 11.

★ 74 ★

Cattle (SIC 0212)

Feed Cattle Producers

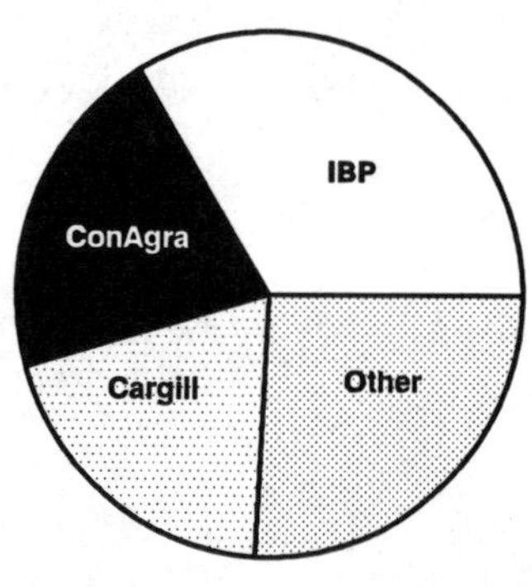

Data are for 1996.

	Heads (mil.)	Share
IBP	9.8	33.6%
ConAgra	6.1	20.9
Cargill	5.8	19.9
Other	7.5	25.7

Source: *Investext,* Thomson Financial Networks, March 7, 1997, p. 54.

★ 75 ★

Cattle (SIC 0212)

Largest Cattle Ranches - Tampa Bay

Ranches are ranked by number of cattle.

Schroder	2,700
Circle B Bar Ranch	2,500
Audubon Ranch	2,400
Hi Hat Ranch	1,500
Berthie Brothers Ranch	1,000
Two Rivers Ranch	1,000
Anclote River Ranch	995
Bexley Brothers Cattle Co.	992
K Bar Ranch	900
Myakka Ranch	750

Source: *Tampa Bay Business Journal*, September 6, 1996, p. 15.

★ 76 ★

Milk Cows (SIC 0212)

Milk Cows by County

County	Cows
Tulare, CA	247,500
San Bernadino, CA	162,400
Merced, CA	155,000
Stanislaus, CA	133,400
Riverside, CA	122,700
Maricopa, AZ	103,000
Kings, CA	98,000
Lancaster, PA	95,000
Erath, TX	90,400
San Joaquin, CA	78,500

Source: *Milwaukee Journal Sentinel*, October 4, 1996, p. A10, from National Agricultural Statistics Service.

★ 77 ★

Hogs (SIC 0213)

Hog Production by State

Breeding herds are shown in thousands of heads.

Iowa	1,250
North Carolina	980
Illinois	560
Minnesota	560
Missouri	520
Indiana	450
South Dakota	450
Ohio	220
Nebraska	185
Oklahoma	160

Source: *Wallace's Farmer*, November 1996, p. C10.

★ 78 ★

Hogs (SIC 0213)

Largest Pork Producers

Companies are ranked by number of sows in production in 1996.

Murphy Family Farms	260,300
Smithfield Foods	112,000
Carroll's Foods	111,400
Tyson Foods	110,000
Premium Standard Farms	105,000
Prestage Farms	102,200
Cargill	90,000
Seaboard Corporation	90,000
DeKalb Swine Breeders	72,000
Iowa Select Farms	62,000
Goldsboro Milling Company	54,000
Continental Grain Company	52,000
Heartland Pork Enterprises	36,400
National Farms	34,000
Sand Systems	27,000

Source: *Successful Farming*, October 1996, p. 28.

★ 79 ★

Poultry (SIC 0251)

Egg Layers by State

Data show number of layers as of August 1996.

California	24,623
Ohio	23,748
Indiana	20,497
Pennsylvania	19,350
Iowa	18,800
Texas	12,631
Minnesota	11,445
Georgia	10,670
Nebraska	9,030
Florida	8,136
Missouri	5,705
North Carolina	5,446
Arizona	4,933
Maine	4,929

Source: *Egg Industry*, November 1996, p. 9.

★ 80 ★

Poultry (SIC 0251)

Largest Poultry Producers

Firms are ranked by average weekly ready-to-cook production in millions of pounds during the past year.

Tyson Foods Inc.	124.50
Gold Kist Inc.	49.40
Perdue Farms Inc.	46.96
ConAgra Poultry Company	31.70
Hudson Foods Inc.	30.26
Pilgrim's Pride Corporation	30.00
Wayne Poultry/Continental Grain	22.79
Cagle's Inc.	16.03
Seaboard Farms Inc.	14.20
Foster Farms	13.47
Townsend's Inc.	12.76
Fieldale Farms Corporation	12.44
Sanderson Farms Inc.	12.37
Wampler Foods Inc. (Chicken Div.)	11.50
Allen Family Foods Inc.	10.90

Source: *Broiler Industry*, January 1997, p. 22C.

★ 81 ★

Poultry (SIC 0251)

Top Broiler States - 1995

Production is shown in millions of dollars.

Georgia	$ 1,772
Arkansas	1,769
Alabama	1,438
North Carolina	1,162
Mississippi	992
Texas	646
Delaware	474
Maryland	462
Virginia	401
California	383

Source: *Broiler Industry*, January 1997, p. 22E, from United States Department of Agriculture.

★ 82 ★

Poultry (SIC 0251)

U.S. Broiler Producers

Data are for 1996.

	Lbs. (bil.)	Share
Tyson	6.47	25.6%
Gold Kist	2.57	10.2
Perdue/Showell	2.44	9.6
ConAgra	1.65	6.5
Hudson Foods	1.58	6.2
Pilgrim's Pride	1.56	6.2
Cont. Grain	1.19	4.7
Other	7.84	31.0

Source: *Investext,* Thomson Financial Networks, March 7, 1997, p. 54.

★ 83 ★

Eggs (SIC 0252)

1996 Egg Sales

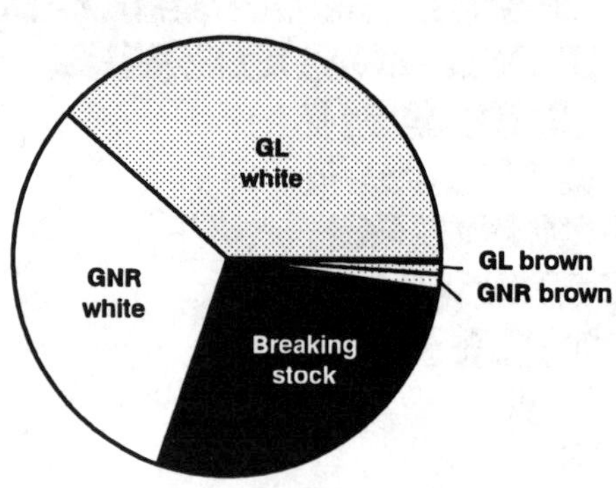

Egg sales are shown by type based on the 8,861 loads traded.

GL white	38.9%
GNR white	31.0
Breaking stock	28.0
GNR brown	1.4
GL brown	0.9

Source: *Egg Industry*, March 1997, p. 20, from United States Department of Agriculture.

★ 84 ★

Eggs (SIC 0252)

Shell Egg Sales

Sales of all shell eggs in the United States in 1995.

Retail (cartoned)	51.0%
Egg products	27.7
Foodservice (loose)	19.7
Export	1.6

Source: *Egg Industry*, August 1996, p. 5.

★ 85 ★

Eggs (SIC 0252)

Top Egg Liquid Processors

Companies are ranked by millions of pounds of liquid processed for foodservice and retail markets. Shares are shown based on 1.66 billion pounds of liquid eggs.

	(mil.)	Share
Papetti's Hygrade Egg Products	576.0	34.7%
Classic Egg Products	250.0	15.1

Continued on next page.

★ 85 ★ *Continued*

Eggs (SIC 0252)

Top Egg Liquid Processors

Companies are ranked by millions of pounds of liquid processed for foodservice and retail markets. Shares are shown based on 1.66 billion pounds of liquid eggs.

	(mil.)	Share
Sunny Fresh Foods	150.0	9.0%
Deb-El Foods Corp.	65.0	3.9
Echo Lake Farm	62.0	3.7
Brown Produce	61.5	3.7
National Egg Products	60.0	3.6
Wabash Valley Produce	50.0	3.0
Oskaloosa Foods Products Corp.	46.0	2.8
Other	339.5	20.5

Source: *Egg Industry*, January 1997, p. 4.

★ 86 ★

Eggs (SIC 0252)

Top Egg Producers

Data show millions of layers in production as of December 31, 1996. Shares are shown based on 190.6 million layers in production at the top 61 companies.

	(mil.)	Share
Cal-Maine Foods Inc.	15.9	8.3%
Michael Foods Inc.	15.2	8.0
Rose Acre Farms Inc.	12.7	6.7
DeCoster Egg Farms	9.7	5.1
Agri-General Corp.	9.0	4.7
Fort Recovery Equity	7.1	3.7
ISE America	5.9	3.1
Papetti Hygrade Eggs	5.1	2.7
Mahard Egg Farms	4.8	2.5
Hillandale Farms	4.4	2.3
Dutchland Farms	4.3	2.3
Midwest Poultry Services	4.2	2.2
Other	92.3	48.4

Source: *Egg Industry*, January 1997, p. 3.

★ 87 ★

Eggs (SIC 0252)

Top Shell Egg Processors

Data show the leading companies involved in breaking shell eggs into liquid. Figures are in millions of dozens of eggs broken in 1996. Shares are shown based on 1.269 billion dozen eggs processed into liquid by the top 38 firms.

	(mil.)	Share
Papetti's Hygrade Egg Products	360.0	28.4%
Sonstegard Foods Inc.	150.0	11.8
Daybreak Foods	67.5	5.3
Rose Acre Farms	50.0	3.9
National Egg Products	46.8	3.7
Echo Lake Farm	46.0	3.6
Other	548.7	43.2

Source: *Egg Industry*, January 1997, p. 3.

★ 88 ★

Turkeys (SIC 0253)

Turkey Production by State

North Carolina	20.9%
Minnesota	13.8
Arkansas	8.9
Virginia	8.0
Missouri	7.7
California	7.5
India	4.9
Other	28.3

Source: *Turkey Hatchery*, January 1996, p. 3, from National Agricultural Statistics Service.

★ 89 ★

Turkeys (SIC 0253)

U.S. Turkey Producers

Data are for 1996.

	Lbs. (bil.)	Share
ConAgra	925	17.8%
WRL/Cuddy	770	14.8
Hormel	573	11.0
Carolina	462	8.9
Rocco	503	9.7
Cargill	488	9.4
Sara Lee	430	8.3
Other	1,055	20.3

Source: *Investext,* Thomson Financial Networks, March 7, 1997, p. 54.

★ 90 ★

Horses (SIC 0272)

Horse Registrations - 1996

Quarter horses
Paint horses
Thoroughbred
Appaloosa
Arabian
Standardbred
Tennessee Walking Horse
Anglo & Half-Arab
Saddlebred
Morgan Horse

Figures are estimated.

Quarter horses	114,000
Paint horses	40,300
Thoroughbred	35,700
Appaloosa	12,500
Arabian	12,500
Standardbred	10,000
Tennessee Walking Horse	10,000
Anglo & Half-Arab	4,200
Saddlebred	3,300
Morgan Horse	3,100

Source: *Equus,* November 1996, p. 34, from associations.

★ 91 ★

Horses (SIC 0272)

Thoroughbred Foal Crop by State

Data are for 1994.

Kentucky	20.30%
Florida	10.12
California	10.02
Texas	6.67
Oklahoma	4.23
Louisiana	4.18
Illinois	3.37
New York	3.34
Maryland	3.31
Washington	3.28
Pennsylvania	2.30
Ohio	2.07
Other	19.40

Source: *Equus,* November 1996, p. 37.

★ 92 ★

Honey (SIC 0279)

Top Honey Producing States - 1996

States are ranked by production in thousands of pounds. Total production reached 198,095,000 pounds.

California	27,300
Florida	25,200
South Dakota	23,280
North Dakota	19,780
Minnesota	11,550
Michigan	8,640
Montana	7,020
Texas	6,806
New York	5,440
Wisconsin	5,382

Source: *American Bee Journal,* April 1997, p. 264, from United States Department of Agriculture.

★93★

Farms (SIC 0291)

Farm Receipts by State

Sales are shown in billions of dollars.

California	$ 18.10
Texas	12.00
Iowa	10.20
California Central Valley	9.20
Nebraska	8.89
Illinois	7.70

Source: *Economic Development Horizon*, April 1996, p. 11, from California Agricultural Statistics Review.

SIC 08 - Forestry

★ 94 ★

Timber (SIC 0811)

Timber Harvest by Region

South Central	29.32%
Southeast	25.58
Pacific Northwest	15.91
North central	9.00
Northeast	8.09
Pacific Southwest	5.57
Rocky Mountains	4.76
Alaska	1.47
Great Plains	0.31

Source: *Pulp & Paper*, September 1996, p. 76.

★ 95 ★

Timber (SIC 0811)

Top Christmas Tree Growing States - 1995

North Carolina
Oregon
Michigan
Pennsylvania
Washington
Wisconsin
California

Top tree growing states are ranked by harvest value in millions of dollars. Oregon, Michigan, and Wisconsin sell a majority of trees wholesale; figures for other states include wholesale and retail. A total of 37.1 million Christmas trees were sold nationwide in 1995.

North Carolina	$ 90.0
Oregon	80.0
Michigan	52.0
Pennsylvania	52.0
Washington	38.0
Wisconsin	32.0
California	27.0

Source: *Business North Carolina*, December 1996, p. 60, from state tree-growers associations and National Christmas Tree Association.

SIC 09 - Fishing, Hunting, and Trapping

★ 96 ★

Fish Hatcheries (SIC 0921)

Catfish Production by State

Data are in thousands of live weight pounds for 1995.

	(000)	Share
Missouri	231.887	66.6%
Alabama	50.883	14.6
Arkansas	38.870	11.2
Louisiana	26.700	7.7

Source: *Catfish Production. National Agricultural Statistics Service*, October 1995, p. 2, from United States Department of Agriculture.

★ 97 ★

Fishing (SIC 0970)

Canadian Recreational Fishing

Data show the most popular types of catches.

Trout	29.0%
Walleye	15.0
Pike	11.0
Bass	10.0
Smelt	8.0

Source: *World Trade*, April 1997, p. 42.

SIC 10 - Metal Mining

★ 98 ★

Taconite (SIC 1011)

Taconite Producers

Production is shown in thousands of long tons.

	(000)	Share
Minntac	13,645	29.2%
Hibbing Taconite	8,469	18.1
LTV Steel Mining Company	7,752	16.6
Eveleth Mines	5,236	11.2
National Steel Pellet Company	5,090	10.9
Northshore Mining	3,751	8.0
Minorca Plant	2,778	5.9

Source: *Corporate Report Minnesota*, September 1996, p. 54, from Michigan State University Department of Resource Development.

★ 99 ★

Copper (SIC 1021)

Top U.S. Copper Mines

Mines are ranked by capacity in thousands of metric tons. Locations are shown in parentheses.

Morenci (Arizona)	400
Bingham Canyon (Utah)	310
San Manuel (Arizona)	170
Chino (New Mexico)	160
Ray (Arizona)	150
Sierrita (Arizona)	135
Bagdad (Arizona)	130
Mission Complex (Arizona)	90
Pinto Valley (Arizona)	90
Tyrone (New Mexico)	70

Source: *Minerals Yearbook: Metals and Materials*, Vol 1, 1994, p. 254, from United States Bureau of Mines.

★ 100 ★

Lead (SIC 1031)

Lead Production by State

Production is shown based on a total of 363 million tons. The Sweetwater mine in Missouri was the largest U.S. producer in 1994.

Missouri	79.9%
Montana	2.7
Other	17.4

Source: *Minerals Yearbook: Metals and Materials*, Vol 1, 1994, p. 453, from United States Bureau of Mines.

★ 101 ★

Silver (SIC 1044)

Silver Production by State - Mexico

Data are in tons.

	Tons	Share
Zacatecas	934	37.4%
Durango	357	14.3
Chihuahua	328	13.1
Sonora	108	4.3
Others	773	30.9

Source: *Latin American Economy & Business*, April 1997, p. 24, from Camara Minera.

★ 102 ★

Uranium (SIC 1094)

U.S. Uranium Production - 1996

Production is shown in millions of pounds.

Highland (Wyoming)	1.25
Crow Butte (Nebraska)	0.79
Kingsville Dome (Texas)	0.70
Rosita (Texas)	0.70
Uncle Sam (Louisiana)	0.70
Irigaray/Christensen (Wyoming)	0.65
White Mesa/Arizona Strip (Utah)	0.60
Donaldsonville (Louisiana)	0.40
El Mesquite (Texas)	0.30
Ambrosia Lake (New Mexico)	0.13

Source: *Engineering and Mining Journal*, March 1997, pp. 42-WW.

★ 103 ★

Palladium (SIC 1099)

Palladium by End Use

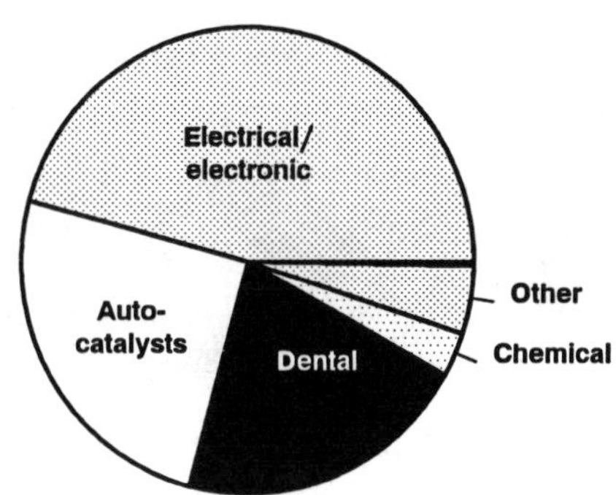

Consumption is shown for 1995.

Electrical/electronic	46.0%
Auto-catalysts	25.0
Dental	21.0
Chemical	3.0
Other	5.0

Source: *Purchasing*, August 15, 1996, p. 32B21, from Johnson Matthey.

SIC 12 - Coal Mining

★ 104 ★

Coal (SIC 1220)

U.S. Coal Producers

Firms are ranked by 1995 coal revenues in millions of dollars.

Peabody Holding	$ 2,100
Consol Coal Group	2,000
Cyprus Amax Coal	1,300
Arco Coal	762
Zeigler Coal Holding	754
Arch Mineral	730
Drummond	725
Interwest Mining	447
Kennecott Energy	377
Kerr-McGee Coal	353

Source: *Forbes*, September 9, 1996, p. 60, from Energy Ventures Analysis Inc. and company reports.

SIC 13 - Oil and Gas Extraction

★ 105 ★

Natural Gas (SIC 1311)

Natural Gas Production by State

Marketed gas production is shown by state in millions of cubic feet per day.

Texas	17,433
Louisiana	14,688
Oklahoma	4,879
New Mexico	4,572
Wyoming	2,075
Kansas	1,961
Colorado	1,386
Alaska	1,303
Alabama	1,054
California	758

Source: *Oil & Gas Journal*, January 27, 1997, p. 66.

★ 106 ★

Oil (SIC 1311)

Leading Oil Firms

Data show revenues in millions of dollars for the third quarter of 1996.

Exxon	$ 33.30
Mobil	20.30
Texaco	11.00
Chevron	10.85
Amoco	9.00

Source: *Financial Times*, October 22, 1996, p. 19, from companies.

★ 107 ★

Oil (SIC 1311)

Offshore Oil Production - North America

Data are in millions of barrels per day.

	1995	2000
Mexican offshore	1.947	2.402
U.S. Gulf of Mexico	1.010	2.027
Offshore California	0.251	0.221
Canadian Atlantic	0.021	0.144
Offshore Alaska	0.134	0.142

Source: *Oil & Gas Journal*, January 27, 1997, p. 38, from International Energy Agency.

★ 108 ★

Oil (SIC 1311)

U.S. Oil Reserves

Proven oil reserves by U.S. based companies are shown in billions of barrels in 1995.

Exxon	5.8
Chevron	4.3
Mobil	3.4
Texaco	2.7
Arco	2.4
Phillips	0.9
Occidental	0.9
USX	0.8
Unocal	0.7
Amerada Hess	0.6

Source: *Investor's Business Daily*, March 3, 1997, p. A2.

★ 109 ★

Oil Well Drilling (SIC 1381)

Rotary Rig Activity by State - 1996

Distribution is shown based on 778 rotary rigs in 1996.

Texas	36.4%
Louisiana	20.0
Oklahoma	13.6
New Mexico	4.4
California	3.5
Wyoming	3.1
Kansas	3.0
Other	16.0

Source: *Oil & Gas Journal*, January 27, 1997, p. 66, from Baker Hughes Inc.

★ 110 ★

Oil Well Drilling (SIC 1381)

Well Drilling by State - 1997

Data show number of exploratory and development wells expected to be drilled in 1997.

California	1,022
Texas	541
Louisiana	408
New Mexico	174
North Dakota	133
Oklahoma	133
Wyoming	44
Utah	34
Colorado	32

Source: *Oil & Gas Journal*, January 27, 1997, p. 66.

★ 111 ★

Oil Well Drilling (SIC 1381)

Well Drilling in Canada - 1997

Data show number of exploratory and development wells expected to be drilled in 1997.

Alberta	466
Northwest Territories	6
British Columbia	2

Source: *Oil & Gas Journal*, January 27, 1997, p. 66.

★ 112 ★

Oil Field Services (SIC 1389)

Leading Oil Field Service Firms

Firms are ranked by sales in millions of dollars for the latest 12 months.

Schlumberger	$ 8,504
Halliburton	6,701
Dresser Industries	6,562
Baker Hughes	3,028
Western Atlas	2,433

Source: *Forbes*, January 13, 1997, p. 143, from Value Line and One Source Information Services.

★ 113 ★

Dimension Stone (SIC 1411)

Dimension Limestone Production by State

Data are in thousands of metric tons.

	(000)	Share
Indiana	173,000	47.4%
Wisconsin	114,000	31.2
Kansas	23,700	6.5
Oklahoma	1,700	0.5
Other	52,900	14.5

Source: *Minerals Yearbook: Metals and Materials*, Vol. 1, 1994, p. 786, from United States Bureau of Mines.

★ 114 ★

Crushed Stone (SIC 1420)

Aggregate Demand by Region

Demand is shown in millions of metric tons for the first three quarters of 1996.

South Atlantic	235.3
East North Central	181.7
East South Central	116.2
West North Central	111.4
Middle Atlantic	109.7
West South Central	108.7
Pacific	63.5
Mountain	26.6
New England	17.1

Source: *Rock Products*, January 1997, p. 18, from U.S. Geological Survey Mineral Industry Surveys.

★ 115 ★

Crushed Stone (SIC 1420)

U.S. Crushed Stone Use

Data are in thousands of metric tons.

	(000)	Share
Limestone	788,000	64.2%
Granite	178,000	14.5
Dolomite	92,700	7.6
Trapock	91,000	7.4
Sandstone/quartzite	34,300	2.8
Calcareous marl	6,190	0.5
Marble	6,090	0.5
Slate	2,730	0.2
Volcanic cider and scoria	2,060	0.2
Other	25,600	2.1

Source: *Minerals Yearbook: Metals and Materials*, Vol. 1, 1994, p. 785, from United States Bureau of Mines.

★ 116 ★

Limestone (SIC 1422)

U.S. Crushed Limestone Use

Data are in thousands of metric tons.

	(000)	Share
Texas	72,000	9.1%
Missouri	64,400	8.2
Florida	64,200	8.2
Kentucky	56,100	7.1
Illinois	47,600	6.0
Pennsylvania	44,000	5.6
Other	439,000	55.8

Source: *Minerals Yearbook: Metals and Materials*, Vol. 1, 1994, p. 786, from United States Bureau of Mines.

★ 117 ★

Marble (SIC 1429)

Marble Production by State

Vermont
Arizona
Pennsylvania
Wyoming
New York
Other

Data are in thousands of metric tons.

	(000)	Share
Vermont	839	13.8%
Arizona	593	9.7
Pennsylvania	476	7.8
Wyoming	93	1.5
New York	87	1.4
Other	4,010	65.8

Source: *Minerals Yearbook: Metals and Materials*, Vol. 1, 1994, p. 786, from United States Bureau of Mines.

★ 118 ★

Clays (SIC 1455)

Ball Clay Use - 1995

Floor and wall tile	30.0%
Sanitaryware	24.0
Fillers/binders	16.0
Pottery	13.0
Refractories and ceramics	7.0
Other	10.0

Source: *Ceramic Industry*, January 1997, p. 32, from United States Geological Survey.

★ 119 ★

Clays (SIC 1455)

U.S. Kaolin Sales by Type

Distribution is shown based on value.

Water-washed	51.0%
Calcined	25.5
Delaminated	15.5
Airfloat	6.7
Unprocessed	1.2

Source: *Minerals Yearbook: Metals and Materials*, Vol 1, 1994, p. 234, from United States Bureau of Mines.

★ 120 ★

Clays (SIC 1459)

Fire Clay Consumption

End users are shown for 1994.

Ohio	39.0%
Missouri	28.1
Alabama	27.3
Other	5.6

Source: *Minerals Yearbook: Metals and Materials*, Vol 1, 1994, p. 232, from United States Bureau of Mines.

★ 121 ★

Clays (SIC 1459)

U.S. Clay/Shale Consumption

Data are in thousands of dollars. Figures do not include Puerto Rico.

	($000)	Share
Alabama	$ 18,900	13.3%
Texas	13,700	9.6
North Carolina	12,500	8.8
Georgia	11,200	7.9
Other	85,700	60.4

Source: *Minerals Yearbook: Metals and Materials*, Vol 1, 1994, p. 238, from United States Bureau of Mines.

★ 122 ★

Potash (SIC 1474)

Potash Sales by State

Data are in metric tons of potash equivalent.

Illinois	607,000
Iowa	455,000
Ohio	447,000
Indiana	403,000
Minnesota	305,000
Missouri	263,000
Wisconsin	239,000

Source: *Minerals Yearbook: Metals and Materials*, Vol 1, 1994, p. 620, from United States Bureau of Mines.

★ 123 ★

Perlite (SIC 1499)

U.S. Perlite Consumption

California	8.4%
Florida	7.4
Pennsylvania	7.0
Mississippi	5.9
Texas	3.8
Other	67.5

Source: *Minerals Yearbook: Metals and Materials*, Vol 1, 1994, p. 593, from United States Bureau of Mines.

SIC 15 - General Building Contractors

★ 124 ★

Building Construction (SIC 1500)

Building Permits by City - Arizona

Cities are ranked by building permits issued in the third quarter of 1996. Values are in millions of dollars.

Chandler	$ 539.0
Phoenix	407.0
Scottsdale	195.0
Mesa	168.0
Gilbert	142.0
Unincorporated Maricopa County	120.0
Tempe	114.0
Tucson	114.0
Unincorporated Pima County	96.0
Glendale	75.0
Peoria	43.0
Flagstaff	43.0

Source: *Arizona Business*, January 1997, p. 8, from Arizona State University.

★ 125 ★

Building Construction (SIC 1500)

Construction Spending - 1997

Data are in billions of dollars.

Nonresidential	$ 199.1
New residential	173.7
Heavy construction	124.6
Institutional	91.3
Industrial	32.0

Source: *Contractor*, December 1996, p. 5, from United States Department of Commerce and Cahners Economics.

★ 126 ★

Building Construction (SIC 1500)

Leading Construction Firms - Alaska

Davis Contractors & Engineers Inc.

Ken Brady Construction Co.

Spinell Homes Inc.

Firms are ranked by revenues in millions of dollars.

Davis Contractors & Engineers Inc.	$ 30.36
Ken Brady Construction Co.	26.94
Spinell Homes Inc.	19.23

Source: *Alaska Business Monthly*, October 1996, p. 101.

★ 127 ★

Building Construction (SIC 1500)

Major Contractors - San Diego, CA

Builders are ranked by 1996 billings in millions of dollars.

Nielsen Dillingham Builders	$ 207.0
Douglas E. Barnhart Inc.	92.0
Centex Rodgers Construction Co.	82.6
Soltek	72.6
Roel Construction Co. Inc.	72.0
Ninteman Construction Co. Inc.	65.9
Lusardi Construction Co.	65.1
C.E. Wytte Construction Co.	48.0
Collins General Contractors	46.6
Hensel Phelps Construction Co.	44.0

Source: *San Diego Business Journal*, October 28, 1996, p. 20, from companies.

★ 128 ★

Building Construction (SIC 1500)

Top Design-Build Firms - 1996

Firms are ranked by revenues in millions of dollars.

Bechtel Group Inc.	$ 7,103.0
Fluor Daniel Inc.	6,742.0
Jacobs Engineering Group Inc.	2,610.0
McDermott International Inc.	1,928.6
Raytheon Engineers & Constructors International	1,646.0
Foster Wheeler Corp.	1,593.6
M.W. Kellogg Co.	1,214.7
ABB Lummus Global Inc.	892.2
Brown & Root Inc.	885.8
Black & Veatch	796.0
Stone & Webster	785.0
Kvaerner Group	674.0
Chicago Bridge & Iron Co.	650.0
OHM Corp.	603.0
Parson's Corp.	473.8

Source: *ENR*, June 16, 1997, p. 50.

★ 129 ★

Building Construction (SIC 1500)

U.S. Construction Market by Segment

Data show the unadjusted values of 1996 construction contracts in millions of dollars.

	($ mil.)	Share
Nonresidential building	$ 115,513	35.6%
Residential building	144,624	44.6
Nonbuilding construction	64,398	19.8

Source: *Pit & Quarry*, March 1997, p. 10.

★ 130 ★

Residential Construction (SIC 1520)

Top Residential Construction Markets

Value are ranked by sales in billions of dollars for the first nine months of 1996.

Phoenix	$ 3.3
Atlanta	3.2
Chicago	2.9
Dallas	2.3
Washington	2.1
Las Vegas	1.9
Detroit	1.7
Mineapolis	1.6
Portland	1.5
Houston	1.5

Source: *Contractor*, December 1996, p. 3, from United States Department of Commerce.

★ 131 ★

Residential Construction (SIC 1521)

Home Builders - Phoenix, AZ

Data show the market share of residential builders based on number of permits.

Builder	Share
Del Webb Corp.	7.15%
Continental Homes Inc.	6.87
Hancock Homes	6.23
UDC Homes	4.85
Shea Homes	4.82
Pulte Homes Corp.	3.69
Trend Homes	3.20
Fulton Homes Corp.	3.13
Lennar Homes	2.24
Richmond America Homes Inc.	2.24

Continued on next page.

★ 131 ★ *Continued*

Residential Construction (SIC 1521)

Home Builders - Phoenix, AZ

Data show the market share of residential builders based on number of permits.

Robson Communities Inc.	2.10%
Other	53.48

Source: *Business Journal*, August 9, 1996, p. 12.

★ 132 ★

Residential Construction (SIC 1521)

Home Construction in Michigan

Data show the number of building permits by community.

Macomb Township	1,094
Shelby Township	815
Pittsfield Township	743
Canton Township	668
Chesterfield Township	549
West Bloomfield Township	487
Orion Township	482
Waterford Township	478
Rochester Hills	469
Novi	461

Source: *Detroit News*, October 27, 1996, p. C3, from Housing Consultants Inc.

★ 133 ★

Residential Construction (SIC 1521)

Home Sales in Chicago

Austin
Palatine
Schaumberg
Arlington Heights
Des Plaines
Belmont Cragin
Ashburn
Portage Park

Data show home sales in 1996.

Austin	2,243
Palatine	2,206
Schaumberg	2,106
Arlington Heights	2,089
Des Plaines	2,011
Belmont Cragin	1,982
Ashburn	1,666
Portage Park	1,656

Source: *Chicago Tribune*, January 28, 1997, p. C1, from Greater Illinois Title Co.

★ 134 ★

Residential Construction (SIC 1521)

Housing Starts in Alaska

Data show the value of residential housing permits in millions of dollars. Figures are for 1995.

Anchorage	$ 145.0
Juneau	37.4
Fairbanks	20.6
Kodiak Island Borough	4.3
Palmer	4.1

Source: *Alaska Business Monthly*, May 1996, p. 43.

★ 135 ★

Residential Construction (SIC 1521)

Housing Starts in Canada

Data are for the fourth quarter of 1996.

Ontario	46,700
Quebec	25,300
British Columbia	24,600
Alberta	18,200
Nova Scotia	4,300
Manitoba	2,700
Newfoundland	2,700
New Brunswick	2,600

Source: *Financial Post*, January 25, 1997, p. 4.

★ 136 ★

Residential Construction (SIC 1521)

Leading Home Builders - 1996

Firms are ranked by number of closings.

Pulte Home Corp.	14,673
Centex Corp.	13,283
A.G. Spanos Cos.	10,799
Kaufman and Broad Home Corp.	10,249
Ryland Group	8,388
U.S. Home Corp.	7,099

Continued on next page.

★136★ *Continued*

Residential Construction (SIC 1521)

Leading Home Builders - 1996

Firms are ranked by number of closings.

JPI Construction	6,445
Del Webb Corp.	6,136
Lennar Corp.	5,968
Beazer Homes USA	5,929

Source: *Wall Street Journal*, May 23, 1997, p. B8, from *Builder*.

★137★

Residential Construction (SIC 1521)

Leading Residential Builders

Firms are ranked by sales in millions of dollars for the latest 12 months.

Centex	$ 3,509
Pulte	2,294
Kaufman & Broad Home	1,745
Ryland Group	1,592
Champion Enterprises	1,588
Del Webb	1,109
Lennar	1,079
Oakwood Homes	974

Source: *Forbes*, January 13, 1997, p. 136, from Value Line and One Source Information Services.

★138★

Residential Construction (SIC 1521)

Leading Single-Family Home Builders - Louisville, KY

Southeast Development
Mareli Development
Hurstborne Ridge
Town & Country Homes
Monsour Builders

Companies are ranked by permits for 1996. There were 5,020 total permits issued for single-family homes.

Southeast Development	95
Mareli Development	53
Hurstborne Ridge	48
Town & Country Homes	47
Monsour Builders	46

Source: *Builder*, May 1997, p. 140, from HBA of Louisville.

★139★

Residential Construction (SIC 1521)

Residential Construction Market by Region

Data are in billions of dollars.

South	$ 41.1
West	28.7
Midwest	23.8
Northeast	9.9

Source: *Contractor*, December 1996, p. 1, from United States Department of Commerce and Cahners Economics.

★140★

Residential Construction (SIC 1521)

Single-Family Housing Permits

Data are for the first two quarters of 1996.

Atlanta, GA	20,000
Phoenix, AZ	16,191
Chicago, IL	12,242
Las Vegas, NV	10,829
Dallas, TX	9,749
Houston, TX	9,088
Detroit, MI	7,914

Continued on next page.

★ 140 ★ *Continued*

Residential Construction (SIC 1521)

Single-Family Housing Permits

Data are for the first two quarters of 1996.

Minneapolis, MN	7,547
Denver, CO	6,829

Source: *Builder*, January 1997, p. 48, from United States Housing Markets.

★ 141 ★

Residential Construction (SIC 1521)

Top Builders - 1996

Companies are ranked by housing revenues in thousands of dollars.

Pulte Home Corp.	$ 2,326,462
Centex Corp.	2,244,995
Kaufman and Broad Home Corp.	1,674,688
Champion Enterprises Inc.	1,640,000
Ryland Group	1,456,600
Fleetwood Enterprises Inc.	1,454,018
U.S. Home Corp.	1,178,938
NVR Inc.	1,045,900
Del Webb Corp.	1,011,829
Lennar Corp.	894,663
M.D.C. Holdings Inc.	880,358
Beazer Homes USA Inc.	868,137
Oakwood Homes Corp.	862,079
A.G. Spanos Cos.	800,000
Hovnanian Enterprises Inc.	764,682

Source: *Professional Builder*, April 1997, p. 130.

★ 142 ★

Residential Construction (SIC 1521)

Top Builders - Atlanta, GA

Shares are shown based on 26,809 units sold in 1996.

Torrey (now D.R. Horton)	4.5%
John Wieland	3.2
Pulte	3.2
Ryland	1.7
Colony	1.2
Beazer	1.0
Bowen & Bowen	0.9
Homeland	0.9
Traton	0.9
West Palm	0.8%
Other	81.7

Source: *Professional Builder*, April 1997, p. 117, from Magellan Information Services Corp.

★ 143 ★

Residential Construction (SIC 1521)

Top Builders - Chicago, IL

Shares are shown based on 18,860 units sold in 1996.

Cambridge Cos.	6.5%
Town & Country	5.2
Lakewood Homes	4.2
Concord Development Corp.	3.5
Kimball Hill Homes	3.5
Sundance Homes	3.5
Pulte	3.0
Neumann Homes	2.8
Pasquinelli Construction	2.5
Pontarelli Builders	2.1
Other	63.2

Source: *Professional Builder*, April 1997, p. 117, from Tracy Cross & Associates Inc.

★ 144 ★

Residential Construction (SIC 1521)

Top Builders - Dallas/Ft. Worth, TX

Shares are shown based on 22,496 starts in 1996.

Centex	7.5%
Highland	6.1
Choice	5.4
Weekley	4.2
Pulte	4.0
D.R. Horton	3.3
Drees	2.4
Lennar	2.4
Legacy	2.2
Sovereign	1.9
Other	60.6

Source: *Professional Builder*, April 1997, p. 117, from American Metro/Study Corp.

★145★

Residential Construction (SIC 1521)

Top Builders - Denver, CO

Richmond American
U.S. Home Corp.
Kaufman and Broad
Melody Homes
Oakwood Homes

Companies are ranked by closings for 1996. There were 12,510 permits issued for single-family homes.

Richmond American	1,721
U.S. Home Corp.	778
Kaufman and Broad	696
Melody Homes	659
Oakwood Homes	604

Source: *Builder,* May 1997, p. 128, from Genesis Group.

★146★

Residential Construction (SIC 1521)

Top Builders - Detroit, MI

Shares are shown based on 24,127 permits issued in 1996.

Bernard Glieberman Cos.	3.2%
Silverman Construction Co.	2.8
Pulte Homes	2.3
Rodney Lockwood Cos.	2.2
Edward Rose Co.	2.0
Singh/Grewal Cos.	2.0
Tri Mount-Vincenti Cos.	1.4
Ford Motor Land Co.	1.2
Anthony Lombardo Cos.	1.0
Moceri Cos.	1.0
Other	80.9

Source: *Professional Builder,* April 1997, p. 117, from Housing Consultants Inc.

★147★

Residential Construction (SIC 1521)

Top Builders - Houston, TX

Shares are shown based on 15,791 units sold in 1996.

MHI	6.9%
Royce	6.2
Village Builders (Lennar)	6.1%
Pulte	4.6
Weekley	4.3
Ryland	4.1
Perry	4.0
Kimball Hill	3.6
Emerald	2.8
General	2.5
Other	54.9

Source: *Professional Builder,* April 1997, p. 117, from American Metro/Study Corp.

★148★

Residential Construction (SIC 1521)

Top Builders - Las Vegas, NV

Shares are shown based on 19,036 units sold for the first three quarters of 1996.

Lewis Homes	8.0%
Del Webb	6.3
American West Homes	4.0
Pardee Construction (Weyerhaeuser)	3.0
Pulte Home Corp.	3.0
Pacific Homes	2.9
Rhodes Homes	2.6
Beazer Homes	2.5
U.S. Home Corp.	2.1
Developers of Nevada	2.0
Other	63.6

Source: *Professional Builder,* April 1997, p. 117, from Meyers Group.

★149★

Residential Construction (SIC 1521)

Top Builders - Minneapolis/St. Paul, MN

Market shares are shown based on 10,610 permits issued in 1996.

The Rottlund Co.	2.6%
Orrin Thompson Homes (U.S. Home)	2.4
Key-Land Homes	2.2
Kenco Construction	2.0
Lundgren Brothers	1.8
Novak-Fleck	1.5
Pulte	1.3
Joe Miller Homes	1.2
McDonald Construction	1.0

Continued on next page.

★ 149 ★ *Continued*

Residential Construction (SIC 1521)

Top Builders - Minneapolis/St. Paul, MN

Market shares are shown based on 10,610 permits issued in 1996.

M.W. Johnson Construction	1.0%
Other	83.0

Source: *Professional Builder*, April 1997, p. 120, from *Keystone Report*.

★ 150 ★

Residential Construction (SIC 1521)

Top Builders - Philadelphia, PA

Companies are ranked by closings for 1996. There were 12,490 permits issued for single-family homes.

Toll Brothers	923
Orleans Builders	519
Pulte Home Corp.	492
Ryan Homes	428
Realen Homes	381

Source: *Builder*, May 1997, p. 128, from Housing Data Reports.

★ 151 ★

Residential Construction (SIC 1521)

Top Builders - Phoenix/Mesa, AZ

Market shares are shown based on 28,065 permits issued in 1996.

Del Webb	8.0%
Continental Homes	7.3
Hancock Homes (Beazer)	6.5
UDC Homes	5.2
Shea Homes	5.0
Pulte Homes	3.7
Fulton Homes	3.3
Trend Homes/Key	3.3
Richmond American	2.6
Homes by Dave Brown	2.3
Other	52.8

Source: *Professional Builder*, April 1997, p. 120, from *R.L. Brown Housing Reports*.

★ 152 ★

Residential Construction (SIC 1521)

Top Builders - Portland/Vancouver

Market shares are shown based on 8,284 permits issued in the first three quarters of 1996.

West Hills Homes Inc.	1.9%
New Tradition Homes	1.8
Centex Real Estate Corp.	1.6
R.M.P. Properties	1.5
Polygon Northwest	1.4
Riverside Homes	1.4
Tenly Properties Corp.	1.2
Sun Country Homes Inc.	1.1
R.C. Olin	1.0
Quail Construction Inc.	1.0
Other	86.1

Source: *Professional Builder*, April 1997, p. 120, from Associated Marketing Resources.

★ 153 ★

Residential Construction (SIC 1521)

Top Builders - Tuscon, AZ

Companies are ranked by unit sales for 1996. There were 5,040 permits issued for single-family homes.

U.S. Home Corp.	406
Estes Homebuilding	370
Pulte Home Corp.	336
Richmond American	310
Robson Communities	290

Source: *Builder*, May 1997, p. 140, from The Meyers Group.

★ 154 ★

Residential Construction (SIC 1521)

Top Single-Family Home Builders - Boston, MA

Companies are ranked by permits for 1996. Figure for Pulte Home Corp. represents closings. There were 5,940 total permits issued for single- family homes.

Toll Brothers	172
Pulte Home Corp.	81
WGB Construction	78
Carruth Capital	37
Buendan Homes	35

Source: *Builder*, May 1997, p. 138, from Dallamora Realtors.

★ 155 ★

Residential Construction (SIC 1521)

Top Single-Family Home Builders - Fort Lauderdale, FL

Companies are ranked by closings for 1996. There were 9,550 permits issued for single-family homes.

Arvida/JMB Partners	928
Lennar Homes	726
G.L. Homes	725
Pulte Home Corp.	605
Westbrooke Communities	559

Source: *Builder*, May 1997, p. 132, from Price Waterhouse.

★ 156 ★

Residential Construction (SIC 1522)

Apartment Building Permits by City

Cities are ranked by multifamily building permits issued through June 30, 1996.

Phoenix	5,625
Las Vegas	5,119
Atlanta	4,445
Washington	4,195
Denver	4,177
Dallas/Fort Worth	3,912
Miami/Fort Lauderdale	3,687
Chicago	3,082
Portland, Oregon	2,722
Houston	2,648
Charlotte	2,564
Seattle	2,547
San Francisco	2,334
Tampa	2,245
Salt Lake City	2,173
Austin	2,055
Nashville	2,015
Jacksonville	1,996
New York/Long Island	1,835
Orange County	1,698

Source: *Urban Land*, November 1996, p. 22, from United States Housing Markets.

★ 157 ★

Residential Construction (SIC 1522)

Largest Markets for Multifamily Construction - 1996

Cities are ranked by value of permits in millions of dollars.

Phoenix	$ 565.4
Chicago	550.4
Las Vegas	520.7
Dallas	500.6
Atlanta	480.5
Seattle	455.4
New York City	453.2
Portland	383.5
Nashville	319.9
Fort Lauderdale	315.7

Source: *Building Design & Construction*, April 1997, p. 21.

★ 158 ★

Nonresidential Construction (SIC 1542)

Commercial Construction - 1996

Distribution is shown based on total spending of $76.5 billion.

Retail	56.0%
Office	30.0
Hotel & motel	14.0

Source: *Building Design & Construction*, November 1996, p. 19.

★ 159 ★

Nonresidential Construction (SIC 1542)

Construction in California

Data are in thousands of dollars for 1995.

Retail	$ 257,445
Office	134,079
Amusements	55,353
Hotels	4,456

Source: *Urban Land*, October 1996, p. 83, from Construction Industry Research Board.

★ 160 ★

Nonresidential Construction (SIC 1542)

Largest Lodging Design Firms

Firms are ranked by lodging design fees in millions of dollars.

Hirsch Bedner Associates	$ 16.39
Wimberly Allison Tong & Goo	15.05
Wilson & Associates	14.15
DiLeonardo International Inc.	10.92
Brennan Beer Gorman/Architects	9.60
Lynn Wilson Associates International	5.50
Daroff Design	4.00
Barry Design	3.40
Concepts 4 Inc.	2.65
The Gettys Group Inc.	2.00

Source: *Hotel & Motel Management*, November 4, 1996, p. 129.

★ 161 ★

Nonresidential Construction (SIC 1542)

Leading Commercial Builders

Firms are ranked by sales in millions of dollars for the latest 12 months.

Fluor	$ 11,015
Foster Wheeler	3,723
Turner	3,311
Jacobs Enginnering	1,799
Perini	1,225
Foster & Wheeler	1,187
Granite Construction	961

Source: *Forbes*, January 13, 1997, p. 136, from Value Line and One Source Information Services.

★ 162 ★

Nonresidential Construction (SIC 1542)

New Office Construction by Region

South Atlantic
Pacific
East North Central
Mountain
West South Central
West North Central
Mid-Atlantic
East South Central
New England

Data are in millions of square feet for 1995-2005.

	(mil.)	Share
South Atlantic	346	26.8%
Pacific	200	15.5
East North Central	152	11.8
Mountain	138	10.7
West South Central	119	9.2
West North Central	99	7.7
Mid-Atlantic	97	7.5
East South Central	91	7.1
New England	48	3.7

Source: *Building Operation & Management*, August 1996, p. 10, from Cognetics Inc.

SIC 16 - Heavy Construction, Except Building

★ 163 ★

Heavy Construction (SIC 1600)

Heavy Construction Contracts - 1997

Contract awards are shown in millions of dollars for 1997.

Highways and streets	$ 23,300
Water use and control	21,100
Sewerage/waste disposal	8,800
Bridges	7,850
Waterworks	7,200
Dams, reservoirs, waterways	5,100
Electric, gas, communications	2,700
Other	11,400

Source: *Engineering News Record*, January 27, 1997, p. 5, from F.W. Dodge division of McGraw-Hill Cos.

★ 164 ★

Highway Construction (SIC 1611)

New Road Construction by State - 1997

Construction is shown in millions of dollars for 1997.

North Carolina	$ 995
Florida	736
Georgia	333
California	325
Mississippi	325
Wisconsin	290
Pennsylvania	268
Missouri	266

Source: *Engineering News Record*, January 27, 1997, p. 52.

★ 165 ★

Bridge Construction (SIC 1622)

New Bridge Construction by State - 1997

Construction is shown in millions of dollars for 1997.

Florida	$ 186
North Carolina	149
Pennsylvania	116
New York	113
West Virginia	80
Wisconsin	77
Oklahoma	76

Source: *Engineering News Record*, January 27, 1997, p. 52.

SIC 17 - Special Trade Contractors

★ 166 ★

Contracting (SIC 1700)

Top Contractors

Contracting firms are ranked by billings in millions of dollars.

Turner Corp.	$ 2,798.0
Fluor Daniel Inc.	2,080.4
Clark Construction Group Inc.	1,332.9
Bovis Inc.	1,277.0
BE&K Inc.	1,160.9
Centex Construction Group	1,008.9
Hoffman Corp.	939.6
McCarthy	831.7
Austin Co.	812.1
Whiting-Turner Contracting Co.	686.2
Perini Corp.	672.8
Bechtel Group Inc.	636.3
Beers Construction Co.	623.2
J.A. Jones Construction Co.	607.0

Source: *Building Design & Construction*, July 1996, p. 26.

★ 167 ★

Contracting - Specialty (SIC 1700)

Top Specialty Contractors

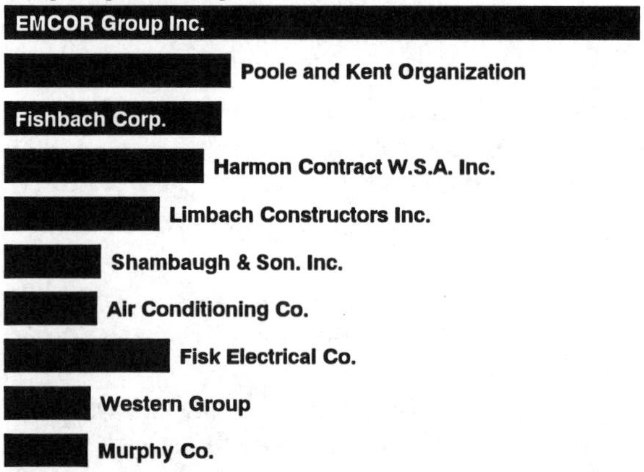

Contractors are ranked by 1995 billings in millions of dollars.

EMCOR Group Inc.	$ 858.0
Poole and Kent Organization	305.0
Fishbach Corp.	291.7
Harmon Contract W.S.A. Inc.	267.9
Limbach Constructors Inc.	207.9
Shambaugh & Son. Inc.	128.6
Air Conditioning Co.	124.0
Fisk Electrical Co.	223.0
Western Group	116.4
Murphy Co.	111.7

Source: *Building Design & Construction*, July 1996, p. 55.

★ 168 ★

Contracting - Mechanical (SIC 1711)

Major Mechanical Contractors

Firms are ranked by 1995 revenues in millions of dollars.

EMCOR Group Inc.	$ 645.8
Fishbach Corp.	319.3
Poole & Kent Co.	309.0

Continued on next page.

★168★ *Continued*

Contracting - Mechanical (SIC 1711)

Major Mechanical Contractors

Firms are ranked by 1995 revenues in millions of dollars.

Limbach Constructors Inc.	$ 218.9
MMC Corp.	204.5
Serv-Tech Inc.	195.7
Corrigan Co.	169.8
Murphy Co. Mech. Contr. & Engineers	153.4
Air Conditioning Co. Inc.	125.0
Southland Industries	121.9

Source: *Engineering News Record*, October 7, 1996, p. 31.

★169★

Contracting - Painting (SIC 1721)

Leading Paint Contractors

Firms are ranked by 1995 revenues in millions of dollars.

Cannon Sline	$ 35.6
J.L. Manta Inc.	29.6
M.L. McDonald Co.	25.5
Robison-Prezloso Inc.	24.7
Avalotis Painting Co. Inc.	23.0
Swanson & Youngdale Inc.	17.1
Fine Painting & Decorating Co. Inc.	15.1
Certified Coatings of California	13.4
Ascher Bros. Co. Inc.	12.7
Hartman-Walsh Painting Co.	11.9

Source: *Engineering News Record*, October 7, 1996, p. 38.

★170★

Contracting - Electrical (SIC 1731)

Largest Electrical Contractors - Cincinnati

Top companies in the tri-state area are ranked by 1995 contract volume in millions of dollars.

Garfield Group	$ 25.0
Mayers Electric Co. Inc.	19.5
Denier Electric Co. Inc.	16.0
Electrical Contractors Inc.	16.0
Edgewood Electric Inc.	15.0
Banta Electrical Contractors Inc.	12.8
Henderson Electric Company	$ 9.5
Sherrer Electrical Contracting Inc.	8.0
Archiable Electric Co.	4.7
T.J. Williams Electric Co.	3.4
Gilkey Electric Co.	2.8
Seco Electric Inc.	2.2

Source: *Cincinnati Business Courier*, August 12, 1996, p. 8C.

★171★

Contracting - Electrical (SIC 1731)

Leading Electrical Contractors

Firms are ranked by 1995 revenues in millions of dollars.

EMCOR Group Inc.	$ 814.3
Fishbach Corp.	314.7
SASCO Group	273.0
MYR Group	251.0
L.K. Comstock & Co.	181.6
Mass. Electric Construction Co.	179.2
Rosendin Electrica Inc.	144.9
Fisk Electric Co.	123.0
Cupertino Electric Inc.	104.9
Morrow - Meadows Corp.	102.0

Source: *Engineering News Record*, October 7, 1996, p. 28.

★172★

Contracting - Masonry (SIC 1741)

Leading Masonry Contractors

Firms are ranked by 1995 revenues in millions of dollars.

Western Group	$ 47.2
Dee Brown Inc.	34.8
Pyramid Masonry Contractors Inc.	28.4
Seedorff Masonry Inc.	26.3
WASCO Inc.	25.5
Thorleif Larsen & Son Inc.	24.7
J.D. Long Masonry Inc.	22.0
Sun Valley Masonry Inc.	21.1
Leonard Masonry Inc.	20.5
Mason Arts Inc.	17.4

Source: *Engineering News Record*, October 7, 1996, p. 32.

★ 173 ★

Contracting - Wall and Ceiling (SIC 1742)

Leading Wall and Ceiling Contractors

Firms are ranked by 1995 revenues in millions of dollars.

Performance Contracting Group Inc.	$ 118.6
Cleveland Construction Inc.	108.0
National Construction Enterprises Inc.	62.5
Anson Industries Inc.	56.7
Nastasi-White Inc.	55.5
Ellason & Knuth Cos. Inc.	54.8
Nastasi & Associates Inc.	50.2
Midwest Dryall Co. Inc.	48.0
Keenan, Hopkins, Schmidt & Stowell Cont. Inc.	43.9
Interior Construction Services Ltd.	37.0

Source: *Engineering News Record*, October 7, 1996, p. 38.

★ 174 ★

Contracting - Roofing (SIC 1761)

Leading Roofing Contractors

Firms are ranked by 1995 revenues in millions of dollars.

Centimark Corp.	$ 140.7
Hartford Roofing Co. Inc.	56.0
Schreiber Corp.	29.0
Campbell Cos.	25.7
J.P. Patti Co. Inc.	24.8
Baker Roofing Co.	24.5
Seyforth Roofing Co. Inc.	22.3
Olsson Roofing Co. Inc.	21.4
W.R. Kelso Co. Inc.	21.3
Birdair Inc.	21.3

Source: *Engineering News Record*, October 7, 1996, p. 34.

★ 175 ★

Contracting - Concrete (SIC 1771)

Top Concrete Contractors

Firms are ranked by 1995 revenues in millions of dollars.

Baker Concrete Construction Inc.	$ 186.0
Miller & Long Co. Inc.	94.8
Ceco Concrete Construction Corp.	82.6
Western Group	66.6
VSL Corp.	$ 54.0
Colasanti Corp.	43.8
Capform Inc.	42.0
T.A.S. Construction Inc.	38.8
Structural Preservation Systems Inc.	35.2
JESCO Inc.	31.5

Source: *Engineering News Record*, October 7, 1996, p. 32.

★ 176 ★

Contracting - Steel Erection (SIC 1791)

Steel Erection Contractors

Firms are ranked by 1995 revenues in millions of dollars.

Broad, Vogt & Conant Inc.	$ 93.3
Schuff Steel Co.	62.1
Williams Group Inc.	57.8
Midwest Steel Inc.	44.3
Interstate Iron Works Corp.	36.0
L.H. Sowles Co.	35.4
J.L. Davidson Co.Inc.	33.7
Derr Construction Co.	30.4
W.O. Grubb Steel Erection Inc.	26.0
Pittsburgh Tank & Tower Co. Inc.	21.7

Source: *Engineering News Record*, October 7, 1996, p. 33.

★ 177 ★

Contracting - Excavation & Foundation (SIC 1794)

Excavating/Foundation Contractors

Firms are ranked by 1995 revenues in millions of dollars.

Layne Christensen Co.	$ 163.5
Hayward Baker Inc.	66.9
Ryan Inc. Central	64.8
Malcolm Drilling Co. Inc.	54.1
Beaver Excavating Co.	51.2
McKinney Drilling Co.	43.6
AGRA Construction Group	43.3
Nicholson Construction Co.	42.7
Berkel & Co. Contractors Inc.	36.0
Case Foundation Co.	33.5

Source: *Engineering News Record*, October 7, 1996, p. 33.

★178★

Contracting - Demolition (SIC 1795)

Leading Wrecking Firms

Firms are ranked by 1995 revenues in millions of dollars.

Penhall International Inc.	$ 83.0
Cleveland Wrecking Co.	62.7
Philip Environmental Services Group	39.0
Bierlein Demolition Contractors Inc.	32.3
U.S. Dismantlement Corp.	30.2
Plant Reclamation/F. Scott Industries	22.1
Midwest Steel Co. Inc.	21.4
Indigo Industries Inc.	20.4
Allied Erecting & Dismantling Co. Inc.	19.5
Olshan Demolishing Inc.	19.5

Source: *Engineering News Record*, October 7, 1996, p. 41.

SIC 20 - Food and Kindred Products

★ 179 ★

Food (SIC 2000)

Best-Selling Grocery Products - 1996

Coke Classic
Pepsi
Campbell's soup
Kraft cheese
Folger's coffee
Diet Coke
Snackwell's cookies
Budweiser beer
Tropicana Pure Premium orange juice

Data show estimated sales in millions of dollars.

Coke Classic	$ 1,784
Pepsi	1,695
Campbell's soup	1,185
Kraft cheese	936
Folger's coffee	927
Diet Coke	846
Snackwell's cookies	810
Budweiser beer	750
Tropicana Pure Premium orange juice	681

Source: *USA TODAY*, December 17, 1996, p. B1, from Information Resources Inc.

★ 180 ★

Food (SIC 2000)

Ethnic Food Market

Retail sales are shown in millions of dollars.

	1996	2001
Pacific Rim	$ 196.0	$ 285.3
Mediterranean Rim	48.3	61.6
Caribbean Basin	27.9	35.9

Source: *Adweek*, March 24, 1997, p. 20.

★ 181 ★

Food (SIC 2000)

Fat-Free Food Market

Data show the market share of fat free or reduced fat items in selected categories.

Yogurt	84.2%
Lunch meat	54.2
Frankfurters	21.0
Breakfast sausage/ham	6.3

Source: *Prepared Foods*, February 1997, p. 48.

★ 182 ★

Food (SIC 2000)

Mexican Food Market - 1996

Distribution is shown based on $1.6 billion in sales.

Salsa	39.0%
Cheese/bean dips	13.0
Refried beans	9.0
Seasoning mix	8.0
Chilies	7.0
Taco shells	7.0
Dinner kits	5.0
Taco sauce	3.0
Enchilada sauce	2.0
Other	7.0

Source: *New York Times*, January 9, 1997, p. C4, from A.C. Nielsen.

★183★

Food (SIC 2000)

Organic Food Market - 1995

Grocery, soyfoods, dairy
Produce
Bulk foods
Herbs
Food service and bakery
Frozen foods
Other

Data show the sales at natural food stores in 1995.

	($ mil.)	Share
Grocery, soyfoods, dairy	512	27.4%
Produce	402	21.5
Bulk foods	231	12.3
Herbs	228	12.2
Food service and bakery	208	11.1
Frozen foods	98	5.2
Other	192	10.3

Source: *New York Times*, October 26, 1996, p. 21, from *Natural Foods Merchandiser* and *New Product News*.

★184★

Food (SIC 2000)

Selected Food Market Sizes

Data show the market sizes of some of the fastest growing supermarket food categories. Figures are in millions of dollars for the year ended June 29, 1996.

Frozen desserts	$ 632
Poultry, frozen	482
Nutritional supplements	373
Snacks, frozen & hors d'oeuvres	335
Olive oil	290
Ale/stout	217
Sweet rolls, refrigerated	194
Breakfast bars	124
Cake mixes, specialty	79
Fruit punch bases and syrups	77

Source: *Grocery Marketing*, January 1997, p. 19, from A.C. Nielsen.

★185★

Food (SIC 2000)

Top Food Companies - 1996

Firms are ranked by revenues in millions of dollars.

Conagra	$ 24,822
Sara Lee	18,624
RJR Nabisco Holdings	17,063
Archer Daniels Midland	13,314
IBP	12,539
CPC International	9,844
Farmland Industries	9,789
H.J. Heinz	9,112
Campbell Soup	7,678
Kellogg	6,677
Tyson Foods	6,454
Ralston Purina	6,114
Borden	5,765
Kash n' Karry Food Stores	1,022
Eagle Food Centers	1,015

Source: *Fortune*, April 28, 1997, p. 50.

★186★

Food (SIC 2000)

Top Grocery Items - Canada

The top brands in supermarkets are ranked by sales in millions of dollars.

Pepsi-Cola	$ 392.1
Coca-Cola	391.8
Campbell's soups	231.3
Tropicana chilled juices	125.3
Christie cookies	121.6
Kraft cheese slices	109.1
Christie crackers	106.8
Minute Maid frozen juices/drinks	94.6
Kraft cheddar	91.3

Source: *Macleans*, February 3, 1997, p. 12, from A.C. Nielsen.

★ 187 ★
Meat Products (SIC 2010)

Best-Selling Meats

Supermarket sales are shown in billions of dollars.

Beef	$ 17.67
Poultry	8.67
Pork	2.87
Lamb	0.71
Veal	0.36

Source: *Supermarket Business*, August 1996, p. 24.

★ 188 ★
Meat Products (SIC 2010)

Canadian Poultry Industry

Data are in thousands of metric tons.

	1995	1996
Pork	1,260	1,245
Chicken	700	680
Turkey	141	142

Source: *World Poultry*, no. 12, 1996, p. 17.

★ 189 ★
Meat Products (SIC 2010)

Hamburger Consumption by Region

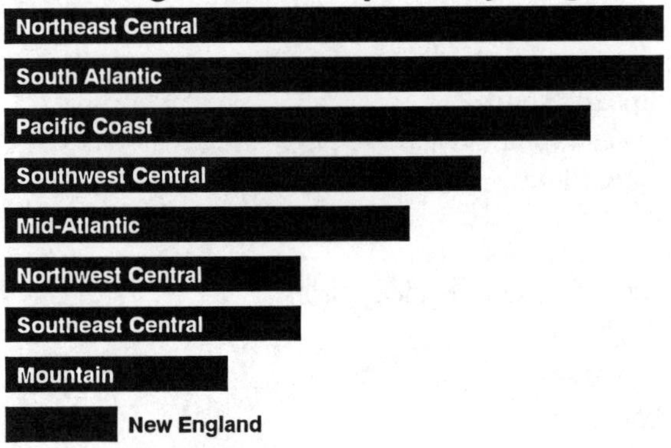

Northeast Central	18.2%
South Atlantic	17.6
Pacific Coast	15.6
Southwest Central	12.8
Mid-Atlantic	10.7
Northwest Central	8.1%
Southeast Central	8.0
Mountain	5.7
New England	3.3

Source: *San Juan Star*, July 4, 1996, p. B22, from National Cattleman's Beef Association and NPD/Crest.

★ 190 ★
Meat Products (SIC 2010)

Top Export Markets for U.S. Broiler Meat - 1996

Data show export value in millions of dollars.

Russian Federation	$ 826.0
Hong Kong	381.3
Japan	142.1
Canada	94.6
Mexico	93.2
Latvia	69.9
China	56.2
Poland	42.5
Singapore	31.2
Leeward - Windward Islands	24.5
Estonia	23.4
South Africa	22.5
Ukraine	15.4
Netherlands	15.3
Netherlands Antilles	15.0

Source: *Broiler Industry*, May 1997, p. 22, from United States Department of Agriculture.

★ 191 ★
Meat Packing (SIC 2011)

Top Beef Packing States

Data are for 1994.

Kansas	20.1%
Nebraska	19.1
Texas	18.1
Colorado	7.1
Iowa	5.1
Wisconsin	4.0
Minnesota	3.1

Continued on next page.

★191★ *Continued*

Meat Packing (SIC 2011)

Top Beef Packing States

Data are for 1994.

Pennsylvania	2.9%
California	2.6
Washington	2.5
Other	15.4

Source: *U.S. News & World Report*, September 23, 1996, p. 43, from United States Department of Agriculture.

★192★

Meat Packing (SIC 2011)

Top Pork Packing States

Data are for 1994.

Iowa	32.5%
Illinois	9.5
Minnesota	7.8
North Carolina	6.9
South Dakota	6.1
Nebraska	6.0
Virginia	4.7
Indiana	3.8
Kentucky	3.0
Pennsylvania	2.3
Other	17.4

Source: *U.S. News & World Report*, September 23, 1996, p. 43, from United States Department of Agriculture.

★193★

Meat Products (SIC 2011)

Meat Snack Sales by Outlet

Sales are shown based on a $631.6 million market in 1995.

Convenience stores	45.0%
Supermarkets	18.9
Mass merchandisers	14.0
Warehouse clubs	8.0
Drugstores	3.1
Vending machines	1.0
Other	10.0

Source: *Discount Store News*, July 15, 1996, p. F50, from Snack Food Association.

★194★

Meat Products (SIC 2013)

Leading Meat Snacks

Brands shares are shown based on supermarket sales. Top producers include Goodmark Foods, Oh Boy! Oberto, and The Turkey Store.

Slim Jim	18.7%
Oberto	14.4
Turkey Store	10.4
Bridgford	9.9
Lowrey's	7.6
Tombstone	5.5
Old Wisconsin Sausage	3.2
Pemmican	2.7
Smokecraft	2.5
Denver Dan	2.2
Jack Link's	1.7
Rustler's	1.4
Other	19.8

Source: *U.S. Distribution Journal*, January/February 1997, p. 39, from Information Resources Inc.

★195★

Meat Products (SIC 2013)

Top Hot Dog Producers

Data show company shares of the $1.4 billion hot dog market. Sara Lee produces Hygrade, Ball Park, Best's, and Bryan Foods brands; ConAgra produces Healthy Choice, Hebrew National, and Armour brands.

Oscar Mayer	19.0%
Sara Lee	15.2
ConAgra	13.2
Others	52.6

Source: *Advertising Age*, April 28, 1997, p. 4, from Information Resources Inc.

★196★

Dairy Products (SIC 2020)

Top Dairy Co-Ops - North America

Groups are ranked by 1995 sales in millions of dollars. Agrifoods International Cooperative Ltd. includes Dairyworld Goods in British Columbia.

Mid-America Dairymen Inc.	$ 1,700.0
Land O'Lakes Inc.	1,512.0
Associated Milk Producers Inc.	1,351.0

Continued on next page.

★ 196 ★ *Continued*

Dairy Products (SIC 2020)

Top Dairy Co-Ops - North America

Groups are ranked by 1995 sales in millions of dollars. Agrifoods International Cooperative Ltd. includes Dairyworld Goods in British Columbia.

Foremost Farms USA Cooperative	$ 820.0
Prairie Farms Dairy Inc.	800.0
Darigold Inc.	785.0
Agropur Cooperative Agro-Alimentaire	741.0
Agrifoods Intl Cooperative Ltd.	657.0
Milk Marketing Inc.	631.0
Dairyman's Cooperative Creamery Assoc.	530.0

Source: *Dairy Foods*, July 1996, p. 14.

★ 197 ★

Dairy Products (SIC 2020)

Top U.S. Dairy Food Producers

Companies are ranked by 1995 sales in millions of dollars. Some figures are estimated.

Kraft Foods	$ 3,340.0
Dean Foods Co.	1,514.0
Leprino Foods Co.	1,150.0
Borden Inc.	1,100.0
Schreiber Foods Inc.	1,000.0
ConAgra Inc.	955.0
Good Humor-Breyers Ice Cream	880.0
BolsWessanen U.S.A. Inc.	840.0
Ault Foods Ltd.	761.0
Stella Foods Inc.	750.0
Dreyers's/Edy's Grand Ice Cream Inc.	679.0
Baskin-Robbins U.S.A. Co.	609.0

Source: *Dairy Foods*, July 1996, p. 11.

★ 198 ★

Whipped Cream (SIC 2023)

Whipped Topping Brands

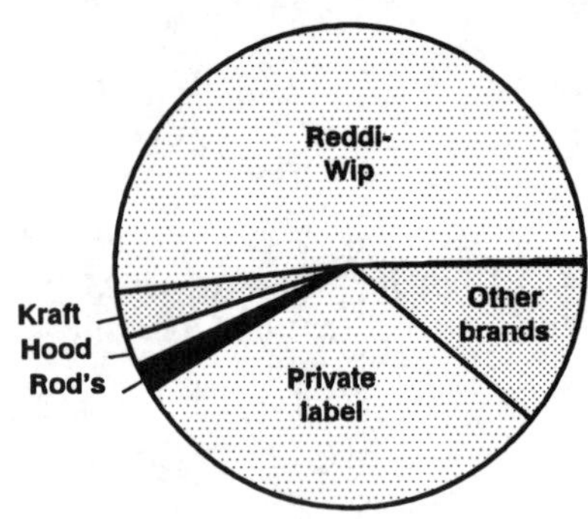

Shares of the $97.5 million aerosol whipped topping market are shown in percent.

Reddi-Wip	51.2%
Kraft	2.5
Hood	2.4
Rod's	2.4
Private label	30.2
Other brands	11.3

Source: *Dairy Foods*, August 1996, p. 33, from Information Resources Inc.

★ 199 ★

Frozen Desserts (SIC 2024)

Frozen Dessert Sales

Total sales reached $10.9 billion in 1995.

Frozen novelties	33.9%
Ice cream, full-fat	31.2
Frozen yogurt	14.7
Ice cream, low-fat	13.8
Sherbet	3.7
Ice cream, non-fat	2.8

Source: *Dairy Foods*, October 1996, p. 12, from International Dairy Foods Association.

★200★

Frozen Yogurt (SIC 2024)

Leading Frozen Yogurt Makers

Shares are shown based on total sales of $535.3 million for the 52 weeks ended June 16, 1996.

Dreyer's/Edy's	15.3%
Marigold	8.5
Ben & Jerry's	8.2
Unilever	7.4
Haagan-Dazs	4.9
Turkey Hill	4.5
Dannon	3.8
Colombo	3.1
Crowley Foods	2.9
Private label	16.6

Source: *Dairy Foods - Industry Planner Supplement*, 1997, p. I, from Information Resources Inc.

★201★

Ice Cream (SIC 2024)

Ice Cream Makers - 1996

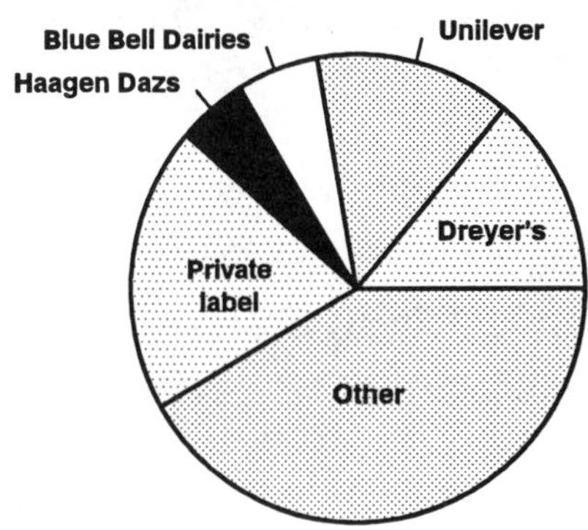

Shares of the $2.9 billion market are shown for the year ended January 21, 1997.

Dreyer's	13.6%
Unilever	13.6
Blue Bell Dairies	6.2
Haagen Dazs	4.8
Private label	20.0
Other	41.8

Source: *Advertising Age*, March 10, 1997, p. 10, from Information Resources Inc.

★202★

Milk (SIC 2026)

Milk Production by County

Data are in millions of pounds.

Tulare, CA	4,970
San Bernadino, CA	3,221
Merced, CA	3,187
Stanislaus, CA	2,785
Riverside, CA	2,434
Kings, CA	1,983
Lancaster, PA	1,767
San Joaquin, CA	1,632
Fresno, CA	1,486
Erath, TX	1,388

Source: *Milwaukee Journal Sentinel*, October 4, 1996, p. A10, from National Agricultural Statistics Service.

★203★

Milk (SIC 2026)

Milk Sales by City

Data show supermarket sales in millions of gallons for the 52 weeks ended July 13, 1996.

Los Angeles	203.9
New York City	155.3
Boston	98.9
Chicago	98.5
San Francisco	91.9

Source: *Dairy Foods*, April 1997, p. 13, from IDFA and A.C. Nielsen.

★204★

Milk (SIC 2026)

Ontario's Milk Market

Market shares are shown in percent. Agropur has recently purchased Ault's milk operations in Ontario. "Other" refers to Agropur and Dairyworld Foods.

Ault Foods	30.0%
Beatrice Foods Inc.	30.0
Neilson Dairy	30.0
Other	10.0

Source: *Marketing Magazine*, February 17, 1997, p. 2.

★ 205 ★

Baby Food (SIC 2032)

Baby Food Makers - 1996

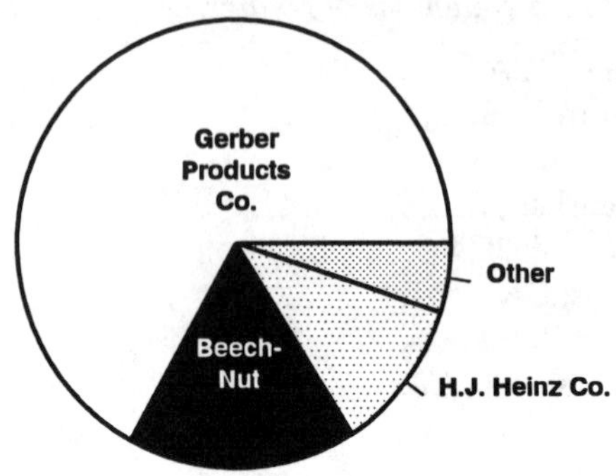

Shares are for the year ended September 8, 1996.

Gerber Products Co.	66.7%
Beech-Nut	16.8
H.J. Heinz Co.	11.1
Other	5.4

Source: *Advertising Age*, October 21, 1996, p. 8, from Information Resources Inc.

★ 206 ★

Baby Food (SIC 2032)

Baby Food Makers - Canada

Heinz	78.0%
Gerber	22.0

Source: *Marketing Magazine*, November 16, 1996, p. 3, from A.C. Nielsen.

★ 207 ★

Canned Food (SIC 2032)

Baked Beans Market - Boston

Shares are shown based on supermarket sales for the year ended November 3, 1996.

B&M	54.4%
Bush's Best	22.0
Campbell's	9.0
Other	14.6

Source: *Brand Marketing*, January 13, 1997, p. 30, from Information Resources Inc.

★ 208 ★

Canned Food (SIC 2032)

U.S. Baked Beans Market

Shares are shown based on supermarket sales for the year ended November 3, 1996.

Bush's Best	32.5%
Van Camps	19.9
B&M	11.2
Other	36.4

Source: *Brand Marketing*, January 13, 1997, p. 30, from Information Resources Inc.

★ 209 ★

Canned Food (SIC 2033)

Canned Pasta Brands

Shares of the $280.4 million market are shown in percent.

Chef Boyardee	59.0%
Franco American	35.0
Other	6.0

Source: *Wall Street Journal*, September 9, 1996, p. A3, from Information Resources Inc.

★ 210 ★

Canned Food (SIC 2033)

Popular Canned Food Brands

Data show the brands of groceries and canned goods preferred by shoppers at discount stores in 1996.

Del Monte	23.0%
Campbell's	13.0
Green Giant	9.0
Libby's	6.0
Folgers	5.0
Chicken of the Sea	3.0
Hunt's	2.0
Frito-Lay	2.0
Kellog's	2.0
Kraft	2.0
Maxwell House	2.0

Source: *Discount Store News*, October 21, 1996, p. 71, from Lee J. Shapiro & Associates.

★211★

Juices (SIC 2033)

Aseptic Juice Sales

Shares are shown based on sales for the year ended August 11, 1996.

	($ mil.)	Share
Capri Sun	$ 171.6	30.0%
Hi-C	127.0	22.2
Kool-Aid Kool Bursts	43.9	7.7
Squeezit	33.9	5.9
Mondo	31.6	5.5
Ocean Spray	18.2	3.2
Hawaiian Punch	16.1	2.8
Lifesavers Squeezit	15.8	2.8
Minute Maid	15.6	2.7
Hi-C Ecto Cooler	11.1	1.9
Other	86.5	15.1

Source: *Beverage Industry*, November 1996, p. 13, from Information Resources Inc. InfoScan.

★212★

Juices (SIC 2033)

Canned Juice Leaders

Shares are shown based on sales for the year ended August 11, 1996.

	($ mil.)	Share
Hawaiian Punch	$ 34.4	30.1%
Hi-C	32.0	28.0
Jumex	7.4	6.5
Kerns	7.0	6.1
Ocean Spray	6.0	5.3
Arizona	4.1	3.6
Hansen's	3.5	3.1
Private label	2.8	2.5
Snapple	2.5	2.2
Gatorade	2.2	1.9
Other	12.3	10.8

Source: *Beverage Industry*, November 1996, p. 13, from Information Resources Inc.

★213★

Juices (SIC 2033)

Chilled Juice Leaders - Canada

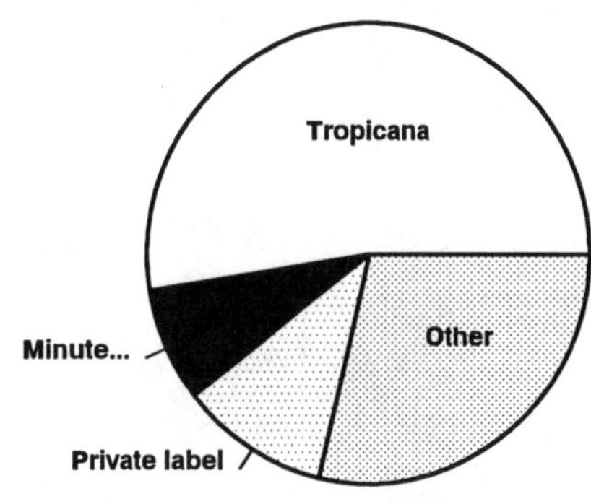

Shares are shown for the year ended October 12, 1996.

Tropicana	52.5%
Minute Maid Canada	8.0
Private label	11.0
Other	28.5

Source: *Marketing Magazine*, December 2, 1996, p. 4.

★214★

Juices (SIC 2033)

Citrus Juice Sales by Type

Data show sales for the four weeks ended July 13, 1996. Figures are in millions of gallons.

Orange juice, ready-to-serve	37.3%
Orange juice, frozen concentrate	13.1
Grapefruit, ready-to-serve	2.1
Grapefruit, canned	0.8
Orange juice, canned	0.5
Other	46.2

Source: *Food Engineering*, September 1996, p. 158, from A.C. Nielsen ScanTrack and Florida Department of Citrus.

★215★

Juices (SIC 2033)

Orange Juice Consumption

Data show the cities drinking the most pulp orange juice as a percent of total gallons sold.

Boise, Idaho	64.5%
Salt Lake City, Utah	61.4
Portland, Oregon	59.7
Roanoke, Virginia	58.9
Spokane, Washington	58.3

Source: *USA TODAY*, February 4, 1997, p. D1, from Tropicana.

★216★

Juices (SIC 2033)

Ready-to-Serve O.J. Leaders

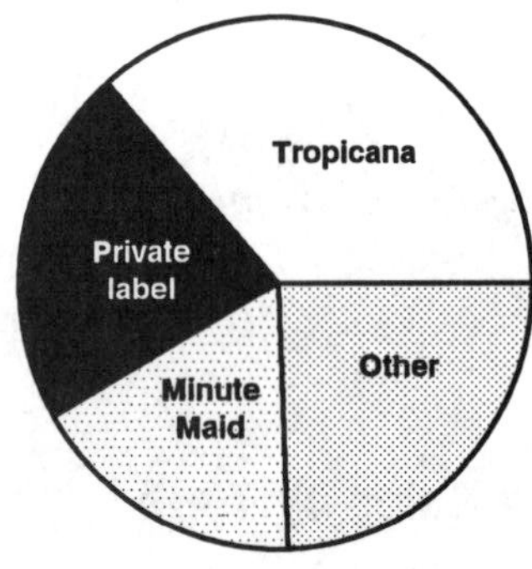

Shares of the $2.2 billion market are shown for the year ended October 6, 1996.

Tropicana	39.8%
Private label	24.0
Minute Maid	19.3
Other	26.9

Source: *Advertising Age*, November 25, 1996, p. 29, from Information Resources Inc.

★217★

Juices (SIC 2033)

Refrigerated Juice Sales

Shares are shown based on supermarket sales for the year ended August 11, 1996.

	($ mil.)	Share
Tropicana Pure Premium	$ 706.2	21.5%
Minute Maid	441.4	13.5
Sunny Delight	$ 343.9	10.5%
Tropicana Season's Best	190.0	5.8
Florida's Natural	178.0	5.4
Dole	76.4	2.3
Minute Maid Premium Choice	66.5	2.0
Tampico	54.0	1.6
Florida Gold	48.4	1.5
Private label	625.0	19.1
Other	550.2	16.8

Source: *Beverage Industry*, November 1996, p. 10, from Information Resources Inc.

★218★

Juices (SIC 2033)

Top Canned Juices - Tucson/Phoenix

Market shares are shown based on $1.14 billion in sales for the year ended June 16, 1996.

Hawaiian Punch	43.1%
Hi-C	13.8
Kerns	11.9
Dole	7.2
Arizona	7.1
Jumex	6.5
Ocean Spray	3.7
Hansens	3.7
Hansens Natural	3.4

Source: *Beverage Industry*, September 1996, p. 31, from Information Resources Inc. InfoScan.

★219★

Soups (SIC 2034)

Condensed Soup Market

Campbell Soup Inc.	90.0%
Other	10.0

Source: *Philadelphia Inquirer*, February 13, 1997, p. C5.

★220★

Soups (SIC 2034)

Wet Soup Market

Shares are shown for the 52 weeks ended August 4, 1996. Campbell Soup is the market leader in other categories such as canned poultry, with its Swanson brand, generating a 53% share; Campbell's and V8 have a 52% share of the vegetable juice market; Godiva has a 50% share of the super premium chocolate market; Vlasic has a 30% share of the pickles market.

Campbell's	79.0%
Other	21.0

Source: *New York Times*, September 6, 1996, p. C5, from Campbell Soup Co. and Information Resources Inc. International.

★221★

Pickles (SIC 2035)

Top Refrigerated Pickle Brands

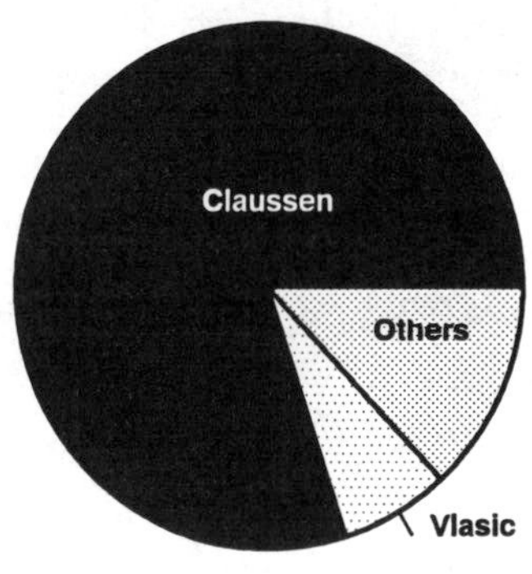

Brand shares are based on a $150.2 million refrigerated pickle market. Vlasic leads the shelf-stable pickle category with a 42.7% share.

Claussen	80.0%
Vlasic	7.0
Others	13.0

Source: *Advertising Age*, April 21, 1997, p. 4, from Information Resources Inc.

★222★

Salad Dressings (SIC 2035)

Top Salad Dressing Brands

Brand sales are shown in millions of dollars for the 52 weeks ended March 2, 1996. Market shares for the same period are shown in percent. Wishbone is produced by Lipton; Hidden Valley Ranch is produced by Clorox Co.

	Sales ($ mil.)	Share
Kraft	$ 416.8	36.9%
Wishbone	205.7	18.2
Hidden Valley Ranch	163.4	14.5
Best Foods/Hellman's	32.9	2.9
Others	281.2	27.5

Source: *Advertising Age*, April 14, 1997, p. 6, from Information Resources Inc.

★223★

Sauces (SIC 2035)

Salsa Producers - 1996

Pillsbury produces Old El Paso and Las Palmas; Campbell's produces Pace; Pepsico produces Tostitos; Nestle produces Ortega; Kraft produces Taco Bell.

Pillsbury	22.0%
Campbell's	13.0
Pepsico	11.0
Nestle	5.0
Kraft	3.0
Other	46.0

Source: *New York Times*, January 9, 1997, p. C1, from A.C. Nielsen.

★224★

Sauces (SIC 2035)

Spaghetti Sauce Market

Volume shares are shown for the year ended July 7, 1996.

Ragu	33.2%
Prego	26.3
Other	40.5

Source: *Advertising Age*, September 16, 1996, p. 12, from Information Resources Inc.

★ 225 ★

Frozen Foods (SIC 2037)

U.S. Frozen Foods Market

Data are in thousands of pounds.

Potato products	8,364.9
Corn products	1,053.6
Green peas	441.5
Green beans	298.5
Broccoli	210.3
Lima beans	105.1
Carrots	314.0
Spinach	185.6
Onions	84.2
Okra	66.2
Brussels sprouts	43.6
Cauliflower	43.1

Source: *Quick Frozen Foods International*, October 1996, p. A17.

★ 226 ★

Frozen Foods (SIC 2038)

Steak Sandwich Market - 1996

Shares are shown for August 14, 1995 - July 14, 1996.

Steak Umm Steaks	53.1%
Quaker Maid Steaks	13.2
Philly Gourmet Steaks	6.9
Other	26.8

Source: *Supermarket News*, January 6, 1997, p. 37, from Information Resources Inc. InfoScan.

★ 227 ★

Frozen Foods (SIC 2038)

Top Frozen Pizza Brands - 1997

Brands are ranked by sales volume in millions of dollars. Shares are shown in percent. Data are for the 52 weeks ending March 2, 1997.

	Sales ($ mil.)	Share
Tombstone	$ 254.9	14.5%
Red Baron	161.0	9.2
DiGiorno	157.2	9.0
Tony's	146.7	8.4
Totino's Party Pizza	139.1	7.9
Stouffers	78.4	4.5
Celeste Pizza for One	62.1	3.5
Jack's Original	$ 57.2	3.3%
Red Baron Super Singles	50.3	2.9
Private label	91.6	5.2
Other	601.5	31.6

Source: *Snack & Bakery Foods*, May 1997, p. 17, from Information Resources Inc.

★ 228 ★

Frozen Foods (SIC 2038)

Top Frozen Pizza Makers

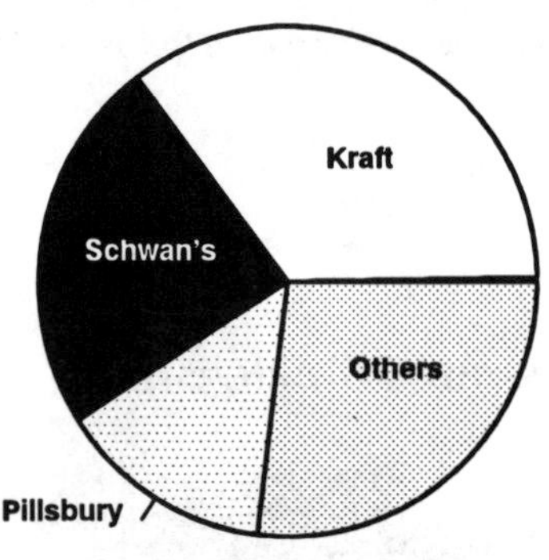

Shares of the $1.8 billion market are shown in percent. Kraft produces DiGiorno and Tombstone. Schwan's produces Tony and Red Baron. Pillsbury produces Totino's.

Kraft	35.1%
Schwan's	23.7
Pillsbury	14.0
Others	27.2

Source: *Advertising Age*, April 28, 1997, p. 16, from Information Resources Inc.

★ 229 ★

Flour (SIC 2041)

Corn Flour Market - Mexico

Grupo Maesca (Gruma)	70.0%
Other	30.0

Source: *Mexico Business*, December 1996, p. 42.

★230★

Cereals (SIC 2043)

Leading Cereal Brands

Shares are shown based on $7.95 billion in supermarket sales in 1995.

Brand	Share
Kellogg's Frosted Flakes	4.24%
General Mills Cheerios	3.66
Kellogg's Corn Flakes	3.03
Kellogg's Rice Krispies	2.77
General Mills Honey Nut Cheerios	2.76
Kellogg's Raisin Bran	2.68
Kellogg's Froot Loops	2.43
Kellogg's Special K	2.11
Kellogg's Corn Pops	2.10
General Mills Lucky Charms	1.99
Other	72.23

Source: *Advertising Age*, September 30, 1996, p. S14, from Information Resources Inc.

★231★

Cereals (SIC 2043)

Top Cereal Brands - 1996

Data are for the year ended September 8, 1996.

Brand	Share
Frosted Flakes	4.1%
Cheerios	3.8
Corn Flakes	2.9
Honey Nut Cheerios	2.8
Rice Krispies	2.7
Other	83.7

Source: *Brandweek*, December 2, 1996, p. 24, from Information Resources Inc.

★232★

Cereals (SIC 2043)

Top Cereal Producers

Kellogg
General Mills
Post
Other

Market shares are shown in percent for the year ended February 23, 1997.

Kellogg	33.3%
General Mills	27.9
Post	16.4
Other	22.4

Source: *Advertising Age*, May 5, 1997, p. 20, from Information Resources Inc.

★233★

Rice (SIC 2044)

Rice Cake Market

Shares shown represent the $225.0 million market.

Quaker Oats Co.	80.0%
Others	20.0

Source: *Forbes*, October 7, 1996, p. 80.

★234★

Pet Food (SIC 2047)

Dog Food Makers - 1996

Shares of the $901.3 million market are for the year ended January 26, 1997.

Kal Kan	39.3%
Grand Metropolitan	27.5
Heinz Co.	20.0
Other	13.2

Source: *Advertising Age*, March 17, 1997, p. 4, from Information Resources Inc.

★ 235 ★

Bakery Products (SIC 2051)

Breakfast Pastry Market - 1996

Shares of the $617.6 million market are shown in percent.

Kellogg's Pop-Tarts	53.5%
Pillsbury Toaster Strudel	17.5
Nabisco	6.4
Private label	22.6

Source: *New York Times*, May 17, 1997, p. 21, from A.C. Nielsen.

★ 236 ★

Bakery Products (SIC 2051)

Fresh Bagel Market

Shares of the $283.3 million market are shown for the year ended November 3, 1996.

	Sales ($ mil.)	Share
Lender's	$ 76.7	27.1%
Private label	41.9	14.8
Sara Lee Corp.	39.1	13.8
Best Foods Baking Corp.	32.5	11.5
Other	93.1	32.9

Source: *Snack & Bakery Foods*, February 1997, p. 54, from Information Resources Inc.

★ 237 ★

Bakery Products (SIC 2051)

Frozen Bagel Market - 1996

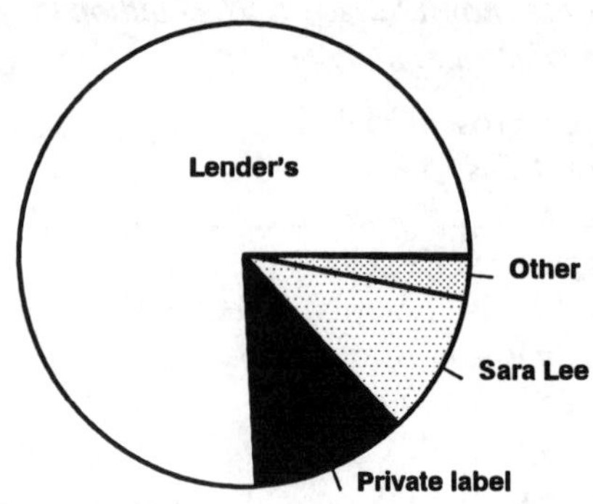

Shares of the $216.9 million market are shown for the year ended November 3, 1996.

	Sales ($ mil.)	Share
Lender's	$ 165.2	76.2%
Private label	22.7	10.5
Sara Lee	21.7	10.0
Other	7.3	3.4

Source: *Snack & Bakery Foods*, February 1997, p. 54, from Information Resources Inc.

★ 238 ★

Bakery Products (SIC 2051)

Leading Muffin Brands

Shares of the $182.4 million market are shown in percent.

Continental Baking	18.2%
Otis Spunkmeyer	15.4
Best Foods Baking	4.5
McKee Baking Co.	4.4
Entenmann's	4.2
Weight Watchers Co.	3.2
McGlynn Bakeries	1.4
Old World Foods	0.7
Private label	31.6
Other	16.4

Source: *Bakery Production and Marketing*, August 15, 1996, p. 42, from Information Resources Inc.

★ 239 ★

Bakery Products (SIC 2051)

Popular Donut Brands

Sales are shown by brand for the year ended May 19, 1996.

	Sales ($ mil.)	Share
Entenmann's	$ 90.1	20.3%
Private label	83.7	18.9
Hostess	74.2	16.7
Dolly Madison	37.5	8.5
Krispy Kreme	32.9	7.4
Merita	9.3	2.1
Freihofer	8.6	1.9
Tastykake	8.5	1.9
Rainbo Break Cake	8.2	1.8
Mrs. Baird	5.8	1.3

Source: *Bakery Production and Marketing*, September 15, 1996, p. 42, from Information Resources Inc.

★ 240 ★

Bakery Products (SIC 2051)

Refrigerated Bagel Market

Shares of the $45.8 million market are shown for the year ended November 3, 1996.

	Sales ($ mil.)	Share
It Works Inc.	$ 19.1	41.7%
Lender's	11.0	24.0
Crystal Farms Inc.	9.4	20.5
Harlan Bakeries	4.3	9.4
Other	2.0	4.4

Source: *Snack & Bakery Foods*, February 1997, p. 54, from Information Resources Inc.

★ 241 ★

Bread (SIC 2051)

Bread Makers

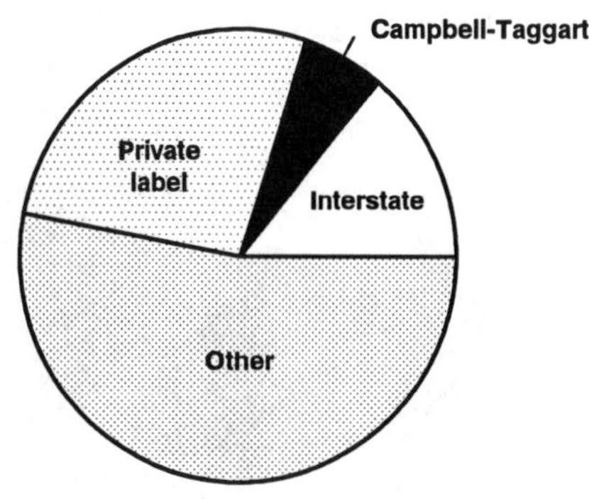

Shares are shown based on sales of $4.9 billion for the 52 weeks ended December 29, 1996.

Interstate	14.4%
Campbell-Taggart	5.7
Private label	27.4
Other	52.5

Source: *Bakery Production and Marketing*, March 15, 1997, p. 45, from Information Resources Inc.

★ 242 ★

Cookies (SIC 2052)

Top Cookie Makers

Shares are shown based on $3.5489 billion in supermarket sales for the year ended October 6, 1996.

	Sales ($ mil.)	Share
Nabisco	$ 1,297.2	36.6%
Private label	441.4	12.4
Keebler	430.1	12.1
Pepperidge Farm	190.4	5.4
Archway	154.1	4.3
Mother's	139.3	3.9
Little Debbie	137.7	3.9
Murray	136.4	3.8
Sunshine	133.0	3.7
Other	489.3	13.8

Source: *Snack & Bakery Foods*, January 1997, p. 14, from Information Resources Inc.

★ 243 ★

Crackers (SIC 2052)

Leading Cracker Brands

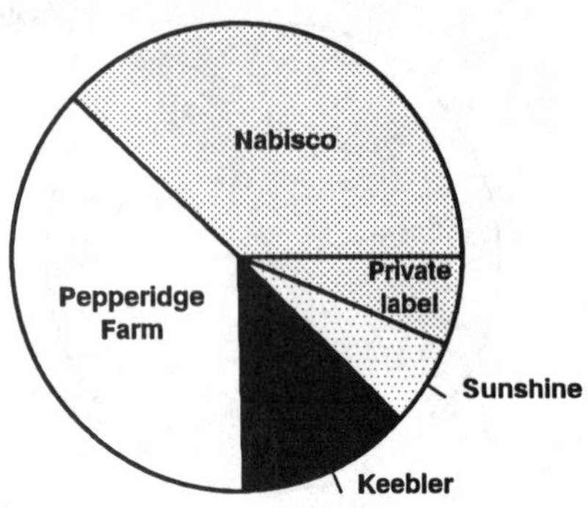

Market shares are shown for the year ended October 6, 1996.

Nabisco	49.3%
Pepperidge Farm	48.0
Keebler	16.0
Sunshine	7.8
Private label	8.4

Source: *Bakery Production and Marketing*, January 15, 1997, p. 60, from Information Resources Inc.

★ 244 ★

Frozen Bakery Products (SIC 2053)

Popular Frozen Pies

Shares are shown based on $258.3 million in supermarket sales for the year ended June 16, 1996.

Mrs. Smith's	51.9%
Sara Lee	23.5
Other	24.6

Source: *Snack Food*, September 1996, p. 32, from Information Resources Inc. InfoScan.

★ 245 ★

Frozen Bakery Products (SIC 2053)

Top Frozen Cheesecake Makers

Companies are ranked by sales in millions of dollars for the 52 weeks ending December 29, 1996. Total sales reached $63.2 million.

	($ mil.)	Share
Sara Lee	$ 39.7	62.8%
Weight Watchers	9.9	15.7
Eli's Chicago Finest	2.5	4.0
Edwards Baking	2.0	3.2
Private label	2.0	3.2
Other	7.1	11.2

Source: *Snack & Bakery Foods*, May 1997, p. 48, from Information Resources Inc.

★ 246 ★

Sugar (SIC 2061)

U.S. Sugar Refiners

Firms are ranked by tons of sugar refined in 1995.

Domino Sugar Corp.	8,000
California and Hawaiian Sugar Co.	3,142
Savannah Foods and Industries Inc.	3,100
Colonial Sugar Inc.	2,150
Refined Sugars Inc.	2,000
Imperial Holly Corp.	1,950

Source: *Sugar & Sweetener. Situation and Outlook Report*, June 1995, p. 18, from Economic Research Service, United States Department of Agriculture.

★ 247 ★

Confectionery Products (SIC 2064)

Hard Sugar Candy Makers

Sales of hard sugar and roll candy reached $87.5 million for the third quarter of 1996. Company shares are shown in percent.

Storck USA	14.4%
Planters/LifeSavers	13.6
Leaf North America	13.4
Hershey Chocolate USA	7.6
Charms Inc.	6.0
Brach and Brock	5.9
Nestle USA	5.7
Private label	5.6
Tootsie Roll Inds. Inc.	5.2

Continued on next page.

★ 247 ★ *Continued*

Confectionery Products (SIC 2064)

Hard Sugar Candy Makers

Sales of hard sugar and roll candy reached $87.5 million for the third quarter of 1996. Company shares are shown in percent.

Farley Candy Co.	3.2%
Other	19.4

Source: *Manufacturing Confectioner*, December 1996, p. 28, from Information Resources Inc.

★ 248 ★

Confectionery Products (SIC 2064)

Leading Breath Fresheners

Sales of breath fresheners reached $54.38 million for the third quarter of 1996. Brand shares are shown in percent.

BreathSavers	31.5%
Tic Tac	30.6
Certs	19.5
Altoids	9.1
Extra Certs Flavor	5.8
Velamints	1.0
Certs Fresh Fruit	0.8
Clorets	0.4
Blitz	0.3
Ice Drops	0.3
Other	0.7

Source: *Manufacturing Confectioner*, December 1996, p. 27, from Information Resources Inc.

★ 249 ★

Confectionery Products (SIC 2064)

Leading Diet Candies

Sweet N Low
LifeSavers Delites
Estee
Sorbee
GoLightly
Sathers
Fifty 50
Square Shooters
Bob's
Private label
Other

Sales of diet candies reached $14.37 million for the third quarter of 1996. Brand shares are shown in percent.

Sweet N Low	14.3%
LifeSavers Delites	14.2
Estee	13.3
Sorbee	10.5
GoLightly	6.0
Sathers	4.9
Fifty 50	4.2
Square Shooters	4.2
Bob's	3.7
Private label	3.4
Other	21.3

Source: *Manufacturing Confectioner*, December 1996, p. 27, from Information Resources Inc.

★ 250 ★

Confectionery Products (SIC 2064)

Leading Gift Box Chocolates

Sales of gift box chocolates reached $143.17 million for the third quarter of 1996. Brand shares are shown in percent.

Russell Stover	43.6%
Whitman's	18.1
Zachary	7.6
Fannie May	6.6
Whitman's Sampler	5.4
Maxfield	2.6
NECCO Masterpieces	2.5
Premiere	2.3

Continued on next page.

★ 250 ★ *Continued*

Confectionery Products (SIC 2064)

Leading Gift Box Chocolates

Sales of gift box chocolates reached $143.17 million for the third quarter of 1996. Brand shares are shown in percent.

Brand	Share
Esther Price	2.2%
Pot of Gold	1.7
Other	7.4

Source: *Manufacturing Confectioner*, December 1996, p. 26, from Information Resources Inc.

★ 251 ★

Confectionery Products (SIC 2064)

Leading Plain Mints

LifeSavers
Can Melles Mentos
Brach's
Brock
Private label
Sathers
Farley's
Richardson After Dinner
Hershey's Tastetations
NECCO
Other

Sales of plain mints reached $39.2 million for the third quarter of 1996. Brand shares are shown in percent.

Brand	Share
LifeSavers	32.1%
Can Melles Mentos	15.0
Brach's	11.1
Brock	9.3
Private label	7.2
Sathers	5.3
Farley's	4.9
Richardson After Dinner	3.1
Hershey's Tastetations	2.1
NECCO	1.3
Other	8.6

Source: *Manufacturing Confectioner*, December 1996, p. 27, from Information Resources Inc.

★ 252 ★

Confectionery Products (SIC 2064)

Leading Specialty Nut/Coconut Candies

Sales of specialty nut and coconut candies reached $17.3 million for the third quarter of 1996. Brand shares are shown in percent.

Brand	Share
Pay Day	29.5%
Brach's	14.8
Private label	7.4
Pearson	5.8
Sophie Mae	4.7
Planters	4.2
Russell Stover	3.5
Lance	3.4
Sathers	2.7
Brown & Haley Almond Roca	2.5
Other	21.5

Source: *Manufacturing Confectioner*, December 1996, p. 26, from Information Resources Inc.

★ 253 ★

Confectionery Products (SIC 2064)

Popular Breath Fresheners

The top 10 fresheners are ranked by unit sales for the 52 weeks ended July 14, 1996. Shares are shown based on unit sales of 26.123 million.

	Units (mil.)	Share
Sweet Breath	13.98	53.6%
Binaca	5.06	19.4
Breath Asure	3.99	15.3
Private label	1.54	5.9
Janar Ranir	0.34	1.3
Other	1.17	4.5

Source: *Supermarket Business*, January 1997, p. 59, from Information Resources Inc. InfoScan.

★254★

Confectionery Products (SIC 2064)

Top Candy Brands

Shares of the $6.667 billion candy and mints market are shown for the year ended November 3, 1996.

	Sales ($ mil.)	Share
M&Ms	$ 162.3	2.4%
Hershey's	152.5	2.3
Reeses	138.5	2.1
Snickers	130.8	2.0
Lifesavers	107.7	1.6
Private label	95.0	1.4
Brachs	87.5	1.3
Kit Kat	87.2	1.3
Farley's	79.9	1.2
Starburst	75.4	1.1
Other	5,550.2	83.3

Source: *Discount Merchandiser*, January 1997, p. 78, from Information Resources Inc.

★255★

Confectionery Products (SIC 2064)

Top Carmel Corn Brands

Shares of the $312.9 million market are shown for the year ended May 19, 1996.

Franklin Crunch & Munch	12.5%
Cracker Jack	11.5
Houston Foods	10.9
Private label	7.4
Smart Food	7.3
Chester's	3.8
Golden Harvest	3.3
Vic's	2.4
Shucks	2.3
Wise	2.1
Other	36.5

Source: *Snack Food*, August 1996, p. 16, from Information Resources Inc.

★256★

Confectionery Products (SIC 2064)

Top Confectionery Makers - 1996

Market shares are shown for the 52 weeks ended December 1, 1996.

Hershey	31.7%
Mars	23.4
Nestle	8.5
Russell Stover	7.1
Brach	5.1
Leaf	3.6
Nabisco	3.4
Other	17.2

Source: *Investext,* Thomson Financial Networks, January 30, 1997, p. 3, from Information Resources Inc. InfoScan.

★257★

Yogurt Bars (SIC 2064)

Popular Granola Bars - 1996

Shares of the $814.3 million market are shown in percent.

	($ mil.)	Share
Kellogg's NutriGrain	$ 145.1	17.8%
Quaker Chewy Granola Bar	117.3	14.4
Kellogg's Rice Krispies Bar	94.3	11.6
Other	456.7	56.1

Source: *Advertising Age*, November 4, 1996, p. 20, from Information Resources Inc.

★ 258 ★

Chocolate (SIC 2066)

Canada's Chocolate Bar Brands - 1996

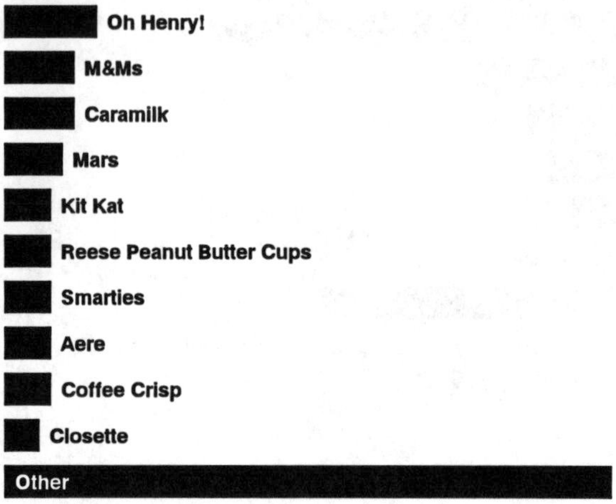

Market shares are shown in percent.

Oh Henry!	7.8%
M&Ms	5.6
Caramilk	5.5
Mars	5.0
Kit Kat	4.4
Reese Peanut Butter Cups	4.4
Smarties	4.0
Aere	3.8
Coffee Crisp	3.8
Closette	3.2
Other	52.6

Source: *Marketing Magazine*, May 26, 1997, p. 11, from industry sources.

★ 259 ★

Chocolate (SIC 2066)

Chocolate Candy Makers - Snack Size

Sales of snack and fun size candy reached $125.1 million for the third quarter of 1996. Company shares are shown in percent.

Hershey Chocolate USA	52.9%
Mars Inc.	32.3
Nestle USA	11.6
Tootsie Roll Industries	1.6
Leaf North	0.7%
Private label	0.3
Goldenberg Candy Co.	0.2
Other	0.4

Source: *Manufacturing Confectioner*, December 1996, p. 28, from Information Resources Inc.

★ 260 ★

Chocolate (SIC 2066)

Chocolate Candy Market Shares

Shares are shown based on sales volume for the year ended March 9, 1996. Figures refer to supermarkets with sales of $2.0 million and over.

Reese's Peanut Butters	13.3%
Snickers	10.2
Kit Kat	9.7
Hershey's Bar	5.4
Hershey's Almond	3.6
Twix Caramel	3.6
M&Ms Plain	3.4
M&Ms Peanut	3.2
Hershey's Kisses	0.8
Brach's	0.7
Other	46.1

Source: *Snack Food*, September 1996, p. 19, from A.C. Nielsen.

★261★

Chocolate (SIC 2066)

Chocolate Product Sales

Data refer to non-confectionery chocolate product sales. Figures are in millions of pounds.

	(mil.)	Share
Cocoa powder, syrup, toppings and other	459	30.1%
Chocolate chips and baking pieces	416	27.3
Chocolate coatings (blocks, wafers, liquid)	355	23.3
Compound coatings (blocks, wafers, liquid)	214	14.0
Chocolate liquors	45	3.0
Cocoa butter	24	1.6
Baking chocolate (bars and blocks)	11	0.7

Source: *Candy Industry*, January 1997, p. A4, from United States Department of Commerce.

★262★

Chocolate (SIC 2066)

Easter Chocolate Market - Canada

Shares of the $40 million market are shown in percent.

Cadbury	65.0%
Other	35.0

Source: *Marketing Magazine*, March 10, 1997, p. 3.

★263★

Chocolate (SIC 2066)

Leading Bite Sized Chocolate Candy Bar Brands

Brand shares are shown based on unit sales.

Snickers	14.6%
Reeses	13.6
Hershey	9.2
Milky Way	7.1
Three Musketeers	6.8
Kit Kat	5.0
Hershey Nuggets	4.9
Butterfinger	4.7
York Peppermint Patty	4.3
M&M's	3.7%
Others	26.1

Source: *Discount Merchandiser*, April 1997, p. 51, from Information Resources Inc.

★264★

Chocolate (SIC 2066)

Leading Box/Bag Chocolate Candy Brands

Brand shares are shown based on unit sales.

M&M's	13.2%
Hershey chocolate bar	7.2
Hershey Kisses	6.7
Snickers	5.8
Reeses	5.4
Kit Kat	4.1
Hershey Sweet Escapes	3.2
Brachs	2.4
Hershey Hugs	1.9
Private label	2.4
Other	47.7

Source: *Discount Merchandiser*, April 1997, p. 52, from Information Resources Inc.

★265★

Chocolate (SIC 2066)

Leading Chocolate Candy Bar Brands

Brand shares are shown based on unit sales of 3.5 ounce chocolate candy bars.

Hershey	11.6%
M&M's	11.3
Snickers	8.2
Reeses	7.9
Kit Kat	6.4
Butterfinger	4.3
Nestle Crunch	3.3
York Peppermint Patty	3.2
Three Musketeers	2.9
Russell Stover	1.8
Other	39.1

Source: *Discount Merchandiser*, April 1997, p. 51, from Information Resources Inc.

★266★

Chocolate (SIC 2066)

Leading Chocolate Candy Box/Bag Brands

Sales of chocolate candy boxes/bags (greater than 3.5 ounces) reached $269.2 million for the third quarter of 1996. Brand shares are shown in percent.

Brand	Share
M&Ms	20.6%
Hershey's Kisses	8.1
Hershey's Candy Bar	7.2
Hershey's Sweet Escapes	5.5
Snickers	5.3
Reeses	5.0
Kit Kat	3.8
Brach's	2.8
Private label	2.5
Farley's	2.2
Other	37.0

Source: *Manufacturing Confectioner*, December 1996, p. 26, from Information Resources Inc.

★267★

Chewing Gum (SIC 2067)

Chewing Gum Producers

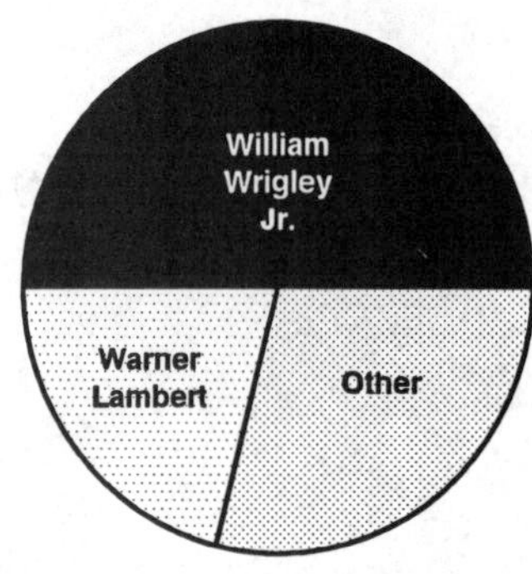

Shares of the $2.0 billion market are shown in percent.

William Wrigley Jr.	50.0%
Warner Lambert	21.0
Other	29.0

Source: *Chicago Tribune*, December 18, 1996, p. C3.

★268★

Chewing Gum (SIC 2067)

Leading Chewing Gum Brands

Sales of chewing gum reached $134.1 million for the third quarter of 1996. Brand shares are shown in percent.

Brand	Share
Wrigley's Double Mint	10.8%
Freedent Regular	9.4
Wrigley's Regular	7.6
Wrigley's Big Red	7.4
Wrigley's Spearmint	6.9
Wrigley's Juicy Fruit	6.6
BreathSavers Ice Breakers	4.8
Bubble Yum	4.6
Cinn-A-Burst	3.9
Bubblicious	3.7
Other	34.3

Source: *Manufacturing Confectioner*, December 1996, p. 27, from Information Resources Inc.

★269★

Chewing Gum (SIC 2067)

Sugarless Chewing Gum Makers

Data are for the year ended October 6, 1996.

Wrigley	39.4%
Warner Lambert	29.8
LifeSavers	21.0
Other	9.8

Source: *Advertising Age*, December 9, 1996, p. B2, from Information Resources Inc.

★270★

Nuts (SIC 2068)

Snack Nut Producers

Sales are shown in millions of dollars for the year ended August 4, 1996.

	($ mil.)	Share
Planters	$ 461.0	37.8%
Blue Diamond Growers	76.3	6.2
John B. Sanfilippo & Son	68.9	5.6
Nutcracker	58.1	4.8
Private label	238.1	19.5

Source: *Snack Food*, December 1996, p. 19, from Information Resources Inc.

★ 271 ★

Fats and Oils (SIC 2079)

Shortening Market

Crisco	65.8%
Other	34.2

Source: *Wall Street Journal*, November 29, 1996, p. B3, from Information Resources Inc.

★ 272 ★

Margarine (SIC 2079)

Top Margarine Producers

Company shares are shown based on a $1.3 billion market. Unilever's top brand is Lipton; Nabisco's top brand is Parkay. Data are for the 52 weeks ended March 30, 1997.

Unilever	50.4%
Nabisco	27.3
Other	22.3

Source: *Advertising Age*, May 5, 1997, p. 4, from Information Resources Inc.

★ 273 ★

Beverages (SIC 2080)

Alcoholic Beverages Market - Mexico

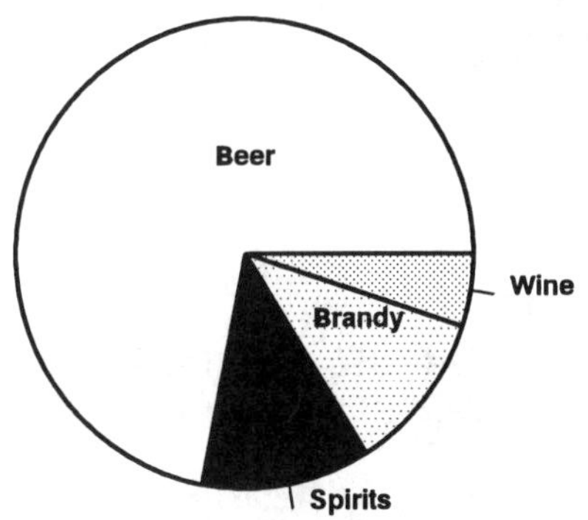

Segment shares are shown based on a $2.8 billion market for 1995.

Beer	72.0%
Spirits	12.0
Brandy	11.0
Wine	5.0

Source: *USA TODAY*, May 22, 1997, p. B1, from Euromonitor.

★ 274 ★

Beverages (SIC 2080)

Beverage Sales in San Diego

Sales are shown in millions of dollars for the 52 weeks ended November 3, 1996. Figures are for food stores only.

Milk	$ 116.5
Carbonated soft drinks	100.0
Beer & ale	71.3
Bottled juices	31.9
Rfg. juices	31.8
Coffee	28.4
Bottled water	18.5
Frozen juices	17.1
Canned juices	10.1
Aseptic juices	6.9
Loose tea & tea bags	4.9
Ready-to-drink tea	4.6
Instant tea mixes	2.1

Source: *Beverage Industry*, February 1997, p. 30, from Information Resources Inc. InfoScan.

★ 275 ★

Beverages (SIC 2080)

Soft Drink Gallonage by Region

Data show 1995 soft drink sales in millions of gallons.

	(mil.)	Share
South	3,672.0	26.7%
East Central	2,640.5	19.2
Northeast	2,420.5	17.6
Southwest	1,705.3	12.4
Pacific	1,678.1	12.2
West Central	1,155.2	8.4
West	481.3	3.5

Source: *Beverage World*, Databank 1997 (Special Issue), p. 10.

★ 276 ★

Beverages (SIC 2080)

Top Beverage Companies - 1996

Firms are ranked by revenues in millions of dollars.

Coca-Cola	$ 18,546
Anheuser-Busch	10,884
Coca-Cola Enterprises	7,921
Whitman	3,111
Adolph Coors	1,732
Brown-Forman	1,544
Canandaigua Wine	987

Source: *Fortune*, April 28, 1997, p. 45.

★ 277 ★

Beverages (SIC 2080)

Top Beverage Firms - North America

Firms are ranked by 1995 sales in millions of dollars.

Coca-Cola Company	$ 18,018.0
PepsiCo	10,548.0
Anheuser-Busch Companies	9,585.9
Seagram Company	6,991.0
Coca-Cola Enterprises	6,773.0
Cadbury Schweppes	4,354.0
Philip Morris Companies	4,304.0
Southern Wine & Spirits of America	2,125.0
Quaker Oats Company	1,959.0
Adolph Coors Company	1,675.4
Whitman Corporation	1,448.7
American Brands	1,288.6

Source: *Beverage World*, July 1996, p. 40.

★ 278 ★

Beverages (SIC 2080)

U.S. Alcohol Sales - 1995

Figures are estimated.

	($ bil.)	Share
Beer	$ 62.60	60.2%
Distilled alcohol	29.48	28.4
Wine	11.81	11.4

Source: *Washington Post*, November 12, 1996, p. C1, from Distilled Spirits Council of America.

★ 279 ★

Beverages (SIC 2080)

U.S. Beverage Market - 1995

Shares of the market are based on consumption by category.

Soft drinks	27.9%
Beer	12.3
Coffee	11.6
Milk	10.3
Bottled water	5.3
Tea	4.1
All other	28.5

Source: *Tea & Coffee Trade Journal*, February 1997, p. 62, from Wheat First Butcher Singer.

★ 280 ★

Beverages (SIC 2080)

U.S. Beverage Sales - 1995

Retail receipts are shown in billions of dollars.

Soft drinks	$ 52.1
Beer	51.6
Spirits	32.4
Fruit beverages	12.5
Wine	12.1
Bottled water	4.0
RTD tea	2.8
Sports drinks	1.8

Source: *Beverage World*, May 1996, p. 48, from industry sources.

★ 281 ★

Beer (SIC 2082)

Beer Market - Houston, TX

Data are for 1995.

Anheuser-Busch	43.5%
Miller	33.9
Other	22.6

Source: *Wall Street Journal*, December 5, 1996, p. A8.

★282★

Beer (SIC 2082)

Beer Market - Mexico

Grupo Modelo	54.0%
Fomento Economico Mexicano (Femsa)	45.0
Imports	1.0

Source: *Wall Street Journal*, January 27, 1997, p. B3C.

★283★

Beer (SIC 2082)

Canadian Beer Market

Market shares are shown in percent.

Labatt	46.5%
Molson	46.1
Other	7.4

Source: *Bizlink. Maclean Hunter Business Magazines Online*, March 24, 1997, p. 1.

★284★

Beer (SIC 2082)

Leaders in the Brewpub Market

Hops Grill and Bar
McMenamin's
Rock Bottom
Mill Brewery Eatery & Bakery
Big Horn Brewing
John Harvard
Gordon Biersch
Wynkoop

Pubs are ranked by the number of outlets.

Hops Grill and Bar	18
McMenamin's	18
Rock Bottom	13
Mill Brewery Eatery & Bakery	11
Big Horn Brewing	6
John Harvard	6
Gordon Biersch	5
Wynkoop	5

Source: *Investext*, Thomson Financial Networks, January 14, 1997, p. 11.

★285★

Beer (SIC 2082)

Leading Ale Brands

Shares are shown based on supermarket sales of $161.5 million for the 52 weeks ended March 9, 1996.

Henry Weinhard's Ale	8.8%
Sierra Nevada Pale Ale	6.7
Pete's Wicked Ale	5.6
Bass Ale	5.1
Samuel Adams Boston Ale	4.3
Henry Weinhard's Ice Ale	4.0
Redhook EDB Ale	3.6
Pete's Wicked Seasonal Ale	3.2
Pyramid Hefeweizen Ale	2.5
Genesee Cream Ale	2.4
Pete's Wicked Red Amber Ale	2.4
Other	51.4

Source: *Beverage World's Periscope*, October 31, 1996, p. 14, from A.C. Nielsen.

★286★

Beer (SIC 2082)

Leading Light Malt Beverage Brands

Shares are shown based on supermarket sales of $2.1 billion for the 52 weeks ended June 8, 1996.

Bud Light	23.1%
Miller Lite	19.0
Coors Light	17.7
Natural Light	9.8
Busch Light Draft	5.3
Michelob Light	4.3
Miller Genuine Draft Light	3.3
Milwaukee's Best Light	3.1
Keystone Light	2.9
Miller Lite Ice	1.8
Other	9.7

Source: *Beverage World's Periscope*, October 31, 1996, p. 12, from A.C. Nielsen.

★ 287 ★

Beer (SIC 2082)

Leading Malt Beverage Brands

Shares are shown based on supermarket sales of $2.8 billion for the 52 weeks ended June 8, 1996.

Brand	Share
Budweiser	27.7%
Miller Genuine Draft	6.7
Busch	5.8
Miller High Life	4.3
Milwaukee's Best	3.9
Corona Extra	3.0
Heineken	2.7
Coors Original	2.5
Michelob	2.4
Old Milwaukee	2.3
Other	38.7

Source: *Beverage World's Periscope*, October 31, 1996, p. 12, from A.C. Nielsen.

★ 288 ★

Beer (SIC 2082)

Microbrew Beer Market - 1995

Market shares are shown in percent.

Boston Beer Co.	25.1%
Pete's Brewing Co.	9.2
Sierra Nevada Brewing Co.	5.3
Redhook Brewing Co.	4.1
Hart Brewing Co.	3.3
Anchor Brewing Co.	2.7
Full Sail Brewing Co.	1.9
Widmer Brewing Co.	1.8
Portland Brewing Co.	1.6
Spanish Peaks Brewing Co.	1.4
Other	43.6

Source: *DM*, August 1996, p. 78.

★ 289 ★

Beer (SIC 2082)

Top Beer Brands - 1996

Shares are shown based on supermarket sales for the year ended October 4, 1996.

Brand	Share
Budweiser	14.0%
Bud Light	9.2
Miller Lite	7.1
Coors Light	6.7
Natural Light	3.6
Miller Genuine Draft	3.5%
Busch	3.0
Busch Light	2.1
Miller High Life	2.1
Corona Extra	1.9
Other	46.8

Source: *Beverage Industry*, January 1997, p. 14, from Information Resources Inc.

★ 290 ★

Beer (SIC 2082)

Top Beer Brands - Canada

Market shares are for 1996.

Brand	Share
Blue	12.3%
Canadian	11.1
Budweiser	7.8
Molson Dry	5.9
Coors Light	5.1
Export	4.7
Kokanoo	2.9
Labatt Genuine Draft	2.5
Labatt Lite	2.3
Wildcat	2.2
Other	43.2

Source: *Marketing Magazine*, May 26, 1997, p. 11, from industry sources.

★ 291 ★

Beer (SIC 2082)

Top Beer Brands - Chicago

Shares are shown in percent.

Brand	Share
Lite	17.7%
Genuine Draft	11.1
Old Style	8.9
Budweiser	7.3
Miller High Life	3.7
Bud Light	3.6
Miller Genuine Draft Light	3.2
Heineken	2.6
Old Style Light	2.5
Corona Extra	1.8
Other	37.6

Source: *Chicago Tribune*, June 12, 1997, p. C3, from Information Resources Inc.

★292★

Beer (SIC 2082)

Top Brewers - 1995

Firms are ranked by number of barrels shipped in 1995. Stroh Brewery and G. Heileman are planning to merge.

	(000)	Share
Anheuser-Busch Inc.	87,500	46.5%
Miller Brewing Co.	45,000	23.9
Adolph Coors Co.	20,312	10.8
Stroh Brewery Co.	13,400	7.1
G. Heileman Brewing Co.	7,900	4.2
Pabst Brewing Co.	6,300	3.4
Genesee Brewing Co.	1,800	1.0
Latrobe Brewing Co.	1,200	0.6
Boston Beer Co.	961	0.5
Pittsburgh Brewing Co.	920	0.5

Source: *Detroit Free Press*, September 9, 1996, p. 6F.

★293★

Beer (SIC 2082)

Top Domestic Beer Brands - 1996

Brand shares are shown based on sales.

Budweiser	20.3%
Bud Light	11.1
Miller Light	8.6
Coors Light	7.2
Busch	4.7
Natural Light	3.5
Miller Genuine Draft	3.3
Miller High Life	2.5
Busch Light Draft	2.4
Milwaukee's Best	2.2
Other	34.2

Source: *Discount Merchandiser*, March 1997, p. 60, from Beverage Marketing Corp.

★294★

Beer (SIC 2082)

Top Specialty Beer Brewers - 1996

Brewers are ranked by shipments in millions of gallons. Specialty brews accounted for 2.5% of the U.S. beer market.

Boston Beer	37.2
Pete's	13.0
Sierra Nevada	8.4
Red Hook (Anheuser-Busch)	7.8
Pyramid	4.0
Widmer	3.8

Source: *USA TODAY*, June 5, 1997, p. B1, from *Beer Marketer's Insights* and Institute for Brewing Studies.

★295★

Beer (SIC 2082)

Top Specialty Brewers - 1996

Market shares are shown in percent.

Boston Beer	24.2%
Pete's Brewing	7.8
D.G. Yuengling	6.9
Others	61.1

Source: *Beverage World*, April 1997, p. 116, from Beverage Marketing Corp.

★296★

Beer (SIC 2082)

U.S. Beer Market - 1996

Company	Share
Anheuser-Busch	44.0%
Miller Brewing	18.5
Adolph Coors	9.1
Stroh Brewery	3.5
Imports	6.4
Others	18.5

Source: *Financial Times*, February 10, 1997, p. 19, from Impact Databank.

★ 297 ★

Beer (SIC 2082)

U.S. Craft Brewing Industry

Total craft brewing industry sales reached $1.0 billion. Regional specialty brewers produce between 15,000 and 2.0 million barrels per year with flagship brands that are all-malt or specialty beers. A microbrewery produces less than 15,000 barrels of beer per year. A brew pub is a restaurant-brewery that brews its beer on site for sale and consumption in the adjacent restaurant or bar. Data show the number of each type of facility operating in the United States.

Brew pubs	691
Microbrewery	361
Regional specialty brewery	34

Source: *Chicago Tribune*, May 13, 1997, p. C1, from Association of Brewers and Institute for Brewing Studies.

★ 298 ★

Wine (SIC 2084)

Best-Selling California Wines

Carlo Rossi
Gallo
Gallo Reserve Cellars
Franzia
Inglenook
Almaden Vineyards
Sutter Home
Robert Mondavi
Paul Masson
August Sebastiani
Kendall-Jackson

Data are in millions of 9-liter case depletions for 1995.

Carlo Rossi	15.4
Gallo	12.0
Gallo Reserve Cellars	10.0
Franzia	9.0
Inglenook	7.8
Almaden Vineyards	7.5
Sutter Home	5.4
Robert Mondavi	5.2
Paul Masson	3.9
August Sebastiani	3.6
Kendall-Jackson	2.1

Source: *New York Times*, January 4, 1997, p. 23, from *Jobson's Wine Marketing Handbook*.

★ 299 ★

Wine (SIC 2084)

Leading Table Wine Brands

Shares of the $1.6 billion market are shown for the year ended June 8, 1996.

E&J Gallo Wine Cellars	7.6%
Gallo Livingston Cellars	7.1
Sutter Home	6.5
Franzia	6.1
Carlo Rossi	5.5
Glen Ellen Proprietor's Reserve	4.4
Robert Mondavi Woodbridge	4.2
Almaden	4.1
Beringer	4.1
Kendall-Jackson	3.7
Inglenook Vineyards	3.6
August Sebastiani	3.3
Fetzer	3.2
Vendange	2.9
Other	33.7

Source: *Beverage World's Periscope*, December 31, 1996, p. 12, from A.C. Nielsen.

★ 300 ★

Wine (SIC 2084)

Leading Wine Advertisers

The leading wine brands are ranked by ad expenditures. Television received the most advertising dollars.

	1994 ($ mil.)	1995 ($ mil.)
Sutter Home	$ 0.5	$ 6.6
Gallo	3.2	5.7
Franzia	3.6	3.9
Meridian	2.7	3.3

Source: *Advertising Age*, October 14, 1996, p. 25, from *Wine Business Monthly* and Steve Barsby & Associates.

★301★

Wine (SIC 2084)

Wine Shipments by Type

Shipments are estimated to increase from 497.5 million gallons in 1996 to 517.3 million gallons in 1997.

	1996	1997
Table wine	83.1%	84.0%
Sparkling wine	6.0	5.7
Other	10.8	10.3

Source: *Wines & Vines*, February 1997, p. 15.

★302★

Liquor (SIC 2085)

Best-Selling Spirit Brands - 1996

Data show the leading brands of premium and superpremium spirits ranked by thousands of 9-liter case depletions in 1996.

Absolut	3,330
Jack Daniels	3,010
Jose Cuervo	2,490
Crown Royal	1,990
Seagram's VO	1,730
Canadian Club	1,575
Dewar's	1,525
Kahlua	1,400
Tanqueray	1,240
Captain Morgan	1,185

Source: *Advertising Age*, January 6, 1997, p. 8, from Impact Databank.

★303★

Liquor (SIC 2085)

Largest Liquor Makers

Data show ad spending in millions of dollars for 1995.

Seagram	$ 55.7
Grand Metropolitan	40.2
Bacardi	24.8
Schieffelin & Somerset	21.2
Brown-Forman	17.5

Source: *Wall Street Journal*, November 8, 1996, p. B2, from Competitive Media Reporting.

★304★

Liquor (SIC 2085)

Leading Distilled Spirits Brands - 1996

Brands are shown ranked by estimated sales in thousands of 9-liter cases.

Bacardi	6,525
Smirnoff	5,951
Seagram's Gin	3,500
Absolut	3,250
Jim Beam	3,250
Jack Daniels Black	3,110
Canadian Mist	2,890
7 Crown	2,850
Popov	2,805
Jose Cuervo/1800	2,495
DeKuyper Cordials	2,216
Crown Royal	2,030
Gordon's Vodka	2,000
E&J	1,890
Black Velvet	1,834

Source: *Beverage Industry*, April 1997, p. 30.

★305★

Liquor (SIC 2085)

Popular Liquor Brands

Brands are ranked by ad spending in millions of dollars for 1995.

Absolut	$ 26.3
Bacardi	21.3
Dewar's	11.0
Jack Daniel's	9.6
Tanqueray	8.8

Source: *USA TODAY*, November 18, 1996, p. B3, from Steve L. Barsby & Associates.

★306★

Liquor (SIC 2085)

Top Liquor Companies in the U.S. Market

GrandMet-Guinness	25.4%
Seagram	12.6
Canandaigna Wine	7.9
Brown-Forman	7.1
Allied Domecq	6.7

Continued on next page.

★ 306 ★ *Continued*

Liquor (SIC 2085)

Top Liquor Companies in the U.S. Market

Company	Share
Bacardi-Martini	5.6%
American brands	12.0
Others	22.7

Source: *Observer*, May 18, 1997, p. 6, from Impact Databank.

★ 307 ★

Bottled Water (SIC 2086)

Top Bottled Water Brands

Market shares are shown for 1996.

Arrowhead	6.9%
Poland Spring	6.8
Evian	5.1
Sparkletts	4.7
Hickley & Schmitt	3.3
Crystal Geyser	2.7
Ozarka	2.7
Zephyrillis	2.5
Deer Park	2.1
Crystal Springs	1.9
Others	61.3

Source: *Beverage World*, April 1997, p. 69, from Beverage Marketing Corp.

★ 308 ★

Bottled Water (SIC 2086)

Top Bottled Water Producers - 1996

Market shares are shown in percent.

Company	Share
Perrier Group	26.7%
Suntory Water Group	9.8
McKesson Corporation	7.5
Great Brands of Europe	5.6
Crystal Geyser	2.7
Culligan	1.9
Glacier Water Services	1.3
Nora Beverages	1.3
Aqua Penn	0.8
Black Mountain	0.8
Others	41.6

Source: *Beverage World*, April 1997, p. 69, from Beverage Marketing Corp.

★ 309 ★

Bottled Water (SIC 2086)

Top Bottled Waters - Tucson/Phoenix

Market shares are shown based on $15.39 billion in sales for the year ended June 16, 1996.

Arrowhead	21.9%
Crystal Fresh	11.7
Evian	4.4
Hinckley & Schmitt	4.2
Arrowhead	3.6
Naya	3.4
Rim Rock	3.1
Aquafina	1.9
Private label	38.5
Other	7.3

Source: *Beverage Industry*, September 1996, p. 31, from Information Resources Inc. InfoScan.

★ 310 ★

Bottled Water (SIC 2086)

Top Carbonated Water Brands

Shares of the $560.3 million market are shown in percent for the year ended May 19, 1996.

	($000)	Share
Canada Dry	$ 68.9	12.3%
Schweppes	49.8	8.9
Clearly Canadian	34.1	6.1
Vintage	34.1	6.1
Perrier	23.9	4.3
Calistoga	14.1	2.5
Polar	11.1	2.0
Poland Spring	10.2	1.8
La Croix	10.1	1.8
Private label	175.5	31.3
Other	128.5	22.9

Source: *Beverage Industry*, September 1996, p. 16, from Information Resources Inc. InfoScan.

★ 311 ★

Bottled Water (SIC 2086)

Top Non-Carbonated Water Brands

Shares of the $900.7 million market are shown in percent for the year ended May 19, 1996.

	($000)	Share
Evian	$ 92.3	10.2%
Arrowhead	68.5	7.6

Continued on next page.

★311★ *Continued*

Bottled Water (SIC 2086)

Top Non-Carbonated Water Brands

Shares of the $900.7 million market are shown in percent for the year ended May 19, 1996.

	($000)	Share
Poland Spring	$ 56.1	6.2%
Sparkletts	30.0	3.3
Zephyrhills	26.0	2.9
Deer Park	24.5	2.7
Hinkley & Schmitz	22.8	2.5
Crystal Geyser	22.7	2.5
Ozarka	19.1	2.1
Private label	226.6	25.2
Other	312.1	34.7

Source: *Beverage Industry*, September 1996, p. 16, from Information Resources Inc. InfoScan.

★312★

Bottled Water (SIC 2086)

U.S. Bottled Water Imports

Data show imports by country. The bottled water market is dominated by the non-sparkling segment with a 84.2% share.

France	61.6%
Canada	25.2
Italy	7.0
Others	6.2

Source: *Beverage World*, September 1996, p. 64, from Beverage Marketing Corp.

★313★

Soft Drinks (SIC 2086)

Corporate Soft Drink Market - Canada

Shares are shown in percent.

Coca-Cola	36.9%
PepsiCo.	34.9
Cadbury	9.8
Other	18.4

Source: *Chief Executive*, July/August 1996, p. 50, from *Beverage Digest* and Coca-Cola Co.

★314★

Soft Drinks (SIC 2086)

Corporate Soft Drink Market - Mexico

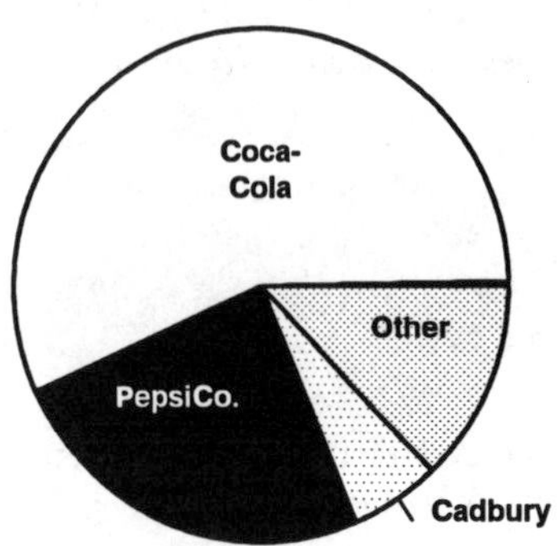

Shares are shown in percent.

Coca-Cola	57.0%
PepsiCo.	24.6
Cadbury	5.7
Other	12.7

Source: *Chief Executive*, July/August 1996, p. 50, from *Beverage Digest* and Coca-Cola Co.

★315★

Soft Drinks (SIC 2086)

Leading Soft Drinks Sold in Restaurants

Brand shares are shown in percent.

Coca-Cola	61.0%
PepsiCola	21.0
Dr. Pepper/7-Up	15.0
Other	3.0

Source: *Restaurants and Institutions*, May 1, 1997, p. 158, from Beverage Marketing Corp.

★316★

Soft Drinks (SIC 2086)

Liquid Tea Brands - Tucson/Phoenix

Market shares are shown based on $5.58 billion in sales for the year ended June 16, 1996.

Lipton Brisk	28.4%
Lipton Original	18.6
Arizona	16.2
Snapple	15.6
Nestea Cool	12.0

Continued on next page.

★ 316 ★ *Continued*

Soft Drinks (SIC 2086)

Liquid Tea Brands - Tucson/Phoenix

Market shares are shown based on $5.58 billion in sales for the year ended June 16, 1996.

Nestea	4.5%
Lipton Brew	1.5
Southwest	0.9
Fruitopia	0.7
Nestea Pitcher Style	0.4
Other	1.2

Source: *Beverage Industry*, September 1996, p. 31, from Information Resources Inc. InfoScan.

★ 317 ★

Soft Drinks (SIC 2086)

Root Beer Market - 1996

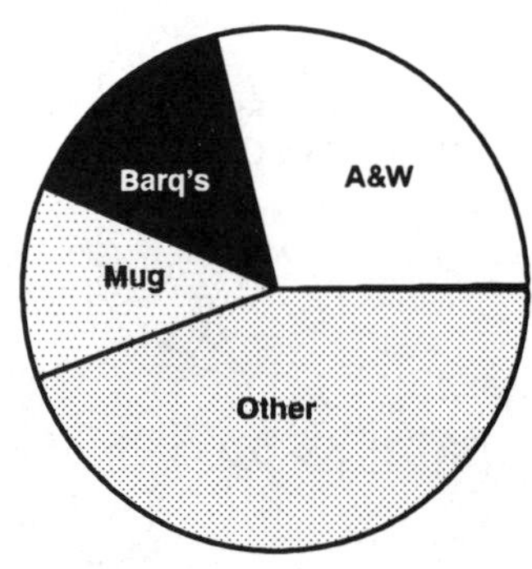

Shares are shown for the first eight months of 1996. Figures are based on supermarket sales. The root beer market is valued at $2.0 billion, approximately 3.5% of the soft drink category.

A&W	29.0%
Barq's	14.5
Mug	12.0
Other	44.5

Source: *Advertising Age*, December 2, 1996, p. 22, from Information Resources Inc.

★ 318 ★

Soft Drinks (SIC 2086)

Soft Drink Market - 1996

Shares of the market are shown in percent.

Coke Classic	20.8%
Pepsi-Cola	14.9
Diet Coke	8.7
Dr. Pepper	5.8
Mountain Dew	5.8
Sprite	5.8
Diet Pepsi	5.7
7UP	2.4
Caffeine-free Diet Coke	1.9
Caffeine-free Diet Pepsi	1.0
Other	27.2

Source: *Atlanta Journal-Constitution*, February 5, 1997, p. C1, from Beverage Digest/Maxwell Report.

★ 319 ★

Soft Drinks (SIC 2086)

Soft Drink Market - Canada

Canada is one of the top 10 soft drink markets in the world. Shares are shown in percent.

Coke	37.0%
Pepsi	24.0
Other	39.0

Source: *Fortune*, October 28, 1996, p. 78, from Andrew Conaway and Morgan Stanley.

★ 320 ★

Soft Drinks (SIC 2086)

Soft Drink Market - Mexico

Market shares are shown for 1995.

Coke	60.0%
Pepsi	21.0
Other	19.0

Source: *Time*, September 2, 1996, p. 49, from Coca-Cola Co.

★321★

Soft Drinks (SIC 2086)

Soft Drink Market - North America

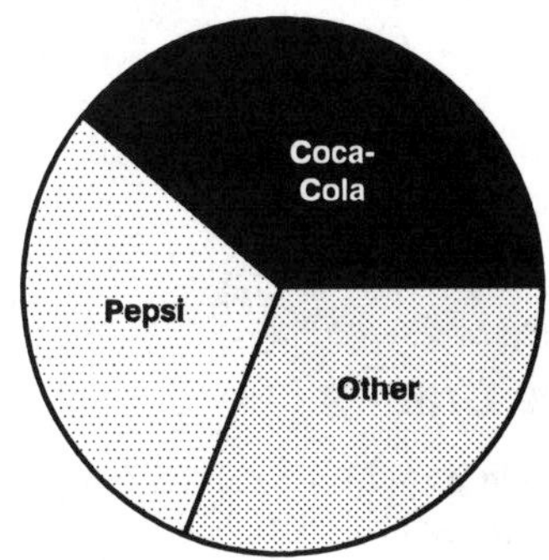

Data are for 1995.

Coca-Cola	39.0%
Pepsi	30.0
Other	31.0

Source: *Wall Street Journal*, January 27, 1997, p. B10, from Morgan Stanley.

★322★

Soft Drinks (SIC 2086)

Sports Drink Market

Gatorade	75.0%
Other	25.0

Source: *Advertising Age*, December 2, 1996, p. 22.

★323★

Soft Drinks (SIC 2086)

Top Diet Soft Drink Brands - 1996

Shares of the diet market are shown in percent.

Diet Coke	35.2%
Diet Pepsi	20.0
Caffeine free Diet Coke	6.8
Caffeine free Diet Pepsi	4.0
Diet Dr. Pepper	3.3
Diet Mountain Dew	2.6
Diet Sprite	2.6
Diet 7Up	2.4%
Diet Rite	1.4
Diet Minute Maid	0.8
Other	20.8

Source: *Beverage World*, March 1997, p. 43, from Beverage Marketing Corporation.

★324★

Soft Drinks (SIC 2086)

Top Root Beer Brands - 1996

Brands are ranked by millions of cases sold.

A&W	75.1
Barq's	67.0
Mug	60.9
Dad's	39.2
Hires	9.9

Source: *Atlanta Journal-Constitution*, May 31, 1997, p. E3, from Maxwell Consumer Report and Wheat First Butcher Singer.

★325★

Soft Drinks (SIC 2086)

U.S. Soft Drink Producers

Market shares are shown in percent.

Coca-Cola Co.	43.1%
Pepsi Cola Co.	31.0
Dr. Pepper/Seven-Up	14.8
Cott Corp.	2.9
National Beverage	1.9
Other	6.3

Source: *Atlanta Journal-Constitution*, May 8, 1997, p. F1, from *Beverage Digest*.

★326★

Syrups (SIC 2087)

Corn Syrup Processors

ADM	30.0%
A.E. Staley	21.0
Cargill	19.0
CPC	19.0
American Fructose	8.0
Other	3.0

Source: *Chicago Tribune*, February 27, 1997, p. 3-1, from NatWest Securities.

★ 327 ★
Seafood (SIC 2091)

Canned Tuna Market

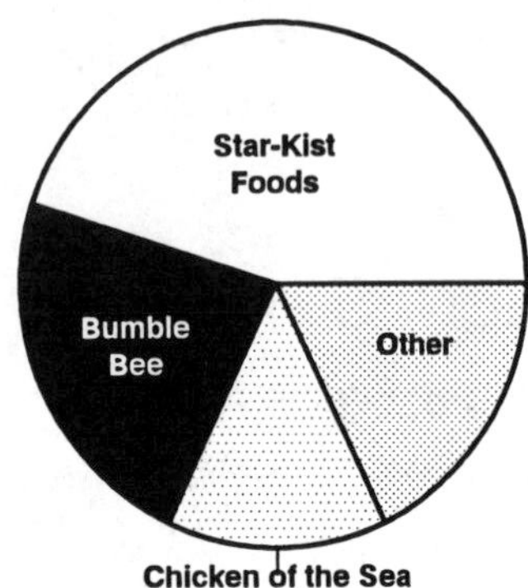

Shares are shown in percent.

Star-Kist Foods	45.0%
Bumble Bee	23.0
Chicken of the Sea	14.0
Other	18.0

Source: *Bangkok Post*, May 5, 1997, p. 2.

★ 328 ★
Seafood (SIC 2091)

Seafood Sales in Supermarkets

Fish	41.0%
Shrimp	30.0
Prepared entrees, cooked	10.0
Prepared entrees, uncooked	10.0
Lobster	3.0
Scallops	2.0
Clams and other	4.0

Source: *Supermarket Business*, November 1996, p. 33.

★ 329 ★
Coffee (SIC 2095)

Largest Coffee Roasters - San Francisco

Data show the thousands of pounds of beans roasted in 1995.

Peat's Coffee & Tea Inc.	3,000
Applets Coffee Co.	1,000
Capricorn Coffee Inc.	800
Hansen Coffee Co.	750
Lappert's Coffee Inc.	745
Pasque Coffee	600
Calle Roma Coffee Roasting Co.	500
Landmark Coffee	500
Jeremiah's Pick Coffee Co.	300

Source: *San Francisco Business Times*, September 13, 1996, p. 24.

★ 330 ★
Coffee (SIC 2095)

Top Coffee Brands

Shares are shown based on $3.38 billion in supermarket sales in 1995.

Folgers	27.4%
Maxwell House	19.2
General Foods Intl. Coffee	4.7
Hills Bros.	4.1
Maxwell House Master Blend	4.1
Tasters Choice	4.0
Chock Full O Nuts	2.2
Folgers Singles	2.0
Yuban	1.9
Private label	7.6
Other	22.8

Source: *Advertising Age*, September 30, 1996, p. S14, from Information Resources Inc.

★ 331 ★
Coffee (SIC 2095)

U.S. Coffee Producers

Shares are estimated for 1995. Regular coffee had sales of 840 million pounds, valued at $2.8 billion, and instant coffee accounted for 88 million pounds valued at $1.1 billion.

Procter & Gamble	34.9%
General Foods	28.8
Nestle	12.2
Chock Full O'Nuts	3.9
Other	20.2

Source: *World Coffee & Tea*, September 1996, p. 28, from Wheat, First Securities Inc.

★332★

Snacks (SIC 2096)

Best-Selling Snacks

Shares are shown based on total sales.

Potato chips	31.9%
Tortilla chips	21.4
Pretzels	8.6
Snack nuts	8.4
Popcorn	8.1
Other	21.6

Source: *USA TODAY*, March 11, 1997, p. D1, from Snack Food Association.

★333★

Snacks (SIC 2096)

Largest Snack Food Makers - 1996

Firms are ranked by snack food sales in millions of dollars. Some of the figures are estimates.

Nabisco Inc.	$ 6,450.0
Frito-Lay Inc.	6,000.0
Hershey Chocolate North America	2,984.0
M&M/Mars	2,500.0
Kraft Foods Inc.	2,395.0
Keebler Corp.	2,100.0
Campbell Soup Co.	1,950.0
Wm. Wrigley Jr. Co.	1,755.0
Nestle USA Inc.	1,697.0
Pillsbury Co.	1,600.0
Sara Lee Bakery Worldwide	965.0
CPC Baking Business	800.0
H.J. Heinz Co.	783.0
Schwan's Sales	764.0

Source: *Snack Food*, December 1996, p. 25.

★334★

Snacks (SIC 2096)

Leading Pork Rind Brands - 1996

Brand shares are shown based on 7.62 million units sold for the year ended March 9, 1996.

	(mil.)	Share
Baken-ets	1,896	24.9%
Golden Flake	407	5.3
Private label	380	5.0
Wise	267	3.5
Villareal	245	3.2
Southern Recipe	231	3.0
Other	4,198	55.1

Source: *Snack Food*, November 1996, p. 19, from A.C. Nielsen.

★335★

Snacks (SIC 2096)

Leading Tortilla Chip Brands

Shares are shown based on sales of $1.57 billion for the year ended April 21, 1996. Frito Lay controls the market with a 76% share.

	Sales ($ mil.)	Share
Doritos	$ 556.0	35.2%
Tostitos	409.0	25.9
Baked Tostitos	144.0	9.1
Santitas	69.0	4.4
Eagle	61.0	3.9
Doritos Thins	23.0	1.5
Mission	23.0	1.5
Padrino's	16.0	1.0
Guiltless Gourmet	13.0	0.8

Continued on next page.

★ 335 ★ *Continued*

Snacks (SIC 2096)

Leading Tortilla Chip Brands

Shares are shown based on sales of $1.57 billion for the year ended April 21, 1996. Frito Lay controls the market with a 76% share.

	Sales ($ mil.)	Share
Private label	$ 74.0	4.7%
Others	191.0	12.1

Source: *Snack Food*, August 1996, p. 22, from Information Resources Inc.

★ 336 ★

Snacks (SIC 2096)

Top 10 Snacks

The top snacks are ranked by percentage of sales to supermarkets and other stores.

Chocolate bars	45.5%
Potato chips, pretzels	22.0
Cookies	9.4
Nonchocolate bars	8.7
Chewing gum	3.4
Filled crackers	2.8
Nuts	2.5
Mints	2.3
Granola bars	1.5
Crackers	1.4
Other	0.5

Source: *Christian Science Monitor*, April 21, 1997, p. 2, from *The Top 10 of Everything*.

★ 337 ★

Snacks (SIC 2096)

Top Potato Chip Brands

Shares are shown based on a $2.3 billion market for the 52 weeks ended December 29, 1996.

Lay's	20.9%
Ruffles	17.4
Pringles	8.3
Baked Lay's	5.2
Pringles Right Crisps	4.5
Wavy Lay's	4.1
Frito Lay	3.8
Ruffles Choice	3.4
Wise	2.3
Private label	7.2%
Other	22.9

Source: *Snack & Bakery Foods*, April 1997, p. 14, from Information Resources Inc.

★ 338 ★

Pasta (SIC 2098)

Top Pasta Makers - 1996

Market shares are shown for the 52 weeks ended December 29, 1996.

Hershey	27.6%
Borden	22.3
CPC International	10.3
Quaker Oats	3.0
ADM	1.2
Private label	16.7
Imports	12.4
Other	6.5

Source: *Investext*, Thomson Financial Networks, January 30, 1997, p. 3, from Information Resources Inc. InfoScan.

★ 339 ★

Food Preparations (SIC 2099)

Lunch Kit Makers

Shares are shown in percent.

Oscar Mayer's Lunchables	72.9%
Jimmy Dean/Hillshire Farms/Bryan Foods brands	19.7
Other	7.4

Source: *Advertising Age*, November 11, 1996, p. 8, from Information Resources Inc.

★340★

Food Preparations (SIC 2099)

Weight Control Products

Total weight control product sales reached $720 million. Shares are shown for the year ended September 8, 1996.

	($ mil.)	Share
Ensure	$ 169.8	23.6%
Ensure Plus	129.7	18.0
Boost	29.7	4.1
Sustacal	12.4	1.9
Other	378.4	52.4

Source: *Nonfoods Merchandising*, December 1996, p. 24, from Information Resources Inc.

★341★

Popcorn (SIC 2099)

Microwave Popcorn Brands

Shares of the $611.13 million market are shown for the year ended May 19, 1996.

Orville Redenbacher	17.8%
Orville Redenbacher Reden Budders	12.6
Act II	12.4
Pop Secret	11.7
Private label	9.9
Orville-Redenbacher Smart-Pop	7.7
Pop Weavers	5.5
Pop Secret Light	4.0
Pop Secret by Request	2.9
Healthy Choice	2.2
Other	13.3

Source: *Snack Food*, August 1996, p. 16, from Information Resources Inc.

★342★

Popcorn (SIC 2099)

Top Kernel Popcorn Brands

Shares of the $59.9 million market are shown for the year ended May 19, 1996.

Orville Redenbacher	36.2%
Private label	22.1
Jolly Time	15.3
Jiffy Pop	9.8
Pops Rite	2.0
Cousin Willie's	1.8
Act II	1.3
Spee Dee Pop	1.1%
Newman's Own	1.0
Pop Weaver's	0.8
Other	9.6

Source: *Snack Food*, August 1996, p. 16, from Information Resources Inc.

★343★

Salads (SIC 2099)

Bagged Salad Market

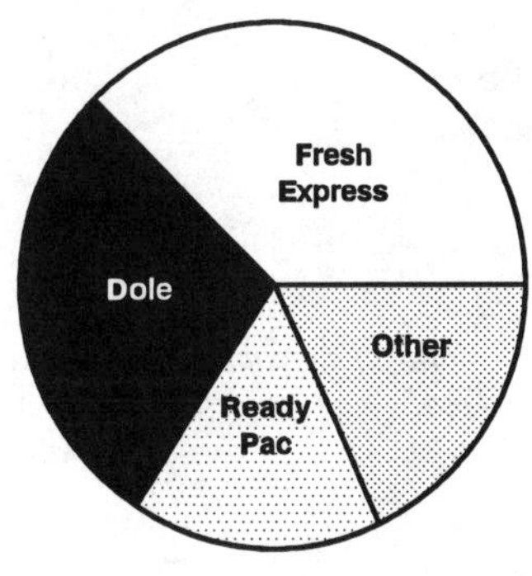

Sales are shown by brand for the year ended September 8, 1996.

	($ mil.)	Share
Fresh Express	$ 294.4	37.3%
Dole	223.0	28.2
Ready Pac	129.0	16.3
Other	143.6	18.2

Source: *Brandweek*, November 11, 1996, p. 25, from Information Resources Inc.

★344★

Syrup (SIC 2099)

Syrup Production by State - 1996

Production is shown in thousands of gallons.

Vermont	550
New York	208
Maine	167
Wisconsin	103
Ohio	90
New Hampshire	89

Source: *USA TODAY*, October 24, 1996, p. A1, from United States Agricultural Statistics Service.

★ 345 ★

Tea (SIC 2099)

Leading Tea Bag Brands

Shares are shown based on supermarket sales of $477.5 million for the 52 weeks ended March 9, 1996.

Lipton	44.1%
Tetley	10.3
Luzianne	9.1
Bigelow	9.0
Twinning	4.8
Red Rose	3.3
Salada	1.9
Lipton Special Blend	1.4
Celestial Seasonings	0.7
Stash	0.7
Private label	10.0
Other	1.4

Source: *Beverage World's Periscope*, October 31, 1996, p. 12, from A.C. Nielsen.

★ 346 ★

Tea (SIC 2099)

Tea Market - 1996

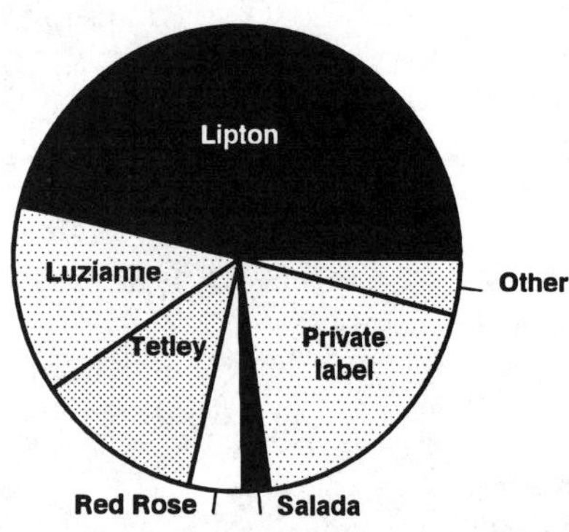

Shares are shown for the year ended May 26, 1996.

Lipton	45.8%
Luzianne	13.2
Tetley	11.6
Red Rose	4.4
Salada	2.3
Private label	18.8
Other	3.9

Source: *Tea & Coffee Trade Journal*, August 1996, p. 36, from Information Resources Inc.

★ 347 ★

Tortillas (SIC 2099)

Tortilla Sales by Region

Sales are in millions of dollars.

	($ mil.)	Share
West	$ 663	31.6%
North Central	568	27.1
South Central	454	21.6
South	225	10.7
Northeast	187	8.9

Source: *Bakery Production and Marketing*, November 15, 1996, p. 42, from Tortilla Industry Association.

SIC 21 - Tobacco Products

★ 348 ★

Cigarettes (SIC 2111)

Canada's Top Cigarette Brands - 1996

Market shares are shown in percent.

Player's Light Regular	12.6%
Du Maurier King Size	9.4
Du Maurier Regular	5.5
Player's Light King Size	4.9
Export A Regular	4.6
Player's Regular	4.4
Du Maurier Light King Size	3.9
Export A Medicin	3.2
Rothmans Kings	3.1
Du Maurier Light Regular	2.8
Other	45.7

Source: *Marketing Magazine*, May 26, 1997, p. 11, from industry sources.

★ 349 ★

Cigarettes (SIC 2111)

Cigarette Market by Segment - 1996

Data show sales in billions of units.

	(bil.)	Share
Plain	345.82	71.6%
Mentholated	122.47	25.3
King	7.97	1.6
Regular	4.51	0.9
Charcoal	2.53	0.5

Source: *Discount Merchandiser*, April 1997, p. 52, from Maxwell Consumer Reports.

★ 350 ★

Cigarettes (SIC 2111)

Discount Cigarette Market

Market shares are shown for the year ended September 1996.

Brown & Williamson	34.9%
R.J. Reynolds	32.0
Philip Morris	26.6
Liggett-Myers	4.9
Lorillard	1.6

Source: *Discount Merchandiser*, January 1997, p. 79, from Maxwell Consumer Reports.

★ 351 ★

Cigarettes (SIC 2111)

Leading Cigarette Brands - 1996

Brands are ranked by sales in billions of units. Shares are shown in percent.

	Units (bil.)	Share
Marlboro	156.21	32.3%
Newport	29.30	6.1
Doral	28.57	5.9
GPC	26.10	5.8
Winston	25.40	5.3
Basic	23.17	4.8
Camel	22.47	4.6
Salem	17.33	3.6
Kool	17.21	3.6
Virginia Slims	11.57	2.4
Merit	11.33	2.3
Benson Hedges	11.10	2.3

Source: *Discount Merchandiser*, April 1997, p. 53, from Maxwell Consumer Reports.

★ 352 ★

Cigarettes (SIC 2111)

Leading Cigarette Makers - 1996

Data show sales in billions of units.

	(bil.)	Share
Philip Morris	230.84	47.8%
R.J. Reynolds	119.08	24.6
Brown & Williamson	83.35	17.2
Lorillard	40.40	8.4
Liggett	8.95	1.9
Others	0.68	0.1

Source: *Discount Merchandiser*, April 1997, p. 52, from Maxwell Consumer Reports.

★ 353 ★

Cigarettes (SIC 2111)

Premium Cigarette Market

Market shares are shown for the year ended September 1996.

Philip Morris	55.9%
R.J. Reynolds	22.0
Lorillard	11.0
Brown & Williamson	10.4
Liggett-Myers	7.0

Source: *Discount Merchandiser*, January 1997, p. 79, from Maxwell Consumer Reports.

★ 354 ★

Cigarettes (SIC 2111)

Top Cigarette Brands

Shares are shown for the year ended June 30, 1996.

Marlboro	31.1%
Doral	5.8
GPC	5.8
Newport	5.8
Winston	5.5
Basic	4.8
Camel	4.6
Salem	3.7
Kool	3.6
Virginia Slims	2.4
Merit	2.3
Benson & Hedges	2.3
Others	22.3

Source: *Nonfoods Merchandising*, January 1997, p. 16, from Maxwell Consumer Reports.

★ 355 ★

Cigarettes (SIC 2111)

U.S. Cigarette Market - 1997

Shares are shown for the first quarter of 1997.

Philip Morris	47.6%
R.J. Reynolds	25.6
Brown & Williamson	15.9
Lorillard	7.8
Liggett	1.6
Other	1.5

Source: *USA TODAY*, June 23, 1997, p. B1, from Emanuel Goldman, PaineWebber, and Wheat First Butcher Singer.

★ 356 ★

Cigars (SIC 2121)

Top Cigar Makers

Market shares are shown in percent.

Swisher International	31.0%
Consolidated	23.0
Havatampa	19.0
Culbro	12.0
Other	15.0

Source: *Investext*, Thomson Financial Networks, January 14, 1997, p. 5.

★ 357 ★

Smokeless Tobacco (SIC 2131)

Moist Snuff Market - 1996

Market shares are shown in percent as of November 2, 1996.

UST	79.9%
Conwood	13.2
Swisher	4.1
Pinkerton	2.2

Source: *Investext*, Thomson Financial Networks, January 23, 1997, p. 2.

SIC 22 - Textile Mill Products

★ 358 ★

Textiles (SIC 2200)

Leading Textile Makers

Firms are ranked by sales in millions of dollars for the latest 12 months.

Burlington Industries	$ 2,182
WestPoint Stevens	1,692
Unifi	1,631
Interface	922
Guilford Mills	830
Cone Mills	808

Source: *Forbes*, January 13, 1997, p. 136, from Value Line and One Source Information Services.

★ 359 ★

Textiles (SIC 2200)

Top Textile Companies - 1996

Companies are ranked by revenues in millions of dollars.

Shaw Industries	$ 3,201
Springs Industries	2,243
Burlington Industries	2,182
Mohawk Industries	1,795
Westpoint Stevens	1,724
Unifi	1,603
Triarc	1,097
Fieldcrest Cannon	1,092
Interface	1,002

Source: *Fortune*, April 28, 1997, p. 62.

★ 360 ★

Textiles (SIC 2200)

U.S. Textile Imports

Data are in millions of square meters for January 1996.

Canada	136
Mexico	71
Pakistan	57
Taiwan	56
South Korea	51
China	47
India	46
Thailand	37
Japan	20
Germany	17

Source: *Textile Asia*, May 1996, p. 14.

★ 361 ★

Carpets (SIC 2273)

Carpet Construction - 1994

Percent of 1.63 billion square yards produced in 1994.

Tufted	91.0%
Knitted, braided	7.0
Woven	2.0

Source: *Contract Design*, August 1996, p. 78.

★ 362 ★

Carpets (SIC 2273)

Carpet Shipments by Type - 1996

The.table shows shipments in millions of square yards. Data are estimated.

Broadloom	1,300
Automotive, industrial	65
Tufted woven	25
Artificial grass	20
Needlepunch, other	105
Rugs, other	85

Source: *Textile World*, May 1997, p. 64, from U.S. Department of Commerce and Carpet & Rug Institute.

SIC 23 - Apparel and Other Textile Products

★ 363 ★

Apparel (SIC 2300)

Designer Jeans Market

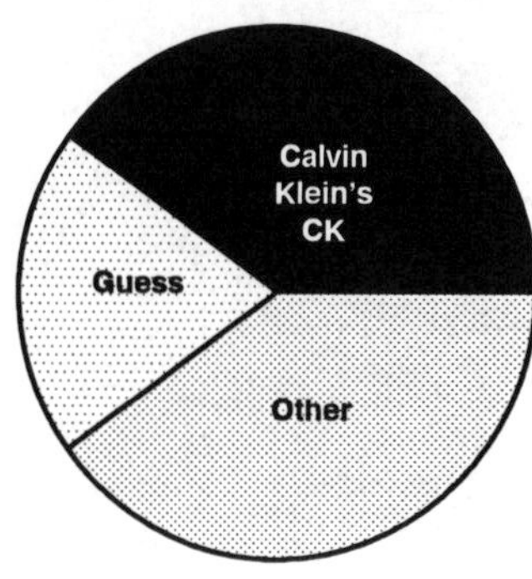

Designer jeans have an estimated 10% share of the $10 billion jeans market. "Other" includes Lucky Brand, Tommy Hilfiger, Ralph Lauren, DKNY, and Diesel.

Calvin Klein's CK	40.0%
Guess	20.0
Other	40.0

Source: *Fortune*, October 14, 1996, p. 140.

★ 364 ★

Apparel (SIC 2300)

Discount Apparel Sales by Segment

Sales at discount stores are shown in percent. Total sales reached $37.94 billion.

Men's	27.1%
Women's	25.8
Girl's	10.2
Boy's	8.7
Infant's	7.8
Intimates	7.2%
Accessories	6.5
Shoes	5.5
Other	1.2

Source: *Discount Store News*, August 5, 1996, p. 60.

★ 365 ★

Apparel (SIC 2300)

Jeans Market Leaders - 1996

Shares are shown based on a $10.6 billion market.

VF	27.0%
Levi	20.0
Guess	10.0
Other	43.0

Source: *New York Times*, March 14, 1997, p. C15, from Morgan Stanley.

★ 366 ★

Apparel (SIC 2300)

Licensed Sports Apparel Sales

Total sales reached $2.571 billion in 1995. Figures are in millions of dollars.

T-shirts	$ 981
Fleece tops	627
Jackets	428
Knit shirts	223
Caps/hats	182
Shorts	78
Fleece bottoms	52

Source: *Sportstyle*, January 1997, p. 6, from National Sporting Goods Association.

★ 367 ★

Apparel (SIC 2300)

Popular Children's Wear Brands

Data show the brands of children's apparel preferred by shoppers at discount stores in 1996.

OshKosh	25.5%
Hanes	14.1
Levi's	11.4
Fruit of the Loom	9.2
Lee	7.6
Carter	6.0
Healthtex	6.0
Wrangler	4.3
Nike	4.3
Gerber	2.2

Source: *Discount Store News*, October 21, 1996, p. A36, from Lee J. Shapiro & Associates.

★ 368 ★

Apparel (SIC 2300)

Sportswear Sales by Sport

Sales are shown in millions of dollars.

Swimming	$ 1,777.5
Golf	1,461.3
Camping	1,131.8
Hunting	942.5
Skiing/alpine	799.6
Bicycling	745.5
Aerobic exercising	705.3
Fishing	701.6
Running/jogging	$ 513.1
Bowling	511.9
Tennis	266.6
Skiing/cross country	142.4

Source: *Discount Merchandiser*, February 1997, p. 90, from National Sporting Goods Association.

★ 369 ★

Apparel (SIC 2300)

Top Beach/Lifestyle Apparel - 1996

Firms are ranked by sales in millions of dollars.

Quiksilver	$ 122.0
Mossimo	108.6
No Fear	80.0
Ocean Pacific	67.0
Gotcha	66.0
Big Dog Sportswear	62.0
Rusty	50.0
Sideout Sport	40.0
Billabong	37.0
O'Neill	35.0

Source: *Sportstyle*, May 1997, p. 36.

★ 370 ★

Apparel (SIC 2300)

Top Designer Apparel Makers

Firms are ranked by estimated 1996 sales in millions of dollars.

Liz Claiborne	$ 2,000
Ralph Lauren	1,300
DKNY	554
Tommy Hilfiger	478
Nautica	303

Source: *Sporting Goods Business*, November 1996, p. 43.

★ 371 ★

Apparel (SIC 2300)

Top Jeans Brands - 1995

Brand shares are shown based on sales.

Levi	26.42%
Lee	10.07
Wrangler	9.11
Rustler	5.32

Continued on next page.

★371★ *Continued*

Apparel (SIC 2300)

Top Jeans Brands - 1995

Brand shares are shown based on sales.

J.C. Penney	5.21%
Riders	2.20
Brittania	1.81
Kmart	1.67
Sears	1.29
Wal-Mart	1.03
Girbaud	0.42
Dockers	0.24
Maverick	0.18

Source: *Investext*, Thomson Financial Networks, June 5, 1996, p. 7, from NPD Group Inc.

★372★

Apparel (SIC 2300)

Top Licensed Apparel Makers

Firms are ranked by estimated 1996 sales in millions of dollars.

Starter	$ 345.0
Champion	245.0
VF Knitwear	230.0
Logo Athletic	228.0
Fruit of the Loom	220.0
Russell	120.0
Nike	100.0
Mighty Mac	75.0
Sports Specialties	60.0
Winning Ways	60.0

Source: *Sporting Goods Business*, November 1996, p. 36.

★373★

Apparel (SIC 2300)

Top Performance Apparel Makers - 1996

Firms are ranked by sales in millions of dollars.

Speedo (Authentic Fitness)	$ 162.0
Champion Jogbra	60.0
Pearl Izumi	25.0
Tyr	24.0
Insport	17.0
Diadora	14.4
The Finals	$ 12.0
Dolfin	11.5
Asics	10.5
Hind (Hyde)	10.0

Source: *Sportstyle*, May 1997, p. 26.

★374★

Apparel (SIC 2300)

Top Sports Apparel Makers

Firms are ranked by sales in millions of dollars for 1996.

Russell	$ 254.0
Umbro	64.6
Wilson	42.0
Don Alleson Athletic	35.7
DeLong	34.0
Bike Athletic	31.5

Source: *Sportstyle*, May 1997, p. 58.

★375★

Apparel (SIC 2300)

Top Team Sports Apparel Makers

Firms are ranked by estimated 1996 sales in millions of dollars.

Spalding	$ 152.0
Wilson	145.0
Rawlings	142.0
Hillerich and Bradsby	113.0
Franklin	100.0
Easton	99.0
Mizuno	77.0
Russell	60.0
CCM	55.0
Bike	53.0

Source: *Sporting Goods Business*, November 1996, p. 38.

★ 376 ★

Apparel (SIC 2300)

U.S. Apparel Imports

Data are for the first seven months of 1996.

	($ mil.)	Share
Hong Kong	$ 2,043	10.0%
Mexico	1,887	9.3
China	1,844	9.0
Taiwan	1,045	5.1
Dominican Republic	930	4.6
Philippines	874	4.3
Korea	789	3.9
Indonesia	723	3.5
Honduras	641	3.1
Bangladesh	614	3.0
Caribbean Basin	614	3.0
Rest of world	8,375	41.1

Source: *World Trade*, February 1997, p. 24, from United States Department of Commerce.

★ 377 ★

Apparel (SIC 2300)

U.S. Jeans Market

VF Corp.	30.1%
Levi Strauss	16.0
Other	53.9

Source: *USA TODAY*, March 17, 1997, p. B6.

★ 378 ★

Apparel (SIC 2320)

Men's Apparel Consumption

Slacks

Coats

Jackets

Suits

Data are in millions of pieces.

Slacks	427.0
Coats	52.7
Jackets	19.7
Suits	12.8

Source: *National Trade Data Bank*, August 26, 1996, p. ISA9606, from *Wool Facts* and International Wool Secretariat.

★ 379 ★

Apparel (SIC 2320)

Men's Designer Apparel Sales

Data show sales at collection sportswear shops for the third quarter of 1996.

Ralph Lauren	29.0%
Tommy Hilfiger	27.0
Nautica	14.0
Guess	7.0
CK Jeanswear	6.0
Claiborne	5.0
Tommy Jeans	5.0
Other	7.0

Source: *DNR*, February 17, 1997, p. 14, from NYD POSTS Department Stores.

★ 380 ★

Apparel (SIC 2320)

Men's Dress Shirt Makers - Canada

Shares of the $30 million market are shown in percent. Data refer to shirts $55-and-up.

Hathaway Canada	55.0%
Other	45.0

Source: *Marketing Magazine*, January 27, 1997, p. 4.

★ 381 ★

Apparel (SIC 2320)

Men's Sportswear Sales by Type

Percentages are shown based of sales in men's designer shops for July - September 1996.

Knit shirts	47.5%
Woven sport shirts	16.4
Shorts	11.7
Jeans	9.2
Slacks	8.3
Outerwear	2.9
Fleece	1.7
Sweaters	1.0
Other	1.3

Source: *DNR*, February 17, 1997, p. 16, from NPD POSTS Department Stores.

★382★

Apparel (SIC 2320)

Popular Men's Wear Brands

Data show the brands of men's apparel preferred by shoppers at discount stores in 1996.

Hanes	29.5%
Levi's	23.5
Fruit of the Loom	19.5
Wrangler	9.4
Lee	6.7
Haggar	4.0
Arrow	3.4
BVD	2.7
Rustler	2.7
Wilson	2.0

Source: *Discount Store News*, October 21, 1996, p. A36, from Lee J. Shapiro & Associates.

★383★

Apparel (SIC 2330)

Popular Women's Wear Brands

Hanes
Levi's
Jaclyn Smith
Lee
L'eggs
Fruit of the Loom
Playtex
Kathie Lee
Chic
No Nonsense

Data show the brands of women's apparel preferred by shoppers at discount stores in 1996.

Hanes	19.0%
Levi's	7.7
Jaclyn Smith	7.7
Lee	7.2
L'eggs	6.7
Fruit of the Loom	5.6
Playtex	5.1
Kathie Lee	2.6
Chic	2.1
No Nonsense	2.1

Source: *Discount Store News*, October 21, 1996, p. A36, from Lee J. Shapiro & Associates.

★384★

Apparel (SIC 2339)

Leading Bodywear/Activewear Producers - 1996

Firms are ranked by sales in millions of dollars.

Sara Lee Bodywear	$ 200.0
Jacques Moret	92.0
Danskin	87.0
Rainbeau/Flyte	82.6
Marika	36.0
Gilda Marx	23.0
S.F. City Lights	20.0

Source: *Sportstyle*, May 1997, p. 24.

★385★

Lingerie (SIC 2341)

Leading Bra Brands

Shares of the $3.6 billion market are estimated in percent.

Playtex	15.0%
Victoria's Secret	7.0
Warner's	7.0
Other	71.0

Source: *Advertising Age*, May 19, 1997, p. 14, from NPD Group Inc.

★386★

Lingerie (SIC 2341)

Lingerie Sales by Type - 1996

Bras	43.0%
Panties	21.0
Robes	11.0
Sleepwear	10.0
Daywear	8.0
Shapewear	5.0
Thermal	2.0

Source: *Women's Wear Daily*, April 28, 1997, p. 4, from Fairchild Strategic Information Services and NPD Group Inc.

★ 387 ★

Homefurnishings (SIC 2392)

Designer Textile Producers

Designers are ranked by estimated sales in millions of dollars.

Ralph Lauren	$ 250
Laura Ashley	130
Calvin Klein	50
Liz Claiborne	50
Adrienne Vittadni	30

Source: *HFN*, April 14, 1997, p. 87, from industry estimates.

★ 388 ★

Homefurnishings (SIC 2392)

Popular Linen Brands

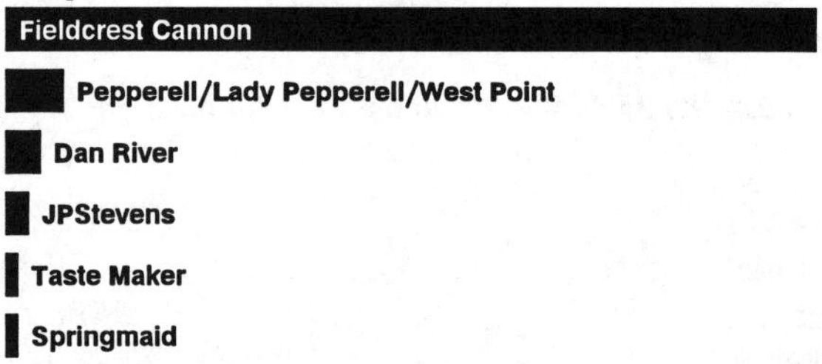

Data show the brands of linens preferred by shoppers at discount stores in 1996.

Fieldcrest Cannon	71.0%
Pepperell/Lady Pepperell/West Point	5.0
Dan River	3.0
JPStevens	2.0
Taste Maker	1.0
Springmaid	1.0

Source: *Discount Store News*, October 21, 1996, p. 65, from Lee J. Shapiro & Associates.

SIC 24 - Lumber and Wood Products

★ 389 ★

Wood Products (SIC 2400)

U.S. Wood Product Exports

Japan	44.8%
Canada	17.5
Germany	4.5
South Korea	4.4
Mexico	3.2
U.K.	3.2
Italy	2.8
Taiwan	2.1
Rest of world	17.6

Source: *Construction Review*, Spring/Summer 1996, p. 7.

★ 390 ★

Fire Logs (SIC 2411)

Best-Selling Fire Logs

Shares are shown based on supermarket sales of $62.1 million for the 52 weeks ended December 9, 1995.

	($ mil.)	Share
Duraflame	$ 32.6	52.4%
Pine Mountain	5.9	5.8
Starterlogg	3.6	5.8
Northland	3.3	5.3
Hearthside	2.0	3.2
Private label	10.9	17.6
Other	3.8	9.9

Source: *Supermarket Business*, August 1996, p. 79, from A.C. Nielsen.

★ 391 ★

Logging (SIC 2411)

Logging Firms by State

State	Firms
Georgia	2,500
North Carolina	2,500
Arkansas	2,000
Kentucky	2,000
Pennsylvania	1,800
Alabama	1,700
Minnesota	1,500
Oregon	1,500
Tennessee	1,500

Source: *Journal of Forestry*, July 1996, p. 10.

★ 392 ★

Lumber (SIC 2426)

Treated Lumber Market - Mexico

The market is shown by end use. Data include stakes for tomatoes, tobacco, grape cultivation, playground equipment, decks, and walkways.

Industrial	35.0%
Agricultural	30.0
Marine and tourism	25.0
Residential	10.0

Source: *Business Mexico*, July 1996, p. 40.

★ 393 ★

Tropical Wood (SIC 2429)

Tropical Wood Market - Mexico

Production is estimated by company.

Chiapas	24.0%
Oaxaca	17.0
Campeche	13.0
Quintana Roo	12.0
Other	34.0

Source: *National Trade Data Bank*, October 3, 1996, p. ISA960801.

★ 394 ★

Cabinets (SIC 2434)

Popular Cabinet Woods

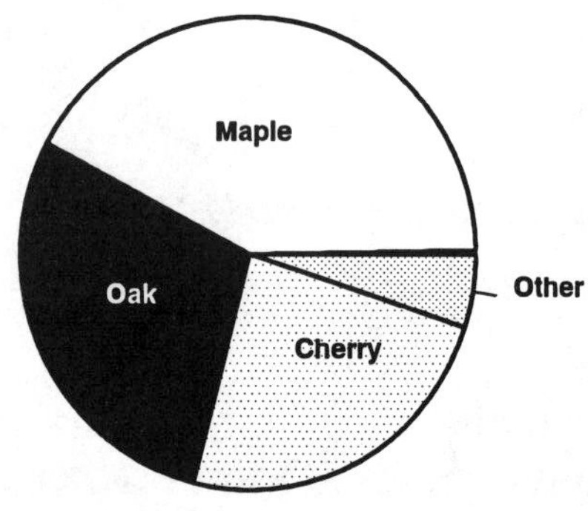

Maple	42.0%
Oak	29.0
Cherry	24.0
Other	5.0

Source: *Custom Builder*, Nov. - Dec. 1996, p. 16, from National Kitchen and Bath Association.

★ 395 ★

Pallets (SIC 2448)

Texas Pallet Production

Pine	49.1%
Oak	35.0
Other hardwood	15.9

Source: *Forest Products Journal*, February 1997, p. 28.

★ 396 ★

Mobile Homes (SIC 2451)

Mobile Home Sales by State - 1995

States are ranked by unit sales.

Texas	33,406
North Carolina	32,297
Georgia	20,412
South Carolina	19,644
Alabama	17,478
Florida	16,172
Tennessee	15,966
Kentucky	12,372
Michigan	11,513
Mississippi	11,212

Source: *Christian Science Monitor*, May 20, 1997, p. 4, from Manufactured Housing Institute.

★ 397 ★

Particleboard (SIC 2493)

Particleboard Market

End use is shown based on 4.8 billion square feet.

Ready-to-assemble	49.0%
Kitchen & bath cabinets	28.0
Home building	9.0
Non-ready-to-assemble furniture	8.0
Industrial	6.0

Source: *Wood Digest*, May 1997, p. 31.

SIC 25 - Furniture and Fixtures

★ 398 ★

Furniture (SIC 2500)

Largest Furniture/Bedding Markets - 2000

Data show estimated sales in millions of dollars.

Chicago	$ 2,567.1
Washington D.C.	1,886.4
New York City	1,487.2
Atlanta	1,309.2
Detroit	1,261.7
Los Angeles/Long Beach	1,230.6
Philadelphia	943.9
Phoenix/Mesa	907.6
Greensboro/Winston Salem/High Point	893.1

Source: *Furniture Today*, December 30, 1996, p. 34.

★ 399 ★

Furniture (SIC 2500)

Leading Furniture Companies - 1996

Firms are ranked by revenues in millions of dollars.

Leggett & Platt	$ 2,466
Furniture Brands International	1,697
Herman Miller	1,284
Hon Industries	998

Source: *Fortune*, April 28, 1997, p. 52.

★ 400 ★

Furniture (SIC 2500)

Leading Furniture Makers - 1996

Data show furniture shipments in millions of dollars.

LifeStyle Furnishings International	$ 1,733.3
Furniture Brands International	1,696.8
La-Z-Boy	985.2
Klaussner	657.0
Ladd	497.5
Sauder	475.0
Bassett	$ 450.7
Ethan Allen	448.0
Ashley	442.0
O'Sullivan	301.1
Bush Furniture	248.6
Natuzzi	237.7
Sunbeam	227.5
Stanley	201.9
Chromcraft Revington	175.9

Source: *Furniture Today*, May 19, 1997, p. 9.

★ 401 ★

Furniture (SIC 2500)

Prison Furniture Industry

Sales are in millions of dollars.

	1997	1999
Systems furniture	$ 100	$ 120
Office casegoods	45	60

Source: *Wood & Wood Products*, March 1997, p. 15, from Federal Prison Industries.

★ 402 ★

Furniture (SIC 2500)

Ready-to-Assemble Furniture Makers - 1996

Producers are ranked by sales in millions of dollars. Shares of the group are shown in percent.

	Sales ($ mil.)	% of Group
Sauder	$ 500.0	42.7%
O'Sullivan	301.1	25.7
Bush	256.3	21.9
Ameriwood	114.5	9.8

Source: *Furniture Today*, May 19, 1997, p. 16, from company reports.

★ 403 ★
Furniture (SIC 2510)

Household Furniture Market

Upholstered furniture	36.7%
Wooden furniture	31.7
Mattresses, spring bases and frames	14.1
Other indoor wood furniture	11.3
Metal and other furniture	6.2

Source: *HFN*, May 19, 1997, p. 20, from U.S. Department of Commerce and U.S. Bureau of Labor.

★ 404 ★
Furniture (SIC 2520)

Top Contract Furniture Makers

Companies are ranked by sales in millions of dollars.

Steelcase Inc.	$ 2,600
Herman Miller	1,374
Haworth Inc.	1,365
HON Industries	998
Knoll Inc.	625
Kimball International	580
Krueger International	425
Virco Manufacturing Corp.	224
Allsteel	180
Shelby Williams	172
Falcon Products	111
American Seating	110
GF Office Furniture	100
American of Martinsville	80
Trendway Corp.	76

Source: *Wood & Wood Products*, May 1997, p. 42.

★ 405 ★
Fixtures (SIC 2540)

Top Store Fixture Producers

Firms are ranked by 1995 sales in millions of dollars. Data refer to North America.

Ontario Store Fixtures	$ 206.0
Madix Store Fixtures Inc.	144.0
RHC Spacemaster Corp.	139.0
Hamilton Fixture	70.0
Excell Store Fixtures	55.0
Mil Inc.	51.0
Ready Metal Mfg. Co.	50.0
Met Merchandising Concepts	50.0
Goer Manufacturing Co.	$ 46.0
Store Kraft Mfg. Co.	39.0
ABC/Spectrum	38.0

Source: *VM + SD*, October 1996, p. 39.

★ 406 ★
Fixtures (SIC 2541)

Top Architectural Woodworking & Store Fixture Makers - 1996

Data show sales in millions of U.S. dollars. Figures for Ontario Store Fixtures and Valley City Manufacturing show sales in millions of Canadian dollars. Figures for Imperial Woodworking show 1995 sales.

Ontario Store Fixtures	$ 216.0
Hamilton Fixture	76.0
Oklahoma Fixture Co.	75.0
Store Kraft Manufacturing Co.	40.0
Monarch Ind.	30.1
Imperial Woodworking	27.0
Russell William Ltd.	25.0
Tarrant Interiors	25.0
Rodgers-Wade Manufacturing	23.0
Valley City Manufacturing Co.	20.0

Source: *Wood & Wood Products*, March 1997, p. 52.

★ 407 ★
Furniture (SIC 2599)

Casino Furniture Makers

Paul-Son	60.0%
Other	40.0

Source: *Investor's Business Daily*, February 25, 1997, p. A4.

SIC 26 - Paper and Allied Products

★ 408 ★

Paper (SIC 2600)

U.S. Paper Firms - 1996

Firms are ranked by net earnings in millions of dollars.

Weyerhaeuser	$ 463.8
International Paper	303.0
Bowater	200.2
Georgia Pacific	156.0
Jefferson Smurfit	112.0

Source: *Financial Times*, January 23, 1997, p. 22, from companies.

★ 409 ★

Paper (SIC 2611)

Mexican Paper Market

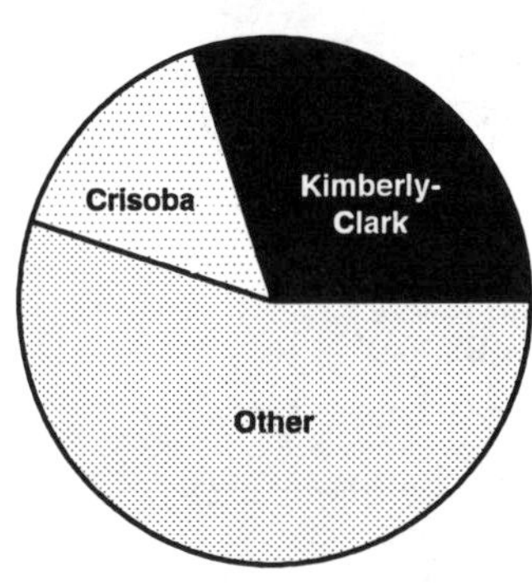

Shares are shown in percent. Crisoba is to complete its merger with Kimberly-Clark in March 1997.

Kimberly-Clark	30.0%
Crisoba	15.0
Other	55.0

Source: *Investext*, Thomson Financial Networks, January 13, 1997, p. 2, from company estimates.

★ 410 ★

Paper (SIC 2621)

Tissue Paper Producers - North America

Shares are shown based on a total capacity.

Kimberly-Clark	22.0%
Fort Howard	16.2
James River	14.0
Procter & Gamble	13.0
Georgia-Pacific	8.0
Chesapeake	4.0
Scott Paper Ltd.	3.7
Cascades	2.2
Jomar Management	2.0
Potlatch	2.0
Irving	1.6
Others	11.3

Source: *Pulp & Paper*, February 1997, p. 13, from Canadian Pulp & Paper Association and American Pulp & Forest Association.

★ 411 ★

Paper (SIC 2621)

Top Corrugated Paper Makers - Mexico

Market shares are shown in percent.

Durango	50.0%
JSG	16.0
Gondi	12.0
Other	22.0

Source: *Investext*, Thomson Financial Networks, June 10, 1996, p. 3, from JSG.

★ 412 ★

Paper (SIC 2621)

Top Newsprint Makers - North America

Total North American capacity reached 16.079 billion metric tons in 1996.

Abitibi-Price Inc.	11.8%
Stone Consolidated Corp.	8.9
Avenor Inc.	8.4
Donohue	8.4
Bowater Inc.	7.8
Kruger Inc.	5.8
Fletcher Challenge Canada	4.8
Champion International Corp.	4.3
North Pacific Paper Group	4.3
Smurfit Newsprint Corp.	4.3
Other	31.2

Source: *Pulp & Paper*, December 1996, p. 13, from Canadian Pulp & Paper Association and *Pulp & Paper Week*.

★ 413 ★

Paper (SIC 2621)

U.S. Paper Mills - 1996

Firms are ranked by sales in thousands of dollars.

International Paper	$ 20.1
Kimberly-Clark	13.1
Georgia Pacific	13.0
Weyerhaeuser	11.1
Champion International	5.8
James River	5.6
Boise Cascade	5.1
Stone Container	5.1
Mead	4.7
Union Camp	4.1

Source: *Pulp & Paper*, April 1997, p. 27.

★ 414 ★

Paper (SIC 2621)

Writing & Printing Paper Consumption

Uncoated free-sheet
Coated groundwood
Uncoated groundwood
Coated free-sheet

Consumption is shown by type in millions of tons.

	1995	1996	1997
Uncoated free-sheet	13.51	13.69	14.06
Coated groundwood	5.24	4.45	5.02
Uncoated groundwood	4.97	4.66	5.02
Coated free-sheet	4.48	4.29	4.65

Source: *Purchasing*, February 13, 1997, p. 77, from American Forest & Paper Association.

★ 415 ★

Containerboard (SIC 2631)

Top Boxboard Makers - Mexico

Market shares are shown in percent.

Ponderosa	50.0%
Cosmos (Estrella)	20.0
JSG	19.0
Other	11.0

Source: *Investext*, Thomson Financial Networks, June 10, 1996, p. 3, from JSG.

★ 416 ★

Containerboard (SIC 2631)

Top Containerboard Makers - Mexico

Market shares are shown in percent.

Durango	24.0%
JSG	18.0
Gondi	16.0
Other	42.0

Source: *Investext*, Thomson Financial Networks, June 10, 1996, p. 3, from JSG.

★ 417 ★

Paperboard (SIC 2650)

U.S. Bleached Paperboard Makers

Shares are shown based on a total annual capacity of 7.15 million tons.

International Paper Co.	21.5%
Federal Paper Board Co.	13.5
Westvaco Corp.	13.5
Temple-Inland Inc.	11.0
Potlatch Corp.	8.0
Georgia Pacific Corp.	5.2
Champion International	4.0
James River Corp.	3.8
Gulf States Paper Corp.	3.5
Weyerhaeuser Corp.	3.2
Other	11.2

Source: *Pulp & Paper*, October 1996, p. 13.

★ 418 ★

Paperboard (SIC 2652)

Top Linerboard Makers - North America

Market shares are shown in percent.

Stone Container	13.7%
Georgia-Pacific	9.1
International Paper	8.3
Temple-Inland	7.7
Union Camp	6.6
Jefferson Smurfit/CCA	6.0
Weyerhaeuser	6.0
Tenneco Packaging	4.8
Willamette Industries	4.5
Gaylord Container	4.4
Other	28.9

Source: *Pulp & Paper*, January 1997, p. 13.

★ 419 ★

Folding Boxes (SIC 2657)

Top Folding Carton Makers - Mexico

Market shares are shown in percent.

Cosmos (Estrella)	18.0%
JSG	16.0
Impresos Automaticos	8.0
Other	58.0

Source: *Investext*, Thomson Financial Networks, June 10, 1996, p. 3, from JSG.

★ 420 ★

Folding Boxes (SIC 2657)

Top Producers of Folding Cartons - 1995

Companies are ranked by sales in millions of dollars. Shares of the $4.525 billion market are shown in percent.

	Sales ($ mil.)	Share
Jefferson Smurfit	$ 686	15.2%
James River	640	14.1
Rock-Tenn	375	8.3
Shorewood	357	7.9
International Paper	320	7.1
Field Container	300	6.6
Waldorf	275	6.1
Universal	200	4.4
Gulf States	182	4.0
Others	1,190	26.3

Source: *Investext*, Thomson Financial Networks, November 5, 1996, p. 7, from CS First Boston.

★ 421 ★

Paper Products (SIC 2670)

Consumer Paper Products Market

Market shares are shown in percent. Shares reflect market after James River merged with Fort Howard; the new company is listed as Fort James.

Procter & Gamble	32.0%
Kimberly-Clark	26.0
Fort James	23.0
Other	19.0

Source: *USA TODAY*, May 6, 1997, p. 3B, from Robert W. Baird.

★ 422 ★

Coated Paper (SIC 2672)

Coated Free-Sheet Paper Makers

Total North American capacity was 5.47 million short tons.

S.D. Warren	20.28%
Westvaco	11.80
Champion International	10.82
Mead	9.59
Consolidated Papers	9.13
Repap	6.67
Potlatch	6.21
International Paper Co.	5.48
Simpson Paper	4.75
Appleton Papers	2.37
Other	13.00

Source: *Pulp & Paper*, March 1997, p. 13.

★ 423 ★

Coated Paper (SIC 2672)

Top Coated Groundwood Paper Producers - North America

Data show thousands of tons.

	(000)	Share
Consolidated Papers	855	16.1%
Champion International	760	14.3
International Paper	650	12.2
Repap Enterprises	508	9.6
Bowater	489	9.2
Blandin Paper	460	8.6
All others	1,597	30.0

Source: *Investext*, Thomson Financial Networks, June 7, 1996, p. 3.

★ 424 ★

Uncoated Paper (SIC 2674)

Uncoated Free-Sheet Producers - North America

Companies are ranked by annual capacity in thousands of tons. Total North American capacity was 15.858 million tons in 1996. Figures are estimated.

	Tons (000)	Share
International Paper Co.	2,510	15.8%
Georgia Pacific Corp.	2,131	13.4
Champion International	1,523	9.6
Boise Cascade Corp.	1,215	7.7
Union Camp Corp.	1,210	7.6
Willamette Industries	969	6.1
Weyerhaeuser Co.	860	5.4
Domtar Inc.	843	5.3
Appleton Papers Inc.	575	3.6
James River Corp.	495	3.1
Noranda Forest Inc.	417	2.6
P. H. Glatfelter Co.	411	2.3
Other	2,775	17.5

Source: *Pulp & Paper*, April 1997, p. 11.

★ 425 ★

Uncoated Paper (SIC 2674)

Uncoated Groundwood Producers

Shares are shown based on a total annual capacity of 5.52 million tons in North America.

Stone Consolidated	17.0%
Abitibi-Price	11.0
Champion International	10.0
MacMillan Bloedel	9.0
Bowater	7.0
Fletcher Challenge Canada	5.0
Tripap	5.0
Consolidated Papers	4.0
Daishowa	4.0
Madison Paper	4.0
Other	26.0

Source: *Pulp & Paper*, September 1996, p. 13.

★ 426 ★

Diapers (SIC 2676)

Diaper Makers - 1996

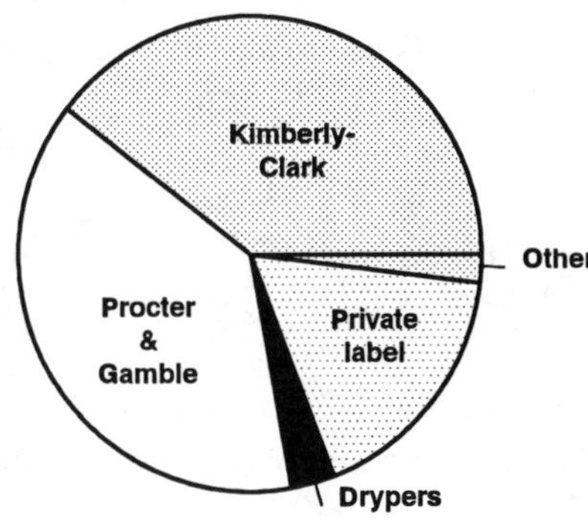

Market shares are shown as of September 1996.

Kimberly-Clark	39.1%
Procter & Gamble	38.3
Drypers	3.3
Private label	17.1
Other	2.2

Source: *Advertising Age*, November 18, 1996, p. 22, from Dean Witter Reynolds.

★ 427 ★

Diapers (SIC 2676)

Mexican Diaper Market

Shares are shown in percent.

Kimberly-Clark	60.0%
Other	40.0

Source: *Investext*, Thomson Financial Networks, January 13, 1997, p. 2, from company estimates.

★ 428 ★

Diapers (SIC 2676)

Top Diaper Brands

Shares are shown in percent for the year ended December 29, 1996.

Huggies	40.6%
Pampers	24.9
Luvs	12.5
Drypers	3.1
Fitti	1.1
Cuddles	0.2
Baby Choice	0.1
Comfees	0.1%
Snuggems	0.1
Private label	16.7

Source: *Supermarket Business*, April 1997, p. 52, from Information Resources Inc.

★ 429 ★

Diapers (SIC 2676)

Top Diaper Brands by Unit Sales

Shares are shown in percent for the year ended December 29, 1996.

Huggies	35.9%
Pampers	20.0
Luvs	13.9
Drypers	4.3
Fitti	1.8
Cuddles	0.3
Baby Choice	0.1
Comfees	0.1
Snuggems	0.1
Private label	22.5

Source: *Supermarket Business*, April 1997, p. 52, from Information Resources Inc.

★ 430 ★

Diapers (SIC 2676)

U.S. Diaper Brand Leaders

Market shares are shown for the year ended April 13, 1996.

Huggies	31.7%
Pampers	26.5
Private label	21.0
Luvs	14.2
Other	6.6

Source: *Wall Street Journal*, July 6, 1996, p. B4, from A.C. Nielsen.

★ 431 ★

Feminine Hygiene Products (SIC 2676)

Feminine Napkin Brands - 1996

Data show the change in unit market share for the last three quarters of 1996.

	2Q 1996	3Q 1996	4Q 1996
Tampax	49.5%	50.6%	52.1%
Playtex	25.0	22.1	20.4
Kotex	11.8	11.6	11.1
O.B.	8.6	10.3	10.4
Private label	5.0	5.5	6.0

Source: *Investext*, Thomson Financial Networks, January 30, 1997, p. 2, from A.C. Nielsen.

★ 432 ★

Feminine Hygiene Products (SIC 2676)

Feminine Product Makers

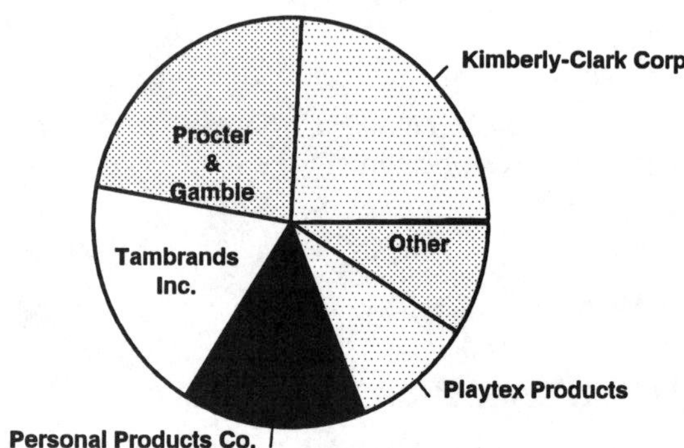

Shares of the $1.7 billion market are shown for the year ended March 2, 1997.

Kimberly-Clark Corp.	24.0%
Procter & Gamble	23.0
Tambrands Inc.	19.0
Personal Products Co.	15.0
Playtex Products	10.0
Other	9.0

Source: *Boston Globe*, April 11, 1997, p. B1, from Information Resources Inc.

★ 433 ★

Feminine Hygiene Products (SIC 2676)

Feminine Protection Market - Canada

Company shares are for 1996. Procter & Gamble recently acquired Tambrands, which will give it a 53.0% share of the Canadian market.

Procter & Gamble	36.0%
Tambrands Canada	17.0
Kimberly-Clark Canada	16.0
Johnson & Johnson	14.0
Playtex	11.0
Shoppers Drug Mart	6.0

Source: *Marketing Magazine*, April 21, 1997, p. 5, from industry sources.

★ 434 ★

Feminine Hygiene Products (SIC 2676)

Leading Sanitary Pad and Liner Market

Shares are shown based on a $1.063 billion market.

Procter & Gamble	37.0%
Kimberly-Clark	32.0
Johnson & Johnson	20.0
Private label	11.0

Source: *New York Times*, April 10, 1997, p. C2, from Information Resources Inc.

★ 435 ★

Feminine Hygiene Products (SIC 2676)

Leading Tampon Brands

Shares are shown based on a $643.8 million market for the year ended March 2, 1997.

	Sales ($ mil.)	Share
Tampax	$ 319.6	49.8%
Playtex	161.8	25.2
OB	69.1	10.8
Kotex	66.4	10.3
Private label	25.1	3.9

Source: *Wall Street Journal*, April 10, 1997, p. A3, from Information Resources Inc.

★ 436 ★

Feminine Hygiene Products (SIC 2676)

Leading Tampon Makers

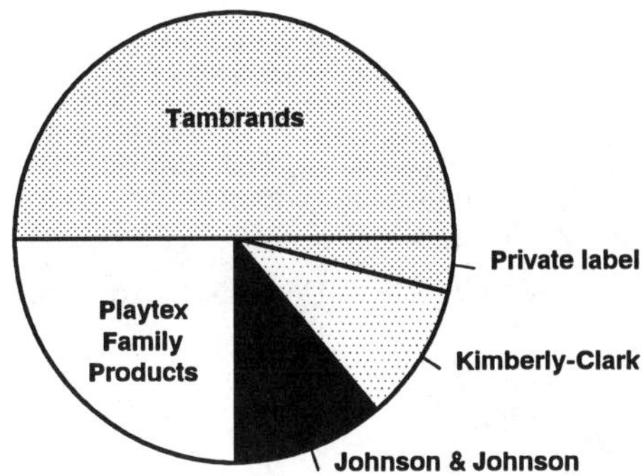

Shares are shown based on a $644 million market. Tambrands is to be acquired by Procter & Gamble.

Tambrands	50.0%
Playtex Family Products	25.0
Johnson & Johnson	11.0
Kimberly-Clark	10.0
Private label	4.0

Source: *New York Times*, April 10, 1997, p. C2, from Information Resources Inc.

★ 437 ★

Feminine Hygiene Products (SIC 2676)

Mexican Feminine Care Market

Shares are shown in percent.

Kimberly-Clark	45.0%
Crisoba	30.0
Other	25.0

Source: *Investext,* Thomson Financial Networks, January 13, 1997, p. 2, from company estimates.

★ 438 ★

Feminine Hygiene Products (SIC 2676)

Tampon Market in the Pacific Northwest

Shares are shown for March 1997.

Tampax	46.9%
Playtex	16.1
O.B.	16.0
Kotex	9.4
Private label	6.4
Other	5.2

Source: http:// biz.yahoo.com/prnews/97/04/11/ufem_y0022_1.html, April 11, 1997, p. 1.

★ 439 ★

Feminine Hygiene Products (SIC 2676)

Top Sanitary Pad and Panty Liner Brands

Shares are shown based on a $1.063 billion market for the year ended March 2, 1997.

	Sales ($ mil.)	Share
Always	$ 396.5	37.3%
Kotex	255.1	24.0
Stayfree	139.1	13.1
New Freedom	81.8	7.7
Carefree	54.1	5.1
Sure & Natural	17.6	1.7
Private label	111.6	10.5
Other	7.2	0.7

Source: *Wall Street Journal*, April 10, 1997, p. A3, from Information Resources Inc.

★ 440 ★

Sanitary Paper Products (SIC 2676)

Adult Care Product Makers

Shares are shown for the year ended December 21, 1996. Popular brands include Depend and Poise.

Kimberly-Clark	53.3%
Procter & Gamble	4.7
Others	42.0

Source: *Forbes*, March 24, 1997, p. 101, from A.C. Nielsen.

★ 441 ★

Sanitary Paper Products (SIC 2676)

Baby Wipes Market - 1996

Shares of the $545 million market are shown in percent.

Kimberly-Clark	31.2%
Procter & Gamble	31.2
Other	36.6

Source: *Advertising Age*, February 24, 1997, p. 87, from Information Resources Inc.

★ 442 ★

Sanitary Paper Products (SIC 2676)

Bathroom Tissue Makers

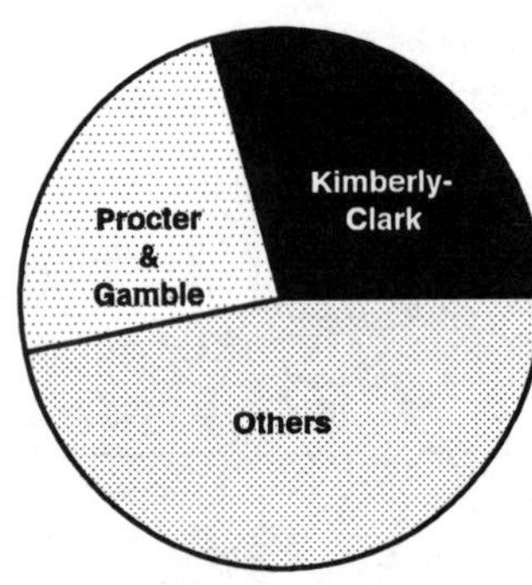

Shares are shown for the year ended December 21, 1996.

Kimberly-Clark	28.8%
Procter & Gamble	23.8
Others	47.4

Source: *Forbes*, March 24, 1997, p. 101, from A.C. Nielsen.

★ 443 ★

Sanitary Paper Products (SIC 2676)

Facial Tissue Makers

Shares are shown for the year ended December 21, 1996.

Kimberly-Clark	48.9%
Procter & Gamble	27.2
Others	23.9

Source: *Forbes*, March 24, 1997, p. 101, from A.C. Nielsen.

★ 444 ★

Sanitary Paper Products (SIC 2676)

Incontinence Product Sales

Total market was valued at $440.7 million.

Undergarments	30.0%
Briefs	27.0
Guards/shields	19.1
Bladder control pads	18.9
Underpants and other	5.0

Source: *NARD Journal*, December 1996, p. 48.

★ 445 ★

Sanitary Paper Products (SIC 2676)

Leading Baby Wipes Brands

Shares are shown for the year ended December 21, 1996.

Huggies	28.4%
Baby Fresh	22.7
Wash-a-Bye-Baby	4.5
Others	44.4

Source: *Forbes*, March 24, 1997, p. 102, from A.C. Nielsen.

★ 446 ★

Sanitary Paper Products (SIC 2676)

Leading Training/Youth Pants Makers

Shares are shown for the year ended December 21, 1996. Popular brands include Pull-ups, Goodnites, and Pampers Trainers.

Kimberly Clark	73.8%
Procter & Gamble	8.5
Others	17.7

Source: *Forbes*, March 24, 1997, p. 102, from A.C. Nielsen.

★ 447 ★

Sanitary Paper Products (SIC 2676)

Mexican Cigarette Paper Market

Shares are shown in percent. Crisoba is to complete its merger with Kimberly-Clark in March 1997.

Kimberly-Clark	90.0%
Other	10.0

Source: *Investext,* Thomson Financial Networks, January 13, 1997, p. 2, from company estimates.

★ 448 ★

Sanitary Paper Products (SIC 2676)

Mexican Facial Tissue Market

Shares are shown in percent. Crisoba is to complete its merger with Kimberly-Clark in March 1997.

Kimberly-Clark	75.0%
Crisoba	25.0

Source: *Investext,* Thomson Financial Networks, January 13, 1997, p. 2, from company estimates.

★ 449 ★

Sanitary Paper Products (SIC 2676)

Mexican Napkin Market

Shares are shown in percent. Crisoba is to complete its merger with Kimberly-Clark in March 1997.

Crisoba	35.0%
Kimberly-Clark	35.0
Other	40.0

Source: *Investext,* Thomson Financial Networks, January 13, 1997, p. 2, from company estimates.

★ 450 ★

Sanitary Paper Products (SIC 2676)

Paper Towel Makers

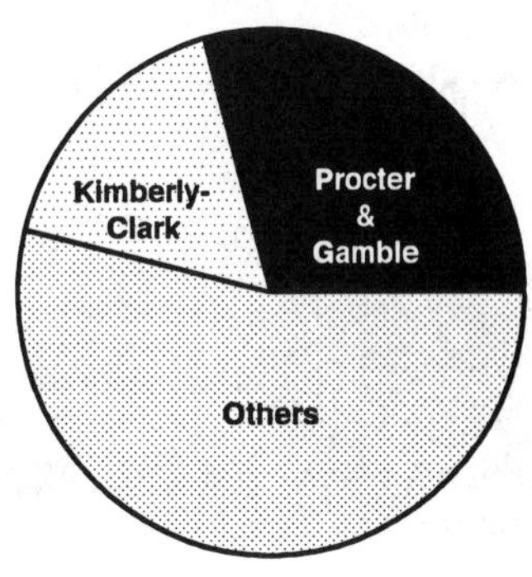

Shares are shown for the year ended December 21, 1996.

Procter & Gamble	29.0%
Kimberly-Clark	16.6
Others	54.4

Source: *Forbes*, March 24, 1997, p. 101, from A.C. Nielsen.

★ 451 ★

Sanitary Paper Products (SIC 2676)

Top Adult Diaper Brands

Brand shares are shown based on a $440.9 million market for the 52 weeks ending December 29, 1996.

Depend	39.3%
Private label	23.2
Poise	15.3
Serenity	14.0
Attends	6.6
Other	1.6

Source: *Supermarket Business*, March 1997, p. 102, from Information Resources Inc.

★ 452 ★

Sanitary Paper Products (SIC 2676)

Top Adult Diaper Brands by Unit Sales

Shares are shown in percent for the year ended December 29, 1996.

Depend	29.3%
Poise	20.1
Serenity	17.1
Attends	4.8
Private label	26.7

Source: *Supermarket Business*, April 1997, p. 52, from Information Resources Inc.

★ 453 ★

Sanitary Paper Products (SIC 2676)

U.S. Tissue Makers - 1996

Market shares are shown in percent.

Kimberly-Clark	25.0%
Fort Howard	17.9
James River	15.9
Procter & Gamble	14.6
Chesapeake	4.5
Potlatch	2.3
Marcal	1.4
Mosinee	1.4
Other	17.0

Source: *Investor's Business Daily*, May 8, 1997, p. A4, from Salomon Brothers.

★ 454 ★

Stationery (SIC 2678)

Popular Stationery Brands

Data show the brands of stationery and accessories preferred by shoppers at discount stores in 1996.

Bic	29.0%
Mead	22.0
Papermate	8.0
Hallmark	8.0
Crayola	7.0
Scotch/3M	4.0

Source: *Discount Store News*, October 21, 1996, p. 75, from Lee J. Shapiro & Associates.

SIC 27 - Printing and Publishing

★ 455 ★

Printing (SIC 2700)

Leading Printing Markets - 1997

Categories are ranked by estimated market size in billions of dollars.

Computer software	$ 9.3
Healthcare services	7.8
Motor vehicles	6.9
Beverages	6.8
Publishing	6.8
Home improvements	5.7
Telecommunications equipment/services	5.7
Medical products/pharmaceuticals	5.4
Packaged foods	5.4
Financial services	4.1
Fashion	3.7
Leisure activity	3.0
Consumer electronics	2.9
Travel/hospitality	2.7
Amusements	1.9

Source: *American Printer*, December 1996, p. 35, from PB/BA Acquisitions Corp.

★ 456 ★

Publishing (SIC 2700)

Top Publishing & Printing Companies - 1996

Data show revenues in millions of dollars.

R.R. Donnelley & Sons	$ 6,599
Gannett	4,665
Times Mirror	3,401
Reader's Digest Association	3,098
McGraw-Hill	3,075
Knight-Ridder	2,775
New York Times	2,615
Dow Jones	2,482
Tribune	2,406
American Greetings	2,012
Deluxe	$ 1,896
Washington Post	1,853
World Color Press	1,641
E.W. Scripps	1,392
K-III Communications	1,374

Source: *Fortune*, April 28, 1997, p. 59.

★ 457 ★

Publishing (SIC 2700)

U.S. Publishing Revenues

The paper-based publishing market generated $78 billion in revenues.

Newspapers	43.8%
Books	28.2
Magazines	27.9

Source: *Telecommunications*, September 1996, p. 34.

★ 458 ★

Newspapers (SIC 2711)

Daily Newspaper Groups by Ad Revenues - Canada

Shares are shown based on advertising revenues for 1996.

Southam Newspapers	31.8%
Thomson Newspapers	12.3
Sun Media	11.2
Hollinger	9.6
Quebecer	8.6
Power Corporation	5.7
Irving Group	2.6
Newfoundland Capital Corp.	1.0
Independents	17.2

Source: *Marketing Magazine*, May 26, 1997, p. 15, from Canadian Newspaper Association.

★ 459 ★

Newspapers (SIC 2711)

Largest Newspapers - San Diego

Newspapers are ranked by circulation in 1996.

San Diego Union-Tribune	376,511
North County Times	84,527
Southern Cross	20,752
Daily Californian	17,057
San Diego Jewish Times	15,382

Source: *San Diego Business Journal*, October 14, 1996, p. 20.

★ 460 ★

Newspapers (SIC 2711)

Newspaper Circulation - Chicago

Data show daily circulation for March 1996.

Chicago Tribune	667,908
Chicago Sun-Times	501,115
Copley Chicago Newspapers	143,851
Daily Herald	130,185
Munster Times	88,349
Gary Post-Tribune	66,355
Daily Southtown	57,179

Source: *Crain's Chicago Business*, July 1996, p. F34, from Audit Bureau of Circulations.

★ 461 ★

Newspapers (SIC 2711)

Top Media Firms by Newspaper Revenues

Firms are ranked by 1995 revenues in millions of dollars.

Gannett Co.	$ 3,226.2
Knight-Ridder	2,250.2
New York Times Co.	2,161.4
Advance Publications	2,108.0
Times Mirror Co.	2,057.6
Tribune Co.	1,304.0
Dow Jones & Co.	1,191.8
Cox Enterprises	976.0
Hearst Corp.	824.0
Thomson Corp.	770.0

Source: *Advertising Age*, August 19, 1996, p. S4.

★ 462 ★

Newspapers (SIC 2711)

Top Newspapers - 1997

Wall Street Journal
USA TODAY
New York Times
Los Angeles Times
Washington Post
Daily News
Chicago Tribune
Newsday
Houston Chronicle
San Francisco Chronicle

Data show average weekday circulations for the reporting period ended March 31, 1997. Figure for USA TODAY represents Monday through Thursday circulation.

Wall Street Journal	1,837,194
USA TODAY	1,662,060
New York Times	1,107,168
Los Angeles Times	1,068,812
Washington Post	818,231
Daily News	728,107
Chicago Tribune	664,586
Newsday	559,233
Houston Chronicle	549,856
San Francisco Chronicle	494,093

Source: *New York Times*, May 6, 1997, p. C8, from Audit Bureau of Circulations.

★ 463 ★

Magazines (SIC 2721)

Consumer Magazines by Ad Revenues - Canada

Shares are shown based on advertising revenues.

	1995	1996
Maclean's	9.7%	9.2%
Chatelaine	10.1	8.9
Canadian Living	6.9	6.5
TV Guide	5.6	5.8
Time	5.1	5.1
Reader's Digest	4.6	4.7
TV Times	2.8	3.9
Report On Business Magazine	3.3	3.2
Homemaker's	3.2	3.1

Continued on next page.

★ 463 ★ *Continued*

Magazines (SIC 2721)

Consumer Magazines by Ad Revenues - Canada

Shares are shown based on advertising revenues.

	1995	1996
Flare	3.0%	2.9%
Others	45.7	46.6

Source: *Marketing Magazine*, May 26, 1997, p. 15, from Leading National Advertisers Canada.

★ 464 ★

Magazines (SIC 2721)

Non-Paid Circulation Leaders - 1996

Data are for the first six months of 1996.

Disney Channel Magazine	5,356,962
Rx Remedy	2,022,988
U - The National College Magazine	1,570,138
Healthy Kids	1,503,856
American Baby	1,393,637
Fantastic Flyer Magazine	1,171,128
Baby Talk	1,101,066
Microsoft Magazine	1,091,178

Source: *Advertising Age*, August 26, 1996, p. 25, from Audit Bureau of Circulations and BPA International.

★ 465 ★

Magazines (SIC 2721)

Top Circulating Magazines

Magazines are ranked by average monthly circulation for the six month period ended June 30, 1996.

Modern Maturity	20,673,063
Reader's Digest	15,150,822
TV Guide	13,076,790
National Geographic	9,184,878
Better Homes and Gardens	7,616,270
Good Housekeeping	5,032,901
Cable Guide	5,022,477
Family Circle	5,003,227
Ladies' Home Journal	4,705,020
Woman's Day	4,501,612
McCall's	4,284,939
Time	4,131,676
Sports Illustrated	3,384,328
People	3,364,252
Prevention	3,251,851

Source: *Advertising Age*, October 14, 1996, p. S14, from Audit Bureau of Circulations and BPA International.

★ 466 ★

Magazines (SIC 2721)

Top Farm Journal Publications

Farm Journal

Top Producer

Beef Today

Dairy Today

Hogs Today

Data show monthly figures for the last six months of 1996.

Farm Journal	640,328
Top Producer	218,763
Beef Today	165,957
Dairy Today	107,267
Hogs Today	76,712

Source: *Philadelphia Inquirer*, April 11, 1997, p. C1, from Audit Bureau of Circulations.

★ 467 ★

Magazines (SIC 2721)

Top Magazine Advertisers - 1995

Companies are ranked by ad spending in millions of dollars.

General Motors Corp.	$ 412.0
Philip Morris Cos.	373.8
Ford Motor Co.	254.3
Procter & Gamble Co.	251.5
Chrysler Corp.	231.1
Toyota Motor Corp.	121.1
Time Warner	119.9
Unilever NV	109.5
IBM Corp.	109.2
L'Oreal	98.4
Johnson & Johnson	85.3
Joh. A. Benckiser GmbH	77.8
Walt Disney Co.	76.7
Sony Corp.	73.3
B.A.T. Industries	70.4

Source: *Advertising Age*, October 14, 1996, p. S14, from Competitive Media Reporting.

★ 468 ★

Magazines (SIC 2721)

Top Magazines - 1996

Magazines are ranked by average paid circulation, in millions.

Reader's Digest	15.072
TV Guide	13.013
National Geographic	9.025
Better Homes and Gardens	7.605
Family Circle	5.239
Good Housekeeping	4.951
Ladies Home Journal	4.544
Woman's Day	4.317
McCall's	4.290
Time	4.102
People Weekly	3.449
Prevention	3.311
Playboy	3.236
Newsweek	3.194
Sports Illustrated	3.173

Source: *Mediaweek*, March 3, 1997, p. 25, from Competitive Media Reporting.

★ 469 ★

Magazines (SIC 2721)

Top Magazines by Ad Pages - 1996

Magazines are ranked by total ad pages.

PC Magazine	6,069.80
Forbes	4,548.18
Business Week	3,885.10
People	3,708.27
Fortune	3,336.59
Bride's	3,062.18
TV Guide	3,038.87
Sports Illustrated	2,870.06
Economist	2,830.83
Windows Magazine	2,788.25
Modern Bride	2,723.84
PC Computing	2,665.15
Vogue	2,545.91
Newsweek	2,533.30
New York Magazine	2,491.92
Time	2,392.92
American Way	2,151.01
U.S. News & World Report	2,083.59
New Yorker	2,038.62
Home PC	1,916.92
Bridal Guide	1,899.77
Entrepreneur	1,894.28
Entertainment Weekly	1,847.92
Elle	1,841.04
Rolling Stone	1,825.12

Source: *Advertising Age*, January 20, 1997, p. 37, from Publishers Information Bureau.

★ 470 ★

Magazines (SIC 2721)

Top Magazines by Ad Revenues - 1996

Magazines are ranked by revenues in millions of dollars.

People Weekly	$ 525.6
Sports Illustrated	522.3
Parade	494.0
Time	439.6
TV Guide	403.0
Newsweek	383.8
Better Homes and Gardens	335.5
PC Magazine	318.0
Business Week	298.8
USA Weekend	228.6
U.S. News & World Report	227.5
Forbes	224.4
Woman's Day	216.9
Reader's Digest	201.6
Fortune	198.9

Source: *Mediaweek*, March 3, 1997, p. 25, from Competitive Media Reporting.

★ 471 ★

Magazines (SIC 2721)

Top Magazines by Revenues - 1995

Magazines are ranked by gross revenues in millions of dollars.

TV Guide	$ 1,068.8
People	801.2
Sports Illustrated	697.4
Time	672.6
Reader's Digest	529.7
Parade	515.6
Newsweek	480.5
Better Homes & Gardens	406.6
PC Magazine	391.3
Good Housekeeping	339.0

Continued on next page.

★ 471 ★ *Continued*

Magazines (SIC 2721)

Top Magazines by Revenues - 1995

Magazines are ranked by gross revenues in millions of dollars.

U.S. News & Word Report	$ 316.4
Business Week	313.5
Woman's Day	288.0
Ladies Home Journal	261.8
Family Circle	255.2

Source: *Advertising Age*, October 14, 1996, p. S14.

★ 472 ★

Magazines (SIC 2721)

Top Magazines Publishers - 1996

Firms are ranked by revenues in millions of dollars.

Time Inc.	$ 2,397.4
Conde Nast	860.4
Hearst Magazines	833.7
Hachette Filpacchi	812.7
Meredith Corp.	636.3
Parade Publications	494.0
Ziff-Davis	465.1
Gruner + Jahr	459.7
News America	403.0
Newsweek Inc.	383.8
New York Times Co.	333.5
K-III Communications	305.4
McGraw-Hill	298.8
Times Mirror	287.7
Reader's Digest	254.0

Source: *Mediaweek*, March 3, 1997, p. 25, from Competitive Media Reporting.

★ 473 ★

Books (SIC 2731)

Bible Sales by Translation

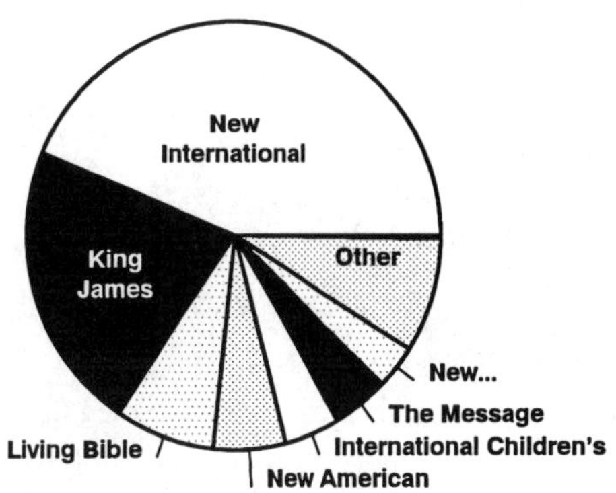

New International	40.0%
King James	20.0
Living Bible	7.0
New American	5.0
International Children's	4.0
The Message	3.5
New Revised Standard	3.0
Other	7.5

Source: *USA TODAY*, December 24, 1996, p. D1, from Zondervan Publishing.

★ 474 ★

Books (SIC 2731)

Book Publishing in Mexico

Data are for 1994.

	Titles	Share
Technical/scientific books	2,428	20.0%
Textbooks	2,243	18.0
Humanities/social sciences	2,067	17.0
Practical books	1,896	15.0
Literature	1,781	14.0
Children/juvenile books	986	8.0
Religion	616	5.0
Reference	240	2.0
Other	212	1.0

Source: *National Trade Data Bank*, March 1, 1996, p. ISA960301.

★ 475 ★

Books (SIC 2731)

Book Sales - 1996

Sales are shown in millions of dollars.

Trade	
Adult hardcover	$ 2,530.4
Adult paperback	1,616.4
Juvenile hardcover	909.1
Juvenile paperback	570.1
Religious	
Bibles	298.2
Other religious	806.0
Professional	3,994.6
Elhi	2,607.6
Higher education	2,485.8
Mass market paperback	1,533.3
Book clubs	1,091.8
Subscription reference	706.1
Mail order	579.5
University press	349.3
Standardized tests	178.7
Other	493.2

Source: *Publishers Weekly*, March 3, 1997, p. 11, from Association of American Publishers.

★ 476 ★

Books (SIC 2731)

Children's Book Sales

Regions are ranked by share of the children's book market.

Mid-Atlantic	20.0%
East North Central	19.0
Pacific	15.0
South Atlantic	15.0
West South Central	9.0
Mountain	6.0
New England	6.0
East South Central	5.0
West North Central	5.0

Source: *USA TODAY*, May 28, 1997, p. D1, from Book Industry Study Group.

★ 477 ★

Books (SIC 2731)

Consumer Book Spending

Total spending is expected to grow from $24.8 billion in 1996 to $27.4 billion in 1998.

	1996	1998
Hardbound	59.0%	58.8%
Paperbound	41.0	41.2

Source: *High Volume Printing*, December 1996, p. 34, from *Book Industry Trends*.

★ 478 ★

Books (SIC 2731)

Fiction Book Sales

General fiction
Children/youth
Horror
Mystery
Romance
Sci-fi fantasy

Fiction accounts for an estimated two-thirds of book sales. Data show the best-selling forms.

General fiction	49.0%
Children/youth	20.0
Horror	9.0
Mystery	8.0
Romance	8.0
Sci-fi fantasy	6.0

Source: *USA TODAY*, December 24, 1996, p. D8, from *USA TODAY's Best-Selling Books List*.

★ 479 ★

Books (SIC 2731)

Leading Hardcover Publishers

Data show the publisher's share of the 1,560 hardcover bestseller positions in 1996.

Random House	20.4%
Bantam Doubleday	16.1
Harper Collins	14.4
Time Warner	12.8

Continued on next page.

★ 479 ★ *Continued*

Books (SIC 2731)

Leading Hardcover Publishers

Data show the publisher's share of the 1,560 hardcover bestseller positions in 1996.

Simon & Schuster	11.3%
Putnam Berkley	8.7
Penguin USA	4.2
Other	12.1

Source: *Publishers Weekly*, January 6, 1997, p. 46.

★ 480 ★

Books (SIC 2731)

Leading Paperback Publishers

Data show the publisher's share of the 1,560 paperback bestseller positions in 1996.

Random House	22.3%
Bantam Doubleday	15.4
Penguin USA	12.1
Simon & Schuster	11.8
Putnam Berkley	8.3
Time Warner	6.3
Health Communications	6.2
Other	17.6

Source: *Publishers Weekly*, January 6, 1997, p. 46.

★ 481 ★

Books (SIC 2731)

Top Children's Trade Publishers

Firms are ranked by net sales in millions of dollars.

Golden Books	$ 260.0
Scholastic	138.0
Random House	125.0
HarperCollins	99.5
Simon & Schuster	95.0
Putnam/Grosset	82.0
Penguin USA	75.0
Disney Juvenile Publishing	62.0
Bantam Doubleday Dell	55.0
Hearst (Morrow/Avon)	43.0

Source: *Publishers Weekly*, October 28, 1996, p. 34.

★ 482 ★

Books (SIC 2732)

Book Printing in Mexico

Data show the kinds of printing in 1994.

	Titles	Share
Reprints	6,633	53.0%
First edition	4,674	38.0
Subsequent editions	1,162	9.0

Source: *National Trade Data Bank*, March 1, 1996, p. ISA960301.

★ 483 ★

Books (SIC 2732)

Book Printing Market - 1997

The size of leading book printing sectors is shown in millions of dollars.

	($ mil.)	Share
General trade books, print & bind	$ 1,550.5	25.4%
Tech, scientific, professional print & bind	1,387.3	22.7
Textbooks, print & bind	853.9	14.0
Pamphlets, print & bind	498.4	8.2
Religious, print & bind	270.5	4.4
Book printing only, no binding	133.8	2.2
Other books, print & bind	812.3	13.3
All other book printing	605.6	9.9

Source: *American Printer*, March 1997, p. 10.

★ 484 ★

Commercial Printing (SIC 2752)

Largest Commercial Printers - Tampa Bay

Companies are ranked by number of employees.

Better Business Forms	420
Eva-Tone Inc.	375
Newspaper Printing Co.	210
Marketing Response Group & Laser Co. Inc.	175
Copy Control Center	168
Hillsboro Printing Co.	130
Feather Fine Printing and Direct Mail Services	103
MGA-A Sandy Alexander Co.	100

Continued on next page.

★ 484 ★ *Continued*

Commercial Printing (SIC 2752)

Largest Commercial Printers - Tampa Bay

Companies are ranked by number of employees.

Interprint Web and Sheet Fed	80
Promocom Printing	56

Source: *Tampa Bay Business Journal*, August 22, 1996, p. 19.

★ 485 ★

Commercial Printing (SIC 2752)

Top Printing Markets by Region - 1997

The total commercial printing market reached $78.3 billion.

North Central	23.8%
North Mid-Atlantic	15.8
South eastern	14.5
Pacific	13.8
Midwest	11.9
South Central	6.0
New England	5.5
South Mid-Atlantic	5.1
Mountain	3.6

Source: *American Printer*, December 1996, p. 30.

★ 486 ★

Commercial Printing (SIC 2752)

U.S. Label Sales by Segment

Data show sales in billions of dollars for 1996 and estimated sales for 2001. Shares are shown based on 2001 sales. Total shipments were valued at $8.875 billion in 1996 and are expected to reach $12.6 billion in 2001.

	1996	2001	Share
Pressure sensitive	$ 5.925	$ 8.840	70.2%
Glue-applied	2.070	2.505	19.9
Other	0.880	1.255	10.0

Source: *Packaging Digest*, April 1997, p. 6, from Freedonia Group.

★ 487 ★

Business Forms (SIC 2761)

U.S. Business Form Sales

The market is expected to fall from $6.9 billion in 1996 to $6.77 billion in 1997.

	1996 ($ mil.)	1997 ($ mil.)	Share
Custom continuous	$ 3,046	$ 2,955	30.4%
Unit sets	1,350	1,303	13.4
Cutsheet	1,119	1,187	12.2
Stock continuous	1,106	1,040	10.7
Salesbooks/pegbooks	300	286	2.9
Form/label combinations	255	285	2.9
Multi-part mailers	230	224	2.3
Other custom continuous	2,562	2,445	25.1

Source: *Purchasing*, October 17, 1996, p. 98, from International Business Forms Institute.

★ 488 ★

Greeting Cards (SIC 2771)

Greeting Card Producers

Shares are estimated.

Hallmark Inc.	45.0%
American Greetings Corp.	35.0
Gibson Greetings Inc.	8.0
Other	12.0

Source: *Wall Street Journal*, August 27, 1996, p. B5.

★ 489 ★

Greeting Cards (SIC 2771)

Top Occasions for Greeting Card Sales - 1997

Sales are shown in millions of cards.

Christmas	2,600
Valentine's Day	900
Mother's Day	150
Easter	120
Father's Day	95
Graduation	60

Continued on next page.

★ 489 ★ *Continued*

Greeting Cards (SIC 2771)

Top Occasions for Greeting Card Sales - 1997

Sales are shown in millions of cards.

Thanksgiving	30
Halloween	25
St. Patrick's Day	15
Jewish New Year	10

Source: *USA TODAY*, June 12, 1997, p. B1, from Greeting Card Association.

SIC 28 - Chemicals and Allied Products

★ 490 ★

Chemicals (SIC 2800)

Auto Maintenance Chemicals

Sales are shown in millions of dollars by product.

Antifreeze	$ 760.0
Protectants	300.0
Fluids	195.0
Wax/polish	190.0
Greases/sealers	115.0
Car washes	110.0

Source: *Discount Merchandiser*, February 1997, p. 65, from *APAA 1997 Aftermarket Factbook.*

★ 491 ★

Chemicals (SIC 2800)

Canada's Chemical Industry

The Canadian chemical industry had a market value of $24.8 billion in 1995.

Industrial chemicals	30.7%
Plastics/synthetic resins	18.0
Pharmaceuticals/resins	17.1
Agricultural chemicals	8.0
Paint and varnishes	5.8
Soaps/cleaning compounds	5.6
Toilet preparations	3.5
Other	11.4

Source: *Canadian Chemical News*, October 1996, p. 10, from Strategies and Institute for Manufacturing Research.

★ 492 ★

Chemicals (SIC 2800)

Flame Retardent Market

Bromine based	32.0%
Antimony oxide	20.0
Chlorine based	17.0
Phosphorous based	17.0
Alumina trihydrate	11.0
Other	3.0

Source: *Chemical & Engineering News*, February 24, 1997, p. 20, from Business Communications Co.

★ 493 ★

Chemicals (SIC 2800)

Largest Chemical Firms - 1996

Sales are in billions of dollars for the first nine months of the year.

Dow Chemical	$ 15.15
Monsanto	7.05
Union Carbide	4.59
Eastman Chemical	3.66
Praxair	3.29
Air Products	3.06
Rohm and Haas	3.01
Arco Chemical	2.97
W.R. Grace	2.65
IMC Global	2.27

Source: *Chemical & Engineering News*, November 18, 1996, p. 12.

★ 494 ★

Chemicals (SIC 2800)

Paper Chemicals by Type - 1996

The $1.0 billion end market is shown in percent.

Sizing	24.0%
Wet strength	15.0

Continued on next page.

★ 494 ★ *Continued*
Chemicals (SIC 2800)

Paper Chemicals by Type - 1996

The $1.0 billion end market is shown in percent.

Defoaming	13.0%
Retention & drainage	13.0
Biocides	12.0
Deposit control	11.0
Dry strength	3.0
Others	9.0

Source: *Chemicalweek*, January 22, 1997, p. 28, from Kline & Co.

★ 495 ★
Chemicals (SIC 2800)

Pulping Chemicals Consumption

Consumption is shown in kilotons for the first nine months of 1996.

Lime	265.0
Sodium hydroxide	264.0
Sulphur	76.0
Sodium sulphate	73.0
Sulphur dioxide	18.0

Source: *Pulp & Paper Canada*, January 1997, p. 21, from Canadian Pulp & Paper Association.

★ 496 ★
Chemicals (SIC 2800)

Specialty Chemical Market

U.S. sales are shown by product. Shares are in percent.

	Sales ($ bil.)	Share
Industrial coatings	$ 8.10	10.1%
Agricultural chemicals	7.50	9.4
Adhesives & sealants	6.10	7.6
I&I cleaners	6.00	7.5
Electronic chemicals	5.10	6.4
Plastic additives	4.40	5.5
Specialty polymers	4.30	5.4
Food ingredients	3.10	3.9
Construction chemicals	2.70	3.4
Dyes & pigments	2.70	3.4
Water management	2.50	3.1
Specialty surfactants	1.90	2.4
Flavor & fragrances	1.80	2.3
Lubricants & additives	$ 1.80	2.3%
Other	21.89	27.4

Source: *Chemicalweek*, January 8, 1997, p. 24, from Strategic Analysis Inc.

★ 497 ★
Chemicals (SIC 2800)

Textile Chemical Demand

Total sales reached $2.91 billion in 1996.

Dyeing/printing	41.6%
Finishing	20.5
Coating	17.8
Preparation/sizing/other	20.1

Source: *Chemical & Engineering News*, January 13, 1997, p. 15, from Freedonia Group.

★ 498 ★
Chemicals (SIC 2800)

Top Chemicals Firms - 1996

Revenues are shown in millions of dollars.

E.I. Du Pont de Nemours	$ 39,689
Dow Chemical	20,053
Occidental Petroleum	10,557
Monsanto	9,262
Sunbeam	1,212
Pittway	1,112
Vishay Intertechnology	1,098
Tracor	1,083
Scientific-Atlanta	1,074
Diebold	1,030
Sensormatic Electronics	995
Read-Rite	991

Source: *Fortune*, April 28, 1997, p. 45.

★ 499 ★

Chemicals (SIC 2800)

Top Water Treatment Companies - 1995

Shares are shown based on total sales of $1.924 billion.

Nalco Chemical	23.0%
BetzDearborn	22.0
Calgon Corp.	7.0
Allied Colloids	5.0
Drew Industrial	5.0
Cytec Industries	4.0
CPS Chemical	3.0
Rohm and Haas	3.0
Dow Chemical	2.0
Other	21.0

Source: *Chemicalweek*, May 7, 1997, p. 31, from SRI Consulting.

★ 500 ★

Chemicals (SIC 2800)

U.S. Aerosol Production

Production is shown by segment.

Personal care products	34.0%
Household products	30.0
Automotive/industrial	14.0
Paints & varnishes	12.0
Food	8.0
Other	2.0

Source: *Spray Technology & Marketing*, November 1996, p. 23.

★ 501 ★

Chemicals (SIC 2800)

U.S. Petrochemical Production

Data show petrochemicals produced by hydrocarbon oxidation. Figures are in millions of pounds per year.

Vinyl chloride	12,910
Terephthalic acid/dimethyl terephthalate	7,791
Ethylene oxide	7,751
Phenol	4,168
Propylene oxide	3,850
Acrylonitrile	3,040
Vinyl acetate	2,915
Caprolactam	1,437
Phthalic anhydride	1,040
Butadeniol	690

Source: *Chemical Engineering Progress*, November 9, 1996, p. 67.

★ 502 ★

Alkalies and Chlorine (SIC 2812)

Leading Chlorine Producers

Production capacity is shown in thousands of tons per year.

	(000)	Share
Dow Chemical	3,900.0	27.2%
OxyChem	3,300.0	23.0
PPG Industries	1,650.0	11.5
Formosa Plastics	850.0	5.9
Olin	800.0	5.6
Vulcan	607.0	4.2
Pioneer	500.0	3.5
Georgia Gulf	230.0	1.6
LaRoche	200.0	1.4
Other	2,308.0	16.1

Source: *Chemicalweek*, February 26, 1997, p. 56.

★ 503 ★

Alkalies and Chlorine (SIC 2812)

Potassium Carbonate Producers

Shares are estimated based on a 183,000 ton capacity in 1996.

Armand Products	58.0%
Ashta Chemical	14.0
Vicksburg Chemical	14.0
Vulcan Chemical	14.0

Source: *Chemicalweek*, September 18, 1996, p. 45, from Armand Products.

★ 504 ★

Alkalies and Chlorine (SIC 2812)

Sodium Bicarbonate Makers

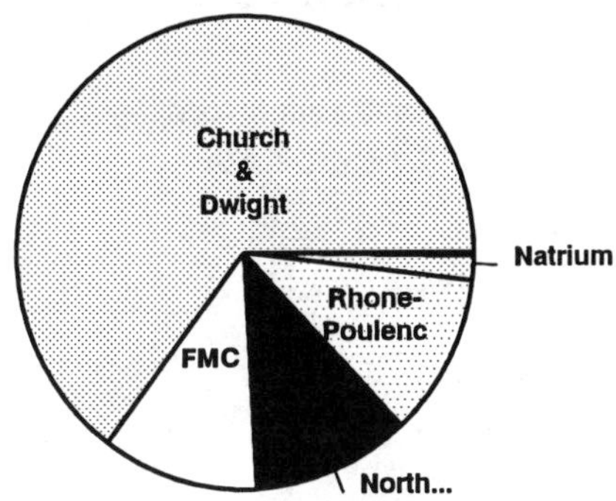

Shares are shown based on total capacity of 657,000 tons produced per year.

Church & Dwight	65.0%
FMC	11.0
North American Chemical Co.	11.0
Rhone-Poulenc	11.0
Natrium	2.0

Source: *Chemicalweek*, October 9, 1996, p. 51, from Church & Dwight.

★ 505 ★

Alkalies and Chlorine (SIC 2812)

Top U.S. Soda-Ash Producers - 1996

Nameplate capacity is shown in millions of short tons.

FMC Corp.	3.55
General Chem.	2.40
OCI	2.30
Solvay Minerals	2.30
TG Soda Ash	1.30
North American	1.25

Source: *Engineering and Mining Journal*, March 1997, p. 36.

★ 506 ★

Alkalies and Chlorine (SIC 2812)

U.S. Chlorine Demand - 1996

Demand is shown in thousands of tons by end use.

	(000)	Share
Ethylene dichloride/vinyl chloride	5,600.0	41.6%
Organic chemicals	3,050.0	22.6
Inorganic chemicals	2,350.0	17.4
Pulp & paper	920.0	6.8
Water treatment	590.0	4.4
Other	960.0	7.1

Source: *Chemical & Engineering News*, January 6, 1997, p. 13, from Consulting Resources.

★ 507 ★

Industrial Gases (SIC 2813)

U.S. Helium Consumption

Consumption is shown based on 75.4 million cubic meters used in 1994.

Cryogenics	24.0%
Welding	20.0
Pressure/purge	19.0
Controlled atmosphere	11.0
Leak detection	5.0
Breathing mixtures	3.0
Other	18.0

Source: *Minerals Yearbook: Metals and Materials*, Vol 1, 1994, p. 364, from United States Bureau of Mines.

★ 508 ★

Industrial Gases (SIC 2813)

U.S. Industrial Gas Producers

Total capacity reached 57,000 tons per day.

	(000)	Share
AGA Gas Inc.	3,600	6.3%
MG Industries	2,800	4.9
Tri-Gas Inc.	1,800	3.2
Holox Inc.	800	1.4
Other	48,000	84.2

Source: *Chemical Market Reporter*, October 28, 1996, p. 16, from J.R. Campbell & Associates.

★ 509 ★

Alumina (SIC 2819)

U.S. Alumina Producers

Shares are shown based on a total production of 5.57 million metric tons.

Aluminum Co. of America	30.7%
Reynolds Metals Co.	28.9
Kaiser Aluminum & Chemical Corp.	18.1
Virgin Islands Alumina	11.5
Ormet Corp.	10.8
Other	0.1

Source: *Minerals Yearbook: Metals and Materials*, Vol 1, 1994, p. 98, from United States Bureau of Mines.

★ 510 ★

Inorganic Chemicals (SIC 2819)

Auto Catalysts Market

Shares are shown based on 70 million units.

Engelhard	30.0%
AlliedSignal	23.0
Johnson Matthey	22.0
Degussa	11.0
Captive	9.0
Other	5.0

Source: *Chemicalweek*, October 9, 1996, p. 48, from Engelhard.

★ 511 ★

Inorganic Chemicals (SIC 2819)

Hydrogen Peroxide Makers - North America

Companies are ranked by production in metric tons.

FMC	211
DuPont	176
Solvay Interox	115
Degussa	78
Oxysynthese	73
Eka Nobel	35

Source: *Chemicalweek*, February 26, 1997, p. 38.

★ 512 ★

Inorganic Chemicals (SIC 2819)

Leading Producers of Phosphorus Trichloride

Firms are ranked by annual production capacity in short tons as of February 3, 1997.

Monsanto	220,000
Albright & Wilson	55,000
FMC	30,000
Akzo Nobel	22,000
Rhone-Poulenc	17,000
Zeneca	15,000

Source: *Chemical Market Reporter*, February 3, 1997, p. 49.

★ 513 ★

Inorganic Chemicals (SIC 2819)

Phosphorus Production Leaders

Production capacity is shown in tons per year.

FMC	135,000
Monsanto	120,000
Purified Acid	52,500
Rhone-Poulenc	35,000

Source: *Chemical Market Reporter*, January 20, 1997, p. 33.

★ 514 ★

Inorganic Chemicals (SIC 2819)

Sodium Chlorate Makers - Canada

Sterling Chemical
CXY
Eka Nobel Canada
B.C. Chemicals
Saskatoon Chemical
ICI Canada
St. Anne Chemical

Capacity is shown in short tons per year.

Sterling Chemical	361,000
CXY	296,000
Eka Nobel Canada	260,000
B.C. Chemicals	78,000
Saskatoon Chemical	52,000
ICI Canada	24,000
St. Anne Chemical	11,000

Source: *Chemical Marketing Reporter*, June 17, 1996, p. 41.

★ 515 ★

Inorganic Chemicals (SIC 2819)

U.S. Ammonia Makers

Shares are shown based on 23.5 billion tons produced per year.

CF Industries	13.0%
Farmland	12.0
Terra	12.0
PCS	11.0
Agrium	7.0
Viridian	7.0
Unocal	6.0
Koch	5.0
Mississippi Chemical	4.0
Other	23.0

Source: *Chemicalweek*, October 16, 1996, p. 36, from Blue, Johnson & Associates.

★ 516 ★

Inorganic Chemicals (SIC 2819)

U.S. Phosphate Makers

Shares are shown based on 12.7 billion tons produced per year.

IMC Global	32.0%
PCS	20.0
Cargill	14.0
CF Industries	7.0
Farlmand	5.0
Mississippi Chemical	3.0
Viridian	3.0
Agrium	2.0
Other	14.0

Source: *Chemicalweek*, October 16, 1996, p. 36, from Blue, Johnson & Associates.

★ 517 ★

Inorganic Chemicals (SIC 2819)

U.S. Potash Makers

Shares are shown based on 16.1 billion tons produced per year.

PCS	47.0%
IMC Global	31.0
Agrium	6.0
Mississippi Chemical	5.0
Other	11.0

Source: *Chemicalweek*, October 16, 1996, p. 36, from Blue, Johnson & Associates.

★ 518 ★

Inorganic Chemicals (SIC 2819)

U.S. Zeolite Demand

	1995	2000
Powdered household detergents	70.3%	67.9%
Petroleum refining	15.6	15.2
Other cleaners	0.2	0.9
Other catalyst	1.0	2.2
Other markets	12.9	13.8

Source: *Chemical Engineering*, July 1996, p. 57, from Freedonia Group.

★ 519 ★

Plastics (SIC 2821)

1996 Composites Shipments

Shipments are shown by industry in millions of dollars.

	($ mil.)	Share
Transportation	$ 994.1	30.7%
Construction	645.0	19.9
Corrosion-resistant equipment	402.4	12.4
Marine	374.4	11.5
Electrical/electronic	326.0	10.1
Consumer products	195.3	6.0
Appliances, business equipment	170.8	5.3
Aircraft, aerospace, defense	23.6	0.7
Other	110.8	3.4

Source: *Chemical & Engineering News*, September 9, 1996, p. 19, from Society of the Plastics Industry's Composites Institute.

★ 520 ★

Plastics (SIC 2821)

Acrylic Market - 1996

Extruded sheet	36.5%
Molding	30.0
Cast sheet	24.1
Dispersions for kitchen/bathroom wares	9.4

Source: *Modern Plastics*, January 1997, p. 78.

★ 521 ★

Plastics (SIC 2821)

Canada's Plastics Consumption

Data are in millions of pounds. LDPE stands for low-density polyethylene; PVC stands for polyvinyl chloride; PP stands for polypropylene; HDPE stands for high-density polyethylene.

	1995	1996
LDPE	1,408	1,256
PVC	1,005	1,186
PP	790	825
HDPE	759	693

Source: *Modern Plastics*, January 1997, p. 80.

★ 522 ★

Plastics (SIC 2821)

Canadian Plastics Markets - 1995

Housewares	32.0%
Automotive	20.0
Electrical material	10.0
Packaging	9.0
Telecommunications	9.0
Toys	8.0
Other	12.0

Source: *Canadian Plastics*, July 1996, p. 23, from ICEP.

★ 523 ★

Plastics (SIC 2821)

Composite Shipments - 1997

Data are in millions of pounds.

	(mil.)	Share
Transportation	1,001.1	30.6%
Construction	665.8	20.3
Corrosion-resistant equipment	404.2	12.3
Marine	361.6	11.0
Electrical/electronic	326.2	10.0
Consumer products	207.3	6.3
Appliance/business equipment	173.1	5.3
Aircraft/aerospace/defense	24.1	0.7
Other	112.7	3.4

Source: *Plastics News*, February 3, 1997, p. 5, from SPI Composites Institute.

★ 524 ★

Plastics (SIC 2821)

Elastomer Market - North America

	1995	2000
Transportation equipment	34.3%	35.6%
Industrial machinery & equipment	22.1	21.9
Footwear	16.0	13.7
Appliances & business machines	9.4	10.2
Wire & cable	6.6	6.0
Medical products	4.7	5.6
Construction	1.8	2.2
Other	5.0	4.9

Source: *Chemical & Engineering News*, August 5, 1996, p. 13, from Freedonia Group.

★ 525 ★

Plastics (SIC 2821)

HDPE Market - 1996

Data are in millions of pounds.

	(mil.)	Share
Blow molding	3,966	29.6%
Extrusion	3,686	27.5
Injection molding	2,135	15.9
Export	1,900	14.2
Resellers and compounders	1,182	8.8
Rotomolding	125	0.9
Other	402	3.0

Source: *Modern Plastics*, January 1997, p. 76.

★ 526 ★

Plastics (SIC 2821)

HDPE Production - North America

Quantum
Exxon-Paxon
Phillips
Solvay
Lyondell
Chevron
Formosa
Fina
Nova
Dow Chemical

Companies are ranked by high-density polyethylene (HDPE) production shown in millions of pounds per year.

Quantum	1,935
Exxon-Paxon	1,920
Phillips	1,700
Solvay	1,630
Lyondell	1,575
Chevron	1,340
Formosa	440
Fina	420
Nova	420
Dow Chemical	125

Source: *Chemicalweek*, February 5, 1997, p. 18, from Schroder Wertheim, Dean Witter and company reports.

★ 527 ★

Plastics (SIC 2821)

Largest Acrylamide Producers

Production capacity is shown in millions of pounds per year.

Cyted Industries	90.0
Dow	65.0
Nalco	35.0

Source: *Chemical Market Reporter*, October 21, 1996, p. 53.

★ 528 ★

Plastics (SIC 2821)

Mexican Plastic Production

Containers and packaging	38.7%
Consumer	19.4
Construction	16.0
Furniture	7.0
Industrial	5.9
Electrical/electronics	5.1
Adhesives	2.4
Transportation	2.3
Agriculture	2.2
Medical	1.0

Source: *Business Mexico*, June 1996, p. 14, from IMPI.

★ 529 ★

Plastics (SIC 2821)

Nylon Market - 1996

Transportation	30.7%
Electrical/electronics	9.6
Film	9.2
Industrial	5.9
Wire & cable	4.7
Consumer products	4.1
Filaments	3.3
Sheet, rod, tube	3.3
Appliances/power tools	2.4
Other	26.7

Source: *Modern Plastics*, January 1997, p. 76.

★ 530 ★

Plastics (SIC 2821)

Ohio's Plastics Market

Automotive
Packaging
Construction
Consumer
Appliances
Electrical/electronics
Medical
Industrial
Other

The end market is shown for 1995.

Automotive	32.0%
Packaging	21.0
Construction	13.0
Consumer	8.0
Appliances	5.0
Electrical/electronics	4.0
Medical	4.0
Industrial	2.0
Other	11.0

Source: *Site Selection*, August 1996, p. 2, from Plastics Technology Center.

★ 531 ★

Plastics (SIC 2821)

Polypropylene Market - 1996

Data are in millions of pounds.

Extrusion	
Fibers and filaments	3,216
Film	1,348
Sheet (over 10 mil.)	241
Coating	11
Wire & conduit	11
Other	95
Injection molding	
Consumer products	1,242
Rigid packaging	1,150
Transportation	408
Appliances	305
Other molding	288
Blow molding	175
Other	3,693

Source: *Modern Plastics*, January 1997, p. 77.

★ 532 ★

Plastics (SIC 2821)

Polypropylene Market by End Use

The 9.8 billion pound market is shown by end market for 1995. "Other" includes pipe fittings, battery cases, drinking straws, foams, and wire and cable insulation.

Fibers	33.0%
Consumer products	13.0
Rigid packaging	13.0
Film	10.0
Transportation	9.0
Appliances	3.0
Other	19.0

Source: *Chemical & Engineering News*, July 15, 1996, p. 19, from SRI Consulting.

★ 533 ★

Plastics (SIC 2821)

Polyurethane End Use Market

Transportation	20.5%
Construction	20.1
Furniture	19.1
Carpet	11.0
Appliances	4.8
Bedding	4.7
Packaging	4.6
Tanks & pipes	3.6
Textiles & fibers	2.1
Machinery	1.2
Marine	1.2
Other	6.9

Source: *Rubber World*, July 1996, p. 11, from Society of the Plastics Industry.

★ 534 ★

Plastics (SIC 2821)

PVC Market - 1996

Data are in millions of pounds.

Extrusion	
Pipe & conduit	5,360
Siding	1,740
Wire & conduit	450
Windows & doors	355
Packaging	342
Non-packaging	77

Continued on next page.

★ 534 ★ *Continued*

Plastics (SIC 2821)

PVC Market - 1996

Data are in millions of pounds.

Other	562
Exports	1,335
Calendering	1,230
Molding	562
Coatings	420
Other	955

Source: *Modern Plastics*, January 1997, p. 77.

★ 535 ★

Plastics (SIC 2821)

PVC Sales in Canada - 1996

Distribution of polyvinyl chloride sales is shown based on 690,000 tons.

Pipe & fittings	21.0%
Rigid profiles	14.0
Siding	14.0
Flexible film & sheet	7.0
Flexible profiles	6.0
Wire & cable	4.0
Flooring	3.0
Rigid packaging	2.0
Exports	27.0
Other	2.0

Source: *Canadian Plastics*, January 1997, p. 27, from CHEMinfo services and The Geon Company.

★ 536 ★

Plastics (SIC 2821)

Top Blow Molders

Crown Cork & Seal Company Inc.
Johnson Controls Inc.
Continental PET Technologies Inc.
Owens-Brockway Plastic Products
Graham Packaging Co.
Plastipak Packaging Inc.
Southeastern Container Inc.
Continental Plastic Containers Inc.
Silgan Plastics Corp.
ABC Group Inc.

Firms are ranked by sales in millions of dollars.

Crown Cork & Seal Company Inc.	$ 925
Johnson Controls Inc.	662
Continental PET Technologies Inc.	550
Owens-Brockway Plastic Products	540
Graham Packaging Co.	490
Plastipak Packaging Inc.	420
Southeastern Container Inc.	300
Continental Plastic Containers Inc.	270
Silgan Plastics Corp.	230
ABC Group Inc.	225

Source: *Plastics News*, November 4, 1996, p. 1.

★ 537 ★

Plastics (SIC 2821)

Top Engineering Plastics Companies

Shares are shown based on annual production of 3.2 million metric tons.

GE Plastics	22.0%
DuPont	12.0
Hoechst	11.0
Bayer	9.0
BASF	5.0
Mitsubishi Gas Chemical	4.0
Asahi	3.0
Dow Chemical	3.0
Toray	3.0
AlliedSignal	2.0
Teijin	2.0
Other	24.0

Source: *Chemicalweek*, May 28, 1997, p. 28, from Hoechst Technical Polymers.

★ 538 ★

Plastics (SIC 2821)

U.S. Composite Shipments

Data are in millions of pounds for 1996.

	(mil.)	Share
Transportation	994.1	30.7%
Construction	645.0	19.9
Corrosion resistant equipment	402.4	12.4
Marine	374.4	11.5
Electrical/electronic	326.0	10.1
Consumer products	195.3	6.0
Appliance/business equipment	170.8	5.3
Aerospace/defense	23.6	0.7
Other	110.8	3.4

Source: *Modern Plastics*, October 1996, p. 16, from SPI Composites Institute.

★ 539 ★

Plastics (SIC 2821)

U.S. Medical Plastics - 1995

Medical product component	56.9%
Medical packaging	43.1

Source: *Assembly*, April 1997, p. 16, from Freedonia Group Inc.

★ 540 ★

Plastics (SIC 2821)

U.S. Plastics Recycling

The market for recycling disposable plastics is shown for 2000.

Rigid/other packaging	74.6%
Flexible packaging	16.0
Foam packaging	9.4

Source: *Plastics News*, February 3, 1997, p. 3, from Business Communications Co. Inc.

★ 541 ★

Plastics (SIC 2821)

U.S. Resin Production - 1996

Production is shown in millions of pounds. PVC stands for polyvinyl chloride, HDPE stands for high-density polyethylene, PP stands for polypropylene, LDPE stands for low-density polyethylene, LLDPE stands for linear low-density polyethylene, PS stands for polystyrene, PET stands for polyethylene terephthalate, ABS stands for acrylonitrile butadiene styrene, and SAN stands for styrene acrylonitrile.

	(mil.)	Share
PVC	13,184.0	20.1%
HDPE	12,170.0	18.5
PP	11,913.0	18.1
LDPE	7,750.0	11.8
LLDPE	6,404.0	9.8
PS	5,973.0	9.1
PET	4,036.0	6.1
ABS	1,505.0	2.3
Nylons	1,112.0	1.7
SAN	123.0	0.2
Other synthetics	1,497.0	2.3

Source: *Chemical Market Reporter*, December 16, 1996, p. 19, from Society of the Plastics Industry.

★ 542 ★

Synthetic Rubber (SIC 2822)

Synthetic Rubber - 2000

Data are for North America.

Styrene butadiene	29.2%
Carboxylated latex	20.6
Polybutadiene	17.8
Ethylene propylene	9.0
Styrene butadiene latex	3.0
Nitrile solid	2.9
Polychlorprene	2.3
Nitrile latex	1.2
Other	14.1

Source: *Chemical & Engineering News*, August 5, 1996, p. 13, from Freedonia Group.

★543★

Fibers (SIC 2823)

Canadian Fiber Exports

Data are in millions of pounds in 1995.

Synthetic filament	161.1
Synthetic staple	100.5
Cellulose staple and low	50.5
Cellulose filament	19.7

Source: *America's Textile International*, January 1997, p. 2, from Fiber Economics Bureau.

★544★

Fibers (SIC 2824)

U.S. Fiber Consumption

Data refer to mill consumption.

Polyester	40.8%
Nylon	28.2
Olefin	24.3
Rayon acetate	4.9
Acrylic	1.9

Source: *Textile Asia*, May 1996, p. 69.

★545★

Vitamins (SIC 2833)

Herbal Supplement Market

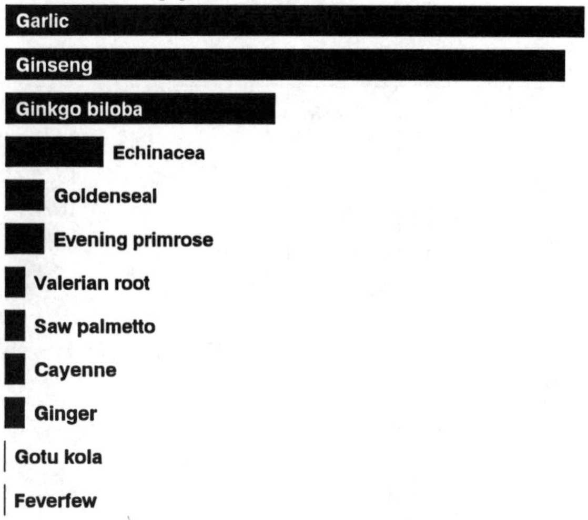

Shares are shown based on discount store sales of herbal supplements. Data are for the 52 weeks ended November 5, 1995, and the 52 weeks ended November 3, 1996.

	1995	1996
Garlic	40.6%	29.6%
Ginseng	36.9	29.3
Ginkgo biloba	1.9	13.7
Echinacea	3.2	5.4
Goldenseal	1.8	2.0
Evening primrose	1.4	2.0
Valerian root	0.7	1.2
Saw palmetto	0.1	1.1
Cayenne	0.7	0.8
Ginger	0.4	0.5
Gotu kola	0.2	0.4
Feverfew	0.1	0.3

Source: *Discount Store News*, February 17, 1997, p. 41, from Information Resources Inc.

★ 546 ★

Vitamins (SIC 2833)

Top Children's Multivitamins

Shares are shown based on revenues.

	($ mil.)	Share
Flintstones	$ 17.5	37.7%
Private label	9.8	21.2
Bugs Bunny	5.7	12.3
Centrum Jr.	4.8	10.4
Sesame Street	3.7	8.1
Sunkist	2.4	5.1
Other	56.1	5.1

Source: *Supermarket Business*, August 1996, p. 66, from A.C. Nielsen.

★ 547 ★

Vitamins (SIC 2833)

Top Multivitamin Brands

Shares are shown based on supermarket sales for the 52 weeks ended March 9, 1996.

Centrum	26.6%
Private label	23.9
One-A-Day	12.0
Centrum Silver	11.3
Nature Made	4.9
Theragran-M	4.8
Your Life	2.9
Geritol	2.6
Ocuvite	1.4
Protegra	1.3
Sundown	0.7
Theragran	0.7
Other	6.9

Source: *Supermarket Business*, August 1996, p. 66, from A.C. Nielsen.

★ 548 ★

Drugs (SIC 2834)

Anti-Psychotic Drug Brands

Haloperidol
Risperdal
Mellaril
Clozaril
Other

Brand shares are shown based on U.S. sales as of August 1996.

Haloperidol	20.0%
Risperdal	17.8
Mellaril	16.0
Clozaril	9.8
Other	36.4

Source: *Wall Street Journal*, October 14, 1996, p. B6, from company reports.

★ 549 ★

Drugs (SIC 2834)

Anti-Ulcer Drug Brands

Shares are shown for the month of October 1996.

Zantac	27.7%
Prilosec	24.0
Pepcid	11.0
Cimetidine	10.6
Propulsid	8.0
Axid	7.5
Prevacid	5.5
Carafate	2.4
Other	4.4

Source: *Drug Topics*, January 6, 1997, p. 24, from Prescription Audit and Scott-Levin.

★ 550 ★

Drugs (SIC 2834)

Baldness Treatment Market

Total sales of baldness remedies reached $111.6 million as of December 1, 1996.

Rogaine	87.0%
Other	13.0

Source: *Wall Street Journal*, January 27, 1997, p. B1, from Information Resources Inc.

★ 551 ★

Drugs (SIC 2834)

Best-Selling Antacids

Shares are shown based on supermarket sales for the year ended March 9, 1996.

Pepcid AC	16.4%
Pepto-Bismol	12.3
Mylanta	12.0
Tagamet HB	8.7
Rolaids	8.5
Tums	8.5
Tums EX	8.0
Private label	6.8
Maalox Plus	6.2
Tums Ultra	3.1
Other	9.5

Source: *Nonfoods Merchandising*, November 1996, p. 24, from A.C. Nielsen.

★ 552 ★

Drugs (SIC 2834)

Canada's Antacid Market

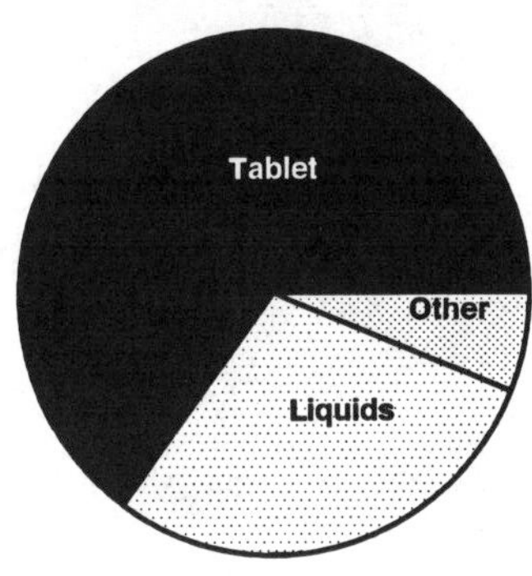

Sales are shown by type.

Tablet	65.0%
Liquids	29.0
Other	6.0

Source: *Marketing Magazine*, March 24, 1997, p. 3, from A.C. Nielsen.

★ 553 ★

Drugs (SIC 2834)

Cough/Cold Remedy Brands

Data show the leading brands of cough or cold remedies without analgesics. Figures are for oral solid forms only.

Claritin D 12hr.	38.9%
Seldane-D	11.7
R-Tannate	3.5
Trinalin	2.7
Claritin D 24 hr.	2.4
Semprex-D	2.1
Chlorophenir/Pseudo	1.6
Bromfed-PD	1.4
Poly-Histine-D	1.4
Other	34.3

Source: *Drug Topics*, January 6, 1997, p. 24, from Prescription Audit and Scott-Levin.

★ 554 ★

Drugs (SIC 2834)

Generic Drug Market - Canada

Company shares are shown based on sales of $986 million for 1996.

Apotex Inc.	30.7%
Novopharm Ltd.	26.0
Altimed Pharma Inc.	7.7
Pharmascience Inc.	6.7
Other	30.0

Source: *Globe and Mail's Report on Business Magazine*, May 1997, p. 72.

★ 555 ★

Drugs (SIC 2834)

Leading Beta Blockers

Shares are shown in percent for May 1996.

Atenolol	35.7%
Metoprolol Tartrate	17.6
Propranolol HCl	10.5
Propranolol LA	6.9
Toprol XL	6.9
Lopressor	4.6
Tenomin	4.6
Nadolol	3.7
Inderal LA	1.9
Inderal	1.8

Continued on next page.

★ 555 ★ *Continued*

Drugs (SIC 2834)

Leading Beta Blockers

Shares are shown in percent for May 1996.

Corgard	1.7%
Sectral	1.1
Other	3.1

Source: *Drug Topics*, August 5, 1996, p. 26, from Source Prescription Audit and Scott-Levin Associates.

★ 556 ★

Drugs (SIC 2834)

Leading Cholesterol Fighters - 1996

Shares are for the first seven months of 1996.

Zocar	30.6%
Mevacor	18.5
Pravachol	17.8
Lescol	12.6
Questran/Questran Light	3.6
Other	16.9

Source: *St. Louis Post-Dispatch*, September 28, 1996, p. B14, from Montgomery Securities.

★ 557 ★

Drugs (SIC 2834)

Leading Diabetes Drugs

Monthly brand shares are shown in percent.

Glyburide	30.7%
Glucophage	19.0
Glucotrol XL	14.1
Glipixide	10.8
Glynase Prestab	7.3
Diabeta	4.7
Other	13.4

Source: *Drug Topics*, September 2, 1996, p. 19, from Source Prescription Audit and Scott-Levin Associates.

★ 558 ★

Drugs (SIC 2834)

Leading Diuretics

Data show brand share for April 1996.

Furosemide oral	29.4%
Triamterene w/HCTZ	21.5
Hydrochlorothlazide	15.7%
Dyazide	5.0
Lasix oral	4.7
Lozol	3.4
Indapamide	2.8
Spironolacatone	2.1
Bumetadiene	2.0
Other	13.4

Source: *Drug Topics*, July 8, 1996, p. 24, from Source Prescription Audit.

★ 559 ★

Drugs (SIC 2834)

Leading Generic Drug Advertisers

Firms are ranked by share of total ad spending in 1996.

Watson	10.9%
Mylan	7.7
Dey	4.9
Alpharma	4.6
Creighton	4.4
Apothecon	4.2
Teva	4.1
Novopharm	4.0
Roxane	3.8
Barr	3.6
ESI Lederle	3.4
Zenith/Goldline	3.3
Copley	3.0
Taro	3.0
Other	35.1

Source: *Medical Marketing & Media*, March 1997, p. 44.

★ 560 ★

Drugs (SIC 2834)

Leading Pharmaceuticals - 1996

The leading prescription pharmaceuticals are ranked by 1996 sales in thousands of dollars at pharmacy acquisition cost. Data represent sales to independents, chains, clinics, HMOs, long-term care pharmacies and federal facilities. Leading producers include Glaxo, Astra-Merck, Amgen, Roenig, Pfizer, Abbott, and Merck.

Zantac	$ 920,938
Prozac	805,196

Continued on next page.

★ 560 ★ *Continued*

Drugs (SIC 2834)

Leading Pharmaceuticals - 1996

The leading prescription pharmaceuticals are ranked by 1996 sales in thousands of dollars at pharmacy acquisition cost. Data represent sales to independents, chains, clinics, HMOs, long-term care pharmacies and federal facilities. Leading producers include Glaxo, Astra-Merck, Amgen, Roenig, Pfizer, Abbott, and Merck.

Prilosec	$ 779,193
Epogen	548,799
Zoloft	523,183
Procardia XL	494,071
Zocor	440,587
Vasotec	425,018
Mevacor	395,931
Biaxin	370,836

Source: *Medical Marketing & Media*, November 1996, p. 58, from *Retail Perspective* and *Provider Perspective*.

★ 561 ★

Drugs (SIC 2834)

Leading Prescription Pharmaceuticals - 1996

Data show sales volume at pharmacy acquisition costs in millions of dollars. Companies are listed in parentheses.

Zantac (Glaxo)	$ 1,761
Prilosec (Astra-Merck)	1,742
Prozac (Dista)	1,685
Epogen (Amgen)	1,184
Zoloft (Roerig)	1,098
Zocor (Merck)	1,015
Procardia XL (Pfizer)	962
Vasotec (Merck)	866
Mevacor (Merck)	792
Premarin (Wyeth-Ayerst)	768
Biaxin (Abbott)	760
Cardizem CD (Hoechest Marion Roussel)	734
Lupron Depot (TAP)	725
Norvasc (Pfizer)	723
Paxil (SmithKline Beecham)	696

Source: *Medical Marketing & Media*, April 1997, p. 80, from *Retail Perspective* and *Provider Perspective*.

★ 562 ★

Drugs (SIC 2834)

Leading Protease Inhibitor Brands

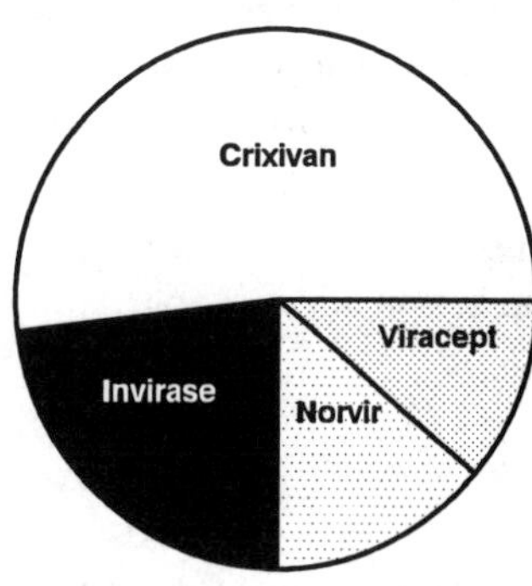

Brand shares are shown in percent. Company names are listed in parentheses.

Crixivan (Merck)	52.0%
Invirase (Roche)	23.0
Norvir (Abbott)	14.0
Viracept (Agouron)	11.0

Source: *Business Week*, June 9, 1997, p. 80, from Paine Webber.

★ 563 ★

Drugs (SIC 2834)

Leading Stomach Remedies

Brand shares are shown for the 52 weeks ended December 29, 1996.

Pepcid AC	15.5%
Tums	10.4
Mylanta	9.0
Zantac 75	8.1
Imodium	7.2
Pepto Bismol	5.9
Tagamet HB	5.3
Maalox	5.2
Alka Seltzer	4.3
Private label	9.2
Other	19.9

Source: *Discount Merchandiser*, April 1997, p. 61, from Information Resources Inc.

★ 564 ★

Drugs (SIC 2834)

Leading Therapeutic Classes - 1996

Figures show thousands of prescriptions dispensed. Data represent sales to independents, chains, clinics, HMOs, long-term care pharmacies and federal facilities.

Calcium channel blockers	44,987
Codeine & Comb, non injectionable	44,512
Antispasmodics	37,950
Amoxicillin	37,567
Systemic antiarthritics	37,339
Ace inhibitors	35,268

Source: *Medical Marketing & Media*, November 1996, p. 58, from NPA Plus.

★ 565 ★

Drugs (SIC 2834)

Major Pharmaceutical Companies - 1996

Company shares are shown based on sales at pharmacy acquisition cost. Ciba and Sandoz merged to form Novartis.

Glaxo Wellcome	6.8%
American Home Products	6.2
Johnson & Johnson	6.2
Bristol-Myers Squibb	6.0
Merck	5.9
Pfizer	5.3
Novartis	4.4
Lilly	4.2
SmithKline Beecham	4.2
Abbott	4.0
Schering-Plough	3.8
Hoechst Marion Roussel	2.9
Hoffman-LaRouche	2.7
Amgen	2.2
Bayer	2.2
Astra Merck	2.1
Pharmacia & Upjohn	1.9
Warner-Lambert	1.5
Zeneca	1.5
Searle	1.3
Other	24.7

Source: *Medical Marketing & Media*, April 1997, p. 84, from *Retail Perspective* and *Provider Perspective*.

★ 566 ★

Drugs (SIC 2834)

Mexican Pharmaceutical Market

Sales are shown in millions of dollars for 1995 and 1996.

	1995	1996	Share
Ethical	$ 754.7	$ 792.4	46.6%
Public	709.3	780.2	45.9
Popular	119.3	126.5	7.4

Source: *Business Mexico*, April 1997, p. 38.

★ 567 ★

Drugs (SIC 2834)

Multiple Schlerosis Drugs

Shares are shown for the week of Thanksgiving 1996.

Avonex	53.0%
Betaseron	47.0

Source: *Wall Street Journal*, December 19, 1996, p. B8, from IMS America.

★ 568 ★

Drugs (SIC 2834)

Nasal Spray Market

The precription market reached sales of $723.8 million in 1996. Flonase is manufactured by Glaxo Wellcome.

Flonase	72.0%
Other	28.0

Source: *Advertising Age*, April 9, 1997, p. 16, from IMS America.

★ 569 ★

Drugs (SIC 2834)

Pharmaceutical Purchases by Type

Total sales for the first 11 months of 1996 reached $54.054 billion.

Central Nervous System	18.8%
Alimentary/Metabolism	16.4
Cardiovascular	14.5
Respiratory	10.4
Anti-infectives	9.6
Genito-urinary	6.4

Continued on next page.

★569★ *Continued*

Drugs (SIC 2834)

Pharmaceutical Purchases by Type

Total sales for the first 11 months of 1996 reached $54.054 billion.

Blood agents	5.2%
Others	18.8

Source: *Financial Times*, February 3, 1997, p. 4, from IMS International.

★570★

Drugs (SIC 2834)

Pharmaceutical Purchases by Type - Canada

Total sales for the first 11 months of 1996 reached $3.42 billion.

Cardiovascular	19.2%
Central Nervous System	16.9
Alimentary/Metabolism	15.5
Respiratory	9.7
Blood agents	7.4
Anti-infectives	7.0
Genito-urinary	5.6
Others	18.7

Source: *Financial Times*, February 3, 1997, p. 4, from IMS International.

★571★

Drugs (SIC 2834)

Prescription Allergy Relief Market - 1996

Shares of the $1.8 billion market are shown as of November 1996.

	Sales ($ mil.)	Share
Claritin	$ 597.0	33.2%
Seldane	189.0	10.5
Zyrtec	120.4	6.7
Other	893.6	49.6

Source: *Advertising Age*, January 20, 1997, p. 14, from IMS America.

★572★

Drugs (SIC 2834)

Prescription Nasal Sprays

Sales of prescription nasal sprays reached $362.7 million in 1995. Data show the top sellers.

	($ mil.)	Share
Vancenase	$ 54.4	12.3%
Beconase	39.0	8.8
Nasalcrom	35.3	8.0
Other	312.0	70.8

Source: *Advertising Age*, October 7, 1996, p. 64, from IMS America.

★573★

Drugs (SIC 2834)

Smoking Cessation Market

Total sales reached $270.5 million as of December 1, 1996.

	($ mil.)	Share
NicoDerm CQ	$ 66.9	24.7%
Nicotrol	35.2	13.0
Other	168.4	62.3

Source: *Advertising Age*, January 20, 1997, p. 48, from Information Resources Inc.

★574★

Drugs (SIC 2834)

Top Cholesterol Fighters

Data show share of new prescriptions for the week ending April 18, 1997.

Zocor	33.9%
Pravachol	21.3
Lipitor	17.3
Mavacor	14.0
Lescol	13.5

Source: *Investor's Business Daily*, April 30, 1997, p. 4, from company reports.

★ 575 ★

Drugs (SIC 2834)

Top Stomach Remedy Brands

Pepcid AC
Tums
Mylanta
Tagamet
Pepto-Bismol
Maalox
Alka-Seltzer
Rolaids
Other

Shares are shown based on $1.48 billion in sales for the 52 weeks ended June 30, 1996.

Pepcid AC	17.2%
Tums	10.8
Mylanta	10.1
Tagamet	8.5
Pepto-Bismol	6.6
Maalox	5.7
Alka-Seltzer	4.5
Rolaids	4.4
Other	32.2

Source: *NARD Journal*, October 1996, p. 145, from Information Resources Inc.

★ 576 ★

Drugs (SIC 2834)

U.S. Pharmaceutical Makers

Firms are ranked by 1996 net income in millions of dollars.

Merck	$ 3,881.3
Johnson & Johnson	2,887.0
Bristol-Myers Squibb	2,850.0
Pfizer	1,929.0
American Home Products	1,883.4
Schering-Plough	1,212.8

Source: *Financial Times*, January 29, 1997, p. 16, from companies.

★ 577 ★

Diagnostic Kits (SIC 2835)

Fertility Test Kit Sales

Pregnancy kits	86.7%
Ovulation kits	13.3

Source: *DM*, December 1996, p. 59, from Packaged Facts.

★ 578 ★

Biotechnology (SIC 2836)

Biotechnology Industry Sales

Sales are shown by category in millions of dollars for 1996 and 2001.

	1996 ($ mil.)	2001 ($ mil.)
Human therapeutics	$ 7,150	$ 12,050.0
Human diagnostics	1,760	2,700.0
Agriculture	290	680.0
Specialties	275	650.0
Nonmedical diagnostics	225	320.0

Source: *Chemicalweek*, January 8, 1997, p. 27, from Consulting Resources.

★ 579 ★

Biotechnology (SIC 2836)

Largest Biotech/Biopharmaceutical Firms - San Francisco

Firms are ranked by market capitalization in millions of dollars as of July 1, 1996.

Genentech Inc.	$ 6,344.7
Chiron Corp.	4,240.5
Alza Corp.	2,315.5
Gilead Sciences Inc.	714.0
Target Therapeutics	588.5
Sequus Pharmaceuticals	563.8
Neurex Corp.	490.0
Athena Neurosciences Inc.	473.7
Incyte Pharmaceuticals	388.6
Matrix Pharmaceutical Inc.	370.1

Source: *San Francisco Business Times*, September 27, 1996, p. 16.

★ 580 ★

Biotechnology (SIC 2836)

Leading Biotech Firms

Sales are shown in millions of dollars for the second quarter of 1996.

Amgen	$ 571
Chiron	316
Genentech	229
Alza	116
Genzyme	116
Mycogen	80
Life Technologies	78
Genetics Institute	65
Immunex	42
Biogen	35

Source: *Chemicalweek*, August 28, 1996, p. 58, from Standard & Poor's.

★ 581 ★

Detergent Chemicals (SIC 2840)

U.S. Surfactant Demand

	1994	2000
Anionic	64.5%	63.8%
Nonionic	25.4	25.5
Cationic	9.4	9.8
Amphoteric	0.7	0.9

Source: *Chemicalweek*, August 28, 1996, p. 40, from Freedonia Group.

★ 582 ★

Detergents (SIC 2841)

Leading Automatic Dishwasher Detergent Brands

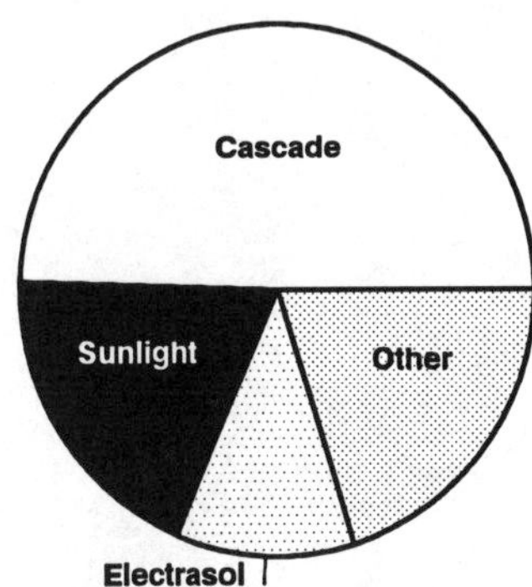

Brand shares of the $490 million category are shown for the 52 weeks ended April 27, 1997. Companies are provided in parentheses.

Cascade (Procter & Gamble)	49.0%
Sunlight (Lever Bros.)	19.3
Electrasol (Benckiser Consumer Products)	11.4
Other	20.3

Source: *Advertising Age*, May 26, 1997, p. 42, from Information Resources Inc.

★ 583 ★

Detergents (SIC 2841)

Leading Liquid Detergent Brands

Dollar shares are shown for the 52 weeks ended October 27, 1996.

Tide	13.8%
All	5.6
Wisk	5.3
Era	3.4
Purex	3.3
Cheer	3.0
Xtra	1.8
Surf	1.5
Private label	1.4
Arm & Hammer	1.1
Other	59.8

Source: *Household and Personal Products Industry*, January 1997, p. 66, from Information Resources Inc.

★ 584 ★

Detergents (SIC 2841)

Leading Powdered Detergent Brands

Dollar shares are shown for the 52 weeks ended October 27, 1996.

Tide	22.8%
Cheer	5.3
Surf	4.3
Gain	3.6
Arm & Hammer	2.8
Wisk	2.6
Purex	2.2
Private label	1.5
Bold	1.4
All	1.3
Other	52.2

Source: *Household and Personal Products Industry*, January 1997, p. 66, from Information Resources Inc.

★ 585 ★

Detergents (SIC 2841)

U.S. Detergent Market

Shares of the 3.86 million metric ton market are shown in percent.

Procter & Gamble	57.0%
Lever Brothers	21.0
Dial	6.0
Church & Dwight	4.0
Colgate-Palmolive	4.0
Other	8.0

Source: *Chemicalweek*, January 29, 1997, p. 32, from Information Resources Inc.

★ 586 ★

Soaps (SIC 2841)

Canada's Leading Soap Brands - 1997

Shares are shown based on estimated sales of $226 million.

Dove	21.6%
Oil of Olay	12.0
Ivory	10.5
Jergens	8.8
Lever 2000	8.0
Zest	6.9
Irish Spring	6.0%
Dial	3.9
Others	22.3

Source: *Marketing Magazine*, June 9, 1997, p. 4, from industry sources.

★ 587 ★

Soaps (SIC 2841)

Personal Soap Market

Lever Bros.	31.1%
Procter & Gamble	25.0
Others	43.9

Source: *Advertising Age*, March 3, 1997, p. 39, from Dean Witter Equity Research.

★ 588 ★

Cleaning Preparations (SIC 2842)

Auto Protectant Market

Brand shares are shown in percent for 1996.

Armor All	60.0%
Other	40.0

Source: *Advertising Age*, April 21, 1997, p. 22.

★ 589 ★

Cleaning Preparations (SIC 2842)

Carpet Cleaner Sales

Sales of the $422 million category are shown for the year ended December 29, 1996.

	($ mil.)	Share
Reckitt & Colman	$ 101.4	24.0%
S.C. Johnson & Son	67.6	16.0
Church & Dwight Co.	40.8	9.7
Other	212.2	50.3

Source: *Advertising Age*, March 10, 1997, p. 6, from Information Resources Inc.

★ 590 ★

Cleaning Preparations (SIC 2842)

Glass Cleaner Market - Canada

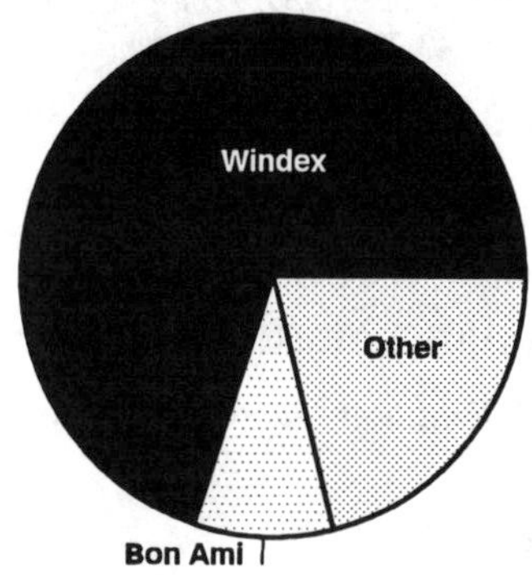

Shares of the $30 million market are shown in percent.

Windex	70.0%
Bon Ami	9.0
Other	21.0

Source: *Marketing Magazine*, December 23, 1996, p. 1.

★ 591 ★

Cleaning Preparations (SIC 2842)

Leading Household Cleaners - 1996

Shares are shown based on sales of $431.8 million for the year ended June 30, 1996.

	($ mil.)	Share
Pine Sol	$ 112.1	26.0%
Lysol	79.6	18.4
Mr. Clean	60.0	13.9
Spic & Span	35.8	8.3
Clorox Clean-Up	28.0	6.5
Other	116.3	26.9

Source: *Household and Personal Products Industry*, November 1996, p. 71, from Information Resources Inc.

★ 592 ★

Cleaning Preparations (SIC 2842)

Leading Laundry Pretreatment Brands

Dollar shares are shown for the 52 weeks ended October 27, 1996.

Shout	35.4%
Spray n Wash	34.5
Stain Out	5.8
Calgon	5.6
Wisk Away	5.0
Zout	2.7
Arm & Hammer	2.0
Magic Goo Gone	1.2
Easy Wash	0.9
Rite White Wash	0.7
Other	6.2

Source: *Household and Personal Products Industry*, January 1997, p. 66, from Information Resources Inc.

★ 593 ★

Cleaning Preparations (SIC 2842)

Oven Cleaner Market

Easy Off	54.4%
Other	45.6

Source: *Brandweek*, December 16, 1996, p. 5, from Information Resources Inc.

★ 594 ★

Cleaning Preparations (SIC 2842)

Popular Cleaning Products

Data show the sales of cleaning products in supermarkets for the year ended March 9, 1996.

	($ mil.)	Share
Non-disinfectant liquid cleaners	$ 332.6	22.4%
Toilet bowl cleaners	227.9	15.4
Bathroom cleaners	166.9	11.2
Liquid disinfectant cleaners	154.3	10.4
Window cleaners	119.9	8.1
Rug cleaners	106.2	7.2
Disinfectant sales	95.8	6.5
Powder abrasive cleaners	71.7	4.8
Liquid abrasive cleaners	59.8	4.0
Oven cleaners	39.4	2.7
Floor cleaners	31.9	2.1
Ammonia sales	26.4	1.8
Metal cleaners	18.8	1.3
Septic tank cleaners	16.2	1.1
Rust removers	9.7	0.7
Upholstery cleaners	7.0	0.5

Source: *Household and Personal Products Industry*, November 1996, p. 68, from A.C. Nielsen.

★ 595 ★

Cleaning Preparations (SIC 2842)

Popular Floor Wax Brands

Brands are ranked by supermarket sales in millions of dollars for the 52 weeks ended March 31, 1996. The market reached $109.55 million in all outlets.

Mop & Glo	$ 14.8
Future	12.3
Step Saver	4.1
Johnson	2.1
Private label	1.0

Source: *Household and Personal Products Industry*, September 1996, p. 43, from A.C. Nielsen.

★ 596 ★

Cleaning Preparations (SIC 2842)

Popular Furniture Polish Brands

Brands are ranked by supermarket sales in millions of dollars for the 52 weeks ended March 31, 1996. The market had sales of $130.9 million.

	($ mil.)	Share
Pledge	$ 64.5	49.3%
Endust	19.1	14.6
Old English	15.8	12.1
Scott's Liquid Gold	7.5	5.7
Favor	6.4	4.9
Behold	2.8	2.1
Kleen Guard	1.8	1.4
Guardsman	1.3	1.0
Jubilee	1.3	1.0
Private label	3.0	2.3
Other	7.4	5.7

Source: *Household and Personal Products Industry*, September 1996, p. 43, from A.C. Nielsen.

★ 597 ★

Cleaning Preparations (SIC 2842)

Wood Finishing Market - Canada

Shares of the $50 million market are shown in percent.

Thomson Minwax Ltd.	60.0%
Other	40.0

Source: *Marketing Magazine*, October 14, 1996, p. 6.

★ 598 ★

Baby Care (SIC 2844)

Baby Product Sales

Shares are shown based on $357.4 million in sales for the year ended June 16, 1996.

Baby powder	24.9%
Petroleum jelly	18.1
Ointments	17.5
Baby oils	15.0
Lotions	12.6
Baby soaps	11.9

Source: *DM*, August 1996, p. 21, from Information Resources Inc.

★ 599 ★

Baby Care (SIC 2844)

Leading Baby Ointment Brands

Shares are shown based on supermarket sales for the 52 weeks ended March 9, 1996. Supermarkets had 38.1% of total retail sales.

Desitin	44.4%
White A&D	23.1
Balmex	11.3
Daily Care	5.5
Johnson & Johnson	5.2
Private label	4.2
Other	6.3

Source: *Supermarket Business*, August 1996, p. 61, from A.C. Nielsen.

★ 600 ★

Baby Care (SIC 2844)

Leading Baby Powder Brands

Shares are shown based on supermarket sales for the 52 weeks ended March 9, 1996. Supermarkets lead the overall retail market with 37.3% of sales.

Johnson & Johnson	34.5%
J&J Baby Powder	23.7
Private label	20.3
Caldesene	5.6
Suave Baby Creme	4.2
Diaprene	3.5
Other	8.2

Source: *Supermarket Business*, August 1996, p. 61, from A.C. Nielsen.

★ 601 ★

Baby Care (SIC 2844)

Leading Bottle/Nipple Brands

Shares are shown based on supermarket sales for the 52 weeks ended March 9, 1996. Mass merchandisers lead with a 47% share, followed by supermarkets with a 36% share.

Playtex	31.2%
Gerber	27.0
Evenflo	17.4
Johnson's Baby	8.7
NUK	4.6
Private label	4.3
Cherubs	3.1
Other	3.7

Source: *Supermarket Business*, August 1996, p. 61, from A.C. Nielsen.

★ 602 ★

Cosmetics (SIC 2844)

Cosmetics Leaders - 1996

Shares of the $2.48 billion market are shown for the year ended June 30, 1996.

	Sales ($ mil.)	Share
Cosmair	$ 680.3	27.0%
Procter & Gamble	672.7	27.0
Revlon	657.5	26.0
Other	473.9	20.0

Source: *Discount Store News*, November 4, 1996, p. 7, from Information Resources Inc.

★ 603 ★

Cosmetics (SIC 2844)

Cosmetics Sales by Segment

Sales at discount stores are shown in percent. Total sales reached $2.54 billion.

Women's fragrances	25.6%
Face makeup	13.8
Lip makeup	11.4
Eye makeup	8.7
Men's fragrances	7.1
Other	33.5

Source: *Discount Store News*, August 5, 1996, p. 63.

★ 604 ★

Cosmetics (SIC 2844)

Eye Color Makeup Producers

Shares of the $679.9 million market are shown for the year ended June 30, 1996.

Cosmair	45.0%
Procter & Gamble	28.0
Revlon	20.0
Other	7.0

Source: *Discount Store News*, November 4, 1996, p. 7, from Information Resources Inc.

★ 605 ★

Cosmetics (SIC 2844)

Face Makeup Brands - 1996

Shares are shown for the year ended June 30, 1996. Maybelline figures exclude sales of Shades of You.

Cover Girl	33.08%
Revlon	18.08
Maybelline	11.78
L'Oreal	10.16
Max Factor	8.94
Almay	6.87
Coty	2.38
Corn Silk	1.89
Physician's Formula	1.12
Flame Glow	0.99
Other	5.00

Source: *Discount Store News*, November 4, 1996, p. 7, from Information Resources Inc.

★ 606 ★

Cosmetics (SIC 2844)

Face Makeup Producers

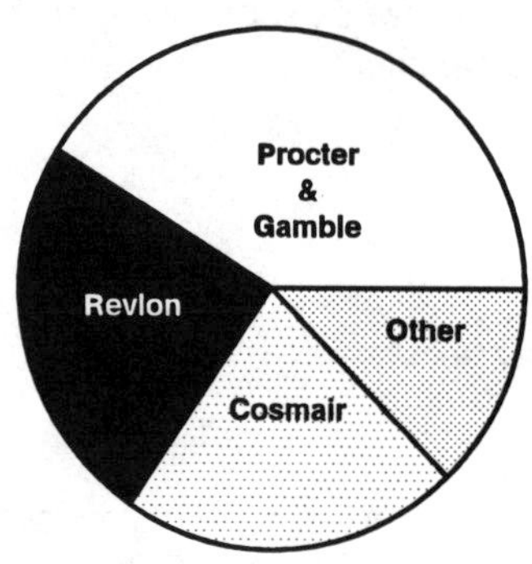

Shares are shown for the year ended June 30, 1996.

	Sales ($ mil.)	Share
Procter & Gamble	$ 345.0	42.0%
Revlon	204.8	25.0
Cosmair	180.1	22.0
Other	91.1	13.0

Source: *Discount Store News*, November 4, 1996, p. 7, from Information Resources Inc.

★ 607 ★

Cosmetics (SIC 2844)

Leading Cosmetics in Dept. Stores

Estee Lauder	42.0%
L'Oreal	14.0
Other	44.0

Source: *Forbes*, December 16, 1996, p. 96.

★ 608 ★

Cosmetics (SIC 2844)

Leading Eye Makeup Brands

Shares are shown for the year ended June 30, 1996.

Maybelline	33.0%
Cover Girl	22.0
L'Oreal	12.0
Revlon	12.0
Other	21.0

Source: *Nonfoods Merchandising*, December 1996, p. 27, from Information Resources Inc.

★ 609 ★

Cosmetics (SIC 2844)

Leading Lip Makeup Brands

Shares are shown for the year ended June 30, 1996.

Revlon	37.0%
L'Oreal	15.0
Cover Girl	12.0
Maybelline	10.0
Other	26.0

Source: *Nonfoods Merchandising*, December 1996, p. 27, from Information Resources Inc.

★ 610 ★

Cosmetics (SIC 2844)

Lip Makeup Producers

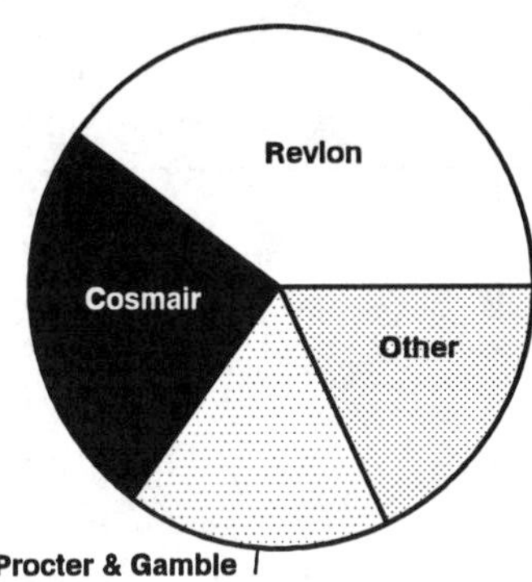

Shares are shown for the year ended June 30, 1996.

	Sales ($ mil.)	Share
Revlon	$ 205.8	40.0%
Cosmair	128.8	25.0
Procter & Gamble	85.4	17.0
Other	89.6	18.0

Source: *Discount Store News*, November 4, 1996, p. 7, from Information Resources Inc.

★ 611 ★

Cosmetics (SIC 2844)

Top Cosmetics Brands by Unit Sales

Unit shares are shown in percent for the year ended December 29, 1996.

Cover Girl	21.6%
Maybelline	14.0
Revlon	13.1
Wet n Wild	8.2%
L'Oreal	7.8
Sally Hansen	4.4
Almay	4.1
Max Factor	3.9
Bonne Bell	1.9
Revitalizing	1.2
Other	19.8

Source: *Supermarket Business*, April 1997, p. 50, from Information Resources Inc.

★ 612 ★

Cosmetics (SIC 2844)

Top Eye Makeup Brands - 1995

Brand shares are shown based on a $647.7 million market for 1995.

Maybelline	33.1%
Cover Girl	22.8
L'Oreal	12.6
Revlon	11.0
Max Factor	6.9
Almay	6.5
Wet N Wild	1.4
Artmatic	0.9
Physicians Formula	0.8
Loveye	0.5
Other	3.5

Source: *Advertising Age*, September 30, 1996, p. S12, from Information Resources Inc.

★ 613 ★

Deodorants (SIC 2844)

Leading Deodorant Brands

Shares are shown for the year ended November 24, 1996.

Secret	14.5%
Right Guard	10.1
Mennen	7.7
Arrid	7.6
Sure	7.2
Degree	7.0
Ban	5.8
Old Spice	4.8
Ladies Mennen	4.7
Soft & Dry	4.7
Suave	4.4

Continued on next page.

★ 613 ★ *Continued*

Deodorants (SIC 2844)

Leading Deodorant Brands

Shares are shown for the year ended November 24, 1996.

Dry Idea	3.6%
Mitchum	3.4
Brut	2.7
Gillette Series	2.6
Other	9.2

Source: *Supermarket Business*, February 1997, p. 83, from Information Resources Inc.

★ 614 ★

Feminine Hygiene Products (SIC 2844)

Top Yeast Infection Remedies - Canada

Shares are shown based on sales.

	1995	1996
Monistat	55.0%	52.0%
Canesten	35.0	35.0
Gynecure	8.0	12.0

Source: *Marketing Magazine*, May 26, 1997, p. 12, from industry sources.

★ 615 ★

Foot Care (SIC 2844)

Top Foot Care Products

Dr. Scholl's Foot Care
Dr. Scholl's Air Pillow
Dr. Scholl's Foam Ease
Private label
Dr. Scholl's Flexo
Dr. Scholl's Workday
Dr. Scholl's Smooth Touch
Professional Foot Care
Dr. Scholl's Zino
Johnson Odor Eaters

The top selling items are ranked by sales in millions of dollars for the year ended October 6, 1996.

Dr. Scholl's Foot Care	$ 244.04
Dr. Scholl's Air Pillow	101.15
Dr. Scholl's Foam Ease	$ 21.52
Private label	21.09
Dr. Scholl's Flexo	13.39
Dr. Scholl's Workday	12.70
Dr. Scholl's Smooth Touch	7.80
Professional Foot Care	6.31
Dr. Scholl's Zino	5.68
Johnson Odor Eaters	4.92

Source: *Supermarket Business*, February 1997, p. 58, from Information Resources Inc.

★ 616 ★

Fragrances (SIC 2844)

Best Selling Women's Fragrances

Brands are ranked by sales for the 52 weeks ended March 30, 1997. The total market had sales of $603.5 million.

	Sales ($ mil.)	Share
Vanilla Fields	$ 20.7	3.4%
Vanderbilt	16.2	2.7
White Diamonds	14.7	2.4
Jovan Musk	13.5	2.3
Lady Stetson	13.3	2.2
Jovan White Musk	12.6	2.1
Exclamation	12.6	2.1
Sand & Sable	11.6	1.9
Vanilla Musk	11.4	1.9
Private label	10.6	1.8

Source: *Advertising Age*, May 12, 1997, p. 8, from Information Resources Inc.

★ 617 ★

Fragrances (SIC 2844)

Leading Unisex Fragrances - 1996

Data are for the first six months of 1996.

Ck One	5.3%
Estee Lauder Pleasures	3.3
Estee Lauder Beautiful	3.1
Eternity For Men	2.6
Tommy	2.6
Other	83.1

Source: *Household and Personal Products Industry*, November 1996, p. 100, from Beauty/Trends.

★ 618 ★

Fragrances (SIC 2844)

Top Fragrances for Men

Old Spice
Stetson
Preferred Stock
Jovan
Brut
Skin Bracer
Aspen
Gillette Series
Drakar Noir
Polo
Other

Market shares are shown in percent for the year ended December 29, 1996.

Old Spice	10.3%
Stetson	9.8
Preferred Stock	9.6
Jovan	5.9
Brut	5.4
Skin Bracer	5.2
Aspen	4.6
Gillette Series	4.1
Drakar Noir	3.7
Polo	3.1
Other	38.3

Source: *Supermarket Business*, April 1997, p. 47, from Information Resources Inc.

★ 619 ★

Fragrances (SIC 2844)

Top Fragrances for Men by Unit Sales

Unit shares are shown in percent for the year ended December 29, 1996.

	(mil.)	Share
Old Spice	8.8	12.8%
Skin Bracer	6.2	9.0
Gillette Series	5.4	7.9
Brut	5.3	7.7
Stetson	4.8	6.9
Jovan	2.8	4.1
Preferred Stock	2.7	3.9
Aspen	1.7	2.5
Drakar Noir	0.7	0.9%
Polo	0.5	0.8

Source: *Supermarket Business*, April 1997, p. 47, from Information Resources Inc.

★ 620 ★

Fragrances (SIC 2844)

Top Mass Market Fragrances

Brand shares are shown based on a $1.3 billion market. Women's fragrance sales reached $799.2 million; men's fragrance sales reached $508.8 million.

Old Spice (men)	3.95%
Stetson (men)	3.88
Vanilla Field (women)	2.85
Jovan (women)	2.56
Jovan (men)	2.12
Other	84.64

Source: *Advertising Age*, September 30, 1996, p. S12, from Information Resources Inc.

★ 621 ★

Fragrances (SIC 2844)

Top Men's Fragrance Makers - 1996

Company shares are shown based on value.

Calvin Klein	21.3%
Ralph Lauren	17.2
Estee Lauder	12.8
Lancaster	11.3
L'Oreal	8.9
Clinique	5.8
Lagerfeld	3.9
Paul Sebastian	3.6
Giorgio Beverly Hills	2.1
Dior	2.0
Compar	1.9
Haltson	1.9
Other	7.3

Source: *Household and Personal Products Industry*, April 1997, p. 80, from Datamonitor Cosmetics & Toiletries Database.

★ 622 ★

Fragrances (SIC 2844)

Top Prestige Market Fragrances

Brand shares are shown based on a $918 million market for the first seven months of 1996. Women's fragrance sales reached $569 million; men's fragrance sales reached $236 million; unisex fragrance sales reached $50 million.

Ck One (unisex)	5.40%
Estee Lauder Pleasures (women)	3.30
Estee Lauder Beautiful (women)	3.10
Tommy (men)	2.70
Calvin Klein Eternity (men)	2.60
Other	82.90

Source: *Advertising Age*, September 30, 1996, p. S12, from NPD Group Inc.

★ 623 ★

Hair Care (SIC 2844)

Black Hair Care Market

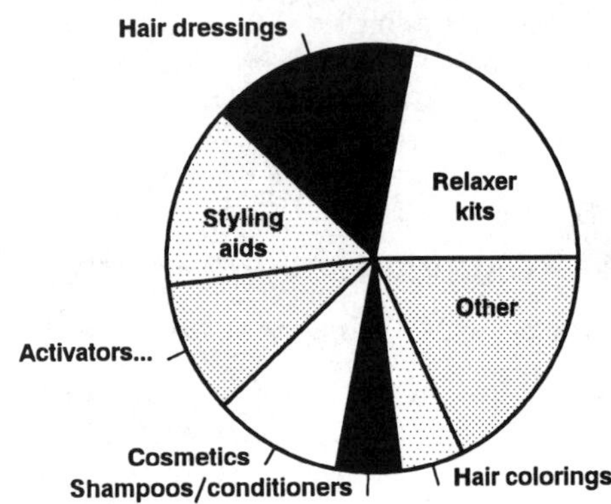

The market is shown for May 1996.

Relaxer kits	21.9%
Hair dressings	15.8
Styling aids	13.9
Activators, moisturizers	10.2
Cosmetics	10.2
Shampoos/conditioners	5.2
Hair colorings	4.6
Other	17.8

Source: *Dallas Morning News*, December 11, 1996, p. D1, from Information Resources Inc.

★ 624 ★

Hair Care (SIC 2844)

Ethnic Comb Out/Oil Sheen Market

Market shares are shown in percent.

Johnson Products	43.5%
African Pride	24.2
Proline	5.8
Other	21.5

Source: *Investext*, Thomson Financial Networks, December 23, 1996, p. 14, from Towne-Oller and DLJ estimates.

★ 625 ★

Hair Care (SIC 2844)

Ethnic Curl/Wave Market

Market shares are shown in percent.

Proline	19.8%
Carson	11.7
Johnson Products	4.3
Soft Sheen	2.2
Other	62.0

Source: *Investext*, Thomson Financial Networks, December 23, 1996, p. 14, from Towne-Oller and DLJ estimates.

★ 626 ★

Hair Care (SIC 2844)

Ethnic Hair Care Product Makers

The black hair care market is shown by producer for May 1996.

Soft Sheen Products Inc.	16.0%
Carson Products Co.	11.2
Luster Products Inc.	10.1
Pro-Line Corp.	7.2
Johnson Products Co. Inc.	6.8
Shark Products Inc.	6.7
Realistic Div./Revlon Inc.	6.0
Other	36.0

Source: *Dallas Morning News*, December 11, 1996, p. D1, from Information Resources Inc.

★ 627 ★

Hair Care (SIC 2844)

Ethnic Hair Coloring Market

Market shares are shown in percent.

Carson	72.5%
Soft Sheen	20.5
Johnson Products	1.4
Other	5.6

Source: *Investext,* Thomson Financial Networks, December 23, 1996, p. 14, from Towne-Oller and DLJ estimates.

★ 628 ★

Hair Care (SIC 2844)

Ethnic Relaxer Market

Market shares are shown in percent for December 1995.

Dark & Lovely	14.8%
Optimum (Soft Sheen)	13.7
Gentle Treatment	10.1
Soft & Beautiful	8.4
African Pride (Shark Products)	6.1
Creme of Nature (Revlon)	6.0
Just For Me	5.8
Revlon Realistic	5.7
TCB (Alberto-Culver)	4.9
Excelle	4.7
Luster PCL	4.3
Pink	3.7
Raveen	2.8
Beautiful Beginnings	2.3
Other	6.7

Source: *Investext,* Thomson Financial Networks, December 23, 1996, p. 14, from Towne-Oller and DLJ estimates.

★ 629 ★

Hair Care (SIC 2844)

Hair Care Sales by Segment

Retail sales are shown in millions of dollars.

	($ mil.)	Share
Shampoo	1,500	35.3%
Hair coloring	921	21.7
Conditioners	803	18.9
Hair sprays	595	14.0
Styling products	430	10.1

Source: *Spray Technology & Marketing*, November 1996, p. 28, from National Retail Auditing Service.

★ 630 ★

Hair Care (SIC 2844)

Hair Coloring Market

Shares of the $994 million market are shown in percent.

Clairol	80.8%
Combe	7.6
Revlon	6.9
Other	4.7

Source: *Advertising Age*, May 19, 1997, p. 3, from Information Resources Inc.

★ 631 ★

Hair Care (SIC 2844)

Hair Spray Producers

Chesebrough-Pond's	21.9%
Helene-Curtis	18.4
Gillette	11.1
Procter & Gamble	9.0
Alberto Culver	7.9
Redmond	6.0
Clairol	4.7
Lamaur	2.7
Cosmair	2.2
Conair	2.1
Demert & Dougherty	1.4
Playtex	1.4
Dep	1.3
Other	9.9

Source: *Spray Technology & Marketing*, November 1996, p. 30, from National Retail Auditing Service.

★ 632 ★

Hair Care (SIC 2844)

Top Conditioner Brands

Shares are shown based on sales for the 52 weeks ended June 30, 1996.

Pantene	13.9%
Alberto	8.2
Suave	7.4
Salonsel	5.2
Infusi23	4.7
Finesse	4.5
L'Oreal	4.2
Clairol	3.7
Aussie	3.6
Vidal Sassoon	3.5
Other	41.1

Source: *Supermarket Business*, October 1996, p. 80, from Information Resources Inc. InfoScan.

★ 633 ★

Hair Care (SIC 2844)

Top Hair Coloring Brands

Shares are shown in percent for the year ended December 29, 1996.

L'Oreal Pref.	16.1%
Clairol Nice N Easy	12.3
L'Oreal Excellence	10.3
Just For Men	6.3
Clairol Natural Instincts	6.0
Clairol Loving Care	5.3
Clairol Ultress	4.7
L'Oreal Casting	4.4
Revlon	3.5
Miss Clairol	2.8
Other	28.3

Source: *Supermarket Business*, April 1997, p. 52, from Information Resources Inc.

★ 634 ★

Hair Care (SIC 2844)

Top Hair Coloring Brands by Unit Sales

Unit shares are shown in percent for the year ended December 29, 1996.

L'Oreal Pref.	14.1%
Clairol Nice N Easy	13.1
L'Oreal Excellence	8.7
Clairol Loving Care	6.1
Revlon	6.0
Just For Men	5.9
Clairol Natural Instincts	5.0
Clairol Ultress	4.1
L'Oreal Casting	3.8
Miss Clairol	2.8
Other	30.4

Source: *Supermarket Business*, April 1997, p. 52, from Information Resources Inc.

★ 635 ★

Hair Care (SIC 2844)

Top Shampoo Brands

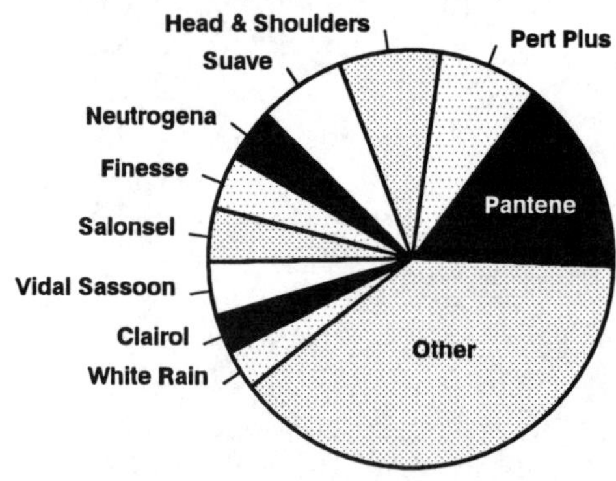

Shares are shown based on sales for the 52 weeks ended June 30, 1996.

Pantene	14.9%
Pert Plus	8.4
Head & Shoulders	7.8
Suave	7.4
Neutrogena	4.3
Finesse	3.8
Salonsel	3.8
Vidal Sassoon	3.5
Clairol	3.4

Continued on next page.

★ 635 ★ *Continued*

Hair Care (SIC 2844)

Top Shampoo Brands

Shares are shown based on sales for the 52 weeks ended June 30, 1996.

White Rain	3.4%
Other	39.4

Source: *Supermarket Business*, October 1996, p. 80, from Information Resources Inc. InfoScan.

★ 636 ★

Hair Care (SIC 2844)

Top Shampoo Brands by Unit Sales

Unit shares are shown in percent for the year ended December 29, 1996.

Suave	15.7%
Pantene	11.6
White Rain	8.7
Pert Plus	5.7
Head & Shoulders	5.3
Salon Selectives	4.7
Clairol	3.2
Finesse	3.1
Vidal Sassoon	2.9
Other	39.1

Source: *Supermarket Business*, April 1997, p. 50, from Information Resources Inc.

★ 637 ★

Hair Care (SIC 2844)

U.S. Hair Coloring Market

Clairol	47.0%
L'Oreal	42.0
Revlon	6.0
Other	5.0

Source: *Forbes*, October 7, 1996, p. 55.

★ 638 ★

Nail Care (SIC 2844)

Nail Care Brands

The market reached $306.2 million in 1995.

Revlon	21.3%
Sally Hansen	20.8
L'Oreal	10.9
Cover Girl	7.5
Cutex	5.6
Wet N Wild	5.6
Maybelline	5.1
Max Factor	3.0
Artmatic	2.9
Flame Glo	1.6
Other	15.7

Source: *Advertising Age*, September 30, 1996, p. S41, from Information Resources Inc.

★ 639 ★

Nail Care (SIC 2844)

Nail Color Makers

Shares of the $247.60 million market are shown for the year ended June 30, 1996.

	Sales ($ mil.)	Share
Revlon	$ 62.6	25.0%
Cosmair	44.4	18.0
Procter & Gamble	26.6	11.0
Other	114.0	46.0

Source: *Discount Store News*, November 4, 1996, p. 7, from Information Resources Inc.

★ 640 ★

Oral Care (SIC 2844)

Denture Products

Data show sales of denture products for the year ended November 3, 1996.

	($ mil.)	Share
Denture adhesives	$ 190.0	48.9%
Denture cleanser/tablets	146.3	37.6
Denture cleanser/paste/ powder	26.3	6.8
Denture cushions	26.0	6.7

Source: *Drug Topics*, January 6, 1997, p. 66, from Information Resources Inc.

★ 641 ★

Oral Care (SIC 2844)

Leading Dentifrice Brands

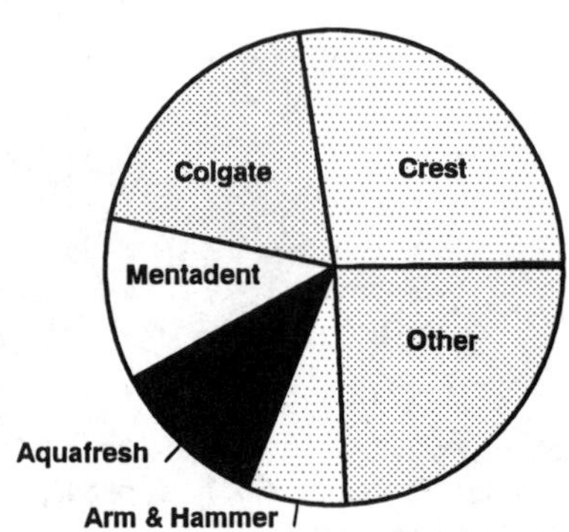

Data are for the 52 week period ending February 23, 1997. Total market sales during that period reached $1.453 billion.

	Sales ($ mil.)	Share
Crest	$ 395.8	27.2%
Colgate	276.4	19.0
Mentadent	163.5	11.3
Aquafresh	156.3	10.8
Arm & Hammer	106.0	7.3
Other	355.1	24.4

Source: *Advertising Age*, April 21, 1997, p. 16, from Information Resources Inc.

★ 642 ★

Oral Care (SIC 2844)

Leading Toothpaste Brands

Shares are shown based on sales of $1.5 billion for the 52 weeks ended May 25, 1997.

Crest	26.3%
Colgate	19.6
Aquafresh	11.2
Mentadent	11.0
Arm & Hammer	7.5
Sensadyne	3.3
Rembrandt	3.1
Listerine	2.8
Close-up	2.2
Ultra Brite	1.8
Other	11.2

Source: *New York Times*, June 20, 1997, p. C4, from Information Resources Inc.

★ 643 ★

Oral Care (SIC 2844)

Oral Care Sales by Segment

Data are for the year ended April 21, 1996.

Toothpaste	47.9%
Toothbrush/dental accessories	25.4
Mouthwash	11.9
Denture products	13.8
Breath fresheners	1.0

Source: *DM*, July 1996, p. 52, from Information Resources Inc.

★ 644 ★

Oral Care (SIC 2844)

Top Mouthwash Brands

Shares are shown in percent for the year ended December 29, 1996.

Listerine	41.0%
Scope	17.4
Plax	7.5
Mentadent	3.0
Act	2.3
Cepacol	1.6
Peroxyl	1.1
Viadent	1.1
Act For Kids	1.0

Continued on next page.

★ 644 ★ *Continued*

Oral Care (SIC 2844)

Top Mouthwash Brands

Shares are shown in percent for the year ended December 29, 1996.

Private label	19.3%
Other	5.7

Source: *Supermarket Business*, April 1997, p. 50, from Information Resources Inc.

★ 645 ★

Oral Care (SIC 2844)

Top Mouthwash Brands by Unit Sales

Unit shares are shown in percent for the year ended December 29, 1996.

Listerine	30.9%
Scope	18.7
Plax	6.8
Mentadent	3.0
Act	2.0
Cepacol	1.8
Act For Kids	0.9
Viadent	0.8
Peroxyl	0.6
Other	34.5

Source: *Supermarket Business*, April 1997, p. 50, from Information Resources Inc.

★ 646 ★

Oral Care (SIC 2844)

Top Toothpaste Brands - Canada

Shares are shown based on sales.

	1995	1996
Colgate	29.4%	35.4%
Crest	34.6	33.7
Aqua Fresh	14.2	14.3
Close-Up	6.0	4.4
Macleans	7.2	4.3
Aim	3.0	2.4
Arm & Hammer	2.3	2.3
Pepsodent	0.3	0.3
Others	3.0	3.0

Source: *Marketing Magazine*, May 26, 1997, p. 12, from industry sources.

★ 647 ★

Personal Care Products (SIC 2844)

Children's HBC Product Makers

Share of HBC (health & beauty care) products for children are shown for 1995.

Johnson & Johnson	16.5%
American Home Products	14.9
Sandoz Pharmaceuticals	11.8
Warner-Lambert	8.8
Procter & Gamble	8.3
Schering-Plough	5.2
Tsumara International	4.5
Bonne Bell	3.7
Dial	2.9
Other	23.4

Source: *Nonfoods Merchandising*, September 1996, p. 12, from Packaged Facts and Information Resources Inc.

★ 648 ★

Personal Care Products (SIC 2844)

Children's HBC Product Market

The HBC (health & beauty care) market for children had sales of $615.5 million for 1995.

OTC remedies	$ 432.2
Cough/cold/flu	383.7
First aid	30.3
Internal analgesics	18.2
Toiletries	83.3
Bubble bath	36.8
Soap	28.7
Hair care	17.8
Oral hygiene	37.7
Toothpaste	20.6
Toothbrushes	16.8
Other	0.3
Sun care	35.3
Cosmetics/fragrances	27.0

Source: *Nonfoods Merchandising*, September 1996, p. 12, from Packaged Facts and Information Resources Inc.

★ 649 ★

Shaving Preparations (SIC 2844)

Shaving Cream Makers - 1996

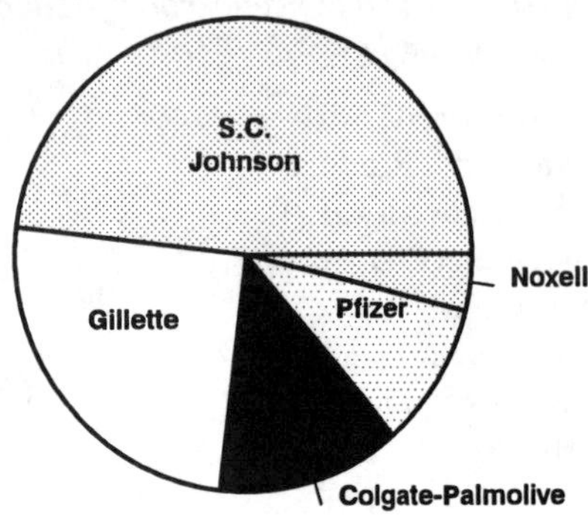

Shares are shown based on sales of $276.3 million for the year ended December 1, 1996.

	Sales ($ mil.)	Share
S.C. Johnson	$ 123.6	47.5%
Gillette	65.1	25.0
Colgate-Palmolive	34.8	13.4
Pfizer	25.9	10.0
Noxell	10.7	4.1

Source: *Supermarket Business*, March 1997, p. 105, from Information Resources Inc.

★ 650 ★

Skin Care (SIC 2844)

Popular Hand/Body Cream Brands

Shares are shown based on sales of $806 million at drug stores.

Vaseline Intensive Care	14.5%
Lubriderm	8.7
Eucerin	7.1
Nivea	6.3
Jergens	6.1
Curel	3.8
Keri	3.4
Suave	2.8
Private label	8.3
Other	39.0

Source: *NARD Journal*, September 1996, p. 56.

★ 651 ★

Skin Care (SIC 2844)

Top Face Care Brands

Brand shares are shown in percent. Manufacturers are listed in parentheses.

Oil of Olay (Procter & Gamble)	18.3%
Ponds (Unilever)	12.8
Plenitude (L'Oreal)	11.7
Noxema (Procter & Gamble)	8.1
Neutrogena (Johnson & Johnson)	7.8
Almay (Revlon)	3.9
Clean & Clear (Johnson & Johnson)	3.8
Alpha Hydrox (Neoteric)	3.6
St. Ives (Alberto Culver)	3.4
Sea Breeze (Bristol-Myers)	3.0
Revlon (Revlon)	2.2
Other	21.4

Source: *Wall Street Journal*, April 9, 1997, p. B1, from A.C. Nielsen Corp. and Revlon.

★ 652 ★

Skin Care (SIC 2844)

Top Facial Cleanser Brands

Shares of the $359.9 million market are shown for the year ended September 29, 1996.

Noxzema	18.5%
Ponds	9.8
Olay	8.0
Clean & Clear	7.1
Seabreeze	7.1
Neutrogena	5.9
St. Ives	5.5
Cetaphil	4.5
Loreplen	3.7
Almay	3.3
Other	26.6

Source: *Supermarket Business*, February 1997, p. 80, from Information Resources Inc.

★ 653 ★

Skin Care (SIC 2844)

Top Facial Cleansers by Unit Sales

Market shares are shown in percent for the year ended December 29, 1996.

Noxzema	21.5%
Clean & Clear	8.7

Continued on next page.

★ 653 ★ *Continued*

Skin Care (SIC 2844)

Top Facial Cleansers by Unit Sales

Market shares are shown in percent for the year ended December 29, 1996.

Olay	7.8%
Ponds	7.4
Seabreeze	7.3
St. Ives	7.1
Freeman	5.2
Neutrogena	4.8
Cetaphil	2.0
Loreal Plentitude	2.0
Other	26.2

Source: *Supermarket Business*, April 1997, p. 47, from Information Resources Inc.

★ 654 ★

Skin Care (SIC 2844)

Top Facial Moisturizer Brand Sales

Unit shares are shown in percent for the year ended December 29, 1996.

Olay	27.1%
Ponds	15.2
L'Oreal Plentitude	12.4
Neutrogena	5.7
Visage	4.5
Alpha Hydroxy	3.9
Almay	3.7
St. Ives	2.8
Sudden Change	2.1
Private label	4.3
Other	18.3

Source: *Supermarket Business*, April 1997, p. 47, from Information Resources Inc.

★ 655 ★

Skin Care (SIC 2844)

Top Facial Moisturizers

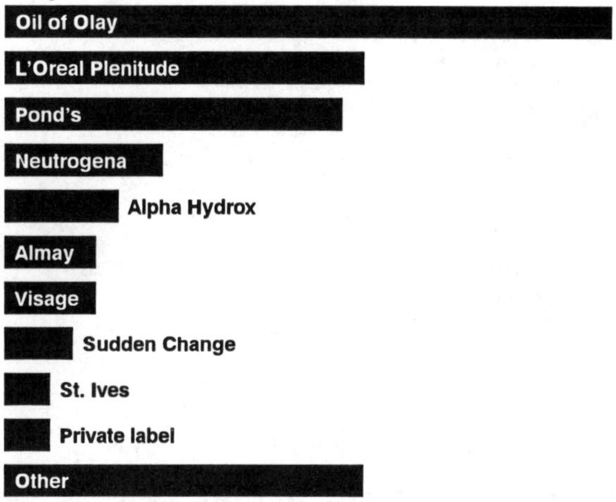

Shares are shown based on sales for the year ended June 30, 1996.

Oil of Olay	26.8%
L'Oreal Plenitude	15.6
Pond's	14.9
Neutrogena	6.6
Alpha Hydrox	5.0
Almay	4.4
Visage	4.4
Sudden Change	2.6
St. Ives	1.5
Private label	2.4
Other	15.8

Source: *Discount Store News*, September 16, 1996, p. 13, from Information Resources Inc.

★ 656 ★

Skin Care (SIC 2844)

Top Hand/Body Lotion Brand Sales

Unit shares are shown in percent for the year ended December 29, 1996.

Vaseline	19.8%
Jergens	12.3
Suave	11.1
St. Ives Swiss	5.8
Lubriderm	5.3
Nivea	3.8

Continued on next page.

★ 656 ★ *Continued*

Skin Care (SIC 2844)

Top Hand/Body Lotion Brand Sales

Unit shares are shown in percent for the year ended December 29, 1996.

Curel	3.3%
Eucerin	1.9
Neutrogena	1.5
Other	35.2

Source: *Supermarket Business*, April 1997, p. 47, from Information Resources Inc.

★ 657 ★

Skin Care (SIC 2844)

Top Hand/Body Lotion Brands

Shares are shown based on total sales of $806.2 million for the 52 weeks ended October 6, 1996.

	Sales ($ mil.)	Share
Vaseline Intensive Care (Chesebrough-Ponds)	$ 139.0	17.2%
Jergens (KAO)	85.9	10.7
Lubriderm (Warner-Lambert)	59.8	7.4
Suave (Helene-Curtis)	46.4	5.8
Nivea (Beiersdorf)	45.6	5.7
Other	429.5	53.3

Source: *Nonfoods Merchandising*, January 1997, p. 46, from Information Resources Inc.

★ 658 ★

Skin Care (SIC 2844)

Top Hand/Body Lotions

Shares are shown based on supermarket sales for the 52 weeks ended March 9, 1996.

Lubriderm	9.8%
Vaseline Reg.	9.0
Suave	8.2
Jergens Ultra	6.1
Curel	5.8
Vaseline Aloe	5.5
St. Ives	5.2
Nivea	4.7%
Vaseline Extra Str.	4.1
Private label	4.0
Other	37.6

Source: *Supermarket Business*, August 1996, p. 77, from A.C. Nielsen.

★ 659 ★

Sun Care (SIC 2844)

Sun Care Brand Leaders

Shares are shown based on $391.7 million for the 52 weeks ended June 16, 1996. Data refer to sales at all supermarkets, drug stores, and discount stores.

	($ mil.)	Share
Coppertone	$ 53.9	13.8%
Banana Boat	49.3	12.6
Private label	34.1	8.7
Hawaiian Tropic	26.6	6.8
Bain de Soleil	24.3	6.2
No-Ad	17.5	4.5
Coppertone Sport	17.4	4.4
Coppertone Water Babies	16.0	4.1
Coppertone Kids	12.6	3.2
Neutrogena	11.6	3.0
Other	128.4	32.8

Source: *Nonfoods Merchandising*, October 1996, p. 28, from Information Resources Inc.

★ 660 ★

Sun Care (SIC 2844)

Sun Care Market - Canada

Shares are shown for the year ended July 1996.

Coppertone	32.0%
Hawaiian Tropic	13.0
Ombrelle	11.0
Bain de Soleil	9.0
Banana Boat	7.0
Private label	5.0
Other	23.0

Source: *Marketing Magazine*, March 17, 1997, p. 3, from A.C. Nielsen.

★ 661 ★

Sun Care (SIC 2844)

Top Sun Lotion Brands

Table shows retail dollar shares for the 52 weeks ending November 1996.

Coppertone	25.6%
Banana Boat	12.7
Hawaiian Tropic	7.0
Neutrogena	6.6
Bain de Soleil	4.7
No-Ad	4.7
Private label	8.8
Others	29.9

Source: *Drug Topics*, February 17, 1997, p. 82, from Information Resources Inc.

★ 662 ★

Sun Care (SIC 2844)

Top Sun Tan Lotions by Unit Sales

Unit shares are shown in percent for the year ended December 29, 1996.

Banana Boat	14.3%
Coppertone	11.9
Hawaiian Tropic	6.2
No Ad	5.7
Bain de Soleil	3.7
Coppertone Sport	3.3
Coppertone Water babies	2.9
Neutrogena	2.7
Neutrogena Glow	2.5
Private label	13.2
Other	33.6

Source: *Supermarket Business*, April 1997, p. 47, from Information Resources Inc.

★ 663 ★

Paints and Coatings (SIC 2851)

Coatings Demand by Type

	1995	2000
Waterborne/high-solids	50.6%	69.8%
Solventborne	32.4	3.3
Other	17.0	26.9

Source: *Industrial Paint & Powder*, January 1997, p. 12, from Freedonia Group.

★ 664 ★

Paints and Coatings (SIC 2851)

Mexican Paint Market - 1994

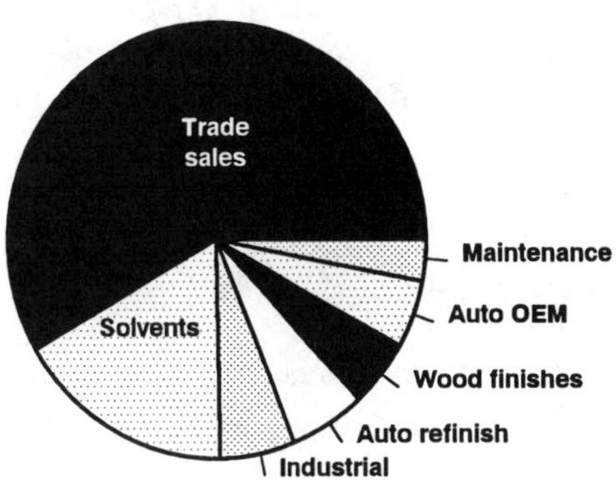

Shares are estimated in percent.

Trade sales	58.9%
Solvents	16.6
Industrial	6.4
Auto refinish	5.5
Wood finishes	5.1
Auto OEM	4.9
Maintenance	2.7

Source: *Canadian Chemical News*, May 1997, p. 16.

★ 665 ★

Paints and Coatings (SIC 2851)

Overprint Coatings Sales

Sales of clear overprint coatings are shown in millions of dollars for 1995.

Water-based	$ 155
Ultraviolet	75
Solvent/press varnish	65
Catalyzed	10

Source: *American Ink Maker*, November 1996, p. 58.

★ 666 ★

Paints and Coatings (SIC 2851)

Paint Chemicals Demand

Distribution is shown based on a total demand of 9.84 billion chemicals in 1995. The demand for resins is expected to exceed that of solvents by the year 2000.

Solvents	36.0%
Resins	33.0
Pigments	15.0
Fillers/extenders	13.0
Additives and modifiers	3.0

Source: *Chemical & Engineering News*, October 14, 1996, p. 52, from Freedonia Group.

★ 667 ★

Paints and Coatings (SIC 2851)

Powder Coatings Market - 1995

The market reached 257 million pounds.

General metal finishing	55.4%
Appliances	16.9
Automotive	16.0
Lawn & garden	7.4
Architectural	4.3

Source: *Chemicalweek*, August 21, 1996, p. 49, from Powder Coatings Institute.

★ 668 ★

Paints and Coatings (SIC 2851)

U.S. Paint Makers

Market shares are shown in percent.

Sherwin-Williams	30.0%
ICI	15.0
Benjamin-Moore	7.0
Valspar	5.0
Duron	3.0
K Moore	3.0
PPG	3.0
Behr	2.0
SICO	1.0
700 others	31.0

Source: *Investext*, Thomson Financial Networks, November 4, 1996, p. 9, from ICI.

★ 669 ★

Organic Chemicals (SIC 2861)

Largest Phenol Producers

Shares are shown based on on 4.46 billion pounds produced each year.

	(mil.)	Share
AlliedSignal	945	21.3%
GE Plastics	690	15.6
Shell	660	14.9
Aristech	630	14.2
Georgia Gulf	600	13.5
Dow	580	13.1
Texaco	125	2.8
JLM	95	2.1
Kalama	70	1.6
Merichem	35	0.8

Source: *Chemical Marketing Reporter*, August 26, 1996, p. 41.

★ 670 ★

Organic Chemicals (SIC 2865)

Aroma Chemical Production

	1995	2000
Fragrance blends	34.0%	34.2%
Aroma chemicals	21.0	21.1
Essential oils	13.5	12.0
Other	31.5	32.7

Source: *Chemicalweek*, October 2, 1996, p. 24, from Freedonia Group.

★ 671 ★

Organic Chemicals (SIC 2865)

Largest Aniline Makers

Capacity is shown in millions of pounds.

	(mil.)	Share
Rubicon	500	35.0%
DuPont	260	18.2
First Chemical	240	16.8
Aristech	200	14.0
BASF	190	13.3
Bayer	40	2.8

Source: *Chemical Marketing Reporter*, July 1, 1996, p. 37.

★ 672 ★

Organic Chemicals (SIC 2865)

Largest Nitrobenzene Makers

Capacity is shown in millions of pounds.

	(mil.)	Share
Rubicon	650	37.1%
First Chemical	500	28.6
DuPont	350	20.0
BASF	250	14.3

Source: *Chemical Marketing Reporter*, July 8, 1996, p. 33.

★ 673 ★

Organic Chemicals (SIC 2865)

Largest Styrene Producers - North America

Capacity is shown in thousands of metric tons.

Arco Chemical	1,145
Cos-Mar	962
Chevron	772
Sterling Chemicals	772
Dow Chemical	716
Huntsman	644
Amoco	450
Shell Canada	450
Nova Chemical	272
Petroleos Mexicanos	181

Source: *Chemicalweek*, August 21, 1996, p. 53, from Chemical Market Associates Inc. and SRI International.

★ 674 ★

Organic Chemicals (SIC 2865)

Leading Phthalic Anhydride Producers

Companies are ranked by production capacity in millions of pounds. Shares are shown based on total production of 1.33 billion pounds.

	(mil.)	Share
Aristech	320	24.1%
Exxon	300	22.6
Koppers	240	18.0
Stepan	240	18.0
Sterling	230	17.3

Source: *Chemical Market Reporter*, February 24, 1997, p. 14.

★ 675 ★

Organic Chemicals (SIC 2865)

Synthetic Organic Dye Production

Production is shown in thousands of kilograms.

	(000)	Share
Direct dyes	19,708	13.4%
Disperse dyes	14,646	10.0
Vat dyes	12,278	8.3
Solvent dyes	7,112	4.8
Acid dyes	6,615	4.5
Basic dyes	6,082	4.1
Other	80,700	54.8

Source: *American Ink Maker*, June 1996, p. 80, from United States International Trade Commission.

★ 676 ★

Organic Chemicals (SIC 2865)

Toluene Diisocyanate Makers

Capacity is shown in millions of pounds per year. Shares are shown based on a total of 930 million pounds.

	(mil.)	Share
Bayer	260	28.0%
Olin	250	26.9
BASF	220	23.7
Dow	140	15.1
ICI	60	6.5

Source: *Chemical Marketing Reporter*, October 7, 1996, p. 45.

★ 677 ★

Organic Chemicals (SIC 2865)

U.S. Cumene Production

Production is shown in millions of pounds per year.

Georgia Gulf	1,500.0
Shell	1,100.0
Koch Refining	950.0
Citgo	825.0
Ashland	540.0
Chevron	450.0
Sun	450.0
Texaco	135.0
Coastal	130.0
JLM Chemical	130.0
Amoco	50.0

Source: *Chemical Marketing Reporter*, August 12, 1996, p. 27.

★ 678 ★

Organic Chemicals (SIC 2869)

Acetone Makers

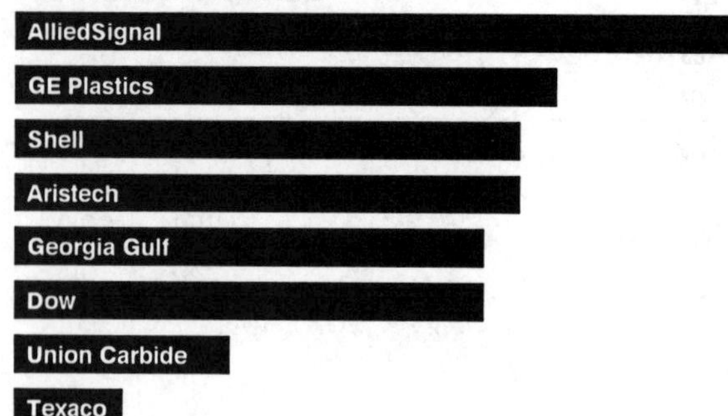

Capacity is shown in millions of pounds per year. Shares are shown based on a total of 2.82 million pounds.

	(mil.)	Share
AlliedSignal	575	20.4%
GE Plastics	420	14.9
Shell	400	14.2
Aristech	390	13.8
Georgia Gulf	370	13.1
Dow	355	12.6
Union Carbide	170	6.0
Texaco	85	3.0
JLM Chemicals	57	2.0

Source: *Chemical Marketing Reporter*, September 2, 1996, p. 37.

★ 679 ★

Organic Chemicals (SIC 2869)

Activated Carbon by End Use

Data are in millions of pounds.

	1995 (mil.)	2000 (mil.)	Share
Water treatment	118.0	152.0	38.0%
Sweetener processing	50.0	60.0	15.0
Solvent recovery	22.0	29.0	7.3
Air purification	21.0	27.0	6.8
Motor vehicle	14.0	22.0	5.5
Other end uses	89.0	110.0	27.5

Source: *Chemical & Engineering News*, December 9, 1996, p. 22, from Freedonia Group.

★ 680 ★

Organic Chemicals (SIC 2869)

BHT Makers

Shares are shown based on a total capacity of 27 million pounds per year.

Rhone-Poulenc	44.4%
PMC	37.0
Uniroyal	18.5

Source: *Chemical Marketing Reporter*, July 29, 1996, p. 37.

★ 681 ★

Organic Chemicals (SIC 2869)

Methylene Diisocyanate Makers

Shares are shown based on a total capacity of 1.21 billion pounds per year.

Dow	32.1%
ICI	27.2
Bayer	26.3
BASF	14.4

Source: *Chemical Marketing Reporter*, September 30, 1996, p. 37.

★ 682 ★

Organic Chemicals (SIC 2869)

Monochlorobenzene Makers

Capacity is shown in millions of pounds per year.

	(mil.)	Share
Monsanto	175	47.3%
Standard Chlorine	150	40.5
PPG	45	12.2

Source: *Chemical Marketing Reporter*, September 23, 1996, p. 41.

★ 683 ★

Organic Chemicals (SIC 2869)

U.S. Acetic Acid Demand - 2000

Vinyl acetate monomer	55.6%
Terephthalic acid	15.2
Acetic acid esters	6.7
Direct use	3.4
Other derivatives	19.0

Source: *Industrial Paint & Powder*, December 1996, p. 11, from Freedonia Group.

★ 684 ★

Organic Chemicals (SIC 2869)

U.S. Tartaric Acid Consumption

Consumption is shown by end use.

Food	27.0%
Datem esters	22.0
Wine	17.0
Pharmaceuticals	13.0
Antacids	11.0
Other	10.0

Source: *Chemical Marketing Reporter*, September 23, 1996, p. 14, from *Chemical Economics Handbook* and SRI Consulting.

★ 685 ★

Phosphates (SIC 2874)

Industrial Phosphate Consumption

Consumption is shown by end use in percent.

Detergent builders & cleaners	44.0%
Food & beverage	19.0
Metal treatment	6.0
Water treatment	5.0
Other	26.0

Source: *Chemical Market Reporter*, December 30, 1996, p. 13, from SRI Consulting.

★ 686 ★

Agrichemicals (SIC 2875)

Fertilizer Makers

Sales are shown in millions of dollars for the second quarter of 1996.

Farmland Industries	$ 2,669
Terra Industries	1,086
Potash of Sask	352
Arcadian	344
Scotts Company	248
Freeport-McMoran Res. Partners	243
Mississippi Chemical	125
Terra Nitrogen	106

Source: *Chemicalweek*, August 28, 1996, p. 58, from Standard & Poor's.

★ 687 ★

Insecticides (SIC 2879)

Insecticide Sales - 1996

Sales are shown in thousands of dollars for the 52 weeks ended March 9, 1996.

	($000)	Share
Ant & roach, regular aerosol	$ 75,606	23.2%
Ant & roach, other	46,108	14.1
Indoor fogger	40,835	12.5
Insect repellents	25,770	7.9
Rodenticides	17,827	5.5
Flea & tick, aerosol	17,109	5.2
Wasp & hornet	16,651	5.1
Flying insect, aerosol	12,675	3.9
Mouse, rat & male traps	9,040	2.8
Ant traps	9,025	2.8
House & garden, aerosol	8,751	2.7
Ant & roach, liquid	6,164	1.9
Other	40,842	12.5

Source: *Nonfoods Merchandising*, October 1996, p. 35.

★ 688 ★

Insecticides (SIC 2879)

Roach Insecticide Sales by City

Los Angeles
New York City
Houston
Dallas/Ft. Worth
San Antonio
Miami/Ft. Lauderdale
Other

Sales of roach removal products reached $293 million in 1996. Figures are shown in millions of dollars.

	($ mil.)	Share
Los Angeles	$ 16.8	5.7%
New York City	9.8	3.3
Houston	6.7	2.3
Dallas/Ft. Worth	6.1	2.1
San Antonio	6.0	2.0
Miami/Ft. Lauderdale	5.6	1.9
Other	242.0	82.6

Source: *USA TODAY*, November 14, 1996, p. D1, from Information Resources Inc. InfoScan for Combat.

★ 689 ★

Adhesives (SIC 2891)

Adhesives/Sealants Market - 1995

Distribution is shown based on a $9.2 billion market.

General purpose	51.0%
Binders	12.0
Hot melts	11.0
Pressure sensitive	10.0
Engineering	8.0
Adhesive films	4.0
Aerosols	2.0
Conductive	1.0
Dental/medical	1.0
Radiation cured	1.0

Source: *Assembly*, September 1996, p. 12, from Impact Marketing Consultants Inc.

★ 690 ★

Explosives (SIC 2892)

Industrial Explosive Sales

Consumption of industrial explosives and blasting agents is shown for 1994.

Unprocessed ammonium nitrate	64.2%
Ammonium nitrate-fuel oil blasting agents	20.0
Water gels, slurries, amulsions	14.1
Permissibles	1.5
Other high explosives	0.2

Source: *Minerals Yearbook: Metals and Materials*, Vol 1, 1994, p. 279, from United States Bureau of Mines.

★ 691 ★

Printing Ink (SIC 2893)

Flexographic Ink Use by Application

Sales are shown by application in millions of dollars. Flexible packaging includes paper, films, and laminates.

	($ mil.)	Share
Flexible packaging	$ 375	47.8%
Corrugated containers	160	20.4
Household paper, wall coverings, labels, rigid plastics, and others	85	10.8
Commercial and newsprint	65	8.3
Food containers	60	7.6
Multiwall bags	40	5.1

Source: *American Ink Maker*, March 1997, p. 32, from Fishman Incorporated.

★ 692 ★

Printing Ink (SIC 2893)

Printing Ink Use - North America

Data show the value of printing ink consumed by each segment of the market. Shares are shown in percent.

	Sales ($ mil.)	Share
Lithography (offset)	$ 1,725	45.4%
Flexography	785	20.7
Gravure	705	18.6
Specialty	485	12.8
Letterpress	100	2.6

Source: *American Ink Maker*, February 1997, p. 25.

★ 693 ★

Printing Ink (SIC 2893)

Top Printing Ink Manufacturers - North America

Companies are ranked by 1996 sales in millions of U.S. dollars. Data for Flint Ink and Wickoff Color are estimates. Shares of the group are shown in percent.

	Sales ($ mil.)	% of Group
Sun Chemical	$ 900	33.6%
Flint Ink Corp.	700	26.2
INX International Ink Co.	271	10.1
The Ink Company	120	4.5
Progressive Ink Co.	110	4.1
Nazdar Company	85	3.2
Siegwerk, Inc.	80	3.0
Superior Printing Ink Co., Inc.	70	2.6
Heritage Inks International	65	2.4
Sicpa Securink	60	2.2
Van Son Holland Ink Corp. of America	50	1.9
Wickoff Color	46	1.7
Borden Chemical, Inc.	40	1.5
Handschy Industries Co.	40	1.5
Braden Sutphin	38	1.4

Source: *American Ink Maker*, February 1997, p. 32.

★ 694 ★

Carbon Black (SIC 2895)

Carbon Black Market

Tires	71.0%
Industrial rubber	23.0
Specialty	6.0

Source: *American Ink Maker*, June 1996, p. 32.

★ 695 ★

Salt (SIC 2899)

U.S. Salt Use

Highways	62.0%
Chemicals	13.0
Water conditioning	11.0
Agriculture	8.0
Food grade	6.0

Source: *Financial Times*, January 10, 1997, p. 30, from United States Salt Institute.

SIC 29 - Petroleum and Coal Products

★ 696 ★

Fuels (SIC 2911)

U.S. Refined Products

Data are in thousands of barrels. LRG stands for liquified refinery gas.

Gasoline	204,495
Distillate	131,120
Natural gas liquids and LRG	99,568
Unfinished oils	85,153
Residual	39,016
Kerosine jet fuel	38,100
Kerosine	5,908
Special naphthas	2,080
Naphtha jet fuel	1,995
Other refined products	55,533

Source: *Oil & Gas Journal*, January 27, 1997, p. 38.

★ 697 ★

Petroleum Refining (SIC 2911)

Top Petroleum Refining Companies - 1996

Companies are ranked by revenues in millions of dollars.

Exxon	$ 119,434
Mobil	72,267
Texaco	44,561
Chevron	38,691
Amoco	32,726
USX	21,076
Atlantic Richfield	19,169
Phillips Petroleum	15,807
Ashland	12,301
Coastal	11,920
Tosco	9,923
Sun	9,875
Amerada Hess	8,930
Unocal	8,588
Ultramar Diamond Sham.	8,208
Valero Energy	$ 4,991
MAPCO	3,474
Pennzoil	2,436
Murphy Oil	2,110
Kerr-McGee	1,931

Source: *Fortune*, April 28, 1997, p. 58.

★ 698 ★

Petroleum Refining (SIC 2911)

U.S. Petroleum Refining

Shares are shown based on capacity.

Chevron	6.8%
Shell	6.7
Amoco	6.6
Exxon	6.5
Texaco	6.4
Mobil	6.3
BP	4.5
Other	56.2

Source: *USA TODAY*, October 8, 1996, p. B3, from NatWest Securities.

★699★

Lubricants (SIC 2992)

Top Selling Conventional Oils

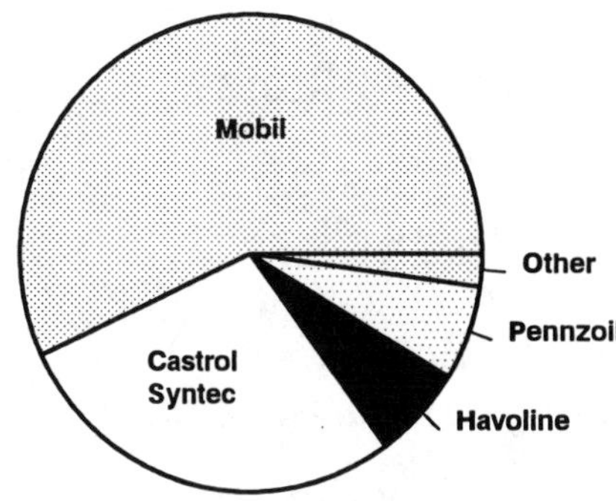

Market shares are shown in percent.

Mobil	53.1%
Castrol Syntec	26.0
Havoline	6.4
Pennzoil	6.4
Other	1.6

Source: *Discount Merchandiser*, April 1997, p. 47, from Information Resources Inc.

★700★

Lubricants (SIC 2992)

Top Selling Synthetic Oils

Market shares are shown in percent.

Pennzoil	22.8%
Havoline	21.1
Castrol	17.6
Valvoline	11.8
Quaker State	10.2
Mobil	6.6
Other	18.9

Source: *Discount Merchandiser*, April 1997, p. 47, from Information Resources Inc.

SIC 30 - Rubber and Misc. Plastics Products

★ 701 ★

Tires (SIC 3011)

Canadian Tire Shipments

Replacement shipments are in thousands of units for the first nine months of 1996.

	(000)	Share
Passenger	9,400,131	75.5%
Truck/bus	2,297,815	18.5
Inner tubes	746,143	6.0

Source: *Rubber & Plastics News*, January 27, 1997, p. 16.

★ 702 ★

Tires (SIC 3011)

Largest Tire Facilities - Canada

Production is shown in units per day.

Goodyear Canada Inc.	42,600
Michelin North America Inc.	22,000
Uniroyal Goodrich Tire Manufacturing	17,000
Bridgestone/Firestone Canada Inc.	12,500
United Tire & Rubber Co.	250

Source: *Tire Business*, December 9, 1996, p. 13.

★ 703 ★

Tires (SIC 3011)

North American Tire Market

Market shares are shown for 1995.

Goodyear/K-S	27.8%
Michelin/UGTC	24.7
Bridgestone/Firestone	21.8
Continental-Genl	7.5
Cooper	6.5
Dunlop	3.4
Titan	1.9
Pirelli-Armstrong	1.6
Yokohama	1.3
Toyo	0.9%
Other	2.6

Source: *European Rubber Journal*, Global Tire Report 1996-97, p. 22.

★ 704 ★

Tires (SIC 3011)

Passenger Car Tire Makers - North America

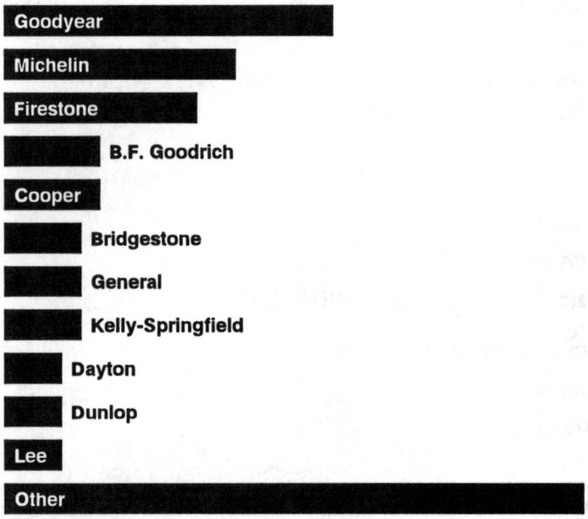

Goodyear leads the light truck tire market with a 14% share and commands a 22% of the highway truck tire market.

Goodyear	17.0%
Michelin	12.0
Firestone	10.0
B.F. Goodrich	5.0
Cooper	5.0
Bridgestone	4.0
General	4.0
Kelly-Springfield	4.0
Dayton	3.0
Dunlop	3.0

Continued on next page.

★ 704 ★ *Continued*

Tires (SIC 3011)

Passenger Car Tire Makers - North America

Goodyear leads the light truck tire market with a 14% share and commands a 22% of the highway truck tire market.

Lee	3.0%
Other	30.0

Source: *Tire Business*, December 9, 1996, p. 12.

★ 705 ★

Tires (SIC 3011)

Tire Makers - North America

Shares of the $19.5 billion market are for 1995.

Goodyear	29.2%
Michelin/Uniroyal/B.F. Goodrich	22.1
Bridgestone/Firestone	19.7
Continental General Tire	6.2
Cooper	6.2
Others	16.6

Source: *Tire Business*, December 9, 1996, p. 12.

★ 706 ★

Tires (SIC 3011)

U.S. Tire Shipments

Data are in thousands of units for the first nine months of 1996.

	(000)	Share
Passenger	191,659	76.4%
Light truck	26,985	10.8
Inner tubes	18,420	7.3
Truck/bus	13,727	5.5

Source: *Rubber & Plastics News*, January 27, 1997, p. 16.

★ 707 ★

Athletic Footwear (SIC 3021)

Mexico's Sports Shoe Market

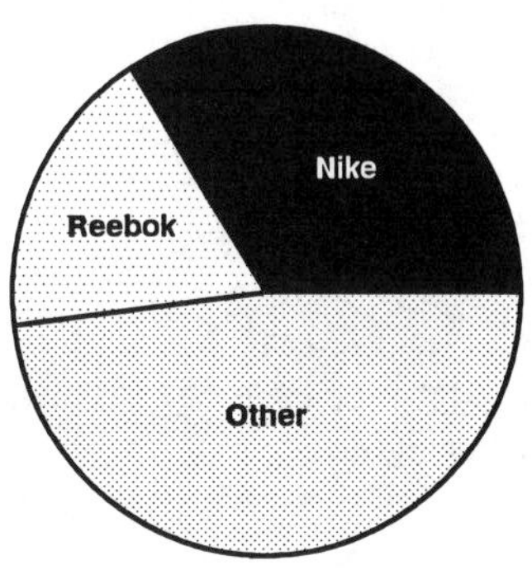

Company shares are shown in percent. "Other" refers primarily to the shares of Adidas and Fila.

Nike	34.0%
Reebok	18.0
Other	48.0

Source: *Latin Trade*, May 1997, p. 34.

★ 708 ★

Athletic Footwear (SIC 3021)

Sports Shoe Leaders - 1996

Market shares are estimated.

Nike	42.2%
Reebok	16.7
Fila	8.0
Adidas	5.8
Airwalk	3.0
Keds	2.6
Converse	2.4
L.A. Gear	2.1
Other	17.2

Source: *Investext*, Thomson Financial Networks, August 23, 1996, p. 5.

★ 709 ★

Athletic Footwear (SIC 3021)

Sports Shoe Market - 1995

Nike	36.8%
Reebok	20.5
Adidas	6.2
Fila	5.8

Continued on next page.

★ 709 ★ *Continued*

Athletic Footwear (SIC 3021)

Sports Shoe Market - 1995

Keds	3.6%
LA Gear	3.0
Converse	2.9
Airwalk	2.7
New Balance	2.2
Asics	1.8
Other	14.5

Source: *USA TODAY*, September 17, 1996, p. B3, from Sporting Goods Intelligence.

★ 710 ★

Athletic Footwear (SIC 3021)

Sports Shoe Sales by Segment

Sales are in millions of dollars for 1995.

Basketball	$ 1,825
Cross-training/fitness	1,450
Walking	1,075
Hiking/outdoor	625
Running/jogging	615

Source: *DM*, November 1996, p. 3, from Sporting Goods Manufacturers Association.

★ 711 ★

Athletic Footwear (SIC 3021)

Sports Shoe Sales by Type

Retail sales are shown in billions of dollars for 1995.

Walking	$ 2.8
Gym shoes/sneakers	1.7
Cross training	1.2
Running	1.1

Source: *Footwear News*, February 1997, p. 2, from National Sporting Goods Association.

★ 712 ★

Athletic Footwear (SIC 3021)

Who Buys Sports Shoes

Data are in millions of pairs.

	1995	1996	Share
Women	46.9	45.5	55.4%
Men	33.7	36.6	44.6

Source: *Sporting Goods Business*, October 1996, p. 13, from Athletic Footwear Association.

★ 713 ★

Plastic Products (SIC 3080)

Largest Pipe/Tubing Extruders

The largest pipe, profile and tubing extruders in North America are ranked by most recent year sales in millions of dollars.

CertainTeed Corp.	$ 432.0
JM Manufacturing	420.0
Alcoa Building Products	382.0
Royal Plastics Group Ltd.	360.6
North American Pipe/North American Profiles	285.0
Standard Products Co.	280.0
Lamson & Sessions Co.	224.0
Pacific Western	222.0
Jannock Inc.	221.5

Source: *Plastics News*, December 30, 1996, p. 52.

★ 714 ★

Plastic Products (SIC 3080)

Plastic Uses in Packaging

Low-density polyethylene	33.0%
High-density polyethylene	31.0
Polyethylene terephthalate	15.0
Polypropylene	12.0
Polyvinyl chloride	6.0
Polystyrene	3.0

Source: *Chemical & Engineering News*, November 4, 1996, p. 22, from American Plastics Council.

★715★

Plastic Products (SIC 3080)

Rotomolding Market by Segment

Data are based on a survey of 135 companies in 1994.

Toys	41.0%
Tanks	19.0
Containers	9.0
Automotive	8.7
Materials handling	3.6
Housewares/consumer	2.6
Playground equipment	2.3
Other	10.6

Source: *Plastics News*, December 30, 1996, p. 68, from Plastics Custom Research Service.

★716★

Plastic Products (SIC 3080)

Top Stretch Film Processors

Company shares are shown based on production capacity for 1995-96.

AEP Industries	19.0%
Tenneco Packaging	18.0
Atlantis Plastics	17.0
Huntsman Packaging	12.0
Sigma Stretch Film	9.0
ITW-Mima	6.0
Others	19.0

Source: *Modern Plastics*, April 1997, p. 12, from Moore Associates.

★717★

Plastic Products (SIC 3080)

Video Cassette Shell Production

Data show who supplied the United States with the shells for blank consumer video tapes. China controls 82.0% of the home video tape shell market.

China	55.0%
U.S.	30.0
Other	15.0

Source: *Plastics News*, February 24, 1997, p. 3, from International Recording Media Association.

★718★

Plastic Foam (SIC 3086)

Plastic Foam Demand

Data are for 1995 based on 5.75 billion pounds.

Polyurethanes	54.5%
Polystyrenes	28.4
Polyvinyl chlorides	14.7
Polyolefins	2.4

Source: *Plastics News*, November 18, 1996, p. 3, from Business Communications Co.

★719★

Baby Seats (SIC 3089)

Booster Seat Makers - 1996

Market shares are shown in percent as of May 31, 1996.

Cosco	54.0%
Gerry	26.0
Century	13.0
Fisher Price	4.0
Evenflo	3.0
Kolcraft	1.0

Source: *Investext*, Thomson Financial Networks, July 24, 1996, p. 4, from NPD Group.

★720★

Baby Seats (SIC 3089)

Convertible Seat Makers - 1996

Market shares are shown in percent as of May 31, 1996.

Evenflo	40.0%
Century	33.0
Cosco	19.0
Gerry	3.0
Kolcraft	3.0

Source: *Investext*, Thomson Financial Networks, July 24, 1996, p. 4, from NPD Group.

★ 721 ★

Baby Seats (SIC 3089)

Infant Seat Makers - 1996

Market shares are shown in percent as of May 31, 1996.

Evenflo	54.0%
Century	24.0
Cosco	8.0
Kolcraft	8.0
Gerry	6.0
Fisher Price	1.0

Source: *Investext,* Thomson Financial Networks, July 24, 1996, p. 4, from NPD Group.

★ 722 ★

Condoms (SIC 3089)

Popular Condom Brands in Supermarkets

Shares are shown based on $41.7 million in supermarket sales for the 52 weeks ended March 9, 1996. Drug stores command a 61.4% share of the retail market.

Trojan	30.7%
Trojan-Enz	22.5
LifeStyles	14.1
Sheik Super	4.6
Class-Act	3.2
Sheik Classic	3.0
NaturaLamb	2.4
Other	19.5

Source: *Supermarket Business,* August 1996, p. 74, from A.C. Nielsen.

★ 723 ★

Condoms (SIC 3089)

Top Condom Brands - Canada

Brand shares are shown based on $31.7 billion Canadian dollars in sales for 1996.

Trojan	32.0%
Durex Ramses	23.8
Durex Sheik	20.5
Ortho Shields	11.2
Durex Titan	4.0
Ortho Supreme	2.8
Ortho Legend	0.5
Other Julius Schmid brands	0.6%
Others	4.6

Source: *Marketing Magazine,* May 26, 1997, p. 12, from industry sources.

★ 724 ★

Coolers (SIC 3089)

Insulated Jug Market

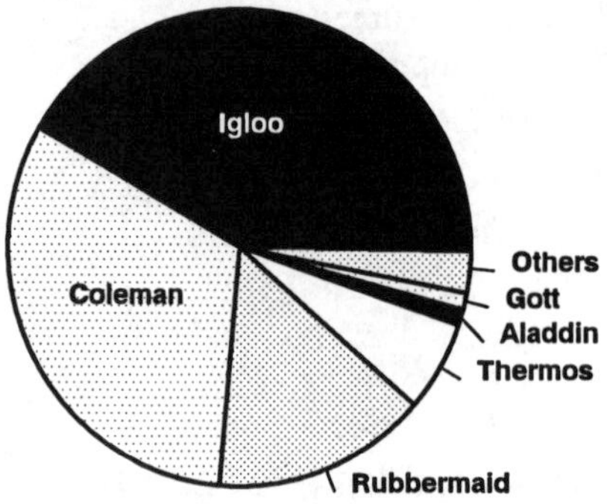

Brand shares are shown in percent.

Igloo	41.6%
Coleman	32.1
Rubbermaid	15.3
Thermos	5.6
Aladdin	1.4
Gott	1.3
Others	2.7

Source: *Discount Store News,* August 5, 1996, p. 105, from Sports Marketing Research Group.

★ 725 ★

Coolers (SIC 3089)

Top Ice Chest/Cooler Brands

Brand shares are shown in percent.

Igloo	43.3%
Coleman	31.8
Rubbermaid	13.6
Thermos	5.1
Arctic Zone	2.0
Other	4.2

Source: *Discount Store News,* August 5, 1996, p. 105, from Sports Marketing Research Group.

SIC 31 - Leather and Leather Products

★ 726 ★

Leather (SIC 3111)

Leather Upholstery Makers - 1996

Firms are ranked by total shipments in millions of dollars. Leather upholstery commanded 18% of the fabric market in 1996.

Klaussner	$ 225
Natuzzi	225
La-Z-Boy	78
Viewpoint	70
Action	66
Leather Trend	62
Palliser	57
Soft Line	48
Thomasville	45
Leather Center	42

Source: *Furniture Today*, November 25, 1996, p. 8.

★ 727 ★

Footwear (SIC 3140)

Casual Footwear Producers

Companies are ranked by sales in millions of dollars. Figures for Rockport, Dexter, Hush Puppies, and Birkenstock are estimated.

Rockport	$ 386
Timberland	364
Dexter	300
Keds	198
Airwalk	175
Sketchers	134
Hushpuppies	130
Vans	100
Birkenstock	68
Sperry	45

Source: *Sportstyle*, May 1997, p. 46.

★ 728 ★

Footwear (SIC 3140)

Rugged Footwear Producers - 1996

Companies are ranked by sales in millions of dollars. Figures for Nike ACG, Adidas, and Merrell are estimated.

Nike ACG	$ 200.0
Wolverine	145.0
LaCrosse	85.9
Rocky	79.5
Hi-Tec USA	52.0
Reebok	42.0
Adidas	33.0
Vasque	31.0
Merrell	28.0
Danner	21.5

Source: *Sportstyle*, May 1997, p. 46.

SIC 32 - Stone, Clay, and Glass Products

★ 729 ★

Glass (SIC 3211)

Flat Glass Market - Mexico

Grupo Vitro	90.0%
Other	10.0

Source: *Mexico Business*, December 1996, p. 53.

★ 730 ★

Glass Containers (SIC 3221)

Glass Container Makers

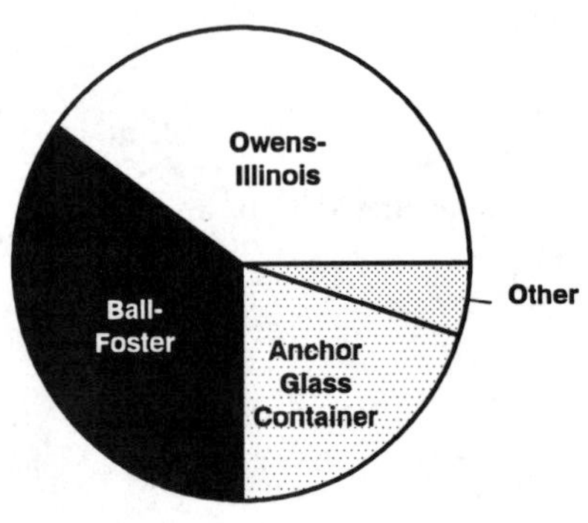

Shares are estimated.

Owens-Illinois	40.0%
Ball-Foster	35.0
Anchor Glass Container	20.0
Other	5.0

Source: *Glass Industry*, November 1996, p. 8.

★ 731 ★

Glass Containers (SIC 3221)

Glass Container Market - Mexico

Grupo Vitro	80.0%
Other	20.0

Source: *Mexico Business*, December 1996, p. 53.

★ 732 ★

Glass Containers (SIC 3221)

Glass Container Market by Segment

Dristribution is forecast for 1997. Production is projected to reach 10 million tons of glass for the entire year.

Beer	46.0%
Food	35.0
Soft drinks	5.0
Wine	5.0
Liquor	4.0
Other	5.0

Source: *USA TODAY*, June 4, 1997, p. B1, from Salomon Brothers.

★ 733 ★

Glass Containers (SIC 3229)

Specialty Glass Market

Data are shown by application for 1995.

Electronics	61.7%
Optical fibers	32.5
Medical/dental	3.8
Aerospace	2.5

Source: *Ceramic Industry*, August 1996, p. 48, from Business Communications Co.

★734★

Ceramics (SIC 3250)

Ceramic Components Market

The U.S. market is shown by type of component for 1995 and 2000.

	1995	2000
Electronic ceramics	76.2%	75.4%
Ceramic coatings	10.4	10.8
Structural ceramics	9.1	9.2
Environmental/industrial ceramics	4.3	4.6

Source: *Ceramic Industry*, October 1996, p. 43, from Business Communications Co. Inc.

★735★

Bricks (SIC 3251)

Brick Market by Region

Shipments are shown for 1995.

Southeast	52.0%
Midwest	19.3
Northeast	5.2
West	2.6
Other	20.9

Source: *Ceramic Industry*, August 1996, p. 34, from Brick Industry of America.

★736★

Bricks (SIC 3253)

Brick Production by Type

Face brick	96.9%
Paver	3.0
Thin	0.1

Source: *Ziegelindustrie*, July 1996, p. 509.

★737★

Ceramics (SIC 3253)

Ceramics Products Market - Mexico

Data are in millions of dollars for 1996.

	($ mil.)	Share
Bathroom, sanitary ware	$ 174.6	35.0%
Ceramic floor/wall coverings	125.8	25.2
Tableware incl. porcelain	89.9	18.0
Advanced ind. ceramic prod.	79.9	16.0
Artistic and decorative items	29.1	5.8

Source: *National Trade Data Bank*, February 6, 1997, p. ISA960301.

★738★

Refractories (SIC 3255)

Clay Refractory Market

Data are for 1994.

High alumina brick	31.3%
Fireclay brick	22.9
Castable refractories	19.5
Plastic refractories	8.8
Fireclay guning mixes	5.9
Insulating brick	5.5
Mortar	3.0
Other unshaped	3.0

Source: *Ceramic Industry*, August 1996, p. 59, from United States Department of Commerce.

★739★

Plumbing Fixtures (SIC 3261)

Vitreous Plumbing Fixtures - 1995

Distribution is shown based on shipments.

Water closet bowls	46.8%
Flush tanks	35.2
Lavoratories	16.5
Other	1.4

Source: *Ceramic Industry*, August 1996, p. 30, from United States Department of Commerce.

★ 740 ★

Cookware (SIC 3262)

Popular Cookware/Kitchen Storage Brands

Data show the brands of housewares preferred by shoppers at discount stores in 1996.

Corelle	25.0%
Corning	19.0
Libbey	15.0
Pyrex	13.0
Rubbermaid	8.0
Anchor Hocking	7.0
Tupperware	2.0
Visions	2.0

Source: *Discount Store News*, October 21, 1996, p. 65, from Lee J. Shapiro & Associates.

★ 741 ★

Dishware (SIC 3263)

Popular Dinnerware Brands

Data show the preferred brands of everyday dishware.

Corelle	32.0%
Pfaltzgraff	11.9
Handmade	10.7
Syracuse	5.1
Johnson Brothers	4.7
Wedgwood	4.0
Melmac	0.8
Other	30.9

Source: *American Ceramic Society Bulletin*, May 1997, p. 62.

★ 742 ★

Abrasives (SIC 3291)

Scouring Pad Brands

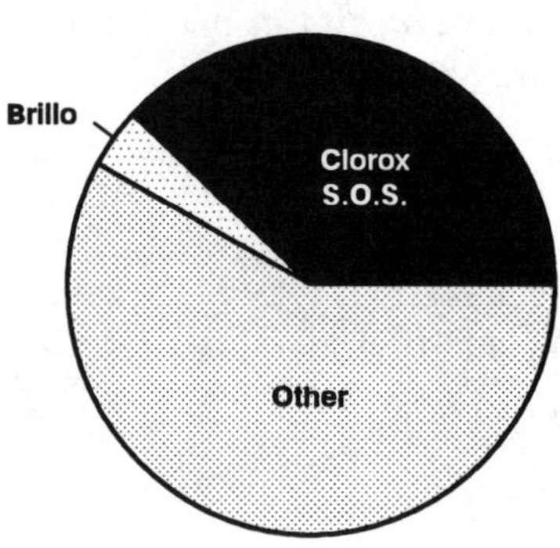

Sales are shown in millions of dollars.

	($ mil.)	Share
Clorox S.O.S.	$ 56.0	37.6%
Brillo	6.0	4.0
Other	87.0	58.4

Source: *Brandweek*, November 25, 1996, p. 9, from Information Resources Inc.

SIC 33 - Primary Metal Industries

★ 743 ★

Metals (SIC 3300)

Top Metals Companies - 1996

Companies are ranked by revenues in millions of dollars.

Alcoa	$ 13,128
Reynolds Metals	7,016
Bethlehem Steel	4,679
Inland Steel Industries	4,584
LTV	4,135
Allegheny Teledyne	3,816
Phelps Dodge	3,787
Nucor	3,647
Alumax	3,159
Maxxam	2,543
Commercial Metals	2,322
AK Steel Holding	2,302
Armco	1,724
Walter Industries	1,486
Worthington Industries	1,478
Weirton Steel	1,383
Essex Group	1,332
Rouge Steel	1,307
WHX	1,233

Source: *Fortune*, April 28, 1997, p. 57.

★ 744 ★

Steel (SIC 3312)

Annual Steel Output - Mini-Mills

Data show the annual steel tonnage of the leading mills.

Nucor/Berkeley	800,000
BHP/North Star	600,000
Trico	500,000
Steel Dynamics	400,000
Gallatin	300,000

Source: *American Metal Market*, November 26, 1996, p. 22A.

★ 745 ★

Steel (SIC 3312)

Steel Market Shipments

Data are for 1996.

	Share
Mills	57.0%
Distributors	26.0
Imports	17.0

Source: *Purchasing*, November 7, 1996, p. 32B.

★ 746 ★

Steel (SIC 3312)

Steel Production by State

Data are in millions of tons for 1995.

	(mil.)	Share
Indiana	22.8	21.7%
Ohio	16.4	15.6
Pennsylvania	9.2	8.8
Other	56.5	53.9

Source: *Business First - Columbus*, August 2, 1996, p. 8, from American Iron and Steel Institute.

★ 747 ★

Steel (SIC 3312)

Steel Shipments by Market

Shipments are shown in thousands of tons for the first nine months of 1996.

Service centers/distributors	16,895
Automotive	10,803
Construction	9,624
Converting/processing	6,015
Containers/packaging	3,002
Oil, gas, petrochemical	2,291
Electrical equipment	1,750
Machinery	1,389
Appliances, utensils, cutlery	1,273

Continued on next page.

★ 747 ★ *Continued*

Steel (SIC 3312)

Steel Shipments by Market

Shipments are shown in thousands of tons for the first nine months of 1996.

Rail transportation	848
Other	21,341

Source: *New Steel*, January 1997, p. 48, from American Iron and Steel Institute.

★ 748 ★

Steel (SIC 3312)

U.S. Steel Makers

Firms are ranked by sales in millions of dollars for the latest 12 months.

USX - U.S. Steel	$ 6,429
Bethlehem Steel	4,682
LTV	4,162
Allegheny Teledyne	3,922
Nucor	3,604
National Steel	2,928
Commercial Metals	2,310

Source: *Forbes*, January 13, 1997, p. 174, from Value Line and OneSource Information Systems.

★ 749 ★

Metal Tubing (SIC 3317)

Metal Tubing by Type

The estimated tubing market is shown for 1997 in thousands of net tons.

	(000)	Share
Mechanical steel	4,049.0	58.9%
Structural steel	1,943.0	28.3
Copper & brass	556.0	8.1
Aluminum	192.0	2.8
Press use steel	78.0	1.1
Stainless steel	57.0	0.8

Source: *Purchasing*, February 13, 1997, p. 28B5, from Metal Market Strategies.

★ 750 ★

Aluminum (SIC 3334)

Aluminum Product Distribution

Distribution is based on new orders received for the first nine months of 1996. Figures are in millions of pounds.

	(000)	Share
Sheet, plate, other	3,509.2	35.1%
Extruded products	1,937.4	19.4
Rod, bar & wire	347.2	3.5
Other	4,193.2	42.0

Source: *American Metal Market*, November 6, 1996, p. 6A, from National Association of Aluminum Distributors.

★ 751 ★

Aluminum (SIC 3334)

Aluminum Shipments by Industry

Distribution of 1995 net shipments is shown for the United States.

Transportation	27.2%
Containers & packaging	24.1
Exports	13.7
Building & construction	12.7
Electrical	6.9
Consumer durables	6.5
Machinery & equipment	6.0
Other domestic	2.9

Source: *Light Metal Age*, October 1996, p. 71, from Aluminum Association.

★ 752 ★

Metal Pellets (SIC 3339)

Iron Ore Pellet Makers

Production is shown for 1996 in gross tons.

	Tons	Share
Minntac	13.70	22.2%
Hibbing Taconite	8.30	13.5
Empire Iron Mining Partnership	8.00	13.0
LTV Steel Mining Co.	7.80	12.7
Tilden Mining	6.30	10.2
National Steel Pellet Co.	5.30	8.6
Eveleth Mines	5.20	8.4
Northshore Mining	4.20	6.8
Inland Steel Mining Co.	2.80	4.5

Source: *Skillings Mining Review*, July 27, 1996, p. 23.

★753★

Metal Pellets (SIC 3339)

Iron Ore Pellet Makers - Canada

Production is shown for 1996 in gross tons.

	Tons	Share
Iron Ore Co. of Canada	9.64	41.1%
Quebec Cartier Mining Co.	8.13	34.6
Wabush Mines	5.70	24.3

Source: *Skillings Mining Review*, July 27, 1996, p. 23.

★754★

Nonferrous Metals (SIC 3339)

Magnesium Metal Makers

Firms are ranked by annual capacity in metric tons.

Dow Chemical Co.	65,000
Magnesium Corp. of America	38,000
Northwest Alloys Inc.	38,000

Source: *Minerals Yearbook: Metals and Materials*, Vol 1, 1994, p. 487, from United States Bureau of Mines.

★755★

Nonferrous Metals (SIC 3350)

U.S. Nonferrous Metals Makers

Firms are ranked by sales in millions of dollars for the latest 12 months.

Broken Hill	$ 15,360
Alcoa	12,911
Alcan Aluminum	7,999
Reynolds Metals	7,093
Phelps Dodge	3,867
Inco	3,374
Alumax	3,202
Engelhard	3,059

Source: *Forbes*, January 13, 1997, p. 174, from Value Line and OneSource Information Systems.

★756★

Gold (SIC 3356)

U.S. Gold Use - 1996

Jewelry	39.0%
Exports	30.0
Electronics	16.0
Coins	6.0
Other	9.0

Source: *USA TODAY*, April 3, 1997, p. A1, from Gold Institute/Gold Fields Mineral Services.

SIC 34 - Fabricated Metal Products

★ 757 ★

Metal Cans (SIC 3410)

Food Can Shipments

Distribution is shown based on 17.78 million three-piece cans.

Vegetables/juice	42.7%
Fruit/juice	12.6
Pet food	10.3
Dairy	4.9
Coffee	3.3
Baby food	3.2
Meat/poultry	3.1
Seafood	1.7
Other	18.2

Source: *Prepared Foods*, October 1996, p. 96, from Can Manufacturers Institute.

★ 758 ★

Razor Blades (SIC 3421)

Razor Blade Makers

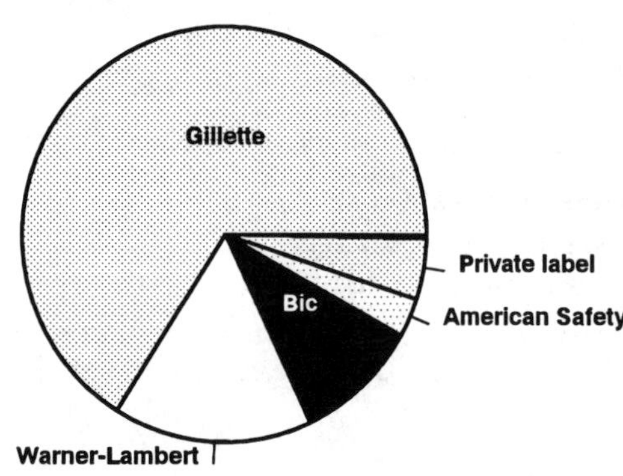

Shares are shown based on sales of $1.06 billion for the year ended March 2, 1997.

	Sales ($ mil.)	Share
Gillette	$ 708.0	66.7%
Warner-Lambert	166.1	15.6
Bic	105.5	9.9
American Safety	28.2	2.7
Private label	53.8	5.1

Source: *Supermarket Business*, March 1997, p. 105, from Information Resources Inc.

★ 759 ★

Prefabricated Buildings (SIC 3448)

Metal Building Sales by Segment - 1995

Shares of the $2.2 billion market are shown in percent.

Manufacturing	40.0%
Commercial	36.0
Community	12.0
Other	12.0

Source: *Building Design & Construction*, April 1997, p. 57, from Metal Building Manufacturers Association.

★ 760 ★

Metal Services (SIC 3470)

Leading Metal Service Companies - 1996

Companies are ranked by sales in millions of dollars.

Ryerson Tull Inc.	$ 2,390.0
Thyssen Inc.	1,750.0
Vincent Metal Goods	1,300.0
Edgcomb Ferro	1,100.0
Earle M. Jorgensen Co.	1,060.0
Russel Metals Inc.	1,020.0
Worthington Steel	820.0
Reynolds Aluminum Supply Co.	800.0
Reliance Steel & Aluminum Co.	786.7
Castle & Co.	725.0
O'Neal Steel Inc.	660.0
Carpenter Steel	650.0

Source: *Purchasing*, April 1, 1997, p. 32B6, from Analytical Computer.

★ 761 ★

Powdered Metal (SIC 3499)

P/M Market by End Use

The market for powdered metal (P/M) is shown by end use for 1995.

Automotive	66.5%
Recreation, hand tools, & hobby	11.6
Household appliances	5.3
Industrial motors, controls, hydraulics	3.7
Hardware	2.3
Business machines	1.6
All other	9.0

Source: *WARD's Auto World*, September 1996, p. 63, from Powder Metallurgy Parts Association.

★ 762 ★

Industrial Equipment (SIC 3500)

Top Industrial and Farm Equipment Manufacturers - 1996

Companies are ranked by revenues in millions of dollars.

Caterpillar	$ 16,522
Deere	11,229
Ingersoll-Rand	6,703
Dresser Industries	6,562
American Standard	5,805
Case	5,409
Cummins Engine	5,257
Black & Decker	4,914
Dover	4,076
Parker Hannifin	3,586
York International	3,219
Baker Hughes	3,028
Harnischfeger Industries	2,888
Western Atlas	2,583
Timken	2,395
Agco	2,317
Nacco Industries	2,273
Trinova	2,033
Detroit Diesel	1,963
Crane	1,848

Source: *Fortune*, April 28, 1997, p. 54.

★ 763 ★

Engines (SIC 3519)

Diesel Engine Manufacturers - Ontario

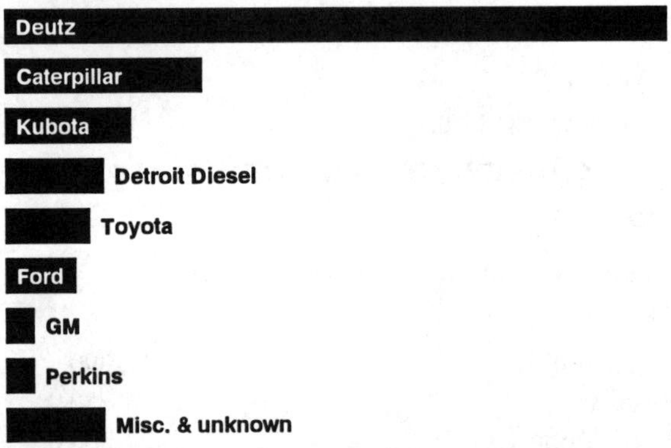

Manufacturers are ranked by installed engines in Ontario mines.

Deutz	47.0%
Caterpillar	14.0
Kubota	9.0
Detroit Diesel	7.0
Toyota	6.0
Ford	5.0
GM	2.0
Perkins	2.0
Misc. & unknown	7.0

Source: *Canadian Mining Journal*, February 1997, p. 9, from Canadian Ministry of Labor.

★764★

Farm Equipment (SIC 3523)

Farm Wheel Tractor Sales

Retail unit sales are for the year ended June 1996.

2WD 0-40 HP	26,034
2WD 40-100 HP	20,899
2WD 100+ HP	11,942
Self-propelled	3,167
4WD	2,494

Source: *Implement & Tractor*, July/August 1996, p. 38, from Equipment Manufacturers Institute.

★765★

Farm Equipment (SIC 3523)

Farm Wheel Tractor Sales - Canada

Retail unit sales are for the year ended June 1996.

2WD 40-99 HP	2,927
2WD 100+ HP	1,964
2WD 0-40 HP	1,293
4WD	1,012
Self-propelled	799

Source: *Implement & Tractor*, July/August 1996, p. 38, from Equipment Manufacturers Institute and Canadian Farm and Industrial Equipment Institute.

★766★

Farm Equipment (SIC 3523)

Tractor and Farm Equipment Sales

Unit sales are shown through July 1996. Two wheel drive tractors are shown by horsepower.

Under 40 hp.	30,400
40 to 99 hp.	24,289
100 hp. & over	12,879
Combines	3,697
4 wheel-drive	2,649

Source: *Successful Farming*, November 1996, p. 32, from Equipment Manufacturers Institute.

★767★

Lawn & Garden Equipment (SIC 3524)

Hand-Held Gasoline Powered Equipment Shipments

Products are ranked by units shipped in 1995.

Trimmers/brushcutters	4,493,000
Chain saws	1,898,600
Hand-held blowers	1,144,800
Hedge trimmers	254,100
Backpack blowers	173,300
Cut-off saws	81,700

Source: *Appliance*, October 1996, p. 37, from Portable Power Equipment Manufacturers Association.

★768★

Lawn & Garden Equipment (SIC 3524)

Lawn & Garden Sales by Segment

Sales at discount stores are shown in percent. Total sales reached $6.06 billion.

Lawn care	28.2%
BBQ	16.7
Lawn furniture	14.7
Live nursery	11.9
Yard tools	11.2
Other	17.3

Source: *Discount Store News*, August 5, 1996, p. 81.

★769★

Lawn & Garden Equipment (SIC 3524)

Outdoor Power Equipment Shipments

Data are in thousands of units.

	1996	1997
Walk-behind power mowers	5,650.0	6,036.7
Front-engine riding mowers	1,187.4	1,264.2
Rotary tillers	340.3	353.3
Riding garden tractors	212.0	244.0
Rear-engine riding mowers	159.7	149.1

Source: *Discount Store News*, July 15, 1996, p. 39, from Outdoor Power Equipment Institute.

★ 770 ★

Construction Equipment (SIC 3531)

Articulated Hauler Purchases by Region - 1996

Southeast	435
Midwest	252
Northeast	137
Southwest	99
West	66

Source: *ENR*, February 3, 1997, p. 33, from Equipment Data Associates Inc.

★ 771 ★

Construction Equipment (SIC 3531)

Construction Equipment Shipments

Shipments are estimated for 1996.

Skd. steer loaders	46,400
Wheel loaders	10,980
Loader/backhoes	10,450
Hyd. excavators	7,690
Crawler tractors	6,950
Rgh. terrain forklift	5,270

Source: *Implement & Tractor*, June 1996, p. 13, from Machinery Outlook.

★ 772 ★

Construction Equipment (SIC 3531)

Earthmoving Machinery Sales - 1997

Data are for North America.

	Units	Share
Skid-steer loaders	44,000	36.5%
Backhoes/loaders	24,500	20.3
Wheel loaders	12,500	10.4
Crawler excavators	11,800	9.8
Crawler dozers	9,600	8.0
Ditchers/trenchers	6,800	5.6
Motor graders	3,675	3.1
Mini-excavators	2,100	1.7
Crawler loaders	1,600	1.3
Articulated haulers	1,125	0.9
Scrapers	975	0.8%
Rigid haulers	820	0.7
Wheeled excavators	600	0.5
Wheeled dozers	325	0.3

Source: *Diesel Progress Engines & Drives*, December 1996, p. 18, from Yengst Associates and Off-Highway Research.

★ 773 ★

Construction Equipment (SIC 3531)

Scraper Purchases by Region - 1996

Southeast	89
Midwest	73
West	36
Southwest	22
Northeast	7

Source: *ENR*, February 3, 1997, p. 33, from Equipment Data Associates Inc.

★ 774 ★

Construction Equipment (SIC 3531)

Skid Steer Loader Market - North America

Shares are shown for 1995.

Melroe Company	46.0%
Case J.I. - Wichita	19.0
New Holland	10.0
Gehl Farm Equip	8.0
Mustang Manufacturing Co. Inc.	8.0
Thomas Equipment Ltd.	6.0
Others	3.0

Source: http://www.powersys.com/oelink.html, June 10, 1997, p. 1.

★ 775 ★

Cranes and Hoists (SIC 3536)

Telescopic Material Handler Producers

Shares are shown for the North American market.

Omniquip	40.0%
Gradall	16.0
JCB	14.0
Pettibone	10.0

Continued on next page.

★ 775 ★ *Continued*

Cranes and Hoists (SIC 3536)

Telescopic Material Handler Producers

Shares are shown for the North American market.

Gehl	8.0%
Caterpillar	4.0
Ingersoll-Rand	3.0
Others	5.0

Source: *Investor's Business Daily*, May 19, 1997, p. A4, from Credit Suisse First Boston.

★ 776 ★

Lift Trucks (SIC 3537)

Lift Truck Market - 1995

Production is shown by type for 1995.

	No.	Share
Internal combustion engine	72,685	47.0%
Electric rider	44,087	28.5
Motorized hand	37,746	24.4

Source: *Beverage World*, August 1996, p. 66.

★ 777 ★

Machine Tools (SIC 3540)

U.S. Machine Tool Consumption by Region

Regions are ranked by the value of orders in millions of dollars. Data are for 1996.

	($ mil.)	Share
Midwest	$ 2,600	46.5%
Central	912	16.3
Northeast	867	15.5
South	641	11.5
West	566	10.1

Source: *Assembly*, April 1997, p. 10, from *U.S. Machine Tool Consumption Report*.

★ 778 ★

CPI Equipment (SIC 3541)

CPI Equipment Makers

Sales are shown in millions of dollars for the second quarter of 1996.

Fluor	$ 2,582
Foster Wheeler	971
Univar	576
Jacobs Engineering Corp.	437
Morrison Knudsen	353
Stone & Webster	269
Millipore	162
Blount Intl.	142

Source: *Chemicalweek*, August 28, 1996, p. 58, from Standard & Poor's.

★ 779 ★

Machine Tools (SIC 3541)

Cutting Tool Market by End Use

Data show the top markets for cutting tools in the Northeast Central region. Figures are in millions of dollars.

Construction machinery	$ 46.4
Internal combustion engines	42.8
Motor vehicle parts & accessories	37.2
Industrial machinery	29.3
Special dies, tools, jigs & fixtures	26.2

Source: *Industrial Distribution*, January 1997, p. 107, from Industrial Market Information, Inc.

★ 780 ★

Paper Machinery (SIC 3554)

Capital Spending on Paper Machinery

Data are in millions of dollars.

	($ mil.)	Share
South Atlantic	$ 2,757	27.4%
East South Central	2,155	21.4
East North Central	1,554	15.4
New England	1,290	12.8
Mid-Atlantic	787	7.8
Mountain Pacific	657	6.5
West South Central	575	5.7
West North Central	300	3.0

Source: *Pulp & Paper*, January 1997, p. 69.

★ 781 ★

Paper Machinery (SIC 3554)

Capital Spending on Paper Machinery - Canada

Data are in millions of Canadian dollars.

	($ mil.)	Share
Quebec	$ 1,701	36.1%
Maritimes	1,052	22.3
British Columbia	899	19.1
Ontario	817	17.3
Central	247	5.2

Source: *Pulp & Paper*, January 1997, p. 69.

★ 782 ★

Paper Machinery (SIC 3554)

Leading Paper Automation Makers - North America

Shares are estimated.

Measurex	70.0%
Valmet	8.0
Other	22.0

Source: *Investext*, Thomson Financial Networks, October 28, 1996, p. 3, from MX and Smith Barney estimates.

★ 783 ★

Paper Machinery (SIC 3554)

Paper Machinery Market

Market shares are estimated in percent.

Beloit	40.0%
Valmet	35.0
Voith	15.0
Other	10.0

Source: *Investext*, Thomson Financial Networks, August 12, 1996, p. 7, from Smith Barney estimates.

★ 784 ★

Printing Machinery (SIC 3555)

Wide-Format Printing Uses

Sign making	24.0%
Banners/posters	22.0
Presentations	16.0
Other	38.0

Source: *Macweek*, November 11, 1996, p. 17, from CK Associates.

★ 785 ★

Forestry Equipment (SIC 3559)

Forestry Equipment Market - North America

Shares are shown for 1995.

Cummins	53.0%
Deere	23.0
CAT	20.0
DET Diesel	2.0
Perkins	1.0
Others	1.0

Source: http:// www.powersys.com/engindata.html, June 10, 1997, p. 1.

★ 786 ★

Packaging Machinery (SIC 3559)

Dairy Packaging Equipment

Data show the types of packaging equipment dairy producers plan to purchase in 1996. Figures are in thousands of dollars.

Extended shelf-life/aseptic fillers	$ 4,405
Case/carton forming, filling sealing	2,136
Paper/gable top fillers	2,085
Case handling equipment	2,009
Plastic bottle fillers	1,436
Palletizers/depalletizers	1,315
Labeling equipment	1,278

Source: *Dairy Foods*, February 1997, p. 64, from *Dairy and Food Industries Supply Assoc. Capital & Supplies Study*.

★ 787 ★

Semiconductor Equipment (SIC 3559)

Chip Processing Gear Market

This table shows the leader in the chip processing machinery market.

PRI Automation Inc.	90.0%
Other	10.0

Source: *Investor's Business Daily*, December 23, 1996, p. A4.

★ 788 ★

Assembly Equipment (SIC 3560)

Assembly Equipment Spending - 1997

Distribution of $2.4 billion in spending in 1997.

Midwest	53.0%
Northeast	15.0
South Central	13.0
Southeast	11.0
Pacific	6.0
Mountain	2.0

Source: *Assembly*, December 1996, p. 19.

★ 789 ★

Pumps (SIC 3561)

Who Uses Pumps in Mexico

Mexcian states/municipalities	43.0%
Manufacturing companies	16.0
Private water treatment plants	14.0
General Directorate of Construction	13.0
Other	14.0

Source: *National Trade Data Bank*, February 6, 1997, p. ISA960901.

★ 790 ★

Business Machines (SIC 3570)

Small/Home Office Market

Data are in thousands of units.

	1995	1996
PCs	8,400	9,825
Electric typewriters	2,650	2,450

Source: *Computer Reseller News*, December 2, 1996, p. 93, from Electronics Industry Association.

★ 791 ★

Computers (SIC 3571)

Canadian PC Market

Market shares are shown based on units in percent.

Compaq	13.0%
IBM	13.0
AST	7.9
NEC	4.3
Acer	2.3
Hewlett-Packard	2.2
Other	57.3

Source: http:// sct.spannet.com/spanfacts/news/ 1995cpu.htm, March 24, 1997, p. 1, from International Data Corp. Canada.

★ 792 ★

Computers (SIC 3571)

Computer Sales by Segment

Medium and large business	31.0%
Home	30.0
Small business	28.0
Government	6.0
Education	5.0

Source: *Investor's Business Daily*, March 31, 1997, p. A6, from International Data Corp.

★ 793 ★

Computers (SIC 3571)

Computer Shipment Leaders

Data compare third quarter shipments for each year.

	3Q 1995	3Q 1996
Compaq	12.2%	14.4%
IBM	8.8	9.1
Packard Bell	11.9	7.8
Apple	13.2	7.3
Dell	4.4	7.3
Other	50.1	54.1

Source: *Computer Reseller News*, November 11, 1996, p. 21, from International Data Corp.

★ 794 ★

Computers (SIC 3571)

Desktop Computer Shipments

Data show desktop computer shipments for the first quarter of 1996. Company shares are shown based on the 4.781 million units shipped during that period.

	Units (000)	Share
Packard Bell	620	13.0%
Compaq	618	12.9
Hewlett-Packard	384	8.0
Apple	330	6.9
Gateway 2000	319	6.7
Dell	298	6.2
IBM	248	5.2
Acer	185	3.9
Micron Electronics	104	2.2
AST	102	2.1
Others	1,573	32.9

Source: *Investext*, Thomson Financial Networks, November 6, 1996, p. 11, from International Data Corporation and Micron Electronics Inc.

★ 795 ★

Computers (SIC 3571)

Handheld Device Shipments

PDA stands for personal digital assistant.

	1996	2000
High-end organizers/PC comp.	74.0%	48.0%
PDAs	21.0	23.0
Personal companions	6.0	29.0

Source: *Reseller Management*, December 1996, p. 114, from International Data Corp.

★ 796 ★

Computers (SIC 3571)

Home PC Market - 1996

Packard Bell
Compaq
IBM
Gateway
Apple
Acer
Other

Data show PC (personal computer) unit sales. The market reached 7.7 million units in 1996.

	Units	Share
Packard Bell	2,100,000	27.3%
Compaq	943,000	12.2
IBM	624,000	8.1
Gateway	604,000	7.8
Apple	570,000	7.4
Acer	466,000	6.1
Other	2,393,000	31.1

Source: *Business Week*, May 26, 1997, p. 134, from Dataquest Inc.

★ 797 ★

Computers (SIC 3571)

How Data Is Lost

Hardware/system malfunction	44.0%
Human error	32.0
Software program malfunction	14.0
Computer virus	7.0
Natural disasters	3.0

Source: *Computer Reseller News*, February 3, 1997, p. 53, from Ontrack Data International Inc.

★ 798 ★

Computers (SIC 3571)

Largest Computer Firms - Minnesota

Firms are ranked by annual revenues in millions of dollars. Some figures are estimated.

IBM Corporation	$ 3,750.0
Imation Corporation	2,245.6
Ceridian Corporation	1,333.0
Cray Research, a Silicon Graphics Co.	676.2
Unisys Corporation	480.0

Continued on next page.

★ 798 ★ *Continued*

Computers (SIC 3571)

Largest Computer Firms - Minnesota

Firms are ranked by annual revenues in millions of dollars. Some figures are estimated.

Control Data System Inc.	$ 454.8
DataCard Corporation	360.0
National Computer Systems Inc.	348.7
Analysts International Corporation	301.9
Seagate Technology Inc.	300.0
Hutchinson Technology Inc.	300.0
AmeriData Inc.	250.0

Source: *Corporate Report Minnesota*, September 1996, p. 64.

★ 799 ★

Computers (SIC 3571)

Leading Computer Firms - 1996

Selected firms are ranked by fiscal year revenues in billions of dollars.

IBM	$ 75.00
Hewlett-Packard	38.50
Compaq	19.00
Digital Equipment	14.56
Dell	7.35
Sun Microsystems	7.09

Source: *Wall Street Journal*, October 25, 1996, p. B4, from Value Line Investment Survey, Baseline, and Disclosure.

★ 800 ★

Computers (SIC 3571)

Macintosh Computer Market

Shares are shown for the first quarter of 1997.

Apple	69.8%
Power Computing	12.0
Motorola	9.2
UMAX	7.2
Other	1.8

Source: *Macweek*, June 9, 1997, p. 32, from Dataquest Inc.

★ 801 ★

Computers (SIC 3571)

Mainframe Computer Shipments

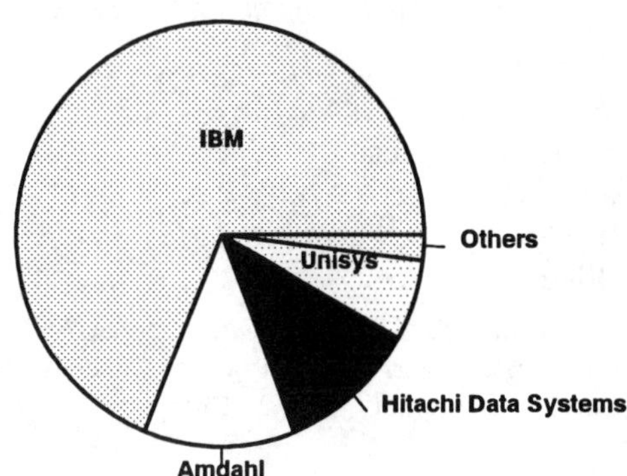

Shares are shown based on 508 mainframes shipped in 1995.

IBM	69.1%
Amdahl	11.8
Hitachi Data Systems	10.8
Unisys	6.3
Others	2.0

Source: *Computerworld*, December 16, 1996, p. 45, from International Data Corp.

★ 802 ★

Computers (SIC 3571)

Network Computer Market

The market is expected to increase from 5.83 million units in 1997 to 45.63 million units in 1999.

	1997	1999
Consumer	52.1%	85.9%
Commercial	45.3	12.6
Education	2.6	1.4

Source: *PC Week*, December 23, 1996, p. A8, from Zona Research.

★ 803 ★

Computers (SIC 3571)

Notebook Market Leaders

Shares are for the second quarter of 1996.

Toshiba	23.7%
IBM	12.9
Texas Instruments	7.8
Compaq	7.3
NEC	6.1
Other	42.2

Source: *Investor's Business Daily*, October 29, 1996, p. A4, from company reports, Forward Concepts/ICE Corp., and International Data Corp.

★ 804 ★

Computers (SIC 3571)

PC Penetration in Schools

Data show the installed base of PCs in schools for 1996-97. Figures are averages.

DOS/Windows	45.0%
MAC	34.0
Apple II	20.0
Other	1.0

Source: *Technology & Learning*, March 1997, p. 22.

★ 805 ★

Computers (SIC 3571)

PC Shipment Leaders - 1997

Shares are shown based on PC (personal computer) unit shipments estimated for the first quarter of 1997.

Compaq	13.2%
Packard Bell-NEC	11.9
Dell	8.8
IBM	8.7
Gateway 2000	6.9
Other	50.5

Source: *Computer Reseller News*, May 12, 1997, p. 21, from Dataquest Inc.

★ 806 ★

Computers (SIC 3571)

Personal and Network Computers Market

Data show the installed base of personal and network computers in the business market. In the consumer market, PCs control 45% of the market, followed by NCs with 5% and the remainder held by such devices as set-up boxes and computer games.

PCs	80.0%
NCs	20.0

Source: *Wall Street Journal*, November 22, 1996, p. B4, from Dataquest Inc. and Gartner Group.

★ 807 ★

Computers (SIC 3571)

Popular Applications on Home PCs

Data show most used applications.

Word processing	64.0%
Games and entertainment	44.0
Home finance	29.0
E-mail	28.0
Educational and reference	28.0
Spreadsheets	25.0
Accounting and finance	24.0
Faxing	23.0
On-line services	23.0
Database	21.0

Source: *Crain's Small Business*, February 1997, p. 18, from *Report to Retailers*.

★ 808 ★

Computers (SIC 3571)

Top Laptop Vendors - 1997

Companies are ranked by units shipped during the first quarter of 1997.

Toshiba	353,000
IBM	184,000
Compaq	147,000
Texas Instruments	80,000
Dell	79,000

Source: *Computerworld*, May 26, 1997, p. 41, from International Data Corp.

★ 809 ★

Computers (SIC 3571)

Top Personal Computer Makers - Canada

Shares are shown based on wholesale revenues for 1996.

IBM Canada	14.8%
Compaq Canada	11.8
Apple Canada	6.5
AST Canada	5.2
Dell Computer	5.0
Toshiba	4.4
NEC	4.2
Hewlett-Packard	2.5
Seanix	2.5
Sidus Systems	2.2
Other	40.9

Source: *Marketing Magazine*, May 26, 1997, p. 14, from International Data Corp.

★ 810 ★

Computers (SIC 3571)

Top PLD Producers

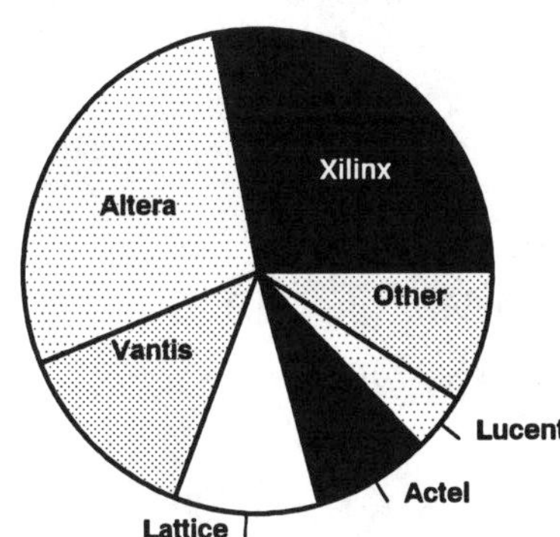

"PLD" stands for Programmable Logic Devices. Data are estimated.

	1996	1997
Xilinx	30.0%	28.0%
Altera	27.0	28.0
Vantis	13.0	13.0
Lattice	11.0	10.0
Actel	8.0	8.0
Lucent	4.0	4.0
Other	7.0	9.0

Source: *Investext*, Thomson Financial Networks, February 27, 1997, p. 18, from DMG estimates and WSTS.

★ 811 ★

Computers (SIC 3571)

Top Video Game Console Systems

Data show shipments in millions of units.

Nintendo Super NES	20.0
Sega Genesis	18.0
Sony Playstation	3.4
Nintendo 64	2.5
Sega Saturn	1.7

Source: *Investor's Business Daily*, May 6, 1997, p. A6, from International Data Corp.

★ 812 ★

Computers (SIC 3571)

U.S. Computer Market - 1996

Market shares are shown in percent.

Compaq	13.3%
Packard Bell-NEC	11.6
IBM	8.7
Dell	6.9
Apple	6.7
Other	52.8

Source: *Investor's Business Daily*, January 30, 1997, p. A6, from Dataquest Inc.

★ 813 ★

Computers (SIC 3571)

U.S. Organizer Makers

Data are for 1995.

Sharp	71.2%
Hewlett-Packard	12.8
Psion	8.6
Others	7.4

Source: *PC Week*, October 21, 1996, p. A8, from International Data Corp.

★ 814 ★

Computers (SIC 3571)

U.S. PDA Makers

Data are for 1995. PDA stands for personal digital assistant.

Apple	44.5%
Sony	22.8

Continued on next page.

★ 814 ★ *Continued*

Computers (SIC 3571)

U.S. PDA Makers

Data are for 1995. PDA stands for personal digital assistant.

Motorola	6.9%
Casio	5.3
Tandy	4.4
Sharp	3.5
AST	1.1
Other	11.5

Source: *Computer Reseller News*, December 9, 1996, p. A8, from International Data Corp.

★ 815 ★

Computers (SIC 3571)

Who Uses Multimedia Products - Mexico

Telecommunications companies	27.0%
Computer firms	25.0
Manufacturers	17.0
Financial companies	9.0
Home users	7.0
Government agencies	6.0

Source: *National Trade Data Bank*, September 9, 1996, p. ISA960801.

★ 816 ★

Workstations (SIC 3571)

U.S. Workstation Makers - 1996

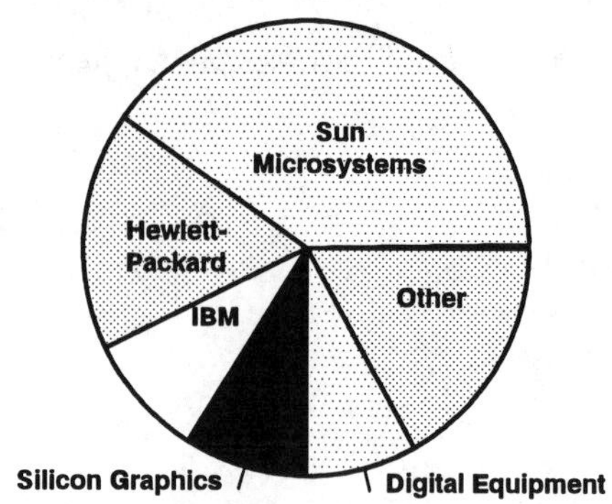

Shares are shown based on 424,6900 units shipped in 1996.

	Units	Share
Sun Microsystems	171.7	40.4%
Hewlett-Packard	71.1	16.7
IBM	40.0	9.4
Silicon Graphics	36.0	8.5
Digital Equipment	33.6	7.9
Other	72.1	17.0

Source: *Wall Street Journal*, October 29, 1996, p. B4, from Dataquest Inc.

★ 817 ★

Computer Data Storage (SIC 3572)

Disk Drive Makers - 1995

Shares are shown based on revenues.

IBM	25.6%
Seagate	19.3
Quantum	14.5
Western Digital	8.9
Conner	8.4
Fujitsu	5.2
Maxtor	4.7
Toshiba	4.2
Hewlett-Packard	2.7
NEC	2.2
Hitachi	1.9
Other	2.7

Source: *Investor's Business Daily*, June 19, 1996, p. A6, from DiskTrend Inc.

★ 818 ★

Computer Data Storage (SIC 3572)

Large Form Factor Market

Data are for 1995.

Philips LMS	41.0%
Sony	35.0
ATG Cygnet	16.0
Hitachi	8.0

Source: *Computer Technology Review*, December 1996, p. 38, from Dataquest Inc.

★ 819 ★

Computer Data Storage (SIC 3572)

Mainframe Storage Leaders

A total of 3,000 bytes was shipped in 1997.

IBM/StorageTek	47.0%
EMC	36.0
HDS	14.0
Amdahl	3.0

Source: *Computerworld*, March 17, 1997, p. 3, from Gartner Group Inc.

★ 820 ★

Computer Data Storage (SIC 3572)

OEM Storage Vendor Makers

OEM stands for original equipment manufacturers.

	Rev. ($ mil.)	Share
Data General	$ 329	30.7%
EMC	217	20.2
Symbios Logic	191	17.8
StorageTek	150	14.0
Digital	74	6.9
Others	112	10.4

Source: *Computerworld*, March 3, 1997, p. 41, from International Data Corp.

★ 821 ★

Computer Data Storage (SIC 3572)

Rigid Disk Drive Vendors - 1996

Market shares are shown based on unit sales.

Seagate Technology	27.5%
Quantum	22.2
Western Digital	18.4
IBM	10.5
Maxtor	5.8
Other	15.6

Source: *Computer Reseller News*, March 31, 1997, p. 19, from Dataquest Inc.

★ 822 ★

Computer Data Storage (SIC 3572)

Tape Storage Systems - 1996

Hewlett-Packard	27.0%
Seagate	18.0
Quantum	16.0
Exabyte	15.0
Tandberg	7.0
Sony	6.0
Iomega	5.0
Others	6.0

Source: *Investor's Business Daily*, January 16, 1997, p. A6, from Freeman Associates Inc.

★ 823 ★

Computer Monitors (SIC 3575)

Computer Monitor Shipments

Color	98.95%
Monochrome	1.05

Source: *Dealerscope*, December 1996, p. 32, from Stanford Resources Inc.

★ 824 ★

Computer Monitors (SIC 3575)

Monitor Shipments by Size

15"	41.27%
14"	31.89
17"	24.16
more than 20"	1.38
20"	1.12
Less than 14"	0.19

Source: *Computer Reseller News*, January 6, 1997, p. 137, from Standard Resources Inc.

★ 825 ★

Computer Terminals (SIC 3575)

Text Terminal Makers - 1995

Wyse	46.0%
SunRiver	35.0
Hewlett-Packard	6.0
Other	13.0

Source: http:// www.sunriver.com/srovr/ sunstrat.htm#two, January 27, 1997, p. 7, from International Data Corp.

★ 826 ★

Computer Peripherals (SIC 3577)

Top CD-R Writer Producers - 1996

Companies are ranked by unit sales.

	Units	Share
Philips	173,000	20.91%
Hewlett-Packard	141,000	17.03
Yamaha	133,000	16.11
JVC	79,000	9.56
Sony	74,000	8.99
Ricoh	50,000	6.08
S&F	44,000	5.31
Pinnacle	33,000	4.01
Other	99,000	12.00

Source: *E-Media Professional*, June 1997, p. 33, from Santa Clara Consulting Group.

★ 827 ★

Computer Printers (SIC 3577)

Color Laser Printer Makers

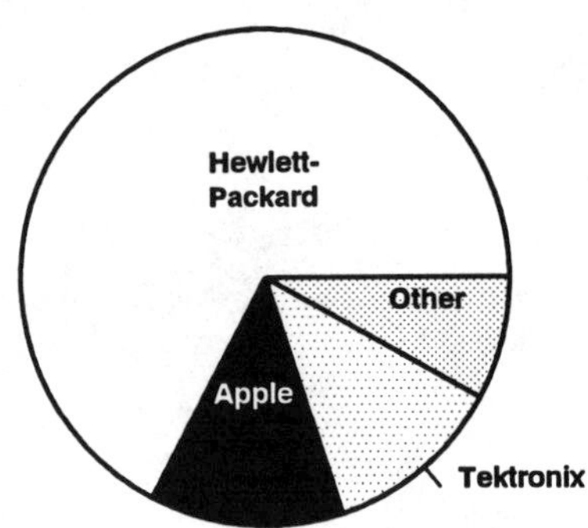

Shares are shown for the first eight months of 1996.

Hewlett-Packard	67.5%
Apple	13.0
Tektronix	12.0
Other	7.5

Source: *Computer Reseller News*, November 11, 1996, p. 181, from Computer Intelligence InfoCorp.

★ 828 ★

Computer Printers (SIC 3577)

Computer Printer Market

Data show who controls the office printer market.

Hewlett-Packard	49.1%
Apple	8.9
Epson	8.0
IBM	7.9
Panasonic	4.9
Canon	2.3
Other	18.8

Source: *Electronic News*, August 26, 1996, p. 44, from Consumer Intelligence Consumer Technology Index.

★ 829 ★

Computer Printers (SIC 3577)

Computer Printer Sales - Canada

Data forecast sales in millions of Canadian dollars for 1997 and 1998. Shares are estimated for 1998.

	1997 ($ mil.)	1998 ($ mil.)	Share
Laser	$ 376	$ 445	64.2%
Inkjet	219	207	29.9
Dot matrix	36	32	4.6
Line impact	10	9	1.3

Source: *Computing Canada*, April 14, 1997, p. 38, from Evans Research.

★ 830 ★

Computer Printers (SIC 3577)

Computer Printer Unit Sales

Data are for the year ended August 1996.

Color ink jet	66.0%
Page/laser/LED	24.0
Dot matrix/24-pin	4.0
Dot matrix/9-pin	4.0
Mono ink jet	3.0

Source: *Dealerscope*, December 1996, p. 32, from Computer Intelligence InfoCorp.

★ 831 ★

Computer Printers (SIC 3577)

Home Printer Market - Canada

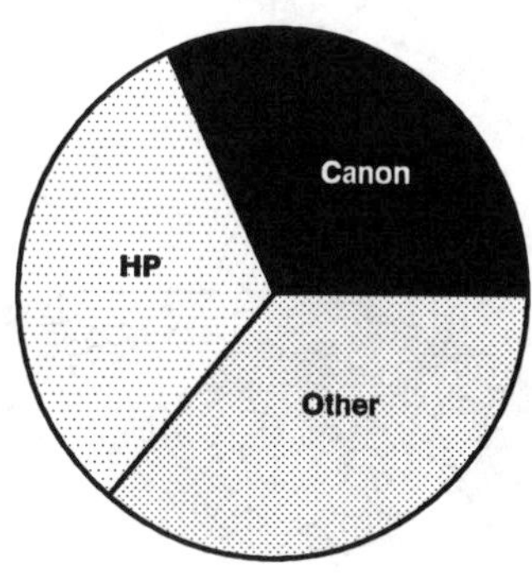

Shares of the $295 million market are shown in percent.

Canon	32.0%
HP	32.2
Other	35.8

Source: *Marketing Magazine*, December 30, 1996, p. 1.

★ 832 ★

Computer Printers (SIC 3577)

Inkjet Printer Shipments - 1995

Shipments of color and monchrome inkjet printers are shown in thousands of units.

Hewlett-Packard	4,100
Canon	2,300
Apple	990
Epson	547
Lexmark	340

Source: *Computer Reseller News*, September 2, 1996, p. 81, from International Data Corp.

★ 833 ★

Computer Printers (SIC 3577)

Mac Inkjet Market - 1995

Apple (Canon)	70.0%
HP Deskwriters	27.0
Others	3.0

Source: *Macweek*, September 16, 1996, p. 1, from Lyra Research Inc.

★ 834 ★

Automated Teller Machines (SIC 3578)

ATM Makers - 1996

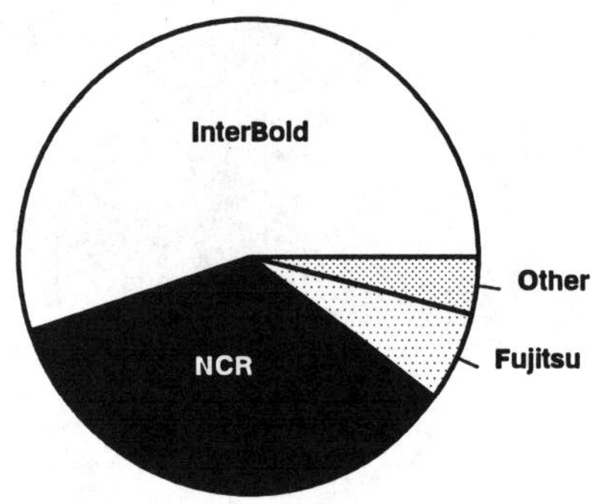

Shares are shown based on units.

InterBold	55.0%
NCR	35.0
Fujitsu	6.0
Other	4.0

Source: *Investor's Business Daily*, April 3, 1997, p. A6, from Mentis Corp.

★ 835 ★

Postage Meters (SIC 3579)

Postage Meter Makers

Pitney Bowes	85.0%
Others	15.0

Source: *Forbes*, February 24, 1997, p. 108.

★ 836 ★

Heating and Cooling (SIC 3585)

A/C Heat Pumps Makers

Shares are shown based on a total of 5,088,061 units shipped in 1995.

Carrier	20.0%
Goodman	16.0
Rheem	13.0
Trane	12.0
Inter-City Products	9.0
York	9.0%
Lennox	5.0
Amana	3.0
Others	3.0

Source: *Appliance*, September 1996, p. 86, from industry sources and market analysts.

★ 837 ★

Heating and Cooling (SIC 3585)

Air Conditioner Sales by Region - 1996

Distribution is shown based on unit sales.

Mid-Atlantic	26.0%
Northeast Central	17.5
South Central	15.9
Soutwest Central	10.6
New England	7.6
Southeast Central	6.8
Northwest Central	6.6
Pacific	5.5
Mountain	3.5

Source: *Dealerscope*, April 1997, p. 32, from Association of Home Appliance Manufacturers.

★ 838 ★

Heating and Cooling (SIC 3585)

Gas Furnace Makers

Shares are shown based on a total of 2,600,967 units shipped in 1995.

Carrier	21.0%
Goodman	14.0
Rheem	13.0
Lennox	11.0
Inter-City Products	10.0
Trane	10.0
York	10.0
Amana	3.0
Consolidated Industries	3.0
Nordyne	3.0
Ducane	2.0

Source: *Appliance*, September 1996, p. 86, from industry sources and market analysts.

★ 839 ★

Heating and Cooling (SIC 3585)

Ice Machine Makers

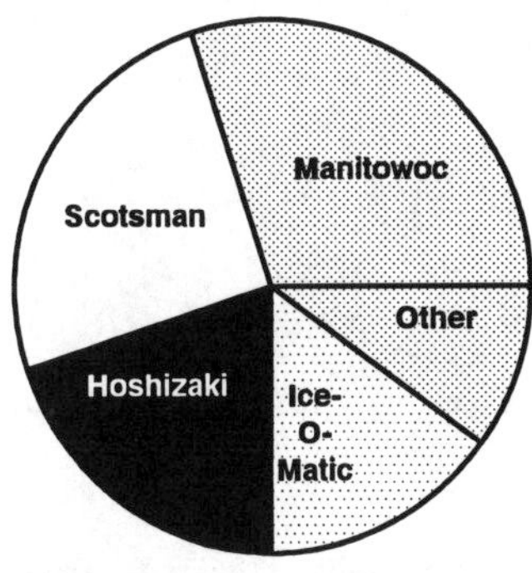

Shares are shown in percent.

Manitowoc	30.0%
Scotsman	25.0
Hoshizaki	20.0
Ice-O-Matic	15.0
Other	10.0

Source: *Air Conditioning, Heating & Refrigeration News*, November 11, 1996, p. 13, from Arthur D. Little Co.

★ 840 ★

Heating and Cooling (SIC 3585)

Largest Beverage Merchandisers

Shares are shown in percent.

Beverage-Air	45.0%
True Mfg.	45.0
Other	10.0

Source: *Air Conditioning, Heating & Refrigeration News*, November 11, 1996, p. 13, from Arthur D. Little Co.

★ 841 ★

Heating and Cooling (SIC 3585)

Leading Room Air Conditioner Brands

Shares are shown based on shipments of 4,824,600 units in 1996.

Fedders	18.1%
Kenmore	17.6
GE/GE Profile	9.8
Whirlpool	9.0%
Emerson Quiet Kool	4.9
Friedrich	4.8
Carrier	4.5
White-Westinghouse	3.9
Amana	3.8
Goldstar	3.0
Panasonic	2.2
Frigidaire	2.1
Sharp	2.1
Montgomery Ward	1.5
Roper	1.3
Airtemp	1.1
Gibson	1.1
Crosley	1.0
Goodman	0.9
Quasar	0.8
Other	6.5

Source: *HFN*, March 10, 1997, p. 67, from Association of Home Appliance Manufacturers.

★ 842 ★

Heating and Cooling (SIC 3585)

Reach-In Display Case Makers

Shares are shown in percent.

True Mfg.	20.0%
Beverage-Air	14.0
Dellfield	10.0
Hobart	6.0
Other	50.0

Source: *Air Conditioning, Heating & Refrigeration News*, November 11, 1996, p. 13, from Arthur D. Little Co.

★ 843 ★

Heating and Cooling (SIC 3585)

Refrigerated Display Case Makers

Shares are shown in percent.

Hussmann	40.0%
Hill/Phoenix	21.0
Kysor/Warren	16.0
Tyler	11.0
Other	12.0

Source: *Air Conditioning, Heating & Refrigeration News*, November 11, 1996, p. 13, from Arthur D. Little Co.

★ 844 ★

Heating and Cooling (SIC 3585)

Refrigerated Vending Machine Makers

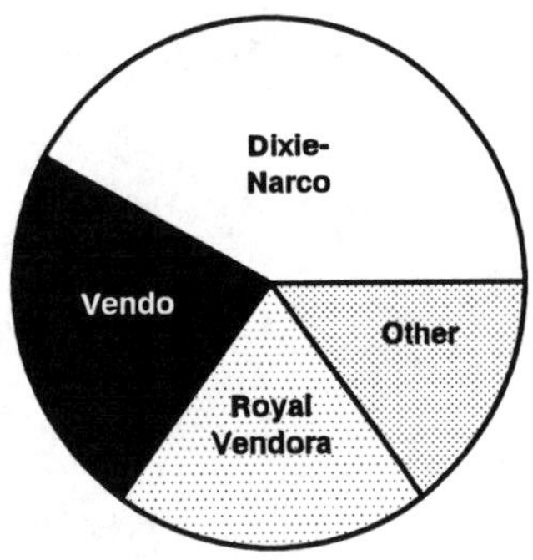

Shares are shown in percent.

Dixie-Narco	42.0%
Vendo	23.0
Royal Vendora	20.0
Other	15.0

Source: *Air Conditioning, Heating & Refrigeration News*, November 11, 1996, p. 13, from Arthur D. Little Co.

★ 845 ★

Heating and Cooling (SIC 3585)

Top Air Conditioner Brands

Shares are shown for the North American market.

Fedders	25.0%
Whirlpool	23.0
Electrolux	22.0
Friedrich	6.0
Matsushita	6.0
Raytheon	6.0
Other	12.0

Source: *Investext,* Thomson Financial Networks, December 4, 1996, p. 30, from *Appliance*.

★ 846 ★

Heating and Cooling (SIC 3585)

U.S. Dehumidifier Makers

Shares are shown based on a total of 1,002,800 units shipped in 1995.

Whirlpool	31.0%
Electrolux (Frigidaire)	29.0
MCD	15.0
Fedders	6.0
W.C. Wood	6.0
Samsung	4.0
Ebco	3.0
Others	6.0

Source: *Appliance*, September 1996, p. 86, from industry sources and market analysts.

★ 847 ★

Industrial Cleaning Equipment (SIC 3589)

Shampooers/Steam Cleaner Market

Shares are shown based a total of 1,825,000 units shipped in 1995.

Bissell	52.0%
Hoover	29.0
Regina	9.0
Sears/Kenmore	8.0
Others	2.0

Source: *Appliance*, September 1996, p. 86, from industry sources and market analysts.

★ 848 ★

Industrial Cleaning Equipment (SIC 3589)

Wet/Dry Vacuum Market

Shares are shown based a total of 3,800,000 units shipped in 1995.

Shop Vac	50.0%
Sears/Kenmore	32.0
Genie	8.0
Hoover	5.0
Royal	3.0
Others	2.0

Source: *Appliance*, September 1996, p. 86, from industry sources and market analysts.

★ 849 ★

Electronics (SIC 3600)

Home Information Products Market - 1996

Distribution is shown based on factory sales.

Personal computers	57.0%
Peripherals	18.0
Software	12.0
Telephones	6.0
Phone answering systems	3.5
Fax machines	2.5
Word processors	1.0

Source: *Investor's Business Daily*, May 21, 1997, p. A6, from Consumer Electronics Manufacturers Association.

★ 850 ★

Household Appliances (SIC 3630)

Appliance Industry Makers

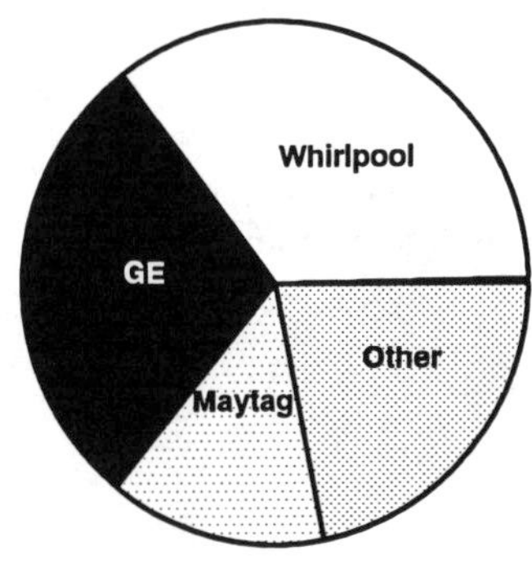

Shares of the $13 billion market are shown in percent.

Whirlpool	35.0%
GE	29.0
Maytag	14.0
Other	22.0

Source: *Forbes*, March 10, 1997, p. 66.

★ 851 ★

Household Appliances (SIC 3630)

Major Appliance Market by Segment - Canada

Data show unit sales estimated for 1997.

Refrigerators	733,000
Microwave ovens	685,000
Automatic washers	577,000
Electric ranges	472,000
Dishwashers	380,000
Freezers	220,000
Disposers	75,000
Room air conditioners	75,000
Gas ranges	52,000
Cooktops	41,000
Gas dryers	32,000

Source: *Appliance Manufacturer*, February 1997, pp. G-23, from Canadian Appliance Manufacturers Association.

★ 852 ★

Household Appliances (SIC 3630)

Top Core Appliance Manufacturers - 1995

Company shares are based on shipments. "Core appliances" include dishwashers, gas and electric dryers, gas and electric ranges, refrigerators, and washers.

Whirlpool	35.1%
General Electric	27.6
Maytag	15.2
Electrolux	13.9
Raytheon	6.5
Other	1.7

Source: *Investext*, Thomson Financial Networks, October 8, 1996, p. 11, from *Appliance Magazine*.

★ 853 ★

Cooking Equipment (SIC 3631)

Leading Electric Range Brands - 1996

Shares are shown based on shipments of 4,280,600 units in 1996.

GE/GE Profile	25.7%
Kenmore	17.1
Whirlpool	14.4
Maytag	5.9
Hotpoint	5.4
Magic Chef	4.9
Amana	4.3
Frigidaire	4.1
Tappan	3.1
Roper	2.7
KitchenAid	2.3
White-Westinghouse	2.2
Caloric	1.5
RCA	1.4
Other	5.0

Source: *HFN*, March 10, 1997, p. 66, from Association of Home Appliance Manufacturers.

★ 854 ★

Cooking Equipment (SIC 3631)

Leading Gas Range Brands - 1996

Shares are shown based on units sold.

General Electric	21.0%
Sears	21.0
Tappan	10.0
Magic Chef	9.0
Whirlpool	6.5
Hotpoint	6.0
Amana	5.0
Maytag	5.0
Caloric	4.0
Frigidaire	2.0
Roper	2.0
Admiral	1.0
Crosley	1.0
Kitchen Aid	1.0
RCA	1.0
White Westinghouse	1.0
Montgomery Ward	0.2
Other	3.3

Source: *Dealerscope*, April 1997, p. 31, from Association of Home Appliance Manufacturers.

★ 855 ★

Cooking Equipment (SIC 3631)

Leading Microwave Oven Brands

Shares are shown based on shipments of 9,318,100 units in 1996.

Sharp	25.8%
GE/GE Profile	14.5
Kenmore	11.8
Panasonic	10.7
Magic Chef	4.8
Samsung	4.6
Goldstar	4.2
Emerson Radio	4.1
Whirlpool	4.0
Tappan	3.5
Amana	2.8
Sanyo	2.3
Quasar	1.0
Other	5.9

Source: *HFN*, March 10, 1997, p. 67, from Association of Home Appliance Manufacturers.

★ 856 ★

Cooking Equipment (SIC 3631)

North America's Gas Range Market

Shares are shown for the North American market.

GE	26.0%
Electrolux	22.0
Maytag	22.0
Raytheon	20.0
Other	10.0

Source: *Investext*, Thomson Financial Networks, December 4, 1996, p. 30, from *Appliance*.

★ 857 ★

Cooking Equipment (SIC 3631)

Outdoor Appliance Market

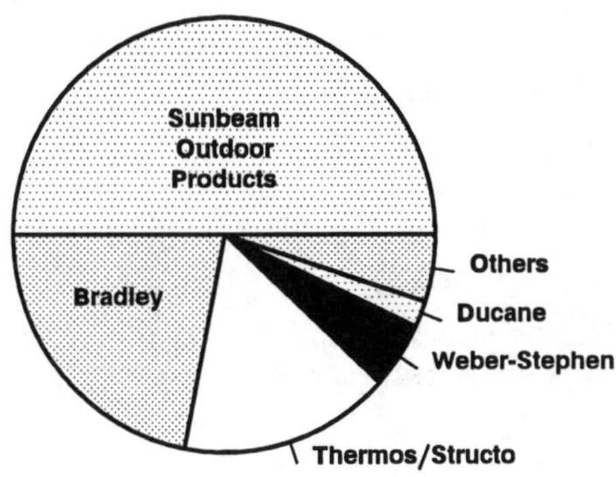

Shares are shown based a total of 4,900,000 units shipped in 1995.

Sunbeam Outdoor Products	50.0%
Bradley	22.0
Thermos/Structo	16.0
Weber-Stephen	5.0
Ducane	2.0
Others	5.0

Source: *Appliance*, September 1996, p. 87, from industry sources and market analysts.

★ 858 ★

Cooking Equipment (SIC 3631)

Range Hood Makers

Shares are shown based a total of 2,740,000 units shipped in 1995.

Broan/Rangaire	73.0%
Nutone	15.0
Watertown Metal Products	11.0
Others	1.0

Source: *Appliance*, September 1996, p. 87, from industry sources and market analysts.

★ 859 ★

Cooking Equipment (SIC 3631)

Top Electric Range Brands

Shares are shown for the North American market.

GE	41.0%
Whirlpool	22.0
Electrolux	14.0
Maytag	14.0
Raytheon	7.0

Source: *Investext*, Thomson Financial Networks, December 4, 1996, p. 30, from *Appliance*.

★ 860 ★

Cooking Equipment (SIC 3631)

Top Gas Range Brands - 1996

Shares are shown based on shipments of 2,830,000 units in 1996.

GE/GE Profile	21.1%
Kenmore	20.8
Tappan	10.1
Magic Chef	8.8
Whirlpool	7.4
Caloric	5.5
Hotpoint	4.9
Maytag	4.9
Amana	2.5
Frigidaire	2.1
Roper	1.6
White-Westinghouse	1.1
Admiral	0.9
Crosley	0.8
KitchenAid	0.8
Premier	0.8
Other	5.9

Source: *HFN*, March 10, 1997, p. 66, from Association of Home Appliance Manufacturers.

★ 861 ★

Cooking Equipment (SIC 3631)

Top Gas Range Manufacturers - Mexico

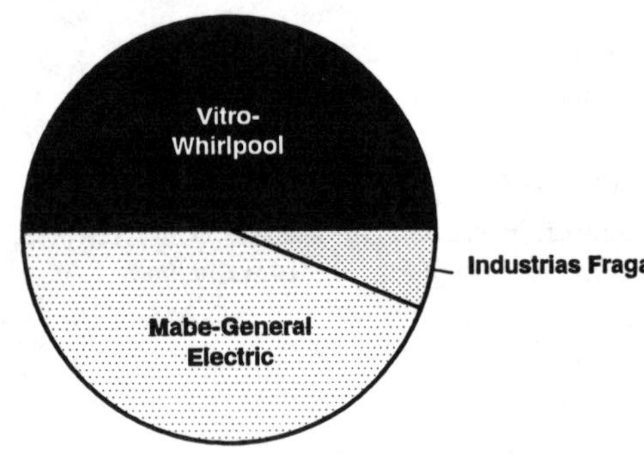

Shares are shown for 1995.

Vitro-Whirlpool	50.0%
Mabe-General Electric	44.0
Industrias Fraga	6.0

Source: *Appliance Manufacturer*, February 1997, pp. G-23, from Consorcio Industrial De Comercio.

★ 862 ★

Cooking Equipment (SIC 3631)

Top Microwave Oven Brands

Shares are shown for the North American market.

Sharp	24.0%
Matsushita	14.0
Samsung	13.0
Goldstar	9.0
MCD	6.0
Sanyo	6.0
Other	28.0

Source: *Investext*, Thomson Financial Networks, December 4, 1996, p. 30, from *Appliance*.

★ 863 ★

Refrigerators and Freezers (SIC 3632)

Industrial Refrigerator Market

Shares are shown based a total of 123,000 units shipped in 1995. Data refer to compact, built-in and undercounter units.

U-Line	58.0%
Marvel Industries	27.0
Sub-Zero Freezer	12.0
Others	3.0

Source: *Appliance*, September 1996, p. 87, from industry sources and market analysts.

★ 864 ★

Refrigerators and Freezers (SIC 3632)

Leading Freezer Brands - 1996

Shares are shown based on unit sales.

Sears/Kenmore	33.0%
GE Appliances	11.5
Frigidaire	8.0
Whirlpool	8.0
Tappan	6.5
White Westinghouse	6.0
Roper	5.0
Kelvinator	4.0
Amana	3.5
Gibson	3.5
W.C. Wood Co.	2.0
Holiday	1.5
Crosley	1.0
Danby Products	1.0
Hotpoint	1.0
Maytag	1.0
Other	3.5

Source: *Dealerscope*, April 1997, p. 33, from Association of Home Appliance Manufacturers.

★ 865 ★

Refrigerators and Freezers (SIC 3632)

Leading Refrigerator Makers - Mexico

Shares are shown for 1995.

Mabe-General Electric	57.0%
Vitro-Whirlpool	43.0

Source: *Appliance Manufacturer*, February 1997, pp. G-23, from Consorcio Industrial De Comercio.

★ 866 ★

Refrigerators and Freezers (SIC 3632)

Refrigerator Brand Leaders

Shares are shown for the North American market.

GE	38.0%
Whirlpool	27.0
Electrolux	15.0
Maytag	10.0
Raytheon	9.0

Source: *Investext,* Thomson Financial Networks, December 4, 1996, p. 30, from *Appliance*.

★ 867 ★

Refrigerators and Freezers (SIC 3632)

Top Refrigerator Brands - 1996

Shares are shown based on shipments of 9,045,000 units in 1996.

Kenmore	23.5%
GE/GE Profile	18.3
Whirlpool	10.9
Amana	10.1
Frigidaire	6.2
Hotpoint	5.5
Maytag	3.5
Admiral	2.9
KitchenAid	2.8
Roper	2.7
Magic Chef	2.2
White-Westinghouse	1.6
Kelvinator	1.3
RCA	1.1
Gibson	0.9
Crosley	0.8
Other	5.7

Source: *HFN*, March 10, 1997, p. 66, from Association of Home Appliance Manufacturers.

★ 868 ★

Refrigerators and Freezers (SIC 3632)

U.S. Compact Refrigerator Market

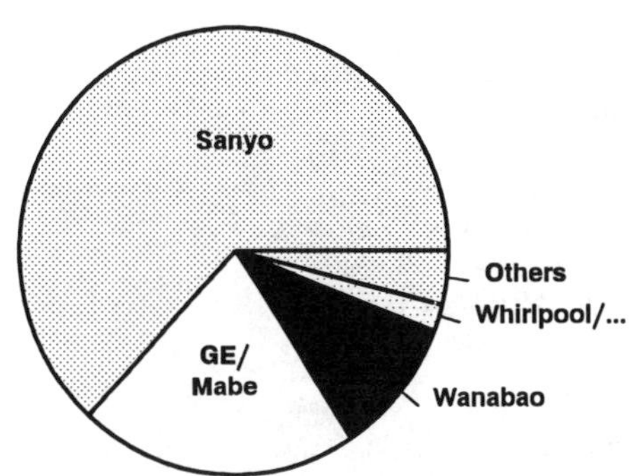

Shares are shown based a total of 1,032,000 units shipped in 1995.

Sanyo	63.0%
GE/Mabe	21.0
Wanabao	10.0
Whirlpool/Consul	2.0
Others	4.0

Source: *Appliance*, September 1996, p. 87, from industry sources and market analysts.

★ 869 ★

Refrigerators and Freezers (SIC 3632)

U.S. Freezer Market

Shares are shown based a total of 1,690,500 units shipped in 1995.

Electrolux (Frigidaire)	67.0%
W.C. Wood	30.0
Sanyo	1.0
Whirlpool	1.0
Others	1.0

Source: *Appliance*, September 1996, p. 87, from industry sources and market analysts.

★ 870 ★

Laundry Equipment (SIC 3633)

Leading Automatic Washer Brands - 1996

Shares are shown based on shipments of 7,128,800 units in 1996.

Kenmore	30.3%
Whirlpool	21.4
Maytag	14.5
GE/GE Profile	13.9
Amana	3.9
Roper	3.1
Frigidaire	2.5
Hotpoint	2.1
White-Westinghouse	1.8
Admiral	1.6
KitchenAid	1.5
Crosley	0.8
Magic Chef	0.8
Speed Queen	0.8
Other	1.0

Source: *HFN*, March 10, 1997, p. 66, from Association of Home Appliance Manufacturers.

★ 871 ★

Laundry Equipment (SIC 3633)

Leading Washing Machine Makers - Mexico

Shares are shown for 1995.

Mabe-General Electric	57.0%
Vitro-Whirlpool	28.0
Hoover Mexicana	12.0
Koblenz Electrica	3.0

Source: *Appliance Manufacturer*, February 1997, pp. G-23, from Consorcio Industrial De Comercio.

★ 872 ★

Laundry Equipment (SIC 3633)

Top Clothes Washer Brands

Shares are shown for the North American market.

Whirlpool	53.0%
GE	17.0
Maytag	17.0
Electrolux	11.0
Raytheon	2.0

Source: *Investext*, Thomson Financial Networks, December 4, 1996, p. 30, from *Appliance*.

★ 873 ★

Laundry Equipment (SIC 3633)

Top Electric Dryer Brands

Shares are shown for the North American market.

Whirlpool	52.0%
GE	19.0
Maytag	15.0
Electrolux	10.0
Raytheon	5.0

Source: *Investext*, Thomson Financial Networks, December 4, 1996, p. 30, from *Appliance*.

★ 874 ★

Laundry Equipment (SIC 3633)

Top Gas Dryer Brands

Shares are shown for the North American market.

Whirlpool	53.0%
GE	15.0
Maytag	14.0
Electrolux	12.0
Raytheon	6.0

Source: *Investext*, Thomson Financial Networks, December 4, 1996, p. 30, from *Appliance*.

★ 875 ★

Laundry Equipment (SIC 3633)

Washing Machine Brand Shares - 1996

Shares are shown based on unit sales.

Sears/Kenmore	29.0%
Whirlpool	22.0

Continued on next page.

★ 875 ★ *Continued*

Laundry Equipment (SIC 3633)

Washing Machine Brand Shares - 1996

Shares are shown based on unit sales.

General Electric	14.0%
Maytag	14.0
Amana	5.0
Roper	2.5
Frigidaire	2.1
Admiral	2.0
Hotpoint	2.0
White Westinghouse	2.0
KitchenAid	1.0
Speed Queen	1.0
Magic Chef	1.0
Gibson	0.7
Tappan	0.5
Montgomery Ward	0.5
Crosley	0.5
Kelvinator	0.2

Source: *Dealerscope*, April 1997, p. 33, from Association of Home Appliance Manufacturers.

★ 876 ★

Household Appliances (SIC 3634)

Blender Market

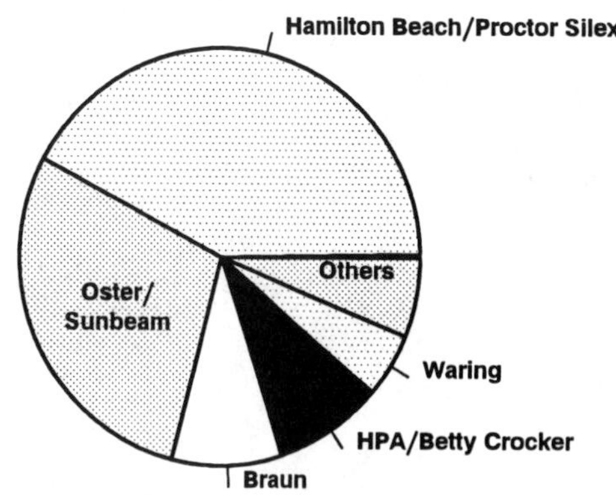

Market shares are shown based on 5,770,000 units shipped in 1995.

Hamilton Beach/Proctor Silex	42.0%
Oster/Sunbeam	29.0
Braun	9.0
HPA/Betty Crocker	9.0
Waring	5.0
Others	6.0

Source: *Appliance*, September 1996, p. 88, from industry sources.

★ 877 ★

Household Appliances (SIC 3634)

Can Opener Manufacturers

Market shares are shown based on 6,810,000 units shipped in 1995.

Rival	26.0%
Hamilton Beach/Proctor Silex	20.0
Black & Decker	15.0
Oster/Sunbeam	13.0
HPA/Betty Crocker	8.0
Presto	4.0
Waring	4.0
Others	10.0

Source: *Appliance*, September 1996, p. 88, from industry sources.

★ 878 ★

Household Appliances (SIC 3634)

Coffee Machine Leaders

Market shares are shown based on 15.5 million units shipped in 1995.

Mr. Coffee	30.0%
Hamilton Beach/Proctor Silex	20.0
Black & Decker	10.0
Braun	10.0
West Bend	7.0
Bunn	5.0
Regal	5.0
Krups	4.0
Others	9.0

Source: *Appliance*, September 1996, p. 88, from industry sources.

★ 879 ★

Household Appliances (SIC 3634)

Electric Knife Leaders

Market shares are shown based on 1.55 million units shipped in 1995.

Black & Decker	29.0%
Hamilton Beach/Proctor Silex	26.0
Toastmaster	19.0
Regal	10.0
HPA/Betty Crocker	7.0
Oster/Sunbeam	5.0
Others	4.0

Source: *Appliance*, September 1996, p. 88, from industry sources.

★ 880 ★

Household Appliances (SIC 3634)

Food Chopper Leaders

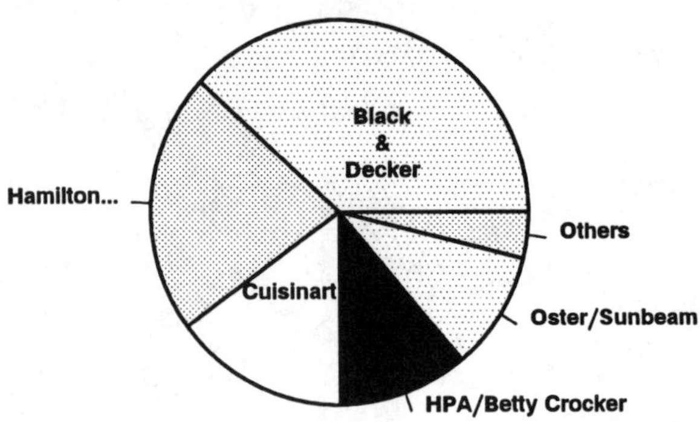

Market shares are shown based on 1.4 million units shipped in 1995.

Black & Decker	38.0%
Hamilton Beach/Proctor Silex	22.0
Cuisinart	15.0
HPA/Betty Crocker	11.0
Oster/Sunbeam	10.0
Others	4.0

Source: *Appliance*, September 1996, p. 88, from industry sources.

★ 881 ★

Household Appliances (SIC 3634)

Hand Mixer Leaders

Market shares are shown based on 5.5 million units shipped in 1995.

Hamilton Beach/Proctor Silex	21.0%
Black & Decker	15.0
Oster/Sunbeam	14.0
HPA/Betty Crocker	11.0
KitchenAid	8.0
West Bend	8.0
Rival	5.0
Toastmaster	5.0
Cuisinart	4.0
Waring	4.0
Others	5.0

Source: *Appliance*, September 1996, p. 88, from industry sources.

★ 882 ★

Household Appliances (SIC 3634)

Kitchen Electrics Sales

Unit sales are for the year ending September 1995 and 1996.

	1995	1996
Coffee makers/espresso makers	13,279	12,610
Irons	11,300	10,439
Toasters	8,595	7,919
Microwave ovens	8,561	7,725
Blenders	5,32	5,260
Mixers	5,499	4,976
Food processors	3,095	2,974
Bread makers	1,648	1,754
Citrus juicers	379	355
Juice extractors	451	314

Source: *Stores*, January 1997, p. 5.

★ 883 ★

Household Appliances (SIC 3634)

Leading Waffle Iron Makers

Market shares are shown in 1995.

Toastmaster	47.0%
Dazey	16.0
Oster/Sunbeam	13.0
Black & Decker	9.0
HPA/Betty Crocker	9.0
Others	6.0

Source: *Appliance*, September 1996, p. 88, from industry sources.

★ 884 ★

Household Appliances (SIC 3634)

Top Toaster Makers

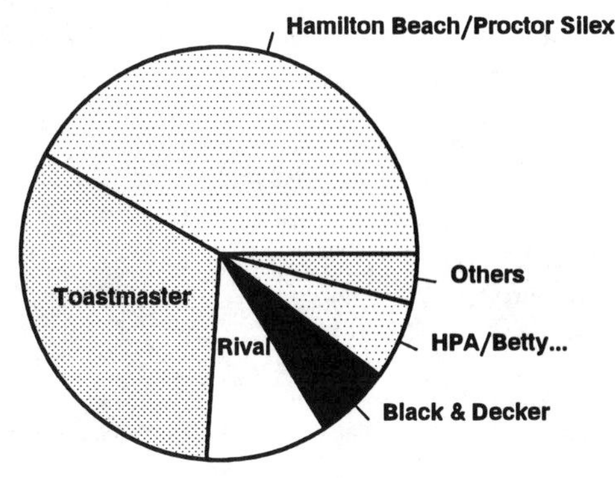

Market shares are shown based on 10,626,000 units shipped in 1995.

Hamilton Beach/Proctor Silex	42.0%
Toastmaster	32.0
Rival	10.0
Black & Decker	6.0
HPA/Betty Crocker	6.0
Others	4.0

Source: *Appliance*, September 1996, p. 88, from industry sources.

★ 885 ★

Household Appliances (SIC 3634)

U.S. Breadmaker Market

Market shares are shown based on 2,678,000 units shipped in 1995.

Welbilt	24.0%
West Bend	15.0
Hitachi	11.0
Oster/Sunbeam	11.0
Toastmaster	11.0
HPA/Betty Crocker	6.0
Regal	6.0
Black & Decker	5.0
Panasonic	5.0
Others	6.0

Source: *Appliance*, September 1996, p. 88, from industry sources.

★ 886 ★

Household Appliances (SIC 3634)

U.S. Iron Makers

Market shares are shown based on 15.58 million units shipped in 1995.

Black & Decker	38.0%
Hamilton Beach/Proctor Silex	30.0
Oster/Sunbeam	16.0
N.A.P.	6.0
Rowenta	3.0
Singer	1.0
Others	6.0

Source: *Appliance*, September 1996, p. 88, from industry sources.

★ 887 ★

Personal Care Appliances (SIC 3634)

Beard/Moustache Trimmer Market

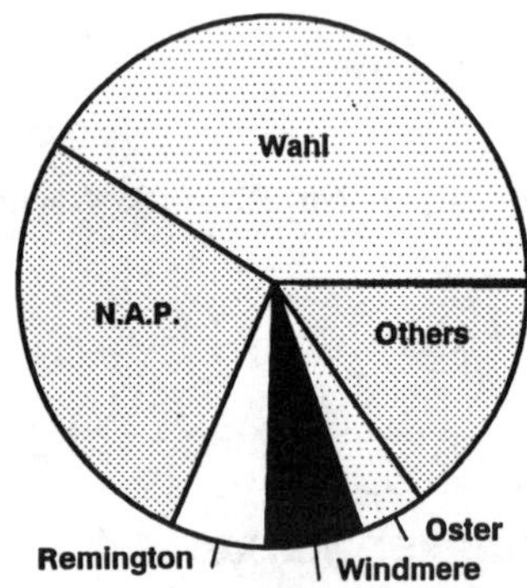

Shares are shown based a total of 2,460,000 units shipped in 1995.

Wahl	41.0%
N.A.P.	27.0
Remington	6.0
Windmere	6.0
Oster	4.0
Others	15.0

Source: *Appliance*, September 1996, p. 87, from industry sources and market analysts.

★ 888 ★

Personal Care Appliances (SIC 3634)

Curling Iron Market

Shares are shown based a total of 13,785,000 units shipped in 1995.

Conair	34.0%
Helen of Troy	18.0
Windmere	16.0
Revlon	6.0
Others	26.0

Source: *Appliance*, September 1996, p. 87, from industry sources and market analysts.

★ 889 ★

Personal Care Appliances (SIC 3634)

Hand-Held Hair Dryer Market

Shares are shown based a total of 21,503,000 units shipped in 1995.

Conair	40.0%
Helen of Troy	25.0
Windmere	11.0
Remington/Clairol	6.0
Revlon	5.0
Others	13.0

Source: *Appliance*, September 1996, p. 87, from industry sources and market analysts.

★ 890 ★

Personal Care Appliances (SIC 3634)

Lighted Make-Up Mirrors Market

Shares are shown based a total of 1.0 million units shipped in 1995.

Remington/Clairol	28.0%
Conair	19.0
Windmere	18.0
Hartman	12.0
Revlon	4.0
Others	19.0

Source: *Appliance*, September 1996, p. 87, from industry sources and market analysts.

★891★

Personal Care Appliances (SIC 3634)

Men's Shaver Market

Shares are shown based a total of 6,940,000 units shipped in 1995.

N.A.P.	52.0%
Remington	24.0
Braun	17.0
Matsushita	8.0
Others	1.0

Source: *Appliance*, September 1996, p. 87, from industry sources and market analysts.

★892★

Personal Care Appliances (SIC 3634)

Personal Care Appliance Sales

Data are for the year ended September 1995 and 1996.

	1995	1996
Electric razors	329,288	309,529
Hair dryers	233,506	205,320
Curling irons	117,893	148,762
Oral care	99,068	99,508
Electric massagers	85,888	83,570

Source: *Stores*, January 1997, p. 7.

★893★

Personal Care Appliances (SIC 3634)

Popular Personal Care Appliance Brands

Data show the personal care appliance brands preferred by shoppers at discount stores in 1996.

Conair	35.0%
Vidal Sassoon	15.0
Norelco	12.0
Remington	10.0
General Electric	9.0
Braun	7.0
Clairol	4.0
Gillette	4.0
Water-Pik	4.0
Schick	3.0
Windmere	3.0

Source: *Discount Store News*, October 21, 1996, p. 83, from Lee J. Shapiro & Associates.

★894★

Personal Care Appliances (SIC 3634)

Women's Shaver Market

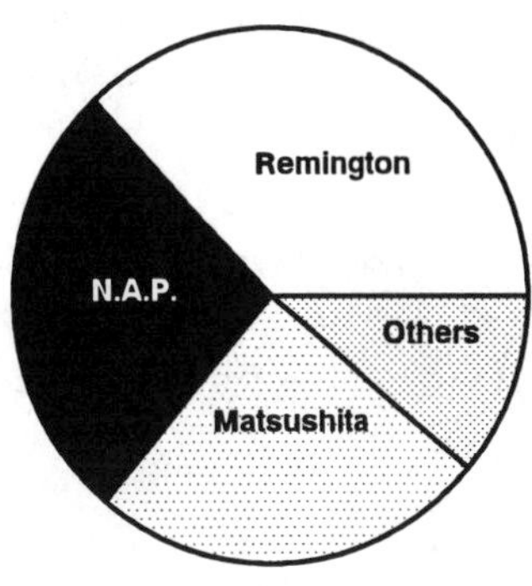

Shares are shown based a total of 2,070,000 units shipped in 1995.

Remington	37.0%
N.A.P.	27.0
Matsushita	25.0
Others	11.0

Source: *Appliance*, September 1996, p. 87, from industry sources and market analysts.

★895★

Vaccum Cleaners (SIC 3635)

Vacuum Cleaner Brand Shares - 1996

Market shares are shown based on unit sales.

Hoover	25.0%
Eureka	20.5
Royal	14.0
Sears/Kenmore	9.0
Oreck	4.5
Fantom	4.0
Kirby	3.5
Singer	3.5
Panasonic	2.5
Sharp	2.0
Shop Vac	2.0
Bissell	1.5
Electrolux	1.5
Rainbow	1.5
Regina	1.0
Black & Decker	0.5
Tri-Star	0.5
Miele	0.3
Amway	0.2

Continued on next page.

★ 895 ★ *Continued*

Vaccum Cleaners (SIC 3635)

Vacuum Cleaner Brand Shares - 1996

Market shares are shown based on unit sales.

Nutone	0.2%
Genie	0.2
Other	2.1

Source: *Dealerscope*, April 1997, p. 32, from Association of Home Appliance Manufacturers.

★ 896 ★

Vacuum Cleaners (SIC 3635)

Vacuum Cleaner Market - Full-Size

Shares are shown based a total of 14,897,000 units shipped in 1995.

Hoover	32.0%
Eureka	23.0
Royal	12.0
Matsushita	10.0
Kirby	4.0
Electrolux	3.0
Ryobi (Singer)	3.0
Bissell	2.0
Regina	2.0
Others	9.0

Source: *Appliance*, September 1996, p. 86, from industry sources and market analysts.

★ 897 ★

Vacuum Cleaners (SIC 3635)

Vacuum Cleaner Market - Hand Held

Shares are shown based a total of 5,520,000 units shipped in 1995.

Royal	45.0%
Black & Decker	38.0
Hoover	7.0
Eureka	4.0
Bissell	3.0
Ryobi (Singer)	2.0
Others	1.0

Source: *Appliance*, September 1996, p. 86, from industry sources and market analysts.

★ 898 ★

Dishwashers (SIC 3639)

Leading Dishwasher Brands - 1996

Shares are shown based on units sold.

Sears/Kenmore	27.0%
General Electric	18.5
Maytag	16.0
Whirlpool	15.0
KitchenAid	7.5
Frigidaire	3.0
Hotpoint	3.0
Magic Chef	2.0
Bosch	1.0
Roper	1.0
Tappan	1.0
White Westinghouse	1.0
Amana	0.7
Jenn-Air	0.7
Gibson	0.5
Other	2.0

Source: *Dealerscope*, April 1997, p. 32, from Association of Home Appliance Manufacturers.

★ 899 ★

Dishwashers (SIC 3639)

Top Dishwasher Brands

Shares are shown for the North American market.

GE	36.0%
Whirlpool	36.0
Maytag	14.0
Electrolux	12.0

Source: *Investext*, Thomson Financial Networks, December 4, 1996, p. 30, from *Appliance*.

★ 900 ★

Garbage Disposals (SIC 3639)

Garbage Disposal Market

Shares are shown based a total of 4,518,900 units shipped in 1995.

In-Sink-Erator	59.0%
Electrolux	36.0
Watertown Metal Products	4.0
Others	1.0

Source: *Appliance*, September 1996, p. 87, from industry sources and market analysts.

★ 901 ★

Trash Compactors (SIC 3639)

Top Trash Compactor Brands

Shares are shown for the North American market.

Whirlpool	92.0%
Braun	8.0

Source: *Investext,* Thomson Financial Networks, December 4, 1996, p. 30, from *Appliance*.

★ 902 ★

Water Heaters (SIC 3639)

Water Heater Market

Shares are shown based a total of 8,370,330 units shipped in 1995.

State Industries	30.0%
Rheem Manufacturing	28.0
SouthCorp.	16.0
A.O. Smith	15.0
Bradford-White	10.0

Source: *Appliance*, September 1996, p. 87, from industry sources and market analysts.

★ 903 ★

Lamps (SIC 3640)

Lamp Shipments by Type

Unit shipments are shown by type. Total lamp shipments are expected to grow from 3.53 billion units in 1994 to 4.12 billion units in 2000. HID stands for high intensity discharge.

	1994 (mil.)	2000 (mil.)	Share
Large incandescents	1,837	2,050	49.8%
Miniature incandescents	1,010	1,215	29.5
Fluorescents	586	770	18.7
HID & other electrical discharge	69	75	1.8
Photographic incandescents	28	10	0.2

Source: *Purchasing*, February 13, 1997, p. 81, from Freedonia Group.

★ 904 ★

Lighting (SIC 3641)

Bulb Use in U.S. Homes

Incandescent

Fluroscent

Compact fluroscent

Halogen

Incandescent	87.0%
Fluroscent	13.0
Compact fluroscent	1.0
Halogen	1.0

Source: *USA TODAY*, April 1, 1997, p. 1, from Energy Information Administration.

★ 905 ★

Consumer Electronics (SIC 3651)

Automobile Electronics Sales

Sales reached $1.313 billion for the 52 weeks ended September 1996.

CD-players, in dash	$ 378,352
Cassette players	323,108
Car stereo speakers	304,924
Amplifiers and equalizers	163,934
Car CD changers	139,869
CD controllers	3,321

Source: *Stores*, January 1997, p. 6.

★ 906 ★

Consumer Electronics (SIC 3651)

Camcorder Sales by Type

8MM	37.0%
VHS-C	36.0
VHS	27.0

Source: *Dealerscope*, August 1996, p. 48, from Hudson Valley Editorial Services.

★ 907 ★

Consumer Electronics (SIC 3651)

Top Camcorder Makers

Shares are shown based on a total of 3,560,497 units shipped in 1995.

Sony	25.0%
Thomson	21.0
Matsushita (Panasonic, Quasar)	17.0
JVC	13.0
Sharp	8.0
Hitachi	4.0
N.A.P.	4.0
Canon	2.0
Sanyo	2.0
Others	4.0

Source: *Appliance*, September 1996, p. 86, from industry sources and market analysts.

★ 908 ★

Consumer Electronics (SIC 3651)

Top CD Player Producers

Shares are shown based a total of 2,800,000 units shipped in 1995.

Sony	30.0%
Pioneer	13.0
Matsushita (Pioneer, Quasar)	11.0
JVC	8.0
Kenwood	8.0
Yamaha	5.0
Onkyo	4.0
RCA	4.0
Denon	3.0
N.A.P.	3.0
Others	11.0

Source: *Appliance*, September 1996, p. 86, from industry sources and market analysts.

★ 909 ★

Consumer Electronics (SIC 3651)

Top Cordless Phone Producers

Shares are shown based a total of 20.3 million units shipped in 1995.

AT&T	27.0%
GE	16.0
Sony	11.0
Uniden	11.0
BellSouth	8.0%
Panasonic	7.0
Radio Shack	4.0
Southwestern Bell	4.0
Cobra	3.0
Others	9.0

Source: *Appliance*, September 1996, p. 86, from industry sources and market analysts.

★ 910 ★

Consumer Electronics (SIC 3651)

Top Television Manufacturers - 1995

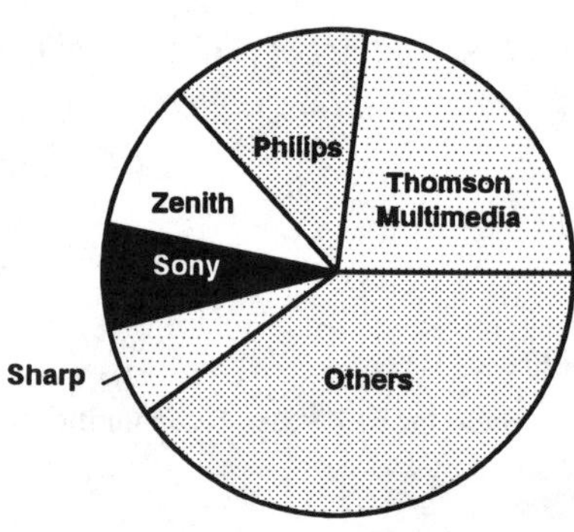

Company shares are shown in percent. The U.S. market sold 40.7 million units in 1995. Thomson Multimedia makes RCA, ProScan, and GE televisions; Philips makes Magnavox televisions.

Thomson Multimedia	23.0%
Philips	14.0
Zenith	10.0
Sony	7.0
Sharp	6.0
Others	40.0

Source: *Investext*, Thomson Financial Networks, July 1, 1996, p. 14, from Euromonitor.

★ 911 ★

Consumer Electronics (SIC 3651)

Top VCR Producers

Shares are shown based a total of 13,562,364 units shipped in 1995.

Thomson	18.0%
N.A.P.	12.0
Matsushita (Panasonic, Quasar)	10.0
JVC	6.0

Continued on next page.

★911★ *Continued*

Consumer Electronics (SIC 3651)

Top VCR Producers

Shares are shown based a total of 13,562,364 units shipped in 1995.

Sanyo/Fisher	5.0%
Sharp	5.0
Sony	5.0
Zenith	5.0
Goldstar	4.0
Hitachi	3.0
Mitsubishi	3.0
Samsung	3.0
Toshiba	3.0
Others	18.0

Source: *Appliance*, September 1996, p. 86, from industry sources and market analysts.

★912★

Consumer Electronics (SIC 3651)

Video Disc Player Market

Shares are shown based a total of 254,970 units shipped in 1995.

Pioneer	65.0%
Sony	15.0
Matsushita	14.0
N.A.P.	5.0
Others	1.0

Source: *Appliance*, September 1996, p. 86, from industry sources and market analysts.

★913★

Prerecorded Music (SIC 3652)

Album Sales - 1996

Modern rock
R&B
Country
Rap
Classical
Jazz

Data show millions of units sold for the first six months of 1996.

Modern rock	48.7
R&B	31.6
Country	29.4
Rap	24.8
Classical	10.0
Jazz	9.3

Source: *USA TODAY*, August 29, 1996, p. 6D, from SoundScan.

★914★

Prerecorded Music (SIC 3652)

Best-Selling Albums - 1996

Sales are in millions of units.

"Jagged Little Pill" by Alanis Morissette	7.4
"Falling Into You" by Celine Dion	6.1
"The Score" by Fugees	4.5
"Tragic Kingdom" by No Doubt	4.4
"Daydream" by Marian Carey	3.1
"All Eyes On Me" by 2Pac	3.0
"Load" by Metallica	3.0
"Secrets" by Toni Braxton	2.9
"The Woman in Me" by Shania Twain	2.8
"What's the Story" by Oasis	2.6

Source: *Entertainment Weekly*, January 17, 1997, p. 34, from *SoundScan*.

★ 915 ★

Prerecorded Music (SIC 3652)

Music Industry Leaders - 1997

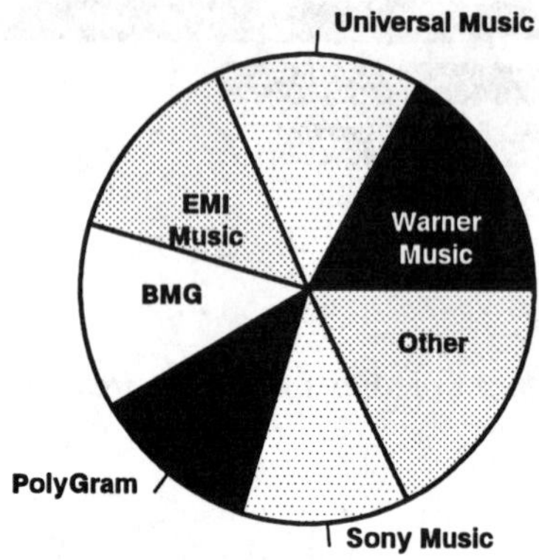

Company shares are shown based on album sales for January 1 through mid-May, 1997.

Warner Music	17.30%
Universal Music	14.91
EMI Music	13.50
BMG	13.21
PolyGram	11.82
Sony Music	11.61
Other	17.65

Source: *Wall Street Journal*, May 29, 1997, p. B4, from SoundScan Inc.

★ 916 ★

Prerecorded Music (SIC 3652)

Music Sales by Region

Sales are shown in percent by region, based on a 1995 survey of 3,065 music buyers.

South	35.3%
Midwest	23.1
West	21.3
Northeast	20.3

Source: http:// www.riaa.com/market/market/releases/demosurv.htm, 1995, p. 1, from Recording Industry Association of America.

★ 917 ★

Prerecorded Music (SIC 3652)

U.S. Music Distributors - 1996

Market shares are shown as of November 17, 1996.

Time Warner	21.9%
Sony	14.9
PolyGram	13.3
BMG	10.4
MCA	9.8
EMI	8.6
Independents	21.1

Source: *USA TODAY*, November 27, 1996, p. 2B, from *Soundscan*.

★ 918 ★

Prerecorded Music (SIC 3652)

U.S. Music Sales - 1996

Data are based on a survey.

Rock	33.5%
Country	16.7
Urban contemporary	11.3
Pop	10.1
Rap	6.7
Gospel	3.1
Jazz	3.0
Classical	2.9
Other	10.1

Source: *U.S. News & World Report*, November 11, 1996, p. 59, from Recording Industry Association of America.

★ 919 ★

Fax Machines (SIC 3661)

Top Fax Machine Makers

Market shares are shown based on 2,778,000 units shipped in 1995.

Sharp	24.0%
Panasonic	16.0
Brother	14.0
Hewlett-Packard	11.0
Canon	10.0

Continued on next page.

★919★ *Continued*

Fax Machines (SIC 3661)

Top Fax Machine Makers

Market shares are shown based on 2,778,000 units shipped in 1995.

Muratec	6.0%
Pitney-Bowes	2.0
Xerox	2.0
Others	15.0

Source: *Appliance*, September 1996, p. 88, from industry sources.

★920★

Modems (SIC 3661)

Modem Producers - North America

Shares are shown based on unit sales for 1995.

U.S. Robotics	22.0%
Maxtech/GVC	18.0
Hayes	9.0
Boca Research	6.0
Zoom Telephonics	5.0
Other	40.0

Source: *Wall Street Journal*, February 27, 1997, p. A3, from company reports and Dataquest Inc.

★921★

Telecommunications Equipment (SIC 3661)

Frame Relay Makers

Market shares are shown for 1996.

AT&T	37.5%
MCI	19.0
Sprint	17.5
WorldCom	8.4
Other	17.6

Source: *Computerworld*, December 23, 1996, p. 69.

★922★

Telecommunications Equipment (SIC 3661)

U.S. Broadband Access Spending

Total spending is expected to reach $30 billion between 1996-2000.

Hybrid fiber coax cable	32.0%
Set tops	24.0
Cable modem	16.0%
Fiber to the curb	10.0
Hybrid fiber coax-telco	9.0
Cable telephony	6.0
ADSL	5.0
Other	4.0

Source: *Network Computing*, January 15, 1997, p. 23, from company and industry data and Roberson, Stephens & Co.

★923★

Telecommunications Equipment (SIC 3661)

U.S. Videoconferencing Market

Revenues are estimated in billions of dollars.

	1996	1997	1998
Services	$ 4.00	$ 6.46	$ 9.66
Systems	0.74	1.09	1.65

Source: *International Business*, February 1997, p. 10, from Frost & Sullivan.

★924★

Wireless Communications (SIC 3663)

PCS Market Leaders

Personal communication systems (PCS) market shares are shown in percent.

Lucent	51.0%
Ericsson	16.0
Nortel	16.0
Motorola	13.0
Other	4.0

Source: *Investor's Business Daily*, November 7, 1996, p. A6, from SBC Warburg Inc. and company reports.

★925★

Wireless Communications (SIC 3663)

Portable Phone Makers

Ericsson	55.7%
Nokia	33.0
Motorola	8.0
Qualcomm	2.9
Others	0.4

Source: *Investor's Business Daily*, March 10, 1997, p. A6, from Dataquest Inc.

★ 926 ★

Wireless Communications (SIC 3663)

Potential Wireless Data Markets

Public safety	58.0%
Trucking	49.0
Utility	38.0
Petroleum	36.0
Insurance	22.0

Source: *Communications News*, October 1996, p. 8, from MTA-EMCI and Zsigo Wireless Data Consultants.

★ 927 ★

Wireless Communications (SIC 3663)

U.S. Cellular Phone Market

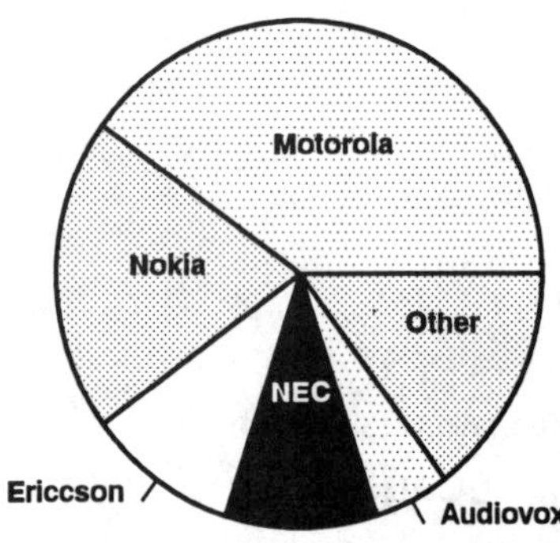

Market shares are shown in percent.

Motorola	40.0%
Nokia	20.0
Ericcson	10.0
NEC	10.0
Audiovox	5.0
Other	15.0

Source: *Investor's Business Daily*, February 20, 1997, p. A6.

★ 928 ★

Wireless Communications (SIC 3663)

U.S. Cellular Phone Sales

Data show the types of digital phones sold in the United States, based on total sales of 16 million units.

	Units	Share
Analog	14.6	92.0%
Digital	1.4	8.0

Source: *Chicago Tribune*, February 26, 1997, p. 3-1.

★ 929 ★

Wireless Communications (SIC 3663)

Why We Purchase Cellular Phones

Safety	45.3%
Business use while commuting	34.3
Stay in touch with friends/family	20.6

Source: *Consumer Reports*, February 1997, p. 11, from MTA-EMCI.

★ 930 ★

Wireless Communications (SIC 3663)

Wireless Office Market - North America

Percentage of total revenues is shown for 1997.

United States	89.3%
Canada	8.6
Mexico	2.1

Source: *Computer Reseller News*, December 23, 1996, p. 23, from Frost & Sullivan Inc.

★ 931 ★

Wireless Communications (SIC 3663)

Wireless Office Market by Segment

The North American market is shown for 1997.

Health care	29.9%
Education	15.1
Retail	14.5
Manufacturing and warehousing	13.5
Other	27.0

Source: *Computer Reseller News*, December 9, 1996, p. 19, from Frost & Sullivan.

★ 932 ★

Data Communications (SIC 3669)

Campus Backbone Market - 1996

Shared FDDI	42.7%
155-Mbps ATM	35.1
Switched FDDI	13.6
Fast ethernet	8.0
VG-AnyLAN	0.6

Source: *Business Communications Review*, March 1997, p. 10, from Allied Business Intelligence.

★ 933 ★

Data Communications (SIC 3669)

Internetworking Market

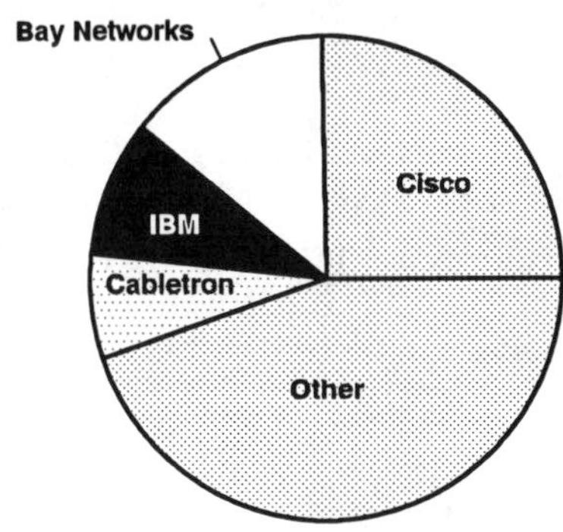

Market shares are shown based on sales of $18.0 billion. Market includes hubs, switches, remote access, and network management.

Cisco	21.9%
Bay Networks	11.6
IBM	8.3
Cabletron	6.0
Other	39.4

Source: *Informationweek*, September 16, 1996, p. 19, from Strategic Networks Consulting.

★ 934 ★

Data Communications (SIC 3669)

Leading Network Equipment Makers - 1996

Shares are shown based on a $28 billion market.

3Com/U.S. Robotics	22.0%
Cisco Systems	20.0
Bay Networks	7.0
Cabletron	4.0
Ascend Communications/Cascade Communications	4.0
Other	43.0

Source: *USA TODAY*, May 6, 1997, p. 2B, from International Data Corp.

★ 935 ★

Data Communications (SIC 3669)

Low-End Router Market

Shares are shown for the third quarter of 1996.

Cisco	64.3%
Bay	10.2
3Com	7.0
IBM	4.5
Other	14.0

Source: *Computer Reseller News*, February 17, 1997, p. 1, from Dell'Oro Group Inc.

★ 936 ★

Data Communications (SIC 3669)

NIC Market by Media

Data are based on revenues. NIC stands for Network Interface Card.

10Mbps Ethernet	62.3%
Token ring	28.3
FDDI	3.8
10/100-Mbps Ethernet	3.6
Other	1.9

Source: *Network Computing*, July 15, 1996, p. 23, from Dataquest Inc.

★ 937 ★

Data Communications (SIC 3669)

Paging Transmitter Makers - North America

Market shares are estimated for 1995.

Glenayre	50.0%
Motorola	30.0
Ericsson	10.0
NEC	5.0
Other	5.0

Source: *Investext,* Thomson Financial Networks, September 5, 1996, p. 5, from company reports.

★ 938 ★

Data Communications (SIC 3669)

Remote Access Market - 1996

Firms are ranked by sales in millions of dollars.

	Sales ($ mil.)	Share
U.S. Robotics	$ 514.1	26.1%
Ascend	448.4	22.7
Cisco	225.6	11.4
Shiva	161.1	8.2
3Com	122.4	6.2
Other	499.6	25.3

Source: *Computer Reseller News,* March 31, 1997, p. 79, from Dell'Oro Group.

★ 939 ★

Data Communications (SIC 3669)

Router Market - 1996

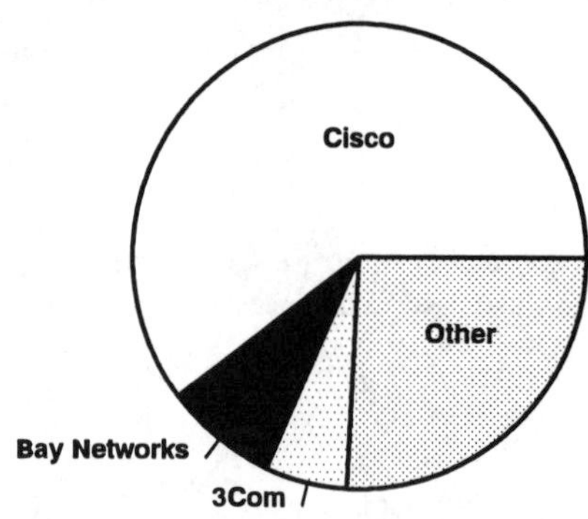

Shares are shown based on unit shipments.

Cisco	61.0%
Bay Networks	7.7
3Com	5.8
Other	25.5

Source: *PC Week,* November 18, 1996, p. A6, from Dow Jones.

★ 940 ★

Data Communications (SIC 3669)

Token Ring Switch Market - 1996

Shares are shown based on shipments of 57,000 units.

IBM	55.0%
Bay Networks	30.0
Cisco	3.0
Madge Networks	3.0
3Com	1.0
Other	8.0

Source: *Investor's Business Daily,* May 20, 1997, p. A6, from Sage Research Inc.

★ 941 ★

Data Communications (SIC 3669)

Top Producers of Ethernet Adapters - 1996

Companies are ranked by units sold.

3Com Corp.	12,150,000
D-Link Systems Inc.	2,841,610
Intel Corp.	2,267,000

Continued on next page.

★ 941 ★ *Continued*

Data Communications (SIC 3669)

Top Producers of Ethernet Adapters - 1996

Companies are ranked by units sold.

Standard Microsystems Corp.	2,042,694
IBM	707,566
Xircom Inc.	500,550
Microdyne Corp.	471,045
Digital Equipment Corp.	303,046
Hewlett-Packard Co.	250,664
Compaq Computer Corp.	212,841
Olicom USA Inc.	147,991

Source: *PC Week*, April 28, 1997, p. 139, from In-Stat.

★ 942 ★

Data Communications (SIC 3669)

Top Producers of Fast Ethernet Adapters - 1996

Companies are ranked by units sold.

3Com Corp.	1,765,000
Intel Corp.	1,645,000
Standard Microsystems Corp.	214,862
Compaq Computer Corp.	197,858
IBM	125,169
Microdyne Corp.	100,756
Digital Equipment Corp.	72,116
D-Link Systems Inc.	68,780
Xircom Inc.	45,600
Olicom USA Inc.	35,936
Hewlett-Packard Co.	28,695

Source: *PC Week*, April 28, 1997, p. 139, from In-Stat.

★ 943 ★

Fiber Optics (SIC 3669)

Fiber-Optic Optoelectronics Market - North America

Applications are ranked by sales in millions of dollars for 1996.

	Sales ($ mil.)	Share
Telecommunications	$ 780	65.0%
Premises	160	13.0
Cable TV	130	11.0
Military/Aerospace	70	6.0
Specialty	60	5.0

Source: *Lightwave*, March 1997, p. 23.

★ 944 ★

Security Equipment (SIC 3669)

Top Carbon Monoxide Detector Makers

Market shares are shown based on 6.6 million units shipped in 1995.

BRK/First Alert	64.0%
American Sensors (Dicon)	19.0
Jameson (Coleman)	5.0
Others	12.0

Source: *Appliance*, September 1996, p. 88, from industry sources.

★ 945 ★

Security Equipment (SIC 3669)

Top Smoke Detector Makers

Market shares are shown based on 18.2 million units shipped in 1995.

BRK/First Alert	48.0%
Jameson (Coleman)	33.0
Fyrnetics	10.0
American Sensors (Dicon)	9.0

Source: *Appliance*, September 1996, p. 88, from industry sources.

★ 946 ★

Components (SIC 3670)

Components Market by Region

The estimated market is shown by region.

San Francisco	$ 2,664
Los Angeles	1,602
New England	1,113
Dallas	444
Long Island	441
South New Jersey/Philadelphia	437
Chicago	433
Florida	431
Baltimore/Washington	400
Huntsville/Atlanta	389

Source: *Electronic News*, December 2, 1996, p. 36.

★ 947 ★

Components (SIC 3670)

Network and Midrange Arrays

Data show estimated shipments in single units for 1996 and 1997.

	1996	1997	Share
Subsystems	370,170	506,360	50.5%
Boards	257,715	367,745	36.7
Software	111,210	128,005	12.8

Source: *Computer Technology Review*, February 1997, p. 48, from Disk/Trend.

★ 948 ★

Components (SIC 3670)

Single-Mode Connector Market - North America

United States	89.0%
Canada	6.0
Mexico	5.0

Source: *Photonics Spectra*, March 1997, p. 62.

★ 949 ★

Components (SIC 3670)

U.S. Component Sales

Connectors	35.7%
Capacitors	18.3
Chokes/coils/transformers	14.3
Microwave components	11.9
Resistors	11.1
Crystals/filters/piez	8.7

Source: *Electronic Design*, October 14, 1996, p. 64, from Freedonia Group Inc.

★ 950 ★

Semiconductors (SIC 3674)

3-D Graphic Chip Makers

Data compares the market shares for the second and third quarter of 1996.

	2Q	3Q
S3	48.4%	51.1%
ATI	13.7	16.0
Other	37.9	32.9

Source: *Wall Street Journal*, November 25, 1996, p. B4, from Jon Pedie Associates.

★ 951 ★

Semiconductors (SIC 3674)

Digital Signal Processing

Shares are estimated for 1996.

Texas Instruments	47.0%
Lucent	26.0
Motorola	12.0
Analog Devices	11.0
Other	4.0

Source: *Investor's Business Daily*, October 29, 1996, p. A4, from company reports, Forward Concepts/ICE Corp., and International Data Corp.

★ 952 ★

Semiconductors (SIC 3674)

DRAM Leaders - 1995

DRAM stands for Dynamic Random Access Memory.

Samsung	16.0%
NEC	12.0
Hitachi	11.0
Hyundai	9.0
Toshiba	9.0
LG Semicon	7.0
Micron	6.0
Fujitsu	5.0
Mitsubishi	5.0
Other	12.0

Source: *Investor's Business Daily*, October 29, 1996, p. A4, from company reports, Forward Concepts/ICE Corp., and International Data Corp.

★ 953 ★

Semiconductors (SIC 3674)

DSP Market Leaders

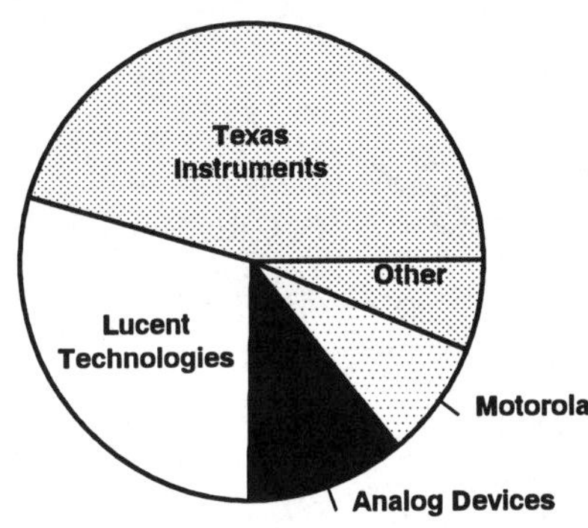

Digital signal processor (DSP) market shares are shown for 1996. Figures are estimates.

Texas Instruments	45.0%
Lucent Technologies	29.0
Analog Devices	11.0
Motorola	8.0
Other	6.0

Source: *Wall Street Journal*, March 26, 1997, p. B1, from Forward Concepts Inc.

★ 954 ★

Semiconductors (SIC 3674)

Embedded RISC Chip Market

Figures are estimated for 1995.

Motorola	26.0%
Mitsubishi	8.6
NEC	7.7
Hitachi	6.8
Intel	6.8
Philips	5.0
Microchip	5.0
Toshiba	4.6
Other	30.0

Source: *Electronic News*, February 10, 1997, p. 16, from Dataquest Inc.

★ 955 ★

Semiconductors (SIC 3674)

How We Use Semiconductors - 1995

Computers	63.0%
Communications	14.2
Industry	8.8
Automobile	5.8
Consumer	5.7
Government	2.5

Source: *Solid State Technology*, November 1996, p. 40, from Electronics Industry Association of Japan.

★ 956 ★

Semiconductors (SIC 3674)

Leading CPLD Makers - 1995

Shares of the $530 million CPLD (complex programmable-logic devices) market are shown in percent.

Altera	64.1%
AMD	17.8
Lattice	10.6
Cypress	3.4
Others	4.1

Source: *Computer Design*, December 1996, p. 91, from In-Stat.

★ 957 ★

Semiconductors (SIC 3674)

PC Microprocessor Market - 1997

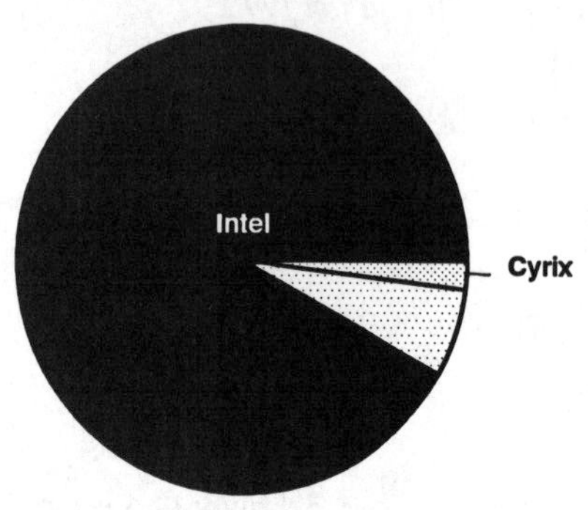

Companies are ranked by sales of Intel-compatible microprocessor chips in millions of units. Figure for Advanced Micro Devices is estimated.

	(mil.)	Share
Intel	70.0	92.1%
Advanced Micro Devices	4.5	5.9
Cyrix	1.5	2.0

Source: *Wall Street Journal*, May 30, 1997, p. B4, from Dataquest Inc. and Baseline.

★ 958 ★

Semiconductors (SIC 3674)

PC Processor Market - 1996

Shares are shown in percent.

Intel	85.3%
AMD	8.6
Cyrix	3.8
Others	2.3

Source: *Investor's Business Daily*, April 1, 1997, p. 4A, from International Data Corp.

★ 959 ★

Semiconductors (SIC 3674)

PC Sales by Microprocessor

Pentium	81.2%
Power PC-601	4.3
486 DX2	4.3
Power PC 603	3.8
486DX4	3.0
Power PC 604	1.3
68040	0.9%
Pentium Pro	0.3
486SX	0.1
486SX2	0.1
486DX	0.1
68030	0.0
Other	0.4

Source: *Dealerscope*, December 1996, p. 32, from Computer Intelligence InfoCorp.

★ 960 ★

Semiconductors (SIC 3674)

RISC System Market - 1996

Market is shown by type of processor.

PA-RISC	29.6%
PowerPC	27.4
SPARC	17.0
MIPS	15.9
Alpha	8.9
Other	1.2

Source: *Computerworld*, February 3, 1997, p. 41, from *Inside the New Computer Industry*.

★ 961 ★

Semiconductors (SIC 3674)

Top Flash Chip Producers - 1996

Company shares are shown in percent.

Intel/Sharp	41.3%
AMD/Fujitsu	36.0
Atmel	9.0
Others	13.7

Source: *Electronic Business Today*, February 1997, p. 59, from Dataquest Inc.

★962★

Semiconductors (SIC 3674)

Top PC Graphics Controller Brands

Brand shares are shown for the third quarter of 1996.

S3	30.0%
Cirrus Logic	26.0
Trident	14.0
ATI	11.0
Other	19.0

Source: *Electronic Business Today*, March 1997, p. 39, from Mercury Research Inc.

★963★

Capacitors (SIC 3675)

Capacitor Sales by Type

Ceramic	45.1%
Tantalum	25.1
Paper and film	16.3
Aluminum	9.8
Other	3.8

Source: *Ceramic Industry*, August 1996, p. 38, from Electronic Industries Association.

★964★

Switches (SIC 3679)

Paging Switch Makers - North America

Market shares are estimated for 1995.

Glenayre	85.0%
Motorola	10.0
Other	5.0

Source: *Investext*, Thomson Financial Networks, September 5, 1996, p. 5, from company reports.

★965★

Batteries (SIC 3691)

Battery Market by Brand

Brand shares are shown for the 52 weeks ended March 9, 1996. Data are based on sales at food stores.

Duracell	43.5%
Energizer	38.7
Eveready Super Heavy Duty	3.7
Rayovac Alkaline	2.7%
Rayovac CB Z HD	1.4
Eveready Classic	1.3
Panasonic	1.0
Duracell Mallory	0.6
Kodak Supralife	0.6
Eveready Overtime	0.5
Private label	4.4
Other	1.6

Source: *Nonfoods Merchandising*, September 1996, p. 14, from A.C. Nielsen.

★966★

Batteries (SIC 3691)

Supermarket Battery Sales by Category

Shares are shown ranked by units sold in supermarkets for the year ended December 7, 1996.

AA	39.9%
9 volt	15.0
AAA	14.9
D	14.7
C	11.5
1.5 volt	1.5
6 volt	1.0
3 volt	0.8
1.4 volt	0.5

Source: *Supermarket Business*, May 1997, p. 140, from A.C. Nielsen.

★967★

Batteries (SIC 3691)

U.S. Battery Market

Shares are shown based on revenues. "Other" includes private label.

Duracell	48.0%
Everready	36.0
Rayovac	8.0
Other	6.8

Source: *Wall Street Journal*, September 13, 1996, p. A3.

★ 968 ★

Recording Media (SIC 3695)

Recording Media Sales

Supermarket sales are shown in millions of dollars for 1995.

	($ mil.)	Share
Videotapes, prerecorded	$ 620.16	75.4%
Videotapes, blank	179.47	21.8
Audiotapes, blank & prerecorded	21.65	2.6
Other	1.11	0.1

Source: *Progressive Grocer*, August 1996, p. 104.

★ 969 ★

Lasers (SIC 3699)

Laser Market by End Use - Canada

Automotive	40.0%
Electronics	25.0
Aerospace	20.0
Other	15.0

Source: *National Trade Data Bank*, October 10, 1996, p. ISA960901.

★ 970 ★

Autos & Trucks (SIC 3710)

Car and Light Truck Market Leaders - 1996

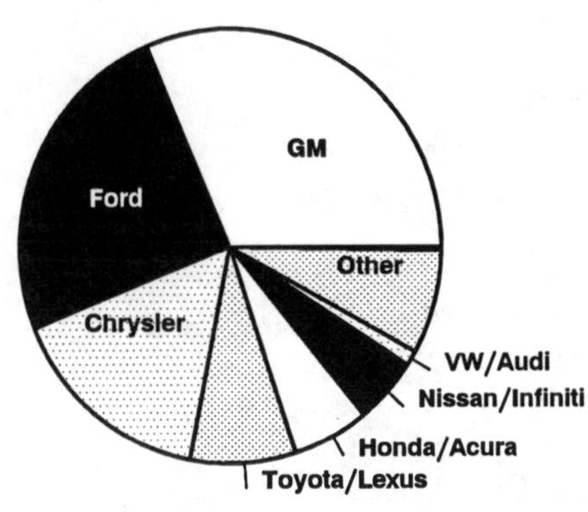

Market shares are shown for the top 1996 models.

GM	32.1%
Ford	25.1
Chrysler	15.9
Toyota/Lexus	7.6
Honda/Acura	5.5
Nissan/Infiniti	5.0
VW/Audi	1.0
Other	7.8

Source: *Automotive News*, October 7, 1996, p. 1, from Automotive News Data Center.

★ 971 ★

Autos & Trucks (SIC 3710)

Car & Truck Sales - Canada

Unit sales are shown by year.

	1995	1996	Share
GM	384,270	380,223	32.2%
Ford	261,774	275,432	23.3
Chrysler	225,122	239,514	20.3
Honda	66,785	73,717	6.2
Toyota	67,956	73,548	6.2
Nissan	32,024	32,290	2.7%
Volkswagen	23,175	27,067	2.3
Mazda	25,325	25,081	2.1
Hyundai	18,424	17,176	1.5
Suzuki	7,764	7,772	0.7
Volvo	7,814	7,264	0.6
Subaru	4,183	5,822	0.5
BMW	5,245	5,725	0.5
Mercedes	4,255	5,033	0.4
Lada	1,855	1,695	0.1
Jaguar	945	1,051	0.1
Land Rover	816	921	0.1
Porsche	307	373	0.0

Source: *Toronto Star*, January 7, 1997, p. D1, from company reports.

★ 972 ★

Autos & Trucks (SIC 3710)

North American Vehicle Production - 1996

Data are for the first 11 months of the year.

General Motors	32.5%
Ford Motor Co.	28.1
Chrysler Corp.	18.0
Honda of America	5.1
Nissan Motor Manufacturing	3.6
Toyota Motor Manufacturing	3.2
New United Motor Manufacturing	2.4
Volkswagen	1.4
Mitsubishi Motor Manufacturing Inc.	1.3
Subaru-Isuzu Manufacturing Inc.	1.3
CAMI Automotive Inc.	1.0
Auto Alliance International	0.8
Navistar International Inc.	0.5
Other	0.8

Source: *Automotive News*, December 2, 1996, p. S4.

★ 973 ★

Autos & Trucks (SIC 3710)

North American Vehicle Sales - 1996

	Units	Share
U.S. cars	8,526,753	50.2%
U.S. trucks	6,929,591	40.8
Canada cars	660,522	3.9
Canada trucks	541,632	3.2
Mexico cars	200,102	1.2
Mexico trucks	133,818	0.8

Source: *WARD's Automotive International*, February 1997, p. 10.

★ 974 ★

Autos & Trucks (SIC 3710)

Top Vehicle Markets

California
Florida
Texas
New York
Illinois
Michigan
Ohio
Pennsylvania
New Jersey
Georgia

Data show the number of vehicle registrations in 1995.

California	1,476,713
Florida	1,191,861
Texas	1,124,430
New York	753,119
Illinois	731,887
Michigan	714,206
Ohio	689,298
Pennsylvania	676,487
New Jersey	510,965
Georgia	471,102

Source: *Detroit News*, October 18, 1996, p. A1, from Polk and Chrysler reports.

★ 975 ★

Autos (SIC 3711)

Auto Auction Chains

Chains are ranked by number of outlets in North America. Manheim includes Greater Mobile (Ala.) Auto Auction. ServeNet is a network of independently owned auctions.

Manheim Auctions	63
ADT Automotive	29
ADESA Corp.	20
ServeNet	17
Canadian Auto Auction Group	10

Source: *Automotive News*, July 22, 1996, p. 6.

★ 976 ★

Autos (SIC 3711)

Best-Selling Autos - 1996

Ford Taurus	401,049
Honda Accord	382,298
Toyota Camry	359,433
Ford Escort	284,644
Saturn	278,574
Honda Civic	278,562
Chevrolet Cavalier	277,222
Chevrolet Lumina	237,973
Pontiac Grand Am	222,477
Toyota Corolla	209,048

Source: *New York Times*, February 2, 1997, p. 36, from Automotive News Data Center.

★ 977 ★

Autos (SIC 3711)

Best-Selling Cars - Santa Clara

Data show units sold in Santa Clara County, California, for 1995.

Honda Civic	3,586
Honda Accord	3,444
Ford Taurus	3,165
Toyota Camry	2,871
Toyota Corolla	1,800
Volkswagen Jetta	1,612

Continued on next page.

★ 977 ★ *Continued*

Autos (SIC 3711)

Best-Selling Cars - Santa Clara

Data show units sold in Santa Clara County, California, for 1995.

Acura Integra	1,432
Saturn SL	1,423
BMW 300/500	1,274
Nissan Maxima	914

Source: *San Jose and Silicon Valley Journal*, May 13, 1996, p. 12, from R.J. Polk & Co.

★ 978 ★

Autos (SIC 3711)

Best-Selling Sports Cars - 1998

Corvette
Mazda Miata
Mitsubishi 3000GT
Mercedes SLK
BMW 23/25
Porsche Boxster
Porsche 911/996
Dodge Viper

Sales are estimated. The top vehicle in 1995 was the Mazda Miata, selling 20,174 units.

Corvette	20,000
Mazda Miata	16,000
Mitsubishi 3000GT	10,000
Mercedes SLK	7,000
BMW 23/25	6,000
Porsche Boxster	6,000
Porsche 911/996	4,000
Dodge Viper	1,500

Source: *Automotive Industries*, October 1996, p. 61.

★ 979 ★

Autos (SIC 3711)

Car Sales in Canada - 1996

Brand shares are shown based on 660,667 units sold.

General Motors Cavalier	6.6%
Honda Civic	5.6
General Motors Sunfire	5.5
Ford Escort	5.2
Chrysler Neon	4.4%
Toyota Corolla	4.4
Ford Taurus	3.8
General Motors Grand Am	3.6
Chrysler Intrepid	3.5
Honda Accord	3.1
Others	54.3

Source: *Marketing Magazine*, May 26, 1997, p. 17, from DesRosiers Automobile Consultants.

★ 980 ★

Autos (SIC 3711)

European Luxury Car Sales

	1995	2000
Volkswagen	133,000	163,000
BMW	100,000	145,000
Mercedes-Benz	77,000	135,000
Volvo	88,500	134,000
Saab	26,000	35,000

Source: *WARD's Automotive International*, September 1996, p. 12, from DRI/McGraw-Hill.

★ 981 ★

Autos (SIC 3711)

Light Vehicle Makers - 1996

North American market shares are for the first 11 months of 1996.

General Motors	31.6%
Ford	25.2
Chrysler	16.3
Other	26.9

Source: *Financial Times*, January 15, 1997, p. 13, from Datastream, *WARD's Automotive Yearbook and Report*, and J.P. Morgan.

★ 982 ★
Autos (SIC 3711)

Light-Vehicle Market - Mexico

Market shares are shown for the first 10 months of 1996.

GM	29.8%
Ford	20.0
Chrysler	17.4
Volkswagen	16.2
Nissan	15.4
Other	1.2

Source: *Automotive News*, December 16, 1996, p. 3, from Mexican Automobile Industry Association.

★ 983 ★
Autos (SIC 3711)

Luxury Car Makers - 1996

Figures are for the first six months of the year.

BMW	80,149
Mercedes	66,132
Lexus	58,238
Acura	44,871
Infiniti	42,290
Audi	19,731

Source: *WARD's Automotive International*, November 1996, p. 16, from *WARD's Automotive Yearbook*.

★ 984 ★
Autos (SIC 3711)

Luxury Car Sales

Data show unit sales in 1995 and share of the car market.

	Sales	Share
Lincoln/Mercury	512,129	5.9%
Buick	471,819	5.5
Oldsmobile	371,725	4.3
Cadillac	180,504	2.1
Chrysler	46,462	0.5

Source: *New York Times*, September 26, 1996, p. C18, from *WARD's Automotive Yearbook*.

★ 985 ★
Autos (SIC 3711)

Mexico's Luxury Car Sales

Data are for the first six months of 1996.

Cadillac De Ville	824
Mercedes Benz	572
BMW	365
Lincoln Town Car	108
Lincoln Mark VII	11

Source: *Business Mexico*, October 1996, p. 38, from Asociacion Mexicoana de la Industria Automtriz.

★ 986 ★
Autos (SIC 3711)

Minivan Sales in Canada - 1996

Models are ranked by unit sales during the 1996 model year to date. The model year to date was October 1, 1995 to February 28, 1996.

Chrysler Voyager/Caravan	26,501
Ford Windstar	9,691
General Motors Venture/Trans Sport	8,205
General Motors Astro/Safari	7,385
Ford Aerostar	4,055
Ford Villager	1,769
Nissan Quest	1,149
Honda Odyssey	783
Chrysler Town and Country	436
Toyota Previa	420
Mazda MPV	374
Volkswagen Bus/Transporter	107
Volkswagen Camper	73
Nissan Axxess	59
Volkswagen Eurovan	41

Source: *Financial Post*, March 29, 1997, p. 13, from DesRosiers Automotive Consultants Inc.

★ 987 ★
Autos (SIC 3711)

Passenger Car Market - 1995

Shares are shown based on 8,636,048 units sold in 1995.

Ford Taurus	4.2%
Honda Accord	4.0
Toyota Camry	3.8
Honda Civic	3.4
Saturn	3.3

Continued on next page.

★ 987 ★ *Continued*

Autos (SIC 3711)

Passenger Car Market - 1995

Shares are shown based on 8,636,048 units sold in 1995.

Ford Escort	3.3%
Dodge/Plymouth Neon	2.8
Pontiac Grand Am	2.7
Chevy Lumina	2.5
Toyota Corolla	2.5
Other	67.6

Source: *Advertising Age*, September 30, 1996, p. S26, from *Automotive News Market Data Book*.

★ 988 ★

Autos (SIC 3711)

Top Car Models

Auto sales are shown for the first six months of 1996.

Taurus	191,263
Accord	185,034
Camry	179,573
Escort	150,618
Civic	150,263
Cavalier	145,814
Lumina	142,998
Saturn	140,818
Grand Am	115,870
Corsica/Beretta	106,465

Source: *WARD's Auto World*, August 1996, p. 14, from WARD's Auto Infobank.

★ 989 ★

Autos (SIC 3711)

Top Mid-Sized Sellers

Data are for the first 10 months of 1996.

Ford Taurus	332,060
Honda Accord	320,609
Toyota Camry	304,262
Chevrolet Lumina	204,048
Dodge Intrepid	123,850

Source: *Automotive News*, November 25, 1996, p. 6, from Automotive News Data Center.

★ 990 ★

Autos (SIC 3711)

U.S. Passenger Car Market

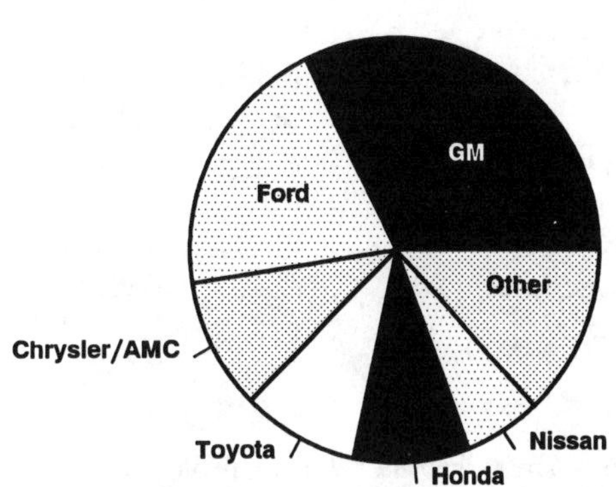

Market shares are shown in percent.

GM	32.3%
Ford	20.4
Chrysler/AMC	9.8
Toyota	9.3
Honda	9.2
Nissan	5.9
Other	13.1

Source: *Investor's Business Daily*, January 30, 1997, p. B1, from Ford Motor Co.

★ 991 ★

Buses (SIC 3713)

Transit Bus Market

Data refer to U.S. transit buses 35-40 feet long. Shares are for 1991-95.

TMC	22.9%
Flxible	21.3
BIA	17.8
Gillig	13.9
New Flyer	8.4
Ikarus	5.3
Neoplan	3.8
MCI	2.7
AVS	0.1
Thomas	0.1
Other	3.7

Source: *Metro Magazine Fact Book*, (annual) 1997, p. 14, from American Public Transport Association.

★ 992 ★
Trucks (SIC 3713)

Best-Selling Trucks - 1996

Ford F-Series pickup	780,838
Chevrolet C/K pickup	550,594
Ford Explorer	402,663
Dodge Ram pickup	383,960
Dodge Caravan	300,117
Ford Ranger	288,393
Jeep Grand Cherokee	279,195
Chevrolet Blazer	246,307
Ford Windstar	209,033
Chevrolet S-10	190,178

Source: *New York Times*, February 2, 1997, p. 36, from Automotive News Data Center.

★ 993 ★
Trucks (SIC 3713)

Class 8 Heavy Truck Market - 1996

Company shares are based on retail sales. The U.S. Class 8 retail truck market sold 170,009 units.

Freightliner	29.4%
Navistar	16.7
Mack	12.1
Peterbilt	11.6
Kenworth	10.4
Volvo GM	9.1
Ford	9.0
Western Star	1.1
Other	0.7

Source: *Financial Times*, April 15, 1997, p. 15, from American Automobile Manufacturers Association.

★ 994 ★
Trucks (SIC 3713)

Class 8 Truck Industry

U.S. industry shown is a forecast for 1997. Ford's figure is expected to reach 145,000-155,000 units.

Navistar	154,000
Kenworth	150,000
Volvo GM	150,000
Freightliner	145,000
Peterbilt	145,000
Mack	134,000

Source: *Automotive News*, December 23, 1996, p. 10.

★ 995 ★
Trucks (SIC 3713)

Heavy-Duty Diesel Truck Makers - North America

Shares of the 1995 market are shown in percent.

Cummins	35.5%
DDC	26.2
CAT	25.2
Mack	12.2
Other	0.9

Source: *Investext*, Thomson Financial Networks, February 7, 1997, p. 12.

★ 996 ★
Trucks (SIC 3713)

Medium Duty Truck Makers

Data refer to class 4-7 trucks. A total of 157,455 trucks are expected to be produced in 1997.

	Units	Share
Navistar	60,568	38.5%
Ford	47,405	30.1
GMC	30,008	19.1
Freightliner	18,740	11.9
Volvo/GM	625	0.4
Paccar	110	0.1

Source: *Financial Times*, December 10, 1996, p. 4, from *World Truck Industry Forecast Report*.

★ 997 ★

Trucks (SIC 3713)

Sports Utility Vehicle Sales in Canada - 1996

Brand shares are shown based on 98,400 units sold.

General Motors SU/Blazer/Jimmy	16.9%
Chrysler Jeep Grand Cherokee	16.5
Ford Explorer	15.9
General Motors Blazer/Yukon	8.8
Nissan Pathfinder	7.7
GM Suburban	5.3
Toyota 4Runner	5.2
Chrysler Jeep YJ/TJ	4.9
Suzuki Sidekick	4.4
Ford Expedition	2.7
Other	11.7

Source: *Marketing Magazine*, May 26, 1997, p. 17, from DesRosiers Automobile Consultants.

★ 998 ★

Trucks (SIC 3713)

Top Light Truck Manufacturers - 1997

Shares are estimated.

Ford	31.7%
General Motors	31.2
Chrysler	24.2
Toyota	5.0
Nissan	3.6
Honda	0.9
Other	3.4

Source: *Investext*, Thomson Financial Networks, July 30, 1996, p. 5, from company data and PaineWebber estimates.

★ 999 ★

Trucks (SIC 3713)

Top Light Vehicle Brands - 1996

Sales are shown for the model year ended September 30, 1996.

Ford F-Series Pickup	731,393
Chevy C-K Pickup	519,578
Ford Explorer	404,658
Ford Taurus	378,144
Dodge Ram Pickup	369,073
Honda Accord	367,137
Toyota Camry	354,035
Dodge Caravan	299,814
Ford Escort	292,900
Honda Civic	290,843

Source: *Detroit Free Press*, October 4, 1996, p. 1C, from WARD's AutoInfoBank.

★ 1000 ★

Trucks (SIC 3713)

Top Truck Brands - 1995

Shares are shown based on 6,130,406 units sold in 1995.

Ford F-series pickup	11.3%
Chevy C/K pickup	8.8
Ford Explorer	6.4
Ford Ranger	5.0
Dodge Ram pickup	4.4
Dodge Caravan	4.3
Jeep Grand Cherokee	4.1
Ford Windstar	3.6
Chevy Blazer	3.5
Chevy S10 pickup	3.4
Other	45.1

Source: *Advertising Age*, September 30, 1996, p. S26, from *Automotive News Market Data Book.*

★ 1001 ★

Trucks (SIC 3713)

U.S. Truck Makers - 1997

A total of 303,741 trucks are expected to be produced in 1997.

	Units	Share
Navistar	74,048	24.4%
Ford	63,165	20.8
Freightliner	62,644	20.6
Paccar	35,958	11.8
GMC	30,008	9.9
Mack	20,080	6.6
Volvo/GM	16,949	5.6
Other	890	0.3

Source: *Financial Times*, December 10, 1996, p. 4, from *World Truck Industry Forecast Report.*

★ 1002 ★

Auto Parts (SIC 3714)

Auto Accessory Market

Exterior car care accessories	25.9%
Child safety seats	20.5
Interior accessories	20.4
Mechanical security devices	11.2
Windshield wipers	10.6
Mirrors	7.2
Utility racks	3.0
Antennas	1.2

Source: *Stores*, October 1996, p. 109, from Frost & Sullivan.

★ 1003 ★

Auto Parts (SIC 3714)

Top OEM Conveyor Firms

Shares are estimated, based on a $1.0 - 1.2 billion market. OEM stands for original equipment manufacturer.

Jervis Webb	40.0%
Dearborn Midwest	25.0
ASI Systems	15.0
Others	30.0

Source: *Investext*, Thomson Financial Networks, August 1, 1996, p. 10, from industry sources and CS First Boston.

★ 1004 ★

Auto Parts (SIC 3714)

Top OEM Suppliers to North America - 1996

Companies are ranked by sales in millions of dollars. Ford Automotive Products Operations ranked second, but its sales figure was unavailable.

Delphi Automotive Systems	$ 21,100
Lear Corp.	4,400
Delco Electronics Corp.	4,350
Johnson Controls Inc.	4,209
Dana Corp.	4,135
Magna International Inc.	3,940
TRW Inc.	3,500
Robert Bosch Corp.	2,900
DuPont Automotive	2,800
Chrysler Component Operations	2,600
Denso International America Inc.	2,500
Eaton Corp.	$ 2,500
ITT Automotive	2,500
G.E. Automotive	2,300
UT Automotive	2,200

Source: *Automotive News*, April 14, 1997, p. 22.

★ 1005 ★

Recreational Vehicles (SIC 3715)

Top Recreational Vehicle Makers

Data show company shares for the first ten months of 1996.

Fleetwood Enterprises	28.30%
Winnebago Industries	16.02
Coachman Industries	10.18
Monaco Coach	8.66
National R.V.	6.02
Thor Industries	5.33
Damon Corporation	4.94
SMC Corp.	4.63
Tiffin Motor Home	4.31
Newmar Corporation	3.99
Rexhall Industries	2.50
Gulfstream Coach	2.49
Forest River	0.92
Foretravel Inc.	0.62
Others	1.09

Source: *Investext*, Thomson Financial Networks, January 13, 1997, p. 2.

★ 1006 ★

Aircraft (SIC 3721)

Large Cabin Aircraft Providers - 1995

Market shares are shown in percent.

Gulfstream	26.0%
Bombardier	24.0
Dassault	10.0
Other	40.0

Source: *Investext*, Thomson Financial Networks, December 5, 1996, p. 16, from Gulfstream and GAMA.

★ 1007 ★

Boats (SIC 3731)

Fiberglass Boat Registrations

Data show the number of boats registered by makers in 1995.

Carolina Skiff	1,348
Bayliner	982
Pro-Line	884
Key West	645
Gheen (Canoes)	592
Wellcraft	505
Boston Whaler	459
Sunbird	404
Grady White	385
Aqua Sport	359

Source: *Boating Industry*, July 1996, p. 16, from John C. Landon & Associates Inc.

★ 1008 ★

Railroad Equipment (SIC 3743)

Freight Car Market

The market is shown by type for 1997.

	No.	Share
Small covered hoppers	10,000	24.0%
Tank cars	9,000	21.6
Large covered hoppers	6,600	15.9
Coal cars	6,000	14.4
Intermodal	3,000	7.2
Boxcars	2,000	4.8
Centerbeam/89-foot flats	2,000	4.8
Mill gons/coil cars	2,000	4.8
Other types	1,000	2.4

Source: *Railway Age*, January 1997, p. 24.

★ 1009 ★

Railroad Equipment (SIC 3743)

U.S. Railcar Deliveries - 1997

Figures are estimated.

Covered hopper	
3,500-5,500 cf	9,000
Over 5,500 cf	7,000
Under 3,500 cf	1,700
Gondolas	
(GT) aluminum	3,500
(GB) steel	1,200
(GT) steel	1,000
Flat cars	
Intermodal	2,000
Non-intermodal	2,000
Open hoppers	3,250
Boxcars	1,500
Tanks	8,500

Source: *Railway Age*, April 1997, p. 1, from American Railway Car Institute and Economic Planning Associates Inc.

★ 1010 ★

Bicycle Parts (SIC 3751)

Leading Bike Shock Parts

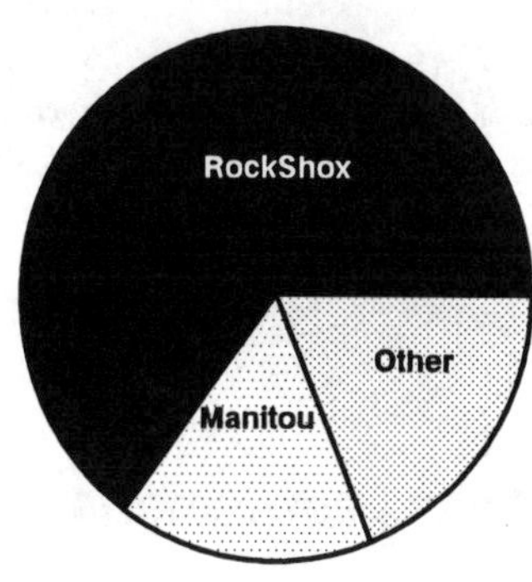

Data show preferred brands of bicycle shocks.

RockShox	65.0%
Manitou	16.0
Other	19.0

Source: *Investor's Business Daily*, March 3, 1997, p. A4, from *Bicycling Magazine* and Jefferies & Co.

★ 1011 ★

Bicycles (SIC 3751)

Bicycle Market by Type - 1994

Shares are shown based on units.

26"	64.0%
20"	19.0
700C	12.0
24"	3.0
27"	0.5
Other	1.5

Source: http:// www.bikenet.com.tw/bikint/report/e-inter.htm, June 4, 1997, p. 6.

★ 1012 ★

Bicycles (SIC 3751)

Specialty Bike Market

Mountain bikes

Children's

Hybrids

Traditional road

Other

The market is shown by type.

Mountain bikes	63.0%
Children's	20.0
Hybrids	10.0
Traditional road	1.0
Other	6.0

Source: *Los Angeles Times*, April 10, 1997, p. D1, from Bicycle Institute of America, Bicycle Manufacturers Association, Bicycle Dealers Association, and *Bike Shop List*.

★ 1013 ★

Aerospace (SIC 3761)

Canadian Aerospace Exports

Electronic parts	35.0%
Fixed-wing aircraft	24.0
Aircraft engines & parts	20.0
Aircraft systems & parts	13.0
Helicopters	5.0
Flight simulators	3.0

Source: *Financial Times*, May 1, 1997, p. 15, from Statistics Canada.

★ 1014 ★

Aerospace (SIC 3761)

Largest Defense Contractors - Colorado

Data show the value of contracts in millions of dollars.

Lockheed Martin	$ 1,040.0
Loral Corp.	129.0
Kaman Corp.	69.6
Raytheon Co.	53.8
IBM	32.3
Swinerton & Wahlberg Co.	29.5
PRC Inc.	22.0
Ball Corp.	$ 21.0
TRW Inc.	14.8
Boeing Co.	11.3
Eastern JBI Joint Venture	11.0

Source: *Denver Business Journal*, April 5, 1996, p. 23A, from United States Department of Defense, Office of Procurement.

★ 1015 ★

Aerospace (SIC 3761)

Leading Aerospace Companies - 1996

Revenues are shown in millions of dollars.

Lockheed Martin	$ 26,875
United Technologies	23,512
Boeing	22,681
Allied Signal	13,971
McDonnell Douglas	13,834
Textron	9,274
Northrop Grumman	8,071
General Dynamics	3,609
B.F. Goodrich	2,556
Sundstrand	1,521
Sequa	1,459
Coltec Industries	1,342
Alliant Techsystems	1,207
Gulfstream Aerospace	1,064

Source: *Fortune*, April 28, 1997, p. 44.

★ 1016 ★

Aerospace (SIC 3761)

Leading Defense Contractors - 1995

Firms are ranked by business value for fiscal year 1995 in millions of dollars.

Lockheed Martin Corp.	$ 10,482.8
McDonnell Douglas Corp.	8,020.9
Tenneco Inc.	3,709.8
General Motors Corp.	2,993.0
Northrop Grumman Corp.	2,913.1
Raytheon Co.	2,890.4
General Electric Co.	2,103.7
Loral Corp.	1,967.3
Boeing Co.	1,780.3
United Technologies Corp.	1,774.8
General Dynamics Corp.	1,695.3
Litton Industries Inc.	1,237.2

Continued on next page.

★ 1016 ★ *Continued*

Aerospace (SIC 3761)

Leading Defense Contractors - 1995

Firms are ranked by business value for fiscal year 1995 in millions of dollars.

Westinghouse Electric Corp.	$ 1,225.4
Rockwell International Corp.	1,210.0
Textron Inc.	1,069.0

Source: *Aviation Week & Space Technology*, January 13, 1997, p. 260.

★ 1017 ★

Aerospace (SIC 3761)

Military Spending - 1996

Data are in billions of dollars.

	($ bil.)	Share
Aircraft	$ 21.7	27.0%
Ships	9.3	11.6
Electronics/communications	7.3	9.1
Missiles	6.8	8.4
Space	4.9	6.1
Weapons	3.8	4.7
Vehicles	2.9	3.6
Other	23.8	29.6

Source: *New York Times*, December 17, 1996, p. C1, from JSA Research Inc., Electronics Industry Association, and Aerospace Industries Association.

★ 1018 ★

Aerospace (SIC 3761)

Top Military Contractors - 1995

Firms are ranked by 1995 prime contracts awarded in billions of dollars.

Lockhead Martin	$ 12.45
Boeing	9.80
Raytheon	5.91
Newport News Shipbuilding	3.71
Northrop Grumman	2.91
General Electric	2.10
United Technologies	1.77
General Dynamics	1.70
Litton Industries	1.24

Source: *New York Times*, January 17, 1997, p. C6, from Bloomberg Financial Markets and United States Department of Defense.

★ 1019 ★

Snowmobiles (SIC 3799)

Snowmobile Registrations by State

Michigan
Minnesota
Wisconsin
New York
Maine

Data show the number of snowmobiles registered by state. Shares are shown based on the more than 1.3 snowmobiles registered in the United States.

	No.	Share
Michigan	270,266	21.0%
Minnesota	254,510	20.0
Wisconsin	193,184	15.0
New York	89,617	7.0
Maine	76,821	6.0

Source: *USA TODAY*, February 17, 1997, p. C1, from American Council of Snowmobile Associations.

SIC 38 - Instruments and Related Products

★ 1020 ★

Sterilized Chambers (SIC 3821)

U.S. Clean Room Market

Data show the number of cleanrooms operating in each segment of the market.

	No.	Share
Electronics	5,000	30.3%
Medcial devices/hospital	3,500	21.2
Pharmaceutical/biotech	3,000	18.2
Aerospace/auto	1,000	6.1
Other	4,000	24.2

Source: *Chemical Engineering*, January 1997, p. 35, from McIlvane Co.

★ 1021 ★

Control Equipment (SIC 3825)

Motion Control Industry - 1996

Electric motors	19.0%
Controls and sensors	17.0
Air & pneumatic hoses and fittings	13.0
Bearings	9.0

Source: *Industrial Distribution*, April 1997, p. MC10, from PT/MC Navigator.

★ 1022 ★

First Aid Needs (SIC 3841)

First Aid Accessories Sales

Data are for supermarket sales.

	($ mil.)	Share
Tape/bandages/gauze	$ 120.8	71.5%
Diabetes test kits	20.2	12.0
Muscle/body support	13.5	8.0
Personal thermometers	9.7	5.7
Heat/ice packs	3.3	2.0
First aid kits	1.5	0.9

Source: *Supermarket Business*, September 1996, p. 148, from A.C. Nielsen.

★ 1023 ★

First Aid Needs (SIC 3841)

First Aid Leaders

BAND-AID first aid
Johnson & Johnson first aid
Curad first aid
Johnson & Johnson Kling Sterile first aid
3M Active Strips first aid
Steripads first aid
Curity first aid
3M Comfort Strips first aid
BAND-AID Sport Strip first aid
Private label

Data show food store, drugstore, and mass merchandiser sales in millions of dollars for the 52 week period ending March 2, 1997. The $397.5 million market includes tape, bandage, gauze and cotton.

BAND-AID first aid	$ 84.6
Johnson & Johnson first aid	49.5
Curad first aid	25.6
Johnson & Johnson Kling Sterile first aid	19.1

Continued on next page.

★ 1023 ★ *Continued*

First Aid Needs (SIC 3841)

First Aid Leaders

Data show food store, drugstore, and mass merchandiser sales in millions of dollars for the 52 week period ending March 2, 1997. The $397.5 million market includes tape, bandage, gauze and cotton.

3M Active Strips first aid	$ 18.6
Steripads first aid	17.5
Curity first aid	17.4
3M Comfort Strips first aid	11.3
BAND-AID Sport Strip first aid	11.3
Private label	53.1

Source: *Discount Merchandiser*, May 1997, p. 92, from Information Resources Inc.

★ 1024 ★

First Aid Needs (SIC 3841)

Top First Aid Brands

Data show the leading brands of tape, bandages, gauze, and cotton.

	($ mil.)	Share
Johnson & Johnson	$ 221.4	54.0%
Futuro	64.4	15.7
Private label	56.0	13.7
3M	40.0	9.8
American White Cross	7.6	1.9
Other	20.3	5.0

Source: *Supermarket Business*, September 1996, p. 148, from A.C. Nielsen.

★ 1025 ★

Medical Instruments (SIC 3841)

Medical Technology Firms - Minnesota

Firms are ranked by annual revenues in millions of dollars.

3M Company/Life Sciences Sector/ Health Care Products	$ 2,221.0
Medtronic Inc.	2,169.1
St. Jude Medical Inc.	723.5
CPI/Guidant Corporation	452.4
SciMed Life Systems Inc.	300.0
Starkey Laboratories Inc.	266.6
Solvay Animal Health Inc.	$ 122.0
Sims Deltec Inc.	100.0
Chronimec Inc.	90.5
American Medical Systems Inc.	90.0

Source: *Corporate Report Minnesota*, October 1996, p. 54.

★ 1026 ★

Medical Instruments (SIC 3841)

Realtime Image-Processing Systems

Shares are shown based on revenues for 1997.

Computer systems	32.0%
Input devices	23.3
Storage systems	18.8
Image processing equipment	15.7
Output devices	7.1
Software	3.2

Source: *Computer Reseller News*, January 20, 1997, p. 23, from Frost & Sullivan Inc.

★ 1027 ★

Bandages (SIC 3842)

Adhesive Bandage Market

Unit shares are shown for the year ended June 8, 1996.

Johnson & Johnson	40.0%
Curad	22.0
3M	10.0
Private label	19.0
Other	9.0

Source: *Supermarket Business*, November 1996, p. 75, from A.C. Nielsen.

★ 1028 ★

Bandages (SIC 3842)

Children's Bandage Market

Unit shares are shown for the year ended June 8, 1996.

Curad	26.0%
Johnson & Johnson	14.0
3M	13.0
Private label	1.0
Other	46.0

Source: *Supermarket Business*, November 1996, p. 75, from A.C. Nielsen.

★ 1029 ★

Bandages (SIC 3842)

Premium Bandage Market

Unit shares are shown for the year ended June 8, 1996.

Johnson & Johnson	47.0%
3M	17.0
Curad	13.0
Private label	20.0
Other	3.0

Source: *Supermarket Business*, November 1996, p. 75, from A.C. Nielsen.

★ 1030 ★

Medical Products (SIC 3842)

Most Heavily Advertised Medical/ Surgical Brands - 1996

Data show the leading medical/surgical brands ranked by share of total ad spending. Companies are listed in parentheses.

Cozzar & Hyzaar (Merck)	2.61%
Tiazac (Forest Pharmaceuticals)	2.31
Fosamax (Merck)	1.79
Cardizem CD (Hoechst Marion Roussel)	1.76
Ultram Tablets (Ortho & McNeil)	1.63
Norvasc (Pfizer Laboratories)	1.58
Zoloft Tablets (Roerig)	1.46
Naprelan Tablets (Wyeth-Ayerst)	1.44
Adalat CC (Bayer Pharmaceuticals)	1.39
Prilosec (Astra/Merck Group)	1.38
Covera (Searle Pharmaceuticals)	1.30
Miacalcin Spray (Sandoz Consumer)	1.12
Precose Tablets (Bayer Pharmaceuticals)	0.97%
Prozac (Eli Lilly & Company)	0.96
Others	78.30

Source: *Medical Marketing & Media*, March 1997, p. 73, from HCI Journal Ad Review.

★ 1031 ★

Medical Products (SIC 3842)

Top Medical/Surgical Advertisers - 1996

Data show the leading medical and surgical advertisers ranked by share of total ad spending.

Merck	7.99%
Wyeth-Ayerst	5.21
Hoechst Marion Roussel	4.77
Pfizer Laboratories	4.51
Bayer Pharmaceuticals	3.89
Forest Pharmaceuticals	3.49
Glaxo Wellcome	3.09
Zeneca Pharmaceuticals	2.85
Searle Pharmaceuticals	2.78
Bristol-Meyers Squibb	2.72
Sandoz Consumer Pharmaceutical Div.	2.56
SmithKline Beecham	2.56
Schering Corporation	2.48
Ciba-Geigy	2.44
Others	48.66

Source: *Medical Marketing & Media*, March 1997, p. 74, from HCI Journal Ad Review.

★ 1032 ★

Surgical Supplies (SIC 3842)

Powder-free Surgeon Glove Makers - 1996

Shares are as of September 1996.

Regent	83.0%
Ansell-Perry	9.0
Maxxim Medical	3.0
Safeskin	3.0
Baxter Pharmaceutical	1.5
Other	0.5

Source: *OR Manager*, February 1997, p. 12, from Frost & Sullivan.

★ 1033 ★

Surgical Supplies (SIC 3842)

Powdered Surgeon Glove Makers - 1996

Shares are as of September 1996.

Baxter Pharmaceutical	42.0%
J&J Medical Inc.	30.0
Ansell Perry	18.0
Maxxim Medical	8.0
Others	3.0

Source: *OR Manager*, February 1997, p. 12, from Frost & Sullivan.

★ 1034 ★

Surgical Supplies (SIC 3842)

Surgeon Glove Market by Type - 1996

Powder-free gloves	35.0%
Regular powdered gloves	31.0
Hypoallergenic gloves	24.0
Specialty gloves	10.0

Source: *OR Manager*, February 1997, p. 12, from Frost & Sullivan.

★ 1035 ★

Electromedical Equipment (SIC 3845)

U.S. Lithotripsy Market

Market shares are shown based on units.

Prime Medical Services Inc.	15.0%
Coram Healthcare Corp.	9.0
American Kidney Stores	2.0
Medstone International Inc.	2.0
Mobile Technology	2.0
Phymatrix	2.0
Other	68.0

Source: *Investext*, Thomson Financial Networks, October 17, 1996, p. 6.

★ 1036 ★

Optical Goods (SIC 3851)

Top Sports Optics Makers

Firms are ranked by sales in millions of dollars. Shares of the group are shown in percent.

	Sales ($ mil.)	% of Group
Bausch & Lomb	$ 515.0	60.1%
Oakley	218.0	25.4
Gargoyles	33.0	3.9
Smith Optics	32.0	3.7
Scott	30.0	3.5
Bolle	27.0	3.2
Briko	2.0	0.2

Source: *Sportstyle*, May 1997, p. 60.

★ 1037 ★

Optical Goods (SIC 3851)

U.S. Optical Market by Product

Spectacle lenses	49.5%
Frames/sunglasses	37.0
Contact lenses	13.5

Source: *Investext*, Thomson Financial Networks, February 26, 1997, p. 4.

★ 1038 ★

Cameras (SIC 3861)

Popular Camera Brands

Data show the brands of cameras preferred by shoppers at discount stores in 1996.

Kodak	31.0%
Canon	23.0
Eastman	11.0
Minolta	10.0
Nikon	8.0
Polaroid	8.0
Duracell	7.0
Fuji	5.0
Olympus	5.0
Panasonic	1.0
Vivitar	1.0

Source: *Discount Store News*, October 21, 1996, p. 71, from Lee J. Shapiro & Associates.

★ 1039 ★

Photocopiers (SIC 3861)

Photocopier Market

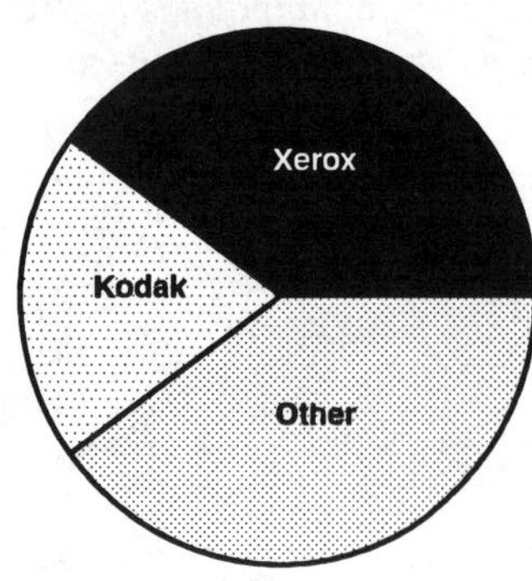

The high-end copier market is shown by company.

Xerox	40.0%
Kodak	20.0
Other	40.0

Source: *Wall Street Journal*, September 6, 1996, p. A5.

★ 1040 ★

Photocopiers (SIC 3861)

Top Photocopier Makers

Market shares are shown based on 1,645,800 units shipped in 1995.

Canon	29.0%
Xerox	23.0
Sharp	13.0
Mita	6.0
Minolta	5.0
Konica	4.0
Lanier	4.0
Ricoh	4.0
Others	12.0

Source: *Appliance*, September 1996, p. 88, from industry sources.

★ 1041 ★

Photographic Film (SIC 3861)

APS Film Market

APS stands for Advanced Photography System. The film is for cameras that can switch between different size photographs on the same roll of film and imprint digital information about the kind of shot, lighting, and the date of the photo.

Advantix	85.0%
Other	15.0

Source: *Forbes*, January 13, 1997, p. 46.

★ 1042 ★

Photographic Film (SIC 3861)

U.S. Film Market

Shares are shown in percent.

Kodak	70.0%
Fuji	10.0
Others	20.0

Source: *Wall Street Journal*, October 16, 1996, p. A5.

SIC 39 - Miscellaneous Manufacturing Industries

★ 1043 ★

Jewelry (SIC 3911)

Fine Jewelry Market

Cartier	20.0%
Tiffany	18.0
Bulgari	7.0
Van Cleef	3.0
Boucheron	2.0
Others	48.0

Source: *Investext,* Thomson Financial Networks, July 26, 1996, p. 2, from company data and C.S. First Boston estimates.

★ 1044 ★

Jewelry (SIC 3915)

Best-Selling Gemstones

Data show the top-selling colored gemstones in the United States, based on a survey.

Sapphires	35.4%
Rubies	16.5
Emeralds	13.5
Amethysts	10.5
Topaz	7.5
Tanzanite	3.8

Source: http:// www.gemstone.org/news.html, February 7, 1997, p. 4, from *National Jeweler.*

★ 1045 ★

Jewelry (SIC 3915)

Jewelry Sales by Type - 1996

Earrings	24.0%
Rings	22.0
Necklaces/neckchains	18.0
Bracelets	11.0
Watches	9.0
Other	16.0

Source: *Michigan Retailer,* March 1997, p. 1, from *Jewelers of America Survey.*

★ 1046 ★

Musical Instruments (SIC 3931)

Grand Piano Sales

Data show unit sales.

5' to 5'5"	10,289
Under 5'0	6,372
5'6" to 5'10"	5,177
5'11" to 6'4"	2,716
6'4" to 7'10"	1,832
7'11" and Over	165

Source: *Music Trades,* April 1997, p. 120.

★ 1047 ★

Musical Instruments (SIC 3931)

Musical Instrument Market

Retail sales are shown in millions of dollars.

Sound reinforcement	$ 729.1
Fretted products	708.2
Acoustic pianos	628.9
School music	606.6
Printed music	425.0
General accessories	355.4
Single unit amplifiers	354.8
Microphones	299.0

Continued on next page.

★ 1047 ★ *Continued*

Musical Instruments (SIC 3931)

Musical Instrument Market

Retail sales are shown in millions of dollars.

Electronic music products	$ 280.6
Percussion products	211.4
Signal processing	153.9
Multi-track recorders	150.8

Source: *Music Trades*, April 1997, p. 101.

★ 1048 ★

Musical Instruments (SIC 3931)

Top Selling Horns

B-flat clarinet
Flute
Trumpet
Alto sax
Piccolos
Tenor trombone
Tenor sax
Baritone horn
French horn
Sousaphone

Data show unit sales.

B-flat clarinet	126,200
Flute	116,000
Trumpet	103,200
Alto sax	79,900
Piccolos	77,300
Tenor trombone	36,300
Tenor sax	13,200
Baritone horn	11,300
French horn	9,900
Sousaphone	1,630

Source: *Music Trades*, April 1997, p. 126.

★ 1049 ★

Musical Instruments (SIC 3931)

Top Suppliers to the Music Trade - 1996

Data show estimated sales in thousands of dollars.

Yamaha Corporation of America	$ 800,000
Harman Int. (Professional Division)	459,773
Peavey Electronics	325,000
Steinway Musical Instruments	257,903
Shure Brothers	200,000
EVI Audio	192,000
Fender Musical Instruments	186,000
Kaman Music	150,000
Roland Corp. USA	130,000
Baldwin Piano & Organ	115,100
Gibson Guitar Corp.	110,000
Kawai America Corporation	103,500
Crown International	98,000
Alesis	88,909
Hal Leonard Corporation	83,000

Source: *Music Trades*, April 1997, p. 146.

★ 1050 ★

Writing Instruments (SIC 3931)

Writing Instrument Sales

Percent of $1.7 billion in sales.

Ballpoint pens	43.0%
Markers/highlights	16.0
Roller pens	14.0
Mechanical pencils	11.0
Coloring markers	6.0
Porous point	4.0
Fountain pens	3.0
Other	3.0

Source: *USA TODAY*, October 14, 1996, p. D1, from Writing Instrument Manufacturers Association.

★ 1051 ★

Toys and Games (SIC 3940)

Popular Licensed Toys - 1996

Data show the licensed or movie tie-in products expected to be best sellers in 1996. Figures are based on a survey.

Star Wars	37.0%
Batman	17.0
Goosebumps	17.0
Hunchback of Notre Dame	13.0
Independence Day	13.0
Space Jam	13.0
101 Dalmations	10.0

Source: *USA TODAY*, December 10, 1996, p. D1, from Duracell Toy Industry Forecast.

★ 1052 ★

Toys and Games (SIC 3940)

Toy Makers - 1995

Mattel

Hasbro

Tyco

Little Tikes

Hallmark

Other

Retail sales of toys reached $17.5 billion in 1995.

Mattel	15.6%
Hasbro	11.8
Tyco	3.2
Little Tikes	2.8
Hallmark	2.1
Other	64.5

Source: *New York Times*, November 19, 1996, p. C1, from NPD Group.

★ 1053 ★

Toys and Games (SIC 3940)

Toys and Game Sales by Segment

Sales at discount stores are shown in percent. Total sales reached $7.78 billion.

Dolls/action figures	28.0%
Games/puzzles	18.4
Vehicles	8.0
Plush toys	5.3
Other	40.4

Source: *Discount Store News*, August 5, 1996, p. 89.

★ 1054 ★

Toys and Games (SIC 3942)

Top Doll Makers - 1996

Shares are shown for the first 11 months of the year.

Mattel	52.5%
Hasbro	6.5
Arco	6.3
Galoob	3.5
Toy Biz	2.4
Tyco	2.1
Other	26.7

Source: *Playthings*, February 1997, p. 22, from NPD Group-TRSTS Report.

★ 1055 ★

Toys and Games (SIC 3944)

Advanced Gaming System Sales

Shares are shown as of November 1996.

	Units	Share
Nintendo	384,000	60.0%
Sony	246,000	31.0
Sega	72,000	9.0

Source: *Globe and Mail*, December 28, 1996, p. B5, from NPD Group Inc.

★ 1056 ★

Toys and Games (SIC 3944)

Arts/Crafts Sales by Segment

Sales at discount stores are shown in percent. Total sales reached $1.89 billion.

Artificial flowers	31.7%
Yarn	7.9
Other	60.3

Source: *Discount Store News*, August 5, 1996, p. 89.

★ 1057 ★

Toys and Games (SIC 3944)

Best-Selling Games - 1996

Uno
Monopoly
Jenga
Candyland
Trouble

Data show unit sales. Manufacturers are shown in parentheses. An estimated 55% of American homes hold an Uno game.

Uno (Mattel Inc.)	1,936,681
Monopoly (Parker Brothers)	1,827,968
Jenga (Milton Bradley)	1,261,539
Candyland (Milton Bradey)	1,101,855
Trouble (Milton Bradley)	1,033,473

Source: *USA TODAY*, December 2, 1996, p. D1, from Trsts and NPD Group Inc.

★ 1058 ★

Toys and Games (SIC 3944)

Canada's Educational Toy Sales

Sales are shown by province. "Other" includes Nova Scotia, Prince Edward Island, New Brunswick, Newfoundland, and Labrador. Leading Canadian firms in the industry include Irwin Toy, Retvik Toys, Canada Games, Wrebbit, Playtoy Industries, Thinkaway Toys, and Bo-Jeux Toys.

Ontario	38.0%
Quebec	28.0
British Columbia	12.0
Alberta	9.0
Other	13.0

Source: *National Trade Data Bank*, October 10, 1996, p. ISA960901.

★ 1059 ★

Toys and Games (SIC 3944)

Popular Video Game Software Brands

Data show the brands of computer software and games preferred by shoppers at discount stores in 1996.

Nintendo/Gameboy	20.0%
Microsoft	19.0
Sega/Genesis	18.0
IBM	10.0
Sony	7.0
Apple	4.0
3M	3.0
Quicken	2.0

Source: *Discount Store News*, October 21, 1996, p. 68, from Lee J. Shapiro & Associates.

★ 1060 ★

Toys and Games (SIC 3944)

Top Child Vehicle Makers - 1996

Shares are shown for the first 11 months of the year.

Tyco	13.6%
Mattel	12.6
Galoob	10.3
Hasbro	6.7
Racing Championships	6.6
New Bright	6.5
Nikko America	4.9

Continued on next page.

★ 1060 ★ *Continued*

Toys and Games (SIC 3944)

Top Child Vehicle Makers - 1996

Shares are shown for the first 11 months of the year.

Funrise	3.1%
Other	35.7

Source: *Playthings*, February 1997, p. 22, from NPD Group-TRSTS Report.

★ 1061 ★

Toys and Games (SIC 3944)

Top Puzzle Makers

Shares of the market are shown for the year ended December 1996.

Milton Bradley	46.0%
Parker Brothers	10.4
Hasbro Toy Group	9.9
Ceaco	9.8
Rose Art	7.7
Patch Products	4.9
Berk	3.6
FX Schmid	2.1
Other	5.6

Source: *Playthings*, March /, 197, p. 20, from NPD Group-TRSTS Report.

★ 1062 ★

Toys and Games (SIC 3944)

U.S. Video Game Market

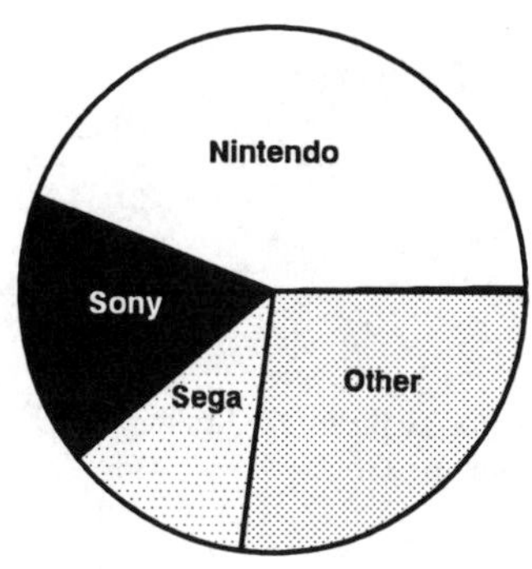

Shares are shown for the $3.3 billion market as of November 1996.

Nintendo	44.0%
Sony	17.0
Sega	12.0
Other	27.0

Source: *Globe and Mail*, December 28, 1996, p. B5, from NPD Group Inc.

★ 1063 ★

Toys and Games (SIC 3944)

Video Game Machine Market

Market shares are shown in percent.

PlayStation	80.0%
Other	20.0

Source: *Forbes*, September 23, 1996, p. 148.

★ 1064 ★

Toys and Games (SIC 3944)

Video Game Market - Canada

Shares of the $171 million market are shown in percent.

Nintendo	50.0%
Sega of Canada	30.0
Sony of Canada	20.0

Source: *Marketing Magazine*, February 24, 1997, p. 2, from Sega.

★ 1065 ★
Sporting Goods (SIC 3949)

Cross-Country Skiing Equipment Purchases

Data show unit sales by year.

	1995	1996
Boots	289,314	366,679
Bindings	231,079	308,867
Poles	240,134	279,158
Skis	224,950	277,854

Source: *Sporting Goods Business*, January 6, 1997, p. 36, from National Sporting Goods Association.

★ 1066 ★
Sporting Goods (SIC 3949)

Popular Sports in Mexico

Data show the largest end-users of the sporting goods market.

Soccer	30.0%
Basketball	18.0
Baseball	15.0
Indoor soccer	9.0
Fitness	7.0
Other	21.0

Source: *National Trade Data Bank*, October 9, 1996, p. ISA960901.

★ 1067 ★
Sporting Goods (SIC 3949)

Skate Sales in Canada

	No.	Share
Hockey	958,000	37.0%
In-line skates	886,000	34.2
Figure skates	570,000	22.0
Roller skates	168,000	6.5
Speed skates	5,000	0.2

Source: *National Trade Data Bank*, August 26, 1996, p. IMI960515, from Canadian Sporting Goods Association.

★ 1068 ★
Sporting Goods (SIC 3949)

Ski Equipment Orders - 1996

Data show wholesale orders.

	1995	1996
Alpine boots	834,240	660,522
Alpine skis	673,668	596,682
Alpine bindings	705,798	574,928

Source: *STN - Skiing Trade News*, October 1996, p. 5, from *Skiing Industries Association's Sales and Order Survey*.

★ 1069 ★
Sporting Goods (SIC 3949)

Sporting Goods Sales

Estimated sales are shown in billions of dollars.

	1995	1996	Share
Equipment	$ 15.0	$ 15.6	41.7%
Footwear	11.4	11.8	31.6
Apparel	9.6	10.0	26.7

Source: *Sporting Goods Business*, June 1996, p. 8, from National Sporting Goods Association.

★ 1070 ★
Sporting Goods (SIC 3949)

Sporting Goods Sales by Category - 1996

Wholesale sales are shown in billions of dollars.

	($ bil.)	Share
Apparel	$ 17.28	41.6%
Equipment	15.18	36.6
Footwear	9.03	21.8

Source: *Sporting Goods Business*, February 24, 1997, p. 8, from Sporting Goods Manufacturers Association.

★ 1071 ★
Sporting Goods (SIC 3949)

Sports Equipment Market - Mexico

Apparel	63.1%
Fitness equipment	23.2
Sports shoes	13.9

Source: *National Trade Data Bank*, December 9, 1996, p. ISA9601.

★ 1072 ★

Sporting Goods (SIC 3949)

Sports Equipment Sales - 1995

Sales are in millions of dollars for 1995.

Golf	$ 2,130
Exercise	1,935
Firearms/hunting	1,675
Camping	1,508
Fishing	1,500

Source: *DM*, November 1996, p. 3, from Sporting Goods Manufacturers Association.

★ 1073 ★

Sporting Goods (SIC 3949)

Top Fitness Gear Makers

Firms are ranked by estimated 1996 sales in millions of dollars.

ICON	$ 747.0
CML/Nordic Track	355.0
DP / Roadmaster	250.0
Life Fitness	155.0
CSA	110.0
Bollinger	80.3
Precor	70.0
Keys Fitness	60.0
Venture Aerobic	57.0
Fitness Master	53.0

Source: *Sporting Goods Business*, November 1996, p. 40.

★ 1074 ★

Sporting Goods (SIC 3949)

Top Inline Skate Makers - 1996

Firms are ranked by sales in millions of dollars. Shares of the group are shown in percent.

	Sales ($ mil.)	% of Group
Rollerblade	$ 210.0	34.0%
First Team (Ultra Wheels)	76.4	12.4
Roller Derby	72.0	11.6
Bauer	50.0	8.1
Variflex	43.2	7.0
Seneca Sports	27.0	4.4
K2	26.0	4.2
Roces	26.0	4.2
Oxygen	21.0	3.4
OCM	$ 18.5	3.0%
National	17.0	2.7
Mission	14.0	2.3
Brookfield	9.4	1.5
California Pro	5.5	0.9
Karhu/Koho	2.5	0.4

Source: *Sportstyle*, May 1997, p. 60.

★ 1075 ★

Sporting Goods (SIC 3949)

Top Outdoor Gear Makers

Firms are ranked by estimated 1996 sales in millions of dollars.

Coleman	$ 476.0
American Recreation	130.0
Nelson/Weather-Rite	120.0
JanSport	118.5
JWA Camping	97.7
Eastpak	52.0
Outdoor Products	43.0
North Face	39.5
High Sierra	35.0
Avid Outdoors	25.0

Source: *Sporting Goods Business*, November 1996, p. 34.

★ 1076 ★

Sporting Goods (SIC 3949)

Top Ski Equipment Makers - 1996

Firms are ranked by sales in millions of dollars. Shares of the group are shown in percent.

	Sales ($ mil.)	% of Group
Salomon	$ 69.0	19.6%
Rossignol	54.7	15.5
Dynastar	35.0	9.9
Marker	33.0	9.4
K2	26.0	7.4
Tecnica	25.0	7.1
Nordica	23.5	6.7
Head USA	18.0	5.1
Elan	16.8	4.8
Volki	10.2	2.9
Olin	9.0	2.6

Continued on next page.

★ 1076 ★ *Continued*

Sporting Goods (SIC 3949)

Top Ski Equipment Makers - 1996

Firms are ranked by sales in millions of dollars. Shares of the group are shown in percent.

	Sales ($ mil.)	% of Group
Alpina	$ 8.9	2.5%
Atomic	8.5	2.4
Fischer	8.2	2.3
Karhu USA	6.2	1.8

Source: *Sportstyle*, May 1997, p. 60.

★ 1077 ★

Sporting Goods (SIC 3949)

Top Snowboard Makers

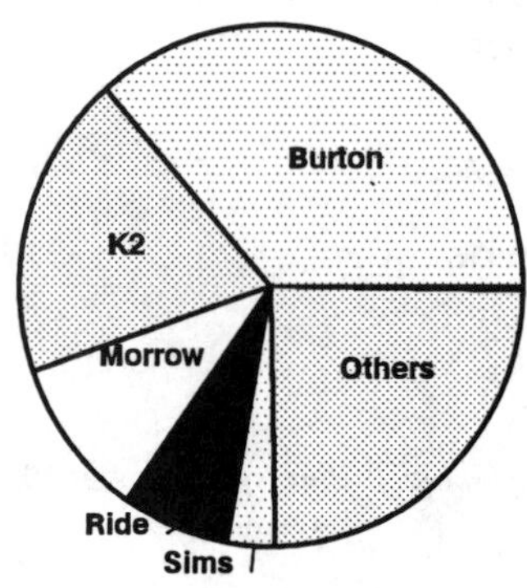

Burton	36.5%
K2	18.5
Morrow	9.5
Ride	7.0
Sims	3.0
Others	24.5

Source: *Sporting Goods Business*, February 24, 1997, p. 27.

★ 1078 ★

Sporting Goods (SIC 3949)

Top Sporting Goods Companies - 1996

Firms are ranked by sales in millions of dollars.

Nike	$ 4,974
Reebok	2,005
Russell	1,244
Spalding	$ 862
Fila	768
VF Corp.	747
Tultex	636
Adidas	570
Bausch & Lomb	515
Coleman	487
Timberland	486
Champion	465
Wilson	400
Starter	357
Benetton	304

Source: *Sportstyle*, May 1997, p. 16.

★ 1079 ★

Sporting Goods (SIC 3949)

Top Team Equipment Makers - 1996

Firms are ranked by sales in millions of dollars.

Spalding	$ 163.0
Rowlings	128.5
Franklin	121.5
Wilson	115.0
Bauer	104.2
Easton Sports	87.0
Hillerich and Bradsby	83.0
Riddell	72.3

Source: *Sportstyle*, May 1997, p. 58.

★ 1080 ★

Sporting Goods (SIC 3949)

Top Tennis Ball Makers - 1996

Firms are ranked by sales in millions of dollars. Shares of the group are shown in percent.

	Sales ($ mil.)	% of Group
Penn	$ 38.00	46.5%
Wilson	33.00	40.4
Dunlop	9.00	11.0
Spalding	1.00	1.2
Gamma	0.50	0.6
Pro Kennex	0.25	0.3

Source: *Sportstyle*, May 1997, p. 60.

★ 1081 ★

Sporting Goods (SIC 3949)

Top Tennis Racquet Makers - 1996

Firms are ranked by sales in millions of dollars.

Wilson	$ 49.0
Prince	32.0
Head	11.5
Dunlop	10.0
Pro Kennex	9.0
Spalding	4.0
Gamma	1.1
Volki	1.0
Yonex	1.0

Source: *Sportstyle*, May 1997, p. 60.

★ 1082 ★

Office Supplies (SIC 3950)

Office Supply Sales

Data are in millions of dollars for the second quarter of 1996.

School, home, office supplies	$ 252.4
Writing instruments	107.2
Drawing/coloring/art supplies	99.0
Tapes	65.5
Mailing supplies and accessories	26.8

Source: *Nonfoods Merchandising*, November 1996, p. 12, from A.C. Nielsen.

★ 1083 ★

Brooms (SIC 3991)

Best-Selling Brooms and Mops

Sales of brooms and mops reached $207.1 million at supermarkets for the 52 weeks ended April 21, 1996. Figures are in millions of dollars. Producers are shown in parentheses.

	Sales ($ mil.)	Share
Quickie (Quickie Mfg.)	$ 25.39	12.3%
Vining (O-Cedar/Vining)	20.35	9.8
Libman (Libman Broom)	15.90	7.7
Private label	14.63	7.1
Empire (Empire Brushes Inc.)	13.41	6.5
Handi Wipe (Colgate-Palmolive)	13.07	6.3
Kellogg (Ekco)	12.15	5.9
Rubbermaid (Rubbermaid)	8.55	4.1
Roll-O-Matic (W.B. Walton)	5.20	2.5
Smart Mop (Direct Marketing Virginia)	$ 1.36	0.7%
Other	77.10	37.2

Source: *Nonfoods Merchandising*, November 1996, p. 10, from Information Resources Inc.

★ 1084 ★

Brooms (SIC 3991)

Push Broom Market

Shares are shown based on unit sales for June 1995 to May 1996.

18" brooms	61.0%
24" brooms	32.0
Other sizes	7.0

Source: *Do-It-Youself Retailing*, January 1997, p. 57, from Vista Sales and Marketing.

★ 1085 ★

Toothbrushes (SIC 3991)

Leading Toothbrush Brands

Market shares are shown in percent.

Oral B	25.0%
Colgate	20.0
Reach	15.0
Crest Complete	10.0
Mentadent	7.0
Butler	4.0
Other	19.0

Source: *Chicago Tribune*, February 25, 1997, p. 3, from Information Resources Inc.

★ 1086 ★

Toothbrushes (SIC 3991)

Top Toothbrush Brands by Unit Sales

Unit shares are shown in percent for the year ended December 29, 1996.

Oral B	21.3%
Colgate	19.8
Reach	13.7
Crest	9.0
Mentadent	5.3
Aqua Fresh	4.4

Continued on next page.

★ 1086 ★ *Continued*

Toothbrushes (SIC 3991)

Top Toothbrush Brands by Unit Sales

Unit shares are shown in percent for the year ended December 29, 1996.

Tek	2.8%
Butler	2.7
Dentax	2.0
Private label	12.3
Other	6.7

Source: *Supermarket Business*, April 1997, p. 50, from Information Resources Inc.

★ 1087 ★

Caskets (SIC 3995)

U.S. Burial Casket Makers

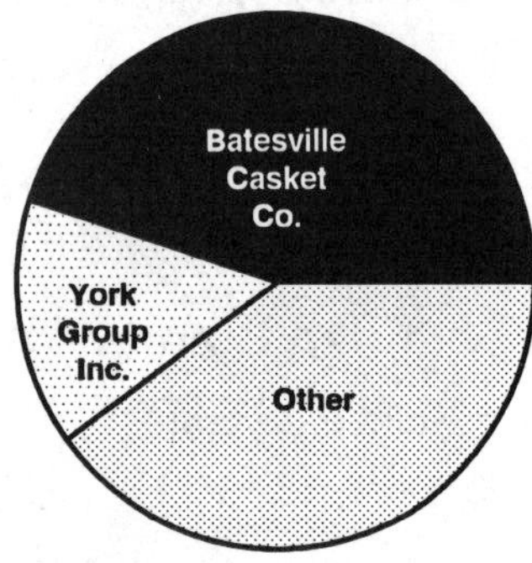

Shares are shown based on 1.9 million caskets sold annually in the United States.

Batesville Casket Co.	45.0%
York Group Inc.	15.0
Other	40.0

Source: *Wall Street Journal*, February 19, 1997, p. B1.

★ 1088 ★

Lighters (SIC 3999)

Refillable Lighter Market

Data show the market by company.

Zippo Manufacturing Co.	40.0%
Other	60.0

Source: *Forbes*, November 18, 1996, p. 214.

★ 1089 ★

Pet Products (SIC 3999)

Pet Product Spending by City

Pet expenditures are shown in millions of dollars for 1995.

New York City	$ 720
Chicago	684
Los Angeles	676
Washington D.C.	449
Philadelphia	442
Detroit	370
Boston	355
Houston	313
Atlanta	302
Dallas	264

Source: *Wall Street Journal*, February 21, 1997, p. B10, from Market Statistics Inc.

★ 1090 ★

Poker Chips (SIC 3999)

Poker Chip Makers

Paul-Son has a 30% share of the dice market.

Paul-Son	80.0%
Other	20.0

Source: *Investor's Business Daily*, February 25, 1997, p. A4.

★ 1091 ★

Slot Machines (SIC 3999)

Slot Machine Makers

International Game Technology	85.0%
Other	15.0

Source: *Wall Street Journal*, February 3, 1997, p. B1.

SIC 40 - Railroad Transportation

★ 1092 ★

Transportation (SIC 4000)

Largest Transportation Companies - Washington D.C.

Firms are ranked by revenues in millions of dollars.

U.S. Airways Group Inc.	$ 8,140.0
WorldCorp Inc.	313.7
World Airways Inc.	309.6
Banner Aerospace Inc.	287.9
Atlantic Coast Airlines Inc.	182.5

Source: *Washington Post*, April 28, 1997, p. 31.

★ 1093 ★

Railroads (SIC 4011)

Eastern Rail Traffic Leaders

Data show the carloads originating from the East as of November 16, 1996.

	No.	Share
CSX	3,300	45.1%
Norfolk Southern	2,200	30.1
Conrail	1,400	19.1
Other	419	5.7

Source: *New York Times*, November 23, 1996, p. 21, from Association of American Railroads.

★ 1094 ★

Railroads (SIC 4011)

Leading U.S. Railroads

The largest railroads are ranked by miles of track operated at the end of 1995. CSX and Conrail are planning to merge.

Union Pacific	60,906
Burlington Northern/Santa Fe	48,463
CSX	31,961
Norfolk Southern	25,236
Conrail	11,635

Source: *New York Times*, October 16, 1996, p. C9, from Association of American Railroads.

★ 1095 ★

Railroads (SIC 4011)

Long-Distance Rail Shipping

Shares of long-distance rail freight shipped in 1995.

Union Pacific	34.73%
Burlington Northern/Santa Fe	30.47
CSX/Conrail	19.33
Other	15.47

Source: *USA TODAY*, October 16, 1996, p. B1, from Association of American Railroads.

★ 1096 ★
Railroads (SIC 4011)

Rail-Freight by Commodity

This table shows the commodity share of the 17.7 million carloads of freight shipped in 1996.

Coal	38.52%
Chemicals	8.98
Grain	6.96
Motor vehicles & equipment	5.73
Metallic ores	5.47
Crushed stone, sand & gravel	4.55
All other carloads	29.79

Source: *Logistics Management*, February 1997, p. 18, from Association of American Railroads.

★ 1097 ★
Railroads (SIC 4011)

Railroad Categories by Freight Revenues

Categories are ranked by freight revenues in thousands of dollars.

Class I lines	$ 31,355,593
Regional lines	1,549,627
Local lines	1,436,811

Source: *Railway Age*, April 1997, p. 66, from *American Association of Railroads Fact Book, 1996.*

★ 1098 ★
Railroads (SIC 4011)

Top Railroad Companies - 1996

Data show revenues in millions of dollars.

CSX	$ 10,536
Union Pacific	10,051
Burlington No. Santa Fe	8,187
Norfolk Southern	4,770
Conrail	3,714

Source: *Fortune*, April 28, 1997, p. 59.

★ 1099 ★
Railroads (SIC 4011)

Top Railroads

Firms are ranked by 1995 revenues in billions of dollars.

CSX	$ 10.5
Union Pacific	7.5
Burlington Northern/Santa Fe	6.2
Southern Pacific	3.2

Source: *American Shipper*, September 1996, p. 28, from American Association of Railroads and individual railroads.

★ 1100 ★
Railroads (SIC 4011)

Top Railroads by Coal Shipments

Market shares are shown based on coal shipments to utilities in 1995.

BNSF	38.0%
UP	38.0
CSX	11.0
NS	6.0
Conrail	3.0
Others	4.0

Source: *Journal of Commerce*, February 3, 1997, p. 1, from RDI.

★ 1101 ★
Railroads (SIC 4011)

Top Railroads by Coal Shipments - Eastern States

Market shares are shown based on coal shipments to utilities in 1995.

CSX	57.0%
NS	26.0
Conrail	16.0
Others	1.0

Source: *Journal of Commerce*, February 3, 1997, p. 1, from RDI.

★1102★

Railroads (SIC 4011)

Top Railroads by Coal Shipments - Western States

Market shares are shown based on coal shipments to utilities in 1995.

BNSF	48.0%
UP	46.0
Others	6.0

Source: *Journal of Commerce*, February 3, 1997, p. 1, from RDI.

★1103★

Railroads (SIC 4011)

Top Transporters of Chemicals

Shares are based on the 139.4 million tons transported in 1995.

UP	42.33%
CSX	17.28
BNSF	14.57
NS	8.60
IC	5.91
Conrail	5.26
KCS	4.02
Soo	1.74
GTW	0.28

Source: *Chemicalweek*, January 8, 1997, p. 29, from American Association of Railroads.

★1104★

Railroads (SIC 4011)

U.S. Freight Leaders - 1996

Shares are shown based on 1.34 trillion ton-miles.

Union Pacific	35.9%
Burlington Northern Santa Fe	30.6
CSX	15.1
Norfolk Southern	12.9
Others	5.5

Source: *Business Week*, March 17, 1997, p. 33, from Association of American Railroads and individual carriers.

SIC 41 - Local and Interurban Passenger Transit

★ 1105 ★

Mass Transit (SIC 4111)

Leading Motorcoach Fleets

The largest companies in the United States and Canada are ranked by fleet size in 1996. The top 10 fleets have an estimated 58.0% of the 100 largest fleets and an estimated 25.0% of the total U.S. and Canada transit fleet.

Greyhound Lines Inc.	2,000
Ryder-ATE	1,120
ATC/Vancom Inc.	1,241
Laidlaw Transit Services	955
Academy Bus Tours Inc.	559
Liberty Lines Transit	419
Greyhound Lines of Canada Ltd.	403
Diversified Transportation Ltd.	350
Suburban Transit Corp.	333
Holland America Line-Westours Inc.	290

Source: *Metro Magazine*, September/October 1996, p. 42.

★ 1106 ★

Mass Transit (SIC 4111)

Top 10 Transit Bus Fleets

The largest companies in the United States and Canada are ranked by fleet size in 1996. The top 10 fleets have an estimated 35.0% of the 100 largest fleets and an estimated 24.0% of the total U.S. and Canada transit fleet.

MTA New York Transit	3,718
New Jersey Transit Corp.	2,943
Los Angeles County MTA	2,020
Chicago Transit Authority	2,000
Toronto Transit Commission	1,508
Southeastern PA Transp. Authority	1,334
Montreal Urban Community Transit Corp.	1,325
Washington Metrop. Area Transit Auth.	1,299
Metropolitan Transit Auth. of Harris Cnty.	1,293
King County Metro	1,145

Source: *Metro Magazine*, September/October 1996, p. 42, from Blue Bird.

★ 1107 ★

Mass Transit (SIC 4111)

Top U.S. & Canadian Bus Firms

Private motorcoach companies are ranked by fleet size in 1996.

Greyhound Lines Inc.	1,894
Ryder-ATE	1,280
ATC/Vancom Inc.	1,241
Laidlaw Transit Services	955
Academy Bus Tours Inc.	585
Liberty Lines Transit	419
Greyhound Canada Transportation Corp.	387
Diversified Transportation Ltd.	350
Suburban Transit Corp.	333
Holland America Line-Westours Inc.	299

Source: *Metro Magazine*, January/February 1997, p. 37, from Blue Bird.

★ 1108 ★

Mass Transit (SIC 4111)

U.S. Motorcoach Business

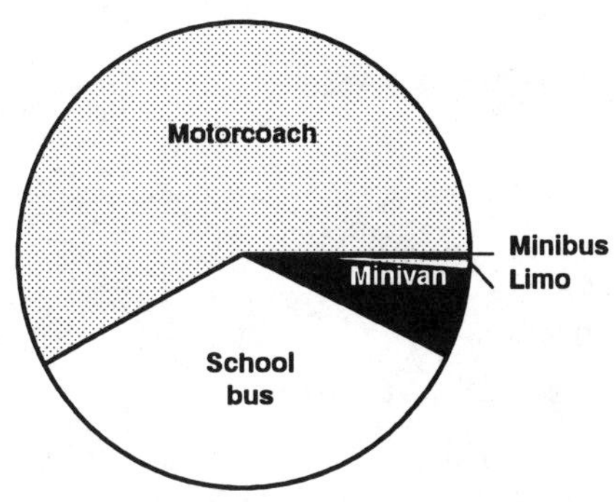

The composition of the U.S. motor fleet is shown in percent.

Motorcoach	58.0%
School bus	35.0
Minivan	6.0
Limo	0.7
Minibus	0.3

Source: *Metro Magazine*, November/December 1996, p. 6, from United Motorcoach Association.

★ 1109 ★

Emergency Transportation (SIC 4119)

Emergency Transportation Industry

Data are for 1995.

Fire department	34.0%
Private	26.0
Private and Fire department	15.0
Hospital based	6.0
Alternative delivery	4.0
Other public	15.0

Source: *Financial Times*, January 31, 1997, p. 25, from *Journal of Emergency Medical Services*.

★ 1110 ★

School Buses (SIC 4151)

School Bus Operators - North America

Firms are ranked by number of buses. Laidlaw has a 25% share of the available contract market.

Laidlaw	35,000
Ryder Systems Inc.	8,000
Vancom	3,500

Source: *Globe and Mail*, January 28, 1997, p. B4.

SIC 42 - Trucking and Warehousing

★ 1111 ★

Trucking (SIC 4210)

Refrigerated Trucking Groups

The leading trucking groups are ranked by 1995 revenues in millions of dollars.

Prime Inc.	$ 270.2
KLLM Inc.	239.7
FFE Transportation Services	234.7
C.R. England & Sons	222.4
Rocor International	209.7
Marten Transport	137.7
Stevens Transport	126.7
Transcontinental Refrigerated Lines	108.0
Midwest Coast Transport	107.1
Willis Shaw Express	104.3

Source: *Transportation Topics*, April 5, 1996, p. 39, from United States Department of Transportation Statistics, Dun & Bradstreet, Trucking Information Services, and annual reports.

★ 1112 ★

Trucking (SIC 4210)

Top Full-Load Carriers

Truckload carriers are ranked by 1995 revenues in millions of dollars.

Schneider	$ 1,709.5
J.B. Hunt	1,194.3
Ryder Dedicated	851.0
Werner	576.0
Swift Trptn.	458.2
Landstar Ranger	366.3
Burlington Motor	359.6
M S Carriers	333.1
Landstar Inway	292.3
Builders	282.5
Prime	276.7
Dart Transit	266.9

Source: *Distribution*, July 1996, p. 26, from Transportation Technical Services Inc.

★ 1113 ★

Trucking (SIC 4210)

Top LTL Truck Lines

Less-than-truckload (LTL) trucking companies are ranked by 1995 revenues in millions of dollars.

Yellow Freight	$ 2,339.0
Roadway Express	2,255.1
CF Motor Freight	4,014.5
A B F	1,005.7
Overnite	976.0
Watkins	471.0

Source: *Distribution*, July 1996, p. 18, from Transportation Technical Services Inc.

★ 1114 ★

Trucking (SIC 4210)

Top Tank Truck Lines

Tank truck carriers are ranked by 1995 revenues in millions of dollars.

Chemical Leaman	$ 244.1
Matlack	236.3
Trimac	228.5
Montgomery Tank	190.1
D S I Transports	190.0
Groendyke	108.3
Miller Transportation	93.7
Bulkmatic	85.9
Koch Services	77.8
Fleet Transport	77.5
Transport Service	76.2
Superior Carriers	67.2
Central Transport	63.9

Source: *Distribution*, July 1996, p. 32, from Transportation Technical Services Inc.

★1115★
Trucking (SIC 4210)

Top Trucking Companies - 1996

Companies are ranked by revenues in millions of dollars.

CNF Transportation	$ 3,662
Yellow	3,073
Caliber System	2,718
Roadway Express	2,373
Consol. Freightways	2,146
Arkansas Best	1,659
J.B. Hunt Transport Services	1,487
USFreightways	1,331
Landstar System	1,284

Source: *Fortune*, April 28, 1997, p. 63.

★1116★
Trucking (SIC 4210)

Top Trucking Groups

Firms are ranked by 1995 revenues in millions of dollars.

Consolidated Freightways Inc.	$ 5,281.1
Yellow Corp.	3,056.6
Caliber System	2,448.2
Ryder System	1,461.1
Arkansas Best Corp.	1,437.3
UniGroup Inc.	1,406.0
J.B. Hunt Transport Services	1,352.2
Landstar System	1,204.7
USFreightways Corp.	1,144.5
NFC plc	1,131.1

Source: *Transportation Topics*, April 5, 1996, p. 33, from United States Department of Transportation Statistics, Dun & Bradstreet, Trucking Information Services, and annual reports.

★1117★
Trucking (SIC 4210)

Top Trucking Groups - Canada

Firms are ranked by 1995 revenues in millions of dollars.

Trimac Transportation System	$ 371.3
Vitran Corp.	269.1
TNT North American	235.3
Westminster Holdings	202.5
Cabanco Kingsway	137.8
Mullen Transportation	134.6

Source: *Transportation Topics*, April 5, 1996, p. 35, from United States Department of Transportation Statistics, Dun & Bradstreet, Trucking Information Services, and annual reports.

★1118★
Trucking (SIC 4210)

U.S. Trucking Companies

Firms are ranked by 1995 revenues in millions of dollars.

United Parcel Service	$ 15,313.8
Yellow Freight System	2,339.0
Roadway Express	2,255.1
CF Motor Freight	2,014.5
Schneider National	1,709.5
RPS	1,290.0
J.B. Hunt Transport	1,194.3
Con-Way Express Carriers	1,049.2
ABF Freight System	1,005.7
Overnite Transportation	976.0
Ryder Dedicated Logistics	851.0
North American Van Lines	625.8
United Van Lines	610.0
Werner Enterprises	576.0

Source: *Transportation Topics*, April 5, 1996, p. 31, from United States Department of Transportation Statistics, Dun & Bradstreet, Trucking Information Services, and annual reports.

★ 1119 ★

Truck Leasing (SIC 4212)

Top Truck Leasing Companies - 1996

Companies are ranked by revenues in millions of dollars.

Ryder System	$ 5,519
Amerco	1,294

Source: *Fortune*, April 28, 1997, p. 63.

★ 1120 ★

Trucking (SIC 4214)

Largest Household Goods Movers

The leading trucking groups are ranked by 1995 revenues in millions of dollars.

North American Van Lines	$ 625.8
United Van Lines	610.0
Allied Van Lines	416.2
Mayflower Transit	315.6
Atlas Van Lines	262.3
Bekins Van Lines Co.	183.6
Graebel Van Lines	139.7
Burnham	104.7

Source: *Transportation Topics*, April 5, 1996, p. 39, from United States Department of Transportation Statistics, Dun & Bradstreet, Trucking Information Services, and annual reports.

★ 1121 ★

Courier Services (SIC 4215)

Letter/Envelope Delivery Service

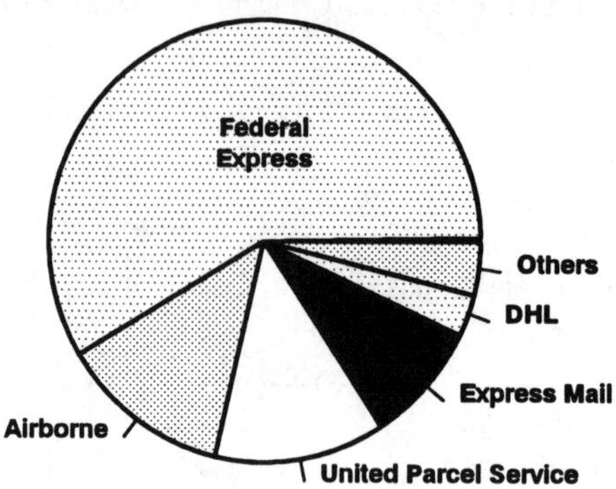

The market for overnight delivery of letters and envelopes two pounds or less reached $5.9 billion in 1995.

Federal Express	59.0%
Airborne	12.8
United Parcel Service	12.8
Express Mail	9.0
DHL	2.6
Others	3.8

Source: *Wall Street Journal*, September 17, 1996, p. B4, from Colography Group and United Parcel Service.

★ 1122 ★

Courier Services (SIC 4215)

Overnight Delivery Market

The market for overnight delivery of packages between 3-70 pounds reached $6.25 billion in 1995.

United Parcel Service	42.5%
Federal Express	40.0
Airborne	8.1
DHL	3.1
Express Mail	2.6
Others	3.7

Source: *Wall Street Journal*, September 17, 1996, p. B4, from Colography Group and United Parcel Service.

★1123★

Storage Facilities (SIC 4225)

Leading Self-Storage Companies - 1996

Firms are ranked by millions of square footage operated.

	(mil)	Share
Public Storage, Inc.	66.32	7.32%
U-Haul International, Inc.	18.17	2.01
Shurgard Storage Centers	18.11	2.00
Storage USA, Inc.	13.32	1.47
Storage Trust Realty	8.20	0.91
Sovran Self-Storage, Inc.	5.05	0.56
Storage Inns, Inc.	5.00	0.55
Derrel's Mini-Storage, Inc.	4.47	0.49
National Self Storage Management, Inc.	4.17	0.46
Private Mini Storage	3.30	0.36
Other	6.82	83.87

Source: *Urban Land*, November 1996, p. 49, from *Mini-Storage Messenger.*

★1124★

Storage Facilities (SIC 4225)

Warehouse Space by Region - 1996

Los Angeles-Long Beach
Chicago
New York City
Atlanta
Dallas
Northern/Central New Jersey
Cleveland
Houston
St. Louis
Miami
Columbus
Memphis
Milwaukee
Philadelphia
Riverside-San Bernadino

Data are in millions of square feet.

Los Angeles-Long Beach	504
Chicago	474
New York City	259
Atlanta	256
Dallas	195
Northern/Central New Jersey	190
Cleveland	169
Houston	135
St. Louis	132
Miami	112
Columbus	106
Memphis	105
Milwaukee	101
Philadelphia	100
Riverside-San Bernadino	99

Source: *Transportation & Distribution*, December 1996, p. 57, from Society of Office and Industrial Realtors, Sales Management, and Corplan Inc.

SIC 44 - Water Transportation

★ 1125 ★

Shipping (SIC 4412)

Top Containerized Exporters - 1996

Companies are ranked by exports in twenty-foot equivalent units.

Weyerhaeuser	91,000
Du Pont	75,000
Philip Morris	50,000
America Chung Nam	46,000
Military Sealift Command	43,000
Westvaco	38,000
Pacific Forest Resources	35,000
IBP	31,000
Chrysler	28,000
Eastman Chemical International	28,000
Union Carbide	25,000
Dow Chemical	23,000
Rayonier	23,000
Caterpillar Tractor	22,000
Dole Food	21,000

Source: *Journal of Commerce*, May 21, 1997, p. 7D.

★ 1126 ★

Shipping (SIC 4412)

Top Containerized Importers - 1996

Companies are ranked by imports in twenty-foot equivalent units.

Chiquita Brands	79,000
Wal Mart Stores	76,000
Sumitomo Amer (& Vendors)	62,000
Dole Food	49,000
Target Stores	47,000
Honda Motor	38,000
J.C. Penney	32,000
Payless Shoe Source	31,000
Canon	23,000
Ford Motor	22,000
Bridgestone/Firestone	21,000
Michelin Tire	21,000
Mattel	20,000
Nissan Motor	16,000
Pier One Imports	16,000

Source: *Journal of Commerce*, May 21, 1997, p. 6D.

★ 1127 ★

Shipping (SIC 4412)

Top Non-Containerized Exporters - 1996

Companies are ranked by exports in thousands of metric tons.

Cargill	21,000
Continental Grain Exports	17,000
Alfred C. Toepfer International	9,000
Consol Sales	9,000
Louis Dreyfus	9,000
Zen Noh Grain	8,000
AMCI Exports	7,000
Marubeni America	7,000
Mitsui & Company	7,000
Peabody Development	5,000
Shell Oil	5,000
Tradigrain	5,000
Pittston Coal Exports	4,500
Massey Coal Exports	4,400
Applied Industrial Materials	4,100

Source: *Journal of Commerce*, May 21, 1997, p. 29D.

★ 1128 ★

Shipping (SIC 4412)

Top Non-Containerized Importers - 1996

Companies are ranked by imports in thousands of metric tons.

Mobil Oil	31,000
Chevron	28,000
Shell Oil	25,000
Citgo	23,000
Amoco	21,000
Exxon	20,000
Star Enterprises	20,000
Bayway Refineries	11,000
Clark Refining	11,000
Lyondell Petrochemical	11,000
Kock Industries	10,000
Phillips 66	9,100
B P Oil	9,000
Ashland Petroleum	8,200
Coastal Petroleum	8,000

Source: *Journal of Commerce*, May 21, 1997, p. 28D.

★ 1129 ★

Shipping (SIC 4412)

Top U.S. Ship Lines

Data are in 20-foot container units of international cargo for the first nine months of the year.

Company	Units
Sea-Land Service	334,275
Evergreen Line	288,450
Maersk	220,654
Hanjin Shipping Co.	180,571
American President Line	171,844
Hyundai Merchant Line	140,985
Orient Overseas Containenr Line	124,410
Nippon Yusen Kaisha	122,044
China Ocean Shipping	116,557
"K" Line (Kawasaki Kisen Kaisha)	113,596
Yangming Maine Line	111,086
Mitsui O.S.K. Line	107,687
Crowley American Transport	75,222
Hapag-Lloyd	70,785
P&O Containers	69,777

Source: *Journal of Commerce*, January 6, 1997, p. 45C, from *Global Container Report*.

★ 1130 ★

Cruise Lines (SIC 4481)

Cruise Destinations in the Caribbean

Data show the number of visitors to each destination from cruise ships.

U.S. Virgin Islands	656,239
Bahamas	643,420
Puerto Rico	441,281
Jamaica	300,812
Cayman Islands	227,746
Barbados	212,440
Antigua & Barbuda	150,211
Grenada	116,066
St. Lucia	90,284
Dominica	71,022
St. Vincent & the Grenadines	39,144
Curacao	24,743
Bonaire	9,537

Source: *Travel Weekly*, October 28, 1996, p. 33, from Caribbean Tourism Organization.

★ 1131 ★

Cruise Lines (SIC 4481)

Cruise Lines by Berths

The leading cruise lines are ranked by number of berths as of May, 1997.

Carnival	20,330
Royal Carribbean	19,770
Princess	12,250
Holland America	10,061
Norwegian	9,556
Celebrity	7,454
Costa	7,180
Cunard	3,131
Seabourn	612
Windstar	444

Source: *USA TODAY*, May 18, 1997, p. 3B, from Carnival and Cruise Lines International Association.

★ 1132 ★

Cruise Lines (SIC 4481)

Leading Cruise Lines

Carnival Corp.
Royal Caribbean Cruise Line
P&O Cruises/Princess
Kloster Cruise Lines
Cunard
Costa Crociere
Chandris/Celebrity

Ranking is based on total berths in 1995. Projected berth availability is shown for 2000.

	1995	2000
Carnival Corp.	26,017	37,716
Royal Caribbean Cruise Line	15,020	24,724
P&O Cruises/Princess	11,130	14,850
Kloster Cruise Lines	9,762	8,805
Cunard	7,983	6,127
Costa Crociere	6,119	9,197
Chandris/Celebrity	5,584	9,224

Source: *Hotels*, November 1996, p. 10.

★ 1133 ★

Ports (SIC 4491)

Largest U.S. Ports - 1996

Data are in 20-foot container units of international cargo for the first nine months of the year.

Long Beach, CA	1,715,255
Los Angeles	1,383,228
New York City	1,144,001
Seattle	702,096
Oakland, CA	610,620
Charleston, CA	594,882
Hampton Roads, VA	534,945
Houston	403,000
Tacoma, WA	380,554
Miami, FL	375,337

Source: *Journal of Commerce*, January 6, 1997, p. 45C, from Port Import/Export Reporting Services.

★ 1134 ★

Ports (SIC 4491)

Leading Ports - 1995

Data show value of cargo in millions of dollars.

Los Angeles/Long Beach	$ 156,985
New York/New Jersey	67,211
Seattle	37,113
Baltimore	20,827
Philadelphia	7,058
Boston	3,640
San Diego	667

Source: *Wall Street Journal*, January 3, 1997, p. A2, from American Association of Port Authorities.

★ 1135 ★

Ports (SIC 4491)

Leading West Coast Ports

Volume of traffic is shown in thousands of twenty-foot equivalent units.

	1995	1996
Long Beach	2,116	2,325
Los Angeles	1,869	1,890
Seattle	993	939
Oakland	919	802
Tacoma	545	505

Source: *Journal of Commerce*, February 21, 1997, p. 1, from Port Import/Export Reporting Service.

★ 1136 ★

Marine Services (SIC 4499)

Leading Marine Service Companies - 1996

Companies are ranked by revenues in millions of dollars.

APL	$ 2,739
Alexander & Baldwin	1,233

Source: *Fortune*, April 28, 1997, p. 56.

SIC 45 - Transportation by Air

★ 1137 ★

Airlines (SIC 4512)

Airline Market - Denver, CO

Shares are shown based on paid departures on U.S. airlines. Passengers departing on foreign airlines are excluded.

United	69.94%
Delta	5.08
American	4.83
Continental	3.89
Air Wisconsin	2.78
Northwest	2.50
TWA	1.66
USAir	1.63
Markair	1.61
Frontier	1.61
America West	1.53
Other	2.94

Source: *Travel Weekly*, October 14, 1996, p. 39, from Salomon Brothers.

★ 1138 ★

Airlines (SIC 4512)

Airline Market - Kennedy Airport

Shares are shown based on paid departures on U.S. airlines. Passengers departing on foreign airlines are excluded. Data are for 1995.

American	32.33%
TWA	22.51
Delta	19.15
United	10.94
Tower Air	6.23
Other	8.84

Source: *Travel Weekly*, October 28, 1996, p. 33, from Salomon Brothers.

★ 1139 ★

Airlines (SIC 4512)

Airline Market - LaGuardia Airport

Shares are shown based on paid departures on U.S. airlines. Passengers departing on foreign airlines are excluded. Data are for 1995.

Delta	26.19%
USAir	21.66
American	18.15
United	8.39
Shuttle Inc.	7.29
Northwest	6.72
Other	11.60

Source: *Travel Weekly*, October 28, 1996, p. 33, from Salomon Brothers.

★ 1140 ★

Airlines (SIC 4512)

Airline Market - Las Vegas, NV

Market shares are shown for the first six months of 1996.

Southwest	31.19%
America West	21.79
United	12.07
Delta	8.97
American	5.13
Northwest	3.88
Others	16.97

Source: *Investext*, Thomson Financial Networks, February 6, 1997, p. 3, from *Aviation Daily*.

★ 1141 ★

Airlines (SIC 4512)

Airline Market - Philadelphia, PA

Market shares are shown for the first six months of 1996.

USAir	55.42%
American	8.71
Other	35.87

Source: *Investext,* Thomson Financial Networks, February 6, 1997, p. 3, from *Aviation Daily.*

★ 1142 ★

Airlines (SIC 4512)

Airline Market - Phoenix, AZ

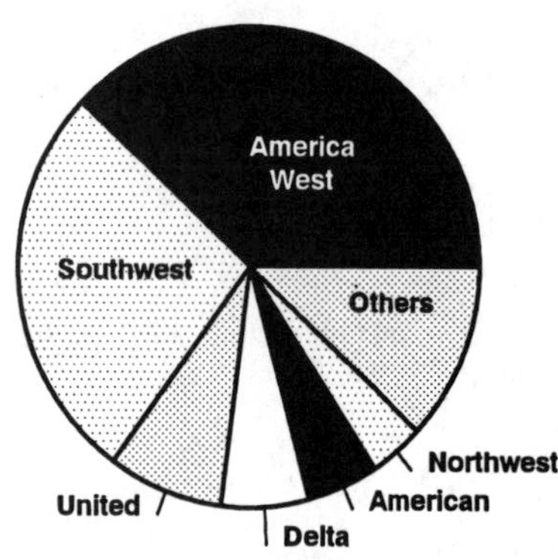

Market shares are shown for the first six months of 1996.

America West	38.14%
Southwest	27.05
United	8.30
Delta	5.70
American	4.82
Northwest	3.91
Others	12.06

Source: *Investext,* Thomson Financial Networks, February 6, 1997, p. 3, from *Aviation Daily.*

★ 1143 ★

Airlines (SIC 4512)

Airline Market - St. Louis, MO

Market shares are shown for the first six months of 1996.

TWA	69.36%
Southwest	13.21
Other	17.43

Source: *Investext,* Thomson Financial Networks, February 6, 1997, p. 3, from *Aviation Daily.*

★ 1144 ★

Airlines (SIC 4512)

Airline Market - Salt Lake City, Utah

Market shares are shown for the first six months of 1996.

Delta	69.64%
Southwest	11.18
Other	19.18

Source: *Investext,* Thomson Financial Networks, February 6, 1997, p. 3, from *Aviation Daily.*

★ 1145 ★

Airlines (SIC 4512)

Airline Market - San Francisco, CA

Market shares are shown for the first six months of 1996.

United	59.30%
American	6.64
Other	34.06

Source: *Investext,* Thomson Financial Networks, February 6, 1997, p. 3, from *Aviation Daily.*

★ 1146 ★

Airlines (SIC 4512)

Airline Market Leaders

Delta/Continental	24.3%
United	21.0
American	18.0
Northwest	12.0
USAir	12.0
Other	12.7

Source: *Business Week*, December 16, 1996, p. 33, from Avitas Inc.

★ 1147 ★

Airlines (SIC 4512)

Airline Travel to Florida

Data show the airlines that flew travelers from the Midwest and Northeast to Florida.

USAir	28.0%
Delta	16.0
Northwest	10.0
American	8.0
Amer. Trans. Air	6.0
TWA	5.0
United	5.0
Carnival	2.0
ValuJet	1.0
Others	7.0

Source: *USA TODAY*, October 8, 1996, p. B9.

★ 1148 ★

Airlines (SIC 4512)

Canada's Leading Airlines - 1996

Shares are shown based on sales of $6.03 million Canadian dollars.

Air Canada	57.0%
Canadian Airlines International	42.0
Others	1.0

Source: *Marketing Magazine*, May 26, 1997, p. 17, from industry sources.

★ 1149 ★

Airlines (SIC 4512)

Largest Airline City Pairs

Data show millions of passengers in 1995.

New York/Los Angeles	2.99
New York/Chicago	2.98
Honolulu/Kahului	2.76
New York/Miami	2.67
New York/Boston	2.49
Dallas/Houston	2.20
New York/San Francisco	2.18
New York/Washington	2.18
New York/Orlando	2.00
Los Angeles/Las Vegas	1.95

Source: *Travel Weekly*, August 19, 1996, p. 33, from Air Transport Association.

★ 1150 ★

Airlines (SIC 4512)

Largest Airlines - Atlanta, GA

Shares are for the first six months of 1996.

Delta	75.8%
ValueJet	6.9
Atlantic Southeast Airlines	4.3
Other	13.0

Source: *USA TODAY*, December 6, 1996, p. B1, from Avitas.

★ 1151 ★

Airlines (SIC 4512)

Largest Airlines - Chicago, IL

Data show millions of passengers transported in 1995.

United Airlines	29.3
American Airlines	22.3
Southwest Airlines	4.8
American Eagle/Simmons	2.7
Northwest Airlines	2.3
Delta Air Lines	1.8
Continental Airlines	1.7

Source: *Crain's Chicago Business*, June 17, 1996, p. 26.

★ 1152 ★

Airlines (SIC 4512)

Largest Airlines - Dallas/Fort Worth, TX

Data are for the first six months of 1996.

American Airlines	63.8%
Delta	18.2
Simmons	6.6
Other	11.4

Source: *USA TODAY*, December 24, 1996, p. B1, from Avitas.

★ 1153 ★

Airlines (SIC 4512)

Largest U.S. Airlines - 1995

Data show millions of passengers.

Delta	86.9
American	79.5
United	78.7
USAir	56.7
Southwest	50.0
Northwest	49.3
Continental	35.0
Trans World	21.6
America West	16.8
Alaska	10.1

Source: *Philadelphia Inquirer*, December 5, 1996, p. C1, from Air Transport Association.

★ 1154 ★

Airlines (SIC 4512)

Leading Airlines

Shares are shown for July 1996 based on revenue-passenger-miles generated.

American Airlines	18.5%
United Airlines	18.5
Delta	18.0
Northwest	10.3
USAir	9.2
Continental	7.6
Southwest	6.5
TWA	5.3
America West	3.6
Alaska	2.5

Source: *Interavia*, November 1996, p. 33.

★ 1155 ★

Airlines (SIC 4512)

Leading Airlines - 1997

United
American
Delta
Northwest
Continental
Other

Shares shown are based on February revenue passenger miles.

United	20.6%
American	17.4
Delta	16.9
Northwest	12.3
Continental	7.9
Other	24.9

Source: *USA TODAY*, April 9, 1997, p. 1B, from *Aviation Daily*.

★ 1156 ★

Airlines (SIC 4512)

Leading Canadian Airlines

Data show operating revenues of selected airlines for the three months ended June 30, 1996. Figures are in millions of dollars.

Air Canada	$ 1,212.0
Canadian	786.9

Source: *Air Transport World*, September 1996, p. 14, from airline reports.

★ 1157 ★

Airlines (SIC 4512)

Leading National/Start-Up Airlines

Data show operating revenues of selected airlines for the three months ended June 30, 1996. Figures are in millions of dollars.

Reno Air	$ 90.9
World	86.6
ValuJet	81.2
Midwest Express	76.8
Kiwi	53.4
Frontier	28.1

Source: *Air Transport World*, September 1996, p. 14, from airline reports.

★ 1158 ★

Airlines (SIC 4512)

Los Angeles Intl. Flight Market

Shares are for the first six months of 1996.

United	29.0%
Delta	14.6
Southwest	13.7
Other	43.3

Source: *USA TODAY*, January 3, 1997, p. B1, from Avitas.

★ 1159 ★

Airlines (SIC 4512)

Popular Aircraft for Regional Airlines

Data show percent of total seating capacity.

Saab 340	13.8%
Embraer Brasilia	12.5
Bombardier Dash 8-100/200	9.7
Beech 1900	9.6
Aerospatiale ATR-42	8.6
Jetstream J31/J32	7.1
Aerospatiale ATR-72	6.2
Avro/BAe RJ/146	4.3
Fairchild Metro/23	3.6
Bombardier CRJ	3.5
Shorts 300	2.3
Other	18.8

Source: *Travel Weekly*, June 20, 1996, p. 19, from Regional Airline Association.

★ 1160 ★

Airlines (SIC 4512)

Top Regional Airlines

Shares are shown based on 14.478 million passengers transported during the first quarter of 1996.

Simmons	9.46%
Comair	7.53
Mesa	7.15
Continental Express	6.14
Horizon Air	5.97
Atlantic Southeast	5.78
Flagship	5.15
Piedmont	4.44
SkyWest	4.27
Trans States	3.30
Other	40.81

Source: *Business & Commercial Aviation*, September 1996, p. C1, from AvStat Association of the Regional Airline Association.

★ 1161 ★

Airlines (SIC 4512)

Trans-Atlantic Airline Market

Shares are shown based on U.S. airline departures for October through December, 1996.

Delta	31.0%
American	25.0
United	16.0
TWA	9.0
Northwest	7.0
Continental	7.0
US Airways	5.0

Source: *USA TODAY*, June 17, 1997, p. B1, from Avitas.

★ 1162 ★

Airlines (SIC 4512)

U.S. Airlines by RPMs - 1995

Airlines are ranked by billions of revenue passenger miles generated in 1995.

United	111.5
American	102.7
Delta	85.1
Northwest	65.5
USAir	37.6

Continued on next page.

★ 1162 ★ *Continued*
Airlines (SIC 4512)

U.S. Airlines by RPMs - 1995

Airlines are ranked by billions of revenue passenger miles generated in 1995.

Continental	35.2
TWA	24.9
Southwest	23.3
American West	13.3
Alaska	8.5
American Trans Air	4.6
Cont'l Micronesia	4.5
Tower	3.7
Hawaiian	3.2
Valuejet	2.7

Source: *Travel Weekly*, October 17, 1996, p. 33, from Air Transport Association.

★ 1163 ★
Airlines (SIC 4512)

Washington National Airport Flight Market

Shares are for the first six months of 1996.

USAir	28.4%
Delta	18.0
American	13.5
Other	40.1

Source: *USA TODAY*, January 14, 1997, p. B1, from Avitas and *Aviation Daily*.

★ 1164 ★
Airlines (SIC 4512)

Who Flew Business Travelers in 1996

Data are for the first five months of 1996.

Delta	16.0%
United	15.0
American	13.0
Southwest	13.0
Other	43.0

Source: *USA TODAY*, August 29, 1996, p. B4, from D.K. Shifflet & Associates.

★ 1165 ★
Air Cargo (SIC 4513)

Air Cargo Airports

Data show millions of cargo tons enplaned and deplaned.

Memphis	1.71
Los Angeles	1.59
Miami	1.58
New York Kennedy	1.57
Louisville	1.35
Chicago O'Hare	1.23
Anchorage	0.98

Source: *Distribution*, July 1996, p. 58, from Air Transport Association.

★ 1166 ★
Air Cargo (SIC 4513)

Air Cargo Transporters - 1995

North American firms are ranked by air cargo revenues in millions of dollars.

Federal Express	$ 4,023.5
United	756.9
Northwest Airlines	751.2
American Airlines	667.9
DHL	567.8
Delta	536.5
Air Canada	323.0
United Parcel Service	305.2
Canadian	266.7
Polar Air Cargo	217.0

Source: *Distribution*, July 1996, p. 58, from Air Transport Association.

★ 1167 ★
Air Cargo (SIC 4513)

Air Freight Market - Kansas City

Data show the shares of the air freight market at Kansas City Airport for August 1996.

Burlington Air Express	22.8%
United Parcel Service	13.6
Emery Worldwide	10.9
DHL	9.9
Other	42.8

Source: *Journal of Commerce*, October 15, 1996, p. 1, from Kansas City International Airport.

★ 1168 ★

Air Cargo (SIC 4513)

Cargo Traffic in Mexico

Airports are in millions of kilos for 1995.

Benito Juarez	97.8
Don Miguel Hidalgo y Costilla	11.7
Abelardo L. Rodriguez	6.7
Mariano Escobedo	5.5
Manuel Marquez de Leon	3.7

Source: *Trade & Culture*, September 1996, p. 4.

★ 1169 ★

Air Cargo (SIC 4513)

Largest Cargo Airports - 1996

Data are in metric tons.

Memphis, TN	173,829
Los Angeles, CA	143,351
Miami, FL	139,287
New York City, NY	133,964
Louisville, KY	115,836
Chicago, IL	104,882
San Francisco, CA	37,583
Boston, MA	35,713

Source: *Asiaweek*, October 1, 1996, p. 12, from Airports Council International.

SIC 46 - Pipelines, Except Natural Gas

★ 1170 ★

Pipelines (SIC 4600)

Top Pipeline Companies - 1996

Data show revenues in millions of dollars.

Enron	$ 13,289
Panenergy	7,537
NGC	7,260
Noram Energy	4,788
Williams	3,531
Sonat	3,395
El Paso Natural Gas	3,010
Enserch	2,143
Tejas Gas	2,108
Western Gas Resources	2,091
Equitable Resources	1,862
KN Energy	1,443

Source: *Fortune*, April 28, 1997, p. 59.

★ 1171 ★

Pipelines (SIC 4612)

Top Liquid Pipelines

Firms are ranked by miles of pipeline in 1996.

Amoco Pipeline Co.	10,976
Chevron Pipe Line Co.	8,085
Mid-America Pipeline Co.	7,619
Williams Pipe Line Co.	7,389
Mobil Pipe Line Co.	7,216
Exxon Pipeline Co.	6,621
Marathon Pipe Line Co.	6,446
Texaco Pipeline Inc.	6,379
Conoco Pipe Line Co.	6,173
Colonial Pipeline Co.	5,340

Source: *Pipeline & Gas Journal*, September 1996, p. 20.

SIC 47 - Transportation Services

★ 1172 ★

Tourism (SIC 4720)

Leading Spenders in the United States

Data show the home country of foreign tourists ranked by 1995 spending in billions of dollars.

Japan	$ 16.8
United Kingdom	8.0
Canada	7.5
Germany	5.5
Mexico	5.4

Source: *World Trade*, November 1996, p. 74, from United States International Trade Administration.

★ 1173 ★

Tourism (SIC 4720)

U.S. International Tourist Industry

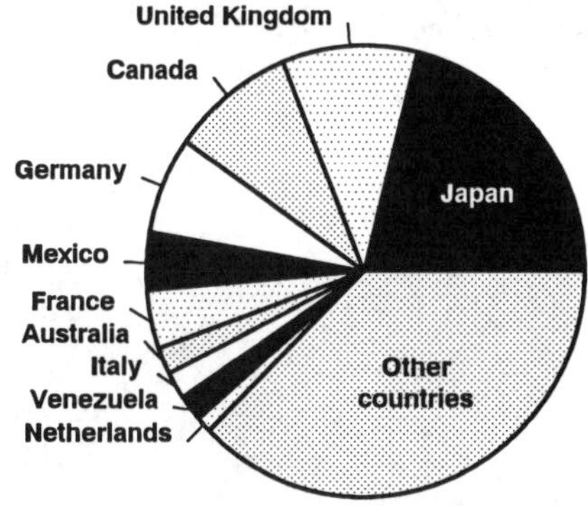

Share of the $79.7 billion industry is shown by country of origin.

Japan	21.1%
United Kingdom	10.0
Canada	9.4
Germany	6.9
Mexico	4.3
France	3.5
Australia	2.4
Italy	2.1%
Venezuela	2.1
Netherlands	1.2
Other countries	36.9

Source: *Association Management*, November 1996, p. 78, from Tourism Industries, International Trade Administration and Bureau of Economic Analysis.

★ 1174 ★

Tourism (SIC 4720)

Visitors to Alaska

Data show origins of the estimated 1 million visitors for the summer of 1995.

Western U.S.	37.0%
Southern U.S.	20.0
Midwestern U.S.	15.0
Eastern U.S.	11.0
Canada	10.0
Overseas	6.0
Unknown	1.0

Source: *Alaska Business Monthly*, December 1996, p. 68, from University of Alaska Center for Economic Development.

★ 1175 ★

Travel Agencies (SIC 4724)

Travel Agencies by State - 1996

States are ranked by number of travel agencies. Figures include home offices, branch offices, independent agencies, and others.

California	6,948
New York	4,098
Florida	3,230
Texas	3,212
Illinois	2,780
New Jersey	2,009
Pennsylvania	1,896

Continued on next page.

★ 1175 ★ *Continued*

Travel Agencies (SIC 4724)

Travel Agencies by State - 1996

States are ranked by number of travel agencies. Figures include home offices, branch offices, independent agencies, and others.

Massachusetts	1,718
Ohio	1,597
Georgia	1,496
Michigan	1,332
Virginia	1,184
Colorado	1,052
Washington	1,032
North Carolina	924

Source: *Travel Weekly*, March 17, 1997, p. 49, from Airlines Reporting Corp.

★ 1176 ★

Tour Operators (SIC 4725)

Tour Operator Market - Canada

Market shares are shown in percent.

Air Transat	31.0%
Sunquest	18.0
Signature	15.0
Regent	5.0
Air Canada	3.0
Globespan Group	3.0
Mont Royal	3.0
Nolitour	3.0
Nouvelles Frontieres	2.0
Royal Vacations	2.0
Exosol	1.0
Others	7.0

Source: *Investext,* Thomson Financial Networks, August 19, 1996, p. 3, from Transat and CIBC Woody Gundy.

★ 1177 ★

Tour Operators (SIC 4725)

Tour Operator Market - Montreal

Market shares are shown in percent.

Air Transat	46.0%
Mont Royal	11.0
Nolitour	11.0
Nouvelles Frontieres	7.0
Royal Vacations	7.0
Signature Regent	5.0%
Air Canada	4.0
Exosol	4.0
Others	6.0

Source: *Investext,* Thomson Financial Networks, August 19, 1996, p. 3, from Transat and CIBC Woody Gundy.

★ 1178 ★

Tour Operators (SIC 4725)

Tour Operator Market - Toronto

Market shares are shown in percent.

Sunquest	27.0%
Air Transat	23.0
Signature	20.0
Regent	8.0
Conquest Tours	6.0
Globespan Group	5.0
Air Canada	3.0
Others	8.0

Source: *Investext,* Thomson Financial Networks, August 19, 1996, p. 3, from Transat and CIBC Woody Gundy.

★ 1179 ★

Tourism (SIC 4725)

Who Visits Hawaii

Data show who visited Hawaii in 1995.

U.S.	3,582,030
Japan	1,998,860
Canada	295,610
Korea	104,550
Australia	92,310
Germany	89,670
U.K.	73,220
Taiwan	62,760
New Zealand	37,130

Source: *Travel Weekly*, August 8, 1996, p. H18, from Hawaii Visitors and Convention Bureau.

SIC 48 - Communications

★ 1180 ★

Wireless Communications (SIC 4812)

ACD Market

Shares are shown in percent. ACD stands for automatic call distribution.

Lucent	32.8%
Nortel	25.4
Siemens	13.1
Aspect	7.4
Rockwell	4.3
Executone	3.3
NEC	3.3
Mitel	3.0
Fujitsu	2.0
AVT	0.8
Intercom	0.8
Teloquent	0.7
Others	3.3

Source: *Business Communications Review*, May 1997, p. 10, from TEQConsult Group.

★ 1181 ★

Wireless Communications (SIC 4812)

Canada's Wireless Markets - 1997

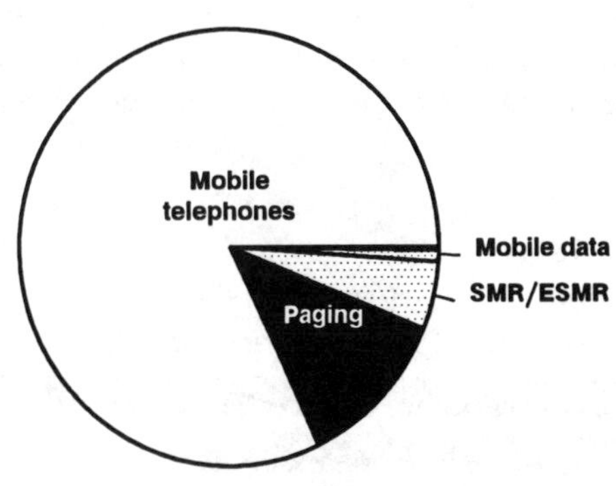

The market generated $3.7 billion in revenues. SMR stands for specialized mobile radio. ESMR stands for enhanced specialized mobile radio.

Mobile telephones	82.5%
Paging	11.6
SMR/ESMR	5.4
Mobile data	0.5

Source: *Globe and Mail*, April 8, 1997, p. C2, from Yankee Group.

★ 1182 ★

Wireless Communications (SIC 4812)

Largest Cellular Service Firms

Data show the millions of people covered by licenses.

AT&T Cellular	70.8
Bell Atlantic NYNEX mobile	54.5
GTE Mobilenet	52.3
AirTouch	42.9
BellSouth	40.5

Source: *Financial Times*, December 16, 1996, p. 17, from Salomon Brothers.

★ 1183 ★

Wireless Communications (SIC 4812)

Largest Pager Firms

Companies are ranked by millions of subscribers.

PageNet	7.8
MobileComm	4.4
Arch Communications	2.8
Metrocall	2.2
PageMart	1.5
ProNet	1.1
Mobile Telecommunications	1.0
American Paging	0.8
A+ Network	0.6

Source: *Forbes*, October 21, 1996, p. 151, from Lehman Brothers Wireless Communications Equity Research.

★ 1184 ★

Wireless Communications (SIC 4812)

Largest PCS Service Firms

Sprint Spectrum
AT&T PCS
NextWave
PCS Primeco
OmniPoint

Data show the millions of people covered by licenses.

Sprint Spectrum	191.8
AT&T PCS	111.7
NextWave	109.2
PCS Primeco	61.0
OmniPoint	40.1

Source: *Financial Times*, December 16, 1996, p. 17, from Salomon Brothers.

★ 1185 ★

Wireless Communications (SIC 4812)

Leading Cellular Phone Companies - Canada

Company shares are shown based on 2,497,000 subscribers for the year ending March 31, 1997.

Rogers Cantel	57.0%
BCE Mobile	43.0

Source: *Marketing Magazine*, May 26, 1997, p. 14, from Loewen Ondaatje McCutcheon Ltd.

★ 1186 ★

Telephone Services (SIC 4813)

Canada's Long-Distance Market - 1997

Shares are estimated.

Stentor Companies	66.0%
Sprint Canada	14.0
AT&T Canada LDS	12.0
Resellers	5.0
Other facilities-based carriers	3.0

Source: *Investext*, Thomson Financial Networks, December 5, 1996, p. 7.

★ 1187 ★

Telephone Services (SIC 4813)

Dial-Around Long-Distance Providers

Shares of the $575 million market are for 1995. Dial around services allow customers to punch in certain access codes to bypass long-distance services.

Telco	40.0%
Vartec	20.0
Frontier Communications	15.0
Matrix	5.0
Startecc	5.0
Other	15.0

Source: *Investor's Business Daily*, October 8, 1996, p. A6, from company reports and Atlantic-ACM.

★ 1188 ★

Telephone Services (SIC 4813)

International Long-Distance Market

Shares are shown based on an estimated $15.4 billion in revenues for 1996 and $16.9 billion in revenues for 2001.

	1996	2001
AT&T	58.0%	45.4%
MCI	28.0	23.4
Sprint	9.0	9.1
Other	5.0	22.1

Source: *Fortune*, May 26, 1997, p. 30, from Sanford C. Bernstein & Co.

★ 1189 ★

Telephone Services (SIC 4813)

Largest Denver-Area Telecom Firms

Companies are ranked by revenues in millions of dollars for 1994 - 1995.

U.S. West Inc.	$ 11,700.0
Tele-Communications Inc.	6,900.0
Jones Intercable Inc.	188.3
EchoStar Communications Corp.	164.0
Triax Communications Corp.	143.2
IntelCom Group Inc.	122.4
Telephone Express	50.0
Integrated Network Services	28.0
T-Netix Inc.	27.8
Krone Inc.	24.0
Executive TeleCard	23.1
PST Inc.	21.0
ITC Media Conferencing	20.0
Voice It Worldwide Inc.	15.6
Cable Television Laboratories Inc.	14.0

Source: *Denver Business Journal*, April 5, 1996, p. 19A.

★ 1190 ★

Telephone Services (SIC 4813)

Largest Telecom Firms - Washington D.C.

Firms are ranked by revenues in millions of dollars.

MCI Communications	$ 18,500.0
LCI International Inc.	1,103.0
Telco Communications	428.6
Nextel Communications	332.9
Primus Telecomm. Group	173.0

Source: *Washington Post*, April 28, 1997, p. 35.

★ 1191 ★

Telephone Services (SIC 4813)

Local Phone Operators - 1995

Firms are ranked by 1995 revenues in millions of dollars.

BellSouth	$ 17.89
Ameritech	13.43
Bell Atlantic	13.43
SBC Communications	12.67
US West Communications	9.50
Pacific Telesis	9.04

Source: *Financial Times*, November 6, 1996, p. 13, from company reports.

★ 1192 ★

Telephone Services (SIC 4813)

Local Telephone Firms - 1996

Firms are ranked by revenues in billions of dollars.

GTE	$ 21.3
BellSouth	19.0
Ameritech	14.9
SBC Comms.	13.9
Nynex	13.5
Bell Atlantic	13.1
Pacific Telesis	9.6

Source: *Financial Times*, January 31, 1997, p. 25, from companies.

★ 1193 ★

Telephone Services (SIC 4813)

Local Telephone Market

Market shares of local phone service are shown for 1995. Total revenues reached $89.5 billion. Data exclude cellular, paging, and other non-local calling revenues.

GTE	14.2%
BellSouth	13.9
Nynex	12.7
Ameritech	11.0
Bell Atlantic	10.3
US West	9.7
SBC Comm.	9.2
Pacific Telesis	8.4
Other	10.6

Source: *Wall Street Journal*, September 16, 1996, p. R14, from Yankee Group and Paul Kagan Associates Inc.

★ 1194 ★

Telephone Services (SIC 4813)

Long-Distance Market

Market shares are shown for 1995. Total revenues reached $89.5 billion. Data exclude AT&T's cellular revenues and Sprint's cellular and local-phone service revenues.

AT&T	60.9%
MCI	20.7
Sprint	10.7
WorldCom	5.0
Frontier	2.0
Other	0.2

Source: *Wall Street Journal*, September 16, 1996, p. R14, from Yankee Group and Paul Kagan Associates Inc.

★ 1195 ★

Telephone Services (SIC 4813)

Long-Distance Telephone Market - British Columbia

Company shares are shown in percent.

BC Tel	75.0%
Other	25.0

Source: *Investext*, Thomson Financial Networks, December 5, 1996, p. 8.

★ 1196 ★

Telephone Services (SIC 4813)

Long-Distance Telephone Market - Newfoundland

Company shares are shown in percent.

Newtel	89.0%
Other	11.0

Source: *Investext*, Thomson Financial Networks, December 5, 1996, p. 8.

★ 1197 ★

Telephone Services (SIC 4813)

Long-Distance Telephone Market - Quebec

Company shares are shown in percent.

Quebec Tel	99.0%
Other	1.0

Source: *Investext*, Thomson Financial Networks, December 5, 1996, p. 8.

★ 1198 ★

Telephone Services (SIC 4813)

Residential Long-Distance Service Market - 1996

Shares are shown in percent.

AT&T	68.4%
MCI	15.3
Sprint	11.4
Other	4.9

Source: *Working Woman*, June 1997, p. 26, from The Yankee Group.

★ 1199 ★

Telephone Services (SIC 4813)

Top Long-Distance Phone Services - Canada

Shares are shown based on revenues.

	1995	1996
Stentor Group of Cos.	79.0%	72.0%
Sprint Canada Inc.	6.5	9.5
AT&T Canada Long Distance Services Co.	6.0	8.0
Fonorola	3.0	3.8
ACC Telenterprises Ltd.	1.7	2.2
Others	3.8	4.5

Source: *Marketing Magazine*, May 26, 1997, p. 14, from NBI and Michael Sone Associates.

★ 1200 ★

Telephone Services (SIC 4813)

Top RBOCs

Bellsouth Corp.
Nynex Corp.
Bell Atlantic Corp.
Ameritech
US West Co.
SBC Communications Corp.
Pacific Telesis Group

Regional bell operating companies (RBOCs) are ranked by revenues in millions of dollars. Pacific Telesis and SBC will merge and become SBC-Pactel.

Bellsouth Corp.	$ 17.9
Nynex Corp.	13.8
Bell Atlantic Corp.	13.3
Ameritech	12.6
US West Co.	11.7
SBC Communications Corp.	11.6
Pacific Telesis Group	9.2

Source: *Data Communications*, September 21, 1996, p. 60.

★ 1201 ★

Data Communications (SIC 4822)

E-Mail Seats - 1997

Estimated millions of seats are shown for 1997.

Microsoft Exchange and Mail	14.1
Lotus Notes and CC:Mail	13.8
Novell GroupWise and MHS Systems	11.6
Other	7.5

Source: *Computerworld*, August 12, 1996, p. 4, from Yankee Group.

★ 1202 ★

Data Communications (SIC 4822)

How We Connect to the Internet

Standard modem over phone lines	50.0%
ISDN phone lines	25.0
Cable modems	15.0
ADSL phone lines	5.0
Satellite	5.0

Source: *USA TODAY*, October 31, 1996, p. B1, from Gartner Group.

★ 1203 ★

Data Communications (SIC 4822)

Internet Access Provider Market - 1995

Companies are ranked by revenues in millions of dollars.

	Rev. ($ mil.)	Share
BBN	$ 71.47	31.2%
UUNET	51.39	22.4
Netcom	47.75	20.8
PSINet	39.71	17.3
Other	18.85	8.2

Source: *Software Magazine*, February 1997, p. 86, from Zona Research Inc.

★ 1204 ★

Radio Broadcasting (SIC 4832)

Largest Radio Stations - Chicago

Stations are ranked by ad revenues in millions of dollars.

WGN-AM	$ 38.3
WUSN-FM	20.2
WGCI-AM/FM	20.0
WJMK-FM	18.2
WLUP-FM	17.9
WLIT-FM	17.8
WMAQ-AM	17.4
WBBM-AM	16.7
WVAZ-FM	15.8
WNUA-FM	14.2

Source: *Chicago Tribune*, February 19, 1997, p. 4, from *Duncan's Radio Market Guide*.

★ 1205 ★

Radio Broadcasting (SIC 4832)

Largest Radio Stations - San Jose

Data show the average 1995 share of the listening audience 12 years and older.

KOG-AM	7.6%
KBAY-FM	5.0
KOME-FM	5.0
KSJO-FM	4.6
KLOK-AM	4.1
KCBS-AM	4.0

Source: *San Jose and Silicon Valley Business Journal*, June 17, 1996, p. 16, from Arbitron Co.

★ 1206 ★

Radio Broadcasting (SIC 4832)

Leading Radio Groups - 1996

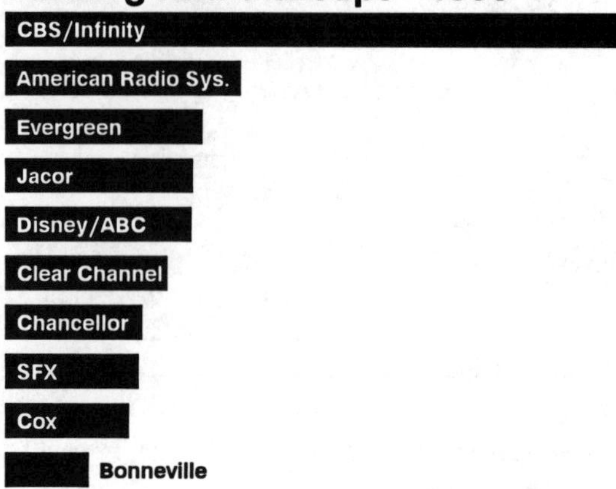

The companies are ranked by estimated 1996 revenues in millions of dollars.

CBS/Infinity	$ 1,033.0
American Radio Sys.	370.0
Evergreen	310.0
Jacor	295.0
Disney/ABC	293.0
Clear Channel	254.0
Chancellor	215.0
SFX	209.0
Cox	194.0
Bonneville	131.0

Source: *Adweek*, September 23, 1996, p. 36, from Washington Research Group.

★ 1207 ★

Radio Broadcasting (SIC 4832)

Mexico's Radio Broadcasters

Data show who controls the Valley of Mexico audience.

Grupo Radio Centro	37.1%
Radiopolis	15.8
Organizacion Radio Formula	11.7
Acir	9.9
MVS	7.2
Nucleo Radio Mil	5.0

Source: *Business Mexico*, August 1996, p. 22.

★ 1208 ★

Radio Broadcasting (SIC 4832)

Popular Radio Formats

Data show the number of stations for each format.

Country	2,613
Adult contemporary	1,052
News/talk	1,036
Oldies	710
Adult standards	470
Spanish	427

Source: *USA TODAY*, April 30, 1997, p. D1, from Interep Research.

★ 1209 ★

Radio Broadcasting (SIC 4832)

Radio Audience by Format

Data show percentage of national listening audience for Winter 1996.

News/talk	15.5%
Adult contemporary	15.0
Country	11.0
R&B	10.7
Album rock	7.7
Top 40	7.2
Oldies	6.5
Spanish	5.6
Modern rock (alternative)	4.4
Classic rock	3.6
Other	12.8

Source: *USA TODAY*, August 29, 1996, p. 6D, from *Billboard*, *Country Airplay Monitor*, and Arbitron.

★ 1210 ★

Radio Broadcasting (SIC 4832)

Top 10 Radio Groups

Firms are ranked by 1995 estimated revenues in millions of dollars.

CBS Radio Station Group	$ 961.0
Evergreen Media Corp.	362.7
Jacor Communications Inc.	359.2
American Radio Systems License Corp.	344.1
ABC Inc.	269.8
Chancellor Broadcasting Co.	262.2
Clear Channel Communications	255.2
SFX Broadcasting Inc.	213.7
Cox Enterprises	$ 181.2
Bonneville International	123.9

Source: *Chicago Tribune*, October 10, 1996, p. C2, from BIA Publications Inc.

★ 1211 ★

Radio Broadcasting (SIC 4832)

Top Media Firms by Radio Revenues

Firms are ranked by 1995 revenues in millions of dollars.

CBS Inc.	$ 880.3
Disney Capital Cities/ABC	406.0
Clear Channel Communications	270.0
Evergreen Media Corp.	248.1
Jacor Communications	244.4
American Radio Systems Co.	194.7
SFX Broadcasting Inc.	190.4
Cox Enterprises	123.6
Viacom	103.4
Gannett Co.	86.2

Source: *Advertising Age*, August 19, 1996, p. S4.

★ 1212 ★

Radio Broadcasting (SIC 4832)

Top Radio Broadcasting Groups - Canada

Shares are shown based on an autumn 1996 survey of 516,108,000 hours tuned in by listeners. Figures are for English language radio stations only.

Standard Broadcasting	8.5%
CHUM Ltd.	6.7
Rogers	6.6
WIC	6.5
Shaw	4.3
Rawlco	3.2
Telemedia	3.2
Others	61.0

Source: *Marketing Magazine*, May 26, 1997, p. 16, from BBM Bureau of Measurement.

★ 1213 ★

Radio Broadcasting (SIC 4832)

Top Radio Stations - 1996

Radio stations are ranked by 1996 sales in millions of dollars. Parent companies are shown in parentheses.

WFAN-AM (CBS)	$ 42.3
WGN-AM (Tribune)	37.9
WINS-AM (CBS)	32.1
KRTH-FM (CBS)	31.0
WCBS-FM (CBS)	30.7
WXRK-FM (CBS)	30.6
WLTW-FM (Viacom)	30.3
KVIL-FM (CBS)	30.0
KGO-AM (Disney)	29.0
KFI-AM (Cox)	28.1
KIIS-FM (Jacor)	28.1

Source: *Fortune*, April 14, 1997, p. 113, from BIA Research.

★ 1214 ★

Radio Broadcasting (SIC 4832)

Top Radio Stations - San Francisco

Broadcasting stations are ranked by average audience share for listeners 12 years and older.

KGO/810 AM	7.1%
KCBS/740 AM	5.0
KMEL/106.1 FM	4.3
KNBR/680 AM	4.0
KOIT/96.5 FM	3.9
KYLD 107.7 FM	3.7
KIOL/ 101.3 FM	3.5
KKSF/103.7 FM	3.4
KFOG/104.5 FM	2.9
KBLX/ 102.9 FM	2.8

Source: *San Francisco Business Journal*, November 7, 1996, p. 31, from Arbitron Co.

★ 1215 ★

Television Broadcasting (SIC 4833)

Chidren's Network Advertising

Data show advertising sales in millions of dollars.

Nickelodeon	$ 240
Fox	170
ABC	50
CBS	46
Kids Well	45

Source: *Broadcasting & Cable*, August 12, 1996, p. 25, from Western International Media.

★ 1216 ★

Television Broadcasting (SIC 4833)

Pay TV Market - 2000

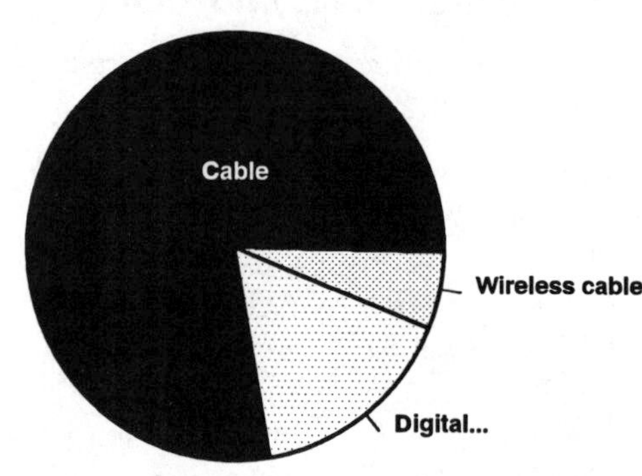

Projected pay-TV market is shown by segment.

Cable	78.0%
Digital broadcast satellite	16.0
Wireless cable	6.0

Source: *Investor's Business Daily*, December 23, 1996, p. A6, from Morgan Stanley & Co.

★ 1217 ★

Television Broadcasting (SIC 4833)

Top Media Firms by TV Revenues

Firms are ranked by 1995 revenues in millions of dollars.

Disney Capital Cities/ABC	$ 4,288.5
NBC-TV	3,659.0
CBS Inc.	3,438.0
News Corp.	1,580.0
Tribune Co.	634.0
Gannett Co.	509.8

Continued on next page.

★ 1217 ★ *Continued*

Television Broadcasting (SIC 4833)

Top Media Firms by TV Revenues

Firms are ranked by 1995 revenues in millions of dollars.

Chris-Craft Industries	$ 454.7
Viacom	385.5
New World Communications Group	376.8
Cox Enterprises	364.0

Source: *Advertising Age*, August 19, 1996, p. S4.

★ 1218 ★

Television Broadcasting (SIC 4833)

Top Television Broadcasting Groups - Canada

Shares are shown based on a spring 1996 survey of 445,425,000 hours tuned in by viewers.

CTV	27.3%
TVA	15.6
CBC	12.8
SRC	10.4
BBS	9.7
Global	7.0
TQS	5.3
BCTV	4.6
ATV	2.5
Tele-Quebec	1.1
Others	3.7

Source: *Marketing Magazine*, May 26, 1997, p. 16, from Television Bureau of Canada.

★ 1219 ★

Television Broadcasting (SIC 4833)

Top Television Groups - 1996

Data show the percent of U.S. homes covered.

CBS/Westinghouse	31.53%
Tribune (Renaissance)	25.71
NBC	24.65
Disney/ABC	24.07
Fox	22.05
Silver King	22.00
Paxson	17.97
Chris Craft	17.70
Gannett	14.08
Univision	12.86
New World	12.78%
Telemundo	10.35
Viacom	10.12
Young	9.08
Sinclair/River City	8.91

Source: *Broadcasting & Cable*, July 8, 1996, p. 12.

★ 1220 ★

Television Broadcasting (SIC 4833)

TV Market - Vancouver

Figures indicate share of viewers, aged 18 and over, 6 to 7 p.m. weekdays.

CHAN	46.0%
UTV	13.0
CBUT	7.0
KVOS	5.0
Others	29.0

Source: *Globe and Mail*, February 1, 1997, p. B5, from Bureau of Broadcast Measurements.

★ 1221 ★

Television Broadcasting (SIC 4833)

TV Network Ratings

Data are for the 1995-96 season.

NBC	10.9%
ABC	9.7
CBS	9.1
Fox	6.5
UPN	2.8
WB	2.4

Source: *New York Times*, September 20, 1996, p. C1.

★ 1222 ★

Cable Broadcasting (SIC 4841)

Largest Audio Services

Data show subscribers in thousands.

Cable Radio Network	10,225
Superaudio	10,000
C-SPAN Audio Network	6,600
AEI Spectra Network	5,000
C-SPAN Audio Network II	3,200
KJAZ Cable Radio Network	2,000

Source: *Cablevision*, August 19, 1996, p. 80, from *Cablevision Subscriber Count Database*.

★ 1223 ★

Cable Broadcasting (SIC 4841)

Largest Interactive/Channel Promotion Services

Data show subscribers in thousands.

Prevue Channel	41,181
Sneak Prevue	29,600
Starnet	23,000
The Dating Network	15,400

Source: *Cablevision*, August 19, 1996, p. 80, from *Cablevision Subscriber Count Database*.

★ 1224 ★

Cable Broadcasting (SIC 4841)

Largest Text Services

Data show subscribers in thousands.

TMS News Plus	3,900
Reuters NewsView	2,437
Story Vision Network	2,200
TMS Business Plus	1,900
EPG	1,678

Source: *Cablevision*, August 19, 1996, p. 80, from *Cablevision Subscriber Count Database*.

★ 1225 ★

Cable Broadcasting (SIC 4841)

Prime Time Cable Stations

The table shows the prime time ratings for 1996. Data are for 8-11 p.m. for Monday-Sunday and include the thousands of viewing households.

	Rtg.	HH (000)
TNT	2.1	1,443
USA	2.0	1,350
WTBS	1.9	1,336
NICK	1.8	1,207
ESPN	1.6	1,116
LIFE	1.5	932
A&E	1.3	828
DISC	1.2	786
FAM	1.2	798
TOON	1.2	330

Source: *Broadcasting & Cable*, January 6, 1997, p. 118, from Turner Broadcasting and other networks.

★ 1226 ★

Cable Broadcasting (SIC 4841)

Top Cable Broadcasting Networks

Networks are ranked by operating cash flow in billions of dollars. Data are estimated for 1998.

ESPN	$ 9.4
QVC	5.3
CNN	4.0
NICK	4.0
HBO	3.9
DIS	3.7
MTV	3.5
TNT	3.4
USA	3.2
TBS	3.0

Source: *Broadcasting & Cable*, May 12, 1997, p. 90, from Wall Street analysts and industry executives.

★ 1227 ★

Cable Broadcasting (SIC 4841)

Top Cable Channels - 1996

Networks are ranked by millions of subscribers.

Learning Channel	54.0
Comedy Central	44.0
E Entertainment TV	42.3

Continued on next page.

★ 1227 ★ *Continued*

Cable Broadcasting (SIC 4841)

Top Cable Channels - 1996

Networks are ranked by millions of subscribers.

ESPN2	40.0
Sci-Fi Channel	37.4
Cartoon Network	31.0
fX	30.3
History Channel	29.0
Bravo	28.0
Court TV	28.0
MSNBC	28.0
Home & Garden TV	22.0
Travel Channel	20.0
TV Food Network	20.0
Fox News Channel	18.0
CNNfn	7.0
CNN/SI	4.5
fXM: Movies From Fox	4.0
ESPNews	1.6

Source: *Mediaweek*, January 6, 1997, p. 13.

★ 1228 ★

Cable Broadcasting (SIC 4841)

Top Cable Companies

Broadcasters are ranked by millions of subscribers.

Tele-Communications	13.9
Time Warner Cable	11.8
U.S. West Media Group	4.2
Comcast Cable Comm.	3.5
Cox Communications	3.2
Cablevision Systems	2.8
Adelphia Communications	1.8
Jones Intercable	1.4
Marcus Cable	1.3
Century Communications	1.2
Falcon Cable TV	1.1
Lenfest Communications	1.1

Source: *Investor's Business Daily*, December 23, 1996, p. A6, from Paul Kagan Associates Inc. and Suhler & Associates Inc.

★ 1229 ★

Cable Broadcasting (SIC 4841)

Top Media Firms by Cable Revenues

Firms are ranked by 1995 revenues in millions of dollars.

Time Warner	$ 7,409.2
Tele-Communications Inc.	5,118.0
Comcast Corp.	1,719.9
US West Media Group	1,657.4
Viacom	1,647.2
Disney Capital Cities/ABC	1,534.0
Cox Enterprises	1,286.2
Cablevision Systems Corp.	1,078.1

Source: *Advertising Age*, August 19, 1996, p. S4.

★ 1230 ★

Satellite Broadcasting (SIC 4841)

Home Satellite Subscribers

Data show subscribers as of October 31, 1996.

C-band	2,314,947
DirecTV, USSB	2,028,000
Primestar	1,500,000
Echostar	235,000
Alphastar	12,000

Source: *Broadcasting & Cable*, November 25, 1996, p. 22, from SBC.

★ 1231 ★

Satellite Broadcasting (SIC 4841)

Largest Satellite Broadcasters

Data show thousands of subscribers.

DirecTV	2,000.0
Primestar	1,500.0
U.S. Satellite Broadcasting	950.0
Echostar	185.0
Alphastar	8.5

Source: *Wall Street Journal*, November 7, 1996, p. A1, from Carmel Group.

★ 1232 ★

Satellite Broadcasting (SIC 4841)

Leading Satellite TV Transponder Holders

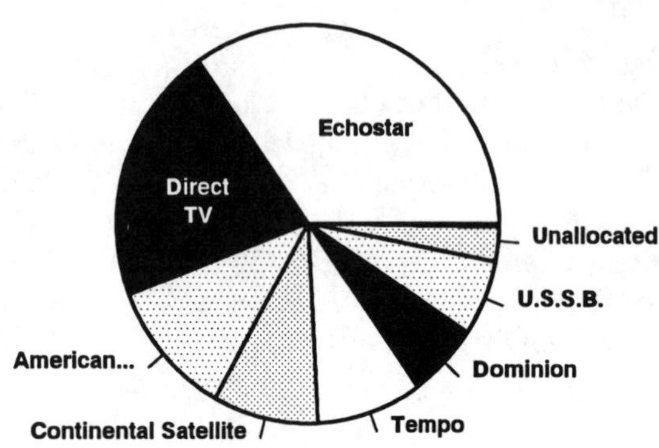

Firms are ranked by share of the 256 satellite transponders that are available for direct TV broadcasting. Tempo refers to TCI Satellite. American Sky Broadcasting refers to News Corporation and MCI.

	No.	Share
Echostar	90	35.2%
Direct TV	54	21.1
American Sky Broadcasting	28	10.9
Continental Satellite	22	8.6
Tempo	22	8.6
Dominion	16	6.3
U.S.S.B.	16	6.3
Unallocated	8	3.1

Source: *New York Times*, February 26, 1997, p. 4, from UBS Securities.

★ 1233 ★

Satellite Broadcasting (SIC 4841)

Mexico's Satellite System

Private operators	32.0%
Trade & industry	30.0
Financial	20.0
Government	10.0
Communication and transportation	5.0
Education	3.0

Source: *Mexico: Building for Growth*, 1996, p. 55, from Telecommunicaciones de Mexico.

★ 1234 ★

Satellite Broadcasting (SIC 4841)

Top Satellite Television Providers - 1996

Company shares are shown in percent. The industry served 6.7 million subscribers.

DirectTV/USSB	35.0%
Large-dish networks	33.0
PrimeStar	25.0
EchoStar	6.0
AlphaStar	1.0

Source: *Investor's Business Daily*, February 25, 1997, p. A6, from SkyReport and Media Business Corp.

SIC 49 - Electric, Gas, and Sanitary Services

★ 1235 ★

Energy (SIC 4900)

Electric Power Generation

Coal	54.7%
Nuclear	22.3
Natural gas	11.0
Hydroelectric	9.7
Petroleum	2.1
Other	0.2

Source: *USA TODAY*, March 7, 1997, p. 10A, from Energy Information Administration.

★ 1236 ★

Energy (SIC 4900)

U.S. Energy Demand

	1996	1997
Oil	39.6%	39.9%
Natural gas	25.1	25.0
Coal	22.7	22.7
Nuclear	8.2	8.1
Hydro & other	4.4	4.2

Source: *Oil & Gas Journal*, January 27, 1997, p. 46.

★ 1237 ★

Utilities (SIC 4911)

Largest Electric Co-ops

Firms are ranked by 1995 revenues in millions of dollars.

Oglethorpe Power Corporation	$ 1,100.0
North Carolina Elec. Membership Corp.	711.0
Seminole Electric Cooperative	535.0
Associated Electric Cooperative	464.0
Tri-State G&T Association	415.0
Basin Electric Power Cooperative	400.0
Old Dominion Electric Cooperative	357.0
Arkansas Electric Cooperative Corp.	340.0
Big River Electric Cooperative	$ 340.0
Central Electric Power Cooperative	336.0
East Kentucky Power Cooperative	329.0

Source: *Rural Electrification*, January 1997, p. 9, from National Cooperative Bank.

★ 1238 ★

Utilities (SIC 4911)

Top Electric Utilities - 1995

Companies are ranked by electric revenues in millions of dollars.

Southern Co.	$ 7,602
Southern California Edison	7,575
Pacific Gas & Electric Co.	7,569
Commonwealth Edison Co.	6,634
TU Electric	5,450
Florida Power & Light Co.	5,325
Consolidated Edison	5,005
Virginia Electric & Power Co.	3,979
Public Service Electric & Gas	3,886
Duke Power Co.	3,800
Baltimore G&E/PEPCO	3,739
GPU Energy	3,618
Houston Lighting & Power	3,493
Detroit Edison Co.	3,482
Peco Energy Co.	3,354

Source: *Philadelphia Inquirer*, June 2, 1997, p. D7, from Edison Electric Institute.

★ 1239 ★

Utilities (SIC 4922)

Largest Energy Firms

Firms are ranked by assets in billions of dollars as of September 1995.

Pacific Gas & Electric	$ 27.8
Southern Co.	27.0
Commonwealth Edison	24.0

Continued on next page.

★ 1239 ★ *Continued*

Utilities (SIC 4922)

Largest Energy Firms

Firms are ranked by assets in billions of dollars as of September 1995.

Entergy	$ 22.6
Edison International	22.4
Texas Utilities	20.9
Public Service Enterprise Group	16.7
American Electric Group	15.7
Constellation Energy	15.1
PECO Energy	15.1

Source: *Washington Post*, December 9, 1996, p. 13.

★ 1240 ★

Utilities (SIC 4922)

Leading Utilities - Northeast

Firms are ranked by sales in millions of dollars for the latest 12 months.

Consolidated Edison	$ 6,856
Public Service Enterprise	6,024
PECO Energy	4,024
Niagara Mohawk Power	3,986
GPU	3,924
Northeast Utilities	3,836

Source: *Forbes*, January 13, 1997, p. 136, from Value Line and One Source Information Services.

★ 1241 ★

Utilities (SIC 4922)

Leading Utilities - Southeast

Firms are ranked by sales in millions of dollars for the latest 12 months.

Southern Co.	$ 10,179
FPL Group	5,963
Dominion Resources	4,782
Duke Power	4,707
Florida Progress	3,114
Carolina Power & Light	3,022

Source: *Forbes*, January 13, 1997, p. 136, from Value Line and One Source Information Services.

★ 1242 ★

Utilities (SIC 4922)

Leading Utilities - West

Firms are ranked by sales in millions of dollars for the latest 12 months.

Pacific G&E	$ 9,137
Edison International	8,401
PacifiCorp.	4,009
Public Service Colo	2,107
Enova	1,913
Pinnacle West	1,785

Source: *Forbes*, January 13, 1997, p. 136, from Value Line and One Source Information Services.

★ 1243 ★

Utilities (SIC 4922)

Top Gas Utilities

The top utilities are ranked by gas sold in millions of cubic feet in 1995.

Noram Energy Corp.	1,121,000
Southern California Gas Co.	337,952
Wisconsin Power & Light Corp.	324,647
Public Service Electric & Gas Co.	306,668
Northern Illinois Gas Co.	301,254
Consolidated Gas Distribution Companies	289,917
Entex	288,840
Pacific Gas & Electric Co.	269,904
Consumers Power Co.	252,248
Michigan Consolidated Gas Co.	206,951

Source: *Pipeline & Gas Journal*, September 1996, p. 20.

★ 1244 ★

Water Services (SIC 4941)

U.S. Water Industry

Distribution is shown based on $75 billion in revenues.

Water utilities	36.0%
Wastewater treatment works	34.0
Water equipment and chemicals	24.0
Consulting and engineering services	5.0
Instruments/analytical services	1.0

Source: *Water Environment & Technology*, October 1996, p. 16, from Environmental Business International Inc.

★ 1245 ★

Refuse Systems (SIC 4953)

Trash Collection Market - Atlanta

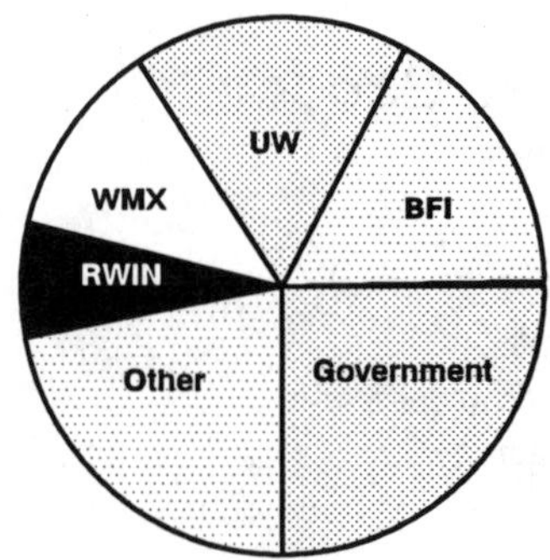

Market shares are shown in percent.

BFI	17.0%
UW	17.0
WMX	12.0
RWIN	7.0
Other	22.0
Government	25.0

Source: *Investext,* Thomson Financial Networks, October 28, 1996, p. 13, from company reports and DLJ.

★ 1246 ★

Refuse Systems (SIC 4953)

Trash Disposal Market - Houston

Market shares are shown in percent. BFI leads the collection market with a 42.0% share.

BFI	35.0%
UW	20.0
WMX	16.0
Government	18.0
Other private	11.0

Source: *Investext,* Thomson Financial Networks, October 28, 1996, p. 13, from company reports and DLJ.

★ 1247 ★

Refuse Systems (SIC 4953)

Trash Disposal Market - Pennsylvania

Market shares are shown in percent. UW controls the collection market with a 28.0% share.

UW	28.0%
WMX	24.0
BFI	19.0
Other private	16.0
Government	13.0

Source: *Investext,* Thomson Financial Networks, October 28, 1996, p. 14, from company reports and DLJ.

★ 1248 ★

Refuse Systems (SIC 4953)

Trash Hauling Industry

Firms are ranked by estimated 1996 revenues in billions of dollars. Allied Waste has a 30% share of the trash industry in Canada. Shares of the group are shown in percent.

	Rev. ($ bil.)	% of Group
WMX Technologies	$ 6.0	42.6%
Browning-Ferris	4.0	28.4
USA Waste Services	2.0	14.2
Allied Waste	1.0	7.1
Republic	0.7	5.0
United Waste Systems	0.4	2.8

Source: *USA TODAY,* September 19, 1996, p. 3B, from CS First Boston.

SIC 50 - Wholesale Trade - Durable Goods

★ 1249 ★

Wholesale Trade (SIC 5000)

Top Management Contract Providers

Data show the providers of integrated supply management contracts. Shares are shown based on a $3.5 billion market in 1996.

Fairmont Supply	11.5%
Cameron & Barkley	7.5
Graybar Electric	5.0
W.W. Grainger	5.0
Strategic Distribution	4.3
GE Supply	3.0

Source: *Purchasing*, October 17, 1996, p. 72, from Frank Lynn & Associates.

★ 1250 ★

Wholesale Trade (SIC 5000)

Wholesale Clubs - 1995

Data show the number of outlets.

Sam's Club	433
PriceCostco	231
BJ's Wholesale Club	71

Source: *DM*, June 1996, p. 55.

★ 1251 ★

Wholesale Trade - Auto Parts (SIC 5013)

Auto Supply Wholesalers

Companies are ranked by number of outlets. Data refer to firms that have over half their sales to professional mechanics.

Genuine Parts	738
General Parts Inc.	610
APS	325
Fisher Auto Parts	235
Hahn Automotive	220
O'Reilly	200
Mid-State Auto	115
Mid-Atlantic Warehouse	109
Crow-Burlingame	107
STRAFCO	102

Source: *Automotive Marketing*, July 1996, p. 29.

★ 1252 ★

Wholesale Trade - Photo Equipment (SIC 5043)

Wholesale Photofinishing Market

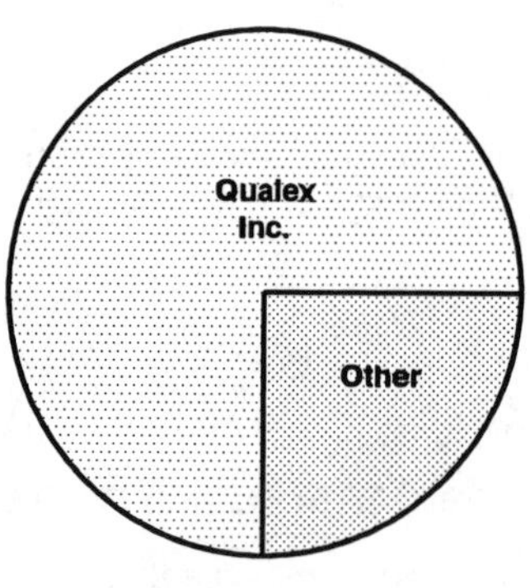

Market shares are shown in percent. Qualex Inc. is a unit of Kodak.

Qualex Inc.	75.0%
Other	25.0

Source: *Wall Street Journal*, September 30, 1996, p. A10.

★ 1253 ★

Wholesale Trade - Computers (SIC 5045)

PC Distribution by Channel

Unit shares are estimated for 1999.

Retail	42.0%
Corporate reseller/aggregator	22.0
Mail order	20.0
VARs/System integrators	15.0
Direct sales	1.0

Source: *Computer Reseller News*, August 26, 1996, p. 107, from International Data Corp.

★ 1254 ★

Wholesale Trade - Computers (SIC 5045)

Top Wholesale Computer Distributors

Data show market shares based on sales.

Ingram Micro	31.5%
Merisel	24.1
Intelligent Electronics	20.6
Tech Data	12.0
MicroAge	11.8

Source: *Investext*, Thomson Financial Networks, December 18, 1996, p. 7.

★ 1255 ★

Wholesale Trade - Electronics (SIC 5045)

Top Active Component Distributors - 1996

Firms are ranked by sales in millions of dollars.

Arrow Electronics Inc.	$ 2,580.0
Avnet Inc.	2,379.0
Wyle Electronics	871.2
Pioneer-Standard Electronics Inc.	711.0
Bell Industries Inc.	453.9

Source: *Purchasing*, April 17, 1997, p. 54.

★ 1256 ★

Wholesale Trade - Electronics (SIC 5045)

Top Computer Product Distributors - 1996

Firms are ranked by sales in millions of dollars.

Arrow Electronics Inc.	$ 1,462.0
Avnet Inc.	780.0
Pioneer-Standard Electronics Inc.	600.4
Wyle Electronics	373.4
Bell Microproducts	217.4

Source: *Purchasing*, April 17, 1997, p. 54.

★ 1257 ★

Wholesale Trade - Electronics (SIC 5045)

Top Electronics Distributors - 1996

Firms are ranked by sales in millions of dollars.

Arrow Electronics Inc.	$ 4.300.0
Avnet Inc.	3,900.0
Future Electronics	1,620.0
Pioneer-Standard Electronics Inc.	1,580.0
Marshall Industries	1,360.0
Wyle Electronics	1,244.5
Bell Industries Inc.	890.0
Premier Farnell	650.0
Kent Electronics Corp.	495.3
Bell Microproducts Inc.	483.0

Source: *Purchasing*, April 17, 1997, p. 54.

★ 1258 ★

Wholesale Trade - Electronics (SIC 5045)

Top Independent Electronics Distributors - 1996

Firms are ranked by sales in millions of dollars.

NECX	$ 376.0
Classic Components	164.0
Smith & Associates	154.5
Real World, The Technology Trading Co.	118.0
Advanced MP Technology	104.7
American IC Exchange	90.0
Legacy Electronics Inc.	30.0
Triangle Electronics Group Inc.	30.0
Accurate Components Inc.	17.1
Orange Coast Components	10.2

Source: *Purchasing*, April 17, 1997, p. 54.

★ 1259 ★

Wholesale Trade - Electronics (SIC 5045)

Top Interconnection Distributors - 1996

Firms are ranked by sales in millions of dollars.

Kent Electronics Corp.	$ 351.7
Avnet Inc.	312.0
Richey Electronics Inc.	151.4
Sterling Electronics Corp.	91.2
The D.A.C. Group Inc.	84.2

Source: *Purchasing*, April 17, 1997, p. 54.

★ 1260 ★

Wholesale Trade - Electronics (SIC 5045)

Top Passive/EM Distributors - 1996

Firms are ranked by sales in millions of dollars.

Avnet Inc.	$ 351.0
TTI Inc.	328.1
Pioneer-Standard Electronics Inc.	268.6
Arrow Electronics Inc.	258.0
Bell Industries Inc.	240.3

Source: *Purchasing*, April 17, 1997, p. 54.

★ 1261 ★

Wholesale Trade - Software (SIC 5045)

Leading Software Distributors

Firms are ranked by 1995 estimated revenues in millions of dollars.

Ingram Micro	$ 12,000
Merisel	5,000
Tech Data	4,500
Access Graphics	1,000
SED	600
D&H Distributing	431

Source: *Computer Reseller News*, January 13, 1997, p. 15.

★ 1262 ★

Wholesale Trade - Dental Products (SIC 5047)

Dental Distribution Market

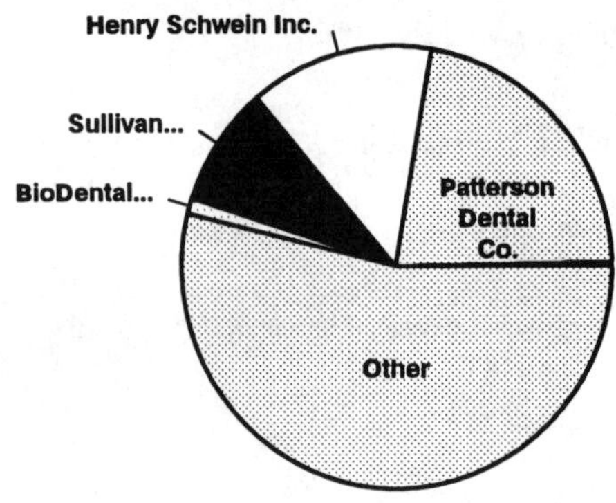

The market reached $2.32 billion in revenues for 1995. Shares are estimated.

	($ mil.)	Share
Patterson Dental Co.	$ 504.5	22.0%
Henry Schwein Inc.	319.5	14.0
Sullivan Dental Products	215.6	9.0
BioDental Technologies Inc.	34.1	1.0
Other	1,248.4	54.0

Source: *Investor's Business Daily*, October 10, 1996, p. A6, from company reports and Volpe, Welty & Co. estimates.

★ 1263 ★

Wholesale Trade - Medical Supplies (SIC 5047)

Top U.S. Medical Supply Distributors

Shares of the estimated $28.525 billion market are shown in percent.

Allegiance Corp.	13.0%
Owens & Minor	11.0
General Medical	5.0
Others	71.0

Source: *Investext*, Thomson Financial Networks, March 3, 1997, p. 6.

★ 1264 ★

Wholesale Trade - Steel (SIC 5051)

Top Importers of Steel to the U.S.

Countries are ranked by millions of tons imported to the U.S. in 1996. Exports from the U.S. reached a total of 100.5 million tons.

	(mil.)	Share
European Union	8.805	30.2%
Canada	4.911	16.8
Mexico	2.905	10.0
Brazil	2.821	9.7
Japan	2.009	6.9
Russia	1.660	5.7
Korea	1.380	4.7
Ukraine	0.803	2.8
China	0.478	1.6
Turkey	0.318	1.1
Others	3.074	10.5

Source: *New Steel*, April 1997, p. 12, from American Iron and Steel Institute.

★ 1265 ★

Wholesale Trade - Electronics (SIC 5060)

U.S. Factory Sales

Data are in millions of dollar for the first six months of each year.

	1995	1996	Share
Electronic components	$ 48,352	$ 56,183	28.6%
Computers & peripherals	24,397	40,822	20.8
Telecommunications	25,460	29,077	14.8
Industrial electronics	16,838	17,438	8.9
Defense communications	14,157	13,339	6.8
Consumer electronics	4,734	5,188	2.6
Electromedical equipment	4,831	5,082	2.6
Other	28,098	29,587	15.0

Source: *TV Digest*, August 12, 1996, p. 16, from Electronics Industry Association.

★ 1266 ★

Wholesale Trade - Lawn & Garden (SIC 5083)

Top Lawn & Garden Buying Groups

Groups are ranked by sales in millions of dollars.

Servistar/Home & Garden Showplace	$ 802.5
Cotter & Co.	672.0
Ace Hardware Corp.	643.2
Growise Centers	602.6
Hardware Wholesalers, Inc.	438.0
Western Independent Nurseries	397.1
Master Nursery Garden Centers	350.0
Garden Master	348.3
Our Own Hardware	23.1
United Hardware Distributing	20.2
SF Services	17.4
Southern States Co-Op, Inc.	11.6

Source: *Nursery Retailer*, March/April 1997, p. 62, from Brantwood Horticultural Research Division.

SIC 51 - Wholesale Trade - Nondurable Goods

★ 1267 ★

Wholesale Trade (SIC 5100)

Top Wholesalers - 1996

Companies are ranked by revenues in millions of dollars.

Fleming	$ 16,487
Supervalu	16,486
McKesson	13,719
Sysco	13,395
Ingram Micro	12,023
Ikon Office Solutions	11,123
Bergen Brunswig	9,943
Cardinal Health	8,862
Arrow Electronics	6,535
Genuine Parts	5,720
Amerisource Health	5,552
Merisel	5,523
Avatex	5,502
Bindley Western	5,319
Avnet	5,208

Source: *Fortune*, April 28, 1997, p. 65.

★ 1268 ★

Wholesale Trade - Drugs (SIC 5112)

Top Distributors in the Pharmaceutical Market

Market shares are shown in percent.

McKesson	17.0%
Bergen Brunswig	14.0
Cardinal Health	12.0
Amerisource	8.0
Other	49.0

Source: *Investext*, Thomson Financial Networks, December 24, 1996, p. 6, from Morgan Stanley Research.

★ 1269 ★

Wholesale Trade - Drugs (SIC 5112)

Top Drug Distributors

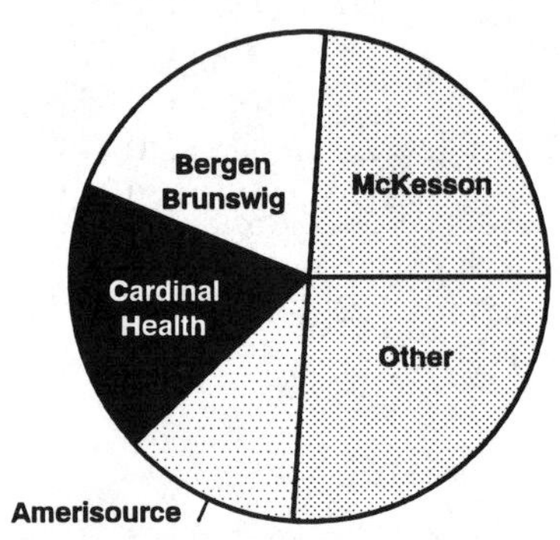

Market shares are shown in percent.

McKesson	24.0%
Bergen Brunswig	20.0
Cardinal Health	18.0
Amerisource	12.0
Other	26.0

Source: *Investext,* Thomson Financial Networks, December 24, 1996, p. 6, from Morgan Stanley Research.

★ 1270 ★

Wholesale Trade - Office Supplies (SIC 5112)

Office Product Shipments - 1996

Wholesalers	22.9%
Large dealers	22.4
Superstores	15.0
Mass market	10.9
Small/medium dealers	9.3
Mail order	4.5
Warehouse clubs	4.1
Direct & government	3.2
Other	7.7

Source: *Purchasing*, October 17, 1996, p. 95, from Business Products Industry Association.

★ 1271 ★

Wholesale Trade - Office Supplies (SIC 5112)

Office Supply Superstores

Firms are ranked by net sales in billions of dollars.

Ofice Depot	$ 6.07
Staples	4.97
OfficeMax	3.18

Source: *Atlanta Journal-Constitution*, March 11, 1997, p. D1, from Bloomberg News.

★ 1272 ★

Wholesale Trade - Office Supplies (SIC 5112)

School/Office Supply Sales by Outlet

Data are for the first quarter of 1996.

Mass merchants	56.1%
Drug stores	28.6
Food stores	11.4
Food/drug combos	3.9

Source: *DM*, September 1996, p. 100, from SHOPA and A.C. Nielsen.

★ 1273 ★

Wholesale Trade - Office Supplies (SIC 5112)

Where Office Supplies Are Shipped

Data show distribution of office supply shipments.

Office superstores	19.0%
Commercial office product wholesalers	18.0
Office product dealers	16.0
Discount stores	12.0
Wholesale	5.0
Drug stores	4.0
Specialty retail	4.0
Wholesalers, distributors & service merchandisers	4.0
Food stores	2.0
Institutional school supply wholesalers	2.0
Mail order	2.0
Office product retailers	2.0
Others	10.0

Source: *Discount Merchandiser*, April 1997, p. 92, from *Strategic Overview and Distribution Trends Report*.

★ 1274 ★

Wholesale Trade - Food (SIC 5140)

Major Wholesale Grocers

Firms are ranked by sales for the latest fiscal year in millions of dollars.

Flemming Cos.	$ 17,502.0
Supervalu Inc.	16,500.0
Wakefern Food Corp.	3,740.0
Penn Traffic Co.	3,536.0
C&S Wholesale Grocers Inc.	3,348.0
Richfood Holdings Inc.	3,097.0
Associated Wholesale Grocers Inc.	2,975.0
Spartan Stores Inc.	2,537.0
Roundy's Inc.	2,488.0
Giant Eagle Co.	2,075.0
Nash Finch Co.	1,969.0
Certified Grocers of California Ltd.	1,823.0
Twin County Grocers	1,200.0
Grocers Supply Co.	1,200.0
United Grocers Inc.	1,200.0

Source: *U.S. Distribution Journal*, September 15, 1996, p. 20.

★ 1275 ★

Wholesale Trade - Bakery Products (SIC 5149)

Top Wholesale Bakery Firms

Companies are ranked by 1995 sales in millions of dollars.

Nabisco Biscuit Co.	$ 3,500.0
Interstate Brands Corp.	3,000.0
CPC Baking Business	1,700.0
Earthgrains Co.	1,490.0
Keebler Co.	1,487.0
Flowers Industries Inc.	1,000.0
Pepperidge Farm Inc.	700.0
McKee Foods Corp.	680.0
Culinar Inc.	593.0
Sunshine Biscuits Inc.	580.0
Sara Lee Bakery	495.0
Lance Inc.	460.0
Metz Baking Co.	451.0
Presidents Baking Co. Inc.	450.0
Western Bakeries Ltd.	420.0

Source: *Bakery Production and Marketing*, July 15, 1996, p. 30.

★ 1276 ★

Wholesale Trade - Candy & Tobacco (SIC 5190)

Convenience Item Distributors

Firms are ranked by 1995 sales in millions of dollars.

McLane Co. Inc.	$ 7,985
Core-Mark International Inc.	2,100
Eby-Brown Co. L.P.	1,550
Eli Witt Co.	1,507
GSC Enterprises Inc.	1,066
S. Abraham & Sons Inc.	644
Fleming Convenience Marketing and Distribution	476
Jos. H. Stomel & Sons	450
Minter-Weisman Co.	401
F.A. Davis & Sons Inc.	390

Source: *U.S. Distribution Journal*, August 15, 1996, p. 26.

★ 1277 ★

Wholesale Trade - Books (SIC 5192)

Where Libraries Buy Books

Data show where the nation's 15,000 public libraries buy their books. Baker & Taylor is the nation's largest book distributor.

Baker & Taylor Inc.	90.0%
Other	10.0

Source: *USA TODAY*, February 4, 1997, p. 3A.

SIC 52 - Building Materials and Garden Supplies

★ 1278 ★

Retailing - Home Improvement (SIC 5211)

Largest Home Improvement Chains

Data show number of chains.

Home Depot	483
Lowe's	402
Payless Cashways	192
Builders Square	168
Menard	128
Hechinger	117
HomeBase	84

Source: *Wall Street Journal*, February 5, 1997, p. B4, from *National Home Center News*.

★ 1279 ★

Retailing - Home Improvement (SIC 5211)

Top Home Improvement Chains

Firms are ranked by 1995 sales in billions of dollars.

Home Depot	$ 15.5
Lowe's Companies	7.1
Menard	2.7
Payless Cashways	2.7
Builders Square	2.6
Hechinger	2.3
Homebase	1.4
Eighty-Four Lumber	1.3

Source: *New York Times*, February 4, 1997, p. C1, from *National Home Center News*.

★ 1280 ★

Retailing - Home Supplies (SIC 5211)

Top Home Improvement Centers - 1996

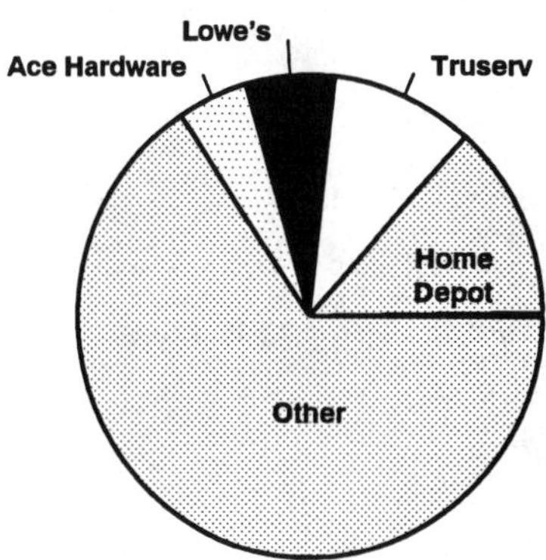

Shares are shown in percent. Figure for Truserv is based on completion of a merger between Cotter & Company and Servistar. Home Depot and Lowe's are mega-stores; Truserv and Ace Hardware are co-operatives.

Home Depot	13.0%
Truserv	10.2
Lowe's	6.1
Ace Hardware	5.3
Other	65.4

Source: *New York Times*, June 11, 1997, p. C7, from *National Home Center News*.

★ 1281 ★

Retailing - Paint & Wallpaper (SIC 5231)

Who Buys Paint and Wallpaper

Data show percent of total annual spending by age.

Age	%
35-44	30.7%
45-54	19.8
25-34	19.5
55-64	12.6
65-74	8.6
75 and over	6.9
Under 25	8.0

Source: *Do-It-Yourself Retailing*, March 1997, p. 97, from New Strategist Publications Inc.

★ 1282 ★

Retailing - Hardware (SIC 5251)

Hardware/Tool Sales by Outlet

Distribution is shown based on sales of $28.37 billion in 1995.

Hardware stores	32.2%
Home centers	26.8
Discount stores	19.8
Wholesale clubs	6.7
Non-store retailing	3.9
Department stores	3.6
Auto/home supply stores	1.7
Drug/proprietary stores	1.5
Supermarkets	1.4
Misc. general merchandise store	1.3
Variety stores	0.6
Household appliance stores	0.5

Source: *DM*, July 1996, p. 32.

★ 1283 ★

Retailing - Hardware (SIC 5251)

Top Hardware Stores - Canada

Shares are shown based on sales for 1996.

Canadian Tire Corp.	29.4%
Home Hardware	10.6
Home Depot	6.2
Beaver Lumber	4.3
Rere Depot	2.7
Revelstoke Home Centres	2.4
Cashway Building Centres	1.7
Lansing Buildall	0.9
Kent Building Supplies	0.9
Lumberland Building Materials	0.8
Other	40.0

Source: *Marketing Magazine*, May 26, 1997, p. 12, from *Hardware Merchandising Magazine's Top 100 Report.*

★ 1284 ★

Retailing - Lawn & Garden (SIC 5261)

Greenhouse/Nursery Receipts By State

Top states are ranked by greenhouse and nursery cash receipts in millions of dollars. The U.S. as a whole earned $10.407 billion in cash receipts.

California	$ 2,172.0
Florida	1,093.0
North Carolina	858.0
Texas	792.0
Ohio	491.0
Minnesota	425.0
Oregon	399.0
Pennsylvania	314.0

Continued on next page.

★ 1284 ★ *Continued*

Retailing - Lawn & Garden (SIC 5261)

Greenhouse/Nursery Receipts By State

Top states are ranked by greenhouse and nursery cash receipts in millions of dollars. The U.S. as a whole earned $10.407 billion in cash receipts.

Oklahoma	$ 264.0
New Jersey	257.0

Source: *Business North Carolina*, December 1996, p. 60, from North Carolina Department of Agriculture.

★ 1285 ★

Retailing - Lawn & Garden (SIC 5261)

Largest Mass Market Plant Sellers

Data show retail space in square feet for 1997. Bay City Flowers figure is estimated. Crops include bedding plants, potted plants, potted foliage, and others.

Color Spot	7,036,000
Kurt Weiss	4,413,000
Baucom's Nursery Co.	3,600,000
Greiling Farms Inc.	3,260,000
Delray Plants Inc.	3,128,516
Neal Robinson Wholesale Greenhouses	3,100,000
Kitayama Brothers	2,950,000
Yoder Brothers	2,924,546
Bay City Flowers	2,730,000
Powell Plant Farm	2,390,000
Hermann Engelmann Greenhouses Inc.	2,200,000
Milgro Nursery Inc.	2,145,000
Matsui Nursery Inc.	2,007,900
Nurserymen's Exchange	2,000,000
Woodburn Nursery & Azaleas	2,000,000
Metrolina Greenhouses Inc.	1,980,000
Paul Ecke Ranch	1,824,348
Bayworth Nurseries	1,742,000

Source: *Greenhouse Grower*, May 1997, p. 17.

★ 1286 ★

Retailing - Lawn & Garden (SIC 5261)

Top Lawn & Garden Retailers

Retailers are ranked by sales in millions of dollars.

Home Depot	$ 1,536.0
Lowe's, Inc.	1,380.0
Kmart	1,200.0
Wal-Mart Stores, Inc.	770.0
Frank's Nursery & Crafts	530.8
Hechinger Company	438.0
Target Stores, Inc.	410.4
Builder's Square	300.0
Price Costco Company	262.0
Menard's Inc.	261.0
Home Base	200.0
Payless Cashway	194.8
Orchard Supply Hardware	178.0
Kroger Company	135.0
Sunbelt Nursery, Inc.	109.0

Source: *Nursery Retailer*, March/April 1997, p. 63, from Brantwood Horticultural Research Division.

★ 1287 ★

Retailing - Nursery Products (SIC 5261)

Home Gardening Sales by Outlet

Data show the millions of households who purchased goods at each outlet in 1995. Total sales reached $22.2 billion.

	(mil.)	Share
Garden centers	32	25.6%
Mass merchandisers	23	18.4
Hardware stores	19	15.2
Home centers	18	14.4
Feed/seed stores	14	11.2
Supermarkets	12	9.6
Mail order companies	7	5.6

Source: *New York Times*, September 28, 1996, p. 21, from National Gardening Association.

★ 1288 ★

Retailing - Nursery Products (SIC 5261)

Top Nurseries - 1996

Companies are ranked by sales in millions of dollars.

Hines Wholesale Nurseries, Inc.	$ 91.9
Monrovia Nursery Company	79.2

Continued on next page.

★ 1288 ★ *Continued*

Retailing - Nursery Products (SIC 5261)

Top Nurseries - 1996

Companies are ranked by sales in millions of dollars.

Color Spot Nurseries, Inc.	$ 75.0
Nurserymen's Exchange, Inc.	67.7
Greenleaf Nursery Company	47.0
Imperial Nurseries, Inc.	46.1
Bear Creek Gardens, Inc.	42.6
Zelenka Nursery, Inc.	42.3
Flowerwood Nursery, Inc.	35.2
Costa Nursery Farms, Inc.	33.3
Powell Plant Farms, Inc.	33.0
Bailey Nurseries, Inc.	32.0

Source: *Nursery Retailer*, February/March 1997, p. 44, from *Nursery Business Grower*.

SIC 53 - General Merchandise Stores

★ 1289 ★

Retailing (SIC 5300)

General Merchandise Companies - 1996

Leading companies are ranked by revenues in millions of dollars. Figure for Bradlees represents revenues for the fiscal year ended January 31, 1996.

Wal-Mart Stores	$ 106,147
Sears Roebuck	38,326
Kmart	31,437
Dayton Hudson	25,371
J.C. Penney	23,649
Federated Department Stores	15,229
May Department Stores	12,601
Dillard Department Stores	6,412
Nordstrom	4,453
Fred Meyer	3,725
Harcourt General	3,290
Mercantile Stores	3,031
Caldor	2,698
Kohl's	2,338
Ames Department Stores	2,162
Dollar General	2,134
Fingerhut	2,027
Saks Holdings	1,945
Bradlees	1,795
Family Dollar Stores	1,715
Venture Stores	1,597
Carson Pirie Scott	1,103

Source: *Fortune*, April 28, 1997, p. 53.

★ 1290 ★

Retailing (SIC 5300)

Holiday Shopping By Teens

Department stores
Clothing stores
Discount stores
Music/video stores
Sporting goods stores
Electronics stores
Shoe stores
Other

Data show where teenagers prefer to shop for holiday gifts. Clothes and apparel were at the top of teenagers' wish lists. The average teenager gets an average of $132 in cash gifts. Teenagers represent over $7.0 billion in holiday shopping power. Figures are based on a survey of 518 respondents.

Department stores	30.0%
Clothing stores	28.0
Discount stores	13.0
Music/video stores	11.0
Sporting goods stores	6.0
Electronics stores	4.0
Shoe stores	3.0
Other	3.0

Source: *Sporting Goods Dealer*, November 1996, p. 6, from Channel One Network.

★ 1291 ★

Retailing (SIC 5300)

Largest Retailers - Washington D.C.

Companies are ranked by revenues in millions of dollars.

Giant Food Inc.	$ 3,881.0
Hechinger Co.	2,199.0
U.S. Office Products Co.	701.9
Dart Group Corp.	678.1
Trak Auto Corp.	344.6

Source: *Washington Post*, April 28, 1997, p. 39.

★ 1292 ★

Retailing (SIC 5300)

Largest Supercenters

Companies are listed by the number of stores in operation.

Wal-Mart	374
Meijer	107
Fred Meyer	103
Super Kmart	97
Smitty's	24
Big Bear	18

Source: *Wall Street Journal*, March 27, 1997, p. B1.

★ 1293 ★

Retailing (SIC 5300)

Leading Single-Price Retailers

Firms are ranked by 1995 sales in millions of dollars.

Dollar Tree Stores	$ 300
99 Cents Only	122
Dollar Bill$	113
All For One/ITZADEAL	106
Everything's A $1	80

Source: *Discount Store News*, July 1, 1996, p. 74.

★ 1294 ★

Retailing (SIC 5300)

Retail Sales by City

Areas are ranked by 1995 retail sales in billions of dollars.

Chicago	$ 71.5
Los Angeles	67.6
New York	52.1
Washington D.C.	45.5
Philadelphia	44.3
Detroit	42.1
Houston	35.3
Atlanta	34.9
Boston	34.1
Dallas	29.9

Source: *Wall Street Journal*, November 8, 1996, p. B10, from Market Statistics.

★ 1295 ★

Retailing (SIC 5300)

Top Chain Stores

Firms are ranked by 1995 revenues in millions of dollars.

Wal-Mart	$ 89.1
Sears, Roebuck & Co.	34.9
Kmart	34.3
Kroger	23.9
Dayton Hudson	23.5
J.C. Penney	21.4
American Stores Co.	18.3
Price/Costco	18.2
Safeway Inc.	16.3
Home Depot	15.4

Source: *Chain Store Age*, August 1996, p. 24A, from company reports and Nordby International.

★ 1296 ★

Retailing (SIC 5300)

Top Close-Out Chains

Firms are ranked by 1995 sales in millions of dollars.

Odd Lots/Big Lots	$ 1,287
MacFrugal's	705
Bud's Warehouse Outlets	570
Tuesday Morning	210
Building #19	95
Universal International	77

Source: *Discount Store News*, July 1, 1996, p. 67.

★ 1297 ★

Retailing (SIC 5300)

Top Retail Firms - North America

Firms are ranked by 1995 sales in millions of dollars.

Wal-Mart	$ 93,627
Sears	34,925
Kmart Corp.	34,389
Dayton Hudson	23,516
Price/Costco	17,900
Melville Corp.	11,516
Toys R Us	9,427
Best Buy	7,200
Circuit City	7,030
Montgomery Ward	7,085

Source: *Discount Store News*, July 1, 1996, p. 53.

★ 1298 ★

Retailing (SIC 5300)

Top Specialty Stores by Sales

Sales are shown in millions of dollars for fiscal year 1995.

Woolworth Corporation	$ 8,224
Limited	7,881
Marmaxx Group	4,448
Gap	4,395
Burlington Coat Factory	1,585
Ross Stores, Inc.	1,426
Talbots, Inc.	$ 981
Stage Stores, Inc.	683
County Seat Stores, Inc.	619
Dress Barn, Inc.	501

Source: *The Apparel Industry and Codes of Conduct*, 1996, p. 24, from U.S. Department of Labor and Bureau of International Labor Affairs.

★ 1299 ★

Retailing (SIC 5300)

Top Supercenters

Firms are ranked by 1995 sales in millions of dollars.

Wal-Mart Superstores	$ 11,500
Meijer	5,600
Super Kmart	3,650
Fred Meyer	3,429
Smitty's	675

Source: *Discount Store News*, July 1, 1996, p. 62.

★ 1300 ★

Retailing (SIC 5300)

Top Supercenters - Indianapolis, IN

Shares are shown based on volume of sales for 1995.

Kroger	25.8%
Marsh	23.7
Supervalu	18.8
Meijer	8.1
Sam's	1.7
Other	21.9

Source: *Investext*, Thomson Financial Networks, November 26, 1996, p. 10, from Metro Market Studies and PaineWebber analysis.

★ 1301 ★

Department Stores (SIC 5311)

Leading Department Stores - Canada

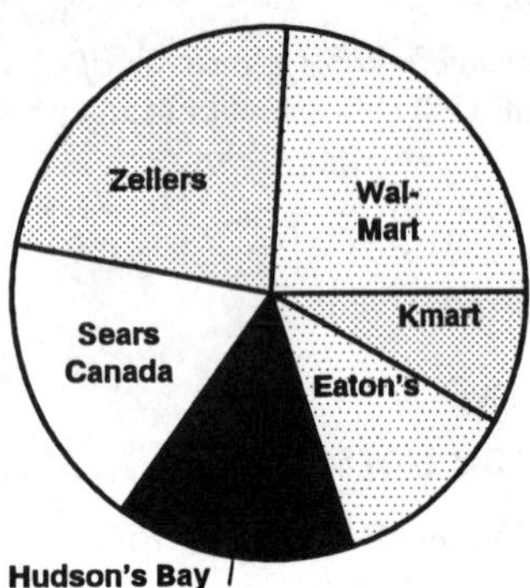

Market shares are shown in percent.

	1995	1996
Wal-Mart	21.0%	24.0%
Zellers	24.0	23.0
Sears Canada	18.0	18.0
Hudson's Bay	16.0	15.0
Eaton's	12.0	12.0
Kmart	9.0	8.0

Source: *Globe and Mail*, April 29, 1997, p. B6, from David Brodie and CIBC Wood Gundy.

★ 1302 ★

Department Stores (SIC 5311)

Top Department Stores

Firms are ranked by 1995 sales in millions of dollars.

Federated Dept. Stores	$ 15,049
May Dept. Stores	10,507
Dayton Hudson	7,709
Dillard	5,918
Nordstrom	4,114
Mercantile Stores	2,944
Neiman Marcus Stores	1,888
Profitt's	1,333
Carson Pirie Scott	1,084
Bon Ton Stores	607

Source: *Chain Store Age*, August 1996, p. 24A, from company reports and Nordby International.

★ 1303 ★

Department Stores (SIC 5311)

Top Department Stores by Sales

Sales are shown in billions of dollars for fiscal year 1995.

Sears Roebuck & Company	$ 31.035
J.C. Penney Company	20.562
Federated Department Stores	15.049
May Department Stores	10.507
Montgomery Ward Holding Company	7.085
Dillard Department Stores	5.918
Nordstrom	4.113
Mercantile Stores Company	2.944
Kohl's Corporation	1.926
Neiman Marcus Group	1.888

Source: *The Apparel Industry and Codes of Conduct*, 1996, p. 23, from U.S. Department of Labor and Bureau of International Labor Affairs.

★ 1304 ★

Convenience Stores (SIC 5331)

Leading Convenience Stores

Firms are ranked by 1995 sales in millions of dollars.

Southland Corp.	$ 6,746
Circle K Corp.	3,516
Super American Group	1,788
National Convenience	906
Dillon Cos.	850
Casey's General Stores Inc.	849

Source: *Chain Store Age*, August 1996, p. 10A, from company reports and Nordby International.

★ 1305 ★

Discount Merchandising (SIC 5331)

Discount Merchandisers - Canada

"Other" includes third place Kmart Canada.

Zellers	45.0%
Wal-Mart	44.0
Other	11.0

Source: *Marketing Magazine*, October 28, 1996, p. 4.

★ 1306 ★

Discount Merchandising (SIC 5331)

Leading Discount Retailers

Firms are ranked by 1995 sales in millions of dollars.

Wal-Mart	$ 54,330
Kmart	26,779
Sears Merchandise	20,132
Sam's Warehouse Club	19,000
Price/Costco	17,900
Target	15,800
Wal-Mart Supercenters	11,500
Best Buy	7,200
Circuit City	7,030
Montgomery Ward	6,219

Source: *Discount Store News*, July 1, 1996, p. 41.

★ 1307 ★

General Merchandising (SIC 5331)

Top Mass Merchandisers by Sales

Sales are shown in billions of dollars for fiscal year 1995.

Wal-Mart Stores	$ 93.627
Kmart Corporation	34.389
Dayton Hudson Corporation	23.516
Price/Costco	17.906
Waban Inc.	3.978
Ames Department Stores	2.120
Venture Stores	1.929
Shopko Stores	1.853
Dollar General Corporation	1.764
Family Dollar Stores	1.547

Source: *The Apparel Industry and Codes of Conduct*, 1996, p. 23, from U.S. Department of Labor and Bureau of International Labor Affairs.

SIC 54 - Food Stores

★ 1308 ★

Grocery Stores (SIC 5411)

Grocery Store Leaders

Sales are shown in billions of dollars.

Kroger	$ 23.9
Safeway/Vons	21.5
American Stores	18.3
Winn-Dixie	13.0
Albertson	12.9

Source: *Wall Street Journal*, October 31, 1996, p. 4A.

★ 1309 ★

Grocery Stores (SIC 5411)

Leading Supercenters - Arkansas

Market shares are shown as of October 1996.

Kroger	35.0%
Harvest	26.0
Other	39.0

Source: *Arkansas Business*, December 9, 1996, p. 22, from *Shelby Report*.

★ 1310 ★

Grocery Stores (SIC 5411)

Leading Supermarket Chains - California

Market shares are shown in percent.

Lucky	19.0%
Vons	13.8
Ralphs	9.4
Safeway	7.8
Alpha Bets	5.4
Other	44.6

Source: *Agribusiness*, March/April 1997, p. 129, from Food Marketing Policy Center.

★ 1311 ★

Grocery Stores (SIC 5411)

Leading Supermarket Chains - Florida

Market shares are shown in percent.

Publix	35.2%
Winn-Dixie	27.6
Albertsons	9.2
Kash N Karry	5.7
Food Lion	5.1
Other	17.2

Source: *Agribusiness*, March/April 1997, p. 129, from Food Marketing Policy Center.

★ 1312 ★

Grocery Stores (SIC 5411)

Leading Supermarket Chains - Northeast

Market shares are shown in percent. "Northeast" refers to Washington D.C., Baltimore, Pennsylvania, New York, and New England.

A&P	12.4%
Pathmark	8.0
Giant Food Inc.	5.5
Acme (Jewel)	4.7
Stop & Shop	4.2
Other	65.2

Source: *Agribusiness*, March/April 1997, p. 129, from Food Marketing Policy Center.

★ 1313 ★

Grocery Stores (SIC 5411)

Leading Supermarkets - Chicago

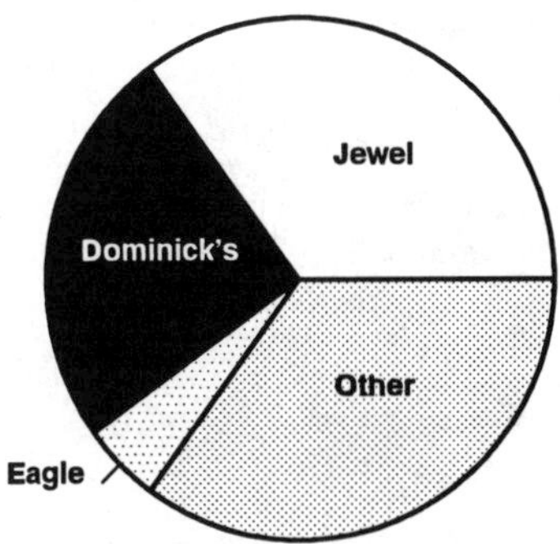

Market shares are shown in percent. Figure for Dominick's includes its Omni operation.

Jewel	35.0%
Dominick's	25.0
Eagle	5.0
Other	35.0

Source: *Chicago Tribune*, May 21, 1997, p. 4.

★ 1314 ★

Grocery Stores (SIC 5411)

Leading Supermarkets - Southern California

Ralphs	27.0%
Vons	19.0
Other	54.0

Source: *Los Angeles Business Journal*, December 2, 1996, p. 4A.

★ 1315 ★

Grocery Stores (SIC 5411)

Major Grocers

Shares are shown based on sales of $336.5 billion by the top 75 companies.

Kroger Co.	7.4%
Safeway	6.7
American Stores Co.	5.6
Supervalu	5.2
Wal-Mart Supercenters	5.2
Fleming Cos.	4.9
Albertson's	4.1
Winn-Dixie Stores	3.9%
Ahold USA	3.3
Publix Super Markets	3.1
Food Lion	3.0
A&P	3.0

Source: *Supermarket News*, January 20, 1997, p. 82.

★ 1316 ★

Grocery Stores (SIC 5411)

Ontario's Grocery Leaders

Ontario represents 39% of the $70 billion Canadian grocery market.

Loblaw	31.0%
A&P	13.0
Oshawa	12.0
Loeb	9.0
Other	35.0

Source: *Marketing Magazine*, October 14, 1996, p. 6, from International Surveys Ltd. of Toronto.

★ 1317 ★

Grocery Stores (SIC 5411)

Supermarket Leaders - Quebec

Loeb	37.0%
Metro-Richelieu	33.0
IGA	17.0
Other	13.0

Source: *Marketing Magazine*, November 25, 1996, p. 10.

★ 1318 ★

Grocery Stores (SIC 5411)

Top Cities for Grocery Sales

Cities are ranked by grocery sales in thousands of dollars for 1995.

Los Angeles	$ 12,244,027
Chicago	10,193,905
New York	8,825,556
Washington D.C.	7,853,418
Philadelphia	7,438,226
Boston	6,445,298
Houston	6,130,527
Atlanta	5,612,025

Continued on next page.

★ 1318 ★ *Continued*

Grocery Stores (SIC 5411)

Top Cities for Grocery Sales

Cities are ranked by grocery sales in thousands of dollars for 1995.

Detroit	$ 5,340,386
Phoenix	4,912,388

Source: *Wall Street Journal*, May 2, 1997, p. B8, from Market Statistics.

★ 1319 ★

Grocery Stores (SIC 5411)

Top Cities for Supermarkets

Cities are ranked by supermarket sales in thousands of dollars for the 52 weeks ending November 2, 1996.

New York City	$ 13,237,724.4
Los Angeles	12,382,585.5
Chicago	7,051,063.7
Philadelphia	7,000,335.1
Boston	6,420,841.6
San Francisco	5,868,985.8
Washington D.C.	5,208,896.4
Detroit	4,946,902.7
Miami	4,618,911.8
Dallas	4,602,500.4
Houston	4,286,532.8
Tampa	4,012,897.6
Seattle	3,802,635.4
Cleveland	3,717,223.4
Phoenix	3,709,414.3

Source: *Supermarket Business*, March 1997, p. 20, from A.C. Nielsen ScanTrack.

★ 1320 ★

Grocery Stores (SIC 5411)

Top Grocery Chains - Arkansas

Companies are ranked by revenues for 1995. Various figures are estimated.

Wal-Mart Stores Inc.	$ 12,500
Kroger Co.	581
Harvest Foods Inc.	372
Harps Food Stores Inc.	343
Town & Country Supermarkets	120
Mad Butcher Inc.	50
Ellison Enterprises	42
Sexton Food Inc.	40
Jitney-Jungle Stores of America Inc.	$ 38
Knight's Inc.	38
Smitty's Food Stores Inc.	37
Food Plus	35
Lynn Green's Big Star Inc.	34
GES Inc.	33
C.V. FoodDrug Inc.	28

Source: *Arkansas Business*, December 9, 1996, p. 23, from *Chain Store Guide's 1996 Directory*.

★ 1321 ★

Grocery Stores (SIC 5411)

Top Grocery Stores - Canada

Shares are based on sales.

	1995	1996
Loblaw Companies	18.5%	18.7%
Non-grocery stores	11.2	12.1
Canada Safeway	8.1	8.7
IGA	8.6	7.5
Membership Club Stores	7.0	7.5
Metro-Richelieu	6.8	6.6
Provigo	6.4	6.5
Corporate A&P	6.2	4.9
Co-Op	5.0	4.8
Other	24.3	22.7

Source: *Marketing Magazine*, May 26, 1997, p. 12, from *Canadian Grocer*.

★ 1322 ★

Retailing - Candy (SIC 5441)

Candy Sales by Outlet

Percentages are based on daily dollar sales.

Food	46.5%
Mass	29.2
Drug	24.3

Source: *U.S. Distribution Journal*, January/February 1997, p. 36, from National Confectionery Association.

★ 1323 ★

Bakeries (SIC 5461)

Bagel Sales by Outlet

Total sales reached $2.6 billion in 1996.

In-store bakeries	29.2%
Specialty bagel shops	25.3
Retail bakeries	18.5
Fresh or refrigerated wholesales	13.5
Frozen wholesale	7.9
Other	5.6

Source: *Bakery Production & Marketing*, November 15, 1996, p. 51.

★ 1324 ★

Bakeries (SIC 5461)

Largest Bagel Stores

Data show number of outlets as of December 1996. Retail sales of bagels are expected to increase from $1.6 billion in 1995 to $2.3 billion in 1996.

Brueggers	450
Einstein/Noah	300
Manhattan Bagel	287

Source: *New York Times*, December 26, 1996, p. C1, from Bruegger's Corporation, Einstein Noah Bagel Corporation, and Manhattan Bagel Company.

SIC 55 - Automotive Dealers and Service Stations

★ 1325 ★

Retailing - Autos (SIC 5511)

Largest Auto Dealers - Cincinnati

Dealers are ranked by unit sales in 1995.

Kenwood Dealer Group Inc.	13,586
Jeff Wyler Dealer Group Inc.	11,617
Jake Sweeney Automotive Inc.	11,561
DeCastro Auto Group	9,761
McCluskey Chevrolet Inc.	6,105
32 Ford Mercury Inc.	4,655
Bob Townsend Ford Inc.	3,492

Source: *Cincinnati Business Courier*, July 15, 1996, p. 14.

★ 1326 ★

Retailing - Autos (SIC 5511)

New Car Dealerships - Los Angeles

Firms are ranked by unit sales in 1995.

Santa Monica Ford	33,396
Longo Toyota, Lexus	20,444
Puente Hills Mazda	16,198
Galpin Motors Inc.	14,967
Norm Reeves Honda	6,590
Don Kott Auto Center	5,272
Toyota of Cerritos	4,468
Cerritos Ford	3,844
Vista Ford	3,308
Universal City Nissan	3,287

Source: *Los Angeles Business Journal*, December 9, 1996, p. 12.

★ 1327 ★

Retailing - Autos (SIC 5511)

Top Auto Dealers - Dallas County, TX

Dealers are ranked by units sold in 1996.

V.T. Inc.	12,326
Westway Motor Sales	5,852
Bankston Enterprises	5,389
Prestige Ford	5,220
David McDavid Automotive Group	5,171
Sewell Dealerships	4,998
Frank Parra Autoplex	4,916
John Eagle Dealerships	4,720
North Central Ford	4,349
Lute Riley Honda	4,205

Source: *Dallas Morning News*, May 4, 1997, p. 36Q, from *Freeman Auto Report*.

★ 1328 ★

Retailing - Autos (SIC 5511)

Top Auto Dealership Groups

Republic Industries
Hendrick Automotive Group
Ed Morse Automotive Group
V.T. Inc.
United Automotive Group
McCombs Automotive
Potamkin Companies
Bill Heard Enterprises
Dobbs Brothers Management
Don Massey Cadillac Group

Companies are ranked by 1996 auto sales in billions of dollars.

Republic Industries	$ 3.8
Hendrick Automotive Group	2.3
Ed Morse Automotive Group	2.1
V.T. Inc.	2.1

Continued on next page.

★ 1328 ★ *Continued*

Retailing - Autos (SIC 5511)

Top Auto Dealership Groups

Companies are ranked by 1996 auto sales in billions of dollars.

United Automotive Group	$ 1.7
McCombs Automotive	1.3
Potamkin Companies	1.2
Bill Heard Enterprises	0.9
Dobbs Brothers Management	0.9
Don Massey Cadillac Group	0.8

Source: *New York Times*, March 6, 1997, p. C6, from Montgomery Securities, *Automotive News*, and Bloomberg Financial Markets.

★ 1329 ★

Retailing - Autos (SIC 5511)

Top Car Dealers - Detroit

Dealers are ranked by 1995 sales in millions of dollars.

Don Massey Cadillac Inc.	$ 774.1
Troy Motors Inc.	467.8
Mel Farr Automotive Group	382.0
Galeana Group	232.5
Tamaroff Automotive Group	205.0
Meade Group Inc.	181.7
Stewart Managament Group Inc.	162.4
Art Moran Pontiac-GMC Inc.	158.1
Suncare Dealerships	157.7
Jerome-Duncan Ford	130.6

Source: *Crain's Detroit Business*, September 2, 1996, p. 9.

★ 1330 ★

Retailing - Auto Parts (SIC 5531)

Auto Accessory Sales by Outlet

Distribution is shown based on sales of $43.77 billion in 1995.

Auto & home supply stores	73.3%
Discount stores	14.0
Wholesale clubs	4.1
Non-store retailers	2.9
Supermarkets & grocery stores	1.8
Home centers	1.2
Drug/proprietary stores	0.8
Hardware stores	0.7
Misc. general merchandise stores	0.7%
Department stores	0.4
Variety stores	0.1

Source: *DM*, July 1996, p. 32.

★ 1331 ★

Retailing - Auto Parts (SIC 5531)

Top Auto Parts Retailers - 1996

Companies are ranked by number of stores.

AutoZone	1,298
Advance Auto Parts	660
Northern Automotive	566
Western Auto	560
Chief Auto Parts	535
Pep Boys	506
Discount Auto Parts	297
Trak Auto	282
Hi-Lo Automotive	194
Super Shops	164

Source: *USA TODAY*, May 30, 1997, p. B1, from *Automotive Marketing*.

★ 1332 ★

Retailing - Tires (SIC 5531)

Dealerships by State - 1996

Therer were a total of 40,478 outlets in 1996.

	No.	Share
California	3,985	9.8%
Texas	3,108	7.7
Florida	2,344	5.8
Pennsylvania	1,724	4.3
New York	1,578	3.9
North Carolina	1,576	3.9
Ohio	1,562	3.9
Other	24,601	60.8

Source: *Tire Business*, December 9, 1996, p. 20, from American Business Information, American Automobile Manufacturing Association, and United States Department of Transportation.

★ 1333 ★

Retailing - Tires (SIC 5531)

Largest Commercial Dealerships

The largest dealerships in North America are ranked by commercial sales in millions of dollars.

Tire Centers Inc.	$ 204.0
Fletcher's Cobre Tire	185.0
Treadco Inc.	172.0
Brad Ragan Inc.	151.0
Kal Tire	145.2
Purcell Tire & Rubber Co.	103.0
Les Schwab Tire Centers Inc.	100.7
J.W. Brewer Tire Co.	90.0
Southern Tire Mart Inc.	83.0
Pomp's Tire Services Inc.	59.8

Source: *Tire Business*, December 9, 1996, p. 20.

★ 1334 ★

Retailing - Tires (SIC 5531)

Largest Retail Tire Chains

Chains are ranked by number of company-owned stores.

Bridgestone/Firestone Inc.	1,525
Firestone Tire & Service Centers	1,329
Expert Tire	74
Mark Morris	10
Sears, Roebuck & Co.	1,400
Sears Auto Centers	773
Western Auto	351
NTW	151
Tire America	125
Wal-Mart Stores Inc.	1,378
Goodyear	920
Penske Auto Centers	860
Pep Boys - Manny, Moe & Jack	506
Canadian Tire Corp.	424
Montgomery Ward Auto Express	324

Source: *Tire Business*, September 2, 1996, p. 17.

★ 1335 ★

Retailing - Tires (SIC 5531)

Largest Tire Marketing Groups

Groups are ranked by number of outlets operating under common banner.

American Car Care Centers	854
Metro 25 Tire	174
Tire Factory	99
Car America	73

Source: *Tire Business*, September 2, 1996, p. 20.

★ 1336 ★

Retailing - Tires (SIC 5531)

Top Tire Cities - North Carolina

Charlotte
Raleigh
Greensboro
Fayetteville
Winston-Salem
Asheville
Durham
Jacksonville
Wilmington
Greenville

Data show the number of tire stores in each city.

Charlotte	93
Raleigh	63
Greensboro	49
Fayetteville	41
Winston-Salem	38
Asheville	36
Durham	35
Jacksonville	28
Wilmington	28
Greenville	21

Source: *Business North Carolina*, March 1997, p. 68, from *1996-97 North Carolina Business Directory*.

★ 1337 ★

Retailing - Tires (SIC 5531)

Top Tire Dealerships

Firms are ranked by retail sales in millions of dollars.

Discount Tire Co. Inc.	$ 678.0
Les Schwab Tire Centers Inc.	488.0
Penske Auto Centers Inc.	360.0
Tire Kingdom Inc.	204.0
Merchant's Inc.	152.0
Oliver & Winston Inc./Winston Tire Co.	144.0
Tire Centers Inc.	103.0
Morgan Tire & Auto Inc./Don Olson Tire	89.4
AKH Co. Inc./Discount Tire Centers	87.0
Kal Tire	74.3

Source: *Tire Business*, September 2, 1996, p. 19.

★ 1338 ★

Gas Stations (SIC 5541)

Gas Station Leaders - Arizona

Shares are current as of December 1996.

Tosco	22.3%
Texaco	15.2
Arco	13.2
Mobil	13.2
Unocal	6.6
Shell	2.2
Other	27.3

Source: *Wall Street Journal*, June 23, 1997, p. B4, from Lundberg Survey.

★ 1339 ★

Gas Stations (SIC 5541)

Gas Station Leaders - California

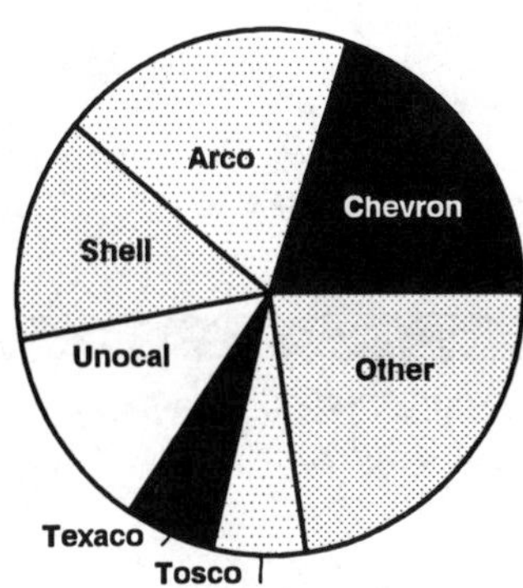

Shares are current as of March 1997.

Chevron	19.5%
Arco	18.9
Shell	14.4
Unocal	12.6
Texaco	6.0
Tosco	5.9
Other	22.7

Source: *Wall Street Journal*, June 23, 1997, p. B4, from Lundberg Survey.

★ 1340 ★

Gas Stations (SIC 5541)

Gas Station Outlets - 1995

Data show the number of outlets.

Citgo	14,054
Texaco	13,023
Amoco	9,600
Shell	8,767
Exxon	8,250
Chevron	7,998
Mobil	7,689
Phillips	7,106
BP America	6,800
Conoco	5,017
Sun	3,861
Sinclair	2,711
Fina	2,631
Uno-Ven	2,395
Marathon	2,380

Source: *National Petroleum News*, July 1996, p. 125.

★ 1341 ★

Gas Stations (SIC 5541)

Gasoline Market - 1995

Shares of the gasoline market are shown based on state-by-state taxable sales.

Shell	7.48%
Amoco	7.15
Mobil	7.04
Texaco and Star Enterprise	6.98
Exxon	6.24
Other	65.11

Source: *New York Times*, October 8, 1996, p. C6, from Lundberg Survey.

SIC 56 - Apparel and Accessory Stores

★ 1342 ★

Retailing - Apparel (SIC 5611)

Boy's & Men's Apparel Sales by Outlet

Distribution is shown based on sales of $54.83 billion in 1995.

Department stores	29.4%
Discount stores	24.0
Family apparel stores	15.2
Men's and boy's wear stores	13.3
Off-price apparel stores	5.9
Non-store retailers	5.0
Sporting goods stores	3.4
Misc. general merchandise stores	1.0
Women's ready-to-wear stores	0.9
Other	1.9

Source: *DM*, July 1996, p. 30.

★ 1343 ★

Retailing - Apparel (SIC 5611)

Men's Designer Apparel Sales - 1996

Market shares are estimated in percent based on department store sales.

Ralph Lauren	35.0%
Tommy Hilfiger	24.0
Nautica	21.0
Liz Claiborne	8.0
Others	13.0

Source: *Investext*, Thomson Financial Networks, December 18, 1996, p. 24, from corporate reports and DLJ estimates.

★ 1344 ★

Retailing - Apparel (SIC 5611)

Men's Underwear Sales by Outlet

Sales are shown by outlet.

Discount stores	52.8%
Mid-tier stores	23.6
Department stores	8.3
Off-price stores	1.4
Mail order	0.7
Other	13.2

Source: *Discount Store News*, February 17, 1997, p. S2.

★ 1345 ★

Retailing - Apparel (SIC 5621)

Where Girls Buy Jeans

Data are estimated for 1997.

Specialty stores	40.7%
Discount stores	19.9
National chains	18.2
Department stores	11.3
Off-pricers	7.1
Catalog/mail order	1.6
Other	1.2

Source: *DM*, August 1996, p. 98.

★ 1346 ★

Retailing - Apparel (SIC 5621)

Where Women Buy Nightgowns - Chicago, IL

Victoria's Secret	22.1%
Carson Pirie Scott	7.9
Marshall Field's	7.4
J.C. Penney	6.8
Other	55.8

Source: *Chain Store Age*, October 1996, p. 20B.

★ 1347 ★

Retailing - Apparel (SIC 5621)

Where Women Buy Suits - Chicago, IL

Carson Pirie Scott	13.6%
Marshall Field's	10.4
J.C. Penney	8.1
Casual Corner	4.7
Other	63.4

Source: *Chain Store Age*, October 1996, p. 20B.

★ 1348 ★

Retailing - Apparel (SIC 5621)

Women's Apparel Sales by Outlet

Distribution is shown based on sales of $114.6 billion in 1995.

Department stores	30.2%
Women's ready to wear stores	24.3
Discount stores	16.4
Off-price apparel stores	10.1
Family apparel stores	9.7
Non-store retailers	4.8
Supermarkets	1.4
Sporting goods	1.0
Variety stores	0.7
Other	1.4

Source: *DM*, July 1996, p. 30.

★ 1349 ★

Retailing - Apparel (SIC 5621)

Women's Apparel Sales by Outlet - Canada

Data are for 1995.

Specialty stores	50.0%
Department stores	25.1
Discount stores	16.5
Other	8.4

Source: *National Trade Data Bank*, October 10, 1996, p. ISA960901.

★ 1350 ★

Retailing - Apparel (SIC 5621)

Women's Casual Designer Sportswear Sales

Market shares are shown in percent based on department store sales.

Liz Claiborne	48.0%
Jones New York	12.0
Nautica	2.0
Tommy	2.0
Other	36.0

Source: *Investext*, Thomson Financial Networks, December 18, 1996, p. 24, from corporate reports and DLJ estimates.

★ 1351 ★

Retailing - Apparel (SIC 5621)

Women's Designer Coats/Suits/ Dresses Sales

Market shares are shown in percent based on department store sales.

Jones New York	28.0%
Liz Claiborne	28.0
Other	45.0

Source: *Investext*, Thomson Financial Networks, December 18, 1996, p. 24, from corporate reports and DLJ estimates.

★ 1352 ★

Retailing - Apparel (SIC 5632)

Lingerie Sales by Outlet - 1996

Total sales reached $10.04 billion.

Non-chain specialty	12.73%
Specialty chains	11.46
Department stores	11.12
Direct mail	9.47
National chains	8.09
Factory outlet	6.23
Off-price	6.21
Other	5.22

Source: *Women's Wear Daily*, April 28, 1997, p. 2, from Fairchild Strategic Information Services and NPD Group Inc.

★ 1353 ★

Retailing - Apparel (SIC 5632)

Top Off-Price Apparel Chains

Firms are ranked by 1995 sales in millions of dollars.

T.J. Maxx	$ 3,897
Marshalls	2,253
Burlington Coat Factory	1,597
Ross Stores	1,426
Kids R Us	732
Goody's Family Clothing	697
Filene's Basement	583

Source: *Discount Store News*, July 1, 1996, p. 61.

★ 1354 ★

Retailing - Apparel (SIC 5632)

Where Women Buy Accessories - Chicago, IL

Marshall Field's
Carson Pirie Scott
Kohl's
Kmart
Other

Marshall Field's	12.7%
Carson Pirie Scott	11.1
Kohl's	7.6
Kmart	6.9
Other	61.7

Source: *Chain Store Age*, October 1996, p. 20B.

★ 1355 ★

Retailing - Apparel (SIC 5632)

Where Women Buy Handbags - Chicago, IL

Carson Pirie Scott	15.2%
Marshall Field's	12.8
J.C. Penney	8.7
Wal-Mart	5.0
Other	58.3

Source: *Chain Store Age*, October 1996, p. 20B.

★ 1356 ★

Retailing - Apparel (SIC 5641)

Children's Underwear Sales by Outlet

Sales are shown by outlet.

Discount stores	67.3%
Mid-tier stores	19.6
Apparel specialty stores	5.6
Department stores	3.7
Off-price stores	0.9
Other	2.9

Source: *Discount Store News*, February 17, 1997, p. S2.

★ 1357 ★

Retailing - Apparel (SIC 5641)

Childrenswear Sales by Outlet

Data are for the first five months of 1996.

	($ bil.)	Share
Discount	$ 3.2	31.7%
Chains	2.1	20.8
Specialty	1.7	16.8
Department stores	1.2	11.9
Off-price	0.7	6.9
Other	1.2	11.9

Source: *Discount Store News*, August 19, 1996, p. A48, from NPD Group Inc.

★ 1358 ★

Retailing - Apparel (SIC 5641)

Infant Apparel Sales by Outlet

Distribution is shown based on sales of $10.03 billion in 1995.

Discount stores	37.1%
Department stores	36.2
Children's & infant's wear stores	13.6
Family apparel stores	8.3
Women's ready-to-wear stores	4.8

Source: *DM*, July 1996, p. 30.

★ 1359 ★

Retailing - Apparel (SIC 5651)

Retail Apparel Market - 1996

Shares of the market are shown in percent.

Specialty stores	21.3%
Discount stores	19.8
Department stores	18.5
Major chains	16.9
J.C. Penney	8.5
Sears	4.2
Mervyn's	2.0
Kohls	1.1
Montgomery Ward	1.1
Other	6.6

Source: *Investext*, Thomson Financial Networks, March 11, 1997, p. 3, from NPD Group Inc.

★ 1360 ★

Retailing - Shoes (SIC 5661)

Where Women Buy Dress Shoes - Chicago, IL

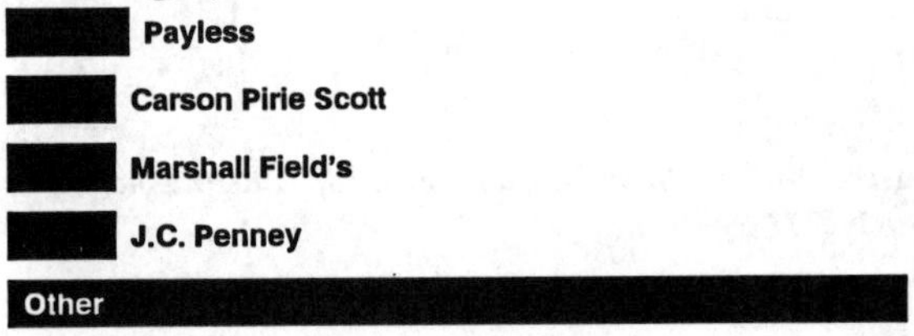

Payless

Carson Pirie Scott

Marshall Field's

J.C. Penney

Other

Payless	9.0%
Carson Pirie Scott	8.2
Marshall Field's	8.0
J.C. Penney	7.6
Other	67.2

Source: *Chain Store Age*, October 1996, p. 20B.

SIC 57 - Furniture and Homefurnishings Stores

★ 1361 ★

Retailing - Furniture (SIC 5712)

Flat-Packed Furniture Sales by Outlet

Distribution is shown based on retail sales of $2.49 billion in 1996. Leading suppliers include Bush, O'Sullivan, and Sauder.

Mass merchants	32.0%
Office superstore/office product dealers	13.0
National chains	11.0
Home centers	10.0
Catalog-showrooms	8.0
Other	26.0

Source: *HFN*, March 17, 1997, p. 13.

★ 1362 ★

Retailing - Furniture (SIC 5712)

Largest Multiregional Furniture Chains

Firms are ranked by 1995 sales in millions of dollars.

Rhodes	$ 430.2
Value City	415.0
Havertys	395.5
Ikea	388.5
Breuner's Home Furnishings Corp.	239.3

Source: *Furniture Today*, December 30, 1996, p. 42.

★ 1363 ★

Retailing - Furniture (SIC 5712)

Largest National Furniture Chains

Firms are ranked by 1995 sales in millions of dollars.

Levitz	$ 1,008.4
Heilig-Meyers	844.2
Pier 1 Imports	459.2
The Bombay Company	309.4
Wickes Furniture	$ 249.0
Mattress Discounters	203.0
Jennifer Convertibles	157.0
Ethan Allen	143.3
This End Up	135.9
Crate & Barrel	97.0

Source: *Furniture Today*, December 30, 1996, p. 42.

★ 1364 ★

Retailing - Furniture (SIC 5712)

Largest Regional Furniture Chains - Midwest

Firms are ranked by 1995 sales in millions of dollars.

Art Van	$ 396.0
Nebraska Furniture Mart	118.0
Slumberland	114.0
Harlem Furniture	61.8
Kittle's	61.0
Darvin	46.0
Steinhafels	42.9

Source: *Furniture Today*, December 30, 1996, p. 42.

★ 1365 ★

Retailing - Furniture (SIC 5712)

Largest Regional Furniture Chains - Northeast

Firms are ranked by 1995 sales in millions of dollars.

Jordan's Furniture	$ 102.4
Raymour & Flanigan	98.9
ABC Carpet & Home	84.0
Good's Furniture	68.0
Sleepy's	63.0
Rockaway Bedding	60.0
Bob's Discount Furniture	46.5

Source: *Furniture Today*, December 30, 1996, p. 42.

★ 1366 ★

Retailing - Furniture (SIC 5712)

Largest Regional Furniture Chains - South

Firms are ranked by 1995 sales in millions of dollars.

Rooms To Go	$ 305.0
W.S. Badcock	300.1
Finger Furniture	112.0
Reliable Stores	108.0
Furnitureland South	98.0

Source: *Furniture Today*, December 30, 1996, p. 42.

★ 1367 ★

Retailing - Furniture (SIC 5712)

Top Furniture Stores - 1995

Companies are ranked by sales of bedding, furniture, and mattresses. Shares of the $47.7 billion market are shown in percent. Data for Federated, J.C. Penney, and May are estimated.

	Sales ($ mil.)	Share
Federated	$ 1,024.4	2.1%
Levits	1,008.4	2.1
Sears	910.0	1.9
Heilig Myers	844.2	1.8
J.C. Penney	800.0	1.7
May	735.5	1.5
Pier 1 Imports	459.2	1.0
Rhodes	430.2	0.9
Value City	$ 415.0	0.9%
Art Van	396.0	0.8

Source: *Investext*, Thomson Financial Networks, December 27, 1996, p. 35, from company reports, Bureau of the Census, and *Furniture Today*.

★ 1368 ★

Retailing - Homefurnishings (SIC 5713)

Machine-Made Rug Sales by Outlet

National chains

Department stores

Home centers

Mass merchants

Specialty stores

Other

Distribution is shown based on retail sales of $1.01 billion in 1996. Leading suppliers include American Rug Craftsmen, Beaulieu, Courtisan, Homemaker, Karastan, Orian, Oriental Weavers, and Shaw Rugs.

National chains	18.0%
Department stores	17.0
Home centers	17.0
Mass merchants	17.0
Specialty stores	13.0
Other	18.0

Source: *HFN*, March 17, 1997, p. 14.

★ 1369 ★

Retailing - Cookware (SIC 5719)

Nonstick Cookware Sales by Channel

Distribution is shown in percent for 1996.

Wal-Mart	14.0%
Kmart	11.0
Department stores	10.0
Wholesale clubs	8.0
Direct mail	7.0
Target	7.0
Sears/Wards/Penney	6.0
Gourmet/Specialty	5.0

Continued on next page.

★ 1369 ★ *Continued*

Retailing - Cookware (SIC 5719)

Nonstick Cookware Sales by Channel

Distribution is shown in percent for 1996.

Supermarkets	5.0%
TV shopping	3.0
Other discount	10.0
Other	14.0

Source: *HFN*, April 28, 1997, p. 50, from National Family Opinion.

★ 1370 ★

Retailing - Homefurnishings (SIC 5719)

Acrylic Tableware Sales

Shares are shown of the $175 million market.

Mass merchants	35.0%
Supermarkets/drug stores	15.0
Specialty stores	14.0
Warehouse clubs	11.0
Department stores	10.0
Ind. gift, gourmet shops	10.0
Casual furniture stores	5.0

Source: *HFN*, February 3, 1997, p. 1.

★ 1371 ★

Retailing - Homefurnishings (SIC 5719)

Bedding Sales by Outlet

Distribution is shown based on retail sales of 6.2 billion in 1996. Leading suppliers include Sealy, Serta, Simmons, and Spring Air.

Furniture stores	45.0%
Sleep shops	22.0
Department stores	11.0
National chains	9.0
Warehouse clubs	5.0
Other	8.0

Source: *HFN*, March 17, 1997, p. 12.

★ 1372 ★

Retailing - Homefurnishings (SIC 5719)

Comforter Sales by Outlet

Mass merchants
Department stores
Specialty stroes
Catalogs
Other

Distribution is shown based on retail sales of $1.9 billion in 1996. Data refer to non-down comforters.

Mass merchants	43.0%
Department stores	23.0
Specialty stroes	19.0
Catalogs	14.0
Other	1.0

Source: *HFN*, March 17, 1997, p. 14.

★ 1373 ★

Retailing - Homefurnishings (SIC 5719)

Foil Pan Sales by Outlet

Total sales reached $179.7 million.

Food	88.0%
Mass merchandisers	8.2
Drug stores	3.7

Source: *Nonfoods Merchandising*, January 1997, p. 12, from Information Resources Inc.

★ 1374 ★

Retailing - Homefurnishings (SIC 5719)

Home Textiles Sales - 1995

Distribution is shown based on $16 billion in sales.

Discounters	37.0%
National chains	21.0
Department stores	18.0
Specialty stores	13.0
Catalog	8.0
Warehouse	3.0

Source: *Investor's Business Daily*, February 5, 1997, p. A4, from Credit Suisse-First Boston.

★ 1375 ★

Retailing - Homefurnishings (SIC 5719)

Houseware Sales by Outlet - 1995

Discount stores	31.5%
Department stores	11.1
Specialty stores	9.1
Other	48.3

Source: *Discount Store News*, November 4, 1996, p. 74, from National Housewares Manufacturers Association.

★ 1376 ★

Retailing - Homefurnishings (SIC 5719)

Houseware Sales Leaders

Discount stores
Department stores
Specialty stores
Hardware stores
Supermarkets
Warehouse clubs
Drug stores
Catalog sales
Direct sales
Other

Discount stores	31.5%
Department stores	11.1
Specialty stores	9.1
Hardware stores	8.7
Supermarkets	6.0
Warehouse clubs	4.9
Drug stores	4.6
Catalog sales	4.6
Direct sales	4.5
Other	14.9

Source: *Stores*, December 1996, p. 69, from National Housewares Manufacturers Association.

★ 1377 ★

Retailing - Homefurnishings (SIC 5719)

Top Home Textile Retailers

Market shares are shown based on the top 20 retailers.

J.C. Penney	12.7%
Wal-Mart	12.2
Kmart	7.8
Sears	5.6
Target	5.5
Mervyn's	3.7
Linens 'n Things	2.9
Spiegel	2.8
Montgomery Ward	2.5
Price/Costco	2.2
Fingerhut	1.8
T.J. Max/Marshall's	1.8
Other	38.5

Source: *Investext*, Thomson Financial Networks, January 16, 1997, p. 6.

★ 1378 ★

Retailing - Homefurnishings (SIC 5719)

Top Houseware Retailers

Firms are ranked by 1995 sales in millions of dollars.

Wal-Mart	$ 4,000.6
Kmart	2,339.2
Price/Costco	1,910.3
Sam's Club	1,644.4
Target	1,154.8
Sears	1,139.6
Service Merchandise	1,016.0
Williams-Sonoma	840.0
Spiegel	581.7
Walgreen	464.4

Source: *HFN*, September 16, 1996, p. 46.

★ 1379 ★

Retailing - Lighting Fixtures (SIC 5719)

Lighting Fixture Sales by Outlet

Distribution is shown based on retail sales of $1.9 billion in 1996. Leading suppliers include Catalina Lighting, Cooper/Halo, Feiss Industries, Genlyte, Kichler Lighting.

Hardware stores/home centers	46.0%
Specialty stores	42.0
National chains	7.0
Mass merchants	5.0

Source: *HFN*, March 17, 1997, p. 14.

★ 1380 ★

Appliance Stores (SIC 5722)

Appliance Sales by Outlet - 1997

Distribution is shown in percent. Sales for the group reached an estimated $10.47 billion.

Sears	45.90%
National electronics, appliance, television stores	28.18
Montgomery Ward	12.90
Home centers	4.51
Warehouse clubs	3.63
Home furnishing stores	2.75
Regional electronics, appliance, tv stores	1.36
Military exchange	0.78

Source: *Dealerscope*, May 1997, p. 38.

★ 1381 ★

Appliance Stores (SIC 5722)

Leading Appliance Retailers

Firms are ranked by 1995 sales in millions of dollars.

Sears	$ 5,000
Montgomery Ward	1,000
Circuit City	896
Best Buy	505
Lowe's	373
Fretter	280
Sam's Club	230
Price/Costco	225
Tops	219
ABC Appliance	200

Source: *HFN*, September 16, 1996, p. 90.

★ 1382 ★

Appliance Stores (SIC 5722)

Microwave Oven Sales by Outlet - 1996

Distribution is shown based on unit sales.

Discount department stores	28.0%
Mass merchandisers	26.0
Appliance stores	15.0
Consumer electronics superstores	11.0
Warehouse clubs	4.5
Department stores	3.0
Home builders	2.0
Home centers	2.0
Furniture stores	2.0
Catalog showrooms	1.7
Mail order/direct	1.1
Hardware stores	0.5

Continued on next page.

★ 1382 ★ *Continued*

Appliance Stores (SIC 5722)

Microwave Oven Sales by Outlet - 1996

Distribution is shown based on unit sales.

Kitchen remodelers	0.5%
Other	2.7

Source: *Dealerscope*, April 1997, p. 28, from Association of Home Appliance Manufacturers.

★ 1383 ★

Appliance Stores (SIC 5722)

Refrigerator Sales by Outlet - 1996

Distribution is shown in percent.

Consumer electronics superstores	45.3%
Appliance stores	28.5
Discount department stores	5.3
Furniture stores	3.1
Home centers	3.0
Home builders	2.3
Hardware stores	1.5
Warehouse clubs	1.2
Department stores	1.1
Landlords	1.0
Mass merchandisers	0.5
Catalog showrooms	0.4
Kitchen remodelers	0.3
Mail order/direct	0.2
Other	6.3

Source: *Dealerscope*, April 1997, p. 33, from Association of Home Appliance Manufacturers.

★ 1384 ★

Appliance Stores (SIC 5722)

Top Appliance Retailers

Sears	31.9%
Montgomery Ward	5.0
Circuit City	4.4
Best Buy	2.5
Others	56.3

Source: *Investext,* Thomson Financial Networks, July 18, 1996, p. 6, from *HFN*.

★ 1385 ★

Retailing - Electronics (SIC 5731)

Consumer Electronics Retailers

Firms are ranked by 1995 sales in billions of dollars.

Best Buy	$ 6.7
Circuit City	6.4
CompUSA	3.3
RadioShack	3.2
Sears Merchandise	2.9
Wal-Mart	2.6
OfficeMax	2.5
Kmart	2.5
Office Depot	2.1
Computer City	1.8

Source: *HFN*, September 16, 1996, p. 90.

★ 1386 ★

Retailing - Electronics (SIC 5731)

Where We Buy Cellular Phones

Retailer shares are shown in percent for 1995.

Circuit City	30.0%
Radio Shack	20.0
Best Buy	8.0
Nobody Beats the Wiz	6.0
The Good Guys	4.0
Montgomery Ward/Electric Avenue/ Lechmere	3.0
QVC	2.0
Sears/Brand Central	2.0
Bradlees	1.0
Caldor	1.0
Home Shopping Network	1.0
J.C. Penney	1.0
Kmart	1.0
P.C. Richard	1.0
Target	1.0
YES!/Fretter/Silo	1.0
Other	17.0

Source: *Dealerscope*, August 1996, p. 47, from Hudson Valley Editorial Services.

★ 1387 ★

Retailing - Electronics (SIC 5731)

Where We Buy Projection TVs

Best Buy	10.0%
Circuit City	10.0

Continued on next page.

★ 1387 ★ *Continued*

Retailing - Electronics (SIC 5731)

Where We Buy Projection TVs

Sears/Brand Central	5.0%
The Good Guys	3.0
Montgomery Ward/Electric Avenue/ Lechmere	2.0
Nobody Beats the Wiz	2.0
J.C. Penney	1.0
P.C. Richard	1.0
YES!/Fretter/Silo	1.0
Other	65.0

Source: *Dealerscope*, August 1996, p. 50, from Hudson Valley Editorial Services.

★ 1388 ★

Retailing - Electronics (SIC 5731)

Where We Buy VCRs

Retailer shares are shown in percent for 1995.

Circuit City	15.0%
Best Buy	12.0
Wal-Mart	10.0
Montgomery Ward/Electric Avenue/ Lechmere	8.0
Sears/Brand Central	8.0
Target	6.0
The Good Guys	5.0
Kmart	5.0
Nobody Beats the Wiz	5.0
P.C. Richard	3.0
Radio Shack	3.0
J.C. Penney	2.0
QVC	2.0
Other	16.0

Source: *Dealerscope*, August 1996, p. 47, from Hudson Valley Editorial Services.

★ 1389 ★

Retailing - Computers (SIC 5734)

Computer Sales by Outlet - 1996

Computer superstores	22.0%
Assembly shops	20.0
Electronics stores	18.0
Manufacturers	15.0
Catalogers/resellers	8.0
Mass merchants	7.0
Office superstores	5.0%
Other	5.0

Source: *New York Times*, January 8, 1997, p. C1, from Access Media International and Computer Intelligence InfoCorp.

★ 1390 ★

Retailing - Computers (SIC 5734)

Leading Computer Chains

Firms are ranked by 1995 sales in millions of dollars.

CompUSA	$ 2,813
Computer City	1,800
Software ETC	245

Source: *Discount Store News*, July 1, 1996, p. 79.

★ 1391 ★

Retailing - Computers (SIC 5734)

PC Sales by Outlet - 1996

Distribution is shown based on retail sales of $32.8 billion in 1996.

Catalogs	37.0%
Consumer electronics retailers	22.0
Computer superstores	19.0
Mass merchants	9.0
Office superstores	8.0
Warehouse clubs	5.0

Source: *HFN*, March 17, 1997, p. 46.

★ 1392 ★

Retailing - Computers (SIC 5734)

Printer Sales by Outlet - 1996

Distribution is shown based on retail sales of $6.596 billion in 1996.

Catalogs	34.0%
Computer superstores	26.0
Consumer electronics stores	17.0
Office superstores	14.0
Mass merchants	6.0
Warehouse clubs	3.0

Source: *HFN*, March 17, 1997, p. 46.

★ 1393 ★

Retailing - Music (SIC 5735)

Music Sales by Outlet

Data are shown based on a 1995 survey of 3,065 music buyers.

Record stores	52.0%
Tape/record clubs	14.3
Mail order	4.0
Other stores	28.1

Source: http:// www.riaa.com/market/market/releases/ demosurv.htm, 1995, p. 1, from Recording Industry Association of America.

★ 1394 ★

Retailing - Software (SIC 5735)

Children's Education Software

Bundled with PC or CD-ROM drive	55.0%
Computer superstore	27.0
Mail order	17.0
Software store	17.0
Book stores	2.0
Other	18.0

Source: *Database*, Nov.- Dec. 1996, p. 21, from Inteco.

★ 1395 ★

Retailing - Video Tapes (SIC 5735)

Canadian Sell-Through Video Market

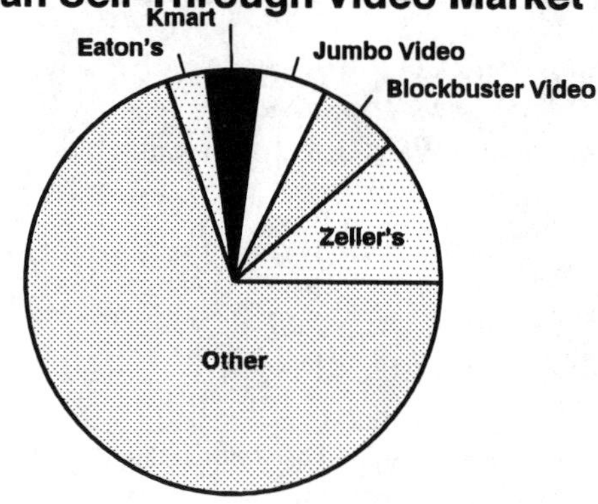

Shares are shown for the month of March 1996.

Zeller's	11.1%
Blockbuster Video	5.7
Jumbo Video	4.8
Kmart	4.0
Eaton's	3.4
Other	67.0

Source: *Bizlink. Maclean Hunter Business Magazines Online*, March 24, 1997, p. 1.

★ 1396 ★

Retailing - Video Tapes (SIC 5735)

Prerecorded Video Retailers

Wal-Mart	25.0%
Blockbuster	6.0
Other	69.0

Source: *Fortune*, November 25, 1996, p. 112.

SIC 58 - Eating and Drinking Places

★ 1397 ★

Catering (SIC 5812)

Largest Caterers - San Diego

Firms are ranked by gross catering sales in thousands of dollars for 1995.

Premier Food Services/Carriage Trade Catering	$ 6,132
Picnic People/Festivities Catering	5,450
French Gourmet Inc.	2,154
Continental Catering	1,300
Party Pros	913
Peartrees Catering Inc.	906
TK & A Custom Catering	900
Crown Point Catering	850
Waters Catering Inc.	660
A Catered Affair	625

Source: *San Diego Business Journal*, July 22, 1996, p. 20.

★ 1398 ★

Foodservice (SIC 5812)

Commercial Foodservice Sales - 1996

Retail sales are shown in billions of dollars.

	($ bil.)	Share
Commercial	$ 75.00	35.5%
Restaurants & bars	61.80	29.3
Quick service	31.70	15.0
Full service	28.40	13.4
Cafeterias & buffets	1.20	0.6
Bars & taverns	0.05	0.0
Recreation	3.2	1.5
Supermarket delis	3.1	1.5
Lodging	3.0	1.4
Convenience stores	1.9	0.9
Other retailers	1.9	0.9

Source: *Restaurant Hospitality*, November 1996, p. 30, from Technomic.

★ 1399 ★

Foodservice (SIC 5812)

F&B Services - Military

Food and beverage (F&B) purchasing is shown by the military in millions of dollars.

U.S. Army Center of Excellence, Subsistence	$ 290.8
Naval Supply Systems Command	224.9
Army & Air Force Exchange Service	114.0
U.S. Air Force Clubs	92.9
U.S. Air Force APF Food Operations	77.3
U.S. Navy MWR Division	71.0
U.S. Marine Corps Food Service	70.4
U.S. Marine Corps MWR Support Activy	54.3
U.S. Army Community & Family Support Centers	53.5
U.S. Navy Exchange Service Command	15.0

Source: *Restaurants & Institutions*, August 1, 1996, p. 74, from individual districts.

★ 1400 ★

Foodservice (SIC 5812)

F&B Services - Prisons

Food and beverage (F&B) spending is shown by prisons in millions of dollars.

California Dept. of Corrections	$ 121.0
Federal Bureau of Prisons	85.0
Texas Dept. of Criminal Justice	80.0
Florida Dept. of Corrections	54.0
New York State Dept. of Corrections	43.0
Michigan Dept. of Corrections	40.0
Ohio Dept. of Corrections	38.0
Pennsylvania Dept. of Corrections	35.0
Illinois Dept. of Corrections	32.6
Georgia Dept. of Corrections	32.0
Virginia Dept. of Corrections	25.6

Source: *Restaurants & Institutions*, August 1, 1996, p. 72, from individual districts.

★ 1401 ★

Foodservice (SIC 5812)

F&B Services - School Districts

Food and beverage (F&B) purchasing is shown by school district in millions of dollars.

New York City Board of Edu.	$ 107.0
Los Angeles Unified School Dist.	73.2
Chicago Public Schools	53.0
Dade County Schools	32.0
Philadelphia School District	24.6
Houston Independent School Dist.	20.0
Broward County Schools	19.4
Hawaii Statewide School Sys.	18.9
Hillsborough County Schools	16.2
Dallas Independent School Dist.	15.1

Source: *Restaurants & Institutions*, August 1, 1996, p. 60, from individual districts.

★ 1402 ★

Foodservice (SIC 5812)

Foodservice Market - 1997

Distribution is shown based on sales of $330.49 billion.

Quick service	33.5%
Full service	30.7
Business and industry	6.0
Schools	5.4
Lodging	4.7
Hospitals	3.7
Colleges/universities	2.7
Corrections	1.8
Nursing homes	1.6
Supermarkets	1.6
Other	8.4

Source: *Restaurants & Institutions*, January 1, 1997, p. 29, from Cahners Bureau of Foodservice Research.

★ 1403 ★

Foodservice (SIC 5812)

Top Foodservice Firms - 1995

Market shares are shown in percent.

Marriott	4.1%
Aramark	3.9
Compass USA	1.3
Service America	0.8
Sodexho	0.8
Delaware North	0.6%
Restaura	0.4
Service Master	0.4
Wood Co.	0.4
Daka Restaurants	0.3
HDS Services	0.2
Morrison's Healthcare	0.2
Restaurant Assoc.	1.0
Other	85.6

Source: *Investext*, Thomson Financial Networks, July 23, 1996, p. 10, from National Restaurant Association and Foodservice Director.

★ 1404 ★

Restaurants (SIC 5812)

Burger Market Leaders - 1995

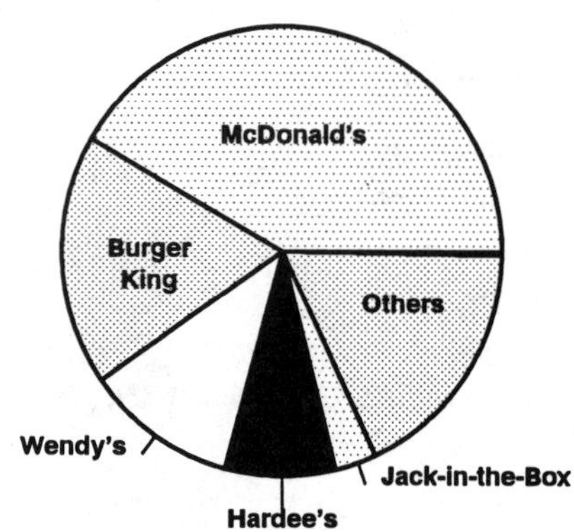

McDonald's	42.3%
Burger King	18.2
Wendy's	10.7
Hardee's	8.3
Jack-in-the-Box	2.9
Others	17.6

Source: *Financial Times*, December 24, 1996, p. 14, from company reports.

★ 1405 ★

Restaurants (SIC 5812)

Eating Place Sales - Midwest States

States are ranked by eating place sales in thousands of dollars for 1997. Total sales for the region reached $60.105 billion.

	($ mil.)	Share
Ohio	$ 11,713.5	19.5%
Illinois	11,492.3	19.1

Continued on next page.

★ 1405 ★ *Continued*

Restaurants (SIC 5812)

Eating Place Sales - Midwest States

States are ranked by eating place sales in thousands of dollars for 1997. Total sales for the region reached $60.105 billion.

	($ mil.)	Share
Michigan	$ 9,119.6	15.2%
Indiana	5,703.6	9.5
Missouri	5,664.5	9.4
Wisconsin	4,712.9	7.8
Minnesota	4,210.5	7.0
Iowa	2,447.5	4.1
Kansas	2,316.4	3.9
Nebraska	1,542.8	2.6
South Dakota	656.2	1.1
North Dakota	525.8	0.9

Source: *Nation's Restaurant News*, January 6, 1997, p. 48, from National Restaurant Association.

★ 1406 ★

Restaurants (SIC 5812)

Eating Place Sales - Southeast States

States are ranked by eating place sales in thousands of dollars for 1997. Total sales for the region reached $57.936 billion.

	($ mil.)	Share
Florida	$ 14,403.7	26.3%
Georgia	6,988.3	12.8
North Carolina	6,717.8	12.3
Virginia	6,606.0	12.1
Tennessee	5,067.9	9.3
Louisiana	3,649.8	6.7
Kentucky	3,417.7	6.3
South Carolina	3,332.4	6.1
Arkansas	1,744.9	3.2
Mississippi	1,598.7	2.9
West Virginia	1,142.4	2.1

Source: *Nation's Restaurant News*, January 6, 1997, p. 48, from National Restaurant Association.

★ 1407 ★

Restaurants (SIC 5812)

Eating Place Sales - Southwest/ Mountain States

States are ranked by eating place sales in thousands of dollars for 1997. Total sales for the region reached $39.524 billion.

	($ mil.)	Share
Texas	$ 16,695.2	47.0%
Arizona	5,336.1	15.0
Colorado	5,126.7	14.4
Oklahoma	1,622.9	4.6
Nevada	2,178.2	6.1
New Mexico	2,071.5	5.8
Utah	1,902.3	5.4
Wyoming	590.8	1.7

Source: *Nation's Restaurant News*, January 6, 1997, p. 48, from National Restaurant Association.

★ 1408 ★

Restaurants (SIC 5812)

Eating Place Sales - Western States

States are ranked by eating place sales in thousands of dollars for 1997. Total sales for the region reached $39.541 billion.

	($ mil.)	Share
California	$ 26,920.9	68.1%
Washington	4,876.1	12.3
Oregon	2,911.5	7.4
Hawaii	1,947.1	4.9
Idaho	1,207.3	3.1
Montana	992.3	2.5
Alaska	685.7	1.7

Source: *Nation's Restaurant News*, January 6, 1997, p. 48, from National Restaurant Association.

★ 1409 ★

Restaurants (SIC 5812)

Fast Food Outlets - Canada

Data show number of outlets.

McDonald's	1,000
A&W	485
Burger King	238
Wendy's	225

Source: *Canadian Business*, December 1996, p. 30.

★ 1410 ★

Restaurants (SIC 5812)

Hamburger Market - 1996

McDonald's	42.1%
Burger King	19.2
Wendy's	11.0
Hardee's	7.2
Jack in the Box	3.1
Others	17.4

Source: *New York Times*, February 27, 1997, p. C5, from Bloomberg, Salomon Brothers, and Technomic Inc.

★ 1411 ★

Restaurants (SIC 5812)

Hamburger Restaurant Leaders - 1996

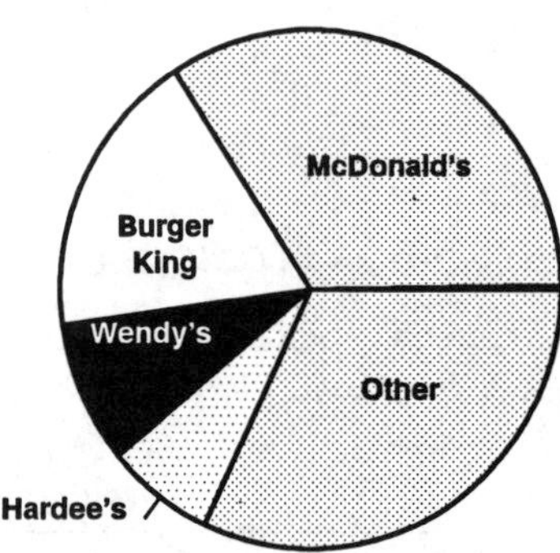

McDonald's	33.8%
Burger King	17.9
Wendy's	8.8
Hardee's	7.1
Other	32.4

Source: *Atlanta-Journal Constitution*, February 27, 1997, p. F1, from *Nation's Restaurant News* and National Restaurant Association.

★ 1412 ★

Restaurants (SIC 5812)

Largest Fast Food Chains - 1995

Sales are shown in billions of dollars.

McDonald's	$ 15.9
Burger King	6.9
Pizza Hut	5.1
Taco Bell	4.4
Wendy's	$ 4.0
KFC	3.7
Hardee's	3.1
Subway	2.6
Dairy Queen	2.4
Domino's	2.2

Source: *Cornell Hotel and Restaurant Administration Quarterly*, June 1996, p. 17, from Technomic and IMP Corp.

★ 1413 ★

Restaurants (SIC 5812)

Leading Family Restaurants

Establishments catering to the dinning-out market are ranked by sales in millions of dollars.

Denny's	$ 1,490.0
Shoney's	1,260.4
Big Boy	970.0
Boston Market	792.9
International House of Pancakes	714.9
Friendly's	649.1
Perkins Family Restaurants	647.0
Coco's	621.7
Cracker Barrell Old Country Store	610.0
Bob Evans Restaurants	590.0
Waffle House	365.3
Village Inn	258.5
Marie Callender's	255.0
Bakers Square	227.0
Country Kitchen	226.9

Source: *Restaurants & Institutions*, July 15, 1996, p. 54.

★ 1414 ★

Restaurants (SIC 5812)

Leading Fast Food Restaurant Chains - Canada

Company shares are shown based on sales of $9.053 billion in Canadian dollars for 1995.

McDonald's Restaurants of Canada	18.7%
Cara Operations Ltd.	11.3
KFC Canada	7.0
Pizza Hut Canada	4.6
Subway Sandwiches and Salads	3.6
A&W Food Services of Canada	3.4
Dairy Queen of Canada	2.9

Continued on next page.

★ 1414 ★ *Continued*

Restaurants (SIC 5812)

Leading Fast Food Restaurant Chains - Canada

Company shares are shown based on sales of $9.053 billion in Canadian dollars for 1995.

Burger King	2.7%
Wendy's Restaurants of Canada	2.6
Les Rotisseries St-Hubert	2.0
Others	41.2

Source: *Marketing Magazine*, May 26, 1997, p. 12, from *Foodservice and Hospitality Magazine* and Canadian Restaurant and Foodservice Association.

★ 1415 ★

Restaurants (SIC 5812)

Leading Specialty Restaurants

Data show the leading snacks and sweets restaurants ranked by sales in millions of dollars.

Dairy Queen	$ 2,484.4
Dunkin' Donuts	1,697.2
Baskin-Robbins	780.0
TCBY Treats	292.0
Starbucks Coffee	290.0
Braum's Ice Cream & Dairy Stores	221.8
Haagen-Dazs Ice Cream Cafe	212.5
I Can't Believe It's Yogurt	150.0
Carvel Ice Cream Bakery	140.7
Cinnabon World Famous Cinnamon Rolls	120.0

Source: *Restaurants & Institutions*, July 15, 1996, p. 94.

★ 1416 ★

Restaurants (SIC 5812)

Leading Steakhouse Chains

Restaurants are ranked by sales in millions of dollars.

Outback Steakhouse	$ 827.0
Sizzler	775.0
Ponderosa	670.0
Golden Corral	618.1
Ryan's Family Steak House	554.0
Lone Star Steakhouse & Saloon	340.9
Western Sizzlin'	340.0
Tony Roma's-A Place for Ribs	296.2
Quincy's Family Steakhouse	$ 294.0
Stuart Anderson's Restaurants	250.0
Bonanza	205.0
Steak and Ale	205.0

Source: *Restaurants & Institutions*, July 15, 1996, p. 116.

★ 1417 ★

Restaurants (SIC 5812)

Pizza Market

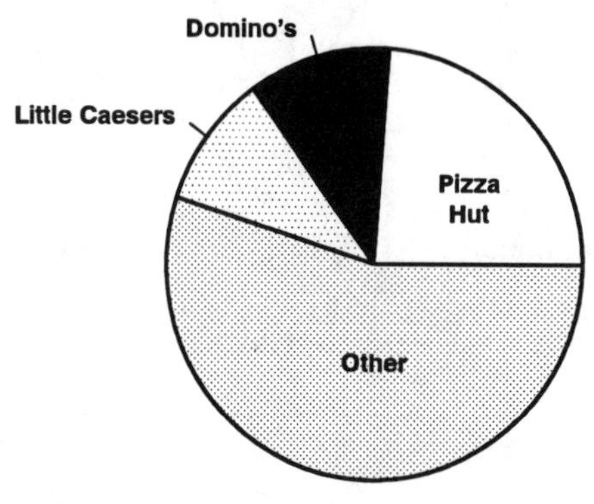

Market shares are shown in percent.

Pizza Hut	24.0%
Domino's	11.0
Little Caesers	10.0
Other	55.0

Source: *USA TODAY*, March 27, 1997, p. B1, from Technomic.

★ 1418 ★

Restaurants (SIC 5812)

Restaurant Market by Segment - Canada

Data show share of revenues.

Quick service	41.1%
Casual	24.8
Family style	21.0
Fine	8.3
Other	4.8

Source: *National Trade Data Bank*, October 10, 1996, p. ISA960901.

★ 1419 ★

Restaurants (SIC 5812)

Submarine Sandwich Market

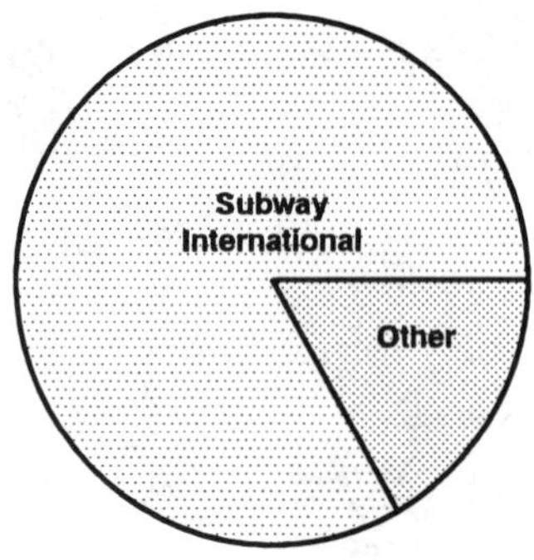

Subway International	83.0%
Other	17.0

Source: *Detroit News*, September 24, 1996, p. B1.

★ 1420 ★

Restaurants (SIC 5812)

Top Fast-Food Restaurants - 1995

McDonald's	7.8%
Burger King	3.4
Pizza Hut	2.5
Taco Bell	2.2
Wendy's	2.0
KFC	1.8
Hardee's	1.5
Subway	1.3
Dairy Queen	1.2
Domino's	1.1
Other	75.2

Source: *Advertising Age*, September 30, 1996, p. S18, from Technomic Inc.

★ 1421 ★

Restaurants (SIC 5812)

Top Independent Restaurants

Establishments are ranked by 1996 sales in millions of dollars.

Rainbow Room (New York)	$ 32.135
Tavern on the Green (New York)	31.700
Smith & Wollensky (New York)	22.287
Bob Chinn's Crabhouse (Wheeling, IL)	21.014
Sparks Steakhouse (New York)	$ 20.400
Official All Star Cafe (New York)	19.500
Joe's Stone Crab (Miami Beach)	17.620
Manor (West Orange, NJ)	14.100
Scoma's Restaurant (San Francisco)	13.605
Four Seasons (New York)	13.600
"21" Club (New York)	13.518
Gladstone's 4 Fish (Pacific Palisades, CA)	12.741

Source: *Restaurants & Institutions*, April 1, 1997, p. 43.

★ 1422 ★

Juice Bars (SIC 5813)

Free-Standing Juice Bars by Region

States are ranked by juice bar outlets as of January 1, 1997. Data does not include juice bars housed inside other retail stores.

California	275
Florida	52
Louisiana	50
Arizona	31
New York	30
Washington State	30
Texas	25
Utah	18
Georgia	17
Oregon	17

Source: *Washington Post*, April 29, 1997, p. C1, from Juice Gallery.

★ 1423 ★

Drug Stores (SIC 5912)

Top Drug Chains

Data show the number of outlets following pending mergers as of October 21, 1996.

Rite Aid	3,500
J.C. Penney (Eckerd/Thrift)	2,800
Revco	2,600
Walgreens	2,190
CVS	1,366
Medicine Shoppe Intl.	1,122
American Drug Stores	832
Longs	328
Drug Emporium	234
K&B Services	194

Source: *Wall Street Journal*, January 2, 1997, p. 12.

★ 1424 ★

Drug Stores (SIC 5912)

Top Drug Stores - Akron, OH

Market shares are shown for 1995.

Revco	23.7%
Marc's	20.2
Albrecht	11.3
Other	44.8

Source: *Investext*, Thomson Financial Networks, July 25, 1996, p. 4, from Metro Market Studies.

★ 1425 ★

Drug Stores (SIC 5912)

Top Drug Stores - Atlanta, GA

Market shares are shown in percent.

Eckerd	24.0%
Big B	15.0
Revco	12.0
Drug Emporium	10.0
Other	39.0

Source: *Atlanta Journal-Constitution*, February 8, 1997, p. D1, from *Chain Store Age*.

★ 1426 ★

Drug Stores (SIC 5912)

Top Drug Stores - Charleston, SC

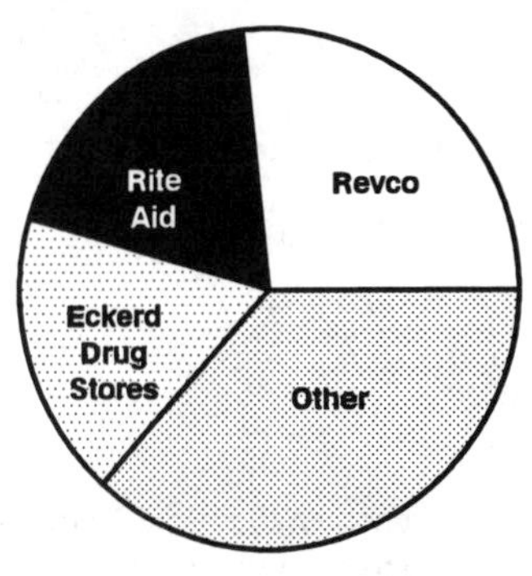

Market shares are shown for 1995.

Revco	26.9%
Rite Aid	18.7
Eckerd Drug Stores	17.8
Other	36.6

Source: *Investext*, Thomson Financial Networks, July 25, 1996, p. 4, from Metro Market Studies.

★ 1427 ★

Drug Stores (SIC 5912)

Top Drug Stores - Dayton-Springfield, OH

Market shares are shown for 1995.

Revco	27.6%
Rite Aid	21.3
Medicine Shoppe	8.5
Other	42.6

Source: *Investext,* Thomson Financial Networks, July 25, 1996, p. 4, from Metro Market Studies.

★ 1428 ★

Drug Stores (SIC 5912)

Top Drug Stores - Evansville, IL

Market shares are shown for 1995.

Revco	30.0%
Walgreens	25.2
OSCO	13.0
Other	31.8

Source: *Investext,* Thomson Financial Networks, July 25, 1996, p. 4, from Metro Market Studies.

★ 1429 ★

Drug Stores (SIC 5912)

Top Drug Stores - Fort Wayne, IN

Market shares are shown for 1995.

Walgreens	31.2%
Revco	23.2
Keltsch Bros.	18.4
Other	27.2

Source: *Investext,* Thomson Financial Networks, July 25, 1996, p. 4, from Metro Market Studies.

★ 1430 ★

Drug Stores (SIC 5912)

Top Drug Stores - Gary-Hammond, IN

Market shares are shown for 1995.

Walgreens	62.2%
OSCO	11.1
Revco	6.3
Other	20.4

Source: *Investext,* Thomson Financial Networks, July 25, 1996, p. 4, from Metro Market Studies.

★ 1431 ★

Drug Stores (SIC 5912)

Top Drug Stores - Greenville, SC

Market shares are shown for 1995.

Revco	44.6%
Rite Aid	15.0
Eckerd Drug Stores	14.5
Other	25.9

Source: *Investext,* Thomson Financial Networks, July 25, 1996, p. 4, from Metro Market Studies.

★ 1432 ★

Drug Stores (SIC 5912)

Top Drug Stores - Indianapolis, IN

Market shares are shown for 1995.

Revco	33.9%
OSCO	25.4
Walgreens	17.0
Other	23.7

Source: *Investext,* Thomson Financial Networks, July 25, 1996, p. 4, from Metro Market Studies.

★ 1433 ★

Drug Stores (SIC 5912)

Top Drug Stores - Knoxville, TN

Market shares are shown for 1995.

Revco	36.1%
Walgreen	32.5
Wal-Mart (DIS)	5.2
Other	26.2

Source: *Investext,* Thomson Financial Networks, July 25, 1996, p. 4, from Metro Market Studies.

★ 1434 ★

Drug Stores (SIC 5912)

Top Drug Stores - Macon, GA

Market shares are shown for 1995.

Revco	25.0%
Big B Drugs	20.3
Eckerd Drug Stores	15.2
Other	39.5

Source: *Investext,* Thomson Financial Networks, July 25, 1996, p. 4, from Metro Market Studies.

★ 1435 ★

Drug Stores (SIC 5912)

Top Drug Stores - Peoria, IL

Market shares are shown for 1995.

Walgreens	37.1%
Revco	30.8
Phar-Mor	10.3
Other	21.8

Source: *Investext,* Thomson Financial Networks, July 25, 1996, p. 4, from Metro Market Studies.

★ 1436 ★

Drug Stores (SIC 5912)

Top Drug Stores - Raleigh-Durham, NC

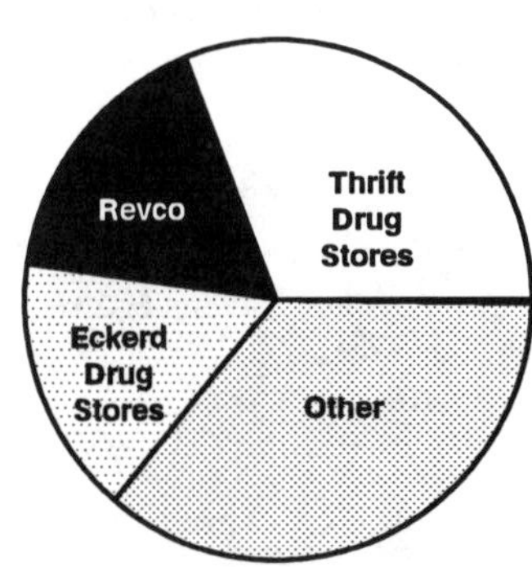

Market shares are shown for 1995.

Thrift Drug Stores	30.9%
Revco	17.4
Eckerd Drug Stores	15.9
Other	35.8

Source: *Investext,* Thomson Financial Networks, July 25, 1996, p. 4, from Metro Market Studies.

★ 1437 ★

Drug Stores (SIC 5912)

Top Drug Stores - Savannah, GA

Market shares are shown for 1995.

Revco	48.6%
Phar-Mor	12.8
Rite Aid	9.2
Other	29.4

Source: *Investext,* Thomson Financial Networks, July 25, 1996, p. 4, from Metro Market Studies.

★ 1438 ★

Retailing - Batteries (SIC 5912)

Battery Sales by Outlet

Total dollar sales reached $1.89 billion for the 52 weeks ended May 19, 1996.

Mass merchandisers	45.7%
Drug stores	28.6
Food stores	25.7

Source: *DM,* August 1996, p. 50, from Information Resources Inc.

★ 1439 ★

Retailing - Contraceptives (SIC 5912)

Contraceptive Sales by Outlet

Sales are shown in percent for the year ended December 29, 1996.

Drug stores	62.0%
Mass merchandisers	20.6
Food stores	17.4

Source: *Supermarket Business,* April 1997, p. 52, from Information Resources Inc.

★ 1440 ★

Retailing - Cosmetics (SIC 5912)

Cosmetics Sales by Outlet

Distribution is shown by outlet for the year ended June 14, 1996. Total sales reached $2.83 billion.

Drug stores	49.4%
Mass merchandisers	35.9
Food stores	14.7

Source: *Supermarket Business,* November 1996, p. 54, from Information Resources Inc.

★ 1441 ★

Retailing - Cosmetics (SIC 5912)

Skin Care Product Sales by Outlet - Canada

Drug stores	60.0%
Supermarkets	12.5
Department stores	10.5
Discount stores	10.0
Other	7.0

Source: *National Trade Data Bank*, October 10, 1996, p. ISA960901.

★ 1442 ★

Retailing - Cough/Cold Medicine (SIC 5912)

Cough/Cold Medicine Sales by Outlet

Distribution is shown by outlet for the year ended June 14, 1996. Total sales reached $1.95 billion.

Drug stores	43.9%
Food stores	34.2
Mass merchandisers	21.9

Source: *Supermarket Business*, November 1996, p. 54, from Information Resources Inc.

★ 1443 ★

Retailing - Deodorants (SIC 5912)

Deodorant Sales by Trade Class

Shares are shown for the year ended November 24, 1996.

Supermarkets	41.0%
Mass merchandisers	36.6
Drug stores	22.4

Source: *Supermarket Business*, February 1997, p. 83, from Information Resources Inc.

★ 1444 ★

Retailing - Detergents (SIC 5912)

Liquid Bleach Sales by Outlet

Total dollar sales reached $513.3 million for the 52 weeks ended September 8, 1996.

Food stores	74.8%
Mass merchandisers	21.5
Drug stores	3.7

Source: *Nonfoods Merchandising*, December 1996, p. 10, from Information Resources Inc.

★ 1445 ★

Retailing - Diapers (SIC 5912)

Diaper Sales by Outlet

Distribution is shown by outlet for the year ended June 14, 1996. Total sales reached $3.58 billion.

Food stores	55.5%
Mass merchandisers	35.5
Drug stores	9.0

Source: *Supermarket Business*, November 1996, p. 54, from Information Resources Inc.

★ 1446 ★

Retailing - Drugs (SIC 5912)

Analgesics Sales by Outlet

Distribution is shown by outlet for the year ended June 14, 1996. Total sales of internal analgesics reached $2.83 billion.

Drug stores	38.8%
Food stores	35.2
Mass merchandisers	26.2

Source: *Supermarket Business*, November 1996, p. 54, from Information Resources Inc.

★ 1447 ★

Retailing - Drugs (SIC 5912)

Most Frequently Dispensed Prescriptions - 1996

Data show sales volume in millions of prescriptions dispensed.

Premarin (Wyeth-Ayerst)	44.8
Trimox (Apothecon)	35.4
Synthroid (Knoll)	33.3

Continued on next page.

★ 1447 ★ *Continued*

Retailing - Drugs (SIC 5912)

Most Frequently Dispensed Prescriptions - 1996

Data show sales volume in millions of prescriptions dispensed.

Lanoxin (Allen & Hansbury)	25.7
Zantac (Glaxo)	23.1
Vasotec (Merck)	21.6
Prozac (Dista)	20.7
Hydrocodone with APAP (Watson)	18.8
Procardia XL (Pratt Pharm)	18.8
Coumadin Sodium (DuPont)	17.5
Zoloft (Roerig)	17.1
Prilosec (Astra Merck)	16.1
Norvasc (Pfizer)	15.6
Albuterol (Warrick)	15.5
Cardizem CD (Hoechst Marion Roussel)	15.5

Source: *Medical Marketing & Media*, April 1997, p. 80, from *NPA Plus*.

★ 1448 ★

Retailing - Drugs (SIC 5912)

Most Frequently Dispensed Therapeutic Classes - 1996

Data show sales volume in millions of prescriptions dispensed.

Calcium channel blockers	90.4
Codeine & comb, non-injectible	90.2
Antispasmodics	76.8
Antiarthritics, systemic	75.7
ACE inhibitors	72.2
Amoxicillin	70.6
O/C estrogen/progesteron	62.6
Benzodiorepine tranquilzers	61.1
Beta blockers	59.5
Estrogens, oral	55.0
Cephalosporins	54.6
Serotonin reuptake inhibitors	50.7
Cholesterol reducers	48.0
Thyroid, synthetic	46.8
Diabetes, oral	45.4

Source: *Medical Marketing & Media*, April 1997, p. 82, from *NPA Plus*.

★ 1449 ★

Retailing - Drugs (SIC 5912)

Pharmaceutical Market by Channel - 1996

Distribution of pharmaceuticals and pharmacy dispensed diagnostics is shown by channel.

Chains	27.7%
Mass merchandisers	11.3
Non-federal hospitals	10.8
Foodstores with a pharmacy	8.0
Mail order	7.7
Clinics	4.6
Foodstores without a pharmacy	3.6
Federal facilities	1.9
Home health	0.8
Independents	11.9
Others	2.5

Source: *Medical Marketing & Media*, April 1997, p. 77.

★ 1450 ★

Retailing - Drugs (SIC 5912)

Top Pharmaceutical Companies by Prescriptions Dispensed

Company shares are shown based on prescriptions dispensed for 1996. Ciba and Sandoz merged to form Novartis.

American Home Products	6.6%
Bristol-Myers Squibb	5.6
Hoechst Marion Roussel	5.5
Novartis	4.8
Mylan	4.5
Glaxo Wellcome	4.2
Schering-Plough	4.0
Merck & Company	3.7
Pfizer	3.7
Teva	3.3
Johnson & Johnson	3.3
IVAX Corporation	3.3
SmithKline Beecham	2.7
Schein Pharm Inc.	2.6
Lilly	2.4
Other	39.8

Source: *Medical Marketing & Media*, April 1997, p. 84, from *Retail Perspective* and *Provider Perspective*.

★ 1451 ★

Retailing - Drugs (SIC 5912)

Where Prescriptions Are Dispensed

Data are for 1996.

Chains	50.8%
Independents	30.4
Food stores	10.2
Long term care	4.6
Mail order	4.1

Source: *Medical Marketing & Media*, November 1996, p. 56, from NPA Plus.

★ 1452 ★

Retailing - Eye Care (SIC 5912)

Contact Lens Product Sales by Outlet

Drug stores
Mass merchandisers
Food stores

Distribution of sales is shown based on a $1.18 billion market.

Drug stores	42.9%
Mass merchandisers	32.0
Food stores	25.1

Source: *Nonfoods Merchandising*, May 1996, p. 20, from Information Resources Inc. InfoScan.

★ 1453 ★

Retailing - Foot Care Products (SIC 5912)

Where Foot Care Products Are Sold

Distribution is shown based on sales of $493.2 million for the 52 weeks ended December 29, 1996.

Drugstores	46.8%
Mass merchandisers	30.5
Supermarkets	22.7

Source: *Discount Merchandiser*, April 1997, p. 56, from Information Resources Inc.

★ 1454 ★

Retailing - Fragrances (SIC 5912)

Men's Cologne Sales by Outlet

Sales are shown in percent for the year ended December 29, 1996.

Mass merchandisers	50.9%
Drug stores	37.0
Food stores	12.1

Source: *Supermarket Business*, April 1997, p. 47, from Information Resources Inc.

★ 1455 ★

Retailing - Fragrances (SIC 5912)

Women's Fragrance Sales by Outlet

Distribution is shown by outlet for the year ended June 14, 1996. Total sales reached $870 million.

Mass merchandisers	50.9%
Drug stores	41.6
Food stores	7.2

Source: *Supermarket Business*, November 1996, p. 54, from Information Resources Inc.

★ 1456 ★

Retailing - Hair Care Products (SIC 5912)

Shampoo Product Sales By Outlet

Sales of the $1.5 billion market are shown by outlet for the year ended May 26, 1996.

Supermarkets	39.0%
Mass merchandisers	37.2
Drug stores	23.8

Source: *DM*, September 1996, p. 64, from Information Resources Inc.

★ 1457 ★

Retailing - Oral Care (SIC 5912)

Mouthwash Sales by Trade Class

Sales are shown in percent for the year ended December 29, 1996.

Food stores	42.9%
Mass merchandisers	32.6
Drug stores	24.5

Source: *Supermarket Business*, April 1997, p. 50, from Information Resources Inc.

★ 1458 ★

Retailing - Sun Care Products (SIC 5912)

Sun Care Product Sales by Outlet

Total dollar sales reached $393 million for the 52 weeks ended February 25, 1996.

Drug stores	44.0%
Mass merchandisers	33.8
Food stores	22.1

Source: *DM*, August 1996, p. 39.

★ 1459 ★

Retailing - Toothpaste (SIC 5912)

Toothpaste Sales by Outlet

Food stores

Mass merchandisers

Drug stores

Distribution is shown by outlet for the year ended June 14, 1996. Total sales reached $1.47 billion.

Food stores	48.6%
Mass merchandisers	30.3
Drug stores	22.9

Source: *Supermarket Business*, November 1996, p. 54, from Information Resources Inc.

★ 1460 ★

Retailing - Vitamins (SIC 5912)

Vitamin Sales by Outlet

Distribution is shown by outlet for the year ended June 14, 1996. Total sales reached $2.01 billion.

Drug stores	50.7%
Mass merchandisers	25.1
Food stores	24.2

Source: *Supermarket Business*, November 1996, p. 54, from Information Resources Inc.

★ 1461 ★

Retailing - Weight Loss Products (SIC 5912)

Diet Product Sales by Outlet

Distribution of sales is shown based on a $672.6 million market.

Food stores	49.4%
Drug stores	23.9
Mass merchandisers	26.8

Source: *Nonfoods Merchandising*, May 1996, p. 20, from Information Resources Inc. InfoScan.

★ 1462 ★

Used Merchandise Stores (SIC 5932)

Second Hand Store Merchandise

Women's apparel	58.0%
Children's apparel	24.0
Durable goods/decorative accessories	8.2
Men's apparel	4.7
Other	5.1

Source: *Entrepeneur*, October 1996, p. 114, from NARTS Industry Overview Report.

★ 1463 ★

Retailing - Bikes (SIC 5941)

Bike Sales by Outlet

There were 12.5 million bikes sold in the United States in 1994. California is the top state for bike shops, having 16% of the 6,992 bike stores nationwide. The top three bike makers, which represent 95% of production, are Huffy Bicycle, Murray Ohio, and Roadmaster.

Mass merchants	72.0%
Independent bike dealers	28.0

Source: http://www.biknet.com.tw/bikint/report/e~us.htm, March 3, 1997, p. 1, from *Business Bike Journal*, Bicycle Manufacturers Association of America, Bicycle Market Research Institute, *Bicycle Retailer & Industry News*, and *Bicycling Magazine*.

★ 1464 ★

Retailing - Sporting Goods (SIC 5941)

Top Sporting Goods Chains

Firms are ranked by 1995 sales in millions of dollars.

Sports Authority	$ 1,046
Sports and Recreation	526
Sportmart	492
Academy Sports	400
Big-5 Sporting Goods	364
Oshman's	343
Herman's World of Sporting Goods	334
Modell's Sporting Goods	230
Dunham's Athleisure	180
Gart Sports	171

Source: *Discount Store News*, July 1, 1996, p. 74.

★ 1465 ★

Retailing - Books (SIC 5942)

Adult Book Sales by Outlet

Adult book sales are shown by retail outlet in percent.

Chain bookstores	26.0%
Independent bookstores	20.0
Book clubs	18.0
Discount stores	7.0
Warehouse clubs	6.0
Food/drug stores	5.0
Mail order	5.0
Used bookstores	4.0
All other	9.0

Source: *Publishers Weekly*, September 16, 1996, p. 24, from *Consumer Research Study on Book Publishing, 1995*.

★ 1466 ★

Retailing - Books (SIC 5942)

Foreign Language Bookstores by City

New York City	101
Los Angeles	61
San Francisco	30
Salt Lake City	28
Chicago	26

Source: *Fortune*, November 11, 1996, p. 140.

★ 1467 ★

Retailing - Books (SIC 5942)

Where Books Are Sold

Data show book sales by retail channel.

Bookstore chains	26.2%
Total mail order	22.8
Independent bookstores	19.5
Discount stores	7.4
Warehouse clubs	6.1
Food/drugstores	4.6
Used-book stores	4.0
Other outlets	9.4

Source: *Discount Merchandiser*, March 1997, p. 82, from American Booksellers Association.

★ 1468 ★

Retailing - Stationery (SIC 5943)

Stationery/Greeting Card Sales by Outlet

Distribution is shown based on sales of $19.62 billion in 1995.

Stationery stores	29.2%
Discount stores	26.4
Wholesale clubs	14.1
Drug/proprietary stores	13.1
Supermarkets	6.1
Non-store retailers	2.8
Department stores	2.6
Bookstores	2.3
Variety stores	2.3
Misc. general merchandise stores	1.1

Source: *DM*, July 1996, p. 38.

★ 1469 ★

Retailing - Writing Supplies (SIC 5943)

Writing Instrument Sales by Outlet

Data are for the second quarter of 1996.

Mass merchants	47.6%
Drug stores	31.6
Food stores	16.1
Food/drug combos	4.7

Source: *DM*, November 1996, p. 68, from SHOPA/ Nielsen Industry Report.

★ 1470 ★

Retailing - Jewelry (SIC 5944)

Jewelry Sales by Outlet - 1996

Independents	33.0%
Multi locations	23.0
Department stores	22.0
Mass merchandiser	6.0
Other	16.0

Source: *Michigan Retailer*, March 1997, p. 1, from *Jewelers of America Survey*.

★ 1471 ★

Retailing - Jewelry (SIC 5944)

Where Women Buy Jewelry - Chicago, IL

Carson Pirie Scott	13.1%
Marshall Field's	11.4
Kohl's	8.3
J.C. Penney	5.5
Other	61.7

Source: *Chain Store Age*, October 1996, p. 20B.

★ 1472 ★

Retailing - Hobby Products (SIC 5945)

Craft Supplies by Outlet

Total sales of craft kits and supplies reached $438.96 million in 1995.

Discount stores	42.0%
National toy chains	11.0
Food drug	4.0
Other toy stores	3.0
Variety stores	3.0
Department stores	2.0%
Catalog showroom	1.0
Other outlets	34.0

Source: *Playthings*, November 1996, p. 37, from NPD Group Inc. and *Toy Market Index*.

★ 1473 ★

Retailing - Hobby Products (SIC 5945)

Hobby Product Sales

Discount stores	52.0%
Toys R Us	8.0
Food and drug stores	2.0
Variety stores	2.0
Department stores	1.0
Other	21.0
Other toy stores	4.0

Source: *Playthings*, October 1996, p. 58, from NPD Group Inc. Toy Market Index.

★ 1474 ★

Retailing - Hobby Products (SIC 5945)

Leading Arts/Crafts Stores

Firms are ranked by revenues in millions of dollars.

Michaels Stores	$ 1,341
Fabri-Centers of America	890
House of Fabrics	277
Tandycrafts	249
Trend-Lines	206
Garden Ridge	197
Old America Stores	131

Source: *Forbes*, March 10, 1997, p. 78, from IBES Inc. and WestCountry Financial.

★ 1475 ★

Retailing - Hobby Products (SIC 5945)

Top Crafts Chains

Firms are ranked by 1995 sales in millions of dollars.

Michaels Stores	$ 1,295
Fabri-Centers of America	835
Frank's Nursery	593
Hobby Lobby	360
House of Fabrics	334

Source: *Discount Store News*, July 1, 1996, p. 70.

★ 1476 ★

Retailing - Sporting Goods (SIC 5945)

Top Sporting Goods Stores - 1996

Firms are ranked by sales in millions of dollars.

Foot Locker	$ 1,900
The Sports Authority	1,270
L.L. Bean	1,040
J.C. Penney Simply for Sports	1,000
Jumbo Sports	624
Champs	577
Footaction	516
Sportmart	514
Athlete's Foot	489
REI	487
Big 5	475
Dick's	450
Lady Foot Locker	385
Academy	367
Oshman's	366

Source: *Sportstyle*, May 1997, p. 18.

★ 1477 ★

Retailing - Toys (SIC 5945)

Doll Sales by Outlet

Distribution of unit sales is shown based on a total of 266,056 dolls sold in 1996.

Discount stores	52.0%
National toy chains	26.0
Food & drug stores	4.0
Department stores	3.0%
Variety stores	3.0
Catalog showrooms	1.0
Other toy stores	3.0
Other	3.0

Source: *Playthings*, April 1997, p. 47, from NPD Group Inc. Toy Market Index.

★ 1478 ★

Retailing - Toys (SIC 5945)

Leading Toy Retailers

Market shares are shown in percent.

Toys R Us	20.3%
Wal-Mart	14.9
Kmart	8.5
Target	6.0
KayBee/Toy Works	4.4
Service Merchandise	1.8
J.C. Penney	1.6
Hills	1.5
Ames	1.2
Meijer	1.2
Other	38.6

Source: *Playthings*, November 1996, p. 22, from NPD Group Inc. and *Toy Market Index.*

★ 1479 ★

Retailing - Cameras (SIC 5946)

Camera Sales by Outlet

Electronics/video store	29.3%
Camera stroes	16.3
Department stores	13.4
Wholesale clubs	13.4
Discount stores	12.4
Mail order	10.8
Catalog showroom	5.7
Drugstores	1.2
Hypermarkets/supermarkets	1.0
Other	5.8

Source: *DM*, September 1996, p. 50, from *PMA U.S. Consumer Photo Buying Report.*

★ 1480 ★

Retailing - Party Goods (SIC 5947)

Party Supply Sales

Data show the types of party goods sold at mass retail outlets. Mass merchandisers lead the market, with card/gift stores and supermarkets tied for the second position.

Juvenile birthday	29.0%
General entertaining	22.0
Keep on hand	22.0
Adult birthday	14.0
Baby shower	5.0
Bridal shower	4.0
Anniversary/wedding	3.0
Other	1.0

Source: *Discount Merchandiser*, January 1997, p. 72, from American Greetings Research.

★ 1481 ★

Fabric Stores (SIC 5949)

Fabric Retailers - 1996

Fabri-Centers
Hancock Fabrics
House of Fabrics
Calico Centers

Data show number of outlets.

Fabri-Centers	915
Hancock Fabrics	473
House of Fabrics	253
Calico Centers	95

Source: *HFN*, December 30, 1996, p. 86.

★ 1482 ★

Mail Order (SIC 5961)

Largest U.S. Mail Order Businesses

Firms are ranked by worldwide mail order sales in millions of dollars.

United Services Automobile Association	$ 5,784.0
Tele-Communications	4,464.5
Dell Computer Corp.	4,042.0
AARP/Prudential	3,584.0
Gateway 2000	3,500.0
J.C. Penney	3,424.0
Time Warner Cable Group	3,371.4
GEICO	$ 2,700.0
AT&T Communications	2,000.0
Fingerhut Catalog	1,743.4
Hewlett-Packard Direct Marketing Division	1,575.0
Comp-U-Card	1,555.0
QVC Network	1,500.0
MCI	1,470.0
DEC Direct	1,350.0

Source: *Direct Marketing*, August 1996, p. 4.

★ 1483 ★

Mail Order (SIC 5961)

Largest U.S. Mail Order Catalog Firms

Firms are ranked by worldwide mail order catalog sales in millions of dollars.

Dell Computer Corp.	$ 4,042.0
Gateway 2000	3,500.0
J.C. Penney	3,424.0
Fingerhut Catalog	1,743.4
Hewlett-Packard Direct Marketing Division	1,575.0
DEC Direct	1,350.0
Micro Warehouse	1,308.0
Federated Department Stores/Macys	1,100.0
Spiegel	1,084.1
W.W. Grainger	1,000.0
Lands' End	959.0
CompUSA	937.7
McMaster Carr	900.0
L.L. Bean	887.8
May Department Stores	850.0

Source: *Direct Marketing*, August 1996, p. 4.

★ 1484 ★

Mail Order (SIC 5961)

Top Catalogers

Firms are ranked by 1995 sales in millions of dollars.

Dell Computer	$ 5,236
J.C. Penney	3,738
Gateway 2000	3,676
Digital	3,000
Fingerhut	1,826
Spiegel	1,751
Micro Warehouse	1,308

Continued on next page.

★ 1484 ★ *Continued*
Mail Order (SIC 5961)

Top Catalogers

Firms are ranked by 1995 sales in millions of dollars.

IBM Direct	$ 1,070
Lands End	1,030
L.L. Bean	846

Source: *Catalog Age*, August 1996, p. 62.

★ 1485 ★
Mail Order (SIC 5961)

Top Mail Order Markets

Data show estimated sales in billions of dollars for 1996.

Women's apparel	$ 7.85
Men's apparel	3.15
Linens & bedding	2.20
Gifts	1.98
Kitchen & tabletop	1.80

Source: *Catalog Age*, July 1996, p. 178.

★ 1486 ★
Vending Machines (SIC 5962)

Popular Vending Machine Products

Can cold drinks
Confections/snacks
Hot drinks
All-purpose foods
Cup cold drinks
Cigarettes
Other

Data show sales by product for 1995. Total sales reached $29.5 billion.

Can cold drinks	38.0%
Confections/snacks	17.8
Hot drinks	7.9
All-purpose foods	7.0
Cup cold drinks	6.8
Cigarettes	6.1
Other	16.4

Source: *Vending Times*, Special Issue, 1996, p. 9.

★ 1487 ★
Vending Machines (SIC 5962)

Vending Sales by Location

Sales are in billions of dollars. Public locations include sports arenas, convention centers and transportation depots.

Public locations	$ 8.3
Office	7.0
Plants and factories	6.8
Colleges and universities	2.8
Hospitals and nursing homes	1.3
Government and military facilities	1.1
Schools	0.7

Source: *Restaurants & Institutions*, October 1, 1996, p. 65, from *Vending Times*.

★ 1488 ★
Vending Machines (SIC 5962)

Vending Snack Sales

Data are for the year ended September 1996. Total snack sales rose from $880 million in 1995 to $985 million in 1996.

	($ mil.)	Share
Chocolate bars	$ 440.0	44.8%
Cookies	120.5	12.3
Non-chocolate bars	98.0	10.0
Pretzels	22.5	2.3
Filled crackers	22.2	2.3
Regular gum	22.0	2.2
Crackers	20.2	2.1
Mints/hard roll candies	19.5	2.0
Nuts	17.8	1.8
Popcorn	15.4	1.6
Granola bars	10.7	1.1
Sugarless gum	8.0	0.8
Meat snacks	6.4	0.7
Other	158.1	16.1

Source: *Manufacturing Confectioner*, December 1996, p. 29, from DEBS and Candi Snacks.

★ 1489 ★

Retailing - Tobacco (SIC 5993)

Cigarette Sales by Outlet

Shares are shown based on total sales of $806.2 million at the three main outlets for the 52 weeks June 29, 1996. Data do not include sales at vending machines or convenience stores.

Food stores	67.0%
Drug stores	17.6
Mass merchandisers	15.4

Source: *Nonfoods Merchandising*, January 1997, p. 46, from Maxwell Consumer Reports.

★ 1490 ★

Retailing - Tobacco (SIC 5993)

Tobacco Product Sales by Outlet

Distribution is shown based on sales of $37.41 billion in 1995.

Supermarkets	57.2%
Gas stations	18.4
Drug/proprietary stores	10.5
Discount stores	3.8
Automatic merchandising machines	3.1
Liquor stores	2.6
Cigar stores/stands	1.8
Wholesale clubs	1.5
Misc. general merchandise stores	0.6
Other	0.5

Source: *DM*, July 1996, p. 38.

★ 1491 ★

Optical Goods (SIC 5995)

U.S. Optical Market by Channel

Optical chains	32.5%
Optometrists	30.5
Opticians	19.0
Opthamologists	13.0
Mass merchants	4.0
Warehouse clubs	1.0

Source: *Investext*, Thomson Financial Networks, February 26, 1997, p. 5, from Jobson Optical Group.

★ 1492 ★

Pet Stores (SIC 5999)

Largest Pet Store Chains

Chains are ranked by number of stores.

PetsMart Inc.	344
Petco Animal Supplies	339
Pet Valu	286
Petland Inc.	143
Pet Supplies "Plus"	130
Petland Discount Centers	101
PetCare Superstores Inc.	83
Pet Supermarket	52
Superpetz	43
Pass Pets	29
Complete Petmart	18
Scamp's Pet Centers	18
Bosley's Pet Food Marts	15

Source: *Pet Product News*, May 1997, p. 25.

★ 1493 ★

Pet Stores (SIC 5999)

Pet Food Sales by Outlet

Grocery stores	55.0%
Pet superstores	13.0
Mass merchants	11.0
Other	21.0

Source: *DM*, July 1996, p. 87, from industry sources.

★ 1494 ★

Pet Stores (SIC 5999)

Top Pet Supply Chains

Firms are ranked by 1995 sales in millions of dollars.

PetsMart	$ 1,030
Petco	271
Pet Supplies Plus	145
Petland Inc.	105
Pet Food Warehouse	101
Pet Care	100
SuperPetz	42

Source: *Discount Store News*, July 1, 1996, p. 76.

★ 1495 ★

Retailing - Baby Products (SIC 5999)

Top Baby Store Chains

Firms are ranked by 1995 sales in millions of dollars.

Baby Superstores	$ 291
Kids Mart	120
Lil Things	90

Source: *Discount Store News*, July 1, 1996, p. 73.

★ 1496 ★

Retailing - Fire Logs (SIC 5999)

Fire Log Sales by Outlet

Shares are shown for the year ended December 1, 1996.

Supermarkets	71.0%
Mass merchandisers	21.0
Drug stores	9.0

Source: *Discount Merchandiser*, March 1997, p. 64, from Information Resources Inc.

★ 1497 ★

Retailing - Health & Beauty Care (SIC 5999)

Health/Beauty Care Product Sales by Outlet

	1995	1996
Drug stores	38.0%	35.0%
Food	34.0	34.0
Mass merchandisers	28.0	31.0

Source: *Supermarket News*, April 27, 1997, p. 59, from Information Resources Inc. InfoScan.

★ 1498 ★

Retailing - Personal Care Products (SIC 5999)

Personal Care Retailers

Bath and Body Works
The Body Shop
Garden Botanika
Crabtree & Evelyn
Aveda
H2O Plus
Nature's Elements

The market for cosmetics, shampoos, and bath oils is a $24.2 billion industry. Data show the major companies ranked by number of outlets.

Bath and Body Works	642
The Body Shop	274
Garden Botanika	186
Crabtree & Evelyn	115
Aveda	100
H2O Plus	62
Nature's Elements	33

Source: *New York Times*, October 5, 1996, p. 21.

SIC 60 - Depository Institutions

★ 1499 ★

Banking (SIC 6020)

Largest Banks - California

Shares are shown based on deposits.

BankAmerica	20.9%
Wells Fargo	14.8
HF Ahmanson	7.6
Great Western Financial	5.8
UnionBancal	4.8
First Nationwide Bank FSB	3.8
Washington Mutual	3.4
Glendale Federal Bank	2.5
Golden West Financial	1.8
Coast Savings Financial	1.7
Other	32.9

Source: *Financial Times*, February 21, 1997, p. 14, from SNL Branch Migration Datasource SNL Securities.

★ 1500 ★

Banking (SIC 6020)

Largest Banks - Canada

Market shares are shown based on $720 billion Canadian dollars in deposits for the year ending October 31, 1996.

Royal Bank of Canada	22.50%
CIBC	17.70
Bank of Montreal	16.50
Bank of Nova Scotia	16.40
Toronto Dominion Bank	12.20
National Bank of Canada	5.60
Laurentian Bank of Canada	1.50
Canadian Western Bank	0.20
Other domestic banks	0.03
Foreign banks	7.40

Source: *Marketing Magazine*, May 26, 1997, p. 18, from Canadian Bankers Association.

★ 1501 ★

Banking (SIC 6020)

Largest Banks - South Florida

Total deposits are shown in billions of dollars.

Barnett Banks Inc.	$ 34.8
First Union Corp. of Florida	29.4
SunTrust Banks of Florida Inc.	17.8
NationsBank Corp.	17.0
Great Western Bank	7.0
Savings of America	4.5
Citizens Federal Bank	3.7
World Savings & Loan	2.4
Citibank Florida	2.2
Chase Federal Bank	2.1

Source: *South Florida Business Journal*, May 3, 1996, p. A16, from Florida Bankers Association.

★ 1502 ★

Banking (SIC 6020)

Largest Banks in Minnesota - 1996

Revenues are shown in millions of dollars. Figure for Minnesota Mutual is estimated.

Norwest Corporation	$ 8,882.9
ITT Hartford Life and Annuity Insurance Company	6,643.0
St. Paul Companies Inc.	5,734.2
American Express Financial Advisors	4,044.0
First Bank System Inc.	3,839.6
Lutheran Brotherhood	2,641.0
Minnesota Mutual	2,500.0
ReliaStar Financial Corporation	2,190.6
Allianz Life Insurance Company of North America	1,735.8
Prudential Insurance Company of America	1,500.0
AgriBank FCB	1,439.0
GE Capital Fleet Services	1,250.0
Green Tree Financial Corporation	924.1

Continued on next page.

★ 1502 ★ *Continued*

Banking (SIC 6020)

Largest Banks in Minnesota - 1996

Revenues are shown in millions of dollars. Figure for Minnesota Mutual is estimated.

Fortis Financial Group	$ 923.7
Federated Mutual Insurance Company	871.0

Source: *Corporate Report Minnesota*, June 1997, p. 81.

★ 1503 ★

Banking (SIC 6020)

Leading Banks - St. Louis

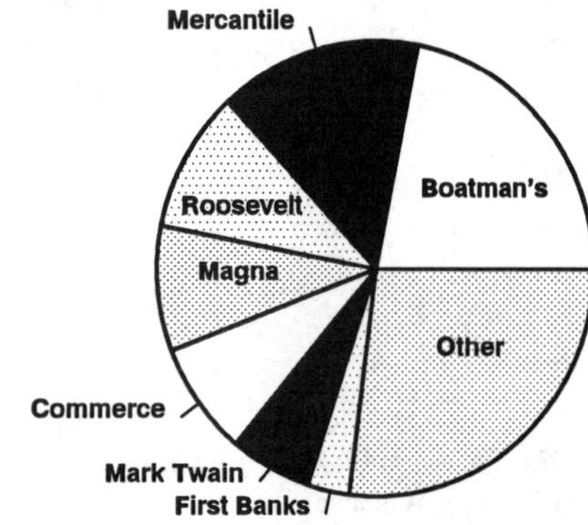

Shares are shown based on deposits.

Boatman's	22.0%
Mercantile	15.0
Roosevelt	10.0
Magna	9.0
Commerce	8.0
Mark Twain	6.0
First Banks	3.0
Other	27.0

Source: *St. Louis Post-Dispatch*, October 29, 1996, p. 6C.

★ 1504 ★

Banking (SIC 6020)

Leading Banks by Income

Banks are ranked by net income for the third quarter of 1996 in millions of dollars.

Citicorp	$ 975
Chase Manhattan	858
NationsBank	625
First Chicago NBD	358
Wells Fargo	321

Source: *Financial Times*, October 16, 1996, p. 20, from agencies.

★ 1505 ★

Banking (SIC 6020)

Major Banks - Madison, WI

Banks are ranked by assets in thousands of dollars as of June 30, 1996.

Firstar Bank Wisconsin	$ 4,294,521
M & I Madison Bank	1,544,608
Bank One Madison	388,319
Associated Bank Madison	158,434
Bank of Sun Prairie	154,453
State Bank of Cross Plains	141,296
First Business Bank of Madison	135,132
Park Bank	123,618
Monona State Bank	99,254
Bankers' Bank	99,096
State Bank of Mount Horeb	92,363
Community National Bank	70,125

Source: *Business Journal Serving Greater Milwaukee*, October 26, 1996, p. 24.

★ 1506 ★

Banking (SIC 6020)

Major U.S. Banking Firms

Firms are ranked by assets in millions of dollars.

Chase Manhattan	$ 331.4
Citicorp	281.0
BankAmerica	250.8
J.P. Morgan	222.0
Bankers Trust	114.9

Source: *Investor's Business Daily*, March 3, 1997, p. A2.

★ 1507 ★

Banking (SIC 6020)

Top Banking Companies - 1996

Data show net income in millions of dollars.

Citicorp	$ 3,788.0
BankAmerica Corp.	2,873.0
Chase Manhattan Corp.	2,461.0
NationsBank Corp.	2,375.0
J.P. Morgan & Co. Inc.	1,574.0
First Union Corp.	1,499.0
First Chicago NBD Corp.	1,436.0
Banc One Corp.	1,426.5
Norwest Corp.	1,153.9
Fleet Financial Group	1,138.8
Wells Fargo & Co.	1,071.0
Bank of New York Co. Inc.	1,020.0
PNC Bank Corp.	992.2
KeyCorp	783.0
CoreStates Financial Corp.	649.1

Source: *Banking Strategies*, March/April 1997, p. 20.

★ 1508 ★

Banking (SIC 6020)

Top Banks - Alaska

Banks are ranked by assets in millions of dollars as of December 31, 1995.

National Bank of Alaska	$ 2,378.1
First National Bank of Anchorage	1,437.1
Key Bank of Alaska	853.5
Bank of America Alaska	235.9
First Bank (Ketchikan)	222.3

Source: *Alaska Business Monthly*, July 1996, p. 46, from Sheshunoff Information Services Inc.

★ 1509 ★

Banking (SIC 6020)

Top Banks - Florida

Shares are shown based on total deposits.

Barnett Banks	19.3%
First Union	17.5
NationsBank	13.1
Sun Trust	9.8
Great Western	3.9
Other	36.4

Source: *Wall Street Journal*, February 24, 1997, p. B4, from Barnett Banks, SNL Securities, and Baseline.

★ 1510 ★

Banking (SIC 6020)

Top Banks - Mexico

Banks are ranked by assets in billions of dollars.

Banamex	$ 26.65
Bancomer	23.86
Serfin	19.31
Mexicano	9.53
Internacional	8.12
Altantico	6.48
Promex	5.86
Bancrecer	5.04
Confia	3.81
Probursa	3.68

Source: *National Trade Data Bank*, February 13, 1997, p. ISA960801, from Banking and Securities National Commission.

★ 1511 ★

Banking (SIC 6020)

Top Banks - Minnesota

Banks are ranked by assets in millions of dollars as of December 31, 1995.

Norwest Bank Minnesota	$ 18,234
First Bank NA	16,376
Firstar Bank of Minnesota NA	2,401
Marquette Bank NA	883
American Bank NA	834
National City Bank of Minneapolis	626

Continued on next page.

★ 1511 ★ *Continued*

Banking (SIC 6020)

Top Banks - Minnesota

Banks are ranked by assets in millions of dollars as of December 31, 1995.

Richfield Bank & Trust	$ 409
Eastern Heights Bank	376
Midway National Bank	337
American Commercial Bank	295

Source: *Corporate Report Minnesota*, June 1996, p. 41, from Minnesota Department of Commerce.

★ 1512 ★

Banking (SIC 6020)

Top Banks - New York City

Shares are shown based on deposits through October 1996.

Chase Manhattan Corp.	29.52%
Citicorp	14.04
Bank of New York Co.	6.91
Republic New York Corp.	5.45
GreenPoint Financial Corp.	4.08
Dime Bancorp	3.28
Other	36.72

Source: *American Banker*, January 2, 1997, p. 4, from Sheshunoff Information Services Inc.

★ 1513 ★

Banking (SIC 6020)

Top Banks - North Carolina

Banks are ranked by assets in millions of dollars as of March 31, 1996.

Nationsbank	$ 74,969.7
First Union	29,890.9
Wachovia	26,310.7
BB&T	15,704.8
First Citizens	7,537.0
Centura	5,546.4
Central Carolina	4,926.4
United Carolina	3,786.0
First Union Home Equity	859.3
Triangle	836.5
Southtrust Bank of Central Carolina	762.5
Southern	502.9

Source: *Business North Carolina*, November 1996, p. 43, from Sheshunoff Information Servies.

★ 1514 ★

Banking (SIC 6020)

Top Banks - West Virginia

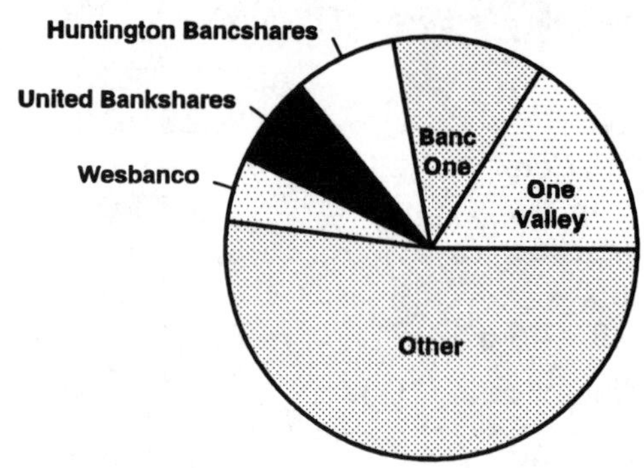

Market shares are shown in percent.

One Valley	15.5%
Banc One	11.6
Huntington Bancshares	8.3
United Bankshares	7.2
Wesbanco	5.1
Other	52.3

Source: *Investext*, Thomson Financial Networks, November 6, 1996, p. 4, from company data and State of West Virginia Division of Banking.

★ 1515 ★

Banking (SIC 6020)

Top Banks by Assets - Atlanta

Banks are ranked by assets in millions of dollars for 1996.

SunTrust Banks	$ 52,468.2
Synovus Financial	8,612.3
First Liberty	1,071.2
Century South Banks	761.1
ABC Bancorp	635.0
Eagle Bancshares	611.5
Fidelity National	605.4
First State	516.5
First Banking Co. of Southeast Georgia	384.0
Habersham Bancorp	310.0

Source: *Atlanta Journal-Constitution*, May 18, 1997, p. E19, from Nordby International Inc.

★ 1516 ★

Banking (SIC 6020)

Top Banks by Deposits - Brooklyn, NY

Shares are shown based on the $25.2 billion deposited in Brooklyn banks.

Chase Manhattan	17.0%
Dime Bancorp	16.2
Republic of New York	15.2
GreenPoint	12.8
Citicorp	8.1
Others	30.7

Source: *Investext*, Thomson Financial Networks, December 6, 1996, p. 34.

★ 1517 ★

Banking (SIC 6020)

Top Banks by Deposits - Indiana

Shares are shown based on deposits at the end of June 1996.

First Chicago/NBD	12.9%
Banc One	10.0
National City	7.3
Old National	4.4
Key Corp	4.0
Others	61.4

Source: *Investext*, Thomson Financial Networks, October 16, 1996, p. 2.

★ 1518 ★

Banking (SIC 6020)

Top Banks by Deposits - Nassau County, NY

Shares are shown based on the $32.1 billion deposited in Nassau County banks.

Chase Manhattan	13.4%
GreenPoint	10.8
Fleet Financial	10.1
Dime Bancorp	8.5
ABN AMRO North America	7.1
Others	50.1

Source: *Investext*, Thomson Financial Networks, December 6, 1996, p. 33.

★ 1519 ★

Banking (SIC 6020)

Top Banks by Deposits - Ohio

Shares are shown based on deposits at the end of June 1996.

National City	11.4%
Banc One	11.0
Key Corp	9.9
Fifth Third	8.6
Huntington	5.4
Others	53.7

Source: *Investext*, Thomson Financial Networks, October 16, 1996, p. 2.

★ 1520 ★

Banking (SIC 6020)

Top Banks by Deposits - Pennsylvania

Shares are shown based on deposits at the end of June 1996.

PNC	16.4%
Corestates	14.5
Mellon	12.5
National City	6.5
First Union	3.7
Others	46.4

Source: *Investext*, Thomson Financial Networks, October 16, 1996, p. 2.

★ 1521 ★

Banking (SIC 6020)

Top Banks in Leveraged Loan Volume

Shares are based on the estimated U.S. dollar value of leveraged loan volume.

Chase	18.0%
NationsBank	9.0
Bankers Trust	8.0
BankAmerica	6.0
Toronto Dominion Bank	6.0
Bank of New York	6.0
Citicorp	5.0
J.P. Morgan	4.0
Bank of Nova Scotia	3.0

Continued on next page.

★ 1521 ★ *Continued*

Banking (SIC 6020)

Top Banks in Leveraged Loan Volume

Shares are based on the estimated U.S. dollar value of leveraged loan volume.

Bank of Boston	3.0%
Others	32.0

Source: *Investext*, Thomson Financial Networks, February 12, 1997, p. 11, from *Investors Dealers' Digest*.

★ 1522 ★

Banking (SIC 6020)

Top Banks in New York, New Jersey, and Connecticut

Market shares are shown in percent.

Chase	14.8%
Fleet Financial	8.1
Citicorp	6.7
Bank of New York	4.4
First Union	3.7
HSBC Holdings	3.6
Summit Bancorp	3.2
Republic of New York	2.6
Dime Bancorporation	2.5
Greenpoint Financial	2.5
KeyCorp	2.3
PNC	2.1
Other	56.5

Source: *Investext*, Thomson Financial Networks, February 12, 1997, p. 14, from *SNL Quarterly Bank Digest* and Prudential Securities.

★ 1523 ★

Banking (SIC 6020)

Top Banks in Syndicated Loan Volume

Shares are based on the estimated U.S. dollar value of syndicated loan volume.

Chase Manhattan	32.0%
J.P. Morgan	18.0
Citicorp	15.0
BankAmerica	14.0
NationsBank	10.0
Deutsche Bank	6.0%
United Bank of Switzerland	6.0
CS First Boston	5.0
NatWest	5.0
Toronto-Dominion	5.0

Source: *Investext*, Thomson Financial Networks, February 12, 1997, p. 11, from *Investors Dealers' Digest*.

★ 1524 ★

Banking (SIC 6020)

Top Banks in Texas

Market shares are shown in percent.

NationsBank	14.1%
Chase Manhattan	9.0
Banc One	8.3
Norwest	4.6
Temple Inland Financial Services	3.7
USAT Holdings Inc.	3.0
Wells Fargo & Company	3.0
BankAmerica	2.9
Compass Bancshares	2.2
Cullen/Frost Bankers	2.2
Other	47.0

Source: *Investext*, Thomson Financial Networks, February 12, 1997, p. 14, from *SNL Quarterly Bank Digest* and Prudential Securities.

★ 1525 ★

Banking (SIC 6020)

Top U.S. Banks

Banks are ranked by assets in billions of dollars as of June 30, 1996.

Chase Manhattan Bank	$ 321.8
Citibank	266.8
BankAmerica	238.8
Nationsbank/Boatmen's Bancshares	233.0
J.P. Morgan	198.8
First Union	139.9
Bankers Trust	114.6
First Chicago NBD Corp.	113.7
Wells Fargo	108.6
Banc One	97.1

Source: *New York Times*, August 31, 1996, p. 23, from *American Banker*.

★ 1526 ★

Banking (SIC 6020)

Top U.S. Banks - 1997

Banks are ranked by assets in billions of dollars as of February 31, 1997.

Chase	$ 340.3
Citicorp	290.4
NationsBank	239.0
First Union	134.9
First Chicago	109.1
Wells Fargo	101.9
Banc One	101.6

Source: *Financial Times*, April 16, 1997, p. 20, from companies.

★ 1527 ★

Community Banks (SIC 6029)

Largest Community Banks - 1996

Banks are ranked by assets in millions of dollars. Figures are for the first six months of 1996.

Bank of Canton of Calif.	$ 771.3
Bank of Granite (N.C.)	479.3
The Palmetto Bank (S.C.)	447.5
Bank of Newport (R.I.)	419.6
First National Bank of Dona Ana City (N.M.)	340.1
Deposit Guaranty of LA.	339.5
United Bank & Trust (MI.)	324.7
First National Bank & Trust Co.	287.7
First National Bank (Minnesota)	224.3
Northwest Georgia Bank (GA)	215.2

Source: *ABA Banking Journal*, September 1996, p. 33.

★ 1528 ★

Savings Institutions (SIC 6035)

Largest Savings and Loans - South Jersey

Firms are ranked by local deposits as of June 30, 1995.

Inter-Boro Savings and Loan Associates	$ 558,999
Collective Federal Savings Banks	544,576
Farmers' & Mechanics' Bank	425,812
Premium Federal Savings Bank	211,440
South Jersey Savings and Loan Association	205,416
Gloucester County Federal Savings Bank	$ 169,865
Haddon Savings Bank	153,609
Hudson City Savings Bank	147,062
Covenant Bank	125,508
Columbia Savings Banks	104,040

Source: *South Jersey Business Journal*, August 23, 1996, p. 22, from annual reports, *McFadden American Financial Directory*, and *Thomson Savings Directory*.

★ 1529 ★

Savings Institutions (SIC 6035)

Leading Savings Institutions - 1996

Institutions are ranked by revenues in millions of dollars.

H.F. Ahmanson	$ 3,767
Great Western Financial Corp.	3,566
Washington Mutual	3,409
Golden West Financial	2,656
California Federal Bank	1,883
Dime Bancorp	1,429
Standard Federal Bancorp.	1,124
Glendale Federal Bank	1,115
Charter One Financial	1,062
Greenpoint Financial	1,031

Source: *Fortune*, April 28, 1997, p. 60.

★ 1530 ★

Credit Unions (SIC 6060)

Top Credit Unions - Denver

Unions are ranked by 1995 assets in millions of dollars.

Bellco First Federal Credit Union	$ 615.3
Colorado State Employees Credit Union	287.1
Univ. of Colorado Federal Credit	208.7
Denver Public School Employees' Credit	196.0
Public Service Credit Union	180.0
Credit Union of Denver	157.6
Gateway Credit Union	104.0
Denver Postal Credit Union	102.4
Safeway Rocky Mountain Federal	98.2
IBM Rocky Mount. Employees	97.6

Source: *Denver Business Journal*, July 18, 1996, p. 216.

★ 1531 ★

Bank Services (SIC 6099)

Largest Bank Leasing Firms

Firms are ranked by 1995 net assets in millions of dollars.

NationsBank Leasing Corp.	$ 4,407.8
Citicorp/Global Equipment Corporation	4,100.2
BankAmerica Leasing & Capital Group	2,734.0
Keycorp Leasing	2,259.7
First Union Leasing	2,100.3
BNY Leasing Corporation	1,999.4
Fleet Credit Corporation	1,819.4
US Bancorp Leasing & Financial	1,732.8
Banc One Leasing Corporation	1,732.2
Banc Leasing Boston	1,354.0

Source: *ABA Banking Journal*, November 1996, p. 46, from *Equipment Leasing Monitor.*

★ 1532 ★

Bank Services (SIC 6099)

On-line Banking Service Plans - 1997

Data show percentage of banks planning to offer each service. Figures are based on a survey.

PC banking	27.0%
Internet	19.0
Telephones	8.0
Screen phones	5.0
Interactive TVs	4.0
ATMs	2.0

Source: *Byte*, December 1996, p. 38, from *Banking Technology*.

★ 1533 ★

Bank Services (SIC 6099)

Popular Bank Services

Data show percentage of U.S. households using each service.

ATMs	55.0%
Direct deposit	53.0
Audio response	30.0

Source: *Credit Union Management*, September 1996, p. 6, from Raddon Financial Group.

★ 1534 ★

Bank Services (SIC 6099)

Transit Check Delivery Market

Shares are for the first quarter of calender year 1996.

U.S. Check (AirNet)	54.0%
ITS (Federal Reserve)	30.0
Other	16.0

Source: *Investext*, Thomson Financial Networks, July 29, 1996, p. 13, from AirNet Systems Inc.

SIC 61 - Nondepository Institutions

★ 1535 ★

Credit Cards (SIC 6141)

Corporate Card Market

Firms are ranked by millions of business cards issued. Shares of the group are shown in percent.

	(mil.)	% of Group
American Express	7.7	63.6%
Diners Club	1.5	12.4
Air Travel Card	1.5	12.4
First Bank	1.0	8.3
GE Capital	0.3	2.5
Elan	0.1	0.8

Source: *American Banker*, August 29, 1996, p. 1, from *Business Travel News*.

★ 1536 ★

Credit Cards (SIC 6141)

Credit Card Accounts

Data show millions of accounts as of April 1, 1996.

Discover	36.7
Citibank	25.6
AT&T Universal	17.9
MBNA America	17.4
Chase Manhattan	16.8
First Chicago	15.6
Household Bank	13.5
Advanta	11.7
First USA	10.7
Capital One	10.1

Source: *USA TODAY*, September 5, 1996, p. B1, from Ram Research.

★ 1537 ★

Credit Cards (SIC 6141)

Credit Card Balances

Outstanding balances are shown in billions of dollars. Figures include old and new charges and interest owed as of August 1, 1996.

Citibank	$ 42.8
MBNA America	29.1
Discover	29.0
Chase Manhattan	23.5
First USA	18.8
First Chicago	17.5
Household Bank	16.7
AT&T Universal	13.2
Advanta National	13.1
Capital One	11.3

Source: *USA TODAY*, September 27, 1996, p. B1, from Bankcard Barometer and Card Management Information Services.

★ 1538 ★

Credit Cards (SIC 6141)

Credit Card Issuers - 1995

Data show estimated millions of seats.

Discover	44.1
Citibank	38.0
American Express	26.7
Chase Manhattan	24.6
AT&T Universal	24.0

Source: *New York Times*, September 18, 1996, p. C4, from Nilson Report.

★ 1539 ★

Credit Cards (SIC 6141)

Gas Credit Card Leaders

Data show the thousands of accounts in 1995. Shares are shown based on 47.87 million accounts held by the top 15 firms.

	(000)	Share
Texaco Credit Card Services	8,888	18.6%
Mobil Oil Credit Corp.	8,000	16.7
Chevron Co. U.S.A.	7,500	15.7
Shell Oil Co.	4,700	9.8
Citgo Petroleum Corp.	4,400	9.2
Unocal Corp.	3,700	7.7
BP America	2,669	5.6
Phillips 66 Co.	2,000	4.2
Sun Co. Inc.	1,830	3.8
Conoco Inc.	1,000	2.1
Gulf Oil	850	1.8
Marathon Petroleum Co.	806	1.7
Diamond Shamrock R & M	782	1.6
Ashaland Oil Co.	375	0.8
Total Petroleum Inc.	374	0.8

Source: *National Petroleum News*, July 1996, p. 124, from *Credit Card News*.

★ 1540 ★

Credit Cards (SIC 6141)

Largest Credit Card Markets

Data show the markets with the largest charge potential. Figures are in billions of dollars.

Insurers	$ 194
Utilities	79
Phone companies	45
Cable TV	37
Publications	37
Associations	10

Source: *American Banker*, August 30, 1996, p. 1, from Payment Systems Inc. and Visa.

★ 1541 ★

Credit Cards (SIC 6141)

Leading Credit Card Firms - 1996

Companies are ranked by receivables in billions of dollars as of September 30, 1996.

Citibank (U.S.)	$ 44.0
MBNA	34.7
Discover	30.2
Chase Manhattan	23.9
First USA	19.9
First Chicago	17.9
Household Bank	16.9
AT&T Universal	13.0
Advanta	12.7
Banc One	12.7
Capital One	12.1

Source: *New York Times*, January 21, 1997, p. C22, from Banc One Corporation and First USA Inc.

★ 1542 ★

Credit Cards (SIC 6141)

Major Credit Cards - 1996

Credit card market shares are shown for 1996.

Visa	50.0%
MasterCard	28.3
American Express	15.8
Discover	6.5

Source: *Wall Street Journal*, February 7, 1997, p. A8, from RAM Research.

★ 1543 ★

Credit Cards (SIC 6141)

Top Credit Card Issuers - Wilmington, Delaware

Banks are ranked by loans in millions of dollars for 1995.

Greenwood Trust Company	$ 31.8
MBNA	25.2
First USA	17.5
FCC National	17.2
Chase Manhattan	12.8
Colonial National Bank and Advanta National Bank	7.9
American Express/Centurion Bank	7.2
Nations Bank of Delaware	4.9
Wachovia Bank Card Services	4.1
Associates National Bank	3.7

Source: http:// www.ci.wilmington.de.us/stats.htm, June 9, 1997, p. 1, from News Journal.

★ 1544 ★

Credit Cards (SIC 6141)

Top Credit Card Processors - 1995

Market shares are shown in percent.

First Data Resources	16.5%
Total System Services	11.7
Merchant Bank Services	11.6
National Processing Co.	8.2
EDS Card Processing Services	6.8
National Bancard Corp.	6.2
JC Penney Business Services	5.4
MasterCard Auto POS	4.2
MBNA Information Services	4.2
Card Establishment Svcs.	3.7
Other	21.5

Source: *Investext,* Thomson Financial Networks, June 28, 1996, p. 5, from *Card Industry Directory*.

★ 1545 ★

Credit Cards (SIC 6141)

Top Merchant Processors

Firms are ranked by bank card sales in billions of dollars in 1995.

First Data	$ 129.6
National Processing	69.0
First USA Paymentech	$ 24.6
Bank of America	17.2
First Bank System	16.1
National Data	15.4
First National Bank of Omaha	13.3
Nova Information Systems	11.0
Fifth Third Bank	10.5
Banc One POS Services	7.7

Source: *American Banker*, September 30, 1996, p. 9, from Nilson Report.

★ 1546 ★

Credit Cards (SIC 6141)

Top Specialty Card Issuers

Firms are ranked by receivables in billions of dollars as of September 30, 1996.

Citibank	$ 44.6
MBNA	34.7
Pro Forma Banc One/First USA	32.6
Discover	30.2
Chase Manhattan	23.9
First Chicago	17.9
Household Bank	16.9
AT&T Universal	13.0
Advanta	12.7
Capital One	12.1

Source: *Financial Times*, March 18, 1997, p. 25, from Nilson Report and FDIC.

★ 1547 ★

Debit Cards (SIC 6141)

Debit Card Market

Check Card	51.0%
MasterMoney	9.0
Other	40.0

Source: *Wall Street Journal*, November 1, 1996, p. B3.

★ 1548 ★

Debit Cards (SIC 6141)

Debit Card Spending - Canada

Gas station/auto repair
Hardware and gardening
Drug stores
Beer/liquor/wine
Utility and government

Data show where consumers have used their debit cards in 1996. Spending is shown in millions of dollars.

Gas station/auto repair	$ 1,500
Hardware and gardening	891
Drug stores	879
Beer/liquor/wine	389
Utility and government	70

Source: *Macleans*, November 4, 1996, p. 14, from Interac.

★ 1549 ★

Factoring (SIC 6153)

Top Factoring Firms - Mexico

Firms are ranked by assets in millions of dollars. Factoring companies are not allowed to receive deposits from the public. They are funded largely from commercial banks and by issuing commercial paper. Factoring companies are required to purchase government securities for an amount equal to 40 percent of their paid-in capital.

Factoraje Serfin	$ 224.3
Factoraje Bancomer	197.5
Banamex Factoraje	166.8
Factoraje Capital	126.2
Factor Quadrum	115.1
Empresarial	105.3
Factoraje Invermexico	91.1
Kapital Haus	78.4
Factoraje Bancrecer	74.7
Factoring Inverlat	70.6

Source: *National Trade Data Bank*, February 13, 1997, p. ISA960801, from Banking and Securities National Commission.

★ 1550 ★

Agricultural Banking (SIC 6159)

Largest Commercial Agricultural Banks

Banks are ranked by loans in millions of dollars for the quarter ending March 31, 1996.

Bank of America Trust & Savings	$ 1,249.0
Wells Fargo	1,178.7
Sanwa Bank California	595.5
Norwest Bank South Dakota	323.2
U.S. Bank of Washington	320.3
Seattle-First National Bank	309.0
NationsBank	274.7
First Union National Bank of Florida	262.2
West One Bank-Idaho	255.9
Key Bank of Washington	253.8
First Bank	223.5
Bank IV	203.3
Key Bank of Idaho	198.1

Source: *Agri Finance*, November 1996, p. 24, from Federal Reserve System.

★ 1551 ★

Leasing (SIC 6159)

Top Leasing Firms - Mexico

Firms are ranked by assets in millions of dollars.

Internacional	$ 508.5
Bancomer	401.4
Banamex	228.6
Invermexico	228.4
Serfin	209.8
Inverlat	153.4
Inbursa	134.8
Capital	132.4
Atlas	119.8
Banobras	81.3

Source: *National Trade Data Bank*, February 13, 1997, p. ISA960801, from Banking and Securities National Commission.

★ 1552 ★

Mortgage Loans (SIC 6162)

Home Mortgage Leaders

Data show who issued the most loans over $500,000 in 1996.

Bank of America	$ 2,346.0
Chase Manhattan	861.0
American Savings	838.0
California Federal	379.0
Merrill Lynch Credit	376.0
First Republic	342.0
Coast Federal Bank	336.0
Citibank	298.0
Norwest Mortgage	257.0
Home Savings	245.0

Source: *Wall Street Journal*, March 7, 1997, p. B10, from Acxiom/DataQuick.

★ 1553 ★

Mortgage Loans (SIC 6162)

Mortgage Lending - Phoenix, AZ

Shares for Phoenix (Maricopa County, AZ) are shown for the first six months of 1996.

Norwest Mortgage	9.30%
Banc One Mortgage	3.28
Union FSB Indianapolis	3.25
Inland Mortgage	2.90
North America Mortgage	2.87
Bank of America FSB	2.42
World Savings	2.40
CH Mortgage	2.18
Chase Manhattan Mortgage	2.15
Fleet Mortgage	1.90
Other	67.75

Source: *American Banker*, September 12, 1996, p. 8, from TRW Redi Property.

★ 1554 ★

Mortgage Loans (SIC 6162)

Mortgage Loans - South Florida

Lenders are ranked by 1995 dollar volume of mortgage originations in millions of dollars.

Barnett Bank, N.A.	$ 455.0
SunTrust Bank, So. FL, N.A.	270.1
NationsBanc Mortgage Corp.	231.8
Vision Mortgage Corp.	173.1
Great Western Bank	$ 173.1
Circle Mortgage Corp.	115.2
BankAtlantic	111.4
Homebanc Mortgage Corp.	110.0
Fidelity Federal Savings Bank of FL	104.3
Home Financing Center Inc.	101.5

Source: *South Florida Business Journal*, August 23, 1996, p. 148.

★ 1555 ★

Mortgage Loans (SIC 6162)

Mortgage Refinancing - Ft. Lauderdale, FL

Shares for Ft. Lauderdale (Broward County, FL) are shown for the first six months of 1996.

Barnett Bank	7.44%
First Union Fla.	4.77
Nationsbank Fla.	4.09
Nationsbank	3.26
Suntrust Bank S. Fla.	3.17
Nationsbanc Mortgage	2.12
Great Western Bank	1.96
Other	73.19

Source: *American Banker*, September 12, 1996, p. 8, from TRW Redi Property.

★ 1556 ★

Mortgage Loans (SIC 6162)

Top Loan Servicers

Data are in billions of dollars as of June 30, 1995.

AMRESCO	$ 11.34
Dorman & Wilson	10.56
Midland Loan Services	10.50
GMAC	10.14
Bankers Trust	8.49
GE Capital	8.38
Reilly Mortgage Group	7.95
Mellon Mortgage Company	6.37
BancOne	4.34
Washington Mortgage Financial Group	4.10

Source: *Mortgage Banking*, October 1996, p. 125, from Mortgage Bankers Association.

★ 1557 ★

Mortgage Loans (SIC 6162)

Top Mortgage Service Providers

Shares are shown based on volume of loans provided in billions of dollars as of March 31, 1996.

Countrywide Credit	3.7%
Fleet Mortgage Group	3.1
Norwest Mortgage	3.0
GE Capital Mortgage	2.9
NationsBanc and affiliates	2.3
GMAC Mortgage Group	2.0
Prudential Home Mortgage	2.0
BankAmerica	1.8
ChemicalBank and affiliates	1.5
Other	77.7

Source: *Investext,* Thomson Financial Networks, July 1, 1996, p. 4, from Inside Mortgage Finance.

★ 1558 ★

Auto Loans (SIC 6163)

Auto Loan Providers

Banks

Credit unions

Other

Banks	42.1%
Credit unions	22.4
Other	35.5

Source: *USBanker,* November 1996, p. 59, from CUNA estimates.

★ 1559 ★

Auto Loans (SIC 6163)

Who Makes Car Loans

Data show the market as of April 1996.

Banks	42.4%
Credit unions	22.5
Finance companies	20.8
Off-book or non-securitized	11.4
Savings institutions	2.9

Source: *Automotive News,* August 12, 1996, p. 8i, from Credit Union National Association.

★ 1560 ★

Loan Arrangers (SIC 6163)

Consumer Installment Loan Providers - 1996

Banks	44.0%
Finance companies	13.5
Credit unions	11.7
Other	30.8

Source: *USBanker,* November 1996, p. 59, from CUNA estimates.

★ 1561 ★

Loan Arrangers (SIC 6163)

Household Savings Loan Providers - 1996

Banks	53.7%
Finance companies	20.3
Credit unions	8.3
Other	17.7

Source: *USBanker,* November 1996, p. 59, from CUNA estimates.

★ 1562 ★

Loan Arrangers (SIC 6163)

Largest Small Business Lenders

Institutions are ranked by outstanding loans in billions of dollars.

NationsBank	$ 4.17
Bank One	3.68
Key Bank	3.66
Norwest Bank	3.12
Bank of America	2.64
NBD Bank	2.04
First Union National Bank	2.03
Chemical Bank	1.96
Comerica Bank	1.89
Fleet Bank	1.89

Source: *Your Company,* May 1996, p. 22, from Sheshunoff Information Services Inc.

★1563★

Loan Arrangers (SIC 6163)

Mexico's Corporate Loan Providers - 1996

Market shares are shown in percent.

Societe Generale SA	5.69%
ING Barings	4.84
Bank of America	3.73
ABN-AMRO Bank NV	3.63
Deutsche Morgan Grenfell	3.18
SBC Warburg	3.15
Bank of Montreal	3.01
WestLB Group	2.76
BFCE	2.63
Union Bank of Switzerland	2.43
Other	64.95

Source: *Latin Finance Corporate Handbook*, Special Issue, 1997, p. 28, from Capital DATA Bondware.

★1564★

Loan Arrangers (SIC 6163)

Top Loan Arrangers - Los Angeles

Data show the dollar value of loans to homebuyers in millions of dollars for the third quarter of 1996.

Norwest	$ 399
American Savings	380
Bank of America	339
World Savings	272
Countrywide	229

Source: *Los Angeles Times*, December 1, 1996, p. K1, from DataQuick Information Systems.

★1565★

Loan Arrangers (SIC 6163)

Top Loan Companies - Canada

Firms are ranked by 1995 receivables in millions of dollars.

Household Finance	$ 1,520
Avco	1,320
Beneficial	933
Trans Canada	700

Source: *Financial Post*, November 9, 1996, p. 18, from company reports.

★ 1566 ★

Investment Banking (SIC 6211)

Canada's Top 10 Underwriters - All Financings

Data show the value of deals in millions of dollars.

RBC Dominion Securities	$ 11,222
CIBC Wood Gundy Securities	8,201
ScotiaMcLeod	6,755
Goldman, Sachs & Co.	6,032
Nesbitt Burns	5,769
Merrill Lynch & Co.	4,299
Levesque Beaubien Geoffrion	2,640
First Marathon Securities	1,684
Midland Walwyn Capital	1,471
Toronto Dominion Securities	1,417

Source: *Financial Post*, January 25, 1997, p. 23.

★ 1567 ★

Investment Banking (SIC 6211)

Canada's Top 10 Underwriters - Corporate

Data show the value of deals in millions of dollars.

RBC Dominion Securities	$ 6,905
Nesbitt Burns	5,684
CIBC Wood Gundy Securities	5,204
ScotiaMcLeod	3,546
Goldman, Sachs & Co.	2,809
Merrill Lynch	2,404
First Marathon Securities	1,684
Midland Walwyn Securities	1,364
Griffiths McBurney & Partners	1,235
Toronto Dominion Securities	1,165

Source: *Financial Post*, January 25, 1997, p. 23.

★ 1568 ★

Investment Banking (SIC 6211)

Canada's Top 10 Underwriters - Corporate Equity

Data show the value of deals in millions of dollars.

RBC Dominion Securities	$ 4,303
Nesbitt Burns	3,738
CIBC Wood Gundy Securities	3,009
ScotiaMcLeod	2,187
First Marathon Securities	1,577
Midland Walwyn Capital	1,109
Richardson Greenshields	772
Yorkton Securities	722
Goldman, Sachs & Co.	690
Gordon Capital Corporation	612

Source: *Financial Post*, January 25, 1997, p. 23.

★ 1569 ★

Investment Banking (SIC 6211)

Canada's Top 10 Underwriters - Government Debt

Data show the value of deals in millions of dollars.

RBC Dominion Securities	$ 4,216
ScotiaMcLeod	3,209
Goldman, Sachs & Co.	2,645
CIBC Wood Gundy Securities	2,543
Levesque Beaubien Geoffrion	1,820
Merrill Lynch	1,282
Lehman Brothers Inc.	1,089
Salomon Brothers International	1,028
Morgan Stanley & Co.	911
CS First Boston Corporation	727

Source: *Financial Post*, January 25, 1997, p. 23.

★ 1570 ★

Investment Banking (SIC 6211)

Corporate Debt Issuers - 1996

Market shares are shown in percent.

Merrill Lynch	17.0%
Goldman Sachs	13.1
Lehman Brothers	10.9
J.P. Morgan	10.5
Morgan Stanley	8.7
Credit Suisse First Boston	5.5
Bear Stearns	3.6
Donaldson, Lufkin & Jenrette	2.9
NationsBank	2.7
Other	25.1

Source: *Financial Times*, January 2, 1996, p. 11, from Securities Data.

★ 1571 ★

Investment Banking (SIC 6211)

Equity Issuers - 1996

Market shares are shown in percent.

Goldman Sachs	14.5%
Merill Lynch	12.3
Morgan Stanley	11.0
Donaldson, Lufkin & Jenrette	7.0
Smith Barney	6.8
Salomon Brothers	5.0
Credit Suisse First Boston	4.9
Alex Brown	4.7
Lehman Brothers	4.0
Other	29.8

Source: *Financial Times*, January 2, 1996, p. 11, from Securities Data.

★ 1572 ★

Investment Banking (SIC 6211)

Health Care Bond Underwriters

Shares are shown for October - December 1995.

Smith Barney	23.7%
PaineWebber	14.8
Merrill Lynch & Co.	11.2
Morgan Stanley & Co.	7.4
Ziegler Securities	5.6
Other	37.3

Source: *Modern Healthcare*, January 15, 1996, p. 35, from Securities Data Co.

★ 1573 ★

Investment Banking (SIC 6211)

IRA Market - 1995

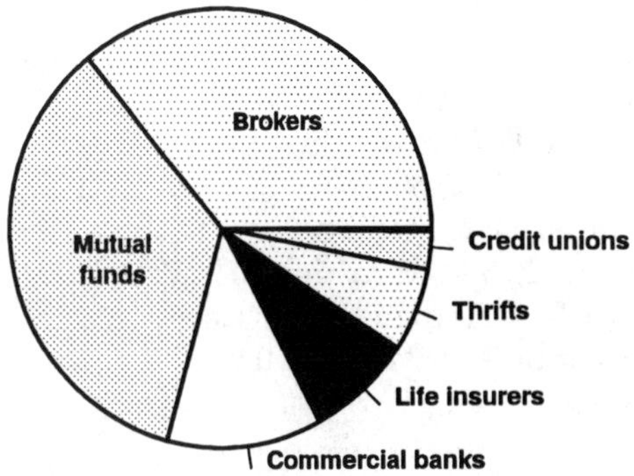

Data show the location of $1.17 billion in IRA (individual retirement account) outstanding assets.

Brokers	35.5%
Mutual funds	35.2
Commercial banks	12.4
Life insurers	8.0
Thrifts	6.1
Credit unions	2.8

Source: *American Banker*, March 26, 1997, p. 18, from Investment Company Institute.

★ 1574 ★

Investment Banking (SIC 6211)

Largest Financial Advisors - 1996

Firms are ranked by value of deals in billions of dollars.

Merrill Lynch	$ 190.3
Morgan Stanley	183.1
Goldman Sachs	123.0
Lazard Houses	115.9
Salomon Brothers	73.7
J.P. Morgan & Co.	65.2
Lehman Bros.	60.6
Credit Suisse First Boston	59.8
Bear Stearns	51.2
Donaldson, Lufkin & Jenrette	38.9

Source: *USA TODAY*, February 28, 1997, p. B3, from Securities Data.

★ 1575 ★

Investment Banking (SIC 6211)

Largest Legal Advisors - 1996

Firms are ranked by value of deals in billions of dollars.

Skadden, Arps, Slate	$ 206.0
Richards, Layton & Finger	134.1
Sullivan & Cromwell	131.5
Shearman & Sterling	130.8
Cravath, Swaine & Moore	104.0
Wachtell Lipton Rosen & Katz	91.3
Simpson Thacher & Bartlett	84.0
Fried, Frank, Harris, Shriver	80.7
Chadbourne & Parke	72.4
Wail Gotshal & Manges	59.5

Source: *USA TODAY*, February 28, 1997, p. B3, from Securities Data.

★ 1576 ★

Investment Banking (SIC 6211)

Largest Long-Term Mutual Funds

Data show assets in millions of dollars as of November 30, 1996.

Fidelity Distributors	$ 301,008.4
Vanguard Group	202,865.6
American Fund Distributors	171,546.3
Franklin Distributors	131,569.8
Putnam Financial Services	109,529.6
T. Rowe Price Investment Services	60,814.4
AIM Distributors	44,710.8
Oppenheimer Investors Services	40,604.8
Janus Funds	33,515.6
Pilgrim Baxter Hoyt Grieg	10,807.9

Source: *Financial Times*, January 22, 1997, p. 13, from Tillinghast, Financial Research Group, Towers Perrin, *Fidelity Mutual Fund Guide*, and Investment Company Institute.

★ 1577 ★

Investment Banking (SIC 6211)

Largest Money Managers

Firms are ranked by assets managed in billions of dollars.

Fidelity	$ 500
Barclays Global	396
State Street Boston	292
Capital Group	246
Mellon Bank	226

Source: *Wall Street Journal*, January 17, 1997, p. C1, from companies.

★ 1578 ★

Investment Banking (SIC 6211)

Largest Mutual Fund Companies - Canada

Firms are ranked by assets in billions of Canadian dollars as of February 1997.

Investors Group	26.9
Trimark	22.4
Royal	20.9
Mackenzie	17.1
TD	11.6
Templeton	11.5
AGF	10.7
CIBC	10.1
Fidelity	8.8
Canada Trust	8.2
Bank of Montreal	8.1
Altamira	6.4
C.I.	6.1
MD	6.1
Scotia	5.8

Source: *Toronto Star*, March 18, 1997, p. B3, from Investment Funds Institute of Canada.

★ 1579 ★

Investment Banking (SIC 6211)

Largest Mutual Fund Managers

Assets are shown in billions of dollars.

Mellon	$ 76.7
PNC	29.6
Wells Fargo	18.8
NationsBank	18.3
Chase Manhattan	15.3

Source: *American Banker*, August 12, 1996, p. 1, from Lippon Analytical Services.

★ 1580 ★

Investment Banking (SIC 6211)

Largest U.S. Investment Banks

Firms are ranked by pre-tax income for the third quarter of 1996. Figures are in millions of dollars.

Merrill Lynch	$ 1,891
Morgan Stanley	1,211
Salomon Brothers	1,131
Lehman Brothers	442

Source: *Banker*, January 1997, p. 12, from company reports.

★ 1581 ★

Investment Banking (SIC 6211)

Largest U.S. Securities Firms

Firms are ranked by capital in billions of dollars.

Merrill Lynch	$ 23.5
Goldman Sachs	18.3
Solomon	17.5
Lehman Bros.	16.5
Morgan Stanley	15.7
Bear Stearns	$ 7.1
CS First Boston	6.2
Paine Webber	4.2
Smith Barney	3.2
Donaldson Lufkin & Jenrette	2.4

Source: *USA TODAY*, February 6, 1997, p. 3B, from Securities Industry Association.

★ 1582 ★

Investment Banking (SIC 6211)

Largest Wall Street Investment Banks

Firms are ranked by net revenues in millions of dollars.

Goldman Sachs	$ 6,140
Morgan Stanley	5,776
Salomon Brothres	4,282
Donaldson, Lufkin & Jenrette	3,491
Lehman Brothers	3,444
Bear Stearns	2,983

Source: *Financial Times*, February 7, 1997, p. 17.

★ 1583 ★

Investment Banking (SIC 6211)

Largest Warehouses - Mexico

Companies are ranked by assets in millions of dollars.

Almacenes Nacionales de Dep Sito	$ 206.7
Almacendora	39.4
Almacenadora Bancomer	33.4
Almacenadora Serfin	14.1
Almacenadora Invermexico	8.9
Almacenadora Tihuana	8.5
Almacenadora Gomez	7.3
Almacenadora Bital	6.3
Almacenadora Comercial America	5.6
Almacenadora Inter Americana	5.2

Source: *National Trade Data Bank*, February 13, 1997, p. ISA960801, from Banking and Securities National Commission.

★ 1584 ★

Investment Banking (SIC 6211)

Leading Mutual Funds

Funds are ranked by net assets in billions of dollars.

Fidelity Magellan	$ 54.0
Investment Co. of America	31.5
Vanguard Index 500	29.9
Washington Mutual Investors	25.7
Fidelity Growth & Income	23.9
Fidelity Contrafund	23.8
Fidelity Puritan	18.5

Source: *Financial Times*, January 6, 1997, p. 21, from Lipper Analytical Services.

★ 1585 ★

Investment Banking (SIC 6211)

Leading On-line Brokerages

Companies are ranked by number of on-line brokerage accounts. Figure for Quick & Reilly is estimated; figure for American Express is estimated and includes telephone accounts.

Charles Schwab	758,000
PC Financial Network	300,000
E*Trade	145,000
Quick & Reilly	90,000
Ameritrade	56,000
Waterhouse Securities	40,000
Jack White	15,000
American Express Financial Direct	10,000

Source: *Wall Street Journal*, May 7, 1997, p. C1, from company reports.

★ 1586 ★

Investment Banking (SIC 6211)

Leading Securities Firms - 1996

Firms are ranked by revenues in millions of dollars.

Merrill Lynch	$ 25,011
Lehman Brothers Holdings	14,260
Morgan Stanley Group	13,144
Salomon	9,002
Paine Webber Group	5,706
Bear Stearns	4,964
Charles Schwabb	1,851
A.G. Edwards	1,454

Source: *Fortune*, April 28, 1997, p. 60.

★ 1587 ★

Investment Banking (SIC 6211)

Leading Securities Underwriting

Data show the value of issuances in millions of dollars.

Merrill Lynch	$ 176.30
Goldman, Sachs	110.16
Lehman Brothers	108.02
Salomon Brothers	103.32
Morgan Stanley	90.56
J.P. Morgan	77.03
Credit Suisse First Boston	64.45
Bear, Stearns	47.66
Donaldson, Lufkin & Jenrette	38.25
Smith Barney	31.73

Source: *New York Times*, February 6, 1997, p. C6, from Securities Data Co.

★ 1588 ★

Investment Banking (SIC 6211)

Leading Technology Underwriters

Firms are ranked by total dollar volume of equity issues since January 1, 1996. Full credit is given to the lead manager. Figures are in billions of dollars.

Morgan Stanley	$ 5.67
Goldman, Sachs	4.32
Merrill Lynch	2.85
Alex. Brown & Sons	2.73
Salomon Brothers	2.15
Hambrecht & Quist	2.02
Montgomery Securities	1.73
Robertson, Stephens	1.34
Smith Barney	1.20

Source: *New York Times*, April 8, 1997, p. C1, from Securities Data Co.

★1589★

Investment Banking (SIC 6211)

Mexico's Equity Issue League Managers - 1996

Market shares are shown in percent.

PaineWebber Inc.	24.99%
Merrill Lynch & Co.	24.43
Morgan Stanley & Co.	15.93
CS First Boston/Credit Suisse	10.76
JP Morgan	9.33
Salomon Brothers Inc.	8.38
Other	6.18

Source: *Latin Finance Corporate Handbook*, Special Issue, 1997, p. 28, from Capital DATA Bondware.

★1590★

Investment Banking (SIC 6211)

Top Asset-Backed Securities Managers - 1996

Shares are shown based on a total of $248.6 billion. Full credit is given to the lead manager.

Lehman Brothers	15.9%
Merrill Lynch	15.1
Credit Suisse First Boston	9.7
Goldman Sachs	7.6
Chase Manhattan	7.2
J.P. Morgan	6.9
Prudential Securities	6.2
Morgan Stanley	6.0
Other	25.4

Source: *Investment Dealers Digest*, January 13, 1997, p. 39.

★1591★

Investment Banking (SIC 6211)

Top Banks in Mutual Funds Custody

Market shares are shown in percent. As of September 30, 1996, total mutual fund assets were approximately $3.3 trillion.

State Street Bank	27.0%
Chase Manhattan	16.0
Bank of New York	13.0
Brown Brothers Harriman	5.0
Investors Fiduciary Trust	4.0
PNC Bank	4.0
Bankers Trust	3.0%
Putnam Fiduciary Trust	3.0
UMB Bank	2.0
Citibank	2.0
Others	21.0

Source: *Investext*, Thomson Financial Networks, December 11, 1996, p. 23, from *Pensions & Investments*.

★1592★

Investment Banking (SIC 6211)

Top Bond Underwriters

Shares for the first nine months of 1996 are for domestic corporate-investment-grade debt.

Merrill Lynch	18.8%
Lehman Brothers	15.4
Salomon Brothers	12.2
J.P. Morgan	11.9
Goldman Sachs	11.4
Morgan Stanley	9.2
CS First Boston	6.6
Other	14.5

Source: *Financial Times*, October 10, 1996, p. 17, from Securities Data Co.

★1593★

Investment Banking (SIC 6211)

Top Bond Underwriters for Commercial Banks - 1996

Shares of the market are shown in percent. Full credit is given to book manager.

J.P. Morgan Securities Inc.	18.4%
Lehman Brothers	17.2
Merrill Lynch & Co.	16.3
Salomon Brothers	15.9
Goldman, Sachs & Co.	8.8
CS First Boston Corp.	5.1
NationsBank Corp.	5.0
Morgan Stanley Group	4.3
Bear Stearns & Co.	2.4
UBS Securities Inc.	1.6
Other	5.0

Source: *USBanker*, February 1997, p. 54, from Securities Data Co. and J.P. Morgan Securities.

★ 1594 ★

Investment Banking (SIC 6211)

Top Collateralized Securities Managers - 1996

Shares are shown based on a total of $248.6 billion. Full credit is given to the lead manager.

Lehman Brothers	16.1%
Merrill Lynch	11.2
Bear Stearns	9.1
Salomon Brothers	8.2
Credit Suisse First Boston	7.2
Morgan Stanley	6.4
Goldman Sachs	6.2
Other	35.6

Source: *Investment Dealers Digest*, January 13, 1997, p. 39.

★ 1595 ★

Investment Banking (SIC 6211)

Top Commercial Backed Mortgage Securities - 1996

Shares are shown based on a total of $29.5 billion. Full credit is given to the book manager.

Lehman Brothers	19.9%
Goldman Sachs	13.9
Nomura Securities	11.3
Donaldson, Lufkin & Jenrette	9.4
Merrill Lynch	6.2
PaineWebber	5.5
Morgan Stanley	5.2
NationsBanc Capital	3.9
Deutsche Morgan Grenfell	3.8
Credit Suisse First Boston	3.7
Other	17.2

Source: *Investment Dealers Digest*, January 13, 1997, p. 39.

★ 1596 ★

Investment Banking (SIC 6211)

Top Domestic Issuers - 1996

Shares are shown based on a total of $954.2 billion. Full credit is given to the lead manager.

Merrill Lynch	16.3%
Lehman Brothers	10.6
Goldman Sachs	10.3
Salomon Brothers	10.1%
Morgan Stanley	8.8
J.P. Morgan	7.2
Credit Suisse First Boston	6.3
Bear Stearns	4.4
Donaldson, Lufkin & Jenrette	3.6
Smith Barney	3.1
Other	19.3

Source: *Investment Dealers Digest*, January 13, 1997, p. 39.

★ 1597 ★

Investment Banking (SIC 6211)

Top Initial Public Offerings Leaders - 1996

Shares are shown based on a total of $50 billion. Full credit is given to the lead manager.

Goldman Sachs	19.8%
Morgan Stanley	14.1
Merrill Lynch	7.2
Smith Barney	6.0
Alex. Brown & Sons	5.0
Donaldson Lufkin & Jenrette	5.0
Lehman Brothers	4.8
Credit Suisse First Boston	3.8
Salomon Brothers	3.3
Montgomery Securities	2.6
Other	28.4

Source: *Investment Dealers Digest*, January 13, 1997, p. 39.

★ 1598 ★

Investment Banking (SIC 6211)

Top Money Managers - Chicago

The largest Chicago companies are ranked by assets managed in millions of dollars.

Northern Investments	$ 119.9
First Chicago NBD Investment Mgmt. Co.	75.3
Zurich Kemper Investments Inc.	74.8
Brinson Partners Inc.	57.9
Van Kampen American Capital Inc.	57.7
John Nuveen Co.	45.4

Continued on next page.

★ 1598 ★ *Continued*

Investment Banking (SIC 6211)

Top Money Managers - Chicago

The largest Chicago companies are ranked by assets managed in millions of dollars.

Lincoln Capital Management Co.	$ 41.7
Stein Roe & Farnham Inc.	24.7
ANB Investment Mgmt & Trust Co.	22.2
Bank of America Illinois	16.8

Source: *Crain's Chicago Business*, August 26, 1996, p. 17.

★ 1599 ★

Investment Banking (SIC 6211)

Top Municipal Bond Issuers - 1996

Shares are shown based on a total of $151.49 billion. Full credit is given to the lead manager.

Smith Barney	10.9%
Goldman Sachs	9.4
Merrill Lynch	9.1
PaineWebber	7.9
Lehman Brothers	6.1
J.P. Morgan	5.1
Bear Stearns	4.7
Morgan Stanley	3.5
Prudential Securities	2.9
A.G. Edwards & Sons	2.0
Other	38.4

Source: *Investment Dealers Digest*, January 13, 1997, p. 46.

★ 1600 ★

Investment Banking (SIC 6211)

Top Mutual Fund Managers - Canada

Shares are shown based on total assets of $234.5 billion Canadian dollars as of March 31, 1997.

Investors Group	11.4%
Trimark Investment Management	9.7
Royal Mutual Funds	9.0
Mackenzie Financial	7.4
TD Asset Management	5.2
Templeton Management	5.1
AGF Management	4.5
CIBC Securities	4.4
Fidelity Investments Canada	3.8
Bank of Montreal	3.7
Others	35.8

Source: *Marketing Magazine*, May 26, 1997, p. 18, from Investment Funds Institute of Canada.

★ 1601 ★

Investment Banking (SIC 6211)

Top Negotiated Issues Leaders - 1996

Shares are shown based on a total of $108.4 billion. Full credit is given to the lead manager.

Smith Barney	12.8%
PaineWebber	9.5
Goldman Sachs	9.3
Bear Stearns	6.0
Merrill Lynch	6.0
Lehman Bothers	5.9
J.P. Morgan	4.0
Morgan Stanley	3.9
A.G. Edwards & Sons	2.6

Continued on next page.

★ 1601 ★ *Continued*

Investment Banking (SIC 6211)

Top Negotiated Issues Leaders - 1996

Shares are shown based on a total of $108.4 billion. Full credit is given to the lead manager.

BankAmerica	1.9%
Other	38.1

Source: *Investment Dealers Digest*, January 13, 1997, p. 46.

★ 1602 ★

Investment Banking (SIC 6211)

Top Thrift Underwriters

Market shares are shown for the first six months of 1996 with full credit given to book manager.

Morgan Stanley	25.5%
Salomon Brothers	20.4
ABN AMRO Hoare Govett	18.0
Goldman, Sachs & Co.	9.6
Merrill Lynch & Co.	9.5
Other	17.0

Source: *US Banker*, August 1996, p. 65, from Securities Data Co.

★ 1603 ★

Investment Banking (SIC 6211)

Top Underwriters for Thrifts - 1996

Underwriters for thrift banks are ranked by market share with full credit given to book managers.

Morgan Stanley	17.4%
ABN AMRO Hoare Govett	17.2
Salomon Brothers	13.8
Goldman, Sachs & Co.	11.3
Merrill Lynch & Co.	8.4
Friedman, Billings, Ramsey & Co.	6.0
Bear Stearns & Co.	5.7
Lehman Brothers	5.1
Deutsche Morgan Grenfell	4.1
Smith Barney Inc.	2.9
Ryan Beck	2.3
NationsBank Corp.	1.7
Piper Jaffray Inc.	1.7
Montgomery Securities	0.8
Other	1.6

Source: *USBanker*, February 1997, p. 53, from Securities Data Co.

★ 1604 ★

Investment Banking (SIC 6211)

Top U.S. Eurobond Issuers - 1996

Shares are shown based on a total of $56.35 billion.

Merrill Lynch	16.2%
Goldman Sachs	9.9
Lehman Brothers	7.7
Morgan Stanley	7.2
Salomon Brothers	6.4
J.P. Morgan	5.4
Deutsche Morgan Grenfell	5.1
SBC Warburg	5.0
Credit Suisse First Boston	3.6
UBS	3.6
Other	29.9

Source: *Investment Dealers Digest*, January 13, 1997, p. 46.

★ 1605 ★

Investment Banking (SIC 6211)

Trusted Equity Fund Market

Market shares among financial advisors are shown for the third quarter of 1996.

Capital Research and Management	19.58%
Franklin Resources Inc.	13.29
Putnam Investments	12.53
Alm Management Group	5.13
OppenheimerFunds Inc.	4.67
Other	44.8

Source: *American Banker*, December 5, 1996, p. 12, from Financial Research Corp.

★ 1606 ★

Venture Capital (SIC 6211)

Venture Capital Spending by Sector - Silicon Valley

Distribution is shown by sector for 1996.

Communications	31.0%
Software	25.0
Biotechnology	18.0
Semiconductors	12.0
Peripherals	7.0
Computers	2.0
Other	5.0

Source: *USA TODAY*, March 13, 1997, p. 2A, from *Joint Venture's Index of Silicon Valley* and *San Jose Mercury News*.

★ 1607 ★

Securities Exchanges (SIC 6231)

Largest Foreign Exchange Houses - Mexico

Companies are ranked by assets in millions of dollars.

Euromex	$ 56.6
Inverlat	37.6
Plus	37.4
Consultoria Internacional	35.4
Monex	18.9
Indicador y Operador Monetario	16.8
Majapara	13.2
C.B.I.	12.2
Aba Divisas	11.9
Invermexico	11.1

Source: *National Trade Data Bank*, February 13, 1997, p. ISA960801, from Banking and Securities National Commission.

★ 1608 ★

Securities Exchanges (SIC 6282)

Largest Stock Brokerages - Mexico

Companies are ranked by assets in millions of dollars.

Operadora de Bolsa Serfin	$ 4,536.7
Inverlat	2,983.2
G.B.M.	2,546.9
Invermexico	1,957.1
BBV - Probursa	$ 1,427.4
Invex	1,010.9
Acciones y Valores	905.1
Multivalores	899.2
Inversora	788.6
Abaco	750.7

Source: *National Trade Data Bank*, February 13, 1997, p. ISA960801, from Mexican Stock Exchange.

SIC 63 - Insurance Carriers

★ 1609 ★

Insurance (SIC 6300)

Apparel Manufacturers Insurance

Apparel firms generate $432 million in insurance premiums. Data show premiums written in millions of dollars by region.

	($ mil.)	Share
Southeast	$ 132.9	30.7%
Northeast	130.5	30.2
West	96.5	22.3
Southwest	47.1	10.9
Midwest	25.3	5.9

Source: *Rough Notes*, September 1996, p. 79, from IMR Corp.

★ 1610 ★

Insurance (SIC 6300)

Hotel/Motel Insurance Market - 1995

Lodging facilities provide an estimated $1.5 billion in premiums in the United States. Data show premiums written by region.

	($ mil.)	Share
West	$ 542.7	36.8%
Northeast	302.4	20.5
Southeast	287.7	19.5
Southwest	185.5	12.6
Midwest	157.5	10.7

Source: *Rough Notes*, July 1996, p. 43, from IMR Corp.

★ 1611 ★

Insurance (SIC 6300)

Illinois Insurance Exchange Syndicates

Firms are ranked by 1995 gross premiums written in thousands of dollars.

Britamco Underwriters Inc.	$ 55,660
First Oak Brook Corp. Syndicate Inc.	34,809
Agora Syndicate Inc.	23,173
Transco Syndicate #1 Ltd.	22,582
First Mercury Syndicate	16,583

Source: *Business Insurance*, September 16, 1996, p. 36, from Illinois Insurance Exchange.

★ 1612 ★

Insurance (SIC 6300)

Insurance Market by Segment - Mexico

Data are for 1996.

Life	32.83%
Automobile	25.81
Fire	10.73
Accident/health	9.68
Marine/transport	8.70

Source: *National Trade Data Bank*, October 10, 1996, p. ISA960801.

★ 1613 ★

Insurance (SIC 6300)

Largest Insurance Wholesalers

Data show 1995 premiums in millions of dollars.

Swett & Crawford Group	$ 633.6
Price Forbes North America	520.0
Tri-City Brokerage	476.5
Alexander Howden North America Inc.	454.9
The Schinnerer Group	442.0

Source: *Business Insurance*, September 14, 1996, p. 3.

★ 1614 ★

Insurance (SIC 6300)

Largest Managers of Hawaii Captives - 1996

Companies are ranked by premium volume in millions of dollars.

M&M Insurance Management Services Inc.	$ 92.1
Becher & Carlson Risk Management Inc.	50.0
Johnson & Higgins Services Inc.	21.6
Willis Corroon Management Ltd.	14.5
Sedgwick Management Services (USA) Ltd.	12.7
Alexander Insurance Managers	8.5
Hawaii Captive Insurance Management Inc./USA Risk Group	2.3
IAS Insurance Management	2.2
50th State Risk Management Services Inc.	0.4

Source: *Business Insurance*, May 14, 1997, p. 63, from Hawaii Insurance Division.

★ 1615 ★

Insurance (SIC 6300)

Largest Managers of Vermont Captives - 1996

Companies are ranked by premium volume in millions of dollars.

Johnson & Higgins Services Inc.	$ 661.6
M&M Insurance Management Services Inc.	633.4
American Risk Management Corp.	428.1
Yankee Captive Management Inc.	273.7
Alexander Insurance Managers	257.8
SB&T Captive Management Co.	129.5
AIG Insurance Management Services Inc.	127.5
Vermont Insurance Management Inc.	115.8
Willis Corroon Management (Vermont) Ltd.	$ 57.9
Skandia International Risk Management (Vermont)	36.4

Source: *Business Insurance*, May 14, 1997, p. 48.

★ 1616 ★

Insurance (SIC 6300)

Largest Mutual Insurers

Companies are ranked by amount of policy surplus in billions of dollars as of Decemebr 31, 1996.

State Farm (IL)	$ 30.05
Prudential (NJ)	9.37
Metropolitan Life (NY)	7.15
Liberty Mutual (MA)	4.87
Nationwide (OH)	4.64
New York Life (NY)	4.01
Northwestern (MN)	3.51

Source: *Wall Street Journal*, April 28, 1997, p. B8, from A.M. Best & Co.

★ 1617 ★

Insurance (SIC 6300)

Membership Organization Insurance

Data show the directly written premiums by region. The total market reached $866 million.

	($ mil.)	Share
Northeast	$ 223.9	25.9%
Midwest	175.9	20.3
West	173.9	20.1
Southeast	162.0	18.7
Southwest	130.0	15.0

Source: *Rough Notes*, August 1996, p. 47, from Insurance Market Research Corp.

★ 1618 ★

Insurance (SIC 6300)

Personal Insurance Market - Canada

Market shares are shown in percent.

AXA Canada	13.9%
ING Canada	11.2
Desjardins	9.6
LA Capitale	8.2
General Accident	5.3

Continued on next page.

★ 1618 ★ *Continued*

Insurance (SIC 6300)

Personal Insurance Market - Canada

Market shares are shown in percent.

Assurance Royale	4.2%
Promutuel	4.2
Guardian	3.4
Uniinroyal	2.8
Lloyd's	2.6
Lombard	2.6
Zurich	2.6
Other	29.4

Source: *Le Devoir*, March 9, 1997, p. 13, from companies.

★ 1619 ★

Insurance (SIC 6300)

Personal Insurance Market - Quebec

Market shares are shown in percent.

Desjardins-Laurentienne	17.7%
Industrielle-Alliance	9.4
Sun Life	6.8
SSQ-Vie	6.0
Standard Life	5.4
La Mutuelle	4.7
La Metropolitaine	4.4
Prudentialle	4.2
ManuVie	3.6
Canada-Vie	3.5
London Life	3.5
Great-West	2.7
Other	28.1

Source: *Le Devoir*, March 9, 1997, p. 13, from companies.

★ 1620 ★

Insurance (SIC 6300)

Top Claims Administrators

Firms are ranked by claims paid for self-insurers in billions of dollars.

First Health Strategies Inc.	$ 5.00
ESIS Inc.	2.50
CoreSource Inc.	2.06
Harrington Services Corp.	2.00
Crawford & Co.	1.96
Sedgwick Claims Management Services Inc.	1.96
Gallagher Bassett Services Inc.	$ 1.81
GAS Robins North America Inc.	1.65
ServCo	1.31
United HealthCare Administrators Inc.	1.20

Source: *Business Insurance*, February 17, 1997, p. 21.

★ 1621 ★

Insurance (SIC 6300)

Top Insurers - Canada

Market shares are shown in percent for 1995.

Manufacturers	13.0%
London Life	12.9
Sun Life	9.0
La Mutuelle	8.4
Canada Vie	7.3
Desjardin-Laurentienne	7.2
Other	42.2

Source: *Le Devoir*, March 9, 1997, p. 13, from *Journal de l'Assurance*.

★ 1622 ★

Insurance (SIC 6300)

Top Mexican Insurers

Market shares are shown in percent for the first six months of 1996.

Comercial America	17.46%
Nacional Provincial	17.06
Asemex	14.16
Monterrey Aetna	12.23
Inbursa	5.03
Tepeyac	3.95
Interamericana	2.18
Genesis	2.17
Atlas	1.72
Serfin	1.47
Allianz	1.23
Abaseguros	1.15
Interacciones	1.10
La Territorial	0.87
Other	18.21

Source: *National Trade Data Bank*, September 12, 1996, p. ISA960801.

★ 1623 ★

Insurance (SIC 6300)

Top Reinsurers - 1995

Insurers are ranked by net premiums written. Data are in thousands of dollars.

General Re	$ 2,964,374
Employers Re	2,391,393
American Re	1,611,509
Transatlantic/Putnam	1,008,781
Swiss Re Group	919,312
Berkshire Hathaway	777,000
St. Paul's Cos.	713,474
Munich Re	713,371
Prudential Re	667,697
Zurich Re Centre	602,269

Source: *Business Insurance*, July 29, 1996, p. 1, from Reinsurance Association of America.

★ 1624 ★

Life Insurance (SIC 6311)

Largest U.S. Life Insurers

Firms are ranked by assets in billions of dollars for the first nine months of the year.

Prudential Inc. Co. of America	$ 182.0
TIAA/CREF	177.4
Metropolitan Life	160.3
New York Life	76.8
Aetna	73.8
Equitable	67.9
ITT Hartford	66.5
CIGNA	64.4
Northwestern Mutual	61.8
John Hancock	56.9

Source: *Best's Review*, January 1997, p. 55, from A.M. Best & Co.

★ 1625 ★

Life Insurance (SIC 6311)

Life Insurance Market - Canada

Market shares are shown based on new annualized premiums at the fourth quarter of 1995.

London Life	13.7%
NN Financial	8.9
Manufacturers Life	8.0
Met Life	6.6
Mutual Life	6.6
Transamerica	5.3%
Sun Life	5.1
Canada Life	4.5
Industrial Alliance	4.5
Maritime Life	4.0
Desjardins-Laurentian Life	3.6
Prudential of America	3.6
Great-West Life	3.2
Aetna Life	3.0
Other	19.5

Source: *Best's Review*, July 1996, p. 62, from Limra Canadian New Business.

★ 1626 ★

Life Insurance (SIC 6311)

Ordinary Life Insurers - 1995

Company shares of the $76,405,977 market are shown in percent.

Prudential Ins. Co.	6.00%
Northwestern Mutual	4.82
Conn General Life	4.73
Hartford Life Ins.	4.47
Metropolitan Life	4.22
New York Life	3.79
State Farm Life	2.25
AIG Life Ins. Co.	2.20
Amer Life Ins. Co.	2.16
Mass Mut. Life	2.13
Equitable Var. Life	1.73
Guardian Life Ins.	1.54
Primerica Life	1.42
John Hancock Mutual	1.34
Transamerica Occid. Life	1.29
Pacific Mutual Life	1.27
New England Mutual	1.22
Phoenix Home Life	1.17
Equitable Life Assur.	0.96
Manufacturers Life	0.96
All other	50.33

Source: *Best's Review*, January 1997, p. 65, from A.M. Best & Co.

★ 1627 ★

Health Insurance (SIC 6321)

Largest Private Practices - Chicago

The largest independent associations are ranked by number of physicians.

Advocate Health Partners	1,789
United Physicians Network Inc.	850
Naperville Physicians Org.	355
Highland Health Care Assn.	349
Evanston Medical Specialties Foundation	322
Family Medical Network	320
Highland Park Ind. Practice Associates	267

Source: *Crain's Chicago Business*, July 23, 1996, p. 21.

★ 1628 ★

Health Insurance (SIC 6321)

Medical Insurers - Oregon

Health and accident insurers direct premiums are shown in millions of dollars.

Blue Cross & Blue Shield of Oregon	$ 755.8
Oregon Dental Service	93.7
ODS Health Plan Inc.	68.8
PACC Health Plans	66.1
Pacif Hospital Assn.dba PacificSource Health Plans	57.7
Standard Insurance Co.	49.2
Pacific Health & Life Insurance Co.	47.5
Klamath Medical Service Bureau	42.9
Prudential Insurance Co. of America	31.6
Continental Assurance Co.	22.4

Source: *Portland Business Journal*, August 16, 1996, p. 12.

★ 1629 ★

Health Plans (SIC 6324)

Dental Plan Enrollment - 1996

Data show the estimated millions of people enrolled in each type of plan.

	(mil.)	Share
Dental indemnity	83.4	67.0%
Dental HMO	23.8	19.0
Dental PPO	16.9	14.0

Source: *Business & Health*, April 1997, p. 15.

★ 1630 ★

Health Plans (SIC 6324)

Dental Plans by Type

Dental indemnity

PPOs

HMOs

Dental indemnity	66.0%
PPOs	34.0
HMOs	21.0

Source: *Human Resource Executive*, August 1996, p. 36.

★ 1631 ★

Health Plans (SIC 6324)

Health Care Providers - Mid-Atlantic

Market shares of the Mid-Atlantic states as of March 31, 1996.

MAMSI	25.6%
Kaiser Permanente	15.4
Blue Cross/Blue Shield	13.9
NYL Care	12.8
Humana	4.6
Other	27.7

Source: *Washington Post*, August 23, 1996, p. A6, from Kaiser Permanente.

★ 1632 ★

Health Plans (SIC 6324)

Health Insurance Leaders - Arkansas

Market shares are shown for 1995.

Arkansas Blue Cross & Blue Shield	42.7%
Prudential Insurance Co. of America	6.3
Hartford Life & Accident Ins. Co.	3.3
Continental Assurance Co. (CNA)	2.3
American Investers Life Ins. Co.	1.6
Travelers Insurance Co.	1.4
John Alden Life Insurance Co.	1.3
Provident Life & Accident Ins.	1.3
Time Insurance Co.	1.2
AFLAC	1.2
Principle Mutual Life Insurance Co.	1.2

Continued on next page.

★ 1632 ★ *Continued*

Health Plans (SIC 6324)

Health Insurance Leaders - Arkansas

Market shares are shown for 1995.

Providential Life Insurance Co.	1.1%
Colonial Life & Accident Ins. Co.	1.0
Golden Rule Insurance Co.	0.9
Other	33.2

Source: *Arkansas Business*, October 28, 1996, p. 25.

★ 1633 ★

Health Plans (SIC 6324)

Health Plan Leaders - Colorado

Kaiser	19.04%
FHP of Colorado	17.79
Blue Cross/Blue Shield	7.54
Prudential	3.85
Rocky Mt. HMO	3.84
HMO Colorado	2.80
Principal	2.63
Other	42.51

Source: http:// bcn.boulder.co.ce/hcp_sidebyside.html, January 22, 1997, p. 1.

★ 1634 ★

Health Plans (SIC 6324)

Heath Care Carriers - Cincinnati

Government health care coverage providers are ranked by contract values in millions of dollars.

Blue Cross/Blue Shield	$ 6,450.0
Mail Handlers Benefit Plan	1,790.0
Govt. Employees Hospital Assn.	982.0
National Assn. of Letter Carriers	651.0
Amer. Postal Workers Union	416.0
Kaiser, Northern California	282.0
Kaiser, Southern California	217.0

Source: *Cincinnati Business Courier*, August 11, 1996, p. 4B.

★ 1635 ★

Health Plans (SIC 6324)

HMO Enrollment - Milwaukee

HMOs (health maintenance organizations) are ranked by members as of September 30, 1996.

PrimeCare Health Plan Inc.	248,638
Compcare Health Services Ins. Co.	142,478
Family Health Plan Cooperative	103,731
Humana/Wisconsin Health Organization	98,743
Emphesys Wisconsin Insurance Co.	31,491
Managed Health Services Ins. Corp.	16,187
Maxicare Health Insurance Co.	15,779
Genesis Health Plan Insurance Corp.	9,587

Source: *Business Journal Serving Greater Milwaukee*, December 7, 1996, p. 8, from Wisconsin Office of the Commissioner of Insurance.

★ 1636 ★

Health Plans (SIC 6324)

Largest Medicare HMOs - 1995

Data show enrollment.

FHP Inc.	362,163
Pacificare of Calif.	352,266
Kaiser Foundation Health Plan	258,110
Humana Medical Plan	209,794
Kaiser Foundation Health Plan	181,608
Health Net	107,875
Keystone Health Plan East	90,712
Aetna Health Plans of Calif.	79,074
Health Insurance Plans of Calif.	77,344
Medica	75,238

Source: *Best's Review*, April 1997, p. 46, from A.M. Best Co.

★ 1637 ★

Health Plans (SIC 6324)

Leading HMOs - Sacramento, CA

Health maintenance organizations (HMOs) are ranked by enrollment in the Sacramento area.

Kaiser Permanente Medical Care Program	410,315
Foundation Health, a CA Health Plane	206,672
Omni Healthcare	64,750
Blue Cross California Care	56,364
FHP/Take Care	55,300

Continued on next page.

★ 1637 ★ *Continued*

Health Plans (SIC 6324)

Leading HMOs - Sacramento, CA

Health maintenance organizations (HMOs) are ranked by enrollment in the Sacramento area.

PacifiCare of California	42,000
Molina Medical Centers	41,500
Blue Shield of California	25,743
Aetna Health Plans of California	2,100

Source: *Business Journal Serving Greater Sacramento*, July 15, 1996, p. 6.

★ 1638 ★

Health Plans (SIC 6324)

Major HMOs - Wisconsin

Wisconsin's largest health maintenance organizations (HMOs) are ranked by enrollment as of March 31, 1996.

PrimeCare Health Plan Inc.	228,914
Dean Health Plan Inc.	151,765
Compcare Health Services	147,476
Family Health Care Cooperative	105,157
Humana Wisconsin Health Org. Ins. Gr.	99,556
Physicians Plus Insurance Corp.	89,790
Security Health Plan of Wisconsin Inc.	76,653
Unity Health Plans	70,808
United Health of Wisconsin	65,643
Network Health Plan	50,142
North Central Health	45,031
Greater Health Coop. of So. Cen. Wisconsin	38,811

Source: *Business Journal Milwaukee*, August 10, 1996, p. 33.

★ 1639 ★

Health Plans (SIC 6324)

Managed-Care Health Plans

Health plans are ranked by millions of members.

United HealthCare	5.13
Aetna	4.86
Humana	4.38
PacifiCare Health Systems	3.98
WellPoint Health Networks	3.26
Cigna/Healthsource	3.16
Foundation Health	3.07
Health Systems International	1.81
Oxford Health Plans	1.49
Trigon Healthcare	1.09

Source: *Wall Street Journal*, March 3, 1997, p. A4, from Sherlock Co.

★ 1640 ★

Health Plans (SIC 6324)

Medicaid Managed Health Plans

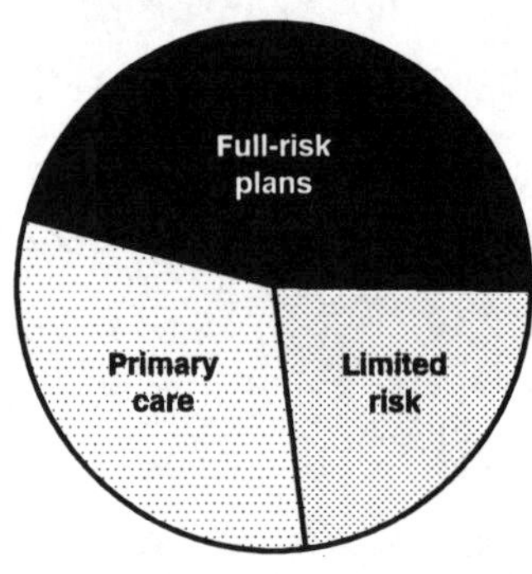

Enrollment is shown by type of coverage.

Full-risk plans	46.0%
Primary care case management plans	31.0
Limited risk prepaid health plans	23.0

Source: *Healthcare Financial Management*, November 1996, p. 45, from HCPA, Medicaid Managed Care Enrollment Report.

★ 1641 ★

Health Plans (SIC 6324)

Privately Insured Health Plans by Type

The table shows the distribution of privately insured individuals and small employers for the first quarter of 1997 and as forecast for 2000. PPO stands for preferred provider organization; HMO stands for health maintenance organization.

	1997	2000
Indemnity	37.0%	20.0%
PPO	25.0	40.0
Point-of-Service	15.0	20.0
HMO	23.0	20.0

Source: *National Underwriter*, April 28, 1997, p. 14.

★ 1642 ★

Health Plans (SIC 6324)

Top Health Care Organizations - Minnesota

Companies are ranked by revenues.

Mayo Foundation	$ 2,147,483,647
Allina Health System	2,123,019,000
Blue Cross and Blue Shield of Minnesota	1,400,000,000
HealthPartners	1,111,058,000
Fairview	440,239,360
HealthSystem Minnesota	382,118,000
HealthEast	335,924,000
Benedictine Health System	269,400,000
North Memorial Health Care	220,626,363
Children's Health Care	178,124,000
CentraCare	145,346,951
St. Mary's Medical Center	139,767,543
Duluth Clinic	114,182,118
St. Luke's Hospital of Duluth	110,126,000
UCare Minnesota	90,467,957

Source: *Corporate Report Minnesota*, November 1996, p. 68.

★ 1643 ★

Health Plans (SIC 6324)

Top Health Plans - Connecticut

Company shares are shown based on the number of members belonging to health plans in Connecticut as of July 1995. At the time, 23.3% of the Connecticut population belonged to health plans.

Physicians Health Services	19.5%
Connecticare	18.9
Kaiser Permanente	14.7
Aetna Health Plans	12.4
Constitution Healthcare	11.6
Health Systems International/M.D. Health Plan	8.0
U.S. Healthcare	5.7
Commodity Health Care Plan	5.2
Cigna HealthCare	1.9
Other HMOs	2.2

Source: *Investext*, Thomson Financial Networks, October 21, 1996, p. 10, from *Interstudy Competitive Edge, 1992-1996, Statistical Abstract of the U.S. 1993-1995*, and DLJ estimates.

★ 1644 ★

Health Plans (SIC 6324)

Top Health Plans - Dallas/Fort Worth

Company shares are shown based on the number of members belonging to health plans in Dallas/Fort Worth as of July 1995. At the time, 24.5% of the Dallas/Fort Worth population belonged to health plans.

Harris Methodist Health Plan	29.5%
Sanus Texas Health Plan	22.1
Kaiser Foundation Health Plan	16.9
PruCare, North Texas	12.3
Aetna Health Plans of North Texas	7.8
MetraHealth/United Healthcare	4.1
Cigna Healthcare of Texas	3.8
Foundation Health Plan	1.5
Humana	0.8
Anthem Health Plans	0.5
Healthsource North Texas	0.4
Exclusive Healthcare/Mutual of Omaha	0.3

Source: *Investext*, Thomson Financial Networks, October 21, 1996, p. 10, from *Interstudy Competitive Edge, 1992-1996, Statistical Abstract of the U.S. 1993-1995*, and DLJ estimates.

★ 1645 ★

Health Plans (SIC 6324)

Top Health Plans - Indiana

Company shares are shown based on the number of members belonging to health plans in Indiana as of July 1995. At the time, 8.5% of the Indiana population belonged to health plans.

M Plan (Methodist Hospital)	19.4%
MaxiCare	15.7
Partners Health Plan	10.5
Physician's Health Plan	10.1
Healthsource	9.8
Welborn HMO	7.3
Physician's Health Network	6.4
Principal Health Care of Indiana	6.4
Blue Cross/Blue Shield	5.7
Arnett HMO	5.4
Other HMOs	3.3

Source: *Investext*, Thomson Financial Networks, October 21, 1996, p. 10, from *Interstudy Competitive Edge, 1992-1996, Statistical Abstract of the U.S. 1993-1995*, and DLJ estimates.

★ 1646 ★

Health Plans (SIC 6324)

Top Health Plans - New Hampshire

Company shares are shown based on the number of members belonging to health plans in New Hampshire as of July 1995. At the time, 19.6% of the New Hampshire population belonged to health plans.

Matthew Thornton Health Plan	50.2%
Healthsource	45.7
U.S. Healthcare	4.1

Source: *Investext*, Thomson Financial Networks, October 21, 1996, p. 10, from *Interstudy Competitive Edge, 1992-1996, Statistical Abstract of the U.S. 1993-1995*, and DLJ estimates.

★ 1647 ★

Health Plans (SIC 6324)

Top Health Plans - New York City Metropolitan Area

Company shares are shown based on the number of members belonging to health plans in the New York City metropolitan area as of July 1995. At the time, 21.0% of the New York City metropolitan area population belonged to health plans.

HIP Health Plans	29.5%
U.S. Healthcare	23.1
Oxford Health Plans	22.2
Aetna Health Plans	7.4
Sanus Health Plans	3.7
Blue Choice/BCBS	2.8
ChoiceCare - Long Island	2.2
United Healthcare/MetraHealth	2.0
Cigna	1.5
Metropolitan Health Plan	1.4
PruCare	1.2
Physicians Health Services	1.1
Independent Health - Hudson/Metro	0.9
ChubbHealth/Healthsource	0.8
Managed Health Inc.	0.3

Source: *Investext*, Thomson Financial Networks, October 21, 1996, p. 10, from *Interstudy Competitive Edge, 1992-1996, Statistical Abstract of the U.S. 1993-1995*, and DLJ estimates.

★ 1648 ★

Health Plans (SIC 6324)

Top HMO Markets

The top market penetrations are shown as of July 1, 1995.

Sacremento, CA	60.5%
Rochester, NY	56.5
Oakland, CA	51.7
Buffalo, NY	49.8
Portland OR-Vancouver, WA	46.1

Source: *OR Manager*, September 1996, p. 36, from InterStudy.

★ 1649 ★

Auto Insurance (SIC 6331)

Auto Insurance Leaders - Massachusetts

Market shares are shown in percent.

Commerce	16.1%
Arbella	12.0
Liberty Mutual	9.6
Met P&C	7.1
Commercial Union	6.5
Safety	6.1
Premier	6.0
Hanover	4.8
Trust	4.3
Plymouth Rock	4.0
Sentry	3.8

Continued on next page.

★ 1649 ★ *Continued*

Auto Insurance (SIC 6331)

Auto Insurance Leaders - Massachusetts

Market shares are shown in percent.

Amica Mutual	3.2%
John Hancock P&C	2.6
USAA	2.5
Other	11.4

Source: http:// www.insure.com/states/ma/auto/share/ html, 1996, p. 1, from Office of Consumer Affairs, Commonwealth of Massachusetts.

★ 1650 ★

Auto Insurance (SIC 6331)

Largest Auto Insurers

Shares are shown based on total premiums of $122.15 billion.

State Farm Group	19.0%
Allstate Ins. Group	10.8
Farmers Ins Group	5.2
Nationwide Group	3.6
USAA Group	2.8
Progressive Group	2.4
Berkshire Hathaway	2.2
Liberty Mutual Group	1.8
CNA Ins. Group	1.7
ITT Hartford Ins Group	1.5
Other	49.0

Source: *Best's Review*, October 1996, p. 32, from A.M. Best Co.

★ 1651 ★

Auto Insurance (SIC 6331)

Private Passenger Auto Insurers

Shares are shown based on total premiums of $104.17 billion.

State Farm Group	21.6%
Allstate Ins. Group	12.2
Farmers Ins Group	5.9
Nationwide Group	3.8
USAA Group	3.2
Berkshire Hathaway	2.5
Progressive Group	2.5
Liberty Mutual Group	1.7
Amer Family Group	1.6
Amer Financial Group	1.4%
Prudential of America Group	1.4
Other	42.2

Source: *Best's Review*, October 1996, p. 32, from A.M. Best Co.

★ 1652 ★

Liability Insurance (SIC 6331)

Liability Insurance Writers

Shares are shown based on total premiums of $24.06 billion.

Amer Intern Group	18.2%
CNA Ins. Group	6.4
Chubb Group of Ins. Cos.	5.6
Zurich Ins. Group - U.S.	4.3
Reliance Ins. Group	3.5
Aetna Life & Casualty Group	3.3
Nationwide Group	3.1
St. Paul Group	3.0
Talegen Ins. Group	2.8
Travelers Ins. Group	2.8
Other	47.0

Source: *Best's Review*, November 1996, p. 26, from A.M. Best & Co.

★ 1653 ★

Malpractice Insurance (SIC 6331)

Malpractice Insurers - Alaska

Market shares are shown in percent.

Norcal Mutual Insuracne Co.	31.7%
Medical Exchange Cal Group	29.0
Other	39.3

Source: *Best's Review*, November 1996, p. 44.

★ 1654 ★

Malpractice Insurance (SIC 6331)

Malpractice Insurers - New York

Market shares are shown in percent.

Medical Liab Mut NY	38.2%
Physicians Rec Insurers	16.4
Other	45.4

Source: *Best's Review*, November 1996, p. 44.

★ 1655 ★

Property Insurance (SIC 6331)

Allied Line Insurers

Shares are shown based on total directly written premiums of $4.8 billion.

Cigna Group	6.6%
State Farm Group	5.5
CNA Ins. Group	5.4
Allstate Ins. Group	3.6
Acceptance Ins Cos.	3.4
Aetna Life & Casualty Group	3.0
Allendale Group	3.0
ITT Hartford Ins. Group	3.0
Zurich Ins. Group	2.7
Amer Inter Group	2.6
Other	61.2

Source: *Best's Review*, December 1996, p. 72, from A.M. Best & Co.

★ 1656 ★

Property Insurance (SIC 6331)

Commercial Multiple-Peril Insurers

Shares are shown based on total directly written premiums of $20.8 billion.

CNA Ins. Group	8.4%
State Farm Group	5.0
ITT Hartford Ins. Group	4.5
Aetna Life & Casualty Group	4.3
Fireman's Fund Cos.	3.9
Chubb Group of Ins. Cos.	3.7
United States F&G Group	3.2
Zurich Ins. Group - U.S.	3.1
Nationwide Group	2.7
Other	61.2

Source: *Best's Review*, December 1996, p. 72, from A.M. Best & Co.

★ 1657 ★

Property Insurance (SIC 6331)

Corporate Property/Casualty Insurers

Firms are ranked by net premiums written in millions of dollars. Total premiums reached $45.556 billion in the first six months of 1996.

American International Group	$ 6,491.8
CNA Financial Group	5,270.0
Nationwide Mutual	4,031.1
ITT Hartford Group Inc.	3,532.0
General Re/Cologne Re Group	2,788.9
Travelers/Aetna P/C Corp.	2,646.7
Liberty Mutual	2,591.6

Source: *Business Insurance*, August 26, 1996, p. 29.

★ 1658 ★

Property Insurance (SIC 6331)

Home Owners Insurance Writers - 1995

Market shares are shown based on total directly written premiums of $25.77 billion in 1995.

State Farm Group	23.5%
Allstate Ins. Group	11.8
Farmers Ins Group	5.9
USAA Group	3.3
Nationwide Group	3.1
Aetna Life & Casualty Group	2.0
Chubb Group of Ins. Cos.	2.0
Prudential of America Group	1.8
Safeco Ins. Companies	1.7
CNA Ins. Group	1.6
Other	43.3

Source: *Best's Review*, December 1996, p. 66, from A.M. Best & Co.

★ 1659 ★

Property Insurance (SIC 6331)

Home Owners Insurance Writers - California

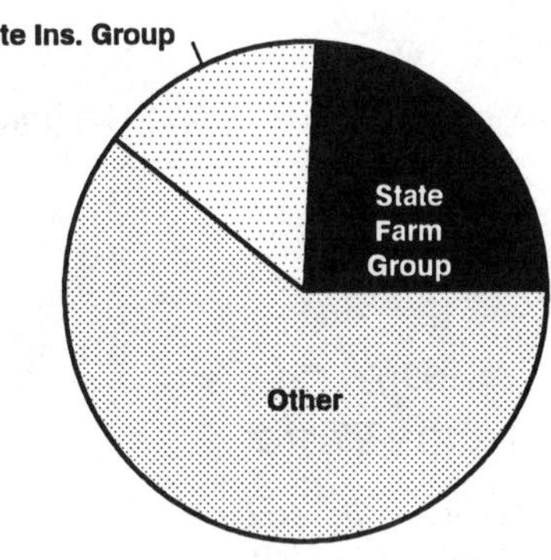

California lead the nation in homeowners multiple-peril insurance, with a total of $2.9 billion in premiums.

State Farm Group	24.4%
Allstate Ins. Group	15.4
Other	60.2

Source: *Best's Review*, December 1996, p. 66, from A.M. Best & Co.

★ 1660 ★

Property Insurance (SIC 6331)

Home Owners Insurance Writers - Missouri

Market shares are shown in percent.

State Farm Group	35.8%
Southern F B Group	20.8
Other	43.4

Source: *Best's Review*, December 1996, p. 66, from A.M. Best & Co.

★ 1661 ★

Property Insurance (SIC 6331)

Largest Property/Casualty Insurers

Data show the value of premiums written for first three quarters of 1996.

Hartford Life	$ 6,713
Teachers Insurance	4,513
Nationwide Life	3,487
Valic	$ 3,000
Lincoln National	2,896
Equitable	2,320
IDS Life	1,999
American Skandia	1,963
Aetna Life & Annuity	1,835
Metropolitan Life	1,732

Source: *National Underwriter*, January 13, 1997, p. 12, from Tillinghast and Towers Perrin.

★ 1662 ★

Property Insurance (SIC 6331)

Maryland's Largest Property Insurers

Companies are ranked by 1995 direct premiums written in millions of dollars.

Government Employees Insurance Co.	$ 1,725.0
U.S. Fidelity & Guaranty Co.	1,356.2
Geico General Insurance Co.	784.6
Maryland Insurance Group	495.5
Fidelity & Deposit Co.	320.9
Geico Indemnity Co.	209.3
Maryland Automobile Insurance Fund	190.8
Geico Casualty Co..	69.5
Montgomery Mutual Insurance Co.	61.4
Hartford Mutual Insurance Co.	56.7

Source: *Baltimore Business Journal*, July 4, 1996, p. 20.

★ 1663 ★

Property Insurance (SIC 6331)

Property & Casualty Insurers

Market shares are shown based on total direct premiums of $263 billion in 1995.

State Farm Group	12.5%
Allstate Ins. Group	6.7
CNA Ins. Group	3.9
Amer Intern Group	3.6
Farmers Ins. Group	3.5
Nationwide Group	3.2
ITT Hartford Ins. Group	2.1
Liberty Mutual Group	2.1
Aetna Life & Cas. Grp.	1.9
Zurich Ins. Group-U.S.	1.9
Other	58.7

Source: *Best's Review*, August 1996, p. 37, from A.M. Best Co.

★ 1664 ★

Property Insurance (SIC 6331)

Top Property and Casualty Companies - Canada

Company shares are estimated. "Other" includes about 225 small companies.

Co-operators	6.5%
General Accident	6.5
ING	6.5
Royal Insurance	6.5
Zurich	6.5
Other	67.5

Source: *Marketing Magazine*, April 28, 1997, p. 1.

★ 1665 ★

Disability Insurance (SIC 6351)

Top Long-Term Disability Insurance Firms in Force Lives

Shares of the $24.5 million segment are shown in percent for 1995.

UNUM	23.0%
Cigna	14.0
Hartford	9.0
Metropolitan	9.0
CNA	6.0
Fortis	5.0
Standard	5.0
Prudential	4.0
Paul Revere	3.0
Reliance	2.0
Others	21.0

Source: *Investext*, Thomson Financial Networks, March 6, 1997, p. 28, from Employee Benefit Plan Review, John Hewitt & Associates, and UNUM.

★ 1666 ★

Fidelity Insurance (SIC 6351)

Fidelity Insurance Leaders

Market shares are shown based on total direct premiums of $927.4 billion in 1995.

CUNA Mut Group	17.0%
Chubb Group of Ins. Cos.	15.2
Amer Intern Group	13.5
Aetna Life & Cas. Group	8.6
Zurich Ins. Group-U.S.	6.6
St. Paul Group	5.5%
CNA Ins. Group	4.8
Reliance Ins. Group	3.2
Capsure Group	3.0
Travelers Ins. Group	2.9
Other	19.7

Source: *Best's Review*, September 1996, p. 117, from A.M. Best Co.

★ 1667 ★

Surety Insurance (SIC 6351)

Surety Insurance Writers

Market shares are shown based on total direct premiums of $2.7 billion in 1995.

CNA Ins. Group	6.0%
Reliance Ins. Group	6.0
Zurich Ins. Group-U.S.	5.9
United States F&G Group	5.7
Amer Express Group	5.5
St. Paul Group	5.1
Aetna Life & Cas. Group	4.5
Amer Intern Group	4.1
Safeco Ins. Companies	3.6
Fireman's Fund Cos.	3.3
Other	50.3

Source: *Best's Review*, September 1996, p. 26, from A.M. Best Co.

★ 1668 ★

Title Insurance (SIC 6361)

Largest Title Firms - Dallas

Firms are ranked by 1995 local title insurance premiums in millions of dollars.

American Title Co.	$ 34.1
Chicago Title Insurance Co.	33.4
Republic Title of Texas Inc.	16.2
Stewart Title North Texas Inc.	12.5
Southwest Land Title Co.	8.9
Trinity-Western Title Co.	7.7
Safeco Land Title of Dallas	6.7
Rattikin Title Co.	5.3
Safeco Land Title of Tarrant County	4.5
Commerce Land Title	3.4

Source: *Dallas Business Journal*, May 31, 1996, p. 8.

★ 1669 ★

Pensions (SIC 6371)

Largest Pension Funds

Assets are shown in millions of dollars.

California Public Employees	$ 102,983
General Motors	79,900
New York Common	78,179
California State Teachers	64,815
Florida State Teachers	55,600
New York State Teachers	55,154
Texas Teachers	51,678
New Jersey	46,280
General Electric	45,324
New York City Retirement	45,022

Source: *Pensions & Investments*, January 20, 1997, p. 24.

★ 1670 ★

Pensions (SIC 6371)

Largest Pension Funds - Detroit

Data show 1995 assets in millions of dollars.

General Motors Corp.	$ 72,000
Ford Motor Co.	34,900
Chrysler Corp.	15,715
City of Detroit Retirement Systems	4,907
Kmart Corp.	2,750
Detroit Edison Co.	1,367
University of Michigan	993

Source: *Crain's Detroit Business*, December 9, 1996, p. 34.

★ 1671 ★

Pensions (SIC 6371)

Top 401(k) Plan Providers

Firms are ranked by 1996 assets in millions of dollars.

Fidelity Investments	$ 119,900
Vanguard Group	68,300
State Street Global	58,400
Merrill Lynch	35,000
Bankers Trust	33,000
Barclays Global Investors	32,800
Prudential	27,000
United Asset Management	25,000
Principal Financial Group	24,500
T. Rowe Price	22,500

Source: *Crain's New York Business*, March 17, 1997, p. 31, from Cerulli Associates.

SIC 64 - Insurance Agents, Brokers, and Service

★ 1672 ★

Insurance Brokers (SIC 6411)

Top Insurance Brokers - 1996

Firms are ranked by gross revenues in millions of dollars. Data are for the first nine months of 1996. Arthur J. Gallagher's figures are restated from 1995.

Marsh & McLennan	$ 3,107.2
Aon Group	2,818.8
Alexander & Alexander	967.4
Acordia	490.0
Arthur J. Gallagher	337.1
Hilb, Rogal & Hamilton	119.6
Poe & Brown	88.8

Source: *Business Insurance*, November 11, 1996, p. 64, from corporate reports.

★ 1673 ★

Insurance Brokers (SIC 6411)

Top U.S. Insurance Brokers

Companies are ranked by estimated 1995 revenues in millions of dollars. Estimates are based on reported percentage of revenues generated by U.S. based clients.

Marsh & McLennan & Co. Inc.	$ 2,409.7
Aon Group Inc.	1,173.7
Johnson & Higgins	858.6
Sedgwick Group P.L.C.	632.1
Alexander & Alexander Services Inc.	602.7
Willis Corroon Group P.L.C.	574.6
Acordia Inc.	554.0
Arthur J. Gallagher & Co.	370.8
Minet Group	215.1
Hilb, Regal & Hamilton Co.	146.6
JIB Group P.L.C.	133.1
Poe & Brown Inc.	$ 106.4
USI Insurance Services Corp.	78.4
Lockton Cos.	70.6
American Phoenix Corp.	63.8

Source: *Business Insurance*, July 22, 1996, p. 3.

★ 1674 ★

Insurance Brokers (SIC 6411)

Top U.S. Retail Brokers

Companies are ranked by estimated 1995 revenues in millions of dollars.

Marsh & McLennan & Co. Inc.	$ 829.1
Aon Group Inc.	739.9
Johnson & Higgins	458.6
Sedgwick Group P.L.C.	408.7
Alexander & Alexander Services Inc.	390.4
Willis Corroon Group P.L.C.	315.8
Arthur J. Gallagher & Co.	211.8
Acordia Inc.	190.6
Hilb, Regal & Hamilton Co.	115.5
JIB Group P.L.C.	74.2

Source: *Business Insurance*, July 22, 1996, p. 10.

SIC 65 - Real Estate

★ 1675 ★

Commercial Real Estate (SIC 6512)

Commercial Real Estate Market - 1997

Shares are shown based on sales of over $14.1 billion. REITs are real estate investment trusts.

REITs	47.5%
Institutional investors	22.0
Individual investors	21.5
Foreign investors	6.4
Building occupants	2.7

Source: *New York Times*, June 17, 1997, p. C1.

★ 1676 ★

Commercial Real Estate (SIC 6512)

Leading Shopping Center Owners

Firms are ranked by total square feet owned.

Simon DeBartolo Group Inc.	111,124,284
Equitable Real Estate Investment Mgmnt. Inc.	65,081,887
Rouse Co.	43,402,000
Heitman Retail Prop/Heitman Capital Mgmnt.	41,588,540
Richard E. Jacobs Group	39,737,413
General Growth Properties Inc.	37,694,819
Westfield Corp. Inc.	36,631,200
Kimco Realty Corp.	33,747,897
WellsPark Group	33,708,800
Cafaro Co.	31,218,709
Corporate Property Investors	30,854,000
Taubman Co.	24,242,000

Source: *Shopping Center World*, January 1997, p. 39.

★ 1677 ★

Commercial Real Estate (SIC 6512)

Office Vacancy Rates - Canada

Data are for 1995.

Victoria	97.9%
Vancouver	90.9
Ottawa	87.1
Calgary	86.0
Montreal	83.9
Edmonton	83.7
Toronto	83.6

Source: *Business Quarterly*, Summer 1996, p. 62.

★ 1678 ★

Commercial Real Estate (SIC 6512)

Rental Property Management Firms - Phoenix, AZ

Firms are ranked by single family residential units managed in the Phoenix area.

Rossmar Management Co. Inc.	45,117
Associated Asset Management Inc.	17,855
City Property Management Co. Inc.	17,146
Graham Management Inc.	15,714
Mutual Management Services Inc.	12,225
Bernard/Finney Management Services Inc.	12,151
Capital Consultants Management Corp.	11,048
Evans Whithycombe Residential Inc.	10,930
Tri-City Property Management Services Inc.	9,200
Lincoln Property Co.	8,831

Source: *Business Journal Serving Phoenix and the Valley of the Sun*, December 20, 1996, p. 22.

★ 1679 ★
Commercial Real Estate (SIC 6512)

Shopping Center Managers

Management firms are ranked by gross leasable area in square feet.

Simon DeBartolo Group Inc.	127,248,770
General Growth Properties Inc.	82,564,272
Urban Retail Properties Co.	54,421,000
Rouse Co.	44,394,000
Richard E. Jacobs Group	40,857,017
Westfield Corp. Inc.	38,731,700
Kimco Realty Corp.	34,541,883
Compass Retail Inc.	31,993,200
Faison	31,825,126
Cafaro Co.	31,218,709
Developers Diversified Realty Corp.	29,741,407
WellsPark Group	29,431,100

Source: *Shopping Center World*, March 1997, p. 24.

★ 1680 ★
Commercial Real Estate (SIC 6512)

Top Outlet Center Managers

Firms are ranked by millions of square feet managed.

Firm	Sq. ft. (mil.)
Horizon Group Inc.	9.24
The Mills Corp.	8.50
Prime Retail Baltimore	5.75
FAC Realty Trust Inc.	5.02
Tanger Factory Outlet Centers	3.80
Chelsea GCA Realty Inc.	3.61
Charter Oak Partners	3.56

Source: *Shopping Center World*, April 1997, p. 64.

★ 1681 ★
Commercial Real Estate (SIC 6512)

Top Outlet Center Owners

Firms are ranked by millions of square feet owned.

Firm	Sq. ft. (mil.)
Horizon Group Inc.	8.91
The Mills Corp.	8.50
Prime Retail Baltimore	5.75
FAC Realty Trust Inc.	4.88
Tanger Factory Outlet Centers	3.80
Chelsea GCA Realty Inc.	3.61
Charter Oak Partners	3.56

Source: *Shopping Center World*, April 1997, p. 64.

★ 1682 ★
Commercial Real Estate (SIC 6512)

Top Shopping Center Managers

The top owners of strip malls are ranked by millions of gross leasable area managed in 1996.

Firm	Area (mil.)
Kimco Realty Corp.	34.54
Koll	30.00
Trammell Crow Co.	27.08
Benderson Development Co. Inc.	25.15
Developers Diversified Realty Corp.	24.92

Source: *Shopping Center World*, August 1996, p. 42.

★ 1683 ★
Commercial Real Estate (SIC 6512)

Top Shopping Center Owners

The top owners of strip malls are ranked by millions of gross leasable area owned in 1996.

Firm	Area (mil.)
Kimco Realty Corp.	33.74
Benderson Development Co Inc.	25.15
Developers Diversified Realty Corp.	21.82
New Plan Realty Trust	18.10
R.D. Management Corp.	17.76

Source: *Shopping Center World*, August 1996, p. 40.

★ 1684 ★
Commercial Real Estate (SIC 6512)

Who Owns Office Space in Los Angeles

Country	Share
United States	49.3%
Japan	32.9
Canada	4.8
Taiwan	3.4
Indonesia	2.1
United Kingdom	2.1
Germany	1.8
Other	4.6

Source: *Los Angeles Business Journal*, May 12, 1997, p. 1, from Cushman Realty Corp.

★ 1685 ★

Real Estate (SIC 6531)

Largest Commercial Developers - St. Louis, MO

Data show total square feet of commercial space developed or under contract in 1996. Commercial space includes office, research and development, hotel, parking, retail, and warehouse structures.

Sansone Group	2,710,000
Duke Realty Investments	800,000
Perkinson Realty	750,000
DESCO Group	582,251
Trammell Crow Co.	500,000
Sverdrup Investments Inc.	400,000
Bakewell Corp.	359,000
Balke Properties	338,000
THF Realty Inc.	299,433

Source: *St. Louis Business Journal*, December 30, 1996, p. 21, from the listed companies.

★ 1686 ★

Real Estate (SIC 6531)

Real Estate Leaders

Firms are ranked by number of offices.

Koll	279
CB Commercial	118
Grubb & Ellis	80
Cushman & Wakefield	42
Galbreath	33

Source: *Wall Street Journal*, November 1, 1996, p. B12.

★ 1687 ★

Real Estate (SIC 6531)

Real Estate Market - Bellingham, WA

Market shares are shown in percent.

Muljat Group	13.94%
Windermere	10.17
ReMax	9.50
CB Miller	9.39
John L. Scott	8.34
Prudential Kelstrup	7.21%
Arnacon	5.01
N.W. Realty	2.24
Other	33.69

Source: http:// www.muljatgroup.com/html/about/ market.html, February 3, 1997, p. 1, from Muljat Group Inc.

★ 1688 ★

Real Estate (SIC 6531)

Top Real Estate Companies - Washington D.C.

Companies are ranked by revenues in millions of dollars.

Ryland Group Inc.	$ 1,580.2
NVR Inc.	1,076.7
Rouse Co.	831.9
NHP Inc.	219.8
Federal Realty Invest. Trust	179.1

Source: *Washington Post*, April 28, 1997, p. 33.

★ 1689 ★

Real Estate (SIC 6531)

Top Real Estate Firms - 1996

Firms are ranked by number of closed transactions ides. A side is either the selling or buying side of a closed deal.

Coldwell Banker	109,759
Weichert Realtors	60,500
Long & Foster Real Estate	43,471
Burnet Financial Group	37,206
Prudential-Jon Douglas Co.	36,832
Edina Realty	30,879
Prudential Florida Realty	26,506
Windermere Real Estate	25,488
Realty Executives	21,389
Realty One	20,071

Source: *Wall Street Journal*, June 20, 1997, p. B8, from *Real Trends Newsletter*.

★ 1690 ★

Real Estate (SIC 6531)

Who Manages Commercial Buildings

Data are in millions of square feet.

New America Network	250.00
Heitman Properties Ltd.	198.50
Holl Management Services Inc.	175.00
Network Management Group Inc.	169.25
COMPASS Mgmt. & Leasing Inc.	148.00
Cushman & Wakefield Inc.	111.64
PM Realty Group	104.30
CB Commercial RE Group Inc.	102.70
Pinnacle Realty Management Co.	81.85
Binswager Co.	80.00

Source: *Buildings*, August 1996, p. 62.

★ 1691 ★

Real Estate (SIC 6550)

Largest Master Planned Communities

Data show the number of acres.

Port St. Lucie	49,000
Ponciana	47,000
Port Malabar	43,000
Palm Coast	42,000
Bella Vista Villa	36,326
Diablo Grande	33,000
Orlandio	32,000
Port LaBelle	31,530
Waikoloa	31,000
King Ranch	30,000

Source: *Wall Street Journal*, November 22, 1996, p. B14, from Urban Land Institute.

SIC 67 - Holding and Other Investment Offices

★ 1692 ★

Bank Holding Companies (SIC 6712)

Leading Bank Holding Companies

Companies are ranked by investments in mortgages and mortgage securities as of September 30, 1996. Figures are in billions of dollars.

Chase Manhattan	$ 59.24
BankAmerica	54.09
First Union	45.13
NationsBank	43.93
Norwest	29.06
Wells Fargo	23.21
PNC	22.94
Banc One	18.47
Citicorp	17.66
Fleet	17.85

Source: *American Banker*, March 4, 1997, p. 12.

★ 1693 ★

Bank Holding Companies (SIC 6712)

Letters of Credit - Top Issuers

The leading bank holding companies are ranked by value of letters of credit issued in millions of dollars.

Chase Manhattan	$ 5,985.0
Citicorp	5,591.0
BankAmerica	4,236.0
Bank of New York	1,671.0
Bank of Boston	1,450.9
CoreStates Financial	1,337.0
NationsBank	922.3
First Chicago NBD	908.0
Republic New York	615.6
Norwest	487.0

Source: *Treasury & Risk Management*, November/December 1996, p. 18, from FED Call Report.

★ 1694 ★

Pension Funds (SIC 6726)

Top Corporate Pension Funds

Funds are shown in millions of dollars.

General Motors	$ 79,900
General Electric	45,324
IBM	43,477
Lucent	39,545
Ford Motor	38,500
DuPont	27,566
Lockheed Martin	27,528
AT&T	26,233
Boeing	21,744
NYNEX	21,286

Source: *Pensions & Investments*, January 20, 1997, p. 44.

★ 1695 ★

Pension Funds (SIC 6726)

Top Public Pension Funds

Funds are shown in millions of dollars.

California Public	$ 102,983
New York Common	78,179
California State Teachers	64,815
Florida State Board	55,600
New York State Teachers	55,154
Texas Teachers	51,678
New Jersey	46,280
New York City Retirement	45,022
Ohio Public Employees	40,335
Wisconsin Investment	39,698

Source: *Pensions & Investments*, January 20, 1997, p. 44.

★ 1696 ★

Pension Funds (SIC 6726)

Top Union Pension Funds

Funds are shown in millions of dollars.

Teamsters, Central States	$ 16,680
Western Teamsters	16,300
IBEW-NECA	6,585
UMWA	6,216
Operating Engineers	4,217
Boilermaker-Blacksmith	4,103
Bakery & Confectionery	3,762
Healthcare Employees	3,657
Sheet Metal Workers	3,278
I.A.M. National	3,240

Source: *Pensions & Investments*, January 20, 1997, p. 44.

★ 1697 ★

Franchises (SIC 6794)

Top Franchise Firms

McDonald's
7-Eleven
Subway
H&R Block
KFC

Firms are ranked by number of outlets.

McDonald's	16,796
7-Eleven	12,800
Subway	12,300
H&R Block	9,900
KFC	8,187

Source: *Christian Science Monitor*, March 17, 1997, p. 7, from International Franchise Association.

★ 1698 ★

Trusts (SIC 6798)

Largest Real Estate Investment Trusts - Dallas/ Fort Worth

Trusts are ranked by assets in millions of dollars.

Crescent Real Estate Equities Co.	$ 1,730.0
FelCor Suite Hotels Inc.	978.0
Patriot American Hospitality Inc.	761.0
Walden Residential Properties Inc.	689.9
Prentiss Properties Trust	596.0
Paragon Group Inc.	$ 529.5
American General Hospitality Corp.	460.0
Columbus Realty Trust	374.6
Continental Mortgage & Equity Trust	250.0
Transcontinental Realty Investors Inc.	245.2

Source: *Dallas Morning News*, May 4, 1997, p. 9Q.

SIC 70 - Hotels and Other Lodging Places

★ 1699 ★

Hotels (SIC 7011)

Extended-Stay Hotel Chains

Data show the firms competing in the extended-stay hotel market. Firms are ranked by number of rooms.

Residence Inn by Marriott	23,000
Homewood Suites	2,881
Villager Lodge	2,400
Hawthorn Suites	2,023
Summerfield Suites	2,000
Woodfin Suites	800

Source: *Real Estate Finance Journal*, Summer 1996, p. 28.

★ 1700 ★

Hotels (SIC 7011)

Highest Hotel Occupancy Rates - 1997

Waikiki	85.0%
New York City	81.0
Boston	80.0
Salt Lake City	79.0
San Francisco	79.0

Source: *USA TODAY*, January 13, 1997, p. B1, from PKF Consulting.

★ 1701 ★

Hotels (SIC 7011)

Hotel Occupancy by City

Data are for 1996.

Honolulu, Hawaii	80.7%
New York City, New York	80.4
Orlando, Florida	80.1
San Francisco, California	78.4
San Jose, California	78.4
Salt Lake City, Utah	77.4
Newark, New Jersey	75.5%
Raleigh-Durham, North Carolina	75.5
Boston, Massachusetts	73.4
Seattle, Washington	73.2

Source: *Hotel & Motel Management*, April 21, 1997, p. 28, from Smith Travel Research.

★ 1702 ★

Hotels (SIC 7011)

Largest Hotels - Chicago

Data show number of rooms.

Hyatt Regency	2,019
Palmer House Hilton	1,639
Chicago Hilton and Towers	1,543
Sheraton Chicago	1,200
Chicago Marriott	1,172
Hyatt Regency O'Hare	1,100

Source: *Chicago Tribune*, February 21, 1997, p. 3-1, from Hotel/Motel Association of Illinois and Chicago Convention and Tourism Bureau.

★ 1703 ★

Hotels (SIC 7011)

Major Hotel Buyers - 1996

The leading hotel acquirors are ranked by millions of dollars invested.

Host Marriott Corp.	$ 1,500.0
Doubletree Hotels Corp.	1,270.0
Starwood Lodging Corp.	880.0
Interstate Hotel Corp.	725.0
Bristol Hotel Co.	665.0
FelCor Suite Hotels Inc.	550.0
Hospitality Properties Trust	484.0
Hilton Hotels Corp.	433.0
Patriot American Hospitality	401.0
Westbrook RE Fund L.P.	265.0
Prime Hospitality Corp.	250.0

Continued on next page.

★ 1703 ★ *Continued*

Hotels (SIC 7011)

Major Hotel Buyers - 1996

The leading hotel acquirors are ranked by millions of dollars invested.

CapStar Hotels	$ 230.0
American General Hospitality	225.0
Wyndham Hotels Corp.	180.0
Olympus Real Estate Corp.	175.0

Source: *National Real Estate Investor*, February 1997, p. 74, from Global Hospitality Resources.

★ 1704 ★

Hotels (SIC 7011)

Top Hotels - Los Angeles, CA

Hotels are ranked by number of rooms.

Westin Bonaventure Hotel Suites	1,368
Los Angeles Airport Hilton & Towers	1,236
Century Plaza & Tower	1,072
Los Angeles Airport Marriott	1,010
Omni Los Angeles Hotel & Centre	900
Sheraton Los Angeles Airport	804
Airport Marina Resort Hotel & Tower	770
Doubletree Hotel Los Angeles Airport	731
Regal Biltmore Hotel	683
Hacienda Hotel	630

Source: *Los Angeles Business Journal*, November 4, 1996, p. 34.

★ 1705 ★

Mobile Home Parks (SIC 7033)

Mobile Home Parks - Arizona

Data show the number of home spaces by area. "Other" refers to total slots outside the Phoenix and Apache junction area.

	No.	Share
Phoenix/Apache Jct. Area	64,500	51.8%
Tucson Area	16,500	13.2
Central region	5,600	4.5
Yuma area	3,900	3.1
Western region	2,400	1.9
Southeast region	1,700	1.4
Other	30,000	24.1

Source: *Arizona Business*, August 1996, p. 2.

SIC 72 - Personal Services

★ 1706 ★

Laundries (SIC 7215)

Equipment Bought by Laundromats

The table shows the percent of laundromat operators planning to buy various kinds of equipment in 1997.

Top loaders	41.6%
Dryers	39.5
Triple loaders	33.3
Double loaders	14.5
Vendors	14.5
Water heaters	10.4
Changers	6.0

Source: *American Coin-Op*, April 1997, p. 12.

★ 1707 ★

Funeral Services (SIC 7261)

Funeral Business Leaders

Firms are ranked by 1995 revenues in millions of dollars for the year ended Semptember 8, 1996.

Service Corp. International	$ 1,650
Loewen Group	600
Stewart Enterprises	320
Prime Succession	82

Source: *Business Week*, October 7, 1996, p. 40, from company reports.

★ 1708 ★

Funeral Services (SIC 7261)

Funeral Market - Houston, TX

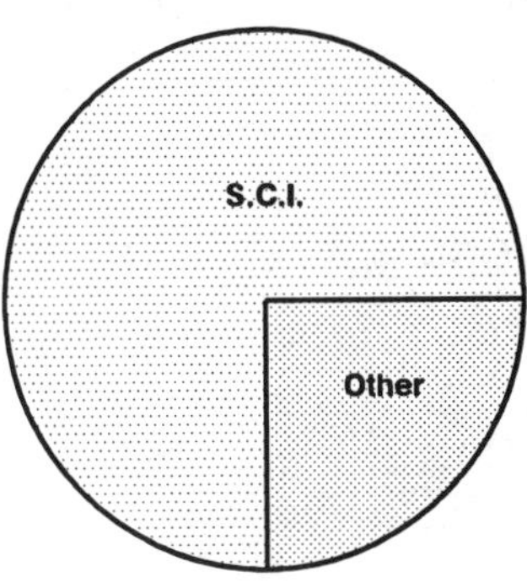

S.C.I.	75.0%
Other	25.0

Source: *Vanity Fair*, March 1997, p. 116.

★ 1709 ★

Funeral Services (SIC 7261)

Funeral Market by State

Data show the share of the funeral market represented by the top two firms, Service Corporation International and Loewen Group., in selected states.

Hawaii	31.0%
Nevada	24.3
Florida	23.4
Texas	21.0
Oregon	19.5
Arizona	16.7
California	16.1
Colorado	14.8
Washington	14.5
Oklahoma	13.6

Source: *New York Times*, September 27, 1996, p. C1, from Raymond-James & Associates and Dun & Bradstreet.

★ 1710 ★

Tax Preparation (SIC 7291)

How Returns Are Filed - 1996

Data show the millions of returns filed by type.

1040	61.1
1040A	18.9
1040EZ	17.2
Electronic	12.1
1040PC	7.1
TeleFile	2.8

Source: *USA TODAY*, January 10, 1997, p. 4B, from Internal Revenue Service.

★ 1711 ★

Tax Preparation (SIC 7291)

Top Tax Preparers - Phoenix

Companies are ranked by number of returns prepared for 1996.

H & R Block	125,000
Jackson Hewitt Tax Service	8,600
Gilman & Clocia	6,000
United Tax Processing Inc.	5,438
Five Star Tax Centers	5,296
Roy Golladay Accounting	2,850
Glenn Allen CPA	2,755
Tax Counselors Association of Arizona	2,100
David C. Rutledge Co.	1,955
A B & P Accounting and Tax Service	1,532
Consultax Inc.	1,523
T & W Tax Service	1,394
Justax Inc.	1,388
ASCOT Tax & Accounting	1,382
Professional Computer Applications	1,046

Source: *The Business Journal - Phoenix*, January 31, 1997, p. 43, from company representatives.

SIC 73 - Business Services

★ 1712 ★

Advertising (SIC 7310)

Ad Spending - 1997

Data show estimated ad spending in millions of dollars.

	($ mil.)	Share
Newspapers	$ 38,413	36.2%
Network TV	13,903	13.1
Magazines	13,774	13.0
Radio	11,150	10.5
Spot-local	10,534	9.9
Spot-national	9,375	8.8
Cable	5,400	5.1
Outdoor	1,841	1.7
Syndication	1,585	1.5

Source: *Adweek*, September 9, 1996, p. 7, from Zenith Media.

★ 1713 ★

Advertising (SIC 7310)

Ad Spending in Canada - 1995

Spending reached $4.643 billion for the top 65 companies.

	($ mil.)	Share
Retail	$ 891.1	19.2%
Automotive	514.4	11.1
Food	395.7	8.5
Business equipment & services	395.0	8.5
Entertainment	300.9	6.5
Financial/insurance services	213.7	4.6
Restaurants	186.9	4.0
Travel & transportation	182.1	3.9
Other	1,563.2	33.7

Source: *Marketing Magazine*, October 21, 1996, p. 21, from A.C. Nielsen.

★ 1714 ★

Advertising (SIC 7310)

Advertising by Medium - Mexico

Television	66.0%
Radio	12.0
Magazines	9.0
Newspapers	6.0
Other	5.0

Source: *National Trade Data Bank*, February 13, 1997, p. IMI960124.

★ 1715 ★

Advertising (SIC 7310)

Top Ad Categories - Mexico

Categories are ranked by ad spending in thousands of dollars for 1996.

Social services	$ 2,294,940
Health/personal hygiene/cosmetics	1,654,460
Food	1,617,510
Commerce	1,479,850
Beverages	1,293,370
Education & media	903,910
Art & culture	888,730
Tobacco	489,370
Household cleaning products	459,810
Finance & insurance	456,900

Source: *Advertising Age*, May 17, 1997, p. I7, from A.C. Nielsen Mexico.

★ 1716 ★

Advertising (SIC 7310)

Top Advertisers - Mexico

Spending is shown in thousands of dollars for 1995.

Videovisa/Videocentro	$ 69,363
Ventel	61,381
Procter & Gamble Co.	58,329

Continued on next page.

★ 1716 ★ *Continued*
Advertising (SIC 7310)

Top Advertisers - Mexico

Spending is shown in thousands of dollars for 1995.

Loteria Nacional	$ 57,879
Televisa	56,838
PepsiCo	54,557
Coca-Cola Co.	46,298
Colgate-Palmolive Co.	45,355
Bacardi Corp.	44,348
Organizacion Bimbo	38,669

Source: *Advertising Age*, May 17, 1997, p. I7.

★ 1717 ★
Advertising (SIC 7311)

Ad Spending by Media

The table shows total measured media spending in millions of dollars for 1996.

Network TV	$ 14,739.6
Spot TV	14,017.7
Newspapers	13,928.8
Magazines	11,213.8
Cable TV networks	4,728.4
Syndicated TV	2,326.1
National spot radio	1,463.9
National newspaper	1,437.0
Outdoor	1,107.4
Sunday magazine	942.4
Network radio	805.9

Source: *Advertising Age*, May 5, 1997, p. 42, from Competitive Media Reporting.

★ 1718 ★
Advertising (SIC 7311)

Golf Equipment - Ad Expenditures

Companies are ranked by media expenditures in millions of dollars.

Titleist/Foot-Joy	$ 22.7
Spalding	12.9
Callaway	10.3
Cobra	9.6
Ping	8.6
Taylor Made	8.2
Maxfli/Dunlop	6.9
Lynx	5.9
Armour/Odyssey	$ 5.7
Wilson	1.6

Source: *Brandweek*, January 20, 1997, p. 36, from Competitive Media Reporting and *Golf Pro*.

★ 1719 ★
Advertising (SIC 7311)

Top Ad Firms - Canada

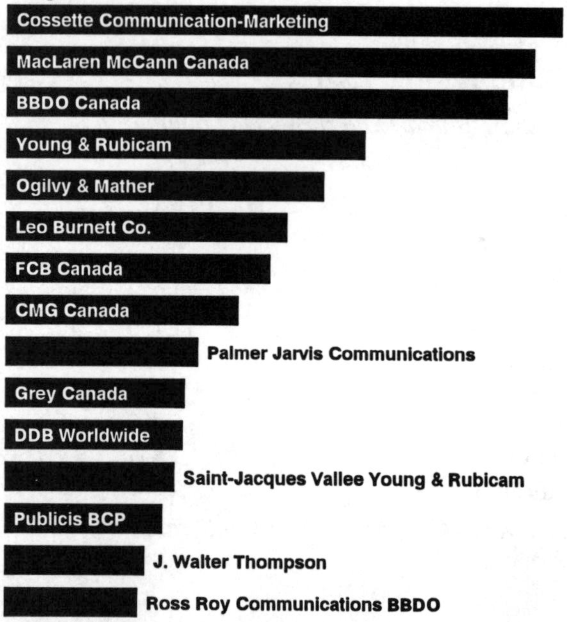

Firms are ranked by 1996 gross income in thousands of U.S. dollars.

Cossette Communication-Marketing	$ 40,905
MacLaren McCann Canada	38,871
BBDO Canada	36,902
Young & Rubicam	26,415
Ogilvy & Mather	23,406
Leo Burnett Co.	20,670
FCB Canada	19,455
CMG Canada	17,075
Palmer Jarvis Communications	14,144
Grey Canada	13,213
DDB Worldwide	13,074
Saint-Jacques Vallee Young & Rubicam	12,476
Publicis BCP	11,561
J. Walter Thompson	10,315
Ross Roy Communications BBDO	9,808

Source: *Advertising Age*, April 21, 1997, p. S28.

★1720★

Advertising (SIC 7311)

Top Ad Firms - Mexico

Firms are ranked by 1996 gross income in thousands of U.S. dollars.

McCann-Erickson Mexico	$ 21,794
Young & Rubicam	11,744
J. Walter Thompson	9,580
Leo Burnett S.A. de C.V.	9,238
Publicidad Ferrer y Asociados	8,532
BBDO/Mexico	8,198
Panamer/Graficoncepto	7,634
Bozell de C.V.	5,492
Ammirati Puris Lintas Mexico	4,981
Grey Mexico	4,488
J. Vale y Asociados	4,483
Noble/D'Arcy Masius Benton & Bowles	4,195
Areliano Publicidad	3,862
Teran TBWA	3,160
Betancourt Barba Euro RSCG	2,473

Source: *Advertising Age*, April 21, 1997, p. S33.

★1721★

Advertising (SIC 7311)

Top Ad Firms - New York

Firms are ranked by local billings in millions of dollars.

Grey Advertising Inc.	$ 2,058.0
Young & Rubicam	1,589.8
Saatchi & Saatchi Advertising	1,447.1
Ogilvy & Mather	1,246.2
McCann-Erickson	1,097.0

Source: *Crain's New York Business*, June 24, 1996, p. 16.

★1722★

Advertising (SIC 7311)

Top Ad Firms - Orange County, CA

Firms are ranked by 1995 billings in millions of dollars.

Alcone Marketing Group	$ 500
Bozell/SMS	240
Foote, Cone and Belding	229
Bates USA	125
Mendoza, Dillon & Asociados	71
G2 Advertising	66
Casanova Pendrill Publiciado	$ 38
Hell-Brice Retail Advertising	30
Pacific Communications	30
Shafer	29

Source: *Adweek*, September 30, 1996, p. 18.

★1723★

Advertising (SIC 7311)

Top Advertising Agencies - Portland, OR

Agencies are ranked by billings in millions of dollars for 1995. Data are estimated.

Wieden & Kennedy	$ 550
KVO	40
Graphic Media	35
Borders, Perrin & Norrander	30
CKS Partners	27
Cole & Weber	25
Young & Roehr	23
Gerber	21
Rosen/Brown Direct	20
INS	16

Source: *Adweek*, February 19, 1996, p. 16.

★1724★

Advertising (SIC 7311)

Top Advertising Categories

Categories are ranked by ad spending in millions of dollars for 1996.

Automotive	$ 5,795.5
Retail	3,243.2
Food	2,355.7
Entertainment, movies & media	2,329.2
Restaurants & fast-food	2,152.2
Personal care, drugs & cosmetics	2,063.9
Telephone	1,975.4
Financial services, insurance & securities	1,317.0
Computer & related products	954.1
Beer	511.7

Source: *Advertising Age*, May 5, 1997, p. 42, from Competitive Media Reporting.

★ 1725 ★

Advertising (SIC 7311)

Top Advertising Firms - Canada

Company shares are shown based on estimated revenues of $1 billion Canadian dollars for 1995.

BBDO Canada	5.5%
Cossette Communication-Marketing	4.9
MacLaren McCann Canada	4.0
Young & Rubicam Group of Cos.	3.2
Leo Burnett Company	2.6
Ogilvy & Mather	2.6
FCB Canada	2.5
Publicis-BCP	2.5
Vickers & Benson Advertising	1.7
Palmer Jarvis Communications	1.6
Others	8.9

Source: *Marketing Magazine*, May 26, 1997, p. 14, from *Marketing Magazine's 1996 Agent Rankings* and industry sources.

★ 1726 ★

Advertising (SIC 7311)

Top Advertising Regions

New York
Chicago
Los Angeles
Detroit
San Francisco
Minneapolis
Boston
Dallas
Connecticut
New Jersey

Markets are ranked by 1996 billings in millions of dollars. Connecticut and New Jersey are top markets but have no dominant cities.

New York	$ 34,208.9
Chicago	10,002.5
Los Angeles	7,256.2
Detroit	5,943.5
San Francisco	4,734.7
Minneapolis	4,259.4
Boston	2,753.2
Dallas	2,679.4
Connecticut	$ 1,674.5
New Jersey	1,411.6

Source: *Advertising Age*, April 21, 1997, p. S24.

★ 1727 ★

Advertising (SIC 7311)

Top Advertising Spenders

Firms are ranked by ad spending in millions of dollars for 1996.

General Motors Corp.	$ 1,710.7
Procter & Gamble Co.	1,493.5
Philip Morris Cos.	1,237.0
Chrysler Corp.	1,089.2
Ford Motor Co.	897.7
Johnson & Johnson	840.5
Walt Disney Co.	773.3
PepsiCo.	768.0
Time Warner	747.0
AT&T Corp.	659.8

Source: *Advertising Age*, May 5, 1997, p. 42, from Competitive Media Reporting.

★ 1728 ★

Advertising (SIC 7312)

Outdoor Advertising Leaders

Firms are ranked by 1996 media billings in millions of dollars.

Leo Burnett Co.	$ 135.3
Grey Advertising	98.6
BBDO Worldwide	72.1
Saatchi & Saatchi Advertising	59.4
DDB Needham Worldwide	57.7
Long Haymes Carr	48.6
Bates Worldwide	48.5
Y&R Advertising	44.0
McCann-Erickson Worldwide	38.9
J. Walter Thompson Co.	28.8

Source: *Advertising Age*, April 21, 1997, p. S41.

★ 1729 ★

Advertising (SIC 7313)

Business Publication Advertising Leaders

Firms are ranked by 1996 media billings in millions of dollars.

Ogilvy & Mather Worldwide	$ 70.2
Ammirati Puris Lintas	66.7
McCann-Erickson Worldwide	65.1
Bernard Hodes Group	58.0
J. Walter Thompson Co.	54.3
Saatchi & Saatchi Advertising	50.3
Anderson & Lembke	49.9
Goldberg Moser O'Neill	28.0
BBDO Worldwide	27.3
CKS Group	25.1

Source: *Advertising Age*, April 21, 1997, p. S41.

★ 1730 ★

Advertising (SIC 7313)

Cable TV Advertising Leaders

Firms are ranked by 1996 media billings in millions of dollars.

Foote, Cone & Belding	$ 346.0
Grey Advertising	251.2
BBDO Worldwide	204.7
Wells Rich Greene BDDP	201.2
Leo Burnett Co.	196.5
D'Arcy Masius Benton & Bowles	191.0
J. Walter Thompson Co.	190.1
Y&R Advertising	185.9
DDB Needham Worldwide	184.4
McCann-Erickson Worldwide	154.5

Source: *Advertising Age*, April 21, 1997, p. S41.

★ 1731 ★

Advertising (SIC 7313)

Consumer Magazine Advertising Leaders

BBDO Worldwide
Grey Advertising
Y&R Advertising
Leo Burnett Co.
McCann-Erickson Worldwide
Saatchi & Saatchi Advertising
J. Walter Thompson Co.
Ogilvy & Mather Worldwide
Foote, Cone & Belding
D'Arcy Masius Benton & Bowles

Firms are ranked by 1996 media billings in millions of dollars.

BBDO Worldwide	$ 317.1
Grey Advertising	288.3
Y&R Advertising	283.1
Leo Burnett Co.	279.4
McCann-Erickson Worldwide	265.5
Saatchi & Saatchi Advertising	262.7
J. Walter Thompson Co.	241.9
Ogilvy & Mather Worldwide	223.1
Foote, Cone & Belding	220.0
D'Arcy Masius Benton & Bowles	203.0

Source: *Advertising Age*, April 21, 1997, p. S41.

★ 1732 ★

Advertising (SIC 7313)

Medical Journal Advertising Leaders

Firms are ranked by 1996 media billings in millions of dollars.

Klemtner Advertising	$ 134.6
Foote, Cone & Belding	33.3
Lyons Lavey Nickel Swift	29.7
Cline, Davis & Mann	28.6
McCann Healthcare	28.2
Harrison & Star	27.5
Kallir, Philips, Ross	20.4
Sudler & Hennessey	20.3
CommonHealth USA	14.6
Abelson-Taylor	13.6

Source: *Advertising Age*, April 21, 1997, p. S41.

★ 1733 ★

Advertising (SIC 7313)

Network Radio Advertising Leaders

Firms are ranked by 1996 media billings in millions of dollars.

Ogilvy & Mather Worldwide	$ 66.0
BBDO Worldwide	51.3
Y&R Advertising	29.8
DDB Needham Worldwide	26.6
J. Walter Thompson Co.	25.9
Leo Burnett Co.	25.3
D'Arcy Masius Benton & Bowles	20.0
Campbell-Ewald	18.9
McCann-Erickson Worldwide	18.5
N.W. Ayer & Partners	16.0

Source: *Advertising Age*, April 21, 1997, p. S41.

★ 1734 ★

Advertising (SIC 7313)

Network TV Advertising Leaders

Firms are ranked by 1996 media billings in millions of dollars.

D'Arcy Masius Benton & Bowles	$ 1,152.0
McCann-Erickson Worldwide	1,051.3
Y&R Advertising	973.9
J. Walter Thompson Co.	967.1
BBDO Worldwide	941.4
Ogilvy & Mather Worldwide	909.3
Saatchi & Saatchi Advertising	886.2
Leo Burnett Co.	843.6
Foote, Cone & Belding	800.0
Grey Advertising	753.5

Source: *Advertising Age*, April 21, 1997, p. S41.

★ 1735 ★

Advertising (SIC 7313)

Newspaper Advertising Leaders

Firms are ranked by 1996 media billings in millions of dollars.

Bernard Hodes Group	$ 425.3
Nationwide Advertising Service	255.7
TMP Worldwide	185.1
McCann-Erickson Worldwide	130.2
Allied Advertising	129.2
Y&R Advertising	123.7
BBDO Worldwide	$ 104.7
DDB Needham Worldwide	102.4
Ogilvy & Mather Worldwide	99.5
Foote, Cone & Belding	95.0

Source: *Advertising Age*, April 21, 1997, p. S41.

★ 1736 ★

Advertising (SIC 7313)

Radio Advertisers - Canada

Eaton's of Canada Ltd.
Government of Canada
Government of Ontario
John Labatt Ltd.
Dairy Farmers of Canada
BCE Inc.
Molson Companies
Government of Quebec
Government of B.C.
Royal Bank of Canada

The top firms are ranked by 1995 advertising expenditures in millions of dollars.

Eaton's of Canada Ltd.	$ 8.11
Government of Canada	7.69
Government of Ontario	5.41
John Labatt Ltd.	5.08
Dairy Farmers of Canada	4.73
BCE Inc.	4.32
Molson Companies	3.91
Government of Quebec	3.43
Government of B.C.	3.01
Royal Bank of Canada	2.94

Source: *Marketing Magazine*, January 13, 1997, p. 11, from *Annual Summary of Advertising Expenditures in Canada* and A.C. Nielsen.

★ 1737 ★

Advertising (SIC 7313)

Spot Radio Advertising Leaders

Firms are ranked by 1996 media billings in millions of dollars.

DDB Needham Worldwide	$ 138.5
BBDO Worldwide	124.2
McCann-Erickson Worldwide	115.6

Continued on next page.

★ 1737 ★ *Continued*

Advertising (SIC 7313)

Spot Radio Advertising Leaders

Firms are ranked by 1996 media billings in millions of dollars.

Foote, Cone & Belding	$ 110.0
Y&R Advertising	102.4
Saatchi & Saatchi Advertising	98.2
Bozell Worldwide	96.6
J. Walter Thompson Co.	88.8
Bates Worldwide	82.1
Campbell Mithun Esty	70.1

Source: *Advertising Age*, April 21, 1997, p. S41.

★ 1738 ★

Advertising (SIC 7313)

Sunday Magazine Advertising Leaders

Firms are ranked by 1996 media billings in millions of dollars.

Ogilvy & Mather Worldwide	$ 18.4
Girgenti Hughes Butler & McDowell	16.6
TBWA Chiat/Day	16.4
BBDO Worldwide	10.0
Foote, Cone & Belding	7.4
D'Arcy Masius Benton & Bowles	6.3
CommonHealth USA	6.3
DraftDirect Worldwide	5.8
Wunderman Cato Johnson	4.4
Bernstein-Rein Advertising	3.6

Source: *Advertising Age*, April 21, 1997, p. S41.

★ 1739 ★

Advertising (SIC 7313)

Syndicated TV Advertising Leaders

Firms are ranked by 1996 media billings in millions of dollars.

D'Arcy Masius Benton & Bowles	$ 224.0
Leo Burnett Co.	128.7
Foote, Cone & Belding	100.0
J. Walter Thompson Co.	83.0
McCann-Erickson Worldwide	80.2
Jordan, McGrath, Case & Taylor	76.8
Ogilvy & Mather Worldwide	70.6
DDB Needham Worldwide	63.7
Y&R Advertising	$ 49.2
Ammirati Puris Lintas	48.8

Source: *Advertising Age*, April 21, 1997, p. S41.

★ 1740 ★

Advertising (SIC 7313)

Yellow Pages Advertising Leaders

Firms are ranked by 1996 media billings in millions of dollars.

TMP Worldwide	$ 640.3
Berry Network	142.4
Foote, Cone & Belding	103.3
Ketchum Directory Advertising	100.2
D'Arcy Masius Benton & Bowles	57.7
Ruppman National Yellow Pages Services	56.4
Bozell Worldwide	23.9
Wunderman Cato Johnson	23.1
Ogilvy & Mather Direct	16.7
Grey Advertising	12.4

Source: *Advertising Age*, April 21, 1997, p. S41.

★ 1741 ★

Advertising (SIC 7319)

Ad Spending in the Gay Press

The table shows the largest ad spending in gay publications. Total ad spending in 138 gay-oriented newspapers, magazines, arts and entertainment guides reached $73.7 million in 1996.

Bars and clubs	14.3%
Phone services	13.5
Classified ads	9.1
Gay events and meetings	5.4
Retail	5.0
Travel, out-of-town gay events	4.6
Other	48.1

Source: *USA TODAY*, March 14, 1997, p. D1, from *Mulryan/Nash's Gay Press Report*.

★ 1742 ★

Advertising (SIC 7319)

Top Web Advertisers - 1996

Firms are ranked by spending in millions of dollars.

Microsoft	$ 13.0
AT&T	7.3
Excite	6.9
IBM	5.9
Netscape	5.7
Infoseek	5.1
Nynex	4.0
Lycos	3.9
Yahoo!	3.9
CNET	2.7

Source: *Advertising Age*, March 17, 1997, p. 32, from Jupiter Communications AdSpend.

★ 1743 ★

Advertising (SIC 7319)

Toy Advertising Market - 1995

Advertising expenditures of the toy industry is shown in millions of dollars by media.

Spot TV	$ 231.08
Network TV	219.01
Syndicated TV	194.14
Cable TV networks	157.13
Magazines	83.37
Newspapers incl. Sunday magazines	4.50
National spot radio	4.43
Network radio	0.95
Outdoor	0.08

Source: *Discount Merchandiser*, February 1997, p. 26, from Competitive Media Reporting and Publishers Information Bureau.

★ 1744 ★

Advertising (SIC 7319)

U.S. Advertising Revenues by Media

Data are for 1995.

Daily newspapers	36.0%
Broadcast television	32.0
Magazines	15.0
Radio	11.0
Cable TV	5.0

Source: *Chicago Tribune*, April 27, 1997, p. C1, from Audit Bureau of Circulation, FCC, Forrester's Research, Morgan Stanley & Co., National Cable Television Association, and Newspaper Association of America.

★ 1745 ★

Advertising (SIC 7319)

Web Advertising by Category

Search engines and directories	36.0%
Entry portals	19.0
Computers & related interests	18.0
News media	11.0
General interests	7.0
Sports/men's interests	4.0
Other	5.0

Source: *PC Week*, September 23, 1996, p. A8, from Jupiter Communications.

★ 1746 ★

Direct Marketing (SIC 7331)

Direct Ad Expenditures by Industry

This table shows the industrial direct marketing ad expenditures made to reach other businesses. The 1995 data are in billions of dollars.

Wholesale trade	$ 7.3
Business services	6.4
Printing & publishing	6.1
Communications	5.9
Transportation services	5.7
Nondepository institutions	4.5
Chemical & allied products	3.2
Insurance carriers & agents	3.0
Electrical machinery & equipment	2.5
Depository institutions	2.5

Source: *Sales & Marketing Management*, January 1997, p. 76, from Direct Marketing Association.

★ 1747 ★

Direct Marketing (SIC 7331)

Direct-Selling Industry

Distribution is shown based on $17.94 billion in retail sales in 1995.

Personal care products	38.8%
Home/family care products	34.4
Misc. services	10.3
Wellness products	9.2
Leisure/educational products	7.3

Source: *Success*, October 1996, p. 75, from Direct Selling Association.

★ 1748 ★

Direct Marketing (SIC 7331)

Largest Direct Response Firms

Revenues are in millions of dollars.

Wunderman Cato Johnson	$ 80.2
Rapp Collins Worldwide	80.0
Bronner Slosberg Humphrey	67.4
DIMAC Direct	52.0
Ogilvy & Mather Direct	52.0
DraftDirect Worldwide	51.6
Barry Blau & Partners	49.8
Customer Development Corp.	34.3
Grey Direct Marketing Corp.	27.9

Source: *Advertising Age*, August 5, 1996, p. S3.

★ 1749 ★

Direct Marketing (SIC 7331)

Top Direct Response Marketing Agencies - 1995

Data show total revenues in thousands of dollars.

Rapp Collins Worldwide	$ 174,729
Wunderman Cato Johnson	171,237
Ogilvy & Mather Direct	164,800
DraftDirect Worldwide	79,238
Bronner Slosberg Humphrey	67,495
DIMAC Direct	64,706
Barry Blau & Partners	49,873
Grey Direct Marketing Group	49,665
McCann Direct	42,750
Customer Development Corp.	34,387

Source: *Advertising Age*, August 5, 1996, p. S6.

★ 1750 ★

Direct Marketing (SIC 7331)

U.S. Marketing Spending

Data show where marketers will spend their dollars, based on a survey of 400 executives.

Trade magazines	49.9%
Internet	40.0
General interest magazines	8.2
Broadcast TV/radio	1.1
Cable TV	0.8

Source: *Sales & Marketing Management*, April 1997, p. 14, from Cahners Business Confidence Index.

★ 1751 ★

Auto Repair Services (SIC 7350)

Automotive Aftermarket

The installer market is valued at $45 billion.

Jobbers	38.0%
Warehouses	21.0
Car dealers	18.0
Retail auto stores	10.0
All others	18.0

Source: *Automotive Marketing*, December 1996, p. 12, from Salomon Brothers.

★ 1752 ★

Rental Services (SIC 7350)

Largest Equipment Rental Firms

Firms are ranked by equipment rental value in millions of dollars.

Hertz Equipment Rental Corp.	$ 700.0
Essex Crane Rental Corp.	400.0
All Erection & Crane Rental	350.0
Prime Equipment	300.0
GE Capital	250.0
American Equipment Co.	241.0
Carlisle Construction Co.	240.0
BET Plant Services (USA)	215.0
Bragg Crane & Rigging Co.	155.0
Morrow Equipment Co.	150.0

Source: *Construction Equipment*, September 1996, p. 52.

★ 1753 ★

Staffing Services (SIC 7360)

Top Service Firms - 1996

Companies are ranked by revenues in millions of dollars.

Keane	$ 426
AccuStaff	400
Analysts International	378
Computer Task Group	365
Cap Gemini America	296
The Registry	267

Source: *Investor's Business Daily*, June 3, 1997, p. 6, from Updata Capital Inc.

★ 1754 ★

Employee Leasing (SIC 7363)

Largest Employee Leasing Firms - Tampa Bay

Firms are ranked by number of total leased employees.

Staff Leasing Group	80,000
T.T.C. Inc.	25,000
Payroll Transfers Inc.	18,000
Professional Employee Management Inc.	11,682
Staff Management Systems	11,000
Paychex Business Solutions	10,000
Southeastern Companies Inc.	5,500
Staffing Concepts International	5,000
Employee Services	3,544
South East Personnel Leasing Inc.	3,268

Source: *Tampa Bay Business Journal*, September 6, 1996, p. 23.

★ 1755 ★

Temp Agencies (SIC 7363)

Largest Temp Firms - San Diego

Firms are ranked by 1995 gross revenues in millions of dollars.

Manpower Temporary Services	$ 41.80
TOPS Staffing Services Inc.	39.20
Volt Temporary Services	37.11
Adla Personnel Services	21.80
The Eastridge Group	20.80

Source: *San Diego Business Journal*, June 24, 1996, p. 18.

★ 1756 ★

Temp Agencies (SIC 7363)

Leading Temp Agencies - 1996

Firms are ranked by revenues in millions of dollars.

Manpower	$ 6,080
Olsten	3,378
Kelly Services	3,302
CDI	1,454
Accustaff	1,449
Interim Services	1,147
Volt Info Sciences	1,049
Norrell	1,014

Source: *Fortune*, April 28, 1997, p. 62.

★ 1757 ★

Temp Agencies (SIC 7363)

Temporary Service Firms - 1996

Data show temporary employee payroll distribution by industry. The industry's revenues reached $43.6 billion.

Office/clerical	38.7%
Industrial	31.8
Technical	14.0
Professional	6.3
Health care	5.0
Marketing	0.6
Other	3.6

Source: *USA TODAY*, April 11, 1997, p. 1B, from National Association of Temporary and Staffing Services.

★ 1758 ★

Software (SIC 7372)

CD-ROM Sales by Type

Arcade/action games	24.0%
Adventure/role playing/interactive drama	18.0
Fight/war simulation games	14.0
Sports games	13.0
Strategy games	8.0
Multiple games	7.0
Card/casino games	5.0
Board games	3.0
Puzzle games	1.0
Other	7.0

Source: *E-Media Professional*, February 1997, p. 14, from SofTrends.

★1759★

Software (SIC 7372)

CD-ROM Titles in U.S. Households

Data show the number of CD-ROM titles in U.S. households. Figures refer to households with an annual income of over $25,000 and having a PC with CD-ROM drive.

Teen/adult games	3.3
Children's games	1.8
Reference	1.8
Business software	1.2
Children's education	1.2
Adult education	1.1
Other	3.2

Source: *Database*, Nov.- Dec. 1996, p. 16, from Inteco.

★1760★

Software (SIC 7372)

Clinical Decision Support Software Suppliers

Shares are shown based on the 296 integrated healthcare delivery systems using decision support.

MEDITECH	26.9%
HBOC	15.0
Self-developed	9.7
SMS	8.7
Transition Systems Inc.	5.5
Cerner	2.7
Accu-Med Services	2.4
Ventech Systems Inc.	2.2
Eclipsys Corporation	1.9
Phamis Inc.	1.7
Other	23.2

Source: *Healthcare Informatics*, May 1997, p. 28, from Dorenfest IDHS 3000+ Surround Database.

★1761★

Software (SIC 7372)

Color Publishing Market

Mac OS	80.0%
Windows	14.0
Proprietary	4.0
Unix	2.0

Source: *Macweek*, September 9, 1996, p. 8, from Griffin Dix Research.

★1762★

Software (SIC 7372)

Computer Software Firms - Milwaukee

Developers are ranked by number of local employees.

Compuware Corp.	615
Catalyst International Inc.	300
Effective Management Systems inc.	250
McHugh Freeman	230
Frontier Technologies Corp.	130
Metrix Inc.	110
Harris Data	65
Data Retrieval Corp.	60
Merge Technologies Inc.	49
PKWare Inc.	35

Source: *Business Journal Milwaukee*, October 19, 1996, p. 31.

★1763★

Software (SIC 7372)

Configuration Management Market

Data show market shares bases on installed configuration management/ version control software.

Intersolv	28.0%
IBM	21.0
Astria	16.0
Computer Associates	14.0
Other	21.0

Source: *Software Magazine*, September 1996, p. 46, from Sentry Market Research.

★ 1764 ★

Software (SIC 7372)

Data Warehousing Market

The market is expected to increase from $1.4 billion in 1995 to $5.5 billion in 2000.

	1995	2000
Data transformation	38.5%	55.1%
Data access	51.0	30.6
Management	10.5	14.4

Source: *InfoWorld*, December 23, 1996, p. 8, from International Data Corp.

★ 1765 ★

Software (SIC 7372)

Desktop Suite Leaders

Unit shares are shown for July 1996.

Corel	48.6%
Microsoft	47.8
Lotus	3.5
Other	0.1

Source: *PC Week*, December 16, 1996, p. A5, from Corel.

★ 1766 ★

Software (SIC 7372)

Directory Service Software

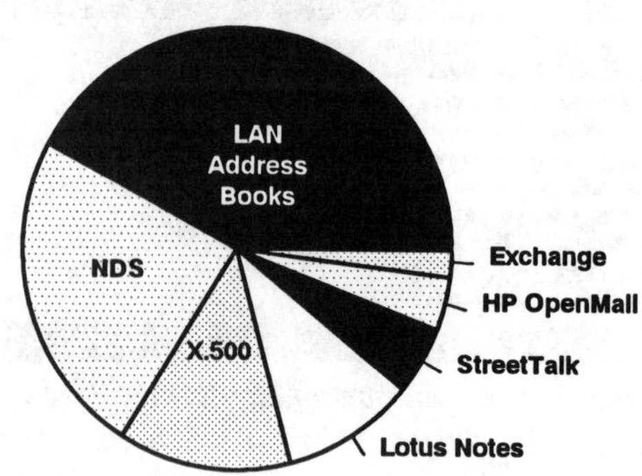

Brand shares are shown in percent for 1996.

LAN Address Books	42.0%
NDS	24.0
X.500	13.0
Lotus Notes	10.0
StreetTalk	5.0
HP OpenMall	4.0
Exchange	2.0

Source: *Network World*, February 17, 1997, p. 15, from Radicati Group.

★ 1767 ★

Software (SIC 7372)

Educational Software Market

Shares are for October 1996.

CUC	22.8%
SoftKey/The Learning Co.	15.7
Other	51.5

Source: *PC Week*, December 23, 1996, p. A6, from PC Data.

★ 1768 ★

Software (SIC 7372)

Internet Server Market

Brand shares are shown based on a survey of 1 million internet sites.

Apache for Unix	42.0%
Servers based on Windows NT	23.0
Microsoft for Unix	14.0
Netscape for Unix	11.0
NCSA for Unix	7.0
Other Unix servers	3.0

Source: *Informationweek*, June 2, 1997, p. 92, from Netcraft.

★ 1769 ★

Software (SIC 7372)

Intranet NOS Market

Data show the network operating systems installed for U.S. corporate intranets.

NetWare	32.0%
Unix	25.0
Windows NT	25.0
OS/2	4.0
Other	14.0

Source: *Datamation*, October 1996, p. 129, from Cowen & Co.

★ 1770 ★

Software (SIC 7372)

Leading Firewall Software

Data are for 1995.

Check Point Software	40.0%
Border Network Technologies	9.0
Trusted Information Systems	6.0
Raptor Systems	3.0
Secure Computing	1.0
Other	41.0

Source: *Informationweek*, November 25, 1996, p. 93, from International Data Corp.

★ 1771 ★

Software (SIC 7372)

Leading Hospital Laboratory Software Vendors

Data show market shares as of October 1995.

Sunquest Information Systems Inc.	18.6%
Medical Information Technology Inc.	17.0
Cerner Corp.	16.0
HBO & Co.	10.3
Citation Computer Systems Inc.	7.3
Shared Medical Systems Corp.	4.2
Dynamic Healthcare Technologies Inc.	3.0
CHC Inc.	2.9
3M Health Information Systems	2.8
Soft Computer Consultants	1.6
Other	16.3

Source: *Health Data Management*, July 1996, p. 36, from Dorenfest 3000+ Database.

★ 1772 ★

Software (SIC 7372)

Leading Software Publishers

Firms are ranked by corporate sales for August 1996 in millions of dollars.

Microsoft	$ 54.85
Symantec	16.83
Lotus	9.45
IBM	6.92
Novell	4.74
Attachmate	4.16
Corel	2.42
McAfee	1.81
Adobe	1.69
Wall Data	1.43
Visio	1.32

Source: *Computer Reseller News*, November 11, 1996, p. 160, from PC Data.

★ 1773 ★

Software (SIC 7372)

Middleware Market - 1995

Data show the message-oriented middleware market for 1995.

Tibco	25.0%
IBM	11.0
Peer Logic	7.0
Isis	5.0
Digital	4.0
Other	48.0

Source: *Network World*, November 25, 1996, p. 19, from International Data Corp.

★ 1774 ★

Software (SIC 7372)

NT Server Backup Market - 1996

The market was valued at $40 million.

Seagate	55.0%
Cheyenne	33.0
Legate	3.0
Other	9.0

Source: *Network World*, November 18, 1996, p. 19, from International Data Corp.

★ 1775 ★

Software (SIC 7372)

Office Suite Market - 1996

Market shares are shown in percent.

	Dol. Share	Unit Share
Microsoft	79.46%	58.97%
Corel	16.26	35.39
Lotus	4.28	5.65

Source: *PC Week*, February 24, 1997, p. 122, from PC Data.

★ 1776 ★

Software (SIC 7372)

Peer-to-Peer Software Market

Peer-to-peer market share is shown based on nodes shipped.

Artisoft LANtastic	42.6%
Windows for Workgroups & Windows 95	37.3
Novell Personal NetWare	14.5
Others	5.4

Source: *Computer Reseller News*, June 17, 1996, p. 67, from International Data Corp.

★ 1777 ★

Software (SIC 7372)

Portable Computer Operating Systems

Data show the preferred brands of operating systems for PC users. Windows 95 and Windows NT are projected to be the leaders by 1999.

Windows 3.1	34.0%
Windows 95	23.0
DOS	8.0
Windows NT	6.0
Unix	6.0

Source: *Computerworld*, December 16, 1996, p. 55, from Yankee Group.

★ 1778 ★

Software (SIC 7372)

Relational Database Market - 1996

The relational database management systems market is shown by company.

Oracle	46.0%
IBM	16.0
Informix	15.0
Sybase	8.0
Microsoft	5.0
Other	10.0

Source: *Infoworld*, March 17, 1997, p. 19, from Gartner Group.

★ 1779 ★

Software (SIC 7372)

Resource Planning Software

The enterprise resource planning software market is estimated to have generated $5.4 billion in revenues in 1996.

SAP	33.0%
Oracle	13.0
System Software Associates	7.7
Bean	6.8
CA	5.6
JBA International	5.1
PeopleSoft	4.8
J.D. Edwards	4.4
Marcam	4.1
D&B Software	3.3
Other	12.2

Source: *Informationweek*, October 28, 1996, p. 28, from Advanced Manufacturing Research.

★ 1780 ★

Software (SIC 7372)

Software in Schools

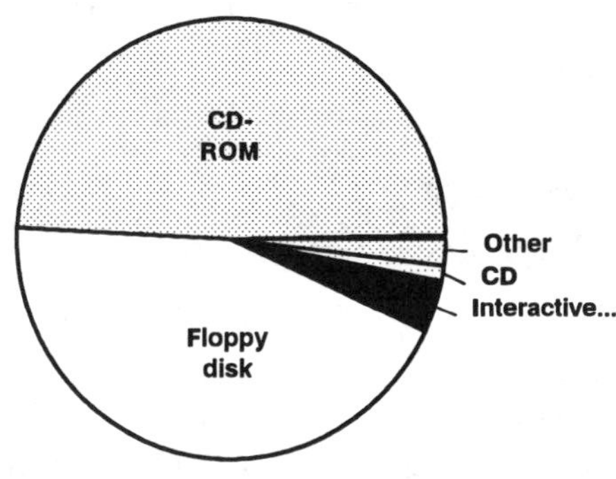

Data show the types of software products purchased by schools for 1996-97.

CD-ROM	49.0%
Floppy disk	44.0
Interactive videodiscs	4.0
CD	1.0
Other	2.0

Source: *Technology & Learning*, March 1997, p. 30.

★ 1781 ★

Software (SIC 7372)

Software Sales by Type

Data show the types of software purchased by PC owners.

Productivity	35.0%
Entertainment	27.0
Educational	17.0
Other	21.0

Source: *Adweek*, August 19, 1996, p. 14, from NPD Group.

★ 1782 ★

Software (SIC 7372)

Storage Management Applications - 1995

Shares are shown based on revenues of $693 million.

Backup	80.0%
Server mirroring	5.4
HSM	4.4
Other	10.2

Source: http:// www.sresearch.com/search/105402.htm, June 10, 1997, p. 1, from 1996 Enterprise Data Management.

★ 1783 ★

Software (SIC 7372)

Supply Chain Software Management Market - 1996

The market was valued at $350 million.

Manugistics	24.0%
12 Technologies	24.0
Numetric	10.0
American Software	5.0
Berclain	4.0
Chesapeake	4.0
Red Pepper Software	4.0
SynQuest	3.0
Other	22.0

Source: *Investor's Business Daily*, April 7, 1997, p. A4, from Advanced Manufacturing Research.

★ 1784 ★

Software (SIC 7372)

Top Budget Software Makers

Unit shares are shown for January 1996. Budget is defined as $20 or less. Figures are based on 9,000 stores, representing over 50% of the retail channel.

Softkey International	16.3%
Expert Software	9.9
Smithalster	9.5
SofSource	4.0
Sierra On-Line	3.5
Electronic Arts	2.8
Lasersoft	2.7
Micro Soft	2.7
WizardWorks	2.6
GT Interactive	2.5
Davidson	2.1
Cosmi	2.0
Digital Systems Research	1.8
Block Financial	1.6
Other	36.0

Source: *Database*, Nov.- Dec. 1996, p. 21, from PC Data.

★ 1785 ★

Software (SIC 7372)

Top CAD/CAM/CAE Resellers - North America

Firms are ranked by 1996 revenues in millions of dollars. The market is expected to exceed $535 million.

Rand Technologies	$ 150
Avcom Group	88
MicroCAD Solutions	60
Visionary Design Systems	40
Professional Control	39
Integrated Systems Tech	35
Workgroup Solutions	34
Strategic Technologies	32
AVCOM Technologies	30
Piedmont CAD/CAM	27

Source: *Electronic Business Today*, September 1996, p. 22, from Daratech Inc.

★ 1786 ★

Software (SIC 7372)

Top CAD/CAM Software Producers - 1996

Parametric Technology
IBM/Dassault
Computervision
SDRC
EDS
Autodesk
Other

Companies are ranked by sales in millions of dollars. "CAD" stands for Computer Aided Design; "CAM" stands for Computer Aided Manufacturing.

	Sales ($ mil.)	Share
Parametric Technology	$ 660.0	18.1%
IBM/Dassault	579.6	15.9
Computervision	290.7	8.0
SDRC	285.3	7.8
EDS	192.2	5.3
Autodesk	189.6	5.2
Other	1,452.6	39.8

Source: *Wall Street Journal*, May 27, 1997, p. B6.

★ 1787 ★

Software (SIC 7372)

Top CD-ROM Categories

Data show shares of total CD-ROM sales.

Suites	11.29%
References	8.52
Presentation	7.42
Images	6.26
Draw	5.75
Role playing	4.54
Maps	3.67
Sports	3.65
Elementary education	3.39
Preschool	3.20
Accounting	2.51
War games	2.21
Other	37.59

Source: *PC Week*, December 9, 1996, p. A14, from G. Meier Inc.

★ 1788 ★

Software (SIC 7372)

Top CD-ROM Sellers - 1996

Data are for the first nine months based on revenues.

Softkey	20.1%
CUC	14.1
Disney	10.8
Broderbund	6.9
Knowledge Adventure	5.8
Softsource	5.2
Microsoft	5.1
Other	32.0

Source: *Business Week*, December 16, 1996, p. 123, from PC Data.

★ 1789 ★

Software (SIC 7372)

Top CD-ROM Titles - 1996

Windows95 upgrade
Myst
Warcraft II
Quicken Deluxe
Duke Nukem 3D

Titles are ranked by units sold at retail. Publishers are shown in parentheses.

Windows95 upgrade (Microsoft)	1,090,693
Myst (Broderbund)	745,423
Warcraft II (CUC Software)	688,307
Quicken Deluxe (Intuit)	543,234
Duke Nukem 3D (GT Interactive)	506,269

Source: *Investor Business Daily*, May 28, 1997, p. A6, from PC Data Inc.

★ 1790 ★

Software (SIC 7372)

Top Publishers of Macintosh-only Software by Unit Shipments

Market shares are shown based on unit shipments of Macintosh-only software in 1996. A total of 7.2 million units were shipped.

CUC Software	15.23%
Learning Co.	10.27
Disney	6.46
Broderbund	6.08
GT Interactive	4.48%
Living Books	2.85
Berkeley	2.84
Intuit	2.18
Adobe	2.04
Maxis	1.97
Other	45.6

Source: *Investor's Business Daily*, April 17, 1997, p. A6, from PC Data Inc.

★ 1791 ★

Software (SIC 7372)

Top Reference CD-ROM Categories

Shares are shown based on unit sales. Figures show the results of a February 1997 survey.

Encyclopedia	24.5%
Travel reference	17.2
Religion	12.3
Medical reference	10.0
Atlases	9.0
Directories	8.8
History reference	4.9
Dictionaries/thesauruses	3.8
Multiple reference	1.9
Sports reference	1.0
Literature	0.3
Business reference	0.1
Other special interest	3.0
All other reference	3.2

Source: *E-Media Professional*, June 1997, p. 28, from SPA and NPD Group.

★ 1792 ★

Software (SIC 7372)

Top Selling Publishers of Macintosh-only Software

Market shares are shown based on retail sales of Macintosh-only software in 1996. Total sales reached $531 million.

CUC Software	10.34%
Learning Co.	8.83
Adobe	7.92
Microsoft	4.94
Broderbund	4.84
Disney	4.34
Quark	3.61

Continued on next page.

★ 1792 ★ *Continued*
Software (SIC 7372)

Top Selling Publishers of Macintosh-only Software

Market shares are shown based on retail sales of Macintosh-only software in 1996. Total sales reached $531 million.

Claris	3.34%
Symantec	3.18
Intuit	2.42
Others	46.24

Source: *Investor's Business Daily*, April 17, 1997, p. A6, from PC Data Inc.

★ 1793 ★
Software (SIC 7372)

Top Selling Server Operating Systems

Brand shares are shown based on 2.65 million server operating systems sold in 1996.

Netware/IntranetWare	37.0%
Windows NT Server	27.0
Unix	23.0
OS/2 Warp Server	13.0

Source: *Informationweek*, April 21, 1997, p. 86, from International Data Corp.

★ 1794 ★
Software (SIC 7372)

Top Software Firms - Canada

Firms are ranked by 1995 worldwide revenues in millions of Canadian dollars.

Corel	270.0
Cognos	168.0
Eicon	74.4
Hummingbird	67.0
Fulcrum	43.0
M3i	21.6
Jetform	20.0
Promis	20.0
Andyne	10.4
Speedware	10.0

Source: *Marketing Magazine*, September 9, 1996, p. 13, from International Data Corp.

★ 1795 ★
Software (SIC 7372)

Top Software Publishers - 1996

	Sales ($ mil.)	Share
Microsoft	$ 931.3	20.3%
CUC	280.9	6.1
Intuit	238.6	5.2
Symantec	191.0	4.2
Broderbund	174.9	3.8
Learning Co. (Softkey)	156.7	3.4
Corel	139.9	3.1
Electronic Arts	121.2	2.6
Adobe	118.2	2.6
GT Interactive	94.0	2.1
Disney	79.0	1.7
Virgin	66.9	1.5

Continued on next page.

★ 1795 ★ *Continued*

Software (SIC 7372)

Top Software Publishers - 1996

	Sales ($ mil.)	Share
Quarterdeck	$ 61.5	1.3%
LucasArts	57.3	1.3
MicroProse	49.4	1.1

Source: *USA TODAY*, February 6, 1997, p. 5D, from PC Data.

★ 1796 ★

Software (SIC 7372)

Utility Software Sales by Platform

Estimated sales are shown in billions of dollars for North America.

Windows 32-bit	$ 70.8
Macintosh	21.5
Windows 16-bit	21.1
PC/MS-DOS	4.1

Source: *Computer Reseller News*, January 20, 1997, p. 97, from Software Publishers Association.

★ 1797 ★

Software (SIC 7372)

Web Browser Market

Data are as of January 1997.

Netscape	70.0%
Microsoft	28.0
Other	2.0

Source: *Wall Street Journal*, January 28, 1997, p. B4, from Zona Research Inc.

★ 1798 ★

Software (SIC 7372)

Web Server Leaders

Netscape	60.0%
Apache	16.0
Microsoft	4.0
NCSA	4.0
Open Market	4.0
Other	10.0

Source: *PC Week*, March 10, 1997, p. A6, from Jupiter Communications.

★ 1799 ★

Software (SIC 7372)

Web Server Market

Data are as of September 1996.

Netscape	75.0%
Microsoft	10.0
Other	15.0

Source: *Wall Street Journal*, January 28, 1997, p. B4, from Zona Research Inc.

★ 1800 ★

Software (SIC 7372)

Word Processing Software Used by Editors

Microsoft Word	59.4%
WordPerfect	29.7
XyWrite	4.0
Other	12.0

Source: *Folio*, October 15, 1996, p. 81.

★ 1801 ★

Software (SIC 7372)

Workflow Market - 1995

Filenet	19.7%
IBM	5.5
DST	4.7
USI	4.4

Continued on next page.

★ 1801 ★ *Continued*

Software (SIC 7372)

Workflow Market - 1995

Wang	4.3%
IA	3.7
ViewStar	3.1
Other	54.7

Source: *Business Communications Review*, July 1996, p. 8, from Delphi Consulting Group.

★ 1802 ★

Integrated Systems (SIC 7373)

Network Sytems Integration Market - 1997

Implementation	51.6%
Management	28.5
Consulting	19.9

Source: *Computer Reseller News*, February 3, 1997, p. 18.

★ 1803 ★

Integrated Systems (SIC 7373)

Top ADC Participants

ADC technology covers all forms of data collection, including printing, inventory management and delivery tracking.

Symbol Technologies	8.1%
Intermec & Norand	7.6
Telxon	6.4
Zebra	2.3
UBI	1.4
PSC	1.1
Eltron	0.9
LXE	0.8
Other	71.4

Source: *Investext,* Thomson Financial Networks, January 29, 1997, p. 6, from Western Atlas.

★ 1804 ★

Networks (SIC 7373)

Client/Server Enterprise Market

Vendor shares are shown based on a $3.5 billion market in 1995.

SAP	32.0%
Oracle	8.0
PeopleSoft	6.0
System Software Associates	6.0
Bean	4.0
Computer Associates	4.0
Other	40.0

Source: *Informationweek*, September 2, 1996, p. 46, from International Data Corp.

★ 1805 ★

Networks (SIC 7373)

Color Printing Leaders

The color server and printer market is shown in percent.

Fiery Color Server	75.0%
Splash	12.0
Other	13.0

Source: *Investor's Business Daily*, January 30, 1997, p. A4.

★ 1806 ★

Networks (SIC 7373)

NT Server Market by Microprocessor

Pentium	76.1%
486	14.6
Alpha	4.9
Pentium Pro	2.4
Other	2.0

Source: *Computer Reseller News*, December 2, 1996, p. 8, from International Data Corp.

★ 1807 ★

Networks (SIC 7373)

PC Server Market - 1996

Data are based on 549,000 units sold for the first six months of 1996.

Compaq	31.0%
Hewlett-Packard	12.0
Acer	5.0
Digital	5.0
Other	33.0

Source: *Informationweek*, October 28, 1996, p. 110, from International Data Corp.

★ 1808 ★

Networks (SIC 7373)

PC Server Software Vendors - Canada

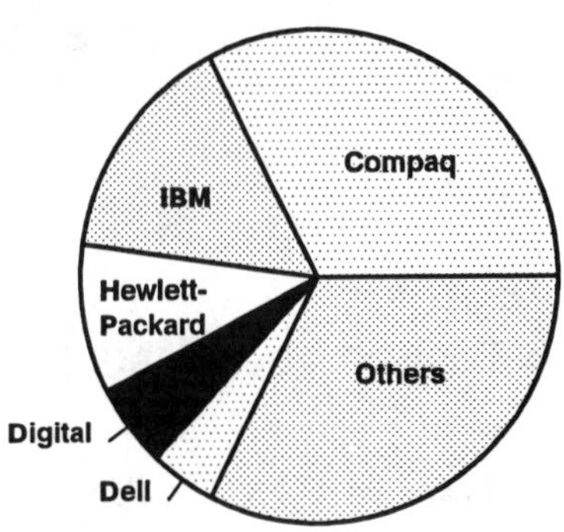

Shares are shown in percent for 1996.

Compaq	30.3%
IBM	14.4
Hewlett-Packard	9.4
Digital	5.3
Dell	4.1
Others	30.3

Source: *Computing Canada*, May 12, 1997, p. 44, from International Data Corp. Canada.

★ 1809 ★

Networks (SIC 7373)

Relational Database Market

Shares of the $2.2 billion market in 1995.

Oracle	44.0%
Sybase	16.9
Informix	15.5
Other	23.5

Source: *Wall Street Journal*, December 2, 1996, p. B4, from company reports, Baseline, Disclosure, and International Data Corp.

★ 1810 ★

Information Technology (SIC 7375)

Electronic Commerce Market by Segment

Data show estimated sales in millions of dollars.

	1996 ($ mil.)	2000 ($ mil.)	Share
Business-to-business	$ 600	$ 66,470	33.9%
Content	5,240	37,280	19.0
Internet access	4,230	33,130	16.9
Infrastructure	4,010	29,510	15.0
Financial services	240	22,580	11.5
Consumer retail	530	7,170	3.7

Source: *PC Week*, November 4, 1996, p. 10, from Forrester Research Inc.

★ 1811 ★

Information Technology (SIC 7375)

Favorite Internet Search Engines

Data show favorite search engines, based on a survey.

Yahoo	45.0%
AltaVista	21.0
Lycos	13.0
HotBot	2.0
Inkitomi	2.0
Other	17.0

Source: *APICS - The Performance Advantage*, November 1996, p. 23.

★ 1812 ★

Information Technology (SIC 7375)

Growth of the Internet by Segment

Data show the Internet market by segment. Figures indicate one-third of the 1.1 million U.S. businesses will be connected to the Internet by 2000. "ISP" stands for internet service provider.

	1996	2000
Content	35.0%	19.0%
ISP Access	28.0	17.0
Infrastructure	27.0	15.0
Business-to-business commerce	4.0	33.0
Retail	4.0	4.0
Financial	2.0	12.0

Source: *PC Week*, May 19, 1997, p. 140, from Forrester Research Inc.

★ 1813 ★

Information Technology (SIC 7375)

How Mexicans Use the Internet

Data show percentage of use.

Research	75.0%
Work	10.0
Socialize	2.0
Play	1.0
Other	12.0

Source: *National Trade Data Bank*, December 10, 1996, p. ISA960301, from Mexican Society of the Internet.

★ 1814 ★

Information Technology (SIC 7375)

How We Use the Web - 1996

Browsing
Entertainment
Education
Work
Business research
Academic research
Shopping

Data are based on a survey of 10,332 respondents.

Browsing	77.0%
Entertainment	64.0
Education	53.0
Work	51.0
Business research	41.0
Academic research	36.0
Shopping	19.0

Source: *Newsweek*, January 27, 1997, p. 34, from Jupiter Communications and Georgia Tech GVU CVenter.

★ 1815 ★

Information Technology (SIC 7375)

Information Techonology Market - 1996

Shares are shown based on a $699.7 billion market.

Information technology services	37.5%
Computers	28.8
Software	14.3
Peripherals	10.1
Telecom equipment	9.3

Source: *PC Week*, April 28, 1997, p. 92, from Dataquest Inc.

★ 1816 ★

Information Technology (SIC 7375)

Internet Hosts by Type of Site

Banks	660
Sex services	451
Credit unions	274
Newspapers	312
U.S. government	47

Source: *Computerworld*, January 6, 1997, p. 3, from Dan Farmer.

★ 1817 ★

Information Technology (SIC 7375)

Internet/Intranet Creation Technology and Services Market - 1996

Market shares are shown in percent.

Page development services	55.0%
Site development services	22.0
Application development	14.0
Development tools	4.0
Authoring tools	3.0
Development languages	1.0
Software developer's kits	1.0

Source: *Infoworld*, April 14, 1997, p. 20, from Zona Research.

★ 1818 ★

Information Technology (SIC 7375)

Internet Services Market

Data show the percentage of revenues by type of service.

	1996	1998	2000
On-line	50.9%	46.6%	46.6%
Internet service provider	40.7	38.4	30.1
Advertising	3.4	9.0	17.1
Host-based	5.0	6.0	6.2

Source: *Computer Reseller News*, January 6, 1997, p. 23, from Frost & Sullivan Inc.

★ 1819 ★

Information Technology (SIC 7375)

Internet Services Market by Segment

	1996	1998	2002
Industry	27.5%	28.7%	31.1%
Business	18.7	19.8	22.0
Government	14.4	13.4	11.4
Commercial	12.1	11.8	11.2
Education	13.5	10.9	7.8
Medical	7.9	7.8	7.7
Other	5.9	5.9	5.7

Source: *Computer Reseller News*, December 2, 1996, p. 19, from Frost & Sullivan.

★ 1820 ★

Information Technology (SIC 7375)

Largest Internet Host Counties

Counties are ranked by the number of Internet hosts as of January 1996.

Santa Clara, CA	554,967
Middlesex, MA	243,765
Los Angeles, CA	159,944
New York, NY	146,371
Fairfax, VA	131,874
Orange, CA	123,685
San Diego, CA	111,981
Cook, IL	110,726
Hennepin, MN	109,047
San Mateo, CA	92,781
Salt Lake, UT	90,693
Alameda, CA	89,851
Washtenaw, MI	82,790
King, WA	79,142
Allegheny, PA	64,616
Philadelphia, PA	62,387
Travis, TX	62,371
Dallas, TX	61,811
Bay, MI	57,726
District of Columbia	55,755

Source: *New York Times*, September 16, 1996, p. C1, from Matrix Information, Directory Services, and Netzwizards Internet Domain via New York University.

★ 1821 ★

Information Technology (SIC 7375)

Leading Internet Service Providers - 1996

Shares are shown based on revenues.

UUnet/MFS	22.0%
MCI	14.0
NetCom	11.0
AT&T	10.0
BBN	10.0
PSInet	8.0
MindSpring	2.0
Other	23.0

Source: *Investor's Business Daily*, June 18, 1997, p. A6, from Zona Reseach Inc.

★ 1822 ★

Information Technology (SIC 7375)

Leading Web Designers

Firms are ranked by 1996 revenues in millions of dollars.

TN Technologies	$ 38.4
Dahlin Smith White	19.0
Strategic Interactive Group	15.0
CKS Group	14.0
Organic Online	10.0

Source: *Adweek*, November 18, 1996, p. 36.

★ 1823 ★

Information Technology (SIC 7375)

On-line Service Companies

America Online
CompuServe
Prodigy
Microsoft Network

Subscribers are shown in millions.

America Online	6.0
CompuServe	5.0
Prodigy	1.2
Microsoft Network	1.0

Source: *Washington Post*, August 9, 1996, p. F2, from Forrester Research Inc.

★ 1824 ★

Information Technology (SIC 7375)

On-line Service Market - 1996

Shares are shown based on revenues.

America Online	39.0%
CompuServe	19.0
Microsoft MSN	9.0
Prodigy	7.0
Other	26.0

Source: *Investor's Business Daily*, June 18, 1997, p. A6, from Zona Reseach Inc.

★ 1825 ★

Information Technology (SIC 7375)

Popular Intranet Applications

Publishing internal information	30.0%
Discussions	16.4
Line-of-business applications	15.9
Collaboration	15.2
Links to partners	9.1
Links to customers	5.9
Electronic commerce	4.5
Other	3.0

Source: *Computerworld*, January 20, 1997, p. 57, from Delphi Computing Group.

★ 1826 ★

Information Technology (SIC 7375)

Preferred On-line Activities

Percentage of on-line service users who do each activity.

E-mail	32.0%
Research	25.0
News/information	22.0
Entertainment	19.0
Education	13.0
Chat-lines/chat rooms	8.0

Source: *Wall Street Journal*, December 9, 1996, p. R5, from Odyssey Ventures Inc.

★ 1827 ★

Information Technology (SIC 7375)

Revenues From the Web

Data show the sources of revenues by source for content providers on the World Wide Web.

	1996	1999
Advertising	43.0%	84.6%
Subscriptions	2.3	8.5
Access providers	54.7	6.9

Source: *Wall Street Journal*, June 17, 1996, p. R25, from Forrester Research Inc.

★ 1828 ★

Information Technology (SIC 7375)

Top Web Publishers

Firms are ranked by revenues in millions of dollars.

Netscape	$ 27.7
Yahoo!	20.6
Infoseek	18.1
Lycos	12.8
Excite	12.2
CNET	11.4
ZDNet	10.2
WebCrawler	7.3
ESPNET SportsZone	6.5
Pathfinder	5.8

Source: *Advertising Age*, March 17, 1997, p. 32, from Jupiter Communications AdSpend.

★ 1829 ★

Information Technology (SIC 7375)

Web Server Spending - 1997

Data are in billions of dollars.

Server software	$ 0.583
Authoring tools	0.330
Browsers	0.312
Shrink wrapped software	0.107
Applets	0.041

Source: *Datamation*, July 1996, p. 16, from Forrester Research Inc.

★ 1830 ★

Information Technology (SIC 7375)

Web Shopping by Sector - 1996

Data are estimated, based on $518 million in on-line spending.

Consumer products	27.0%
Travel	24.3
Adult entertainment	9.9
Apparel	8.9
Gifts/flowers	8.7
Food/drink	7.5
General entertainment	6.5
Other	7.2

Source: *U.S. News & World Report*, August 19, 1996, p. 52, from Forrester Research.

★ 1831 ★

Information Technology (SIC 7375)

What We Shop For On-line

On-line shopping is estimated to have total revenues of $518 million in 1996, $2.37 billion in 1998 and $6.57 billion in 2000.

	1996	1998	2000
Computer products	27.0%	29.6%	32.0%
Travel	24.3	24.1	24.0
Entertainment	16.4	17.7	19.0
Gifts and flowers	8.7	9.4	10.0
Food and drink	7.5	6.3	5.1
Clothes	8.9	6.9	4.9
Other	7.1	6.1	5.0

Source: *Sunday Times*, January 9, 1997, p. 14, from Forrester Research Inc.

★ 1832 ★

Information Technology (SIC 7375)

Who Builds Web Sites

Data are based on a survey of 52 Web masters.

Content creators	55.0%
Programmers	30.0
Webmasters	10.0
Marketers	5.0

Source: *Infoworld*, January 13, 1997, p. 19, from Forrester Research.

★ 1833 ★

Information Technology (SIC 7375)

Who Uses the Web - 2000

By the year 2000, an estimated 25 million adults are expected to use the Web.

Corporate	46.0%
Recreational	27.0
Academic	15.0
Small business	12.0

Source: *Data Communications*, August 1996, p. 20, from Find/SVP Inc.

★ 1834 ★

Computer Services (SIC 7378)

Computer Services Outsourcing - 1996

Shares are estimated.

EDS	40.0%
IBM	25.0
CSC	8.0
Other	27.0

Source: *Investor's Business Daily*, January 13, 1996, p. A6, from Input.

★ 1835 ★

Computer Services (SIC 7379)

What Computer Firms Outsource

Application development
Application maintenance
Mainframe data center
Client/server
Training
Desktop systems
LANs
End-user support
WANs

Data show activities being outsourced, based on a survey of 135 organizations.

Application development	28.0%
Application maintenance	21.0
Mainframe data center	19.0
Client/server	16.0
Training	15.0
Desktop systems	14.0%
LANs	14.0
End-user support	13.0
WANs	13.0

Source: *Computerworld*, September 2, 1996, p. 60.

★ 1836 ★

Security Services (SIC 7382)

Security Equipment Sales by Type - 1996

Shares are shown based on revenues of $13.19 billion.

Burglar alarms	49.2%
Fire detectors	17.9
CCTV	11.4
Access control	9.4
Home systems	5.2
Other	6.9

Source: *Security Distribution & Marketing*, January 1997, p. 66.

★ 1837 ★

Photofinishing (SIC 7384)

Film Processing by Outlet

Shares are shown for the second quarter of 1996.

Discount department store	27.2%
Drugstore/pharmacy	19.4
Supermarket/combination	15.4
Mail order	13.2
Camera store/one hour lab store	10.9
Wholesale club	7.3
Discount drugstore	3.4
Other	3.3

Source: *Photo Marketing*, October 1996, p. 64.

★ 1838 ★

Business Services (SIC 7389)

Check Processing Market

Shares are shown based on prime-pass check volume.

Bank in-house	62.0%
Federal Reserve	26.0
Fiserv	4.4
EDS	4.4
Questpoint	2.8
M&I	1.0

Source: *American Banker*, November 12, 1996, p. 29, from CoreStates.

★ 1839 ★

Business Services (SIC 7389)

Contracted Services in Colleges

Foodservice	74.3%
Vending	65.3
Bookstores	33.7
Custodial/academic buildings	30.7
Laundry	18.6

Source: *AS&U*, September 1996, p. 21.

★ 1840 ★

Business Services (SIC 7389)

Largest Interior Design Firms - Phoenix

Firms are ranked by millions of square feet designed in 1995.

Associates & Architecture & Design Ltd.	2.1
Cornoyer-Hedrick Inc.	2.0
Leo A. Daly Co.	1.8
ADM Group	1.5
HNTB Corp.	1.5

Source: *Business Journal - Serving Phoenix and the Valley of the Sun*, August 9, 1996, p. 29.

★ 1841 ★

Business Services (SIC 7389)

Leading Retail Interior Designers

Firms are ranked by 1996 design fees in millions of dollars.

Pavlik Design Team	$ 23.77
Retail Planning Associates Inc.	17.20
FRCH Design Worldwide	15.50
Design Forum	8.65
Development Design Group Inc.	7.20
Jon Greenberg & Associates Inc.	7.00
Gensler	7.00
Robert Young Associates Inc.	6.80
NBBJ Retail Concepts	6.50
Bergmeyer Associates Inc.	5.60
ELS/Elbasani & Logan Architects	4.50
JPRA Architects	4.30

Source: *VM + SD*, February 1997, p. 66.

★ 1842 ★

Business Services (SIC 7389)

Training Spending - 1996

Training budgets reached $59.8 billion in 1996.

Training staff salaries	71.0%
Facilities/overhead	8.0
Hardware	6.0
Seminars/conference	6.0
Off-the-shelf materials	4.0
Custom materials	3.0
Outside services	3.0

Source: *Training*, October 1996, p. 42.

★ 1843 ★

Conventions (SIC 7389)

Largest Trade Shows - Chicago

Attendance is shown for 1996.

National Restaurant Association	101,000
National Sporting Goods Association	92,744
National Hardware Show	70,000
International Air Conditioning/Heating Expo	61,749
Radiological Society of North America	60,000

Source: *USA TODAY*, August 23, 1996, p. A1, from Chicago Convention and Tourism Bureau and Associated Press.

★ 1844 ★

Mergers & Acquisitions (SIC 7389)

Bank Mergers in California

Data show the number of mergers by size of target.

$0-$150m	17
$150-$500m	7
$500m-$2bn	2
Over $2bn	2

Source: *Financial Times*, February 10, 1997, p. 6, from Sheshunoff.

★ 1845 ★

Mergers & Acquisitions (SIC 7389)

Largest Bank & Thrift Deals

The top deals are ranked by value in millions of dollars. Acquirers are shown in parentheses.

First Interstate Bancorp (Wells Fargo & Co.)	$ 13.70
Chase Manhattan Corp. (Chemical Banking Corp.)	13.28
First Fidelity Bancorp. (First Union Corp.)	6.13
Meridian Bancorp. (CoreStates Financial Corp.)	3.44
Natwest Bank NA (Fleet Financial Group Inc.)	2.70
Integra Financial Corp. (National City Corp.)	2.41
Bay Banks Inc. (Bank of Boston Corp.)	2.30
American Savings Bank (Washington Mutual Inc.)	2.04
First NH Banks (Citizens Financial Group)	1.85
Bank South Corp. (NationsBank Corp.)	1.73

Source: *American Banker*, January 31, 1997, p. 2A, from Sheshunoff International Services Inc.

★ 1846 ★

Mergers & Acquisitions (SIC 7389)

Largest Corporate Acquisitions - 1996

Deals are ranked by value in millions of dollars. Acquirers are shown in parentheses.

NYNEX (Bell Atlantic)	$ 21.34
MCI (British Telecommunications)	21.27
Pacific Telesis (SBC Communications)	16.52
McDonnell Douglas (Boeing)	14.40
MFS Communications (Worldcom)	13.36
Continental Cablevision (US West Media)	11.40
Conrail (Norfolk Southern)	$ 10.50
Conrail (CSX)	9.76
Boatmen's Bancshares (NationsBank)	9.47
US Healthcare (Aetna Life & Casualty)	8.77

Source: *ABA Journal*, March 1997, p. 62, from Securities Data Co.

★ 1847 ★

Mergers & Acquisitions (SIC 7389)

Largest Hotel Buyers

Data show the number of hotel acquisitions by each company.

Host Marriott	9
Starwood	8
Interstone	7
Equistar	4
Felcor	4
HEI Hotels	3

Source: *Real Estate Finance Journal*, Fall 1996, p. 18.

★ 1848 ★

Mergers & Acquisitions (SIC 7389)

Largest Mergers - Canada

Data show the largest mergers in millions of dollars. Acquirers are shown in parentheses.

West Publishing (Thomson)	$ 4,672
Diamond Fields (Inco)	4,500
Laidlaw's solid waste unit (Allied Waste)	2,200
Hemlo Gold (Battle Mountain Gold)	2,048
Viridian (Agrium)	1,300
Arequipa Resources (Barrick Gold)	1,100
Marathon Realty (Oxford Properties & GE Capital)	952
Scott's Hospitality (Laidlaw)	836
Diversey (Unilever Canada)	780
Amerada Hess Canada (Petro-Canada)	731

Source: *Globe and Mail*, January 6, 1997, p. B1.

★ 1849 ★

Mergers & Acquisitions (SIC 7389)

Largest Midwest Bank Mergers

Mergers are ranked by value of transactions in millions of dollars. Acquirers are shown in parentheses.

Boatmen's Bancshares Inc. (NationsBank Corp.)	$ 9,600.0
Homeland Bancshares Corp. (Magna Group Inc.)	216.0
Comerica Bank-Illinois (ABN/AMRO North America)	191.0
Mountain Parks Financial Corp. (Community First Bankshares)	123.0
Texarkana National Bancshares (Hibernia Corp.)	77.0

Source: *Bank News*, September 1996, p. 19.

★ 1850 ★

Mergers & Acquisitions (SIC 7389)

Largest Software Firm Mergers

Value of mergers are shown in millions of dollars. Acquirers are shown in parentheses.

Davidson (CUC)	$ 1,140
Sierra (CUC)	1,060
Learning Company (Softkey)	606
Minnesota Educational Computing (Softkey)	324
Edmark (IBM)	110
Knowledge Adventure (CUC)	90
Humongous (GT)	76

Source: *Business Week*, December 16, 1996, p. 124, from company reports.

★ 1851 ★

Mergers & Acquisitions (SIC 7389)

Largest Utility Mergers

Companies are ranked by size of deal in billions of dollars.

Houston Industries (NorAm Energy)	$ 3.8
Baltimore G&E (Potomac Electric)	3.1
Wisconsin Energy (Northern States)	3.0
Enron (Portland General)	2.1
Atlantic Energy (Delmarva)	2.0
Texas Utilities (Enserch)	1.7
Utilicorp (Kansas City P&L)	1.7

Source: *Christian Science Monitor*, August 15, 1996, p. 6, from Securities Data Co.

★ 1852 ★

Mergers & Acquisitions (SIC 7389)

Leading Oil Mergers - Canada

Mergers are ranked by value in millions of dollars for 1996-97. Acquirers are shown in parentheses.

Clyde Petroleum (Gulf Canada Resources)	$ 972.0
Amerada Hess Canada (Petro Canada)	735.0
Morrison Petroleums (Canadian 88 Energy)	652.0
Sceptre Resources (Canadian Natural Resources)	590.0
Mark Resources (Enerplus Energy Services)	500.0
Morgan Hydrocarbons (Stampeder Explorations)	374.0
Gardiner Oil and Gas (Poco Petroleums)	225.0
Serenpet (Pembina Resources)	110.0

Source: *Globe and Mail*, January 21, 1997, p. B1.

★ 1853 ★

Mergers & Acquisitions (SIC 7389)

Leading U.S. Mergers

Data are in billions of dollars. Acquirers are shown in parentheses.

Nynex (Bell Atlantic)	$ 21.34
MCI (British Telecommunications)	21.27
Pacific Telesis (SBC Communications)	16.52
MFS Communications (WorldCom)	13.56
McDonnell Douglas (Boeing)	13.34

Continued on next page.

★ 1853 ★ *Continued*

Mergers & Acquisitions (SIC 7389)

Leading U.S. Mergers

Data are in billions of dollars. Acquirers are shown in parentheses.

Continental Cablevision (U S West Media)	$ 11.40
Conrail (Norfolk Southern)	10.32
Boatmen's Bancshares (NationsBank)	9.47
U.S. Healthcare (Aetna Life & Casualty)	8.77

Source: *San Francisco Chronicle*, January 2, 1997, p. D1, from Securities Data Co.

★ 1854 ★

Mergers & Acquisitions (SIC 7389)

Mergers by Segment

A total of $658.8 billion in domestic mergers and acquisitions were announced in 1996. Data show by segment.

	($ mil.)	Share
Telecommunications	$ 103.89	15.8%
Electric, gas, water distribution	41.06	6.2
Radio and television broadcasting stations	37.54	5.7
Business services	32.00	4.9
Health services	28.75	4.4
Other	415.56	63.1

Source: *New York Times*, January 2, 1997, p. C3, from Securities Data Co.

★ 1855 ★

Mergers & Acquisitions (SIC 7389)

Mergers in Service Industries

Data are in billions of dollars.

Residential services	$ 45.0
Solid waste	35.0
Eye care	20.0
Motorcoaches	20.0
Funeral homes	15.0
Ambulances	5.0

Source: *Investor's Business Daily*, January 29, 1997, p. A4, from Montgomery Securities.

★ 1856 ★

Mergers & Acquisitions (SIC 7389)

Top Bank Deposit Sales - 1996

Deals are ranked by value of deposits sold in millions of dollars. Acquirers are shown in parentheses.

Household International, Inc. (Harris Bankcorp, Inc.)	$ 2,900.0
First Interstate Bancorp (H.F. Ahmanson & Co.)	2,546.0
C.F.S.B. Corp. (NationsBank Corp.)	1,000.0
BayBanks, Inc. (U.S.T. Corp.)	860.0
Franklin Federal Bancorp, FSB (Norwest Corp.)	550.0
Topa Equities, Ltd. (F.B.O.P. Corp.)	528.0
Meridian Bancorp, Inc. (Commonwealth Savings Bank, M.H.C.)	400.0
Cal Fed Bancorp, Inc. (F.B.O.P. Corp.)	381.3
BankAmerica Corp. (Pacific U.S.A. Holdings Corp.)	330.7
H.F. Ahmanson & Co. (International Bancshares Corp.)	270.0

Source: *Banking Strategies*, March/April 1997, p. 54, from SNL Securities LP.

★ 1857 ★

Mergers & Acquisitions (SIC 7389)

Top Bank Mergers - 1996

Banks are ranked by value of transactions in millions of dollars. Acquirers are shown in parentheses.

First Interstate (Wells Fargo)	$ 14,044
Boatmen's Bancshares (NationsBank)	8,700
California Federal (First Nationwide)	1,200
American Savings (Washington Mutual)	1,200
Fleet Banking (Fleet Financial)	950
United Carolina Bancshares (Southern National)	935
Leader Financial (Union Planters)	505
Center Financial (First Union)	385

Source: *Financial Times*, December 3, 1996, p. 23, from companies.

★ 1858 ★

Mergers & Acquisitions (SIC 7389)

Top M&A's - 1997

The table shows the top announced mergers & acquisitions for the first quarter of 1997. Acquirers are shown in parentheses.

Morgan Stanley Group Inc. (Dean Witter, Discover & Co.)	$ 9.71
U.S. Bancorp (First Bank Systems Inc.)	8.74
First USA Inc. (Banc One Corp.)	7.30
U.S. Robotics Corp. (3Com Corp.)	6.60
Great Western Financial (Washington Mutual)	6.59
ITT Corp. (Hilton Hotels Corp.)	6.40
General Motors Corp. (Raytheon Co.)	4.80
ADT Ltd (Tyco International)	4.10
Cascade Comm. Corp. (Ascend Comm. Inc.)	3.41
Texas Instruments Inc. (Raytheon Co.)	2.95

Source: *Chicago Tribune*, April 2, 1997, p. 3, from Houlihan Lokey's MergerStat.

★ 1859 ★

Mergers & Acquisitions (SIC 7389)

Top M&As in Illinois - 1997

The table shows the top announced mergers & acquisitions for the first quarter of 1997. Acquirers are shown in parentheses.

U.S. Robotics Corp. (3Com Corp.)	$ 6,600
WMX Technologies Inc. (ServiceMaster)	626
Wellsford Res. Property Trust (Equity Res.)	506
Standard Financial Inc. (TCF Financial Corp.)	404
Falcon Bldg. Products Inc. (Investcorp.)	355

Source: *Chicago Tribune*, April 2, 1997, p. 3, from Houlihan Lokey's MergerStat.

★ 1860 ★

Outsourcing (SIC 7389)

Leading Outsourcing Firms - 1996

Fiserv
Alltel
EDS
M&I

Firms are ranked by number of major contracts signed.

	No.	Share
Fiserv	38	42.7%
Alltel	18	20.2
EDS	18	20.2
M&I	15	16.9

Source: *Banking Strategies*, May/June 1997, p. 59, from Computer Based Solutions.

★ 1861 ★

Training (SIC 7389)

How Training Revenues Are Put to Use

Information service spending is shown in billions of dollars. The industry is valued at $60 billion.

	($ bil.)	Share
Training salaries	$ 42.3	70.5%
Overhead	4.6	7.7
Seminars/conferences	3.7	6.2
Hardware	3.6	6.0
Off-the-shelf training	2.2	3.7
Custom materials	1.9	3.2
Outside services	1.7	2.8

Source: *Computerworld*, May 26, 1997, p. 47, from Lakewood Research.

SIC 75 - Auto Repair, Services, and Parking

★ 1862 ★

Auto Rental (SIC 7514)

Auto Rental Leaders by Outlets

Companies are ranked by number of locations in 1996.

Enterprise	2,636
Hertz	1,200
Avis	1,130
Budget	1,052
National	935
Alamo	171

Source: *USA TODAY*, January 13, 1997, p. B7, from *Auto Rental News*.

★ 1863 ★

Auto Rental (SIC 7514)

Largest Auto Rental Firms

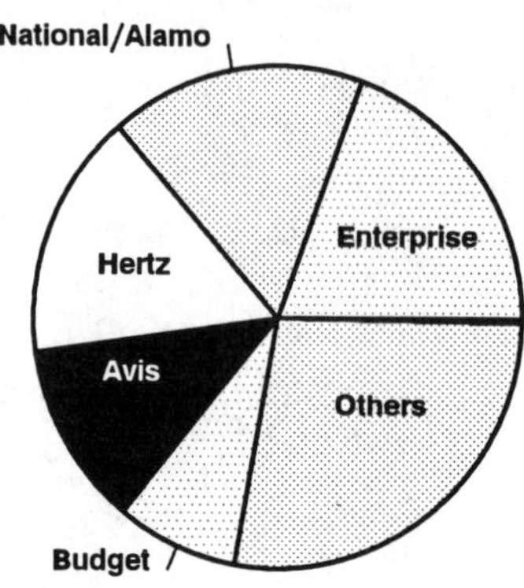

Data show averages size of fleet in 1996. Figures include franchises.

	(000)	Share
Enterprise	315.1	19.8%
National/Alamo	265.0	16.7
Hertz	250.0	15.7
Avis	190.0	12.0
Budget	126.0	7.9
Others	442.1	27.8

Source: *New York Times*, January 7, 1997, p. C1, from *Auto Rental News*.

★ 1864 ★

Auto Rental (SIC 7514)

Top Car Rental Airports

Airports are ranked by car rental revenues in millions of dollars.

Orlando, FL	$ 344.6
Los Angeles, CA	320.6
Miami, FL	265.7
San Francisco, CA	257.3
Dallas/Fort Worth, TX	239.6

Source: *USA TODAY*, June 16, 1997, p. B1, from *Auto Rental News*.

★ 1865 ★

Auto Rental (SIC 7514)

U.S. Rental Car Market - 1996

Hertz
Avis
Alamo
National
Budget
Enterprise
Dollar
Thrifty
Others

Shares are shown based on leisure and business rentals from July 1, 1995 - June 30, 1996.

Hertz	26.0%
Avis	21.0
Alamo	13.0
National	13.0
Budget	11.0
Enterprise	5.0
Dollar	4.0
Thrifty	2.0
Others	5.0

Source: *USA TODAY*, November 8, 1996, p. B3, from D.K. Shifflet.

★ 1866 ★

Auto Repair Services (SIC 7530)

Automotive Repair Market

	($ bil.)	Share
Light vehicle parts	$ 68.0	53.1%
Labor charges	33.0	25.8
Heavy-duty truck parts	27.0	21.1

Source: *Automotive Marketing*, November 1996, p. 43, from Lang Marketing Resources.

★ 1867 ★

Auto Repair Services (SIC 7530)

Collision Repair Market

Data are shown in billions of dollars.

Insurance paid claims	$ 20.3
Customer paid claims	2.6
OE paint warranty	0.3

Source: *Auto Body Repair News*, March 1997, p. 20, from Collision Repair Industry: INSIGHT.

★ 1868 ★

Auto Repair Services (SIC 7530)

Service Plan Shares

Market shares of extended service plan contracts are shown for 1996.

Factory-backed contracts	60.0%
Independent contracts	40.0

Source: *Automotive News*, August 12, 1996, p. 32i, from Association of Finance and Insurance Professionals.

★ 1869 ★

Auto Repair Services (SIC 7530)

Vehicle Aftermarket - 1995

The market reached $127.9 billion.

Truck products	33.7%
Car products	32.6
Purchased service	25.9
Other products	7.8

Source: *Aftermarket Business*, August 1, 1996, p. 1, from Lang Marketing.

★ 1870 ★

Auto Repair Services (SIC 7532)

Body Repair Product Sales by Type of Chain

Distribution is shown in percent.

Automotive chains	76.0%
Discount store chains	15.0
Department store chains	6.0
Non-automotive chains	3.0

Source: *Aftermarket Business*, May 1, 1997, p. 50.

★ 1871 ★

Tire Retreading (SIC 7534)

Largest Off-the-Road Retreaders

The largest firms in North America are ranked by millions of pounds of rubber consumed in 1995.

Brad Ragan Inc.	8.00
NRI Inc.	7.25
Fletcher's Cobre Tire	5.00
Purcell Tire & Rubber Co.	4.85
B.R. Retreading	4.20
Shrader's Inc.	3.30
RDH Tire & Retread Co.	2.40
Goodyear	2.23
H&H Retreading Inc.	1.50
Bridgestone/Firestone Canada Inc.	1.40

Source: *Tire Business*, December 9, 1996, p. 22.

★ 1872 ★

Tire Retreading (SIC 7534)

Largest Passenger/Light Truck Retreaders

The largest firms in North America are ranked by millions of pounds of rubber consumed in 1995.

Les Schwab Tire Centers Inc.	4.90
Achievor Tire L.P.	2.50
Ray Carr Tires Inc.	1.30
White's Tire Service of Wilson Inc.	1.03
C&J Tire Service Inc.	0.92
Goodyear	0.66
Becker Tire & Retreading	0.62

Source: *Tire Business*, December 9, 1996, p. 22.

★ 1873 ★

Tire Retreading (SIC 7534)

Largest Tire Retreaders

The largest firms in North America are ranked by millions of pounds of rubber consumed in 1995. Shares are shown based on consumption by the top 25 firms.

	(mil.)	Share
Goodyear	28.30	19.2%
Treadco Inc.	15.20	10.3
Tire Centers Inc.	8.70	5.9
Southern Tire Mart Inc.	7.30	4.9
Brad Ragan Inc.	6.00	4.1
GCR Truck Tire Centers	5.95	4.0
Purcell Tire & Rubber Co.	5.90	4.0
New Holland Tire Co. Inc.	5.66	3.8
Les Schwab Tire Centers Inc.	5.56	3.8
Pomp's Tire Service Inc.	5.19	3.5
Other	53.74	36.4

Source: *Tire Business*, December 9, 1996, p. 22.

★ 1874 ★

Auto Repair Services (SIC 7538)

Brake Installations by Type

Semimetallic	69.0%
Non-asbestos	23.0
Asbestos	8.0

Source: *Brake & Front End*, June 1996, p. 44.

★ 1875 ★

Auto Repair Services (SIC 7538)

Engine Treatment Product Sales by Type of Chain

Distribution is shown in percent.

Automotive chains	49.0%
Discount store chains	46.0
Non-automotive chains	4.0
Department store chains	1.0

Source: *Aftermarket Business*, May 1, 1997, p. 40.

★ 1876 ★

Auto Repair Services (SIC 7538)

Largest Auto Repair Providers

Chains are ranked by number of service bays.

Pep Boys	4,735
Western Auto	2,119
Super Shops	425
Grand Auto	379
WSR Corp.	341
Tire Warehouse Central	200
Gillman Auto Parts	150
VIP Discount Auto Central	150
All-Car Distributors	135
Big Wheel/Rossi Auto	44

Source: *Automotive Marketing*, July 1996, p. 38.

★ 1877 ★

Carwashes (SIC 7542)

Top Conveyor Car Wash Operators - North America

Companies are ranked by number of outlets.

Petro-Canada	152
Shell Oil Company	96
Imperial Oil Company	46
Prowash/Unocal	39
Sunoco Canada	29
White Glove	29
Ultramar Canada	28
British Petroleum	26
Octopus Car Wash	26
Delta Sonic Car Wash	21
Auto Bell Car Wash	19
Brown Bear Car Wash/Tosco	19
Calibur Carwash/United Petro	17
American Auto Wash	14
Beacon Bay Enterprises	14
Lage Car Washes	14
Regal Auto Wash	14
Turtle Wax	14
Golden Nozzle	13
Mike's Car Wash	13
Terrible Herbst Oil Company	13
Weiss Guys Car Wash	13
Hoffman's Car Wash	12
Kaady Car Wash	12
Sonny's	12

Source: *Auto Laundry News*, April 1997, p. 40, from Power Inc.

SIC 76 - Miscellaneous Repair Services

★ 1878 ★

Maintenance Services (SIC 7699)

Crane Maintenance Providers

Market shares are shown in percent.

Harnishfeger	6.0%
KCI	5.0
Hoist and Crane Service	1.0
Whiting	1.0
Local service companies	13.0
In-house maintenance	74.0

Source: *Investext,* Thomson Financial Networks, June 14, 1996, p. 9, from KCI.

SIC 78 - Motion Pictures

★ 1879 ★

Infomercials (SIC 7812)

Leading Infomercial Categories

Product sales generated by infomercials are shown by category.

Fitness, health, beauty, diet	47.1%
900 number services	12.3
Business opportunities	12.1
Housewares	12.0
Self improvement	7.0
Entertainment	5.0
Hobbies and crafts	2.6
Automotive	2.0

Source: *U.S. News & World Report*, September 9, 1996, p. 44, from AIMA International.

★ 1880 ★

Infomercials (SIC 7812)

Leading Infomercial Products

Ab products

Psychic Friends Network

Power Rider

Health Rider

Tony Robbins Personal Power

The top categories on TV infomercials are ranked by sales for the first nine months of 1996. Ab products figure represents sales of entire category. Tony Robbins Personal Power are motivational tapes. Figures are in millions of dollars.

Ab products	$ 150.0
Psychic Friends Network	70.0
Power Rider	50.0
Health Rider	35.0
Tony Robbins Personal Power	15.0

Source: *USA TODAY*, October 22, 1996, p. 2D, from *Infomercial Marketing Report*.

★ 1881 ★

Motion Pictures (SIC 7812)

Studios that Made the Most Films in 1995

Shares are shown based on the number of films made as a percent of the total made by major studios. Major studios accounted for 41.4% of the 382 films produced by the industry as a whole.

Buena Vista	20.9%
Columbia/TriStar/Sony	17.7
Warner Bros.	15.2
Universal	11.4
MGM/UA	10.1
Paramount	8.9
20th Century Fox	7.0
New Line	7.0
Orion	1.9

Source: *Investext*, Thomson Financial Networks, December 5, 1996, p. 17, from *Encyclopedia of Exhibition*.

★ 1882 ★

Motion Pictures (SIC 7812)

Studios with the Most Box Office Receipts in 1995

Data show box office receipts in millions of dollars and studio shares as a percent of receipts earned by major studios. Major studios accounted for 90.3% of the receipts earned by the industry as a whole.

	($ mil.)	Share
Buena Vista	$ 1,131.4	22.8%
Warner Bros.	895.4	18.0
Universal	729.1	14.7
Columbia/TriStar/Sony	662.8	13.4
Paramount	469.3	9.5
20th Century Fox	417.8	8.4
MGM/UA	372.1	7.5

Continued on next page.

★ 1882 ★ *Continued*

Motion Pictures (SIC 7812)

Studios with the Most Box Office Receipts in 1995

Data show box office receipts in millions of dollars and studio shares as a percent of receipts earned by major studios. Major studios accounted for 90.3% of the receipts earned by the industry as a whole.

	($ mil.)	Share
New Line	$ 280.2	5.6%
Orion	4.0	0.1

Source: *Investext*, Thomson Financial Networks, December 5, 1996, p. 17, from *Encyclopedia of Exhibition*.

★ 1883 ★

Motion Pictures (SIC 7812)

Top Film Studios

Market shares are shown for the first nine months of 1996.

Buena Vista	21.2%
Warner Bros.	15.9
20th Century Fox	13.6
Universal	10.6
Paramount	10.3
Sony	9.4
MGM/UA	7.0
Miramax	3.9
New Line	3.4
Gramercy	1.9
Other	2.8

Source: *Entertainment Weekly*, September 8, 1996, p. 25, from Entertainment Data Inc.

★ 1884 ★

Motion Pictures (SIC 7812)

Top Films - 1996

Films are ranked by box office receipts in millions of dollars.

Film	($ mil.)
Independence Day	$ 306
Twister	242
Mission: Impossible	181
The Rock	134
The Nutty Professor	129
Ransom	129
The Birdcage	124
101 Dalmations	$ 122
A Time to Kill	109
GoldenEye	106

Source: *Financial Times*, May 19, 1997, p. 15, from Veronis, Suhler & Associates, Wilkofsky Gruen Associates, and Paul Kagan Associates.

★ 1885 ★

Motion Pictures (SIC 7812)

Top Horror Films

Pet Semetary

Nightmare on Elm Street IV

Halloween

Nightmare on Elm Street III

Friday the 13th

Data show the top grossing horror films of all time. Figures are in millions of dollars.

Film	($ mil.)
Pet Semetary	$ 57.5
Nightmare on Elm Street IV	49.4
Halloween	47.0
Nightmare on Elm Street III	44.1
Friday the 13th	39.8

Source: *Entertainment Weekly*, January 13, 1997, p. 8, from Exhibitor Relations.

★ 1886 ★

Motion Pictures (SIC 7812)

Top Re-Releases

Figures are in millions of dollars. Data include the year of re-release.

Film	($ mil.)
Star Wars (1997)	$ 125.0
Gone With the Wind (1967)	70.6
101 Dalmations (1991)	60.8
Snow White and the Seven Dwarfs (1987)	46.6
The Jungle Book (1990)	44.6
Star Wars (1978)	43.8
Snow White and the Seven Dwarfs (1993)	41.6
E.T.: The Extra-Terrestrial (1985)	40.3
The Empire Strikes Back (1997)	39.7
Bambi (1988)	39.0

Source: *USA TODAY*, March 3, 1997, p. D1, from Exhibitor Relations Inc.

★ 1887 ★

Motion Pictures (SIC 7812)

Video Production Firms - Denver

Firms are ranked by 1995 revenues in millions of dollars.

Colorado Production Group	$ 2.00
Lumivision Corp.	1.56
Update Productions	0.75
Communi Creations Inc.	0.44
Transtar Productions Inc.	0.31
Audio Video Services	0.30
Video Engagements	0.21

Source: *Denver Business Journal*, June 28, 1996, p. A18.

★ 1888 ★

Motion Pictures (SIC 7812)

Video Sales Leaders

Shares are shown for the top three companies in 1995. Universal Studios Home Video was formerly known as MCA Home Video.

Disney	34.2%
Warner Home Video	14.7
Universal Studios Home Video	11.4
Others	39.7

Source: *Marketing Magazine*, January 6, 1997, p. 7, from Adams Media Research.

★ 1889 ★

Television Production (SIC 7812)

Film Funding in Canada

Data show the thousands of dollars in funding for television and film production in Canada.

SODEC	$ 46,000
Ontario Film Development Corp.	11,500
British Columbia Film	3,000
Alberta Motion Picture Development Corp.	1,000
SaskFILM	1,000
Nova Scotia Film Development Corp.	950
Manitoba Film & Sound Development Corp.	876

Source: *Variety*, September 2, 1996, p. 50.

★ 1890 ★

Television Production (SIC 7812)

Leading Kids Series

Power-Zeo
Aladdin
Bobby's World
Batman & Robin
Timon & Pumbaa
Gargoyles
VR Troopers
Bonkers

Data show the audience share of the leading animated series for children between 2-11 years of age. Shares are for the broadcast time period. Some shows are broadcast daily in the morning or afternoon; some are weekly shows.

Power-Zeo	7.1%
Aladdin	5.1
Bobby's World	4.6
Batman & Robin	4.5
Timon & Pumbaa	4.1
Gargoyles	4.0
VR Troopers	3.8
Bonkers	3.7

Source: *Broadcasting & Cable*, August 12, 1996, p. 31, from Nielsen NSI ratings.

★ 1891 ★

Film Distribution (SIC 7822)

Leading Film Distributors - 1996

Shares refer to U.S. and Canada box office revenues from the period January 1, 1996 - January 1, 1997.

Buena Vista	21.0%
Warner Bros.	15.7
20th Century Fox	12.9
Paramount	12.7
Sony	10.5
Universal	8.3
New Line	5.2
MGM/UA	5.0
Miramax	4.5
Gramercy	1.4
Other	2.8

Source: *Hollywood Reporter*, January 7, 1997, p. 118.

★ 1892 ★

Film Distribution (SIC 7822)

Top Film Distributors - 1997

Shares are shown based on domestic box office earnings from January 6 - April 13, 1997.

Sony	20.6%
Fox	17.5
Universal	13.0
Buena Vista	12.6
Paramount	9.5
Miramax	9.0
New Line	7.8
Warner Bros.	6.0
MGM/UA	1.2
Other	2.8

Source: *Los Angeles Business Journal*, May 21, 1997, p. 1, from Entertainment Data Inc.

★ 1893 ★

Movie Theaters (SIC 7832)

Largest Movie Theaters

Data show number of screens.

Carmike Cinemas	2,518
AMC Entertainment	1,936
Cineplex Odeon	1,551
Regal Cinemas	1,287
GC Companies	1,159

Source: *Forbes*, February 24, 1997, p. 52, from Standard & Poor's and company reports.

★ 1894 ★

Movie Theaters (SIC 7832)

Movie Theaters - Milwaukee

Facilities are ranked by seat capacity.

South Shore Cinemas	3,200
Westown Cinemas	2,899
Northtown Cinemas	2,821
North Shore Cinemas	2,581
Southtown 1-2-3-4-5-6	2,576
Mill Road Theaters	2,500
Northridge Movies 1-2-3-4-5-6	2,500
Ridge Cinemas	2,250
West Point Cinemas	2,190
Capitol Cinemas 12	2,155

Source: *Business Journal Serving Greater Milwaukee*, November 30, 1996, p. 17.

★ 1895 ★

Movie Theaters (SIC 7832)

Top Movie Theater Operators

Carmike Cinemas Inc.
United Artists Theater
AMC Entertainment
Cineplex Odeon
Cinemark USA
General Cinemas
National Amusements
Regal Cinemas
Sony
Act III
Other

Carmike Cinemas Inc.	9.3%
United Artists Theater	8.9
AMC Entertainment	6.3
Cineplex Odeon	5.6
Cinemark USA	5.0
General Cinemas	4.5
National Amusements	3.8
Regal Cinemas	3.7
Sony	3.3
Act III	2.6
Other	47.0

Source: *Investext*, Thomson Financial Networks, June 5, 1996, p. 2.

★ 1896 ★

Video Tape Rental (SIC 7841)

Home Video Market - 1996

Consumer expenditures are shown in billions of dollars.

	($ bil.)	Share
Rentals	$ 9.2	55.8%
Purchases	7.3	44.2

Source: *Wall Street Journal*, January 17, 1997, p. B1, from Adams Media Research.

★ 1897 ★

Video Tape Rental (SIC 7841)

Leading Video Retailers - 1996

Market shares are shown based on percentage of total rental dollars.

Blockbuster	24.5%
Hollywood Video	2.7
Movie Gallery	2.4
West Coast Entertainment	2.0
Other	68.4

Source: *USA TODAY*, May 8, 1997, p. 2B, from Adams Media Research.

★ 1898 ★

Video Tape Rental (SIC 7841)

Top Video Rental Chains - Canada

Company shares are shown in percent. Jumbo is owned by West Coast Video. The rest of the market is comprised of regional companies with significant presence in their individual markets. Players include Video Update of Vancouver, Videotron of Montreal and Ambassador Video of Ontario. The industry generated sales of $2.0 billion.

Blockbuster Video Canada Inc.	11.0%
Rogers Video	9.0
Jumbo	4.0
Independents	70.0
Other	6.0

Source: *Marketing Magazine*, April 21, 1997, p. 2.

★ 1899 ★

Video Tape Rental (SIC 7841)

Top Video Rentals - 1996

Data show rental revenues in millions of dollars.

Braveheart	$ 54.0
Seven	53.3
The Net	43.0
Twister	41.0
Nutty Professor	39.0
Ace Ventura 2	38.6
Jumanji	$ 38.3
Under Siege 2	36.9
Get Shorty	36.4
Executive Decision	36.0

Source: *Hollywood Reporter*, January 7, 1997, p. 1, from VidTrac/Video Software Dealers Association.

★ 1900 ★

Video Tape Rental (SIC 7841)

Video Sell-Thru Leaders

Market shares are shown in percent. Data are as of October 1996.

Blockbuster Video	34.8%
Tower Rec./Video	4.6
Hollywood Video	3.5
Movie Gallery	2.7
West Coast Video	2.5
Moovies Inc.	0.8
Easy Video	0.4
Roadrunner Video	0.4
Video Update	0.4
Family Video	0.3
Movie Warehouse	0.3
Mr. Movies Inc.	0.3
Pick-A-Flick	0.3
Movies Plus	0.2
Other	48.5

Source: *Investext*, Thomson Financial Networks, December 5, 1996, p. 5, from *Video Store Magazine*, VSDA, Paul Kagen Associates, and company reports.

★ 1901 ★

Video Tape Rental (SIC 7841)

Video Tape Rental Leaders

Companies are ranked by video tape rentals in millions of dollars. Data are as of October 1996.

	Rentals ($ mil.)	Share
Blockbuster Video	$ 2,198	25.7%
Hollywood Video	255	3.0
Movie Gallery	252	2.9
West Coast Video	196	2.3
Video Update	87	1.0
Moovies Inc.	73	0.9
Tower Rec./Video	21	0.2
Family Video	20	0.2

Continued on next page.

★ 1901 ★ *Continued*

Video Tape Rental (SIC 7841)

Video Tape Rental Leaders

Companies are ranked by video tape rentals in millions of dollars. Data are as of October 1996.

	Rentals ($ mil.)	Share
Mr. Movies Inc.	$ 18	0.2%
Pick-A-Flick	17	0.2
Roadrunner Video	17	0.2
Movie Warehouse	16	0.2
Easy Video	15	0.2

Source: *Investext,* Thomson Financial Networks, December 5, 1996, p. 5, from *Video Store Magazine*, VSDA, Paul Kagen Associates, and company reports.

★ 1902 ★

Video Tape Rental (SIC 7841)

Video Tape Rental Market - Canada

Shares are shown for the month of March 1996. Total rental volume for teh first quarter reached 97.5 million cassettes.

Blockbuster	12.8%
Jumbo Video	5.4
Rogers Video	4.3
Super Club Videotron	3.0
Videoflicks	1.5
Other	73.0

Source: *Bizlink. Maclean Hunter Business Magazines Online*, March 24, 1997, p. 1.

★ 1903 ★

Video Tape Rental (SIC 7841)

Video Tape Rental Market by Outlets

Data show the number of stores as of October 1996.

	No.	Share
Blockbuster Video	3,348	12.2%
Movie Gallery	969	3.5
West Coast Video	545	2.0
Hollywood Video	453	1.7
Video Update	265	1.0
Moovies Inc.	204	0.7
Tower Rec./Video	103	0.4
Family Video	86	0.3
Movie Warehouse	70	0.3
Mr. Movies Inc.	68	0.2%
Easy Video	47	0.2

Source: *Investext,* Thomson Financial Networks, December 5, 1996, p. 5, from *Video Store Magazine*, VSDA, Paul Kagen Associates, and company reports.

★ 1904 ★

Arts Groups (SIC 7922)

Who Has the Most Arts Groups

Data show the cities with the most performing arts groups.

New York City	153
Los Angeles	53
San Francisco	51
Chicago	48
Washington D.C.	35

Source: *Fortune*, November 11, 1996, p. 138.

★ 1905 ★

Theatrical Entertainment (SIC 7922)

Leading Concert Facilities

Facilities are ranked by ticket grosses in millions of dollars. Data refer to locations with a capacity of 10,001 - 15,000 people.

The Mark of the Quad	$ 3.06
Centrum Worchester	2.99
Ervin J. Nutter Center	1.91
Brisbane Entertainment Center	1.83
Tingley Coliseum	1.44

Source: *Amusement Business*, September 9, 1996, p. 35, from Amusement Business Boxscore.

★ 1906 ★

Theatrical Entertainment (SIC 7922)

Leading Concert Promoters - 1996

Promoters are ranked by gross revenues.

PACE Concerts	$ 42,033,740
Cellar Door	41,008,265
Delsener/Slater Ent.	35,185,245
MCA Concerts	31,620,129
Jam Prods/MAI/Tinley Park Jam Corp.	29,408,026
Belkin Prods.	24,664,023
Varnell Enterprises	24,431,499
Contemporary Prods.	17,215,955
Udo Artists	16,843,137
Bill Graham Presents	16,236,543

Source: *Amusement Business*, September 15, 1996, p. 44, from Amusement Business Boxscore.

★ 1907 ★

Theatrical Entertainment (SIC 7922)

Longest Running Musicals

Data show the number of performances as of December 29, 1996. The longest running plays on Broadway include Master Class, with 423 performances and An Ideal Husband with 272 performances. Musicals account for approximately 80% of Broadway's box office. An estimated 60% of Broadway's audience comes from outside the New York area; the share of foreign tourists has increased to 15%. The 1996-97 season is expected to be the highest grossing ever, with receipts of more than $470 million.

Cats	5,941
Les Miserables	4,026
The Phantom of the Opera	3,726
Miss Saigon	2,380

Source: *New York Times*, January 9, 1997, p. B8, from *Variety*.

★ 1908 ★

Theatrical Entertainment (SIC 7922)

Popular Theaters - Chicago

Data show attendance in 1995.

Auditorium Theater	250,000
Goodman Theater	226,628
Steppenwolf Theater Company	128,894

Source: *Crain's Chicago Business*, July 1996, p. F38, from Chicago Department of Tourism and Museum of Contemporary Art and Auditorium Theater.

★ 1909 ★

Theatrical Entertainment (SIC 7922)

Ticket Sales at Regional Theaters

Data show ticket sales in thousands of units for 1996-97.

Seattle Repertory	20.6
Guthrie Theater	17.8
Arena Stage	15.9
Long Wharf Theater	10.8

Source: *New York Times*, February 27, 1997, p. B1.

★ 1910 ★

Theatrical Entertainment (SIC 7922)

Top Touring Shows - 1996

Shows are ranked by gross sales in millions of dollars for the first six months of 1996.

Phantom of the Opera	10.7
Jesus Christ Superstar	8.1
Ringling Brothers and Barnum & Bailey Circus	5.5
Miss Saigon	5.0
West Side Story	2.8

Source: *USA TODAY*, October 18, 1996, p. D1, from *Performance*.

★ 1911 ★

Entertainers (SIC 7929)

Leading Concert Entertainers - 1996

Kiss
Garth Brooks
Neil Diamond
Rod Stewart
Bob Seger
Jimmy Buffett
Reba McEntire
Alanis Morissette
Hootie & the Blowfish
Ozzy Osbourne

Entertainers are ranked by gross revenues in millions of dollars.

Kiss	$ 43.9
Garth Brooks	34.5
Neil Diamond	32.2
Rod Stewart	29.1
Bob Seger	26.3
Jimmy Buffett	26.2
Reba McEntire	26.1
Alanis Morissette	23.2
Hootie & the Blowfish	21.4
Ozzy Osbourne	21.3

Source: *Detroit Free Press*, December 26, 1996, p. 14A, from Associated Press.

★ 1912 ★

Entertainers (SIC 7929)

Leading Entertainers - 1996

The top entertainers are ranked by 1995-96 incomes in millions of dollars.

Oprah Winfrey	$ 171.0
Steven Spielberg	150.0
Beatles	130.0
Michael Jackson	90.0
Rolling Stones	77.0
Eagles	75.0
Arnold Schwarznegger	74.0
David Copperfield	74.0
Jim Carrey	63.0
Michael Crichton	59.0
Jerry Seinfeld	59.0
Stephen King	56.0

Continued on next page.

★ 1912 ★ *Continued*

Entertainers (SIC 7929)

Leading Entertainers - 1996

The top entertainers are ranked by 1995-96 incomes in millions of dollars.

Garth Brooks	$ 51.0
Andrew Lloyd Webber	50.0
Tom Hanks	50.0
Siegfried & Roy	48.0
Tom Cruise	46.0
Harrison Ford	44.0
Clint Eastwood	44.0
R.E.M.	44.0

Source: *Forbes*, September 23, 1996, p. 165.

★ 1913 ★

Entertainers (SIC 7929)

Top California Concerts - 1996

Data show attendance capacity.

Tibetan Freedom Concert	100,000
Kiss	40,919
Lolapalooza '96	30,616
Kenny G	22,270

Source: *Amusement Business*, February 17, 1997, p. 13.

★ 1914 ★

Entertainers (SIC 7929)

Top Earners - Classical Music

Data show the earnings of the leading performers for the 1995-96 season. Figures are in millions of dollars.

Luciano Pavarotti	$ 18.0
Jose Carreras	10.0
Placido Domingo	10.0
Zubin Mehta	6.0
Itzhak Perlman	5.5
Lorin Maazel	4.5
Daniel Barenbolm	3.0
Vladimir Ashkenazy	2.7
Anne-Sophie Mutter	2.5
Claudio Abbado	2.5

Source: *New York Times*, September 29, 1996, p. C1, from *When the Music Stops*.

★ 1915 ★

Entertainers (SIC 7929)

Top Entertainers - Country Music

Performers are ranked by gross concert receipts.

Garth Brooks	$ 24,507,213
Reba McEntire	18,288,132
George Strait	11,094,137
Alan Jackson	8,879,314
Tim McGraw	7,138,836
Vince Gill	5,922,812
Brooks & Dunn	5,444,451
John Michael Montgomery	3,435,020
Dwight Yoakam	3,225,636
Alabama	2,493,649
Hank Williams Jr.	2,139,758

Source: *Amusement Business*, October 6, 1996, p. 18.

★ 1916 ★

Entertainers (SIC 7929)

Top Grossing Tours of All Time - North America

The top tours are ranked by gross revenues in millions of dollars.

Rolling Stones, 1994	$ 121.2
Pink Floyd, 1994	103.5
Rolling Stones, 1989	98.0
Eagles, 1994	79.4
New Kids On the Block, 1990	74.1
U2, 1992	67.0
Eagles, 1995	63.3
Barbara Streisand, 1994	58.9
Grateful Dead, 1994	52.4
Elton John and Billy Joel, 1994	47.8

Source: *Financial Times*, April 21, 1997, p. 18.

★ 1917 ★

Entertainers (SIC 7929)

Top Touring Acts by Attendance - 1996

Acts are ranked by attendance.

Garth Brooks	1,843,328
Eagles	1,061,321
KISS	1,011,701
Bob Seger	923,829
Alanis Morissette	873,855

Continued on next page.

★ 1917 ★ *Continued*

Entertainers (SIC 7929)

Top Touring Acts by Attendance - 1996

Acts are ranked by attendance.

Neil Diamond	847,655
Reba McEntire	835,042
Ozzy Osbourne	767,916
Jimmy Buffett	621,306
Rod Stewart	599,495

Source: *Brandweek*, February 24, 1997, p. 24, from Amusement Business Boxscore.

★ 1918 ★

Sports (SIC 7941)

American League Baseball Attendance

Data show attendance in 1996 in millions of people.

Baltimore Orioles	3.6
Cleveland Indians	3.3
Texas Rangers	2.9
Seattle Mariners	2.7
Toronto Blue Jays	2.6
Boston Red Sox	2.3
New York Yankees	2.2
California Angels	1.8
Chicago White Sox	1.7
Minnesota Twins	1.4

Source: *Amusement Business*, October 14, 1996, p. 22, from Major League Baseball.

★ 1919 ★

Sports (SIC 7941)

Licensed Merchandise Sales

Retail sales are shown in the United States and Canada in billions of dollars.

NFL	$ 2.7
NBA	2.6
College	2.5
MLB	1.9
NHL	1.0

Source: *Sportstyle*, January 1997, p. 4, from National Sporting Goods Association.

★ 1920 ★

Sports (SIC 7941)

Sports Merchandise Sales

Sales are shown in billions of dollars.

NFL	$ 3.15
NBA	2.65
MLB	1.85
CLC	1.75
NHL	1.00

Source: *Women's Wear Daily*, October 17, 1996, p. 11, from Sporting Goods Manufacturers Association.

★ 1921 ★

Sports (SIC 7941)

Top Professional Sports Leagues by Attendance

Data show attendance for the 1995 - 1996 seasons.

Major League Baseball	60,097,381
National Basketball Association	20,513,218
National Hockey League	17,041,614
National Football League	15,043,562

Source: *Amusement Business*, December 16, 1996, p. 57, from MLB, NBA, NFL and NHL.

★ 1922 ★

Sports Promotion (SIC 7941)

Top Sports Endorsers - 1996

Athletes are ranked by annual endorsement income in millions of dollars. Figure for Tiger Woods is based on 1997 contracts.

Michael Jordan	$ 38.0
Shaquille O'Neal	23.0
Arnold Palmer	16.0
Andre Agassi	15.8
Jack Nicklaus	14.3
Grant Hill	14.0
Tiger Woods	14.0
Joe Montana	12.0
Wayne Gretzky	8.8
Deion Sanders	6.0
Hakeem Olajuwon	5.0

Source: *USA TODAY*, May 20, 1997, p. B1, from *Sports Marketing Letter*.

★ 1923 ★

Racing (SIC 7948)

Top Horse Tracks - 1995

Del Martin
Saratoga
Santa Anita
Hollywood Park
Churchill Downs

Data show the average daily attendance.

Del Mar	33,150
Saratoga	27,344
Santa Anita	27,219
Hollywood Park	25,617
Churchill Downs	16,435

Source: *New York Times*, October 16, 1996, p. C4, from Association of Racing Commissioners International.

★ 1924 ★

Entertainment Facilities (SIC 7990)

Popular Events at Amphitheaters

Concerts	81.0%
Symphonies	5.0
Other	14.0

Source: *Amusement Business*, February 10, 1997, p. 22, from Price Waterhouse.

★ 1925 ★

Entertainment Facilities (SIC 7990)

Top Amphitheaters - 1996

Amphitheaters are ranked by gross revenues in 1996.

Pine Knob Music Theatre	$ 9,236,537
John Beach Theatre	7,976,541
World Music Theatre	6,707,701
Deer Creek Music Center	5,407,216
PNC Bank Arts Center	4,807,671
Coca-Cola Star Lake Amph.	4,489,275
Blockbuster-Sony Music	3,578,858
Universal Amphitheatre	3,537,368
Riverport Amphitheatre	3,461,498
Blossom Music Center	3,436,040

Source: *Amusement Business*, September 15, 1996, p. 44, from Amusement Business Boxscore.

★ 1926 ★

Sports Participation (SIC 7990)

Female Participation in Shooting Sports - 1996

Activities are ranked by thousands of participants.

Target shooting	3,400
Hunting, shotgun and rifle	1,700
Shooting, trap and skeet	363
Shooting, sporting clays	324

Source: *Women's Wear Daily*, May 29, 1997, p. 13, from Women's Shooting Sports Foundation.

★ 1927 ★

Sports Participation (SIC 7990)

Top Participatory Sports - 1996

Participants must have played the sport at least once in the last year.

Bowling	52,179,000
Freshwater fishing	45,903,000
Basketball	45,557,000
Billiards/pool	44,530,000
Free weights	42,817,000

Source: *USA TODAY*, June 2, 1997, p. C1, from American Sports Data Inc.

★ 1928 ★

Health Clubs (SIC 7991)

Health Club Memberships - 1995

Data show millions of members by age.

Under 18	1.2
18-24	2.0
25-34	7.1
35-44	3.3
45-54	2.9
55+	2.7

Source: *Remedy*, Nov./ Dec. 1995, p. 9, from Fitness Products Council and American Sports Data.

★ 1929 ★

Health Clubs (SIC 7991)

Largest Health Clubs - Dallas

Data show active members as of December 1, 1996.

Bally Total Fitness	180,000
Results Health Centers	15,000
Baylor Fitness Center	5,700
YMCA of Metropolitan Dallas	4,900
USA Fitness	4,600
Body Shop for Women	4,400
Fit For Life Center	3,100
Irving Fitness	3,000
Fitness World	2,900
Finley Ewing Cardiovascular & Fitness Center	2,868
Solana Club	2,200
Centrum Sports Club	1,500
North Star Athletic Club	1,500
Victory Gym	1,305
Texas Club	1,000

Source: *Dallas Business Journal*, January 3, 1997, p. 6, from company records.

★ 1930 ★

Golf Courses (SIC 7992)

Golf Courses by City

Philadelphia
Minneapolis
Pittsburgh
Washington D.C.
Atlanta
Cincinnati
Dallas-Fort Worth
Denver
St. Louis
Boston

Data show the number of 18-hole public golf courses in selected cities.

Philadelphia	166
Minneapolis	125
Pittsburgh	112
Washington D.C.	105
Atlanta	102
Cincinnati	94
Dallas-Fort Worth	77
Denver	71
St. Louis	62
Boston	55

Source: *Fortune*, November 11, 1996, p. 135, from *Arthur Andersen's Survey of Major Cities, Demographics USA, National Directory of Performing Arts*, and cities' Chamber of Commerce.

★ 1931 ★

Golf Courses (SIC 7992)

Golf Courses by State

There are over 15,000 golf courses in the United States.

Florida	1,119
California	898
Michigan	855
New York	823
Texas	805
Ohio	770

Source: *USA TODAY*, January 27, 1997, p. C1, from National Golf Foundation.

★ 1932 ★

Amusement Parks (SIC 7996)

Top Amusement Parks in North America - 1996

Parks are ranked by attendance in thousands of visitors. Data are estimated.

Disneyland (Anaheim, CA)	15,000
Magic Kingdom at Walt Disney World (Orlando, FL)	13,803
Epcot at Walt Disney World (Lake Buena Vista, FL)	11,235
Disney-MGM Studios at Walt Disney World (Lake Buena Vista, FL)	9,975
Universal Studios Florida (Orlando, FL)	8,400
Universal Studios Hollywood (Universal City, CA)	5,400
Sea World of Florida (Orlando, FL)	5,100
Busch Gardens Tampa (Tampa Bay, FL)	4,170
Six Flags Great Adventure (Jackson, NJ)	4,000
Sea World of California (San Diego, CA)	3,890

Source: *Amusement Business*, December 16, 1996, p. 80.

★1933★

Amusement Parks (SIC 7996)

Top Aquariums - North America

Living Seas
Sea World of Florida
Sea World of California
Shedd Aquarium
Marine World Africa USA
National Aquarium in Baltimore
Monterey Bay Aquarium
Sea World of Ohio
Sea World of Texas
New England Aquarium

Data show millions of visitors.

Living Seas (Fla)	6.00
Sea World of Florida	4.60
Sea World of California	3.70
Shedd Aquarium (Chicago)	1.84
Marine World Africa USA (Calif)	1.65
National Aquarium in Baltimore	1.63
Monterey Bay Aquarium	1.61
Sea World of Ohio	1.50
Sea World of Texas	1.50
New England Aquarium	1.31

Source: *Business Journal - Serving Greater Milwaukee*, July 27, 1996, p. 22, from American Zoo and Aquarium Association.

★1934★

Amusement Parks (SIC 7996)

Top U.S. Waterparks

Data show attendance in thousands of people. Data are estimated for 1996.

Wet'N Wild (Orlando, FL)	1,380
Typhoon Lagoon (Lake Buena Vista, FL)	1,250
Blizzard Beach (Lake Buena Vista, FL)	1,100
Schlitterbahn (New Braunfels, TX)	775
Raging Waters (San Dimas, CA)	720
Six Flags Wet'N Wild (Arlington, TX)	700
White Water (Marietta, GA)	600
Water Country USA (Williamsburg, VA)	540
Wild Rivers (Irvine, CA)	535
Wet'N Wild (Las Vegas, NV)	500
Adventure Island (Tampa, FL)	490
Hyland Hills Water World (Federal Heights, CO)	425
Six Flags Waterworld (Houston, TX)	400
Splish Splash (Riverhead, NY)	400
Wyandot Lake (Powell, OH)	400

Source: *Amusement Business*, December 16, 1996, p. 84.

★1935★

Expositions (SIC 7999)

Largest Expositions - San Franciso Area

Shows are ranked by expected attendance in 1997.

San Francisco Sport & Boat Show	225,000
Grand National Rodeo, Horse & Stock Show	100,000
East Bay Home & Garden Shows	65,000
International Gem & Jewelry Show	62,000
Macworld Expo	60,000
San Francisco International Gift Fair	52,000
Seybold Seminars San Francisco	45,000
Windows NT Internet Solutions & Support	45,000
Alameda County Home & Garden Shows	44,000
Conta Costa Home & Garden Shows	44,000

Source: *San Francisco Business Journal*, November 14, 1996, p. 13A.

★1936★

Fairs (SIC 7999)

Largest Fairs in North America

Fairs are ranked by attendance for 1996.

State Fair of Texas (Dallas)	3,558,749
Houston Livestock Show & Rodeo (TX)	1,830,265
New Mexico State Fair (Albuquerque)	1,749,275
Canadian National Exhibition (Toronto)	1,706,323
Minnesota State Fair (St. Paul)	1,673,976
State Fair of Oklahoma (Oklahoma City)	1,621,593
Western Washington Fair (Puyallup)	1,364,623
Los Angeles County Fair (Pomona)	1,269,573

Continued on next page.

★ 1936 ★ *Continued*

Fairs (SIC 7999)

Largest Fairs in North America

Fairs are ranked by attendance for 1996.

Tulsa State Fair (OK)	1,107,110
Calgary Stampede (Alberta)	1,100,007
The Big E (West Springfield, MA)	1,078,120
Colorado State Fair (Pueblo)	1,063,067

Source: *Amusement Business*, December 16, 1996, p. 88.

★ 1937 ★

Gambling (SIC 7999)

Leading Lottery Outlets - Buffalo, NY

Data show weekly average sales. Figures are for receipts from March 31 - July 13, 1996.

Tops No. 234	$ 42,569
Carl's Superstore Inc.	37,608
Wilson Farms No. 309	30,978
Wegman's No. 80	30,336
Tops No. 41	28,778
Hertel News & Tobacco	27,536
Dickie's Donuts	27,192

Source: *Business First of Buffalo*, August 12, 1996, p. 12, from New York Lottery.

★ 1938 ★

Leisure Activities (SIC 7999)

Bird Watching Activities

Data show retail sales associated with watching, feeding and photographing birds. Figures are in millions of dollars.

California	$ 623.0
Florida	477.0
Michigan	268.0
Pennsylvania	256.0
Wisconsin	225.0
New York	219.0
Colorado	180.0
Missouri	165.0

Source: *American Demographics*, December 1996, p. 49, from Southwick Associates.

★ 1939 ★

Leisure Activities (SIC 7999)

How Americans Exercise

Data show millions of participants.

Fitness walking	17.2
Free weights	11.3
Running/jogging	9.4
Stationary biking	9.4
Treadmill	7.0
Resistance machines	6.2

Source: *USA TODAY*, February 24, 1997, p. C1, from Fitness Products Council.

★ 1940 ★

Ski Resorts (SIC 7999)

Ski Travel by State

Data show millions of skier visitors in 1995-96.

Colorado	11.403
California	5.597
Vermont	4.506
New York	3.784
Pennsylvania	3.288
Utah	3.004
Michigan	2.585
New Hampshire	2.321
Washington	1.471
Wisconsin	1.460

Source: *Travel Weekly*, October 7, 1996, p. 49, from National Ski Areas Association.

SIC 80 - Health Services

★ 1941 ★

Health Care (SIC 8000)

Largest Health Care Companies - Washington D.C.

Companies are ranked by revenues in millions of dollars.

Manor Care Inc.	$ 1,248.2
Mid Atlantic Medical Services	1,133.7
PHP Healthcare Corp.	203.4
Hanger Orthopedic Group	66.8
Sunrise Assisted Living	47.3

Source: *Washington Post*, April 28, 1997, p. 37.

★ 1942 ★

Health Care (SIC 8000)

Top Doctor Diagnoses

Data show the leading ailments diagnosed in doctors offices, ranked by millions of visitors.

Hypertension	28.3
Acute upper respiratory infection	14.1
Bronchitis	11.7
Chronic sinusitis	11.4
Diabetes mellitus	10.9

Source: *Hospitals & Health Networks*, November 5, 1996, p. 18, from Scott-Levin.

★ 1943 ★

Physicians (SIC 8011)

Major Medical Groups - Chicago, IL

Physician groups are ranked by membership.

University of Chicago Physicians Group	649
UIC Physician Group	460
Northwestern Medical Facility	397
Loyola University Physician Foundation	370
Advocate Medical Group S.C.	225
Midwest Physician Group Ltd.	211
Evanston Medical Specialists	188
Dreyer Medical Clinic S.C.	102
Glen Ellyn Clinic S.C.	90
North Suburban Clinic	79

Source: *Crain's Chicago Business*, July 29, 1996, p. 17.

★ 1944 ★

Physicians (SIC 8011)

Major Medical Groups - Sacramento, CA

Physician groups are ranked by number of members.

Permanente Medical Group Inc.	648
Unversity Faculty Medical Associates	450
MedClinic	130
Sutter Medical Group	103
University of California at Davis Medical Group	86
Woodland Clinic Medical Group	85
Emergency Physicians' Medical Group	73
Central Anesthesis Exchange Medical Group Inc.	62
Foundation Health Medical Group Inc.	58
Radiological Associates of Sacramento Medical Group Inc.	40

Source: *Business Journal Serving Greater Sacramento*, August 19, 1996, p. 26.

★ 1945 ★

Dentists (SIC 8021)

Dentists' Practices by Region in Canada

Provinces are ranked by number of dentists' practices for 1996.

	No.	Share
Ontario	6,285	40.2%
Quebec	3,706	23.7

Continued on next page.

★ 1945 ★ *Continued*

Dentists (SIC 8021)

Dentists' Practices by Region in Canada

Provinces are ranked by number of dentists' practices for 1996.

	No.	Share
British Columbia	2,311	14.8%
Alberta	1,505	9.6
Manitoba	543	3.5
Nova Scotia	434	2.8
Saskatchewan	340	2.2
New Brunswick	255	1.6
Newfoundland	144	0.9
Northwest Territories	51	0.3
Prince Edward Island	47	0.3
Yukon Territories	9	0.1

Source: *National Trade Data Bank*, March 14, 1997, p. ISA960901.

★ 1946 ★

Podiatry (SIC 8043)

Most Common Podiatric Ailments

Data show incidents of podiatric ailments based on a survey of 46,476 U.S. households.

Infections	11,264,000
Toenail problems	11,260,000
Corns or calluses	11,175,000
Injuries	5,588,000
Flat feet/fallen arches	4,621,000
Bunions	4,368,000
Arthritis	3,903,000
Toe/joint deformity	2,515,000

Source: *USA TODAY*, June 12, 1997, p. 5D, from National Health Interview Survey.

★ 1947 ★

Nursing Homes (SIC 8050)

Top Assisted Living Chains

Companies are ranked by number of assisted living beds as of June 30, 1996.

ARV Assisted Living Inc.	4,823
Marriot Senior Living Services	3,939
ManorCare Health Services	3,377
Emeritus Corp.	2,846
Leisure Care Inc.	2,814
Sunrise Assisted Living Inc.	2,800
Alternative Living Services	2,630
Adult Care Management Corp.	2,605
Kapson Senior Quarters Corp.	2,393
Integrated Health Services Inc.	1,812
Assisted Living Concepts Inc.	1,629
Grand Court Lifestyles Inc.	1,610
ServiceMaster Diversified Health Services	1,428
American Care Communities Inc.	1,325
National Health Management Inc.	1,271
Living Centers of America	1,230
United Health Inc.	1,026
Sterling House Corp.	991
CareMatrix Corp.	959
Beverly Enterprises Inc.	815

Source: *Provider*, February 1997, p. 34.

★ 1948 ★

Hospitals (SIC 8060)

Hospital Market Shares - Montana

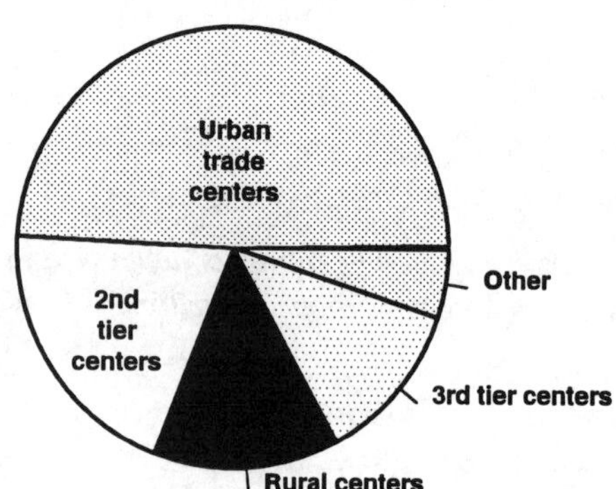

Shares are shown based on 96,488 patients discharged in 1994.

Urban trade centers	49.4%
2nd tier centers	20.0
Rural centers	14.0
3rd tier centers	12.0
Other	4.6

Source: *Montana Business Quarterly*, Summer 1996, p. 22, from Montana Department of Health and Human Services.

★ 1949 ★

Hospitals (SIC 8060)

Largest Hospitals - L.A. County

Hospitals are ranked by 1995 gross revenues in millions of dollars.

L.A.County-USC Medical Center	$ 1,289.9
Cedars-Sinai Medical Center	1,254.9
UCLA Medical Center	857.9
L.A. County-Harbor-UCLA Medical Center	565.3
L.A. County-Martin Luther King Jr. Center	498.7
Long Beach Memorial Medical Center	457.2
Hospital of the Good Samaritan	428.3
Huntington Memorial Hospital	417.6
Pomona Valley Hospital Medical Center	409.7
Northridge Hospital Medical Center	406.8

Source: *Los Angeles Business Journal*, November 18, 1996, p. 4A, from Healthcare Association of Southern California.

★ 1950 ★

Hospitals (SIC 8060)

Leading Hospitals/Hospital Companies in Southeast Michigan

Data show 1996 revenues in millions of dollars.

Mercy Health Services Inc.	$ 2,302.6
Detroit Medical Center	1,923.5
Henry Ford Health System	1,780.0
Sisters of St. Joseph Health System	1,082.7
William Beaumont Hospital	799.4
University of Michigan Health Systems	715.6
Oakwood Healthcare Inc.	639.3
Providence Hospital and Medical Centers	314.8
Detroit-Macomb Hospital Corp.	258.1
St. Mary Hospital	199.8
Botsford General Hospital	169.1
MCG Telesis	165.0
Crittenton Hospital	115.0
Bon Secours of Michigan Healthcare System Inc.	105.0
POH Medical Center	92.8

Source: *Crain's Detroit Business*, May 14, 1997, p. 15.

★ 1951 ★

Surgery (SIC 8060)

Cosmetic Surgery - 1995

Data are in millions of dollars.

Liposuction	$ 94.4
Rhinoplasty	93.3
Eyelid	55.0
Jaw surgery	42.3
Face-lift	33.7
Dermabrasion	33.3
Retin-A treatment	25.8
Chemical peel	25.4

Source: *Fortune*, September 9, 1996, p. 82, from American Academy of Cosmetic Surgery.

★ 1952 ★

Legal Services (SIC 8111)

Canada's Top Law Firms

Firms are ranked by fee income in millions of Canadian dollars.

KPMG	$ 524.7
Deloitte & Touche	499.0
Ernst & Young	415.0
Coopers & Lybrand	333.5
Andersen Worldwide	300.0
Price Waterhouse	279.0
Doane Raymond	202.9
BDO Dunwoody	132.3
Collins Barrow	31.3

Source: *Accountancy*, May 1997, p. 12.

★ 1953 ★

Legal Services (SIC 8111)

Largest Law Firms - Cleveland, OH

Companies are ranked by number of local attorneys as of January 1, 1997.

Jones, Day, Reavis & Pogue	233
Thompson Hine & Flory LLP	160
Calfee, Halter & Griswold LLP	156
Squire, Sanders & Dempsey	154
Baker & Hostetler LLP	149
Benesch, Friedlander, Coplan & Aronoff	109
Arter and Hadden	102
Buckingham, Doolittle & Burroughs LPA	90
Ulmer & Berne LLP	83
Hahn Loeser & Parks LLP	80

Source: *Crain's Cleveland Business*, March 3, 1997, p. 24.

★ 1954 ★

Legal Services (SIC 8111)

Largest Law Firms - Dallas/Fort Worth, TX

Firms are ranked by number of attorneys.

Jones, Day, Reavis & Pogue	1,167
Fulbright & Jaworski	630
Akin, Gump, Strauss, Hauer & Feld	624
Vinson & Elkins	501
Baker & Botts	439
Jenkens & Gilchrist	295
Haynes and Boone	270
Gardere & Wynne	258
Thompson & Knight	230
Strasburger & Price	200
Winstead Sechrest & Minick	195
Locke Purnell Rain Harrell	189
Jackson & Walker	170
Hughes & Luce	140
Cowles & Thompson	105
Vial, Hamilton, Kock & Knox	105
Carringon, Coleman, Sloman & Blumenthal	80
Kelly, Hart & Hallman	76
Cantey & Hanger	74
Thompson, Coe, Cousins & Irons	60

Source: *Dallas Morning News*, May 4, 1997, p. 26Q.

★ 1955 ★

Legal Services (SIC 8111)

Leading Law Firms - Buffalo, NY

Firms are ranked by the number of attorneys in the firm.

Hodgeson Russ Andrews Woods & Goodyear	118
Phillips Lytie Hitchcock Blaine & Huber	116
Saperston & Day	67
Damon & Morey	65

Continued on next page.

★ 1955 ★ *Continued*
Legal Services (SIC 8111)

Leading Law Firms - Buffalo, NY

Firms are ranked by the number of attorneys in the firm.

Jaecide Fleischmann & Mugel	45
Lipitz Green Fahringer Rolls Salisbury & Cambria	45
Spiegel Kelleher & Kahn	43
Kavinoki & Cook	26
Magavern Magavern & Grimm	26
Bouvier O'Connor	23

Source: *Business First Buffalo*, July 22, 1996, p. 18.

★ 1956 ★
Legal Services (SIC 8111)

Top U.S. Law Firms

Skadden, Arps, Slate, Meagher & Flom
Baker & McKenzie
Jones, Day, Reavis & Pogue
Sullivan and Cromwell
Weil, Gotshal & Manges

Firms are ranked by gross fees in millions of dollars.

Firm	Gross fees ($ mil.)
Skadden, Arps, Slate, Meagher & Flom	$ 635
Baker & McKenzie	594
Jones, Day, Reavis & Pogue	400
Sullivan and Cromwell	318
Weil, Gotshal & Manges	306

Source: *Economist*, November 23, 1996, p. 78, from *Legal Business* and *American Lawyer*.

SIC 82 - Educational Services

★ 1957 ★

Education (SIC 8200)

U.S. Students Abroad

Data show where students are studying in 1994-95.

Great Britain	14,910
France	7,872
Spain	7,473
Italy	7,062
Mexico	4,715
Germany	3,504
Australia	3,346
Israel	2,621
Costa Rica	2,302
Japan	2,212
Austria	1,489

Source: *Time*, December 16, 1996, p. 22, from Institute of International Education.

★ 1958 ★

Schools (SIC 8211)

Private Secondary Schools - Buffalo, NY

The largest, private secondary schools are shown based on enrollment for the 1995-96 school year.

St. Joseph's Collegiate Institute	813
St. Francis High School	600
Canisius High School	583
Mount Mercy Academy	490
St. Mary's High School	388
Nicholas School	386
Nardin Academy	384
Cardinal O'Hara High School	377

Source: *Business First of Buffalo*, August 5, 1996, p. 12.

★ 1959 ★

Universities (SIC 8211)

Ivy League Admissions

Applications are for the class of 2001. Princeton's figure was unavailable.

Cornell	19,656
Harvard	16,700
Penn	15,353
Brown	14,826
Columbia	12,983

Source: *Christian Science Monitor*, February 7, 1997, p. 2, from Associated Press and *Boston Globe*.

★ 1960 ★

Universities (SIC 8211)

Largest Colleges/Universities - Bay Area

Data are shown based on Fall 1995 enrollment.

City College of San Francisco	77,000
University of California, Santa Cruz	51,280
De Anza College	30,731
University of California, Berkley	30,000
San Francisco State University	26,791
San Jose State University	25,997
Diablo Valley College	20,000

Source: *San Francisco Business Times*, September 27, 1996, p. 19.

★ 1961 ★

Libraries (SIC 8231)

Largest Public Libraries

Data show the millions of bound volumes in 1994-95.

Chicago Public Library	11.46
Queensborough, New York	9.68
Los Angeles	6.06

Continued on next page.

★ 1961 ★ *Continued*

Libraries (SIC 8231)

Largest Public Libraries

Data show the millions of bound volumes in 1994-95.

Brooklyn, New York	5.94
Los Angeles County, California	5.85
Free Library of Philadelphia	5.12
Cincinnati & Hamilton County	4.65
New York, New York	4.61
Houston, Texas	4.11
Buffalo & Erie County, New York	4.00

Source: *Statesman*, December 2, 1996, p. 8, from *World Almanac of Facts*.

★ 1962 ★

Libraries (SIC 8231)

Public Libraries by City

Boston
Philadelphia
Washington D.C.
Minneapolis
Pittsburgh
Atlanta
Seattle
St. Louis
Baltimore
Dallas-Fort Worth
Cincinnati

Data show the number of public libraries in selected cities.

Boston	240
Philadelphia	216
Washington D.C.	148
Minneapolis	131
Pittsburgh	124
Atlanta	118
Seattle	117
St. Louis	104
Baltimore	102
Dallas-Fort Worth	98
Cincinnati	71

Source: *Fortune*, November 11, 1996, p. 135, from *Arthur Andersen's Survey of Major Cities, Demographics USA, National Directory of Performing Arts*, and cities' Chamber of Commerce.

SIC 83 - Social Services

★ 1963 ★

Child Care Services (SIC 8351)

Largest For-Profit Child Care Organizations - North America

Data show licensed capacity as of January 1, 1997.

KinderCare Learning Centers, Inc.	142,843
La Petite Academy	100,000
Children's World Learning Centers	71,500
Tutor Time Child Care Systems, Inc.	26,996
Children's Discovery Centers	25,601
Childtime Learning Centers	23,169
Kids 'R Kids International	15,500
Nobel Education Dynamics, Inc.	15,500
Bright Horizons Children's Centers, Inc.	13,500
CorporateFamily Solutions	12,000

Source: *Child Care Information Exchange*, May 1997, p. 70.

★ 1964 ★

Charities (SIC 8399)

Largest Charities - 1995

Firms are ranked by total revenues in millions of dollars.

YMCA of the USA	$ 2,060
Catholic Charities USA	1,942
American Red Cross	1,724
Salvation Army	1,421
Shriners Childrens' Hospital	1,254
Goodwill Industries International	1,037
YMCA of the USA	570
United Cerebral Palsy Association	543
Girl Scouts of America	515
Boy Scouts of America	513

Source: *USA TODAY*, November 22, 1996, p. 4B, from *NonProfit Times*.

★ 1965 ★

Charities (SIC 8399)

Largest Foundations - Denver, CO

The largest foundations are ranked by total 1995 assets in millions of dollars.

The Colorado Trust	$ 295.9
Rose Foundation	175.0
Boettcher Foundation	170.9
Adolph Coors Foundation	133.7
Helen K. and Arthur E. Johnson Foundation	110.0
Gates Foundation	108.6
The Denver Foundation	58.2
Temple Hoyne Buell Foundation	56.8
A.V. Hunter Trust	39.5
Bonfila-Stanton Foundation	38.0

Source: *Denver Business Journal*, August 30, 1996, p. A16.

★ 1966 ★

Charities (SIC 8399)

Who Provides Donations

Total donations reached $143.84 billion in 1995.

	($ bil.)	Share
Individual	$ 116.23	80.8%
Foundations	10.44	7.3
Bequests	9.77	6.8
Corporations	7.40	5.1

Source: *Christian Science Monitor*, April 18, 1997, p. 8, from GivingUSA.

SIC 84 - Museums, Botanical, Zoological Gardens

★ 1967 ★

Museums (SIC 8412)

Art Museums by City

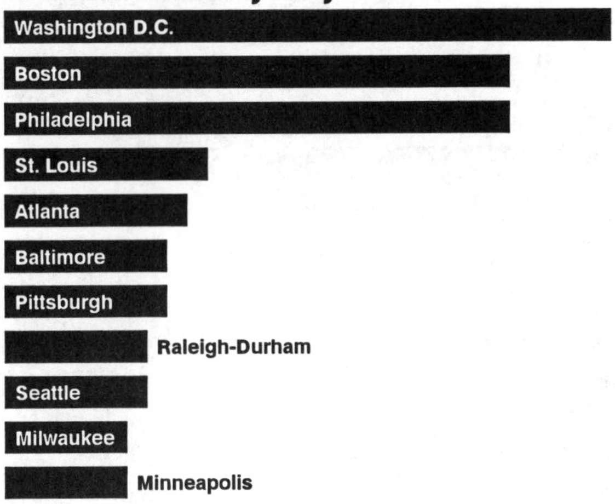

Data show the number of art museums in selected cities.

Washington D.C.	30
Boston	25
Philadelphia	25
St. Louis	10
Atlanta	9
Baltimore	8
Pittsburgh	8
Raleigh-Durham	7
Seattle	7
Milwaukee	6
Minneapolis	6

Source: *Fortune*, November 11, 1996, p. 135, from *Arthur Andersen's Survey of Major Cities, Demographics USA, National Directory of Performing Arts*, and cities' Chamber of Commerce.

★ 1968 ★

Museums (SIC 8412)

Museum Attendance - Chicago, IL

Data are for 1995.

Art Institute of Chicago	2,248,576
Museum of Science and Industry	2,012,284
DuSable Museum of African-American History	220,000
Mexican Fine Arts Center Museum	92,301
Museum of Contemporary Art	88,663

Source: *Crain's Chicago Business*, July 1996, p. F38, from Chicago Department of Tourism and Museum of Contemporary Art and Auditorium Theater.

SIC 86 - Membership Organizations

★ 1969 ★

Professional Organizations (SIC 8621)

Horse Organization Memberships

Figures are estimated.

American Horse Shows Association	65,000
U.S. Dressage Federation	38,923
U.S. Trotting Association	31,000
U.S. Pony Clubs	13,500
Pro Rodeo Cowboys Association	13,000
National Cutting Horse	12,000
U.S. Combined Training Association	10,900
National Reining Horse Association	7,800

Source: *Equus*, November 1996, p. 36, from associations.

★ 1970 ★

Labor Unions (SIC 8631)

Top Labor Union Locals

Locals are ranked by gross receipts in 1995.

UAW Local 600	$ 8,205,815
United Food & Commercial Workers 876	8,131,61
Operating Engineers Local 234	4,825,786
Service Employees Intl. Local 79	4,813,782
Electrical Workers Local 58	4,642,656
Teamsters Local 337	3,666,774
UAW Local 594	3,470,995
UAW Local 900	3,371,684
UAW Local 400	3,181,503
UAW Local 653	3,169,327

Source: *Crain's Small Business Labor Report*, February 1996, pp. L-5.

★ 1971 ★

Membership Organizations (SIC 8641)

Popular Bike Organizations

American Bicycle Association
National Bicycle League
U.S. Cycling Federation
National Off-Road Bicycle Association
League of American Bicyclists
Triathlon Federation/USA

Groups are ranked by memberships.

American Bicycle Association	54,000
National Bicycle League	35,000
U.S. Cycling Federation	34,867
National Off-Road Bicycle Association	33,407
League of American Bicyclists	31,276
Triathlon Federation/USA	20,000

Source: http:// www.biknet.com.tw/bikint/report/ e~us.htm, March 3, 1997, p. 3, from *Business Bike Journal*, Bicycle Manufacturers Association of America, Bicycle Market Research Institute, *Bicycle Retailer & Industry News*, and *Bicycling Magazine*.

★ 1972 ★

Social Organizations (SIC 8641)

Largest Human Service Organizations - Denver, CO

Firms are ranked by operating budget in millions of dollars.

Developmental Disabilities Resource Center	$ 23.7
Volunteers of America	23.4
Visiting Nurse Association	20.5
Rebound Corp.	16.7
Planned Parenthood of the Rocky Mountains	13.7
Arapahoe House Inc.	11.9

Continued on next page.

★ 1972 ★ *Continued*

Social Organizations (SIC 8641)

Largest Human Service Organizations - Denver, CO

Firms are ranked by operating budget in millions of dollars.

Catholic Charities	$ 11.1
Goodwill Industries of Denver	9.5

Source: *Denver Business Journal*, August 30, 1996, p. A13.

SIC 87 - Engineering and Management Services

★ 1973 ★

Engineering Services (SIC 8711)

Leading Construction Engineers

Engineering firms are ranked by billings in millions of dollars.

Fluor Daniels Inc.	$ 233.6
BE&K Inc.	214.7
Dames & Moore	192.0
Burns and Roe Enterprises	57.0
Simons-Eastern Consultants Inc.	56.1
Bechtel Group Inc.	41.6
Syska & Hennessy Inc.	38.0
Fru-Con Engineering Inc.	33.5
Martin Associates Group Inc.	27.6
Parsons Binckerhoff Inc.	26.3

Source: *Building Design & Construction*, July 1996, p. 38.

★ 1974 ★

Architectural Services (SIC 8712)

Largest Architectural Firms

The largest commercial, industrial and institutional architects are ranked by billings in millions of dollars.

Gensler	$ 74.0
NBBJ	43.5
Hillier Group	31.9
Callison Architecture Inc.	24.4
Thompson, Ventulett, Stainback & Associates	18.6
Smallwood, Reynolds Stewart, Stewart & Assoc. Inc.	17.9
Kaplan/McLaughlin/Diaz	15.0
Kohn Pedersen Fox Associates	15.0
Zimmer Gunsul Frasca Partnership	14.8
Anshen & Allen	13.3

Source: *Building Design & Construction*, July 1996, p. 10.

★ 1975 ★

Architectural Services (SIC 8712)

Largest Architectural Firms - Bay Area

Firms are ranked by gross billings in millions of dollars for 1995.

Kaplan McLaughlin Diaz	$ 23.5
Gensler	22.0
Hellmuth, Obata & Kassabaum Inc.	20.5
Skidmore Ownings & Merrill	15.2
Stone Marraccini Patterson	14.0
Anshen & Allen	13.8
The Ratcliff Architects	9.6
RMW Architecture & Design	9.4
DES Architects & Engineers	8.5
Gordon H. Chong & Associates	8.5

Source: *San Francisco Business Times*, September 27, 1996, p. 27.

★ 1976 ★

Architectural Services (SIC 8712)

Largest Architectural Firms - Cleveland, OH

Firms are ranked by local office revenues in millions of dollars for 1995.

Austin Co.	$ 40.0
URS Consultants Inc.	15.3
KA Inc.	9.8
HWH Architects Engineers Planners Inc.	8.5
Osborn Architects and Engineers	6.5
Robert P. Madison International Inc.	6.4
Richard L. Bowen & Associates Inc.	5.6
Collins, Rimer and Gordon, Architects Inc.	5.4
Dorsky Hodgson & Partners Inc.	4.9
van Dijk, Pace, Westlake & Partners, Architects	4.8
G. Herschman Architects	4.0
Braun & Steidl Architects Inc.	2.8

Continued on next page.

★ 1976 ★ *Continued*

Architectural Services (SIC 8712)

Largest Architectural Firms - Cleveland, OH

Firms are ranked by local office revenues in millions of dollars for 1995.

City Architecture Inc.	$ 2.3
Hasenstab & McCarthy Architects Inc.	2.3
Lesko Associates Inc., Architects-Planners	2.2

Source: *Crain's Cleveland Business*, May 20, 1996, p. 20.

★ 1977 ★

Architectural Services (SIC 8712)

Largest Architectural Firms - Sacramento, CA

Firms are ranked by the number of licensed architects based in Sacramento for 1996.

Lionakis-Beaumont Design Group	30
Stafford-King-Wiese Architects	18
Dreyfuss & Blackford Architects	14
LPA Inc.	13
English Harper Reta Architects Inc.	11
Williams + Paddon Architects + Planners Inc.	11
F.K.A. Corp.	10
Murray & Downs AIA Architects Inc.	10
Ehrilch Rominger	9
Forrar Williams Architects	9
Madsen, Flathmann, Dameron & Babcock Architects	9
Caipo/Hom/Macaulay/Dong Architects	8
Nacht & Lewis Architects Inc.	8
Rainforth-Grau-Architects	7
Rauschenbach Marvelli Becker, Architects	7

Source: *Sacramento Business Journal*, January 6, 1997, p. 18.

★ 1978 ★

Accounting Services (SIC 8721)

Accounting Leaders

Firms are ranked by revenues in millions of dollars for fiscal year 1996.

Andersen Worldwide	$ 4,500
Ernst & Young LLP	3,600
Deloitte and Touche LLP	$ 2,900
KPMG Peat Marwick LLP	2,500
Coopers & Lybrand LLP	2,100
Price Waterhouse LLP	2,000
Grant Thornton LLP	266
McGladrey & Pullen, LLP	251
BDO Seidman, LLP	211

Source: *Practical Accountant*, April 1997, p. 24.

★ 1979 ★

Accounting Services (SIC 8721)

Largest Accounting Firms - Detroit, CO

Firms are ranked by number of employees as of January 1, 1997.

Arthur Andersen L.L.P.	884
Deloitte & Touche L.L.P.	694
Plante & Moran L.L.P.	550
Coopers & Lybrand L.L.P.	536
Ernst & Young L.L.P.	402
KPMG Peat Marwick L.L.P.	217
Follmer, Rudzewicz & Co. P.C.	205
Price Waterhouse L.L.P.	200
Doeren Mayhew	148
BDO Seidman L.L.P.	138

Source: *Crain's Detroit Business*, February 17, 1997, p. 24.

★ 1980 ★

Accounting Services (SIC 8721)

Leading Accounting Firms - Phoenix

Firms are ranked by number of professional staff.

Arthur Andersen LLP	312
Ernst & Young LLP	194
Deloitte & Touche LLP	167
Coopers & Lybrand LLP	99
KPMG Post Marwick LLP	89
Price Waterhouse LLP	80
Henry & Horne PLC	64
Tobeck CPAs PC	50
McGledrey & Pullen LLP	44
Miller Wagner & Co. Ltd.	38

Source: *Business Journal Serving Phoenix and the Valley of the Sun*, July 26, 1996, p. 33, from representatives of the firms.

★ 1981 ★

Accounting Services (SIC 8721)

Top Accounting Firms

Andersen Worldwide
Ernst & Young
Deloitte & Touche
KPMG Peat Marwick
Coopers & Lybrand
Price Waterhouse
H&R Block Tax Services
Grant Thornton
McGladrey & Pullen
BDO Seidman
Crowe, Chizek and Co.
Baird Kurtz & Dobson
Plante & Moran
Clifton Gunderson & Co.
Jackson Hewitt

Top accounting firms are ranked by revenues in billions of dollars.

Andersen Worldwide	$ 4,511.0
Ernst & Young	3,571.0
Deloitte & Touche	2,925.0
KPMG Peat Marwick	2,530.0
Coopers & Lybrand	2,115.0
Price Waterhouse	2,020.0
H&R Block Tax Services	750.4
Grant Thornton	266.0
McGladrey & Pullen	251.1
BDO Seidman	211.0
Crowe, Chizek and Co.	86.0
Baird Kurtz & Dobson	81.9
Plante & Moran	74.7
Clifton Gunderson & Co.	68.6
Jackson Hewitt	66.8

Source: *Accounting Today*, March 17, 1997, p. 24.

★ 1982 ★

Accounting Services (SIC 8721)

Top Accounting Firms - Midwest

Firms are ranked by revenues in millions of dollars for fiscal year 1996.

Baird, Kurtz & Dobson	$ 81.6
Larson Allen Weishair	43.1
Mayer Hoffman McCann, L.C.	$ 24.0
Eide Helmeke, P.L.L.P.	17.2
Rubin, Brown, Gornstein & Co. L.L.P.	15.3
Charles Bailly & Co., L.L.P.	14.5
Kennedy & Coe, LLC	14.3
Lurie Beslkof Lapidus & Co., LLP	11.0
Brady Martz & Associates, PC	10.0
Olsen Thielen & Co., Ltd.	9.8
Grace & Co. PC	9.7
Mizer, Houser & Co., PA	8.1
Boulay, Heutmaker, Zibell & Co. P.L.L.P.	7.9
Seim, Johnson, Sestak & Quist	5.8
Donnelly Meiners Jordan Kline, PC	5.4

Source: *Practical Accountant*, April 1997, p. 35.

★ 1983 ★

Accounting Services (SIC 8721)

Top Accounting Firms - Mountain States

Firms are ranked by revenues in millions of dollars for fiscal year 1996.

Galusha, Higgins & Galusha	$ 10.2
Hein + Associates LLP	8.0
Ehrhardt Keefe Steiner & Hottman, PC	7.5
Anderson, ZurMuehlen & Co., P.C.	6.2
Gelfond Hochstadt Pangburn & Co., PC	4.6
Junkermier, Clark, Campanella, Stevens, P.C.	4.5
Brock and Company	3.6
Rudd & Company, PLLC	3.4
Foote, Passey, Griffin & Company	3.1
Hawkins Cloward Simister	2.9
John M. Hanson & Company, P.C.	2.9
Presnell Gage, PC	2.9
Hamilton, Misfeldt & Company, PC	2.8
Hansen, Barnett & Maxwell	2.6
Balukoff, Lindstrom & Co., PA	2.5

Source: *Practical Accountant*, April 1997, p. 37.

★ 1984 ★

Accounting Services (SIC 8721)

Top Accounting Firms - New England

Firms are ranked by revenues in millions of dollars for fiscal year 1996.

Berry, Dunn, McNeil & Parker	$ 14.9
Tofias, Fleishman, Shapiro & Co.	14.1

Continued on next page.

★ 1984 ★ *Continued*

Accounting Services (SIC 8721)

Top Accounting Firms - New England

Firms are ranked by revenues in millions of dollars for fiscal year 1996.

Blum Shapiro & Co.	$ 11.1
Baker, Newman & Noyes LLC	11.0
Feeley & Driscoll, P.C.	8.5
Vitale, Caturano & Co. P.C.	7.9
Koslin Ruffkess & Co. L.L.C.	7.1
Wolf & Company, P.C.	6.8
O'Connor & Drew, P.C.	5.9
Tonneson & Company CPA's P.C.	5.5
Rooney, Plotkin & Willey	5.2
Sansiveri, Kimball & McNamee, L.L.P.	5.2
Ziner & Company, P.C.	5.2
Lefkowitz, Garfinkel, Champi & DeRienzo P.C.	5.1
Macdonald, Page & Co.	5.0

Source: *Practical Accountant*, April 1997, p. 27.

★ 1985 ★

Accounting Services (SIC 8721)

Top Accounting Firms - North Central

Firms are ranked by revenues in millions of dollars for fiscal year 1996.

Crowe Chizek and Company LLP	$ 86.0
Plante & Moran, LLP	74.8
Clifton Gunderson L.L.C.	68.6
George S. Olive & Co. LLC	52.2
Altschuler, Melvoin and Glasser LLP	49.1
Friedman Elsenstein Raemer & Schwartz, LLP	39.9
Wipfli Ulrich Bertelson LLP	26.5
Hausser + Taylor	24.4
Checkers, Simon & Rosner LLP	23.3
Thomas Havey LLP	22.0
Virchow-Krause & Company, LLP	21.1
Schenck & Associates SC	19.3
Rehmann Robson, P.C.	18.0
Follmer, Rudzewicz & Co., P.C.	16.3
Blue & Co., LLC	16.1

Source: *Practical Accountant*, April 1997, p. 33.

★ 1986 ★

Accounting Services (SIC 8721)

Top Accounting Firms - North East

Firms are ranked by revenues in millions of dollars for fiscal year 1996.

Richard A. Elsner & Company, LLP	$ 51.3
Goldstein Golub Kessler & Company, P.C.	44.4
David Berdon & Co. LLP	32.2
Reznick Fedder & Silverman	31.5
Anchin, Block & Anchin LLP	28.0
M.R. Weiser & Co. LLP	27.0
J.H. Cohn LLP	24.0
Campos & Stratis LLP	23.9
Parente, Randolph, Orlando, Carey & Assoc.	23.4
Zelenkofske Axelrod & Co.	22.7
Mahoney Cohen Rashba & Pokart, CPA PC	21.0
Mitchell & Titus, LLP	20.2
Edward Isaacs & Co. LLP	18.0
C.W. Amos & Co., LLC	17.0
Urbach Kahn & Werlin PC	16.4

Source: *Practical Accountant*, April 1997, p. 29.

★ 1987 ★

Accounting Services (SIC 8721)

Top Accounting Firms - South East

Firms are ranked by revenues in millions of dollars for fiscal year 1996.

Cherry, Bekaert & Holland, L.L.P.	$ 23.3
Dixon, Odom & Co., L.L.P.	18.9
Elliot, Davis & Company, L.L.P.	14.0
Hyatt, Imler, Ott & Bount, P.C.	13.3
Joseph Decosimo and Company, LLP	12.9
Mauldin & Jenkins, LLC	12.9
Kaufman Rossin & Co.	12.5
Goodman & Co., L.L.P.	12.4
Habif, Arogeti & Wynne P.C.	12.0
Rachlin Cohen & Holtz	12.0
Morrison, Brown, Argiz & Company	10.6
Crisp Hughes & Co., L.L.P.	9.9
Keiter, Stephens, Hurst, Gary & Shreaves, P.C.	9.7
Horne CPA Group	9.4
Jackson Thorton & Co., P.C.	9.2

Source: *Practical Accountant*, April 1997, p. 31.

★ 1988 ★
Accounting Services (SIC 8721)

Top Accounting Firms - Southwest

Firms are ranked by revenues in millions of dollars for fiscal year 1996.

Weaver and Tidwell, L.L.P.	$ 9.8
Mann Frankfort Stein & Lipp, P.C.	9.3
Postlehwaite & Netterville, APAC	7.3
Lane Gorman Trubitt, L.L.P.	7.2
Henry & Horne, P.L.C.	7.2
Broussard Poche Lewis & Breaux	6.6
Toback CPAs, P.C.	6.1
Padgett, Stratemann & Co., L.L.P.	5.9
Bourgeois Bennett, L.L.C.	5.8
Heard, McElroy & Vestal, L.L.P.	5.3
Johnson Miller & Company, P.C.	5.1
Miller, Wagner & Co.	5.1
Darnall, Sikes, Kolder, Frederick & Rainey	5.0
Brown, Graham & Co., P.C.	4.9
Atkinson & Co. Ltd.	4.7

Source: *Practical Accountant*, April 1997, p. 39.

★ 1989 ★
Accounting Services (SIC 8721)

Top Accounting Firms - West

Firms are ranked by revenues in millions of dollars for fiscal year 1996.

Moss Adams LLP	$ 63.5
LeMaster & Daniels PLLC	16.2
Yergen and Meyer LLP	11.7
Stonefield Josephson	11.7
Nigro, Karlin & Segal	10.8
Hood & Strong	10.7
Kafoury, Armstrong & Co.	10.7
Hemming Morse, Inc.	10.0
Grobstein, Horwath & Co. LLP	9.3
Ireland, San Filippo, LLP	8.8
Singer, Lewalk, Greenhaum & Goldstein LLP	8.6
Windes & McClaughry PC	8.6
Knight Vale & Gregory Inc., P.S.	7.8
Pisenti & Brinker	7.8
Clark Nuber CPAs	7.5

Source: *Practical Accountant*, April 1997, p. 41.

★ 1990 ★
Accounting Services (SIC 8721)

Top CPA Firms

Firms are ranked by 1994 revenues in millions of dollars.

Arthur Andersen & Co.	$ 3,317.2
Ernst & Young	2,543.0
Deloitte & Touche	2,230.0
KPMG Peat Marwick	1,907.0
Coopers & Lybrand	1,783.0
Price Waterhouse	1,570.0
Grant Thornton	229.0
McGladrey & Pullen	208.9
BD0 Seidman	201.0
Kenneth Leventhal & Co.	195.0

Source: *CPA Journal*, July 1996, p. 64.

★ 1991 ★
Accounting Services (SIC 8721)

Top U.S. Accounting Firms - 1996

Firms are ranked by fee income in millions of U.S. dollars.

Andersen Worldwide	$ 3,861
Ernst & Young	2,974
Deloitte & Touche	2,570
KPMG	2,289
Coopers & Lybrand	1,905
Price Waterhouse	1,780
Grant Thornton	240
McGladrey & Pullen	238
BDO Seidman	203
Crowe Chizek	76

Source: *Accountancy*, February 1997, p. 13.

★ 1992 ★
Commercial Research (SIC 8732)

Largest Research Parks

Groups are ranked by number of companies.

Cummings Research Park	170
Stanford Research Park	162
University City Science Center	140
Oakland Technology Park	120
Princeton Forrestal Center	85
Research Triangle Park	71
Central Florida Research Park	70

Continued on next page.

★ 1992 ★ *Continued*

Commercial Research (SIC 8732)

Largest Research Parks

Groups are ranked by number of companies.

Tri-Cities Science & Technology Park	53
University of Utah Research Park	46
University Research Park	29

Source: *World Trade*, April 1997, p. 74, from Association of University Related Research Parks.

★ 1993 ★

Commercial Research (SIC 8732)

Top U.S. Research Firms - 1996

Firms are ranked by total research revenues in millions of dollars. Revenues for all 169 members of the Council of American Survey Research Organizations exceeded $5.5 billion.

A.C. Nielsen Corp.	$ 1,358.6
Cognizant Corp.	1,223.8
Information Resources Inc.	405.6
Arbitron Co.	153.1
PMSI/Source Informatics	152.2
Westat Inc.	146.5
Maritz Marketing Research Inc.	133.6
NFO Research Inc.	109.2
Kantar Group	103.3
NPD Group	99.6
Market Facts Inc.	83.8
Audits & Surveys Worldwide Inc.	60.4
M/A/R/C Group Inc.	55.7
BASES Group	53.3
Opinion Research Corp.	47.3

Source: *Marketing News*, June 9, 1997, p. H4.

★ 1994 ★

Construction Management (SIC 8741)

Construction Management Providers

Construction management firms are ranked by billings in millions of dollars.

Bovis Inc.	$ 2,456.0
URS Consultants Inc.	2,008.0
Heery International Inc.	1,218.0
Gilbane Building Co.	1,197.3
Sverdrup Corp.	866..2
3D/International	738.0
Daniel, Mann, Johnson & Mendenhall	696.0
Barton Malow Co.	$ 619.4
Turner Corp.	554.5
Tishman Realty & Construction Co.	527.4

Source: *Building Design & Construction*, July 1996, p. 25.

★ 1995 ★

Construction Management (SIC 8741)

Leading Construction Management Firms

Firms are ranked by total billings in millions of dollars.

Jacobs Engineering Group Inc.	$ 828.0
Foster Wheeler Corp.	666.2
Raytheon Engineers & Constructors International	612.0
M.W. Kellogg Co.	337.9
Kvaerner Group	318.5
CH2M Hill Cos. Ltd.	306.7
Bechtel Group Inc.	245.0
Huber, Hunt and Nichols Inc.	198.0
Parsons Corp.	186.9
Morrison Knudsen Corp.	159.0
Fluor Daniel Inc.	148.0
Bovis Inc.	140.5
Metcalf & Eddy/AWT Cos.	135.3
Barton Malow Co.	130.0
ICF Kaiser International Inc.	113.1

Source: *ENR*, June 16, 1997, p. 56.

★ 1996 ★

Marketing Services (SIC 8741)

Market Research Funding - Canada

Distribution is shown based on $130 million in total funding.

Private industry	77.9%
Government	9.1
Crown corp's	5.3
Ad agencies	3.9
Other groups	3.7

Source: *Marketing Magazine*, October 14, 1996, p. 20, from Canadian Association of Marketing Research Organization.

★ 1997 ★

Management Consulting (SIC 8742)

Consulting Firms - Columbus, OH

Companies are ranked by consultants in the Columbus area.

Andersen Consulting LLP	265
Compuware Corp.	260
Claremont Technology Group Inc.	160
Maximation Inc.	100
Quick Solutions Inc.	96
Retail Planning Associates LP	72
Deloitte & Touche LLP	58
Ernst & Young	50
Crowe Chizek	45
William M. Mercer Inc.	42
POU Partners	22
Cambridge Technology Partners	20

Source: *Business First Columbus*, November 15, 1996, p. 12.

★ 1998 ★

Management Consulting (SIC 8742)

Top Management Consulting Firms

Firms are ranked by revenues in millions of dollars.

KPMG Peat Marwick	$ 241.5
Andersen Consulting	224.3
Coopers & Lybrand	171.2
Deloitte & Touche	161.6
Booz-Allen & Hamilton	157.0
AMS	114.5
Price Waterhouse	52.9
ICF Kaiser Intl.	48.3
Arthur D. Little	25.9

Source: *Consultants News*, October 1996, p. 4.

★ 1999 ★

Public Relations Services (SIC 8743)

Largest PR Firms - Dallas, TX

Firms are ranked by 1995 fee incomes in millions of dollars.

Publicis Public Relations	$ 2.9
Halcyon Associates	2.6
Edelman Public Relations Worldwide	2.5
Temerlin McClain Public Relations	2.4
Bustin & Co.	1.5
Stern, Nathan & Perryman	1.4
MCCommunications	1.3

Source: *Dallas Business Journal*, May 3, 1996, p. 8, from companies.

★ 2000 ★

Public Relations Services (SIC 8743)

Leading Public Relations Firms

Companies are ranked by 1996 net fees.

Burson-Marsteller	$ 233,344,022
Shandwick	190,700,000
Hill and Knowlton	160,800,000
Porter Novelli International	121,178,280
Edelman Public Rel. Worldwide	111,680,350
Fleishman-Hillard	107,494,000
Ketchum Public Relations	74,836,000
GCI Group including GTFH PR	52,293,330
Ogilvy Adams & Rinehart	48,544,000
Manning, Selvage & Lee	47,925,000
Bozell Sawyer Miller Group	43,900,000
Ruder Finn	41,870,165

Source: *Advertising Age*, March 24, 1997, p. 25.

★ 2001 ★

Public Relations Services (SIC 8743)

Public Relations Firms - South Florida

Companies are ranked by fee income in 1995.

Zynyx Marketing Communications	$ 2,950,000
Rubin Barney & Birger Inc.	2,770,555
Burson-Marsteller	2,462,748
Wragg & Casas Public Relations	2,067,255
Gordon Sloan Diaz-Balart	1,495,000
Bitner.com: The Worldcom Group	1,476,722
Fleischmann-Hillard	1,476,000
JGR & Associates Inc.	1,341,500

Continued on next page.

★ 2001 ★ *Continued*

Public Relations Services (SIC 8743)

Public Relations Firms - South Florida

Companies are ranked by fee income in 1995.

Greenstone Roberts	$ 1,250,000
CreatAbility	1,055,055

Source: *South Florida Business Journal*, June 21, 1996, p. 10C, from company reports and other accounting firms.

★ 2002 ★

Consulting Services (SIC 8748)

Environmental Consulting/ Remediation Market

The $12.5 billion market is shown for 1995.

Remediation consulting	32.0%
Remediation construction	28.0
Water	24.0
Multimedia	8.0
Air	5.0
Solid waste	3.0

Source: *Environmental Management Today*, July/August 1996, p. 22, from Farkas Berkowitz & Co.

★ 2003 ★

Consulting Services (SIC 8748)

Largest Environment Consulting Firms

Firms are ranked by estimated consulting/ engineering revenues in millions of dollars.

CH2M Hill Companies Ltd.	$ 643.0
Metcalf & Eddy	615.8
ICF Kaiser International Inc.	550.2
OHM Remediation Services Corp.	448.0
Montgomery Watson	395.9
Black & Vaatch	372.0
Camp Dresser & McKee Inc.	305.0
Rust International Inc.	300.0
Radian International	257.5
Roy F. Weston Inc.	257.0

Source: *Environmental Management Today*, July/August 1996, p. 24.

★ 2004 ★

Human Resource Consulting (SIC 8748)

Top Benefit Consultants

Firms are ranked by 1996 estimated consulting fees in millions of dollars.

Towers Perrin	$ 476.0
William M. Mercer Cos. Inc.	474.0
Hewitt Associates L.L.C.	464.0
Watson Wyatt Worldwide	354.0
A. Foster Higgins & Co. Inc.	216.0
Coopers & Lybrand L.L.P. Human Res. Adv. Grp.	198.0
Buck Consultants Inc.	169.0
Aon Consulting	121.0
Alexander Consulting Group Inc.	117.0
Deloitte & Touche	108.0

Source: *Business Insurance*, December 9, 1996, p. 18.

★ 2005 ★

Human Resource Consulting (SIC 8748)

Top Employee Benefit Consultants - Silicon Valley

Firms are ranked by number of employees.

Watson Wyatt Worldwide	140
Matrix Cos.	80
PGR Group Inc.	45
Capital Management Group	45
Alburger Basso & DeGreez	40
MGIS Cos.	40
Kaufmann & Goble	25
Lipman Co. Inc. dba TLC Admin.	25
JDN Inc. Pension Consultants	20
Minet Insurance Services Inc.	17

Source: *San Jose and Silicon Valley Business Journal*, June 30, 1996, p. 20.

SIC 91 - Executive, Legislative, and General

★ 2006 ★

Government (SIC 9199)

Federal Government Spending

Expenses are shown as a percent of all Federal Government outlays. Data are estimated for fiscal year 1998.

Social Security & direct benefit payments for individuals	50.0%
Grants to states & localities	15.0
National defense	15.0
Net interest	15.0
Other federal operations	5.0

Source: *State Government News*, May 1997, p. 25.

SIC 92 - Justice, Public Order, and Safety

★ 2007 ★

Crime (SIC 9220)

Frequently Stolen Vehicles

Data are for 1995.

Passenger cars	67.0%
Pickup trucks	14.0
Vans/sports utilities	14.0
Motorcycles	2.0
Boats	1.0
Other	2.0

Source: *USA TODAY*, September 30, 1996, p. A1, from National Insurance Crime Bureau.

★ 2008 ★

Crime (SIC 9220)

Items Most Frequently Shoplifted

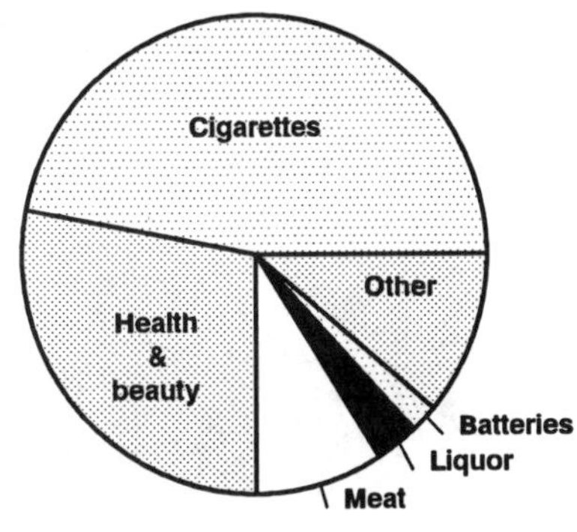

Cigarettes	47.0%
Health & beauty care items	28.0
Meat	9.0
Liquor	3.0
Batteries	2.0
Other	11.0

Source: *Grocery Headquarters*, May 1997, p. 33, from National Retail Security Survey.

★ 2009 ★

Crime (SIC 9220)

Popular Stolen Cars in Mexico

Data show number of thefts in 1995. Figures refer to insured vehicles only.

VW Beetle	5,746
VW Jetta	3,581
Nissan Tauru	3,196
Chrysler Spirit	2,797
VW Golf	1,652
GM pickups	1,332
Chrysler Shadow	1,317
Nissan pickups	1,202
Ford pickups	1,160
Chrysler pickups	1,034

Source: *Automotive News*, August 5, 1996, p. 17, from Association of Mexican Insurance Companies.

★ 2010 ★

Crime (SIC 9220)

U.S. Software/Entertainment Piracy

The table shows the millions of dollars U.S. firms have lost in software and entertainment in foreign countries. Data refer to motion pictures, music, business products, software, and books.

Asia	$ 6,017.0
Western Europe	3,682.8
Latin America and Caribbean	1,847.2
Eastern Europe and Russia	1,829.6
Middle East and Mediterrenean	686.0
Canada	309.5
Africa	267.0

Source: *Financial Times*, February 10, 1997, p. 6, from International Intellectual Property Alliance.

SIC 93 - Finance, Taxation, and Monetary Policy

★ 2011 ★

Government Programs (SIC 9311)

Top Government Stat Programs

Data show the millions of dollars in direct funding as of September 30, 1996.

Bureau of Labor Statistics	$ 343
National Institute of Health	316
Census Bureau	293
Centers for Disease Control	168
Environmental Protection Agency	140

Source: *Journal of Commerce*, November 7, 1996, p. 1, from United States Office of Management and Budget.

★ 2012 ★

Taxation (SIC 9311)

State Tax Revenues - 1995

Revenues are shown by source for fiscal year 1995.

	($ bil.)	Share
General sales	$ 132.7	33.1%
Individual income	126.3	31.5
Corporate income	29.2	7.3
Licenses	26.1	6.5
Motor fuels	25.5	6.4
Alcohol & tobacco	11.0	2.7
Property	10.2	2.5
Insurance	8.6	2.1
Public utilities	8.2	2.0
Death & gift	4.9	1.2
Severance	4.5	1.1
Other	14.3	3.6

Source: *Practical Accountant*, February 1997, p. 6, from Tax Foundation.

SIC 95 - Environmental Quality and Housing

★ 2013 ★

Environmental Services (SIC 9510)

Canadian Environmental Market

The market had sales of $17.6 billion in 1994.

Water & wastewater treatment	27.3%
Solid wastes management	22.7
Air pollution technology & control	18.2
Demand site management	18.2
Other	13.6

Source: *Business America*, October 1996, p. 20, from OECD.

★ 2014 ★

Environmental Services (SIC 9510)

Environmental Service Market

Services are ranked by millions of dollars spent in 1996.

On-site treatment	$ 9,800.0
Treatment and disposal	7,000.0
Remediation construction	2,900.0
Consulting	1,500.0
Remediation consulting	1,500.0
Industrial wastewater	1,400.0
Environmental information	660.0
Air pollution control	600.0
Management services	440.0
Outsourcing	280.0

Source: *Chemicalweek*, January 8, 1997, p. 28, from BTI Consulting Group.

★ 2015 ★

Land Conservation (SIC 9512)

Who Owns U.S. Land

Data show who owned 271 million acres of U.S. land in 1994.

Fish & Wildlife Service	33.92%
National Park Service	30.78
Bureau of Land Management	19.06
National Forest System	16.25

Source: *Pulp & Paper*, September 1996, p. 70.

★ 2016 ★

Land Ownership (SIC 9512)

Who Owns Timberland

Private non-industrial	59.0%
State, local governments	17.0
Forest industry	14.0
Federal government	10.0

Source: *USA TODAY*, March 17, 1997, p. A1, from University of Georgia.

SIC 97 - National Security and International Affairs

★ 2017 ★

Defense (SIC 9711)

U.S. Military Manpower

Data show programmed forces for 1997. Figures for Active and Civilian forces do not include Navy outsourcing initiatives planned prior to the Quadrenial Defense Review.

Active	1,450,000
Reserve	900,000
Civilian	800,000

Source: *Financial Times*, May 20, 1997, p. 6, from Quadrennial Defense Review.

Source Index: Primary

SOURCE INDEX

This index is divided into *primary sources* and *original sources*. Primary sources are the publications where the market shares were found. Original sources are sources cited in the primary sources. Numbers following the sources are entry numbers, arranged sequentially; the first number refers to the first appearance of the source in *Market Share Reporter*. All told, 1120 organizations are listed.

Primary Sources

Original Sources

PLACE NAMES INDEX

This index shows global regions, political entities, states and provinces, regions within countries, and cities. The numbers that follow listings are entry numbers; they are arranged sequentially so that the first mention of a place is listed first. The index shows references to more than 250 places.

PRODUCTS, SERVICES, AND ISSUES INDEX

This index shows, in alphabetical order, references to products, services, and issues covered in *Market Share Reporter*, 8th Edition. More than 2,500 terms are included. Terms include subjects not readily categorized as products and services, including such subjects as *crime* and *welfare*. The numbers that follow each term refer to entry numbers and are arranged sequentially so that the first mention is listed first.

Products, Services, and Issues Index

COMPANY INDEX

The more than 5,450 companies and institutions in this book are indexed here in alphabetical order. Numbers following the terms are entry numbers. They are arranged sequentially; the first entry number refers to the first mention of the company in *Market Share Reporter*. Although most organizations appear only once, some entities are referred to under abbreviations in the sources and these have not always been expanded.

BRANDS INDEX

This index shows more than 1,650 brands—including names of periodicals, television programs, popular movies, and other "brand-equivalent" names. Each brand name is followed by one or more numerals; these are entry numbers; they are arranged sequentially, with the first mention of the brand shown first.

Brands Index

APPENDIX I

SIC COVERAGE

This appendix lists the Standard Industrial Classification codes (SICs) included in *Market Share Reporter*. Page numbers are shown following each SIC category; the page shown indicates the first occurrence of an SIC. *NEC* stands for not elsewhere classified.

Food and Kindred Products

Tobacco Products

Textile Mill Products

Apparel and Other Textile Products

Lumber and Wood Products

Furniture and Fixtures

Paper and Allied Products

Printing and Publishing

Chemicals and Allied Products

Petroleum and Coal Products

Rubber and Misc. Plastics Products

Leather and Leather Products

Stone, Clay, and Glass Products

Primary Metal Industries

Fabricated Metal Products

Industry Machinery and Equipment

Electronic and Other Electric Equipment

Transportation Equipment

Instruments and Related Products

Miscellaneous Manufacturing Industries

Railroad Transportation

Local and Interurban Passenger Transit

Trucking and Warehousing

Water Transportation

Transportation by Air

Pipelines, Except Natural Gas

Transportation Services

Legal Services

8111 Legal services, p. 444

Educational Services

8200 Educational services, p. 446
8211 Elementary and secondary schools, p. 446
8231 Libraries, p. 446

Social Services

8351 Child day care services, p. 448
8399 Social services, nec, p. 448

Museums, Botanical, Zoological Gardens

8412 Museums and art galleries, p. 449

Membership Organizations

8621 Professional organizations, p. 450
8631 Labor organizations, p. 450
8641 Civic and social associations, p. 450

Engineering and Management Services

8711 Engineering services, p. 452
8712 Architectural services, p. 452
8721 Accounting, auditing, & bookkeeping, p. 453
8732 Commercial nonphysical research, p. 456
8741 Management services, p. 457
8742 Management consulting services, p. 458
8743 Public relations services, p. 458
8748 Business consulting, nec, p. 459

Executive, Legislative, and General

9199 General government, nec, p. 460

Justice, Public Order, and Safety

9220 Public order and safety, p. 461

Finance, Taxation, and Monetary Policy

9311 Finance, taxation, & monetary policy, p. 462

Environmental Quality and Housing

9510 Environmental quality, p. 463
9512 Land, mineral, wildlife conservation, p. 463

National Security and International Affairs

9711 National security, p. 464

APPENDIX II

ANNOTATED SOURCE LIST

The following listing provides the names, publishers, addresses, telephone and fax numbers (if available), and frequency of publications for the primary sources used in *Market Share Reporter*.

ABA Banking Journal, Simmons-Boardman Publishing Corp., 345 Hudson St., New York, NY 10014-4502, *Telephone:* (212) 620-7200.

Accountancy, The American Institute of Certified Public Accountants, 1211 Avenue of the Americas, New York, NY 10036, *Telephone:* (212) 596-6200, *Fax:* (212) 596-6213. *Published:* monthly.

Accounting Today, 425 Park Ave., New York, NY 10018, *Telephone*: (212) 756-5155, *Fax:* (212) 756-5175, *Published:* 2x mo.

Advertising Age, Crain Communications, Inc., 220 E. 42nd St., New York, NY 10017, *Telephone:* (212) 210-0725, *Fax:* (212) 210-0111, *Published:* weekly.

Advertising Age- Supplement, Crain Communications, Inc., 220 E. 42nd St., New York, NY 10017, *Telephone:* (212) 210-0725, *Fax:* (212) 210-0111, *Published:* weekly.

Adweek, BPI Communications, Merchandise Mart, Suite 936, Chicago, IL 60654, *Telephone:* (800) 722-6658, *Fax:* (312) 464-8540, *Published:* weekly.

Aftermarket Business, Advanstar Communications, Inc., 7500 Old Oak Blvd., Cleveland, OH 44130-3343, *Published*: monthly.

Agri Finance, Century Publishing Co., 990 Grove St., Evanston, IL 60201-4370, *Telephone:* (708) 491-6440, *Fax:* (708) 647-7055, *Published:* 9x/yr.

Agribusiness, John Wiley and Sons Inc., 605 3rd Ave., New York, NY 10158, *Telephone:* (212) 850-6133, *Fax:* (212) 850-6052, *Published*: 6x/yr.

Air Conditioning, Heating and Refrigeration News, Business News Publishing Co., P.O. Box 2600, Troy MI 48007, *Telephone:* (313) 362-3700, *Fax:* (313) 362-0317.

Air Transport World, Penton Publishing, Inc., 600 Summer St., P.O. Box 1361, Stamford, CT. 06904, *Telephone:* (203) 348-7531, *Fax:* (203) 348-4023. *Published:* monthly.

Alaska Business Monthly, P.O. Box 241288, Anchorage, AK 99524-1288, *Telephone*: (907) 276-4373, *Fax:* (907) 279-2900, *Published:* monthly, *Price:* $21.95.

American Banker, American Banker Inc., 1 State St. , New York, NY 10023,*Telephone:* (212) 408-1480, *Fax:* (212) 943-2984. *Published:* Mon.-Fri.

American Bee Journal, Dadant & Sons Inc., 51 S. 2nd St., Hamilton, IL 62341, *Telephone:* (217) 847 - 3324, *Fax:* (217) 847-3660, *Published:* monthly, *Cost:* $15.60; $24.10 foreign.

American Ceramic Society Bulletin, American Ceramic Society, 735 Ceramic Place, Westerville, OH 43081-8720, *Published:* monthly, *Price:* $50 per year for nonmembers and libraries; included in membership dues.

American Co-Op, American Trade Magazines, Inc., 500 N. Dearborn St., Chicago, IL 60610-4901, *Published:* monthly, *Price:$33* per year.

American Demographics, P.O. Box 68, Ithaca, NY 14851-0068, *Telephone:* (607) 273-6343, *Fax:* (607) 273-3196.

American Fruit Grower, Meister Publishing Co., 37733 Euclid Ave., Willoughby, OH 44094-5992, *Telephone:* (216) 942-2000, *Fax:* (216) 942-0662, *Published:* monthly, *Cost:* $14.

American Ink Maker, MacNair-Dorland Co., 445 Broadhollow Rd., Melville, NY 11747, *Telephone:* (212) 279-4456. *Published:* monthly.

American Metal Market, Capital Cities Media Inc., 825 7th Avenue, New York, NY 10019, *Telephone:* (800) 360-7600. *Published:* daily, except Saturdays, Sundays, and holidays, *Price:* $560 per year (U.S., Canada, and Mexico).

American Printer, Maclean Hunter Publishing Co., 29 N. Wacker Dr., Chicago, IL 60606. *Published:* monthly.

American Shipper, Howard Publications Inc., 33 South Hogan Street, P.O. Box 4728, Jacksonville, FL 32201, *Telephone:* (904) 365-2601. *Published:* monthly, *Price:* $35 per year; $3 per single copy.

American Vegetable Grower, Meister Publishing Co., 37733 Euclid Ave., Willoughby, OH 44094-5992, *Telephone:* (216) 942-2000, *Fax:* (216) 942-0662. *Published:* monthly.

America's Textile International, Billian Publishing, 2100 Powers Ferry NW, Ste. 300, Atlanta, GA 30339, *Telephone:* (404) 955-5656, *Fax:* (404) 952-0669. *Published:* monthly.

Amusement Business, BPI Communications Inc., Box 24970, Nashville, TN 37202, *Telephone:* (615) 321-4250, *Fax:* (615) 327-1575. *Published:* weekly.

Apparel Industry and Codes of Conduct, U.S. Govt. Printing Office, Superintendent of Documents, Washington D.C. 2000, *Telephone:* (202) 783 - 3238.

Appliance, Dana Chase Publications Inc., 1110 Jorie Blvd., CS 9019, Ste. 203, Hinsdale, IL 60521, *Telephone:* (708) 990 - 3484, *Fax:* (708) 990 - 0078, *Published:* monthly, *Cost:* $60.

Appliance Manufacturer, Business News Publishing Co., 755 W. Big Beaver Rd., Ste. 1000, Troy, MI 48084-4900, *Telephone:* (313) 362-3700, *Fax:* (313) 244-6439. *Published:* monthly.

Arizona Business, 3111 N. Central, Phoenix, AZ 85012, *Telephone:* (602) 277-6045, *Published:* weekly.

Arkansas Business, 201 E. Markham, P.O. Box 3686, Little Rock, AR 72203, *Telephone:* (501)372-1443 Fax: (501) 375-3623. *Published:* weekly, *Price:* $38 per year.

AS&U (American School and University), North American Publishing Co., 401 N. Broad St., Philadelphia, PA 19106, *Telephone:* (215) 238-4200, *Fax:* (215) 238-4227. *Published:* monthly.

Asiaweek, 20th Floor, Trust Tower, 58 Johnston Road, Wanchal, Hong Kong, *Published:* weekly.

Assembly, Hitchcock Publishing Co., 191 S. Gary Ave., Carol Stream, IL 60188, *Telephone:* (708) 665 - 1000, *Fax:* (708) 462 - 2225.

Association Management, American Society of Association Executives, 1575 Eye St., Washington DC 20005, *Published:* monthly, *Price:* $24 per year to members, $30 per year for nonmembers.

Atlanta Journal-Constitution, 72 Marietta St., NW Atlanta, GA 30303, *Telephone:* (404) 526 - 5151, *Published:* daily.

Auto Body Repair News, Capital Cities/ABC/Chilton Co., Chilton Wy., Radnor PA 19089, *Published:* monthly.

Auto Laundry News, E.W. Williams Publications Co., 370 Lexington Ave., New York, NY 10017-6658, *Published:* monthly, *Price:* $25 per year.

Automotive Industries, Capital Cities/ABC/Chilton Co., Chilton Way, Radnor PA 19089, *Telephone*: (215) 964 - 4255, *Fax:* (215) 964 - 4251.

Automotive Marketing, Capital Cities/ABC/Chilton Co., Chilton Way, Radnor, PA 19089, *Telephone:* (215) 964-4000, *Fax:* (215) 964 - 4251. *Published:* monthly, *Price:* $36 per year.

Automotive News, Crain Communications Inc., 380 Woodbridge, Detroit, MI 48207 *Telephone:* (313) 446-6000, *Fax:* (313) 446-0347.

Aviation Week & Space Technology, McGraw-Hill, Inc., 1221 Avenue of the Americas, New York, NY 10020, *Telephone:* (212) 512-2294, *Fax:* (212) 869-7799. *Published:* weekly.

Bakery Production and Marketing, Cahners Publishing Co., 455 N. Cityfront Plaza Dr., Chicago, IL 60611, *Telephone:* (312) 222-2000.

Baltimore Business Journal, American City Business Journals, 117 Water St., Baltimore, MD 21202, *Telephone:* (410) 576-1161, *Fax:* (301) 383-3213. *Published:* weekly.

Bangkok Post, Post Publishing Company Ltd., Bankok Post Building, 136 Na Ranong Road, Office Kosa Road, Klong Toei, Bangkok, Thailand 10110, *Published:* daily.

Bank News, 912 Baltimore, Kansas City, MO 64105, *Telephone:* (816) 421-7941, *Fax:* (816) 472-0379, *Published:* monthly, *Cost*: $48.

Banker, Greystoke Place, Feteer Lane, London, England EC4A IND, *Telephone:* (071) 405-6969, *Published:* monthly

Banking Strategies, Bank Administration Institute, One North Franklin, Chicago, IL 60606, *Telephone:* (312) 553-4600, *Cost:* $59.

Best's Review, A.M. Best Co. Inc., Ambest Rd., Oldwick, NJ 08858, *Telephone:* (908) 439-2200, *Fax:* (908) 439-3363. *Published:* monthly.

Beverage Industry, Advanstar Communications, Inc., 7500 Oald Oak Blvd., Cleveland OH 44130, *Telephone:* (216) 243-8100, *Fax:* (216) 891-2651. *Published:* monthly, *Price:* $40 per year.

Beverage World, Keller International Publishing Corp., 150 Great Neck Rd., Great Neck, NY 11021, *Telephone:* (516) 829-9210, *Fax:* (516) 829-5414. *Published:* monthly.

Beverage World's Periscope, Keller International Publishing Corp., 150 Great Neck Rd., Great Neck, NY 11021, *Telephone:* (516) 829-9210, *Fax:* (516) 829-5414. *Published:* monthly.

Boating Industry, Communication Channels, Inc., 6151 Powers Ferry Road, Atlanta, GA 30339, *Telephone:* (404) 955-2500. *Published:* monthly.

Boston Globe, Globe Newspaper Co., P.O. Box 2378, Boston, MA 02107, *Telephone:* (617) 929-2000. *Published:* daily.

Brake & Front End, Babcox Publications Inc., 11 S. Forge St., Akron, OH 44304, *Telephone*: (216) 535-7011, *Price:* $115 per year.

Brand Marketing, Fairchild Publications, 7 W. 34th Street, New York, NY 10001, *Telephone:* (212) 630 - 4750, *Fax:* (212) 630 -4760.

Brandweek, Adweek L.P., 1515 Broadway, New York, NY 10036, *Telephone:* (212) 536-5336. *Published:* weekly, except no issue in the last week of Dec.

Broadcasting & Cable, Cahners Publishing Co., 1705 DeSales Street, N.W., Washington, DC 20036, *Telephone:* (800) 554-5729 or (202) 659-2340, *Fax:* (202) 331-1732.

Broiler Industry, Watt Publishing Co., 122 S. Wesley Ave., Mount Morris, IL 61054-1497, *Telephone:* (815) 734-4171, *Fax:* (815) 734-4201. *Published:* monthly.

Builder, Hanley-Wood Inc., 655 15th St. N.W., Ste. 475, Washington, D.C. 20005, *Telephone:* (202) 737-0717, *Fax:* (202) 737-2439. *Published:* monthly.

Building Design & Construction, Cahners Publishing, 1350 E. Touhy Ave., Des Plaines, IL 60017-5080, *Telephone:* (708) 635-8800. *Published:* monthly.

Building Operation & Management, Trade Press Publishing Corp., 2100 W. Florist Ave., Milwaukee, WI 53209, *Telephone:* (414) 228-7701, *Fax:* (414) 228-1134, *Published:* monthly.

Buildings, Stamats Communications Inc., 427 6th Ave., P.O. Box 1888, Cedar Rapids, IA 52406, *Telephone:* (319) 364-6167, *Fax:* (319) 364-4278, *Published:* monthly, *Price:* $50 per year.

Business America, U.S. Government Printing Office, Superintendent of Documents, Washington D.C. 20402, *Telephone:* (202) 783-3238, *Fax:* (202) 275-0019, *Published:* monthly.

Business & Commercial Aviation, 4 International Drive, Ste. 260, Rye Brook, NY 10573 - 1065, *Telephone:* (914) 939-0300, *Fax:* (914) 939-1100, *Published:* monthly, *Price:* $42.

Business & Health, Medical Economics Publishing Co., 5 Paragon Dr., Montvale, NJ 07645-1184, *Telephone:* (201) 358-7208. *Published:* 14x/yr.

Business Communications Review, BCR Enterprises, Inc., 950 York Rd., Hinsdale, IL 60521, *Telephone:* (800) 227-1324. *Published:* monthly.

Business First Columbus, 200 E. Rich St., Columbus, OH 43215, *Telephone:* (614) 461-4040.

Business First of Buffalo, 472 Delaware St., Buffalo, NY 14202.

Business Insurance, Crain Communications, Inc., 740 N. Rush St., Chicago IL 60611, *Published:* monthly.

Business Journal, American City Business Journals, 2025 N. Summit Ave., Milwaukee, WI 53202.

Business Journal-Serving Greater Milwaukee, American City Business Journals, 2025 N. Summit Ave., Milwaukee, WI 53202, *Telephone:* (414) 278-7788, *Fax:* (414) 278-7028.

Business Journal - Serving Greater Sacramento, 1401 21st St., Sacramento, CA 95814-5221, *Telephone:* (916) 447-7661, *Fax:* (916) 444-7779, *Published:* weekly, *Cost:* $36; $34 corporate.

Business Journal - Serving Phoenix and the Valley of the Sun, 3737 N. 7th St., Ste. 200, Phoenix, AZ 85014, *Telephone:* (602) 230-8400, *Fax:* (602) 230-0955, *Published:* weekly, *Cost:* $46.

Business Mexico, American Chamber of Commerce, A.C., Lucerna 78, Col. Juarez, DEl. Cuauhtemoc, Mexico City, Mexico, *Telephone:* 705-0995. *Published:* monthly.

Business Quarterly, University of Western Ontario, Western Business School, London, ON Canada N6A 3K7, *Telephone:* (519) 661-3309, *Fax:* (519) 661-3838, *Published:* quarterly, *Cost:* $40; $60 foreign.

Business North Carolina, 5435 77 Center Dr., No. 50, Charlotte, NC 28217-0711 *Telephone:* (704) 523-6987 *Published:* monthly.

Business Week, McGraw-Hill Inc., 1221 Avenue of the Americas, New York, NY 10020. *Published:* weekly, *Price:* U.S.: $46.95 per year; Canada: $69 CDN per year.

Byte, Byte Publications, 1 Phoenix Mill Lane, Petersborough, NH 03458, *Telephone:* (212) 512-2000.

Cablevision, Chilton Publications, P.O. Box 7698, Riverton, NJ 08077-7698, *Telephone:* (609) 786-0501. *Published:* twice monthly, *Price:* U.S.: $55 per year, $99 for 2 years; Elsewhere via surface mail: $85 per year, $159 for 2 years.

Canadian Business, CB Media Limited, 70 Esplanade, Second Floor, Toronto MSE IR2 Canada, *Telephone:* (416) 364-4266, *Fax:* (416) 364-2783. *Published:* monthly, *Price:* Canada: $24 per year, $60 for 3 years; Elsewhere: $40 per year, $100 for 3 years.

Canadian Chemical News (L'Actualite Chimique Canadienne), Chemican Publishers Ltd., 130 Slater St., Ste. 550, Ottawa, ON Canada K 1 P 6E2, *Telephone:* (613) 232-6252, *Fax:* (613) 232-5862, *Published:* 10x/yr.

Canadian Mining Journal, Southam Magazine Group, PO Box 1144, Lewiston, NY 14092, *Published:* 4x/yr.

Canadian Plastics, Southam Magazine Group, 4703 Porter Ctr. Rd, Lewiston, NY 14092.

Candy Industry, Advanstar Communications, Inc., 7500 Old Oak Blvd., Cleveland, OH 44130. *Telephone:* (216) 891-2612, *Fax:* (216) 891-2651.

Catalog Age, Cowles Business Media Inc., 911 Hope St., Six River Bend Center, Box 4949, Stanford CT 06907-0949, *Telephone:* (203) 358-9900, *Published:* monthly.

Catfish Production. National Agricultural Statistics Service, Superintendent of Documents, Superintendent of Socuments, U.S. Govt. Printing Office, Washington D.C. 20402, *Telephone*: (202) 783 - 3238.

Ceramic Industry, Business News Publishing Co., 5900 Harper Road, Suite 109, Solon, OH 44139, *Telephone:* (216) 498-9214, *Fax:* (216) 498-9121. *Published:* monthly, *Price:* U.S.: $53 per year; Mexico: $63; Canada: $66.71 (includes postage & GST).

Chain Store Age, Lebhar-Friedman Inc., 425 Park Ave., New York, NY 10022, *Telephone:* (212) 371-9400, *Fax:* (212) 319-4129. *Published:* monthly.

Chemical & Engineering News, American Chemical Society, Dept. L-0011, Columbus, OH 43210, *Telephone:* (800) 333-9511 or (614) 447-3776. *Published:* weekly, except last week in December, *Price:* U.S.: $100 per year, $198 for 2 years; elsewhere: $148 per year, $274 for 2 years.

Chemical Engineering, McGraw-Hill Inc., 1221 Avenue of the Americas, New York, NY 10020, *Telephone:* (212) 512-2000. *Published:* monthly.

Chemical Engineering Progress, American Institute of Chemical Engineers, 345 E. 47th St., New York, NY 10017, Telephone: (212) 705-7576, *Published:* weekly.

Chemical Market Reporter (formerly Chemical Marketing Reporter), Schnell Publishing Co., Inc., 80 Broad St., New York, NY 1004-2203, *Telephone:* (212) 248-4177, *Fax:* (212) 248-4903, *Published:* weekly.

Chemical Marketing Reporter, Schnell Publishing Co., Inc., 80 Broad St., New York, NY 1004-2203, *Telephone:* (212) 248-4177, *Fax:* (212) 248-4903, *Published:* weekly.

Chemicalweek, Chemical Week Associates, P.O. Box 7721, Riverton, NJ 08077-7721, *Telephone:* (609) 786-0401, *Published:* weekly, except four combination issues (total of 49 issues), *Price:* U.S.: $99 per year; Canada: $129 per year. Single copies $8 in U.S. and $10 elsewhere.

Chicago Tribune, 435 N. Michigan Ave., Chicago, IL 60611, *Telephone:* (312) 222-3232. *Published:* daily.

Chief Executive, Macfadden Holdings Inc., 233 Park Ave. S, New York, NY 10003, *Telephone*: (212) 979 - 4810, *Fax:* (212) 979 - 7431, *Published:* 9x/yr. *Cost:* $95.

Child Care Information Exchange, Exchange Press Inc., P.O. 2890, Redmond, WA 98073, *Telephone:* (800) 221-2864, *Published:* bimonthly, *Price:* $35 per year.

Christian Science Monitor, Christian Science Publishing Society, One Norway St., Boston, MA 02115, *Telephone:* (800) 456-2220, *Published:* daily, except weekends and holidays.

Cincinnati Business Courier, Standard Publishing, 4500 Carew Tower, Cincinnati, OH 45202, *Telephone:* (513) 621-6665, *Fax:* (513) 621-2462, *Published:* weekly.

Communications News, Nelson Publishing, 2504 N Tamiami Tr, Nelson Bldg., Nokomis, FL 34275, Telephone: (813) 966-9521, Fax: (813) 966-2590, Published: monthly.

Computer Design, PennWell Publishing Co., 1 Technology Park Drive, Westford, MA 01886, *Telephone:* (508) 692-0700, *Published:* 24x/yr.

Computer Reseller News, CMP Media Inc., One Jericho Plaza, Jericho, New York 11753, *Published:* $199; Canada $224

Computer Technology Review, 924 Westwood Blvd., No. 650, Los Angeles, CA 90024-2910, *Telephone:* (310) 208-1335, *Fax:* (310) 208-1054, *Published:* monthly, *Cost:* $80.

Computerworld, P.O. Box 2043, Marion, OH 43305-2403, *Telephone:* (800) 669-1002, *Published*: weekly.

Computing Canada, Plesman Publications Ltd., 2005 Sheppard Ave. E., 4th Fl., Willowsdale, ON, Canada M2J 5B1, *Telephone:* (416) 497-9562, *Fax:* (416) 497-9427. *Published:* biweekly.

Construction Equipment, Cahners Publishing Co., 1350 E. Touhy Ave., Des Plaines, IL 60018, *Telephone:* (708) 635-8800, *Fax:* (708) 390-2690, *Published:* monthly (with 2 annuals).

Construction Review, U.S. Dept. of Commerce, Superintendent of Documents, USGPO, Washington DC 20402, *Telephone:* (202) 783-3238.

Consultants News, Kennedy Publications, Templeton Road, Fitzwilliam, NH 03447, *Telephone:* (603) 585-6544, *Fax:* (603) 585-6401, Published: monthly, *Price:* $158 per year.

Consumer Reports, Consumers Union of U.S., Inc., 101 Truman Ave., Yonkers, NY 10703-1057, *Telephone:* (914) 378-2000, *Fax:* (914) 378-2900, *Published:* monthly, *Cost:* $18.

Contract Design, Miller Freeman Inc., 1515 Broadway, New York, NY 10036, *Telephone:* (212) 869-1300, *Fax:* (212) 302-6273.

Contractor, Cahners Publishing Co., 44 Cook St., Denver, CO. 80206-5800, *Telephone:* (708) 390-2676, *Fax:* (708) 390-2690, *Published:* monthly.

Cornell Hotel and Restaurant Administration Quarterly, Cornell University of School of Hotel Administration, Statlet Hall, Ithaca, NY 14853, *Telephone:* (607) 255-5093, *Fax:* (607) 257-1204, *Published:* 6x/yr., *Cost:* $62; $102 institutions; $90 foreign.

Corporate Report Minnesota, Corporate Report Inc., 5500 Wayzata Blvd., Suite 800, Minneapolis, MN 55416, *Telephone:* (612) 591-2531. *Published:* monthly, *Price:* $29 per year, $47 for 2 years, $63 for three years. Back issues $3.95 each.

CPA Journal, 535 Metro Pl. S., P.O. Box 1810, Dublin, OH 43017-7810, *Telephone:* (614) 764-2727, *Fax:* (614) 764-5880.

Crain's Chicago Business, Crain Communications Inc., 740 N. Rush St., Chicago, IL 60611, *Telephone:* (312) 649-5411.

Crain's Cleveland Business, Crain Communications, Inc., 1725 Merriman Rd., Ste. 300, Akron, OH 44313-5251, *Telephone:* (216) 836-9180, *Fax:* (216) 836-1005. *Published:* weekly.

Crain's Detroit Business, Crain Communications Inc., 1400 Woodbridge, Detroit, MI 48207-3187, *Telephone:* (313) 446-6000. *Published:* weekly, except semiweekly the fourth week in May.

Crain's New York Business, Crain Communications, Inc., 220 E. 42nd St., New York, NY 10017, *Telephone:* (212) 210-0100, *Fax:* (212) 210-0799. *Published:* weekly.

Crain's Small Business, Crain Communications Inc., 1400 Woodbridge, Detroit, MI 48207-3187, *Telephone:* (313) 446-6000.

Credit Union Management, Credit Union Executives Society, 6410 Enterprise Ln., Ste. 300, Madison, WI 53719-1143, *Telephone:* (608) 271-2664, *Fax:* (608) 271-2303.

Custom Builder, Willows Publishing Group Inc., 38 Lafayette St., P.O. Box 998, Yarmouth, ME 04096, *Telephone:* (207) 846-0970, *Fax:* (207) 846-1561, *Published:* 6x/yr.

Dairy Foods, Gorman Publishing Co., 8750 W. Bryn Mawr Ave., Chicago, IL 60062, *Telephone:* (312) 693-3200. *Published:* monthly, except semimonthly in Aug.

Dairy Foods - Industry Planner Supplement, Gorman Publishing Co., 8750 W. Bryn Mawr Ave., Chicago, IL 60062, *Telephone:* (312) 6933-3200.

Dallas Business Journal, American City Business Journals, American City Business Journals, 4131 N Central Expy, Ste. 310, Dallas, TX 75204, *Telephone:* (214) 520-1010, *Fax:* (214) 528-4686.

Dallas Morning News, 508 Young St., P.O. Box 655237, Dallas, TX 75265, *Telephone:* (214) 977-8222, *Fax:* (214) 977-8776. *Published:* daily.

Data Communications, McGraw-Hill Inc., 1221 Avenue of the Americas, New York, NY 10020, *Telephone:* (212) 512-2699, *Fax:* (212) 512-6833. *Published:* monthly.

Database, 462 Danbury Rd., Wilton, CT 06897-2125, *Published:* 6x/yr.

Datamation, Cahners Publishing Co., 275 Washington Street, Newton, MA 02158, *Telephone:* (617) 558-4281.

Dealerscope, North American Publishing Co., 401 N. Broad St., Philadelphia, PA 19108, *Telephone:* (215) 238-5300, *Published:* semi-monthly.

Denver Business Journal, 1700 Broadway, Ste. 515, Denver, CO 80290, Telephone: (303) 837-3500, Fax: (303) 837-3535, *Published:* weekly.

Detroit Free Press, Knight-Ridder, Inc., 1 Herald Plaza, Miami, FL 33132, *Telephone:* (305) 376-3800, *Published:* daily.

Detroit News, Gannett Co. Inc., 1 Gannett Dr., White Plains, NY 10604-3498, *Telephone:* (914) 694-9300, *Published:* daily.

Diesel Progress Engines & Drives, Diesel & Gas Turbine Publications, 13555 Bishop's Ct., Brookfield, WI 53005-6286, *Telephone:* (414) 784-9177, *Fax:* (414) 784-8133, *Published:* monthly.

Direct Marketing, Hoke Communications Inc., 224 7th St., Garden City, NY 11530, *Telephone:* (516) 746-6700, *Fax:* (516) 294-8141, *Published:* monthly, *Cost:* $56.

Discount Merchandiser, Schwartz Publications, 233 Park Ave. S., New York, NY 10003, *Telephone:* (212) 979-4860, *Fax:* (212) 979-7431, *Published:* monthly.

Discount Store News, Lebhar-Friedman Inc., 425 Park Ave, New York, NY 10022, *Telephone:* (212) 756-5100, *Fax:* (212) 756-5125, *Published:* weekly.

Distribution, Chilton Co., Chilton Way, Radnor, PA 19089, *Telephone:* (215) 964-4000. *Published:* monthly, *Price:* U.S.: $65 per year; Canada: $70 per year, Single issues $5.50, except July issue $45.

DM, Schwartz Publications, 233 Park Ave. S., New York, NY 10003, *Telephone:* (212) 979-4860, *Fax:* (212) 979-7431, *Published:* monthly.

DNR (Digital News & Review), Cahners Publishing Co., 275 Washington St., Newton, MA 02158, *Telephone:* (617) 558-4243, *Fax:* (617) 558-4759, *Published:* 2x/mo.

Do-It-Yourself-Retailing, National Retail Hardware Assn., 5822 W. 74th St., Indianapolis, IN 46278-1756, *Telephone:* (317) 297-1190, *Fax:* (317) 328-4354, *Published:* monthly, *Cost*: $8; $2 single issue.

Drug Topics, Medical Economics Publishing Co., 5 Paragon Dr., Montvale, NJ 07645-1742, *Telephone:* (201) 358-7200, *Published:* semimonthly, only once in December.

E-Media Professional, Online Inc., 462 Danbury Road, Wilton, CT 06897-2126, *Published:* monthly, *Cost:* $55; $98 corporate.

Economic Development Horizon, 3281 E. Guasti Road, Ste. 275, Ontario, California 91764.

Economist, The Economist Bldg, 111 W. 57th St., New York, NY 10019, *Telephone:* (212) 541-5730, *Fax:* (212) 541-9378, *Published:* weekly, *Cost:* $110; $3.50 per single issue.

Egg Industry, Watt Publishing Co., 122 S. Wesley Ave., Mount Morris, IL 61054-1497, *Telephone:* (815) 734-4171, *Fax:* (815) 734-4201, *Published:* bimonthly.

Electronic Business Today, CMP Publications Inc., 8773 South Ridgeline Blvd., Highlands Ranch, CO, 80126-2329, *Telephone:* (516) 562-5000, *Fax:* (516) 562-5409, *Published:* monthly.

Electronic Design, 222 Rosewood Drive, Danvers, MA 01923.

Electronic News, Electronic News Publishing Corp., 488 Madison Ave., New York, NY 10022, *Telephone:* (212) 909-5924, *Published:* weekly, except last week of Dec.

Engineering & Mining Journal, Maclean Hunter Publishing Co., 29 Wacker Dr., Chicago, IL 60606, *Fax:* (312) 726-2574, *Published:* monthly.

Engineering News Record**,** McGraw-Hill Inc., Fulfillment Manager, ENR, P.O. Box 518, Highstown, NJ 08520, *Telephone:* (609) 426-7070 or (212) 512-3549, *Fax:* (212) 512-3150, *Published:* weekly, *Price:* U.S.: $89 per year; Canada: $75 per year. Single copies $5 in U.S.

Entertainment Weekly, Time-Warner Inc., 1675 Broadway, New York, NY 10019, Published: weekly.

Entrepreneur Magazine, Entrepreneur Inc., 2392 Morse Ave., Irvine, CA 92714, *Telephone:* (714) 261-2325, *Fax:* (714) 755-4211.

Environmental Management Today, Springer-Verlag New York Inc., 175 5th Ave., New York, NY 10010, *Telephone:* (212) 460-1500, *Fax:* (212) 473-6272.

Equus, Fleet Street Publishing Corp., 656 Quince Orchard Rd., Gaithersburg, MD 20878, *Telephone:* (301) 977-3900, *Fax:* (301) 990-9015, *Published:* monthly, *Price:* $24 per year.

European Rubber Journal, Crain Communications Ltd., 20-22 Bedford Row, London WC1R 4EW, UK *Telephone:* (071) 831-9511, *Fax:* (071) 430-2176, *Published:* monthly, except August.

Farm Journal, 230 W. Washington Sq., Philadelphia, PA 19106, *Telephone:* (215) 829-4700, *Published:* 13x/yr, *Price:* $14 per year.

Financial Post, The Financial Post Company, 333 King St., East, Toronto M5A 4N2, Canada, *Telephone:* (800) 387-9011. *Published:* monthly with 5-day per week newspaper, *Price:* $182 per year; weekend mail subscription $49.95 includes magazine and annual issues.

Financial Times, FT Publications Inc., 14 East 60th Street, New York, NY 21002, *Telephone:* (212) 752-4500, *Fax:* (212) 319-0704, *Published:* daily, except for Sundays and holidays, *Cost:* $425.

Folio, Cowles Business Media, P.O. Box 4294, Stamford, CT 60907-0294, *Price:* U.S.: 24 issues for $96, 48 issues for $152, 72 issues for $199; Canada/Mexico: 24 issues for $116, 48 issues for $184, 72 issues for $240.

Food Engineering, Chilton Co., One Chilton Way, Radnor, PA 19089, *Telephone:* (215) 964-4000. *Published:* monthly, *Price:* solicited only from professionals in field: $55 per year, $100 for 2 years; educational rate: $28 per year.

Footwear News, Fairchild Publications, 7 West 34th Str., New York, NY 10001-8191.

Forbes, Forbes, Inc., P.O. Box 10048, Des Moines, IA 50340-0048, *Telephone:* (800) 888-9896, *Published:* 27 issues per year, *Price:* U.S.: $54 per year; Canada: $95 per year (includes GST).

Forest Products Journal, Forest Products Society, 2801 Marshall Court, Madison, WI 53705-2295, *Published:* monthly, except combined issues in July/August and November/December, *Price:* U.S.: $115 per year; Canada/Mexico: $125; single copies $12 each plus shipping and handling.

Fortune, Time Inc., Time & Life Building, Rockefeller Center, New York, NY 10020-1393, *Published:* twice monthly, except two issues combined into a single issue at year-end, *Price:* U.S.: $57 per year; Canada: $65 per year.

Fruit Grower, Meister Publishing Co., 37733 Euclid Ave., Willoughsby, OH 44094-5992.

Furniture Today, Cahners Publishing Co., 200 S. Main St., P.O. Box 2754, High Point, NC 27261, *Telephone:* (919) 889-0113, *Published:* weekly.

Glass Industry, Ashlee Publishing Co., Inc., 310 Madison Avenue, New York, NY 10017-6098, *Telephone:* (212) 682-7681, *Fax:* (212) 697-8331, *Published:* monthly, except 2 issues in February, *Price:* U.S./Canada/Mexico: $40 per year, $50 for 2 years, $60 for 3 years.

Global Finance, Global Finance Joint Venture, 11 W. 19th St. 2nd Fl., New York, NY 1011, *Telephone:* (212)337-5900, *Fax:* (212) 697-8331, *Published:* monthly.

Globe and Mail, 444 Front St. W., Toronto, ON, Canada M5V 2S9, *Telephone:* (416) 585-5000, *Fax:* (416) 585-5085, *Published:* Mon.-Sat. (morn.).

Globe and Mail's Report on Business Magazine, 444 Front St. W., Toronto, ON, Canada M5V 2S9, *Telephone:* (416) 585-5000, *Fax:* (416) 585-5085.

Greenhouse Grocer, Meister Publishing Co., 37733 Euclid Ave., Willoughby, OH 44094-5922. *Telephone:* (216) 942-2000, *Fax:* (216) 942-0662, *Published:* 14x/yr.

Grocery Headquarters, Delta Communications Inc., 455 N. Cityfront Plaza Drive, Chicago, IL 60611, *Telephone:* (312) 222-2000, *Fax:* (312) 222-2026, *Published:* monthly.

Grocery Marketing, Delta Communications Inc., 455 N. Cityfront Plaza Drive, Chicago, IL 60611, *Telephone:* (312) 222-2000, *Fax:* (312) 222-2026, *Published:* monthly.

Grounds Maintenance, Intertec Publishing Co., 9800 Metcalf Ave., Overland Park, KS 66212-2215, *Published:* monthly.

Health Data Management, 5350 S. Rosyln St., Englewood, CO 80111-2125.

Healthcare Financial Management, 2 West Corp. Ctr., Ste. 700, Westchester, IL 60154, *Telephone:* (708) 531-9600, *Fax:* (708) 531-0032.

Healthcare Informatics, Wiesner Inc., Englewood, CO 80112, *Published:* monthly.

HFN, 7 E. 12th St., New York, NY 10003. *Published:* weekly.

High Volume Printing, Innes Publishing Co., 425 Huehl Rd., Bldg. 11, Northbrook, IL 60062-2319, *Published:* monthly, *Price:* $45 per year.

Hollywood Reporter, H.R. Industries Inc., 5055 Wilshire Blvd., Los Angles, CA 90036-4396, *Published:* weekly, *Price:* $90.

Hospitals & Health Networks, Chilton Co., 737 North Michigan Avenue, Suite 700, Chicago, IL 60611, *Telephone:* (312) 440-6836, *Published:* monthly.

Hotel & Motel Management, Advanstar Communications, Inc., 7500 Old Oak Blvd., Cleveland, OH 44130, *Telephone:* (216) 826-2839.

Hotels, Cahners Publishing Co., 1350 Touhy Ave., P.O. Box 5080, Des Plaines, IL 60017-5080, *Telephone:* (708) 635-8800, *Fax:* (708) 635-6856.

Household and Personal Products Industry, Rodman Publishing, 17 S. Franklin Turnpike, Box 555, Ramsey, NJ 07446, *Telephone:* (201) 825-2552, *Fax:* (201) 825-0553, *Published:* monthly.

Human Resource Executive, Axon Magazine Group, 747 Dresher Rd., Ste 500, P.O. Box 980, Horsham, PA 19044, *Telephone:* (215) 784-0860.

Implement & Tractor, Farm Press Publications, Inc., PO Box 1420, Clarksdale, MS 38614, *Telephone:* (601) 624-8503, *Fax:* (601) 627-1977. *Published:* monthly, *Price:* $15 per year.

Industrial Distribution, Cahners Publishing Company, 275 Washington Street, Newton, MA 02158, *Telephone:* (617) 964-3030, *Published:* monthly.

Industrial Paint & Powder, Chilton Publications, 191 S. Gary Ave., Carol Stream, IL 60188, *Telephone:* (708) 665-1000, *Fax:* (708) 462-2225, *Published:* monthly.

Informationweek, CMP Publications, Inc., P.O. Box 1093, Skokie, IL 60076-8093, *Published:* weekly, except double issue in the last two weeks of December, *Price:* U.S./Canada: $120 per year; free to qualified persons in field of information management.

Infoworld, Infoworld Publishing Co., 155 Bovet Rd., Ste. 800, San Mateo, CA 94402, *Telephone:* (415) 572-7341, *Published:* weekly.

Interavia, Swissair Centre, 31 Route de l'Aeroport, P.O. Box 437, 1215 Geneva 15, Switzerland, Switzerland, *Telephone*: (902) 788-2788, *Published:* monthly, Price: $128 per year.

International Business, American International Publishing, 500 Mamaroneck Ave., Ste 314, Harrison, NY 10528-1600, *Telephone:* (914) 381-7700, *Fax:* (914) 381-7713, *Published:* monthly, except for double issue in May.

Investext, The Investext Group, 22 Pittsburgh Street, Boston, MA 02210. Investext is an online database of full-text company and industry research reports produced by more than 385 investment banks and brokerage firms around the globe. Approximately 400 new reports are added daily. The Investext database is available on the Investext Group's online and CD-ROM products and via most major online business providers. Reports and research services may also be ordered by phone. Telephone: 800-662-7878 (U.S.), +44-171-815-3860 (U.K./Europe), 852-2522-4159 (Hong Kong), 03-5213-7300.

Investment Dealers Digest, 2 World Trade Center, 18th Fl., New York, NY 10048, *Telephone:* (212)227-1200, *Fax:* (212) 321-3805.

Investor's Business Daily, P.O. Box 661750, Los Angeles, CA 90066-8950, *Published:* daily, except weekends and holidays, *Cost:* $128 per year.

Journal of Commerce, Journal of Commerce, Inc., Two World Trade Center, 27th Floor, New York, NY 10048, *Telephone:* (212) 837-7000, *Fax:* (212) 837-7035.

Journal of Forestry, Society of American Foresters, 5400 Grosvenor Ln., Bethesda, MD 20814-2198, *Telephone:* (301) 897-8720, *Fax:* (301) 897-3690, *Published:* monthly.

Latin American Economy & Business, Latin American Newsletters, 61 Old Street, London EC1V 9hX, England, *Telephone*: (4471) 251 0012, *Published:* monthly.

Latin Finance Corporate Handbook, Reed Publishing, 205 E. 42nd St., Ste. 1705, New York, NY 10017, *Telephone:* (212) 867-2080, *Fax:* (212) 687-6604, *Published:* annually.

Latin Trade, Freedom Communications Inc., 200 South Bicauyne Blvd., Suite 1150, Miami, FL 33131, *Published:* monthly.

Le Devoir, L'Imprimiere Populaire, 211 du SAt. Sacrement, Montreal, PQ, Canada H2Y 1X1, *Telephone:* (514) 985-3333, *Fax:* (514) 985-3360.

Light Metal Age, Fellon Publishing Co., 170 S. Spruce Ave., Ste. 120, South San Francisco, CA 94080, *Telephone:* (415) 588-8832, *Fax:* (415) 588-0901, *Published:* 6x/yr.

Logistics Management, 1924 W. Mall, Vancouver, BC, Canada, V6t 1Zs.

Los Angeles Business Journal, 5700 Wilshire, No. 170, Los Angeles, CA 90010, *Telephone:* (213) 549-5225, *Fax:* (213) 480-0468.

Los Angeles Times, The Times Mirror Company, Times Mirror Square, Los Angeles, CA 90053, *Telephone:* (800) LA TIMES.

Macleans, Maclean Hunter Ltd., 777 Bay St., Toronto, ON, Canada M5W 1A7, *Telephone:* (416) 596-5311, *Fax:* (416) 596-6001, *Published:* weekly.

Macweek, JCI Co., 301 Howard St., 15th Fl., San Francisco, CA 94015, *Telephone:* (415) 243-3500, *Fax:* (415) 243-3651.

Manufacturing Confectioner, The Manufacturing Confectioner Publishing Company, 175 Rock Rd., Glen Rock, NJ 07452, *Telephone:* (201) 652-2655, *Fax:* (201) 652-3419, *Published:* 12 times per year, *Price:* $25 per year, single copies $10 each, except $25 for April and July issues.

Marketing Magazine, Maclean Hunter Canadian Publishing, P.O. Box 4541, Buffalo, NY 14240-4541, *Telephone:* (800) 567-0444, *Fax:* (416) 946-1679, *Price:* Canada: $59.50 per year, $98.50 for 2 years, $125 for 3 years; U.S.: $90 per year.

Marketing News, American Marketing Assn., 250 S. Wacker Dr., Ste. 200, Chicago, IL 60606-5819, *Telephone:* (312) 993-9517, *Fax:* (312) 993-7540, *Published:* biweekly.

Mediaweek, ADWEEK, L.P., P.O. Box 1976, Danbury, CT 06813-1976, *Telephone:* (800) 722-6658, *Published:* weekly, except first week of July, last week of August, and Last two weeks of December, *Price:* U.S.: $95 per year, $170 for 2 years; Canada: $230 per year.

Medical Marketing & Media, CPS Communications, Inc., 7200 West Camino Real, Suite 215, Boca Raton, FL 33433, *Telephone:* (407) 368-9301, *Fax:* (407) 368-7870, *Published:* monthly, *Price:* U.S.: $75 per year; Canada: $90 per year.

Metro Magazine, Bobbit Publishing Co., 2512 Artesia Boulevard, Redondo Beach, CA 90278, *Published:* bimonthly, with an extra issue in October, *Price:* $25 per year.

Metro Magazine Fact Book, Bobbit Publishing Co., 2512 Artesia Boulevard, Redondo Beach, CA 90278.

Mexico Business, 3033 Chimey Rd., Suite 300, Houston, TX 77056, *Published:* monthly, combined issues in Jan./Feb. and July/Aug.

Mexico: Building For Growth, Superintendent of Documents, U.S. Govt. Printing Office, Washington, DC 20402, *Telephone:* (202) 783-3238.

Michigan Retailer, Michigan Retailers Association, 221 North Pine Street, Lansing, MI 48933, *Published:* 10x/yr. *Cost:* $20.

Milwaukee Journal-Sentinel, P.O. Box 371, Milwaukee, WI 53201, *Telephone:* (414) 224-2000, *Fax:* (414) 224-2049.

Minerals Yearbook: Metals and Minerals, Superintendent of Documents, U.S. Govt. Printing Office, Washington, DC 20402, *Telephone:* (202) 783-3238.

Modern Healthcare, Crain Communications, Inc., 740 N. Rush St., Chicago, IL 60611-2590, *Telephone:* (312) 649-5350, *Fax:* (312) 280-3189, *Published:* weekly.

Modern Plastics, McGraw-Hill, Inc., Attn. Fulfillment Manager, P.O. Box 481, Highstown, NJ 08520, *Telephone:* (800) 525-5003, *Published:* monthly, *Price:* U.S.: $41.75 per year, $62.70 for 2 years, $83.50 for 3 years; Canada:$CDN 53 per year, $CDN 80 for 2 years, $CDN 106 for 3 years.

Montana Business Quarterly, Bureau of Business and Economic Research, University of Montana, Missoula, MT 59812, *Telephone:* (406) 243-5113, *Published:* 4x/yr.

Mortgage Banking, Mortgage Bankers Association of America, MBA Dept. 0021, Washington, DC 20073-0021, *Telephone:* (202) 861-6992, *Published:* monthly,

Price: U.S.: $40 per year, $95 for 3 years; Canada: $42 per year.

Music Trades, P.O. Box 432, 80 West St., Englewood, NJ 07631, *Telephone:* (201) 871-1965, *Fax:* (201) 871-0455, *Published:* monthly.

NARD Journal, NARD: The National Association Representing Independent Retail Pharmacy, 205 Daingerfield Rd., Alexandria, VA 22314, *Telephone:* (703) 683-8200, *Fax:* (703) 683-3619, *Published:* monthly, *Cost:* $50.

National Petroleum News, Hunter Publishing Limited Partnership, Circulation Dept., National Petroleum News, 25 Northwest Point Blvd., Suite 800, Elk Grove Village, IL 60007, *Telephone:* (708) 427-9512, *Published:* monthly, except semimonthly in June, *Price:* U.S.: $60 per year for those in petroleum marketing industry, $75 per year for others; Canada: $69 per year for those in petroleum marketing industry, $84 per year for others.

National Real Estate Investor, Communication Channels Inc., 6255 Barfield Rd., Atlanta, GA 30328, *Telephone:* (404) 256-9800, *Fax:* (404) 256-3116, *Published:* monthly.

National Trade Data Bank, STAT-USA, U.S. Department of Commerce, Washington D.C., 20230, *Telephone:* (202) 482-1986, *Fax:* (202) 482-2164.

National Underwriter, The National Underwriter Co., 505 Gest St., Cincinnati, OH 45203, *Telephone:* (800) 543-0874, *Fax:* (800) 874-1916, *Published:* weekly, except last week in December, *Price:* U.S.: $77 per year, $130 for 2 years; Canada: $112 per year, $130 for 2 years.

Nation's Restaurant News, Lebhar-Friedman, Inc., Subscription Dept., P.O. Box 31179, Tampa, FL 33631-3179, *Telephone:* (800) 447-7133. *Published:* weekly on Mondays, except the first Monday in July and the last Monday in December, *Price:* $34.50 per year and $55 for 2 years for professionals in the field; $89 per year for those allied to field.

Network Computing, CMP Publications, Inc., 600 Community Dr., Manhasset, NY 11030, *Telephone:* (708) 647-6834, *Fax:* (708) 647-6838.

Network World, Network World, Inc., 161 Worcester Rd., Framingham, MA 01701-9172, *Telephone:* (508) 875-6400, *Published:* weekly.

New Steel, Chilton Publishing Company, One Chilton Way, Radnor, PA 19089, *Telephone:* (212) 887-8560, *Published:* monthly.

New York Times, New York Times Co., 229 W. 43rd St., New York, NY 10036, *Telephone:* (212) 556-1234. *Published:* daily.

Newsweek, The Newsweek Building, Livingston, NJ 07039-1666, *Telephone:* (800) 631-1040, *Published:* weekly, *Price:* U.S.: $41.08 per year; Canada: $61.88 per year (send to P.O. Box 4012, Postal Station A, Toronto, ON M5W 2K1).

Nonfoods Merchandising, Intl. Thomson Retail Press, 22 W. 21st. St., Box 640, New York, NY 10011, *Telephone:* (212) 741-7210, *Published:* monthly.

Nursery Retailer, Brantwood Publications, Inc., 3023 Eastland Blvd., Ste. 103, Clearwater, FL 34621-4106, *Telephone:* (813) 796-3877, *Fax:* (813) 791-4126, *Published:* 6x/yr.

Observer, Guardian Newspapers Ltd., 119 Farrington Road, London ECR1R ER, *Telephone:* (0171) 278-2332, Published: sundays.

OR Manager, 2170 S. Parker Rd., Ste. 300, Denver, CO 80231-5711, *Telephone:* (303) 755-6300.

Packaging Digest, Delta Communications, 455 N. Cityfront Plaza Drive, Chicago, IL 60611, *Telephone:* (312) 222-2000, *Fax:* (312) 222-2026, Published: monthly, *Cost:* $75.

Paperboard Packaging, Advanstar Communications Inc., 131 West First Street, Duluth, MN 55802, *Telephone:* (218) 723-9477, *Fax:* (218) 723-9437, *Publish-*

ed: monthly, *Price:* U.S.: $39 per year, $58 for 2 years; Canada: $59 per year, $88 for 2 years.

PC Week, Ziff-Davis Publishing Company L.P., Customer Service Dept., PC WEEK, P.O. Box 1770, Riverton, NJ 08077-7370, *Telephone:* (609) 461-210, *Published:* weekly, except combined issue at year-end, *Price:* U.S.: $160 per year; Canada/Mexico: $200 per year.

Pensions & Investments, Crain Communications Inc., 220 E. 42nd St., New York, NY 10017, *Telephone:* (212) 210-0227, *Fax:* (212) 210-0117, *Published:* biweekly

Pet Product News, Fancy Publications, Inc., P.O. Box 6050, Mission Viejo, CA 92690, *Telephone:* (714) 855-8822, *Fax:* (714) 855-3045, *Published:* monthly.

Philadelphia Inquirer, Philadelphia Newspapers Inc., 400 N. Broad St., Box 8263, Philadelphia, PA 19101, *Telephone:* (215) 854-2000, *Published:* daily.

Photo Marketing, Photo Marketing Association International, 3000 Picture Place, Jackson, MI 49201, *Telephone:* (517) 788-8100, *Fax:* (517) 788-8371. *Published:* monthly, *Price:* U.S.: $35 per year/with Newsline $50, $55 for 2 years/$65 with Newsline; Canada: $35 per year/$50 with Newsline, $55 for 2 years/$70 with Newsline (payable in Canadian funds plus GST).

Photonics Spectra, Laurin Publishing Co., Inc., Berkshire Common, PO Box 4949, Pittsfield, MA 01202, *Telephone:* (413) 499-0514, *Fax:* (413) 442-3180, *Published:* monthly.

Pipeline & Gas Journal, Oildom Publishing Co. of Texas, Inc., 3314 Mercer St., Houston, TX 77027, *Telephone:* (713) 622-0676, *Fax:* (713) 623-4768, *Published:* monthly, *Price:* free to qualitifed subscribers; all others $15 per year.

Pit & Quarry, Edgell Communications, Inc., 7500 Old Oak Blvd., Cleveland, OH 44130, *Telephone:* (216) 243-8100, *Fax:* (216) 891-2726, *Published:* monthly.

Plastics News, Crain Communications, 965 E. Jefferson, Detroit, MI 48207-3185, *Published:* weekly.

Playthings, Geyer-McAllister Publications, Inc., 51 Madison Ave., New York, NY 10010, *Telephone:* (212) 689-4411, *Fax:* (212) 683-7929, *Published:* monthly, except semimonthly in May.

Portland Business Journal, American City Business Journals, P.O. Box 14490, Portland, OR 97280, *Telephone:* (503) 274-8733, *Fax:* (503) 227-2650, *Published:* weekly.

Practical Accountant, Faulkner & Gray, Inc., 11 Penn Plaza, 17th Floor, New York, NY 10001, *Telephone:* (800) 535-8403 or (212) 967-7060, *Published:* monthly, *Price:* U.S.: $60 per year; Elsewhere: $79 per year.

Prepared Foods, Cahners Publishing Company, 44 Cook St., Denver, CO 80217-3377, *Telephone:* (303) 388-4511, Published: monthly, except semimonthly in April, *Price:* qualified manufacturers - $41 per year; all others in U.S. - $84 per year.

Professional Builder, Cahners Publishing Co., 1350 E. Touhy Ave., Des Plaines, IL 60018.

Progressive Grocer, 263 Tresser Blvd., Stamford, CT 06901, *Telephone:* (203) 325-3500, *Published:* monthly, *Price:* U.S.: $75 per year; Canada: $86 per year; single copies $9 each.

Provider, American Health Care Association, 5615 W. Cermak Rd., Cicero, IL 60650, *Published:* monthly.

Publishers Weekly, Cahners Publishing Company, ESP Computer Services, 19110 Van Ness Ave., Torrance, CA 90501-1170, *Telephone:* (800) 278-2991, *Published:* weekly, *Price:* U.S.: $129 per year; Canada: $177 per year (includes GST).

Pulp & Paper, Miller Freeman Inc., P.O. Box 1065, Skokie, IL 60076-8065, *Telephone:* (800) 682-8297, *Published:* monthly, *Price:* free to those in pulp, paper, and board manufacturing and paper converting firms; Others in U.S.: $100 per year.

Pulp & Paper Canada, Southam Business Communications Inc., P.O. Box 1144, Lewiston, NY 14092, *Published:* monthly, *Price:* Canada: $55 per year, $66 for 2 years, $78 for 3 years; U.S.: $62 per year, $91 for 2 years.

Purchasing, Cahners Publishing Company, 44 Cook St., Denver, CO 80217-3377, *Telephone:* (303) 388-4511. *Published:* semimonthly, except monthly in January, February, July, August, December, and one extra issue in March and September, *Price:* U.S.: $84.95 per year; Canada: $133.95 per year; Mexico: $124.95 per year.

Quick Frozen Foods International, E.W. Williams Publications Co., 2125 Center Ave., Ste. 305, Fort Lee, NJ 07024, *Telephone:* (201) 592-7007, *Fax:* (201) 592-7171, *Published:* quarterly.

R&D Magazine, Cahners Publishing Company, 275 Washington St., Newton, MA 02158, *Telephone:* (708) 635-8800, *Fax:* (708) 390-2618, *Published*: monthly.

Railway Age, Simmons-Boardman Publishing, 345 Hudson St., New York, NY 10014, *Telephone:* (212) 620-7200, *Fax:* (212) 633-1165, *Published:* monthly.

Real Estate Finance Journal, Warren, Gorham and Lamont, Inc., 1 Penn Plaza, New York, NY 10119, *Telephone:* (212) 971-5225, *Fax:* (212) 971-5024, *Price:* $96 per year.

Real Estate Finance Today, Mortgage Bankers Assn., 1125 15th St., NW, Washington, DC 20005, *Telephone:* (202) 861-6500, *Fax:* (202) 429-9524.

Remedy, Rx Remedy Inc., 120 Post Road West, Wesport, CT 06880, *Telephone:* (203) 341-7000, *Published:* monthly.

Reseller Management, Elsevier Science Publishing Co. Inc., 655 Avenue of the Americas, New York, NY 10010, *Telephone:* (201) 292-5100, *Fax:* (201) 292-0783.

Restaurant Hospitality, Penton Publishing, 1100 Superior Ave., Cleveland, OH 44114, *Telephone:* (216) 696-7000, *Published*: monthly.

Restaurants & Institutions, Cahners Publishing Co., 1350 Touhy Ave., Cahners Plaza, Des Plaines, IL 60017-5080, *Telephone:* (312) 635-8800.

Rock Products, Maclean Hunter Publishing Co., 29 N. Wacker Dr., Chicago, IL 60606, *Telephone:* (312) 726-2802.

Rough Notes, Rough Notes Co. Inc., 11690 Technologies Dr., Carmel, IN 46032-5600, *Published:* monthly, *Cost:* $25.

Rubber & Plastics News, Crain Communications, 1725 Merriman Road, Ste. 300, Akron, OH 44313, *Telephone:* (330) 836-9180, *Fax*: (33) 836-1005, *Published:* weekly.

Rubber World, 1867 W. Market St., PO Box 5485, Akron, OH 44313, *Telephone:* (216) 864-2122, *Fax:* (216) 836-1005.

Rural Electrification, National Rural Electric Coperative, 1800 Massachusetts Ave., NW, Washington D.C. 20036.

Sacramento Business Journal, 1401 21st St., Sacramento, CA 95814-5221, *Telephone:* (916) 447-7661, *Fax:* (916) 444-7779, *Published:* weekly.

Sales & Marketing Management, Times Mirror Magazines, Inc., 2 Park Ave., New York, NY 10016, *Telephone:* (212) 592-6300, *Fax:* (212) 592-6300, Published: 15x/yr.

San Diego Business Journal, 4909 Murphy Canyon Rd., No. 200, San Diego, CA 92123, *Telephone:* (619) 277-6359, *Fax:* (619) 571-3628, *Published:* weekly.

San Diego Business Journal, 4909 Murphy Canyon Rd., No. 200, San Diego, CA 92123, *Telephone:* (619) 277-6359, *Fax:* (619) 571-3628, *Published:* weekly.

San Francisco Business Times, San Francisco Business Times, Inc., Embarcadero Center West, 275 Battery Street, Suite 940, San Francisco, CA 94111. *Published:* weekly, *Price:* $49 per year.

San Francisco Chronicle, 901 Mission St., San Francisco, CA 94103, *Telephone:* (415) 777-1111, *Fax:* (415) 512-8196. *Published:* daily.

San Jose and Silicon Valley Business Journal, 56 N 3rd St., San Jose, CA 95112, *Telephone:* (408) 295-3800, *Fax:* (408) 295-5028, *Published:* weekly.

San Juan Star, P.O. Box, 364187, San Juan PR 00936-4187, *Telephone:* (809) 782-4200, *Fax:* (809) 783-5788, *Published:* daily.

Security Distribution & Marketing, Cahners Publishing Co., 1350 E. Touhy Ave., Des Plaines, IL 60018, *Telephone:* (708) 635--8800, *Fax:* (708) 299-8622.

Shopping Center World, Communications Channels, Inc., 6255 Barfield Rd., Altanta, GA 30328, *Telephone:* (404) 256-9800.

Site Selection, Conway Data, Inc., 40 Technology Park/Atlanta, Norcross, GA 30092-9990, *Telephone:* (404) 446-6996.

Skillings' Mining Review, 1st Bank Pl., Ste. 278, 130 W. Superior St., Duluth, MN 55802, *Telephone:* (218) 722-2310, *Fax:* (218) 722-0134. *Published:* weekly.

Snack & Bakery Foods (formerly Snack Food), Stagnito Publishing Co., 1935 Shermer Rd., Ste. 100, Northbrook, IL 60062-5354, *Telephone:* (708) 205-5660, *Fax:* (708) 205-5680, *Published:* monthly, *Price:* free to qualified subscribers; $45 per year to all others.

Snack Food, Stagnito Publishing Co., 1935 Shermer Rd., Ste. 100, Northbrook, IL 60062-5354, *Telephone:* (708) 205-5660, *Fax:* (708) 205-568,. *Published:* monthly, *Price:* free to qualified subscribers; $45 per year to all others.

Soap/Cosmetic/Chemical Specialties, 455 Broad Hollow Road, Melville, NY 11747-4722.

Software Magazine, Sentry Publishing Co., One Research Drive, Suite 400B, Westborough, MA 01581, *Telephone:* (508) 366-2031. *Published*: monthly.

Solid State Technology, PennWell Publishing Company, 1421 S. Sheridan Road, Tulsa, OK 74112, *Telephone:* (603) 891-0123.

South Florida Business Journal, American City Business Journals, 7950 NW 53 St., Ste. 210, Miami, FL 33166, *Telephone:* (305) 594-2100, *Fax:* (305) 594-1892.

South Jersey Business Journal, P.O. Box 920, Morristown, NJ 07963-0920.

Sporting Goods Business, Gralla Publications, Inc., 1515 Broadway, New York, NY 10036, *Telephone:* (212) 869-1300.

Sporting Goods Dealer, Times Mirror Magazines, Inc., 2 Park Ave., New York, NY 10016, *Telephone:* (212) 779-5000, *Fax:* (212) 213-3540, *Published:* monthly.

Sportstyle, Fairchild Publications, 7 W. 34th St., New York, NY 10001, *Telephone:* (212) 630-4000, *Fax:* (212) 630-3726.

Spray Technology & Marketing, Indsutry Publications, Inc., 389 Passaic Ave., Fairfield, NJ 07004, *Telephone:* (201) 227-5151, *Fax:* (201) 227-921, *Published:* monthly.

St. Louis Business Journal, American City Business Journals, 1 Metropolitan Sq., P.O. Box 647, Saint Louis, MO 63188, *Telephone:* (314) 421-6200, *Fax:* (314) 621-5031.

St. Louis Post-Dispatch, 900 N. Tucker Blvd., Saint Louis, MO 63101, *Telephone:* (314) 340-8000, *Fax:* (314) 340-3050.

State Government News, Council of State Governments, Iron Works Pike, PO Box 11910, Lexington, KY 40578-1910, *Telephone:* (606) 231-1812, *Fax:* (606) 231-1823, *Published:* monthly.

Statesman, Statesman House, 4 Chowringhee Square, Calcutta, India.

STN/Skiing Trade News, Times Mirror Magazines, Inc., 2 Park Ave., New York, NY 10016, *Telephone:* (212) 779-5019, *Fax:* (212) 779-5465, *Published:* 8x/yr. *Price:* $15 per year.

Stores, NRF Enterprises Inc., 100 West 31st St., New York, NY 10001, *Published:* monthly, *Price:* U.S./Canada: $49 per year, $80 for 2 years, $120 for 3 years.

Success, Lang Communications, P.O. Box 3038, Harlan, IA 51537-3038, *Published:* monthly, except January and July, *Price:* U.S.: $19.97 per year, $33.97 for 2 years, $47.97 for 3 years; Canada: add $7 for postage and GST.

Successful Farming, Meredith Corp., 1716 Locust St., Des Moines, IA 50309, *Telephone:* (515) 284-3000, *Fax:* (515) 284-2700.

Sugar & Sweetner. Situation and Outlook Review, Superintendent of Documents, U.S. Govt. Printing Office, Washington, DC 20402, *Telephone:* (202) 783-3238.

Sunday Times, Times Newspapers, P.O. Box 495, Virginia Street, London E19XY.

Supermarket Business, Howfrey Communications, Inc., 1086 Teaneck Rd., Teaneck, NJ 07666, *Telephone:* (201) 833-1900, *Published:* monthly.

Supermarket News, Fairchild Publications, 7 W. 34th St., New York, NY 10001, *Telephone:* (212) 630-4750, *Fax:* (212) 630-4760.

Tampa Bay Business Journal, American City Business Journals, 405 Reo St., Ste. 210, Tampa, FL 33609, *Telephone:* (813) 289-8255.

Tea & Coffee Trade Journal, Lockwood Trade Journal Co., 130 W. 42nd St., Ste. 2200, New York, NY 10036-7802, *Telephone:* (212) 391-2060, *Fax:* (212) 827-0945, *Published:* monthly, *Price:* $29 per year.

Technology & Learning, Peter Li. Inc., 330 Progress Rd., Dayton, OH 45449, *Telephone:* (513) 847-5900, *Fax:* (513) 847-5910, *Published:* 8x/yr.

Telecommunications, Horizon House Publications, Inc., 685 Canton St., Norwood, CA 02062, *Telephone:* (617) 769-9750, *Fax:* (617) 762-9071.

Textile Asia, Tak Yan Commercial Bldg., 11th Fl., 30-32 D'Aguilar St., Hong Kong, *Telephone:* (5) 247467, *Published:* monthly.

Textile World, Maclean Hunter Publishing Co., Circulation Dept., 29 N. Wacker Dr., Chicago, IL 60606, *Price:* U.S./Canada: $45 per year, $75 for 2 years, $105 for 3 years.

Time, Time, Inc., Time & Life Bldg., Rockefeller Center, New York, NY 10020-1393, *Telephone:* (800) 843-8463, *Published:* weekly.

Tire Business, Crain Commincations, Inc., 1725 Merriman Rd., Ste. 300, Akron, OH 44313-5251, *Telephone:* (216) 836-9180, *Fax:* (216) 836-1005.

Toronto Star, One Yong Street, Toronto, Ontario M5E 1E6, Telephone: (416) 367-2000, *Published:* daily.

Trade & Culture, 3500 Bank Street, Baltimore, MD 21224-2303, *Telephone*: (800) 544-5684, *Published*: bimonthly, *Cost:* $20.

Training, American Society for Training and Development Inc., 1640 King Street, P.O. Box 1443, Alexandria, VA 22313-2043, *Telephone*: (703) 683-8100, *Published:* monthly.

Transportation & Distribution, Penton Publishing, 1100 Superior Ave., Cleveland, OH 44114-2543, *Telephone:* (216) 696-7000, *Fax:* (216) 696-4135, *Published:* monthly.

Transportation Topics, American Trucking Assn., 2200 Mill Road, Alexandria, VA 22314, *Telephone*: (703) 838-1770.

Travel Weekly, Reed Travel Group, 500 Plaza Dr., Secaucus, NJ 07096, *Telephone:* (201) 902-2000, *Fax:* (201) 319-1947, *Published:* 2 times/week (Mon. and Thurs.).

Treasury and Risk Management, Economist Bldg, 111 W. 57th St., New York, NY 10019, *Published:* quarterly.

Turkey Hatchery, Superintendent of Documents, U.S. Govt. Printing Office, Washington, DC 20402, *Telephone:* (202) 783-3238.

TV Digest, Warren Publishing Inc., 215 Ward Ct., NW, Washington D.C. 20037.

U.S. Distribution Journal, BMT Publications Inc., 7 Penn Plaza, New York, NY 10001, *Telephone:* (212) 594-4120. *Published:* monthly, plus one additional issue in Dec.

U.S. News & World Report, 2400 N. St. NW, Washington, D.C. 20037, *Telephone:* (202) 955-2000. *Published:* weekly.

Urban Land, Urban Land Institute, 625 Indiana Avenue, N.W., Suite 400, Washington, DC 20004-2930, *Telephone:* (202) 624-7000, *Published:* monthly, *Price:* $60 per year as part of membership.

US Banker, Kalo Communications, 60 E. 42nd St., Ste. 3810, New York, NY 10165, Telephone: (212) 599-3310.

USA TODAY, Gannett Co., Inc., 1000 Wilson Blvd., Arlington, VA 22229, *Telephone:* (703) 276-3400. *Published:* Mon.-Fri.

Vanity Fair, Codne Nast Publications Inc., 350 Madison Ave., Newark, NY 10017, *Telephone*: (212) 880-8800, *Fax:* (212) 880-8289.

Variety, 475 Park Ave., South, New York, NY 10016, *Telephone:* (212) 779-1100, *Fax:* (212) 779-0026. *Published:* weekly.

Vending Times, Vending Times Inc., 545 8th Ave., New York, NY 10018, *Telephone:* (212) 714-0101, *Fax:* (212) 564-0196, *Published:* monthly.

VM + SD (Visual Merchandising and Store Design), ST Publications Inc., 407 Gilbert Ave., Cincinnati, OH 45202, *Telephone:* (513) 421-2050, *Published:* monthly, *Price:* $39 per year.

Wall Street Journal, Dow Jones & Co. Inc., 200 Liberty St., New York, NY 10281, *Telephone:* (212) 416-2000. *Published:* Mon.-Fri.

Wallace's Farmer, Farm Progress Companies, 191 S. Gary Ave., Carol Stream, IL 60188, Telephone: (708) 690-5600, Published: 15x/yr.

WARD's Auto World, Ward's Communications, 28 W. Adams, Detroit, MI 48226, *Telephone:* (313) 962-4456. *Published:* monthly.

WARD's Automotive International, Ward's Communications, 28 W. Adams, Detroit, MI 48226, *Telephone:* (313) 962-4456. *Published:* monthly.

Washington Post (National Weekly Edition), The Washington Post, 1150 15th St., N.W., Washington, DC 20071, *Published:* weekly, *Price:* $48 per year.

Water Environment & Technology, 601 Wythe Street, Alexandria, VA 22314-1994, *Published:* monthly.

Wines & Vines, Hiaring Co., 1800 Lincoln Ave., San Rafael, CA 94901-1298, *Telephone:* (415) 453-9700, *Fax:* (415) 453-2517, *Published:* monthly, *Price:* $32 per year without directory; $77.50 per year including directory.

Wired, 520 3rd St., 4th Fl., San Francisco, CA 94107-1815, Telephone: (415) 276-5000, *Published*: monthly, *Cost:* $39.95; *Corporate* $80.

Women's Wear Daily, Fairchild Publications, 7 E. 12th St., New York, NY 10003, *Telephone:* (212) 741-4000, *Fax:* (212) 337-3225. *Published:* daily.

Wood & Wood Products, Vance Publishing Corp., 400 Knightsbridge Pkway., Lincolnshire, IL 60069, *Telephone:* (708) 634-4347, *Fax:* (708) 634-4379, Published: monthly, except semimonthly in March.

Wood Digest, Johnson Hill Press, 1233 Janesville Ave., Fort Atkinson, WI 53538, *Telephone:* (414) 563-6388, *Fax*: (414) 563-1702.

Working Woman, Lang Communications, 230 Park Ave., 7th Fl., New York, NY 10169, *Published*: monthly.

World Coffee & Tea, CGI Publishing Co. Inc., 1801 Rockville Pike, Ste. 330, Rockville, MD 20852, *Telephone:* (301) 984-7333, *Fax:* (301) 984-7340.

World Poultry-Misset, Misset International, P.O. Box 4, 7000 BA, Doetinchem, the Netherlands, *Telephone:* 31 8340-49562, *Fax:* 31 8340-40515, *Price:* U.S.: $79 per year, $123 for 2 years, $155 for 3 years.

World Trade, Freedom Magazines, 17702 Cowan, Ste. 100, Irvine, CA 92714-6035.

Your Company, Time Inc., 1271 Avenue of the Americas, New York, NY 10020-1393.

Ziegelindustrie, Bauverlag GmbH, D-65173 Wiesbaden, *Telephone:* (0 61 23) 7 00-0.